Management of the Sales Force

Management of the Sales Force

William J. Stanton
University of Colorado

Richard H. Buskirk
University of Southern California

Seventh Edition
1987
IRWIN
Homewood, Illinois 60430

To Imma and Barbara

ISBN 0-256-03635-7

Library of Congress Catalog Card No. 86-82598

Printed in the United States of America

3 4 5 6 7 8 9 0 DO 4 3 2 1 0 9 8 7

Preface

When the first edition of this book was published, our economic growth rate was strong, and jobs for college graduates were plentiful. This new edition (the seventh) comes out in a quite different socioeconomic setting as we move through the late 1980s and prepare for the 1900s. Both our economic growth rate and the birth rate have slowed down considerably. Computers are dramatically changing many aspects of our lives, and foreign competition is seriously affecting many of our industries. The role of women in our society is continuing to change significantly. People's values are changing as we become more concerned about our social and physical environment and our quality of life.

In response to these and other social and economic forces the nature of the outside sales job has changed rather dramatically. A new kind of sales person has been developing—a more professional sales representative, a profit manager of a territory. These changes have been paralleled by a substantial upgrading of the positions of sales-force executives. In the past, these jobs often involved little more than being a field supervisor of the sales force. Today, in contrast, a sales-force executive's job is influenced considerably by the strategic company planning and the strategic marketing planning in his or her firm. Today, these executives must engage in planning sales-force activities and evaluating sales performance, as well as operating a sales force.

In this seventh edition of *Management of the Sales Force,* we have reflected these changing conditions in all parts of the book. Of the many new features in this edition the one that is probably the most immediately noticeable is the physical appearance of the book. Many

v

new figures and other visuals have been added to help make an already good teaching and learning resource even better.

We also have made several changes in the content of the book. Early in our coverage of each sales-force management activity—sales organization, selection, training, compensation, etc.—we discuss the relationship between that activity and strategic marketing planning in recognition of the importance of coordinating sales-force management activites with the organization's strategic marketing planning.

The cases have always been an important part, and one of the main strengths, of this book. In this edition we have generated 30 new cases out of a total of 45. Also new are 5 of the 12 Majestic Glass Company problems. These are day-to-day operating problems of the sort typically faced by sales managers.

Several of the chapters have been substantially rewritten to reflect changing philosophies and new concepts. For example, the chapter on sales organization reflects the growing importance of national-account selling and market-oriented rather than product-oriented sales organizational structures. Chapters on sales-force selection were rewritten to reflect changing opinions on interviewing and testing as selection tools. Leadership and motivation now are covered in the same chapter, thus recognizing the close relationship between these two managerial activities. In the sales-forecasting chapter, key concepts have been clarified and new examples introduced in the section dealing with the application of forecasting methods.

In this edition all the material has been updated. The entire book has been carefully edited to reduce the average sentence length and to reduce the amount of detail in many sections.

At the same time, those who are familiar with the earlier editions will find that we have retained the features that have made this book an outstanding teaching and learning resource. The writing style continues to make the book clear and interesting to read. The section-heading structure makes for easier reading and outlining. We still have the excellent end-of-chapter discussion questions. Most of these questions are thought-provoking and involve the *application* of text material, rather than being answerable "right out of the book." The issue-oriented cases provide an opportunity for problem solving and decision making, rather than being simply a vehicle for long-winded discussions of a company's action.

We also have retained the basic scope, approach, and organization that have made this book the market leader in its field for over 20 years. With respect to its *scope, this book still is concerned specifically with the management of an outside sales force and its activities.* Outside sales people, those who go to the customers, are distinguished here from over-the-counter sales persons to whom the customers come. Therefore, the book deals largely with the management of sales forces of manufacturers and wholesaling middlemen. Thus the scope of this book does *not* include any significant treatment of the broader fields of marketing management or the personal-selling component of promotional management.

It seems appropriate that special attention should be devoted to the management of a sales force. This field should not be neglected by administrators in their preoccupation with strategic *marketing* management. The sales people in the field have the task of properly carrying out the sales plan. In the final analysis, it is this group which brings in the revenue. There is a direct relationship between company profits and the management of the sales force. Furthermore, the cost of administering and operating a sales force usually is by far the largest single marketing expense in a company.

This edition continues the *real-world approach* that has successfully characterized previous editions. We have intentionally avoided the sophisticated mathematical models and behavioral concepts whose limiting assumptions and other impractical features have rendered them essentially valueless for practicing sales managers. Students who learn from this book can talk to sales executives in the business world. And the sales executives can read and understand this book. In fact, this book has been used in many executive development programs for sales managers.

The contents of this book can be valuable to you who are student readers because your use of the knowledge can be fairly immediate. Few of you will become marketing managers soon after graduation. Within a very few years, however, you may well be some type of sales-force managers, perhaps at a district level. Even as sales people, you may be called upon to use material covered in this book. The year following your graduation, you may come back to your alma mater as members of your firm's employee recruiting team. Or you may be called upon for suggestions regarding a proposed compensation, expense, or quota plan.

In its *organization* the text is divided into 5 main parts:

1. *Introduction to Sales-Force Management.* The three chapters in this section include an introductory chapter and one on sales-force organization (Chapter 3). In Chapter 2 we cast sales managers in their true role—that of administrators. We explain the role of strategic sales-force planning as it relates to strategic marketing planning and strategic company planning. Also in Chapter 2, we set forth a basic managerial philosophy which permeates the entire book. We believe that staffing—the selection of personnel at any level from top to bottom in an organization—is the most important function of administrators. It is not their *only* job, but it is their *most important* one.

2. *Staffing and Operating a Sales Force.* This part includes such

topics as selecting, training, and compensating a sales force. Sales operations also includes the topics of motivating and supervising a sales force, as well as sales-force morale.

3. *Sales Planning.* Part 3 covers sales planning activities starting with a forecast of market demand, including sales forecasting. Then we discuss sales department budgeting, the establishing of sales territories, and finally the subject of sales quotas.

4. *Evaluating Sales Performance.* This part deals with sales volume analysis, marketing cost and profitability analysis, and an evaluation of the performance of individual sales people.

5. *A Look-Ahead.* Part 5 includes chapters on the ethical problems and social responsibilities facing sales managers, and on career opportunities in sales management.

Many people contributed directly to the improvements in this edition. Several of the cases were prepared by other professors and students, and in each instance their authorship is identified with the case. The Majestic Glass Company problems were originally written by Phillip McVey when he was at the University of Nebraska-Lincoln. George R. Cook of the Xerox Corporation contributed several ideas as well as supplying us with the Xerox company forms that nicely illustrate several concepts in the sales-force selection chapters.

Many of the changes that we made in this edition were inspired by the in-depth reviews provided by Kenneth R. Evans (Arizona State University), Terrence Kroeten (North Dakota State University), Lynn J. Loudenback (New Mexico State University), and Richard S. Nelson (San Francisco State University).

Through the years, many sales executives, present and past colleagues, and other professors have contributed greatly to this book. Many of these debts are acknowledged in footnotes and other references throughout the text. Perhaps, however, our greatest debt is to our students who have used this text. Their suggestions, constructive criticisms, and yes, sometimes even their complaints have led to many changes and improvements in the book. To all these people we are deeply grateful.

William J. Stanton
Richard H. Buskirk

Contents

Part Two   Sales-Force Staffing and Operations   **95**

4.   Selecting the Sales Force—Determining the Kind of People Wanted   **97**

Sales-Force Selection and Strategic Planning. Importance of a Good Selection Program. Responsibility for Selection. The Law and Sales-Force Selection. Nature of the Sales Job. Scope of the Sales-Force Selection Program. Determining the Number and Type of People Wanted.

Cases

5.   Selecting the Sales Force—Recruiting Applicants   **133**

Recruiting and Strategic Planning. Importance of Planned Recruiting. Find and Maintain Good Recruiting Sources. Sources of Sales Representatives. Factors Influencing Choice of Recruiting Sources. Evaluation of Recruiting Program.

Cases

6.   Selecting the Sales Force—Processing Applicants   **159**

Processing Applicants and Strategic Planning. Legal Considerations. Application Blanks. Personal Interviews. References and Other Outside Sources. Psychological Testing. Physical Examination. Assessment Centers. Coming to a Conclusion about an Applicant.

Cases

15. Sales-Force Morale 414

The Nature of Morale. Morale and Strategic Planning. Effects of Low Sales-Force Morale. Causes of Low Sales-Force Morale. Special Problems in Morale. Determining the Cause of Poor Morale. The Morale-Building Process.

Part Three Sales Planning 441

16. Forecasting Market Demand 443

Market Opportunity Analysis. Explanation of Basic Terms. Need for Consumer Analysis. Determination and Use of Market Factors. Basic Techniques for Deriving Potentials. Territorial Potentials. Sales Forecasting. Examples of Application of Forecasting Methods. Some Guiding Principles for Forecasting.

17. Sales-Department Budgeting 477

Budgeting and Strategic Planning. Management by Percentage. Benefits of Budgeting. Budgets for Sales Department Activities. The Budgeting Process for the Firm. Budget Periods. The Budget-Making Procedure. Reasons Some Firms Do Not Use Budgets. Summary of Criticisms. Managing with Budgets.

Management of the Sales Force

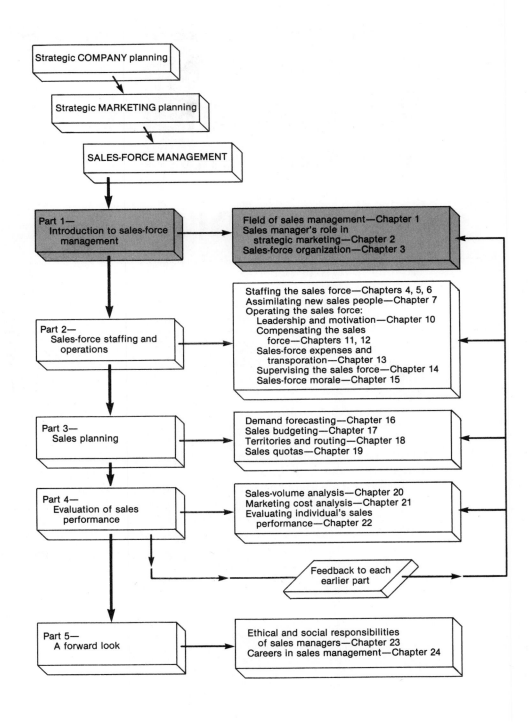

Introduction to Sales-Force Management

For firms with an outside sales force, the activities involved in personal selling typically include more people and cost more money than any other phase of the firm's marketing program. Moreover, the degree of success experienced by the sales people usually is a major—if not *the* most important—factor determining the degree of success enjoyed by the firm. Consequently, sales-force management—the topic of this book—is a very important part of a company's total management effort.

The first part of this book introduces the field of sales management. In Chapter 1 we explain what marketing is and how it has evolved in our socioeconomic system. Then we explain the role of sales-force management in a total marketing program and discuss the distinctive nature and importance of sales management.

Chapter 2 considers the role of sales managers as administrators. The role of sales-force strategy is examined in relation to a firm's marketing strategy and its overall company strategy.

Chapter 3 deals with sales-force organization—the concepts of good organization, the basic types of organizations, and the organizational specialization within a sales department.

1

The Field of Sales Management

Nothing happens until somebody sells something.
ARTHUR H. MOTLEY

As the songwriters say, "then was then and now is now," and "the times they are a-changing." In the 1970s product shortages and the energy crisis focused attention on financial and legal management. Many organizations succumbed to "analysis paralysis." They grew conservative and looked inward as they worked to cut costs, quantified everything, and took forever to make decisions.

Today marketing is the name of the game in both business and nonbusiness organizations. Companies want a president with marketing experience. They want to renew the risk-taking, dynamic, entrepreneurial spirit necessary to grow and be successful.[1] As we anticipate the 1990s, this entrepreneurial spirit is shaped by the realization that:

- Consumers are continuing to demand higher quality and better performing products and services.
- Foreign competition is increasing and intensifying.
- The technology of electronic communication is changing rapidly, spurred on by the developments in the computer field.
- We live in a "spaceship" economy of limited, irreplaceable, and often high-cost resources.
- We continue to develop social values which call for a better quality of life and a pollution-free environment.
- We expect higher standards of social responsibility from our business leaders.

[1] "Marketing: The New Priority," *Business Week*, November 21, 1983, p. 96.

5

These factors present an interesting set of challenges to business management in general and to marketing and sales executives in particular. The success sales executives enjoy during the next decade will depend to a great extent on their ability to meet these challenges. Sales-force management activities must be attuned to our changing social, economic, and political environment.[2]

To introduce the study of sales-force management, let's first review the nature and scope of marketing in our economy. Then let's see where the management of a sales force fits into a company's marketing program.

Marketing in Our Economy

One day early last summer two boys placed written notices in neighborhood mailboxes announcing a window-washing and lawn-care service they had just started. They also went door-to-door to spread the word about their new venture. Whether these young entrepreneurs realized it or not, they were engaging in marketing. At the other end of the size scale, IBM also engages in marketing when it realizes that a major auto producer needs an improved marketing information system to implement its new "just-in-time" inventory control system. IBM then develops, sells, and installs in the auto firm a new marketing information system built around IBM computers.

In a business firm, the marketing department—especially the sales force—generates the revenues that are managed by the financial people and used by the production people in creating products and services. The challenge of marketing is to generate those revenues by satisfying customers' wants profitably and in a socially responsible manner.

Societal Dimensions of Marketing

But marketing is not limited to business. It has a broader, societal dimension that is more meaningful and truly descriptive of marketing today. Whenever you try to persuade somebody to do something—donate to the United Fund, stop littering the highway, lower the stereo sound during study hours in the dorm, accept a date with you (or even marry you)—you are engaging in a marketing activity. So-called nonbusiness organizations—they really are in business but don't think of themselves as business people—also engage in market-

[2] See Rolph E. Anderson and Bert Rosenbloom, "Eclectic Sales Management: Strategic Response to Trends in the Eighties," *Journal of Personal Selling & Sales Management*, November 1982, pp. 41–46.

ing. Their "product" may be a vacation place they want you to visit, a social cause they want you to support, or a cultural event they want you to attend.

As you can see, marketing is a very broad-based activity, and consequently, it calls for a broad definition. The essence of marketing is a transaction—an exchange—intended to set aside human needs and wants. That is, marketing occurs any time one social unit (person or organization) strives to exchange something of value with another social unit. Thus our broad definition is as follows:

Marketing consists of all activities designed to generate and facilitate any exchange intended to satisfy human needs and wants.

In this book the terms **needs** and **wants** are used interchangeably.

Within this broad definition of marketing, then, (1) the marketers, (2) what they are marketing, and (3) their potential markets all assume broad dimensions. The category of **marketers** might include, in addition to business firms, such diverse social units as:

- A politician party trying to market its candidate to the public.
- The director of an art museum providing new exhibits to generate greater attendance and financial support.
- A labor union marketing ideas to its members and to company management.
- Professors trying to make their courses more interesting for their students.

In addition to the range of items normally considered as products and services, a broader sense of **what is being marketed** might include (1) *ideas*, such as reducing air pollution or stopping smoking, (2) *people*, such as a new football coach or a political candidate, or (3) *places*, such as a vacation resort.

In a broad sense, **target markets** include more than the direct consumers of products, services, and ideas. In addition to its faculty and students, a state university's market includes the legislators who provide funds, the citizens living near the university who may be affected by its activities, and the alumni.

Business Dimensions of Marketing

Our broad (or macro) definition of marketing tells us something about the role of marketing in our socioeconomic system. But this is a book about managing a sales force in an individual organization within that system. So let's see what marketing looks like in an organizational context. The organization may be a business firm in the conventional sense of the word "business." Or it may be what is called a nonbusiness or nonprofit organization—a hospital, university, United Way, church, police department, or museum, for example. Both groups—business and nonbusiness—face essentially the same basic marketing problems.

Business definition of marketing. Our micro definition of marketing—applicable in an individual business or nonbusiness organization—is as follows:

> Marketing is a total system of business activities designed to plan, price, promote, and distribute want-satisfying products, services, and ideas to target markets in order to achieve organizational objectives.[3]

> *Marketing is:*
> a system: of business activities
> designed to: plan, price, promote, and distribute
> something of value: want-satisfying products, services, and ideas
> for the benefit of: the target market—present and potential household consumers or industrial users
> to achieve: the organization's objectives.

This definition has significant implications:

- It is a managerial, systems definition.
- The entire system of business activities must be customer oriented. Customers' wants must be recognized and satisfied effectively.
- Marketing is a dynamic business process—a total, integrated process—rather than a fragmented assortment of institutions and functions. Marketing is not any *one* activity, nor is it exactly the *sum* of several. Rather, it is the result of the *interaction* of many activities.

[3] This definition is essentially the same as the one used in all previous editions of this book. We modified our original definition slightly to conform generally with a revised American Marketing Association definition. The AMA definition is as follows: "Marketing is the process of planning and executing the conception, pricing, promotion, and distribution of ideas, goods, and services to create exchanges that satisfy individual and organizational objectives." See "AMA Board Approves New Marketing Definition," *Marketing News,* March 1, 1985, p. 1.

- The marketing program starts with the germ of a product idea and does not end until the customer's wants are completely satisfied, which may be some time after the sale is made.
- To be successful, marketing must maximize profitable sales over the *long run*. Thus, customers must be satisfied in order for a company to get the repeat business that ordinarily is so vital to success.

The Marketing Concept and Marketing Management

As business people have come to recognize that marketing is vitally important to the success of a firm, an entirely new way of business thinking—a new philosophy—has evolved. This is called the **marketing concept**, and it is based on three fundamental beliefs (see Figure 1–1):

1. All company planning and operations should be **customer oriented.**
2. The goal of the organization should be to generate **profitable sales volume over the long run.**
3. All marketing activities in a firm should be **organizationally coordinated.**

In its fullest sense, the marketing concept is a philosophy of business that states that the customers' want-satisfaction is the economic and social justification for the firm's existence. Consequently, all company activities should be devoted to finding out what the customers want and then satisfying those wants, while making a profit over the long run.

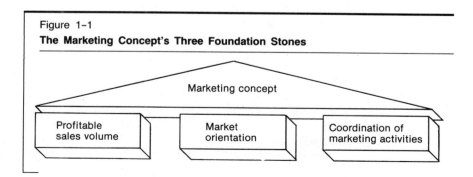

Figure 1–1
The Marketing Concept's Three Foundation Stones

Marketing Management and Its Evolution

For a business enterprise to realize the full benefits of the marketing concept, this philosophy must be translated into action. This means that (1) the marketing activities in a firm must be totally coordinated and (2) the chief marketing executive must play an important role in company planning. As these two moves occur, marketing management begins to develop. ***Marketing management, then, is the marketing concept in action.***

Since the Industrial Revolution, marketing management in American business has evolved through three stages of development. A fourth one is now emerging. Many companies are still in one of the earlier stages. Only a few firms as yet exhibit the managerial philosophies and practices which are characteristic of the most advanced developmental period. The following diagram shows the four stages in the evolution of marketing management:

Stages in evolution of marketing management

Production-orientation stage. During the first stage, a company is typically production oriented. The executives in production and engineering shape the company's objectives and planning. The function of the sales department is simply to sell the production output at the price set by production and financial executives. This is the build-a-better-mousetrap stage. The underlying assumption is that marketing effort is not needed to get people to buy a product which is well made and reasonably priced.

During this period, manufacturers have sales departments—marketing is not yet recognized—headed by a sales manager whose main job is to operate a sales force. This organizational pattern was predominant in the United States until about the start of the Great Depression in the 1930s.

Sales-orientation stage. The Depression made it quite clear that the main problem in our economy was no longer the ability to make or grow enough products. Rather, the problem was selling this output. Just *producing* a better mousetrap was no assurance of market success. Thus we entered a period during which selling and sales executives were given new respect and responsibilities by company management.

Unfortunately, during this same period selling acquired much of its bad reputation. This was the age of the "hard sell." Even today, many organizations—both business and nonbusiness—still believe that they must operate with a hard-sell philosophy. They rarely consider first finding out what the consumer wants. As long as there are companies operating with a hard-sell philosophy, there will be continued (and justified, in our opinion) criticism of selling and marketing. The sales-orientation era generally extended from the 1930s into the 1950s, although no specific dates define any of the four stages.

Marketing-orientation stage. In the third stage, companies embrace the concept of coordinated marketing management directed toward the twin goals of customer satisfaction and *profitable* sales volume. Attention is focused on marketing rather than on selling. The top executive is called a marketing manager or the vice president of marketing. In this stage, several activities that traditionally were the province of other executives become the responsibility of the marketing manager (see Figure 1–2). For instance, inventory control, ware-

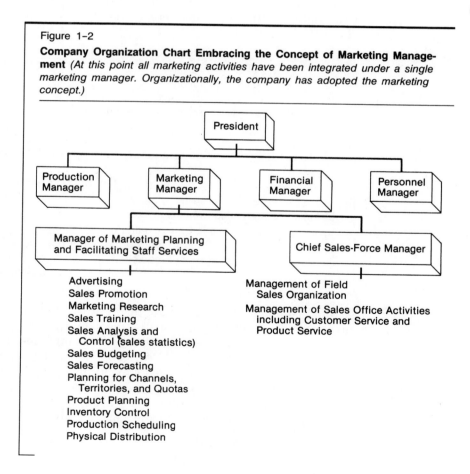

Figure 1–2

Company Organization Chart Embracing the Concept of Marketing Management (At this point all marketing activities have been integrated under a single marketing manager. Organizationally, the company has adopted the marketing concept.)

President

Production Manager | Marketing Manager | Financial Manager | Personnel Manager

Manager of Marketing Planning and Facilitating Staff Services

Chief Sales-Force Manager

Advertising
Sales Promotion
Marketing Research
Sales Training
Sales Analysis and
   Control (sales statistics)
Sales Budgeting
Sales Forecasting
Planning for Channels,
   Territories, and Quotas
Product Planning
Inventory Control
Production Scheduling
Physical Distribution

Management of Field
   Sales Organization

Management of Sales Office Activities
   including Customer Service and
   Product Service

housing, and aspects of product planning are often turned over to the marketing manager. This executive should be brought in at the *beginning*, rather than at the end of a production cycle. In effect, marketing should influence all short-term and long-range company planning.

The key to implementing the marketing concept successfully is a favorable attitude on the part of top management. As an executive at the Chase Manhattan Bank once said, "Marketing begins with top management. Only top management can provide the climate, the discipline, and the leadership required for a successful marketing program."

We are *not* saying that marketing executives should hold the top positions in a company. The marketing concept *does not* imply that the president of a firm must come up through the marketing department. We say only that the president must be marketing-oriented. Interestingly enough, results of a 1985 study of the chief executive officers (CEOs) of America's 500 largest industrial firms (see Figure 1–3) indicate that sales/marketing was the most frequently stated route to the top.

This is a production orientation:
Our attitude toward marketing was that we made solid, competitive bicycles. If people didn't buy these excellent French bicycles, they were stupid.

> William Desazars de Montgailhard chief executive officer, Cycles Peugeot, Paris as quoted in *Sales & Marketing Management*, April 6, 1981, p. 96.

And this is a marketing orientation:
Any company is nothing but a marketing organization.
> (a former president of Burroughs Corporation)

Our business is the business of marketing.
> (a former president of Pepsi-Cola Company)

Most American firms are now in the third stage in the marketing management evolution. The marketing concept has generally been *adopted* by both large- and medium-size companies. But how well many companies have actually *implemented* the marketing concept is still questionable. There are many forms and degrees of market orientation. Probably many companies, although using the appropriate fashionable titles and other external trappings, are still paying little more than lip service to the concept. In many instances, the

---

Figure 1–3
Profile of a CEO

A composite of the chief executive officer (CEO) of a large U. S. corporation.
Note the "route to the top" section in the career path below.

The position:
  Title: Chairman and chief executive officer.
  Compensation: $473,500 salary and bonus plus several benefits.
  Workload: 60 or more hours in an average week.
  Drawbacks: Insufficient time for family and outside interests.

Career path:
  ◆**Route to the top: Sales/marketing.**
  Number of employers: 2.4.
  Years with present company: 23 years.
  Number of locations with present company: No more than 2.

The person:
  Age: 56.6 years.
  Marital status: In first marriage.
  Religion: Protestant.
  Education: Advanced degree.
  Ranking of priorities: Family first, then work, country, and community.

Source: Adapted from a survey of CEOs of *Fortune* 500 companies by Heidrick & Struggles, an executive search firm, as reported in *USA Today*, August 16, 1985, p. 1B.

---

misunderstanding endures that marketing is merely a fancy name for selling.

Social responsibility and human-orientation stage. Social and economic conditions in the 1980s have led to a fourth stage in the evolution of marketing management—a period characterized by a societal orientation. It is increasingly obvious that marketing executives must act in a socially responsible manner if they wish to succeed, or even survive, in this era. External pressures—consumer discontent, concern for environmental problems, and political-legal forces—are influencing marketing programs in countless firms.

This fourth stage may also be viewed more broadly as a human-orientation period—a time in which there is a concern for the management of human resources. We sense a change in emphasis from materialism to humanitarianism in our society. One mark of an affluent society is a shift in consumption from products to services and a shift in cultural emphasis from things to people. In this fourth stage, marketing management must be concerned with creating and delivering a better quality of *life*, rather than only a better material standard of *living*.

Broadening the Marketing Concept

To some people, the wave of consumer protests starting in the 1960s and 1970s indicated that there had been a failure to implement the marketing concept. Others even suggested that the marketing concept, as an operational philosophy, might *conflict* with a company's social responsibility. From one point of view, these charges are true. A firm may totally satisfy its customers (in line with the marketing concept), while at the same time be adversely affecting society. To illustrate, a steel company in Ohio might be satisfying its customers in Texas with the right product, reasonably priced. Yet at the same time, this company is polluting the air and water in Ohio.

The marketing concept and a company's social responsibility can be quite compatible, however. They need not conflict. The key to compatibility lies in extending the **breadth** and **time** dimensions in the definition of the marketing concept.

Regarding *breadth*, we must recognize that a company's market includes more than just the buyers of the firm's products. This market also includes other people directly affected by the firm's operations. Under this broader definition of customers, the marketing concept and the social responsibility of the firm can indeed be compatible. In our example, the Ohio steel mill has several "customer" groups to satisfy: (1) the Texas customers of the steel shipments, (2) the customers of the impure air elements given off by the mill, (3) the recreational users of the local river affected by the mill waste matter, and (4) the community affected by employee traffic driving to and from work. This broadening of the marketing concept is consistent with our previously discussed broad definition of marketing. There we recognized that a given marketer may have several different target markets.

Regarding the extended *time* dimension, we must view consumer satisfaction and profitable business as goals to be achieved *over the long run*. If a company prospers in the long run, it must be doing a reasonably good job of satisfying its customers' current social and economic demands.

We want to make one final point in our broadening of the marketing concept. International competition is making it clear that American firms must devote more attention to product quality and product value. Certainly the idea of producing quality products at competitive prices is compatible with the customer-orientation feature of the marketing concept.

In summary, if the marketing concept and social responsibility are to be realistically compatible, management must strive *over the long run* to balance (1) satisfying the wants of product-buying customers, (2) satisfying the societal wants affected by the firm's activities, and (3) meeting the company's profit goals.

Sales-Force Management and the Total Marketing Program

So far we have been discussing marketing and marketing management. But this is a book about the management of a sales force—that is, the management of the personal selling effort of a firm. So now let's consider the relationship between sales-force management and marketing—and the place of personal selling in a company's total marketing program.

A company must operate its marketing system within a framework of forces that constitute the system's environment. Two sets of these forces are external to the company, and another two sets are internal (see Figures 1–4 and 1–5).

External Environment

Six macroenvironmental forces impinge considerably on any company's marketing system, yet they generally are *not* controllable by management. This set of forces includes:

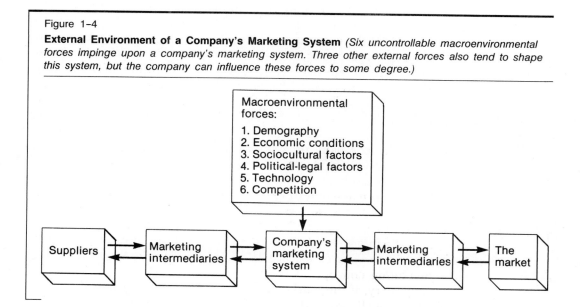

Figure 1–4

External Environment of a Company's Marketing System *(Six uncontrollable macroenvironmental forces impinge upon a company's marketing system. Three other external forces also tend to shape this system, but the company can influence these forces to some degree.)*

Macroenvironmental forces:

1. Demography
2. Economic conditions
3. Sociocultural factors
4. Political-legal factors
5. Technology
6. Competition

Suppliers → Marketing intermediaries → Company's marketing system → Marketing intermediaries → The market

- Demography.
- Economic conditions.
- Sociocultural factors.

- Political-legal factors.
- Technology.
- Competition.

In addition, a company faces a set of three forces which are also external, but which are *directly* a part of the firm's marketing system. These are the company's market, its suppliers, and marketing intermediaries (primarily middlemen). While generally classed as uncontrollable, these three elements are susceptible to a greater degree of company influence than the other six are. Note the two-way flows between the company and these three external elements in Figure 1–4. The company receives products and promotional messages from its suppliers. In return, the company sends payments and marketing information. The same types of exchanges occur between the company and its market. Any of these exchanges can go through one or more middlemen.

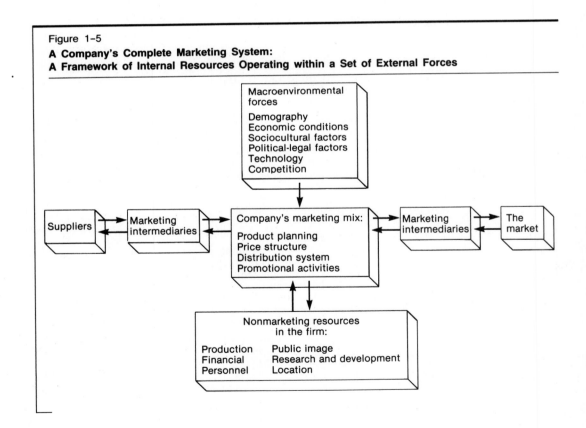

Figure 1–5

A Company's Complete Marketing System:
A Framework of Internal Resources Operating within a Set of External Forces

Internal Variables in Marketing Systems

To reach its marketing goals, management has at its disposal two sets of internal, controllable forces: (1) the company's resources in nonmarketing areas and (2) the components of its **marketing mix**— its product, price structure, promotional activities, and distribution system. Figure 1–5 shows these internal forces combined with the forces in the external environment illustrated in Figure 1–4. The result is the company's total marketing system, set within its environment.

The *marketing mix* is the term used to describe the combination of the four ingredients that constitute the core of a company's marketing system. When these four—product, price, distribution, and promotion—are effectively blended, they form a marketing program designed to provide want-satisfying goods and services to the company's market.

Promotional activities form a separate submix that we call the **promotional mix** or the **communications mix** in the company's marketing program. The major elements in the promotional mix are the company's advertising, sales promotion, and personal selling effort (see Figure 1–6). In the American economy, the most important of these three, by any measure—people employed, dollars spent, sales generated—is the personal selling effort. It is the management of that personal selling effort—the management of the sales force—that is the topic of this book.

Integrating Marketing and Sales Functions

Earlier we observed that many organizations today still pay little more than lip service to the marketing concept. In those companies, unfortunately, sales and marketing activities tend to be separated and sometimes even seem to be competing with each other. In a typical

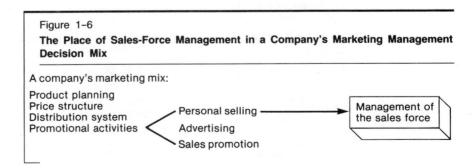

Figure 1–6

The Place of Sales-Force Management in a Company's Marketing Management Decision Mix

A company's marketing mix:

Product planning
Price structure
Distribution system
Promotional activities

Personal selling ⟶ Management of the sales force
Advertising
Sales promotion

marketing department, the marketing staff activities in the home office comprise one function and the field sales force effort is another function. Too often marketing staff executives fail to understand that field sales executives also are a part of the marketing management team. A lack of communication sometimes separates these two groups.

The marketing concept holds that sales activities are a part of marketing. Consequently, a company should do more than simply **coordinate** its sales and marketing activities. Management should fully **integrate** these two functions. One key to successfully implementing the market concept is management's ability to effectively integrate selling—the prime revenue-generating activity—with other marketing activities.[4]

Nature and Importance of Sales Management

Sales management (or sales-force management) is the management of the personal selling component of a company's marketing program. In the administrative structure of most firms, many executive echelons are involved in sales-force management. The term **sales manager** may be applied to any of the following:

- The top marketing executive.
- The head of the field sales force—sometimes called general sales manager.
- A divisional manager responsible for several districts. This sales manager is sometimes called a ''branch manager'' especially when the branch office carries product inventory and performs physical distribution activities.
- The manager of any one of those districts—often called district sales manager.
- An adminstrator in charge of the people who sell only one of the company's product lines.

In contrast, when we speak of executives in advertising or marketing research, we are speaking of relatively few people.

During the early stages of the evolution of marketing management, sales management was viewed quite narrowly. Generally it was limited to such tasks as recruiting and selecting a sales force, and then

[4] Bert Rosenbloom and Rolph E. Anderson, ''The Sales Manager: Tomorrow's Super Marketer,'' *Business Horizons*, March–April 1984, pp. 51–52. Also see Nick Di-Bari, ''Marketing vs. Sales! Is There Really a Difference?'' *Sales & Marketing Management*, November 10, 1984, pp. 51–53; and ''When Sales Meets Marketing,'' *Sales & Marketing Management*, May 13, 1985, p. 59.

training, supervising, and motivating these sales people. Today selling and sales management have taken on new dimensions. Furthermore, we are recognizing that a sales person's job and a sales executive's job are different from other jobs.

New Dimensions of Sales Management and Selling

As marketing management has evolved, the concepts of sales management and personal selling have assumed significantly broader dimensions. Today's top sales-force managers are involved more in setting sales goals, planning a program to reach these goals, and evaluating the results. Their job is to coordinate the field selling with the other elements in their company's total marketing program. Their role is more of a planning executive rather than an operations manager. Although they are still responsible for the general administration of sales-force activities, they spend less of their time in daily routine contacts with sales people.

In a similarly broad vein, today's sales representatives are managers of a market area—their territories. Often they are assigned a profit responsibility in those markets. In line with the marketing concept, the sales reps are trained to identify customers' wants and to help solve customers' problems. They must organize much of their own time and effort. They may participate in recruiting, market planning in their territories, and other managerial activities.[5]

Two other major developments have a considerable impact today in the field of industrial selling and sales management. One is the significant increase in the number of women who are going into industrial selling and sales management. The implications of this trend are discussed later in connection with selection, assimilation, training, and other aspects of operating a sales force. The second development is the growing expertise and sophistication among purchasing agents in business and nonbusiness organizations. These organizations are improving their inventory control systems. Among these systems, the "just-in-time" inventory system especially is gaining wider acceptance. Consequently, today's knowledgeable purchasing agents are looking for different characteristics in the sales people they deal with.

For several years *Purchasing* magazine has conducted an annual survey among its readers (primarily purchasing agents) to determine what attributes buyers most favor in sales people. Over the years the top five most desirable traits (in order of times mentioned) are:

---

[5] The term *sales rep* will be used frequently throughout this book as a short form of *sales representative*. Sales rep is commonly used in business and parallels such titles as *factory rep* or *manufacturer's rep*. We consider *sales rep* synonymous with *sales person, saleswoman,* or *salesman.*

1. Thoroughness and follow through.
2. Knowledge of the product line.
3. Willingness to go to bat for the buyer within the seller's firm.
4. Market knowledge and willingness to keep the buyer posted.
5. Imagination in applying his or her products to the buyer's needs.[6]

In a similar survey by *Sales & Marketing Management* magazine, the following characteristics were the ones that purchasing agents liked most in a sales person:

1. Reliability/credibility.
2. Professionalism/integrity.
3. Product knowledge.
4. Innovativeness in problem solving.
5. Sales presentation and preparation.[7]

To seek and/or develop these traits in a sales force today poses serious challenges to sales executives in their selection, training, compensation, and motivation programs. Technological developments in the computer field have brought an entirely new dimension to the tasks involved in personal selling and sales management. Throughout this book we will point out many personal selling activities in which computer-information technology can provide support for sales reps and improve their performance. Also, in virtually every phase of managing a sales force, we will see opportunities to improve management's performance by using computers and related information technology.[8]

How Sales Jobs Differ from Other Jobs

Why is it useful to study management of a sales force separately from the management of other classes of business personnel? Why are there no courses in the management of accountants or finance personnel? Separate treatment for sales people is warranted largely because a sales job is so different from other jobs and so important to a company's financial well-being. Now let's take a detailed look at some of the key differentiating features of a sales job.

---

[6] Alvin J. Williams and John Seminerio, "What Buyers Like from Salesmen," *Industrial Marketing Management*, May 1985, pp. 75–78.

[7] "PAs (Purchasing Agents) Examine the People Who Sell to Them," *Sales & Marketing Management*, November 11, 1985, pp. 38–41.

[8] For a starter, see Catherine L. Harris, "Information Power: How Companies Are Using New Technologies to Gain a Competitive Edge," *Business Week*, October 4, 1985, p. 110; and William M. Bulkeley, "Better Than a Smile: Salespeople Begin to Use Computers on the Job," *The Wall Street Journal*, September 13, 1985, p. 25.

The sales reps are the ones who generate the revenues that are managed by the financial people and used by the production people. Moreover, it is the sales force that is largely responsible for implementing the firm's marketing strategies in the field.

Sales people represent their company to customers and to society in general. Opinions of the firm and its products are formed on the basis of impressions left by these people in their work and outside activities. The public ordinarily does not judge a company by its factory or office workers. But because sales reps are so visible and available, they are often blamed for mistakes made elsewhere in the firm.

Typically, a factory or office employee works under the close supervisory control of a foreman or office manager. In contrast, sales reps operate with little or no direct supervision. Compared with a sales person, most other employee groups can perform successfully with relatively little stimulation. For success in many selling tasks, however, a sales rep must work hard physically and mentally, be creative and persistent, and show great initiative. These traits require a high degree of motivation.

A sales person needs more tact and social intelligence than other employees on the same level in the organization. Many sales jobs require the rep to mix socially with customers, who frequently are people of high rank in their companies. Considerable social intelligence may be needed in dealing with difficult buyers.

Sales people are among the few employees authorized to spend company funds. They have the responsibility for the proper use of money for entertainment, rooms, food, transportation, and other business expenses. Their effectiveness in discharging this responsibility can have a significant influence on marketing costs and profits.

Sales jobs frequently require considerable traveling and demand much time away from home and family. Being in the field puts sales people in enemy territory, so to speak. They must deal with an apparently endless stream of customers who may seem determined not to buy their products. The reps face mental stresses and disappointments, coupled with the physical demands of long hours, much traveling, strange beds and food, and perhaps heavy sample cases or catalogs. These factors combine to require a degree of mental toughness and physical stamina that is rarely demanded in other types of jobs. Selling is hard work!

How Sales Management Jobs Differ from Other Management Jobs

Some of the factors that make sales jobs different also affect the sales manager's job, which differs from other management jobs in several respects. The geographical deployment of the sales force means that the sales manager cannot directly oversee the work. Nor can the manager control the environment in which this work is done. Other aspects of jobs and careers in sales management are discussed in more detail in Chapter 24.

Importance of Management of the Sales Force

The attention devoted to marketing management in many businesses today should in no way lessen the importance of sales-force management. In fact, top administrators should be careful not to neglect the management of their sales forces in their preoccupation with marketing management.

When marketing management is stressed in a firm, executive attention is devoted to sales and market planning. Such emphasis may be well placed, but ordinarily it takes the sales force in the field to carry out the sales plan. No plan is of much value unless it is implemented properly. If sales people cannot sell successfully because they are improperly selected, trained, or compensated, then the efforts devoted to sales planning are of little value. About the only exceptions are firms that do not rely on their own sales force. Instead they primarily use advertising or agent middlemen, such as brokers or manufacturers' agents, to move the products. Since the sales force is critical to the success of a concern's marketing venture, sound management of these representatives is important.

The cost of managing and operating a sales force typically is the largest single operating expense for most firms. True, it is marketing's responsibility to generate sales-volume revenues. However, these revenues are valuable only if sales expenses incurred in getting the volume are reasonable. The public's attention and criticism are most often directed at advertising and the amounts a firm spends for television or magazine exposure. Yet the firm's total advertising expenditures may be only 3 or 4 percent of net sales. The total expenses related to sales people may be 15 or 20 percent of net sales.

Importance to you, the student.   For students, there is an added dimension to the study of sales-force management, because you soon may be involved in these activities. Within a year or two after graduation, you may well be serving as a sales supervisor or a district sales manager. Even as a sales person, you may engage in managerial activites, such as visiting your alma mater to do employee recruiting. You may be asked to do some sales forecasting for your territory or to offer suggestions regarding a proposed compensation or quota plan.

Sales-Force Managers' Preparation for the 1990s

If sales executives expect to manage their sales forces successfully during the coming decade, there are five areas in which these executives must improve their level of expertise. In preparation for the competitive environment of the 1990s, sales managers must develop:

- A better understanding of buyer behavior.
- Superior leadership and motivation skills.
- Ways to increase sales-force productivity—for example, better expense control and profitability analyses.
- A better understanding of computer-related technology useful in personal selling and sales management.
- An increased appreciation of ethical practices and social responsibility in personal selling and sales management.[9]

Each of these issues is discussed in varying depth periodically throughout this book.

Plan of This Book

Scope of the Book

This book deals specifically with the management of an *outside* sales force and its activities. Outside sales people are those who go to the customers, as distinguished from across-the-counter selling where the customers go to the sales people. Consequently, this book is concerned almost entirely with the management of the industrial sales force of manufacturers and wholesaling middlemen. However, our definition of an outside sales force also includes (1) retail sales people (such as auto dealers) who go to the customers, (2) producers who sell directly to household consumers (for example, insurance firms and in-home sellers such as Avon cosmetics), and (3) outside sales forces of nonbusiness organizations.

Sales-Force Management Model

The management process in any organization—selling or nonselling business or nonbusiness—basically consists of three stages: (1) planning a program, (2) implementing it, and (3) evaluating its results (see Figure 1–7).

The *planning* stage includes setting the goals and planning how to reach them. *Implementation* includes organizing and staffing the organization, and directing the actual operations of the organization according to the plans. The *evaluation* stage is a good example of the interrelated, continuing nature of the management process. That is, evaluation is both a look back and a look ahead. Looking back,

---

[9] Rosenbloom and Anderson, "The Sales Manager: Tomorrow's Super Marketer," pp. 52–56.

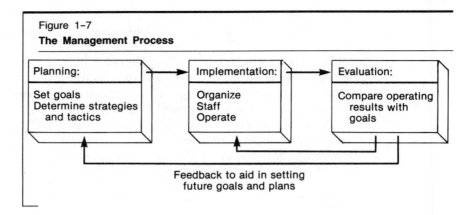

Figure 1–7
The Management Process

Planning:		Implementation:		Evaluation:
Set goals Determine strategies and tactics	→	Organize Staff Operate	→	Compare operating results with goals

Feedback to aid in setting
future goals and plans

management compares the operating results with the plans and goals. Looking ahead, this evaluation is used as an aid in future goal setting and strategic planning.

This book follows the management process as it relates to the strategic management of an outside sales force. The particular model we are using to structure this book is illustrated in Figure 1–8. Note that sales-force management must be placed within the context of marketing strategy and overall company strategy. Two seemingly similar firms in the same industry may come up with different goals, strategic planning, and operational procedures for their sales forces. The reason for these differences is simply that each company's marketing strategies and overall company strategies are different.

As you read through the model in Figure 1–8, you may wonder why sales planning comes so late in the book. If planning is the first stage in the management process, then why doesn't the section on sales planning appear after Chapter 2? Why does planning *follow*, instead of precede, Part 2 on sales staffing and operations and Chapter 3 on sales organization?

There is no question but that *logically* sales planning should follow Chapter 2. But *pedagogically*—that is, from a teaching and learning point of view—we believe it is better to cover sales-force staffing and operations before getting into sales planning. We believe that will make this course and this book far more interesting to you—the student. The topics in staffing and operating typically generate student interest and embody the challenge and dynamism that is modern sales-force management. To start early in the course with sales planning, including demand forecasting and budgeting and territorial design, might suggest that sales management is all statistics and accounting.

There is another basic reason for stressing the importance of staffing and operations. In the 1960s and 70s, both business and aca-

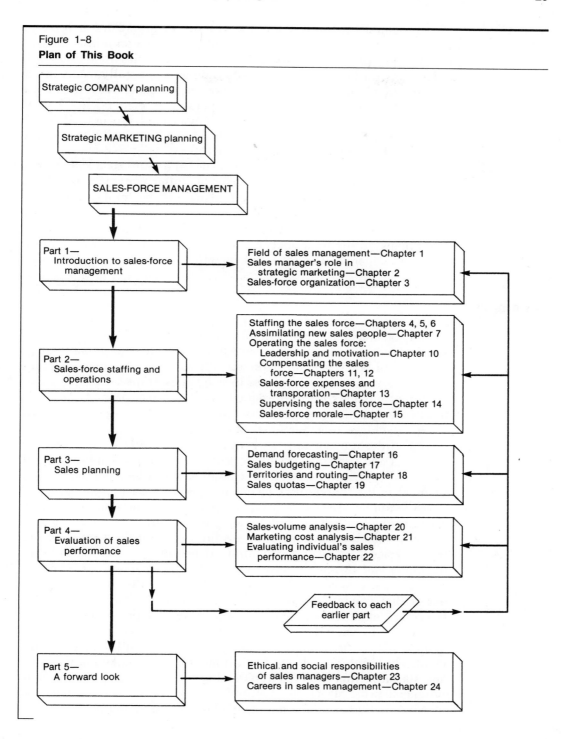

Figure 1–8
Plan of This Book

demia tended to de-emphasize sales-force management in favor of marketing management. Even in the 1980s, much attention is focused on strategic planning in marketing. This book tries to redress this balance. We want to present the situation as it generally exists in the real world of business. Actually, most sales executives spend the bulk of their time on staffing and operational matters, not on the planning or evaluation stages of the management process. Also, the cost of staffing and operating a sales force is usually by far the largest single marketing cost in most firms.

Too often, planning executives leave the impression that they think the job is finished when their planning work is done. They seem to take for granted that their plans will be implemented successfully. However, neither of these generalizations is correct. It takes an effectively managed sales force in the field to carry out these plans. In the final analysis, it is the sales force operating in the field that generates the revenues for most companies.

Summary

In a societal sense, marketing is any exchange activity intended to satisfy human wants. In this context we need to look broadly at (1) who should be classed as marketers, (2) what is being marketed, and (3) who are the target markets. In a business sense, marketing is a system of business action designed to plan, price, promote, and distribute want-satisfying products and services to target markets in order to achieve organizational objectives.

The philosophy of the marketing concept holds that a company should (1) be customer oriented, (2) strive for a profitable sales volume, and (3) coordinate all its marketing activities. Marketing management is the marketing concept in action.

Marketing management has evolved from a production-oriented stage, through a sales-oriented stage, into today's customer-oriented economy of abundance. In this evolution, a fourth stage is emerging—a stage that focuses attention (1) on human and societal relationships and (2) on the need to broaden the marketing concept.

A company operates its marketing system within a framework of forces that constitute the system's environment. Two sets of these forces are external variables that generally cannot be controlled by executives in an individual firm. Another two sets of these forces operate within the firm, and they are largely controllable by management. These internal factors are a company's nonmarketing resources and its marketing mix. This marketing mix—the combination of its products, price structure, distribution system, and promotional activities—is the core of a company's marketing system.

A company's promotional program—its promotional mix—consists of its personal selling, advertising, and sales-promotion activities. The topic of this book—sales management or sales-force management—is the management of the personal selling component of a company's marketing program.

Sales management thus constitutes an important part of a company's strategic marketing planning. As marketing management has evolved, the concepts of personal selling and sales management have taken on significantly broader dimensions. However, sales jobs still are quite different from other jobs, and consequently, sales-management jobs are different from other management jobs.

Questions and Problems

1. For each of the following organizations, describe what is being marketed and what the target market is.
   a. Chicago Bears professional football team.
   b. United Automobile Workers labor union.
   c. Professor teaching a freshman sociology course.
   d. Police department in your city.
2. Identify some of the nonbusiness organizations to which you belong. Then describe some of the ways in which these organizations are engaged in marketing activities.
3. What is the marketing concept?
4. Explain the differences between the production stage and the sales stage in the evolution of marketing management.
5. Carefully distinguish between the sales stage and the marketing stage in the evolution of marketing management.
6. Name some companies that you believe are still in the production stage. In the sales stage. Explain your reasoning in each example.
7. The president of Pepsi-Cola Company has said, "Our business is the business of marketing." How would you explain this idea to a student majoring in accounting, finance, or production management?
8. The quotation at the beginning of the chapter is "Nothing happens until somebody sells something." How would you convince a lawyer, production manager, farmer, banker, or aerospace engineer that the statement is true?
9. Explain how the six macroenvironmental forces listed in Figure 1–4 might influence a company's marketing program.
10. Explain the concept of the marketing mix and its relation to the management of a sales force.

11. Do you agree that "A sales job requires a degree of mental toughness and physical stamina rarely demanded in other types of jobs"? Discuss.

12. Explain why sales-force management should continue to receive executive attention in a firm, even after the company adopts the marketing management concept.

2

Sales Managers and Strategic Marketing

*"And what do you do for your firm?" asked a golfer of
his new acquaintance.
"I'm manager of strategic accounts," was the reply.
"Is that what we used to call key accounts?"
"No. It's those customers who pay their bills!"*

"In all the years I spent in the field selling, I had no idea what the sales manager really did while I was contacting accounts. I thought he was hired mainly to yell at us and keep us working hard. Now I know better. My first six months as sales manager have been largely spent processing paperwork and attending meetings," declared a newly appointed sales manager.

He continued, "The sales reps don't see 90 percent of what I do to make all the right things happen at the right time and what I do to try to avoid many of the bad things as we can."

Let's examine what sales managers do to earn their keep.

A company manages its sales force within the context of its strategic marketing program. Strategic marketing planning, in turn, depends on the overall company planning. Thus, when shaping their sales-force management strategy, sales executives are both limited and guided by their firm's strategic marketing planning and total company planning.

In this chapter we will first explore some of the administrative aspects of a sales manager's job as he or she runs a sales force within this marketing and corporate framework. Then we will apply some of these administrative concepts as we consider the relationships in strategic planning at the corporate, marketing, and sales-force levels.

A Sales Manager as an Administrator

One of the ironies of sales-force management is that the people in charge usually acquire their position on the basis of their talent as sales people, but succeed or fail depending on their administrative skills. These skills may or may not have been developed as the people moved up in the organization. At this point let's examine some managerial concepts as they apply to a sales manager's job.

Administration a Distinct Skill

Only recently has administration been recognized as a separate body of knowledge. The concept of managing people encounters resistance in many circles. Many scholars have refused to recognize management as an acceptable subject for study.[1] Perhaps our reluctance to acknowledge it stems from our cultural distaste for the idea of manipulating people to do what needs to be done. Call it what you want, but this is management. Few things would happen in this world without it.

Technical ability not sufficient. Although many people with outstanding technical abilities do make good administrators, there is considerable evidence that technical talent alone does not necessarily make a good manager. (Witness the sports world, where many successful coaches—administrators—were only average players.)

In the entrepreneurial world, the technical genius who creates the concept around which a new venture is built seldom has the managerial skills needed to make the new enterprise successful. Three other types of managers are needed to make new ventures into large successful corporations: the driving force, the organizer, and the operational manager. The driving force is the person who gathers the resources together to make the enterprise a reality and then drives it to market. As the firm grows, the organizer ensures order with proper control systems and operational procedures. The operational manager is the person who is skilled in keeping the organization functioning efficiently once it is up and running.

In the sales field, it is widely recognized that the best sales person may not make even a passable sales manager. The very factors that create an outstanding sales person often cause failure as an administrator. For example, most highly successful sales people like extensive personal contact with customers in the field. Yet sales managers who try to hold onto their accounts spend too much time in the field and neglect their office work. Moreover, many successful sales people have strong, aggressive personalities, which can be a liability in working closely with other people in the organization. Finally, the

---

[1] One early (1530) writer on administration, Niccolo Machiavelli, consistently has been criticized for his observations on the art of administering the activities of other people, even though his book *The Prince* has endured through the ages.

detail and organizational work most sales personalities detest are essential duties of the sales manager.

But at the same time you should not jump to the opposite conclusion—that top sales producers never make good sales managers. By all means, the firm's top sales people should be given every consideration when an opening in management develops. To do otherwise courts serious morale problems. The rank-and-file sales people would then have good reason to wonder what they have to do to be promoted.

While possession of technical skills does not necessarily make a good administrator, some degree of proficiency is needed. It would be difficult to envision a successful sales manager who had little knowledge of selling. First, a sales manager planning to hire sales people must know what attributes to look for. Second, the manager who lacks technical skills is continually at the mercy of subordinates. He cannot evaluate their competency or the soundness of their recommendations or methods of operation. Third, the sales manager must make the sales force confident that he can lead them. Successful sales experience can inspire such confidence. Finally, a person who is not fairly successful in selling may never get the chance to become a sales manager, no matter how potentially good an administrator he may be.

Universality of management principles. Most of the activities people engage in (such as war, business, sports) are goal directed—the participants seek to achieve something. Individuals join together in the belief that they have the same goals and they are more likely to achieve them as a group. If any semblance of efficiency and orderly progress toward the goals is to be realized, the groups' activities must be managed—that is, planned and controlled.

The fundamental principles underlying success in administering all types of behavior are essentially the same. The memoirs of military leaders and coaches reveal that the basic principles underlying their success were no different than those business leaders have adopted. General Ulysses S. Grant was far more concerned with the qualities of his subordinates than with military strategy and tactics. Coaches attribute their success to subordinates, training programs, recruiting and selection procedures, and team morale.

It is this universality of management principles that allows the executive to transfer administrative abilities from one job to another. The existence of these management principles makes administration a distinct skill separate from technical abilities.

Management can be learned. One top executive of a vigorously growing company, a leader in the Young President's Organization, confessed to a group of business students that he discovered he was a terrible manager in his very first job. He set out to rectify this deficiency by volunteering for charitable work. In this way he learned how to organize people and get them to work together. It was slow going, but he claimed it was well worth the effort.

Another young president reported he had learned a great deal about administration by studying executives and how they behaved in managing their enterprises. Observing the tactical behavior of both successful and unsuccessful managers helped him form some ideas on what and what not to do in managing people. The continuing growth of the huge management development industry is a direct result of the recognition that there is a body of management knowledge that can be taught and learned. The seminar business is booming.

The moral of these tales is that you can learn to manage. There is no inborn managerial trait. But don't be misled; it takes great effort.

What a Sales Manager Does

A glance at the table of contents of this book will provide some idea of the general scope of the sales manager's duties. Chapter 24, "Careers in Sales Management," gives a detailed, personal view of the job.

First, a sales manager is responsible for hiring the sales force, arranging it in some meaningful organizational structure, and deploying it geographically. These activities are focused on maintaining a group of people in the field to sell the company's products and services. But that is only the beginning. Sales people need training, supervision, and motivation. These are the tasks devoted to improving performance of the sales force. The sales people must be compensated by some meaningful scheme. Also the expenses they incur in pursuing the company's business must be reimbursed.

Planning is well recognized as one of management's main functions. A sales manager must analyze markets, develop sales forecasts, formulate budgets, set quotas, establish territories, and plot operational plans. The manager who did not analyze and evaluate sales performance with an eye to improving it would be negligent. These are the obvious activities of the sales manager.

Sales managers also perform numerous tasks that can be described as troubleshooting. Customer relations figure largely in the sales manager's day. Things go wrong. Orders are late or incomplete. The wrong goods are sent. The goods are not what was ordered or are not of the expected quality. The credit department is giving a slow-paying customer a bad time. The list could go on.

A sales manager must also handle competitors, who seldom do what the company would like them to do. They cut prices, invade markets, bring out new products, hire away sales people, and steal accounts or dealers. They can also get rough and use unethical, even illegal, tactics to gain an increased share of the market. The sales manager is expected to handle such competitive developments and prevent the firm from being hurt by them.

Even within the organization the sales manager must cope with problems. The accountant questions expense accounts and can see no reason why the sales department needs more funds. Production is not making the right products; the customers want one model but the production planners produce more of another. The personnel manager insists that the sales department must hire more people from minority groups.

A sales manager's schedule is subject to constant interruption. In the morning mail there is a letter from the Federal Trade Commission accusing the company's sales force of misrepresentation. The manager will have to spend a great deal of time with the firm's lawyers to answer the charge. A college student majoring in marketing appears at the door and asks for an interview. The student's sales-management professor has assigned a term paper in which a sales manager must be interviewed. There goes another afternoon.

Such activities, and many of the things sales managers do, could be classified as fighting fires. Sometimes they have little time left to devote to the basic things they should be doing, such as the topics covered in this book. They usually want to spend more time with the sales force and regret the amount of time they must spend on other things.

The Six Publics of a Sales Executive

A sales manager must be able to handle relationships with numerous other people. In their transactions with a sales manager, these people may be:

- Superiors.
- Equals.
- Subordinates.
- Competitors.
- Members of the community.
- Customers.

Superiors, equals, and subordinates may be people in the manager's own organization or in those of customers or competitors (Figure 2–1).

Each of these six publics requires different applications of strategy and tactics. It is a mistake for an administrator to think that everyone

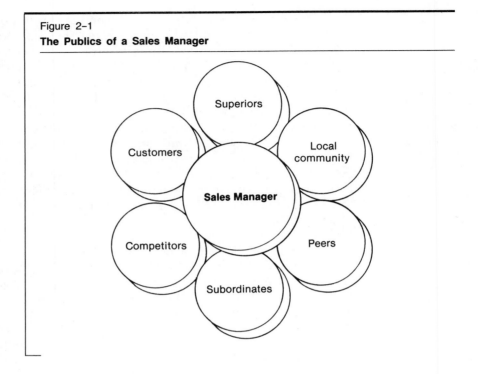

Figure 2–1
The Publics of a Sales Manager

can be handled in the same manner. Obviously, the same approach cannot be used on both superiors and subordinates, nor can the same strategies be used in dealing with competitors and customers. Deception may achieve results when used with a rival, but it can be disastrous if applied to customer relations. Presenting a fait accompli, without allowing further consideration, might be the correct tactic for use within an organization. However, a community could get incensed over its use in some matter involving social welfare.

The Responsibilities of an Administrator

> The fundamental responsibility of an administrator is to staff the organization with the right people.

This statement expresses the basic philosophy of this book regarding managing people. Above all else, the administrator's basic duty in an organization is to staff it properly.

If the right people have been hired, even bad plans may be successful. But more important, the right people will not make bad plans. They eliminate or considerably lessen most of the manager's problems. With competent individuals, training is easier and more effective, compensation plans work as intended, minimum supervision and stimulation are required, and control of efforts poses fewer problems. In short, if competent individuals are hired, life is easier for the manager.

This is particularly important in sales management because marketing is an art of execution. The success of most marketing plans rests not so much with the plan as with the aptness with which it is carried out. Actually, devising proper marketing strategies is not at all difficult. Most of the time, the necessary actions are quite obvious. The success of the endeavor depends on the execution of the plan: how well the advertising is done, how well the sales force does its job, and how well the product is made.

If people are hired who are not able to implement the plans successfully, they can ruin the best of plans. If the right person is not hired for a sales job, training is a major problem. A below-par sales rep requires constant attention and stimulation, and even then may not be able to perform satisfactorily. Morale of the sales force is a critical factor when poorly placed individuals convey their discontent to their fellow workers.

Immediate Subordinates

The sales manager is most concerned with immediate subordinates. If you do a good job picking your subordinates, they will in turn select the right people to serve under them. With the right subordinates, an executive may succeed in spite of himself.

Executives who cannot delegate responsibility and authority to their subordinates are not really administrators. They are just highly paid workers. No organization can grow with one person running it. The capacity of a single individual is too limited. Sooner or later the individual must give way. When that happens, the firm is in trouble if no provison has been made for a successor.

Objectives, Strategies, and Tactics

These three concepts are the heart of strategic planning at any level in an organization's hierarchy. To be an effective administrator, any sales manager should have a thorough understanding of these concepts—what they are and how a manger can use them.

Objectives

Objectives are necessary in planning operations—a plan needs goals. Without them, it is impossible to create any meaningful design in the plan.

The primary goal chosen by the founder of Staar Surgical Company was to make the new enterprise the dominant firm in the emerging small-incision eye surgery industry. That goal dictated its subsequent decisions at every step. It did not invest in any attractive new ventures in eye-care technology that did not fit into the small-incision surgery category. One venture in a portable oxygen generator was so attractive that it was undertaken outside of the Staar organization.

The need for specific, written objectives. In the hurry and confusion of routine business operations, an activity's purpose is easily lost. Written objectives are clearer and easier to keep in mind. Everyone should know them and be able to refer to them.

Objectives must be more than platitudes. Such mouthings as "We should be of service to our customers and treat our employees fairly" are only hazy guideposts for making business decisions. To be useful, objectives must be specific. Then an executive cannot use them to justify whatever decision he or she wants to make.

Alignment of objectives and decisions. Once the firm's objectives are agreed on, all decisions should be in alignment with them. Decisions that are incompatible with objectives serve only to deter realization of goals.[2]

This alignment seems simple and obvious, but it is not easy to achieve. All objectives are not compatible with one another. If a firm aims for a 15 percent return on investment and also wants a 10 percent annual growth rate, these two objectives will eventually clash. Heublein, Inc., encountered this difficulty in acquiring Hamms beer. One of Heublein's objectives was 15 percent rate of return on its investment. It also had ambitious growth objectives. Heublein management had the opportunity to buy Hamms, whose large sales volume nicely fit the company's growth objective. However, profits in the beer business are far less than 15 percent. Hamms was making about a 5 percent return on investment. If Heublein tried to satisfy the growth objective, the profit objective would have to be sacrificed. A few years later Heublein sold Hamms at a loss.

A priority of objectives is necessary to guide managers in making decisions that conflict with one or more objectives while fulfilling

---

[2] For a discussion of the importance of coordinating sales-force tactics with company goals, see Bruce D. Buskirk, "Make Sure Sales Force Tactics, Firm's Goals Don't Conflict," *Marketing News,* March 18, 1983, p. 20.

others. The more objectives management establishes, the more conflicts it will have to resolve. Given too many objectives, managers
may become lost in a sea of goals, throw up their hands, and make
their decisions solely on the basis of personal judgment. Some firms'
objectives are so prolific and conflicting that clever executives can
usually find some goal to use for justifying their decisions.

Strategies

The words **objectives, strategies,** and **tactics** gain more meaning
when viewed in relation to each other as in Figure 2–2. What may be
an objective to a manager of one product may be only part of the
strategy of the president of the company. For instance, the product
manager may be given the dictate to achieve a certain dollar volume
of sales in a coming period. He proceeds to form strategies and tactics to accomplish this goal. However, this sales volume may be only
one small portion of the operating strategy of top management,
whose *objective* may be the realization of a certain amount of profit
or a certain level of operations for the period. No matter what the
objective may be, the *strategy* is the plan of action by which the
administrator hopes to achieve it, and the *tactics* are the details that
activate the plan.

Every organization must have some plan of action—a strategy to
be used—whether it is recognized or unrecognized. If the executive
allows the strategy to go unrecognized, a dangerous situation may
arise. An unrecognized plan of action cannot be evaluated or altered
to meet conditions as they are encountered. The plan must be
brought out into the open before the leaders can obtain maximum

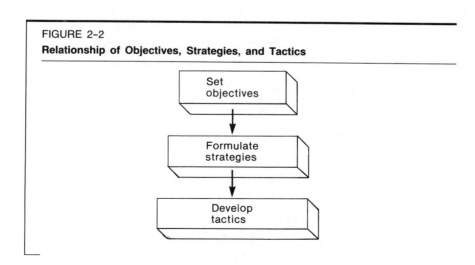

FIGURE 2–2
Relationship of Objectives, Strategies, and Tactics

use of it. If the strategy is not recognized, it will probably be implemented with the wrong tactics.

The strategies chosen should be followed with some degree of perseverance. Some strategies require time to be effective. Impatient managers who are eager for results may not allow certain programs the time to bear fruit. They often take new products off the market before the products have had a fair chance to develop a following. One sales manager fired a representative who had been sent to open up a new territory because dealers were not flocking to the product as fast as the manager had expected. The fault was not that the sales rep was inefficient, but rather that the manager had unrealistic expectations.

Tactics

In both the academic and business worlds, so much attention of late has been focused on the *strategic* aspects of operations that the role of tactics[3] has been often overlooked.

The importance of tactics.　Many fine strategies with highly desirable goals have failed for want of proper tactics. A sales manager formulated a new compensation plan designed to increase both sales and sales people's earnings—worthy goals. But he gave no thought to tactics. When he tried a direct frontal attack, he was soundly defeated by the sales people, who were afraid of the new plan. Other tactics could have carried the day.

Indeed, many ill-advised strategies have been successful due to the use of excellent tactics. For example, a college administrator had developed an organizational plan he wished to have adopted. Unfortunately, it was a very bad plan, as subsequent events made obvious. Through expert tactical moves, he overcame the opposition that would have easily sidetracked the plan under more normal circumstances.

Little has been written about administrative tactics. We do not like the idea of tactics. In our society it is not acceptable to appear as if we are manipulating people, and most tactics focus on manipulating people or structuring situations. Moreover, many tactics, when improperly applied, are considered unethical. Some administrators probably would be more willing to talk about their private lives than about the tactics they use in reaching their goals, and for good reason. It is usually best for other people to remain unaware of the tactics being used on them.

Proper use of tactics.　Tactics themselves are amoral—they are neither good nor bad. They are simply behavior. There are no perfect

---

[3] The material in this section is based on Richard H. Buskirk, *Handbook of Managerial Tactics* (Boston: CBI, 1976).

tactics, and in any situation there is no one *best* tactic that can be used. Many tactics may work, some better than others.

Many administrators mistakenly use the same tactics repeatedly, regardless of the circumstances. They develop such habits because the favored tactics have worked for them previously. Success reinforces the habit of using a tactic. But success can be lulling. There comes a time when the tactic will not work, and that is usually a most critical time.

The classic example of administrative inability to vary tactics is the forceful, hard-hitting executive who uses strong, authoritarian tactics to climb through the ranks. Such an executive will discover that at the top such tactics are not effective in dealing with others of equal ability. New tactics are needed for the new environment. The manager who is unable to make the necessary tactical adjustments fails.

Tactical evaluation of the situation. Tactical evaluation involves deciding which tactics to use in a situation. In making this decision, the manager must decide how to confront the other party in the situation, whether peers, subordinates, customers, or competitors.

An executive faces a number of considerations when deciding on a tactical course of action. In Figure 2–3 are some of the more critical elements in the tactical model.

Personalities. People react to situations in different ways. Some adversaries are belligerent and combative. Any direct action that would antagonize them might prod them into doing exactly what the manager does not want them to do. In such cases it would be better to use indirect tactics. Other people are more passive and less apt to take offense at tactical actions. The relative belligerency of the other person's personality is only one of a multitude of character traits to be considered in making tactical decisions.

One's own personality characteristics must also be recognized. Trying to bluff is folly if one cannot carry through on the acting skills necessary to make the bluff believeable to the other party. Some managers find that their personalities are better suited for dealing with other people on a one-to-one basis rather than in groups. In their tactical maneuvering, they try to avoid group meetings and confrontations.

Stakes. How much money is involved? If the stakes are high, more forceful tactics may be needed than if the matter is inconsequential. On minor issues, many managers might choose to ignore the adversary in the matter.

Power bases. The power held, or perceived to be held, by both parties plays a pivotal role in tactical selection. The manager who has a strong unassailable power base can make forceful tactical moves. Managers who do not have the right to fire subordinates for

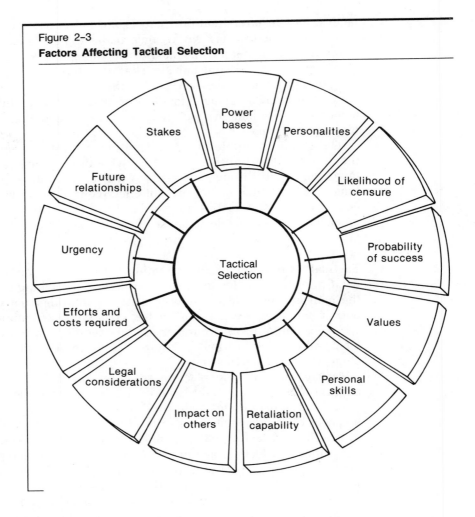

Figure 2–3
Factors Affecting Tactical Selection

example, must use other tactics. As a general rule, managers have less power than they think they do. Power is also elusive. One may have it one day and not the next.

Future relationships.   The manager cannot treat a customer that the firm hopes to do future business with the same way as one who will be served only once. And the firm might be willing to take an errant supplier to court to satisfy a contract but would never do so with a good customer.

Censure.   Certain tactics, if their use is publicly known, can result in censure by others. Tactics rarely remain secret, so those used should be able to bear up under scrutiny. Some managers mistakenly believe that the opinions of subordinates are not important. However, in any such conflict, it may be easier for the firm to fire a manager than a whole sales force.

Retaliation capabilities.   It makes sense to treat people carefully if they are in a position to retaliate. Taxpayers instinctively know they should not give the Internal Revenue Service a bad time, and who would anger a traffic officer?

Urgency.   The time dimensions of the matter must be appraised. If quick action is needed, direct, forceful tactics may have to be used. If there is enough time, more indirect, persuasive tactics may be in order.

Probability of success.   Tactics have different likelihoods of success in different situations. Some managers become so enchanted with a certain tactic they try to use it in situations in which it will not work. A football coach may favor a power running attack so much that he insists on it even when passing tactics are clearly called for. A manager may enjoy communicating with the sales force informally, but may use the tactic when it is inappropriate.

Efforts required.   Some tactics require more managerial effort than others. Often the matter is not worth the effort it would take to handle it a certain way. A customer balks at paying a $2 late charge; merchandise arrives with slight damages costing about $5 to repair. Many managers ignore such issues, since the effort to handle them exceeds the gain to be realized.

Personal skills.   Some people can do certain things easily, others cannot. The manager who finds it difficult to fire people develops other ways of accomplishing the same task. The person who does not talk well resorts to written communications. Managers should use tactics at which they are adept.

Legal considerations.   Some issues are loaded with potential legal liability. If the firm could end up in court on the matter, the selection of tactics should be made carefully. There should be no reason to question their legality. One tactic would be to get the other party to commit itself on paper and to prepare appropriate documents for the firm.

Values.   The manager's personal values should play a key role in tactical selection. You should not do things that you don't feel right about. Some managers will not fire a subordinate. They go out of their way to find some useful place in the organization for the person. Lying is a tactic many people use, to one degree or another. For others, any untruth violates their personal values.

Impact on others.   While the manager may intend for a tactic to be directed at a particular person, often it affects others. One manager hoped to drive out a subordinate with whom he clashed personally by harassing and insulting him. But the subordinate would have none of it; he fought back. The resulting conflict tore apart a previously united organization. The manager had not only badly misjudged his adversary, but he overlooked the conflict's impact on the organization.

In conclusion, the manager has many things to consider in selecting the tactics to use in a certain situation. The greater the issue, the more carefully these factors should be weighed.

An example of tactical decision making. The preceding discussion of tactics has been abstract. A following example of tactical decision making will provide a more concrete idea of what tactics are and do.

Bill Griff had been one of the company's leading salesmen for more than a decade. But his performance was steadily declining because he resorted to alcohol to console himself over his marital difficulties. Since Griff's territory had become a weak spot in the firm's distributive system, Henry Ewald, the sales manager, decided it had to be brought back to its former sales level. Something would have to be done regarding Griff.

Thus Ewald had to make a critical strategic decision—either dismiss Griff or reform him. Since a sober Griff was a proven performer with a great deal of value to the company, Ewald decided to first try to help Griff refrain from drinking. The plan was to keep Griff sober.

The manager mulled over the multitude of tactics open to him but settled on a direct, no-nonsense approach. Past experience had indicated that unless the alcoholic sincerely regretted his situation and desperately wanted to remedy it, there was no hope. So he flew out to talk with Griff. Note that the manager went to see the salesman rather than having the man come to see him. This was a deliberate tactic selected because Ewald wanted to investigate Griff's home situation and examine his present relationships with a few key accounts.

It soon became apparent that Griff was not likely to change. "I can handle my liquor. . . . It's just that competition is tougher these days. . . . I'm just as good as ever!" were the excuses Griff offered.

Ewald knew he should move fast to minimize the damage, since he saw little but grief in Griff's future. He would have preferred to discharge Griff. However, to do so might have created some problems in the home office if Griff were to complain to top management.

Ewald decided he would have to let Griff hang himself (a tactic). Edwald furnished the rope (a tactic) by sending Griff a long letter relating his sales history and clearly telling him that henceforth, if he did not meet all quotas, he would be dismissed. Then the manager touched all bases (a tactic) by informing his superiors of the situation. As a bonus, he projected an image to the sales force (news of such situations always gets around) of being a fair man: "Ewald gave Griff every chance!" Moreover, he bought some time to locate a replacement for Griff.

Had Griff straightened himself out, the problem would have been solved. Since his performance continued to be unsatisfactory, however, he was fired. There were no repercussions; everyone understood. In this case we will never know what the outcome would have been had Griff been fired right after Ewald's visit. It might have been uneventful, but not likely. Firing a formerly good sales rep of long-standing is not to be done casually. No doubt some other tactics would have worked as well. Yet, some would have been disastrous. It all depends on the players and the situation.

Strategic Planning at Company—Marketing— and Sales-Force Levels

Several of the administrative concepts that we just discussed are involved in the strategic planning process for the total company, its marketing program, and its sales-force operations. The strategic planning on all levels in a firm should be well integrated and highly coordinated. In any organization, the planning should start at the top and guide the entire organization. Thus, decisions at the top shape the strategic management of the marketing program. Marketing planning, in turn, determines the strategic course of sales-force management.

Strategic Planning for Total Company

Strategic planning for the total company involves determining (1) the organization's mission, (2) the broad objectives (goals) that will enable the company to fulfill its mission, and (3) the strategies and tactics needed to achieve the objectives.

Thus, strategic planning starts with identifying the organization's broad, fundamental mission—that is, management should decide essentially "What business are we in?" and "What business should we be in?" The answers to these two questions may or may not be the same. A television manufacturer may say it is in the indoor entertainment business. But after further analysis of its market opportunities, management may say its mission is to be in the entertainment and education business.

A company's mission is influenced by the firm's external and internal environments. The external environment consists of elements such as demography, the economy, political-legal influences, technology, and competition. The internal environment refers to the organization's human and financial resources.

Once its mission is determined, management can set broad goals that are consistent with that mission. For example, the company may aim to (1) earn a 20 percent return on investment next year, or (2) increase its market share from the present 8 percent to a level of 20 percent in three years.

The next step is to select the strategy to be used to reach the goal. As examples, consider the following relationships:

Goals	Possible Strategies
1. Earn 20 percent return on investment next year.	A. Reduce production and marketing costs. B. Increase rate of capital turnover.
2. Increase market share from present 8 percent to 20 percent in two years.	A. Intensify marketing efforts in domestic markets. B. Expand into foreign markets.

The tactics selected to implement the strategy would, of course, depend on what strategy was chosen. That is, usually a different set of tactics is needed to implement each different strategy. Thus, if the strategy is to reduce marketing costs, management can use such tactics as (1) cutting advertising expenses by 10 percent or (2) closing two branch offices. To implement the strategy of intensifying the domestic marketing effort, management might (1) add 20 more sales reps or (2) change the compensation plan to provide greater motivation for the sales force.

Strategic Marketing Planning

Once the total company planning process is completed, essentially the same procedure can be repeated for the marketing program. The strategic planning in any of the functional areas (for example, marketing, production) must be integrated with the total corporate planning.

The goals, strategies, and tactics at the marketing level are closely related to those at the corporate level. For example, a corporate strategy often translates into a marketing goal. To illustrate:

Company Goal	Company Strategy (marketing goal)	Marketing Strategy
1. Earn 20 percent return on investment.	Cut marketing costs by 15 percent this year.	Reduce direct selling effort by using wholesalers to reach small accounts.
2. Increase market share from present 8 percent to 20 percent.	Expand into foreign markets. Sales target of $2 million next year.	Establish distribution network in Western Europe.

Sales-Force Strategy

Once the strategic planning process for the entire marketing program has been completed, the role of the sales force has largely been established. That is, the goals, strategies, and tactics adopted by sales managers generally are limited and guided by the strategic marketing plan. To illustrate:

Corporate goal:	Increase market share from 8 to 20 percent in two years.
Corporate strategy: (Marketing goal)	Intensify market efforts in domestic markets so as to increase sales volume by $3 million next year.
Marketing strategy: (Sales-force goal)	A. Enter new geographic markets and sell to new types of customers, or B. Cover existing geographic markets more aggressively.

Now, whether the company elects to pursue marketing strategy (sales-force goal) A or B will make a big difference in the choice of sales-force strategies and tactics. These differences may be illustrated as follows:

Marketing Strategy (sales-force goal)	Sales-Force Strategy	Sales-Force Tactics
A. Enter new markets.	Build long-term customer relations.	1. Stress missionary selling in sales training and supervision. 2. Stress salary element in compensation plan.
B. Sell aggressively in existing markets.	Increase sales-force motivation.	1. Conduct more sales contests. 2. Stress commission feature in pay plan. 3. Increase field supervision.

In many companies, this strategic sales-force planning is continued down the organizational hierarchy. That is, sales-force goals and strategies are established for regional sales divisions, and even for individual sales reps and key accounts.

Summary

Modern sales managers understand that they are but one link in the total marketing strategy for the firm. Moreover, they understand the place of the firm's marketing strategy within their company's total strategic plan.

Administration is a distinct skill separate from operational skills. A great sales producer may not be a good sales manager. Yet the sales manager needs some technical skill in selling in order to recognize good selling, train recruits, and inspire confidence among the sales force.

The key responsibility of the administrator is the staffing of the organization. Selecting subordinates is the single most important function of the sales manager.

The setting of specific, clear-cut objectives is an essential step in the management of a company. Once the company's goals are set, then management can develop appropriate strategies for achieving those objectives. Tactics are the organizational behavior that executes the strategy.

Strategic planning on all levels in a firm should be coordinated. This planning should start at the top and guide the entire organization. Thus, decisions at the top shape the strategic planning in the marketing program. Then the marketing planning determines the strategic course of sales-force management.

Questions and Problems

1. Why do many successful sales people fail to become successful sales managers?
2. Under what circumstances could a successful sales person also become a successful sales manager?
3. Why might a highly paid sales rep accept a reduction in earnings to become a sales manager?
4. Suppose you are a sales person. What traits should a sales manager have to manage you successfully?
5. Some observers have not been overly impressed with the transferability of administrative talents between significantly different organizations. They point to the difficulties many high-ranking military officers have upon retiring in trying to move into corporate management. What are the barriers to moving into corporate management from the government or the armed forces?
6. Why do emotions interfere with good managerial judgment?
7. What causes people to lose confidence in the leadership capabilities of their boss?
8. In what way is the existence of a sales force the reflection of a strategy?
9. Describe a situation in which you prevailed through adept tactical maneuvering.
10. One noted management writer (Stephen Kerr) has observed that it is folly to expect behavior A when rewarding behavior B. How might his insight be applied to the problem of aligning sales-force behavior with corporate goals?

Case 2-1

Executives Insurance Company

Superior Sales Rep Doing Poorly as a Manager

The western regional sales manager of the Executives Insurance Company, Henry Vidmar, was wondering what he should do about what he called the "Paul Kauffman situation." For 10 years Mr. Kauffman had been a member of the million dollar round table in San Francisco, California. (To qualify as a member of this group, in one year an insurance agent had to write insurance policies whose face value totaled at least $1 million.) Over three years ago, at his own request, Mr. Kauffman had been promoted to the position of sales manager in the new office which the company had opened in Salt Lake City, Utah. Since that time, he had not met the company's expectations in recruiting and keeping successful sales representatives (agents). Mr. Vidmar and other executives wanted to correct that situation.

Executives Insurance Company, with headquarters in Dallas, Texas, was licensed to sell in 40 states. Currently, the company carried an A rating (excellent) from the Alfred Best Company, an independent rating organization in the insurance industry. The Executives Company sold both health and life insurance to business executives. It also sold group policies covering all employees in a firm. In recent years Executives had broadened its market to include people not directly working for any firm.

During his years as a salesman, Paul Kauffman had won eight overseas trips, one car, a set of luggage, and various other incentive prizes offered by his company. He said he enjoyed selling tremendously and felt no pressure in selling situations.

About four years ago, Paul began to feel he had more to offer his company than selling. As a professional salesman, he believed that he could transmit this ability to new sales people entering the insurance field. Although lower-level management positions did not pay as much as he could make in full-time selling, Paul felt that the prestige of a management job would overcome the lower salary.

Paul approached Mr. Vidmar and also some executives from the home office to discuss a promotion. He stated that he could produce profitable results in a new district, if he were allowed to recruit and train a new sales force. He also made it quite clear that he would leave the Executives Company for a competitor's offer as a manager, if he was not promoted by Executives.

Mr. Vidmar and the other involved executives then discussed

Kauffman's proposal. They all agreed that being a fantastic sales person did not mean that this same person would necessarily be an outstanding manager. Many of the skills and characteristics needed for success in the two positions were quite different. Mr. Vidmar also pointed out that it is quite difficult for one person to transfer his knowledge and ability in salesmanship to another person. Other executives wondered if Kauffman had the patience and all-around ability to be a good manager.

At the same time, however, one of the older executives expressed the view that million-dollar-round-table sales reps were very hard to find, and the company could not afford to lose Kauffman to a competitor. Therefore, these executives agreed to promote Paul Kauffman to the position of sales manager in the new office to be opened in Salt Lake City. His salary was to be $25,000 a year, plus the usual commissions on any insurance he would sell when time was available.

Paul found that recruiting sales reps in Salt Lake City and other places in the Intermountain region was easy enough. The main problems he ran into were how to train the new agents effectively and how to keep them. At the end of the first year and a half, he had experienced a turnover rate of 90 percent in his sales force. Paul still felt confident in his new situation. He felt he just needed a little more time to get adjusted to his new role as a manager.

As time went by, Paul gradually came to recognize some of the mistakes he was making. He realized he was spending a considerable portion of his time in selling activities. He admitted that—as he put it—"I sometimes tend to fall back into the work that I know best and that is most familiar to me, namely, selling." Some of the new sales trainees complained that Paul sometimes stepped into their sales presentations with customers, especially when a big sale was at stake. They complained that he had an attitude of "I can do it better myself."

After Kauffman had been a sales manager for over three years, there still was a turnover rate of 75–80 percent in his sales force. Yet he was still selling $1 million worth of insurance on his own each year.

Mr. Vidmar finally was convinced that he had to do something quickly regarding Paul Kauffman. The company was experiencing much higher than anticipated costs in hiring and training new sales agents in the Salt Lake City district. Moreover, Mr. Vidmar felt that Paul was not performing his management job adequately.

Unfortunately, when several executives met to decide what to do, several different courses of action were discussed, but there was no general agreement. One executive proposed that Paul be demoted back to a sales position. Another executive objected to the term *de-*

mote. He felt that moving Paul to a sales job was simply a switch or transfer in his duties. He said, "Separate skills are needed in the two jobs (manager and sales rep), but the jobs are on the same grade level."

Mr. Vidmar suggested the idea of training Paul on teaching techniques, so as to improve his ability to transfer salesmanship arts to his trainees. In this way the company would keep its super-salesman as well as having a candidate for a good manager. Still another executive said, "Let's face it—we have wasted a lot of time and money on the guy (Paul), and it's time now to let him go. He has failed us for over three years. There's no way he's going to get his confidence back up to where it was when he was doing such a great job selling for us back in San Francisco."

Question

How should Mr. Vidmar handle the "Paul Kauffman situation?"

3

Sales-Force Organization

Order is a lovely thing.
ANNA BRANCH

In the management process, you must first decide where you want to go and then figure out how to get there. In more formal terms, management should first establish its objectives and then plan the appropriate strategies and tactics to reach those goals. To implement this planning, the activities and people must be properly arranged and effectively coordinated. This is where the concept of organization comes in. The fundamentals of organization are essentially the same, whether we are talking about organizing a sales force, a production department, a football team, an army, or any other group involved in a common effort.

Nature of Sales Organization

The concept of **organization** may seem nebulous or abstract. It will be helpful to differentiate between:

- Organization—as the end product or end result.
- Organizing—as the process, or the means to the end result.

As the end product, an organization is simply an arrangement—a working structure—of activities (functions) involving a group of people. The goal is to arrange these functions so that the people involved can act *together* better than they can *individually*.

Organizational changes have occurred in companies' sales and marketing efforts as firms have found their existing structures were inappropriate to implement the marketing concept. As we noted in Figure 1–1, one foundation stone underlying the marketing concept is that all marketing activities should be organizationally integrated and coordinated. That is, a firm's total marketing activities should be centralized in one department. Then this department's plans and efforts must be organizationally coordinated with those of the other major departments, such as production and finance. Next, all the activities *within* the marketing system must be coordinated. That is, management should integrate all planning and operational policies that involve the personal-selling effort, the advertising program, product development, marketing research, and so on.

Sales-Force Organization and Strategic Planning

A close relationship exists between a company's sales-force organizational structure and its strategic marketing and sales-force planning. The organizational structure has a direct and significant bearing on the **implementation** of strategic planning. The key here is to design an organizational structure that will help, rather than hinder, the successful implementation of the strategic marketing and sales-force planning.

An organizational structure—whether it is for a sales force or any other group involved in a joint effort toward a goal—is a control mechanism. Besides its organizational structure, management has several other mechanisms to control and direct the efforts of its sales force—its compensation plan, training program, and supervisory techniques, among others. But the organizational structure looms large because it typically is set up before these other mechanisms are established. Consequently, any mistakes made in organization can result in reduced efficiencies in selection, compensation, training, and other tools for managerial control and guidance.

Therefore, as a control mechanism, the organizational structure guides the company—or in some cases, the sales-force segment—in carrying out the strategic planning to pursue marketing and sales-force goals. Often a sales force fails to reach its goals because the organizational structure hindered the effective implementation of the strategic sales-force planning.

To illustrate, let's assume that a company's sales goal is to increase its market share to 20 percent next year. The company's key sales strategy is to increase its sales to large, national accounts by 30 percent over last year's level. However, the sales force is structured so that each sales rep's efforts are spread thinly over accounts of all sizes. No key executives are assigned to sell to national accounts.

Under these organizational conditions, it is doubtful that this company will successfully implement its plan. Another company's strategic plan is to open new markets. However, its sales organization is designed to service existing customers in existing markets. Again, the present organizational structure is hindering the implementation of the strategic plan.

Pertinent Concepts in Organization Theory

If sales executives are familiar with the conceptual foundations in organization theory, perhaps they can better understand the organizational relationships and problems in their firms. Let's consider three of these concepts at this point.

The Human Factor in Organization

Consideration of the human factor in administration has experienced some pendulum-like swings in American industry during the 20th century. Early in this century, organizational theory was influenced heavily by Frederick W. Taylor and others who developed their concepts in a mechanistic setting in factories and offices. Work standards and performance quotas were established rationally on the basis of time and motion studies. The emphasis was on the machine—on the task—and not on the individual human being.

The influence of these concepts is reflected in classical organizational theory. Organizational structures were highly formalized, highly authoritarian, and highly centralized. In effect, a worker was just another machine. Sales departments were not immune to this type of organizational thinking. Salesmen often were impersonally treated as little more than pins on a sales map.

In reaction to the impersonal treatment of workers, organizational theory swung to the other extreme in the 1940s and 1950s when the concept of *human relations* became quite fashionable. Writers stressed the importance of interpersonal relationships and the motivation of workers, including sales people. Management became less authoritarian and more participative. Sales executives began to realize that sales people are individuals with emotions, personalities, expectations, and self-concepts.

Current thinking in organizational theory recognizes that neither of these two extremes is effective in optimizing worker productivity and profitability. Today we seek a balance between the formalized, impersonal organizational structure and the human-relations approach to administration.

Centralized versus Decentralized Organization

During the past three decades companies have shifted toward a **decentralized** structure in their sales and marketing organizations—and in other divisions of the firm too. The organizational pattern that emerged is marketing oriented and externally directed, in contrast to the traditional production-oriented and internally-directed structure.

Internal system versus external results. The production-oriented sales organization model is highly formalized and generally inflexible. Much emphasis is placed on the internal system and on procedures. Sales people and field sales managers are expected to follow established procedures. Management seems to be more concerned with the job and the system than with the results the system is supposed to produce.

The decentralized sales organization model is a less formal, more flexible structure. Management relies more on the people—their motivations, personalities, and general knowledge—than on the technical systems and procedures. The system is subordinated to the overall results. *How* you get the job done is not nearly so important as *did* you get it done.

Authority and control. In the traditional sales organization, full authority for all sales-force management activities—selection, training, supervision, setting quotas, and so on—is centralized in the home office. Centralized authority requires close, tight control over the sales force and field sales managers to ensure that the one best system is being followed. In the newer type of sales organization, much of the authority and decision making regarding sales-force activities is decentralized.

The degree of decentralization is related to the span of executive control. (By **span of executive control,** we mean the number of subordinates who report directly to one executive.) A highly centralized organization requires a *short* span of control. The reason for this is that if management is to maintain close and detailed control over a work force, the group must be small.

A direct relationship exists between the span of control and the number of executive levels in a company. The shorter the span of control, the greater the number of layers or echelons of supervision.

This relationship between span of control and number of executive levels has irreconcilable consequences. A company that can keep its span of control short is inevitably plagued with the problems stemming from multiple layers of supervision. Every time another level is added, the cost of executive overhead increases, and so does the red tape. The more levels (links) between the decision

Figure 3–1

Summary of Contrasts between Traditional and Current Models in Organization Theory

Traditional	*Current*
1. More likely to be production oriented.	1. More likely to be marketing oriented.
2. Internally oriented.	2. Oriented toward external environment.
3. Highly formalized and inflexible.	3. Less formalized; more flexible.
4. Centralized authority.	4. Decentralized authority.
5. More levels of supervision and shorter span of control.	5. Fewer levels of supervision and broader span of control.
6. Major concern is toward the system; system becomes an end in itself.	6. Management relies on the workers rather than on the system; system is only a means to an end.
7. Orientation is toward *how* the job is done.	7. Results oriented: *did* you get the job done.

maker and the operator carrying out the decision, the greater the chances for mistakes in executing the decision and the slower the process. Information is misinterpreted as it passes through the channels—*if* it passes through.

In the decentralized model of sales organization, more authority is delegated to the field sales executives. There is a broader span of control. Because field sales executives are allowed to develop their own procedures, they can be more responsive to customers' wants and local competitive situations (see Figure 3–1).

Role of the Informal Organization

A healthy organization is a self-adjusting one. Through its own devices, it finds ways to get a job done with a minimum of effort. A formal organization's well-being is maintained by the system known as the **informal organization** structure. This structure represents how things *really* get done in a company, not how they are supposed to be done according to a formal plan. Most firms rely heavily on their informal structures to get work done efficiently.

The following example shows how an informal organization may actually work. The sales manager's secretary opens a letter from a customer who complains that he was overcharged on an order. If the lines of the formal organization chart were followed, the secretary would refer the letter to her boss, the sales manager. He, in turn, would relay the message up through executive echelons until ultimately it reached the administrator who is over the chief executives in sales and accounting. This top administrator would forward the complaint down through channels in the accounting department to the appropriate person of responsibility in the billing division. The answer would follow the reverse path up and down through channels until the sales manager's secretary received it and could notify the customer. Such procedures are rather ridiculous, and most organizations would not follow them. Instead, the informal structure would be used. The sales manager's secretary would simply telephone or walk over to see a clerk in the billing department to find out what happened to the customer's order.

The informal organization also gives richer meaning to some of the time-honored principles of organization. For instance, a person should have only one boss. Fundamentally, this is a sound generalization. Yet, the informal structure adds dimensions of practicality and flexibility to this principle. Actually, we all have many bosses, each being granted authority over different activities. Consider the example of the billing mistake. When the sales manager's secretary telephoned the billing department, the people in that department granted her a certain amount of authority in that, on her request, they investigated the overcharged order. They realized this was the most efficient way of getting the job done. The sales secretary herself recognizes more than one boss, even in a situation so simple as complying with a janitor's request to close the windows at night.

Characteristics of a Good Organization

In this section we will review six generalizations which typically characterize a good organization. These fundamentals are useful in designing a new organization or revising an existing one.

Organizational Structure Should Reflect Market Orientation

Traditionally, in designing a sales organization, a company would start with the president's office and the sales and marketing activities in the central office. By working from the top down, eventually the sales force and the field-selling operation would be structured. Today, we realize that exactly the opposite procedure should be used. Management should focus attention first on the market and the sales force. Executives should consider the selling and marketing tasks necessary to capitalize on the market demand and to serve the firm's customers. From there, they can work back to the top marketing executive in the central office.

Activities, Not People, Should Be Organized

The major sales activities are sales planning, sales operations, and sales-performance evaluation. The organization should be built around these activities (or functions), and not around the people participating in them. Naturally, workers perform the activities, but ideally these people should be placed *after* the basic duties have been arranged.

In many respects, this generalization is difficult to put into operation. From a practical standpoint, it is almost impossible to avoid organizing around people. Sometimes the vitality and effectiveness of an organization can be increased by adapting the structure to take advantage of people's strengths. The managerial trick is to know how far to go when making these "people adaptations."

Responsibility and Authority Should Be Related Properly

Misunderstandings often occur because someone did not know that he or she was supposed to do a given job. Or, the person was not granted adequate authority to fulfill the responsibility. Responsibility for each activity should be clearly spelled out (preferably in writing) and assigned to some individual. Then the necessary authority should be delegated to that person. If you are going to give a person a job to do, then give him the tools to do it. If branch managers are assigned a sales volume quota (the responsibility), then they should be allowed to select their sales forces (the authority). Suppose a sales representative is given the responsibility for developing a new territory where competition is strong. The rep who cannot quote varying prices to meet this competition without first getting home-office sanction probably does not have enough authority to go along with the responsibility.

Span of Executive Control Should Be Reasonable

An executive must have adequate time to spend with subordinates—guiding their efforts, counseling with them, evaluating their results—in addition to performing other administrative tasks. Just what constitutes a reasonable span of executive control depends on many variables. However, this number should be small—usually not more than 6 or 8 persons or, in rare situations, perhaps 10.

There are a few guidelines for determining the appropriate number. If the subordinates' work is similar or their duties are routine, the span can be relatively wider. Likewise, the higher the ability levels of the executive and the subordinates, the greater the span of control can be.

Organization Should Be Stable, But Flexible

A good organization will be stable but flexible, like a tree. A tree has to be firmly and deeply rooted to withstand extreme blows. But above ground it must be able to give with the wind or it will snap off at its base.

The factor of *stability* in an organization means that the structure can stand losses of managerial personnel at any level and still maintain peak efficiency. The company has trained replacements available. In athletics, this concept is referred to as "depth in all positions."

The concept of *flexibility* in an organization refers more to short-run situations. A flexible structure, for example, will be able to adjust to seasonal fluctuations in needs for workers or to counter the moves of a competitor who brings out a new product. Flexibility can be built into an organization by effectively scheduling executive duties or by subcontracting some of the work. An advertising department, for instance, might lease out the job of preparing the Christmas catalog.

Activities Should Be Balanced and Coordinated

A well-organized company keeps a good *balance* among all its divisions. That is, management does not let any unit become *unduly* more important than another. If an athletic team stresses either the offense or the defense to the neglect of the other, the team is basically unsound because the organization lacks balance. Sales-department activities are tied in with virtually every other major function in business. Consequently, effective *coordination* is needed (1) between sales and nonmarketing departments as well as (2) between sales and other marketing units.

Sales and nonmarketing activities. Here are a few examples of how sales and nonmarketing departments can help each other.

Sales $\longleftrightarrow$ production. The sales department can help the production people by:

- Furnishing an accurate, detailed sales forecast.
- Relaying ideas about color, design, packaging, and new products.

Production, in turn, can provide:

- Dependable production schedules to provide the right quantity and quality of goods at the right time.
- Technical product information.

Introduction to
Majestic Glass Company

A Series of Day-to-Day Operating Problems Facing a Sales Manager

Clyde D. Brion, general sales manager for the Majestic Glass Company, directed 18 sales people, each based in a different city. The company's factory, located in eastern Ohio, manufactured glass bottles, jars, and other glass containers. Bottles for cosmetics and toiletries accounted for the bulk of the sales volume. However, containers for beer, soft drinks, shoe polish, milk, food products, and medicine were also important in the Majestic line.

Orders from large and regular customers were shipped direct from the Majestic factory to users' plants by rail. For smaller and infrequent buyers, stocks of standard bottles and jars were maintained in warehouses owned by public warehouse companies. The warehouse companies leased space to producers and distributors of many types of goods, billing each occupant monthly for the space actually used. Brion also rented desk space for each of his sales representatives at these warehouses. Telephone and basic secretarial services were also available. This arrangement provided Majestic with regional sales branches, with stocks in 18 cities.

Rivalry was keen in the container industry. More than a dozen large firms were engaged in the manufacture of glass bottles and jars. Increasing competition was also provided by containers made of plastic, metal, and paper. It was especially important that the Majestic sales force be alert to new business possibilities, that they follow up leads and market tips quickly, and that they offer maximum service. It was Majestic's policy to meet competitor's prices, but not to undercut a competitor willfully in order to steal business. Instead, the company relied on various original features of its containers to outsell competitors.

Each sales person was paid a commission of 10 percent on all sales in the territory in which he was located. He received an additional 5 percent on orders from new customers, provided the order was larger than a specified minimum quantity. A sales person could also draw on anticipated commissions, up to a limit determined by Brion. Usually this equalled the sales representative's average commission earnings for a good month's business in his territory.

At the time you are studying this case, Brion faced several problems in the operation of his sales force. He was anxious to solve each problem correctly. At the same time, he also wanted to establish safeguards against a recurrence of the same problem if possible. If recurrence was thought to be probable, he wanted to establish a workable policy for dealing with the problem in the future.

Twelve of these operating problems facing Brion appear at various places in this text. In each instance, the particular problem is located at a relevant place in the chapter. The first in the series is a problem in organizational conflict, and it follows right after this introduction.

Note: This series of problems was written by Professor Phillip McVey, then at the University of Nebraska-Lincoln. Reproduced with permission.

A day-to-day operating problem in the
Majestic Glass Company (A)

Conflict between Production and Sales Departments

Mr. Brion's secretary handed him an intracompany memorandum form, on which this message was mimeographed:

> To all Majestic salesmen:
> Because factory capacity is severely overtaxed, no new production orders will be accepted until further notice.
>
> B. K. Morley
> Vice-President of Manufacturing

A penciled note was attached, reading: "C.D.B.—I have copies of this ready to mail out, but thought you should see it first. Too bad it has to be this way. B. M."

Mr. Brion went immediately to Mr. Morley's office to learn the reasons for this order. It would shut down all sales activity of the firm, except for sales from present warehouse stocks of standard containers. Warehouse inventory levels were normally maintained at approximately two weeks' supply of these items. However, it was known that the stocks of some popular items were nearly zero.

Although Mr. Morley and Mr. Brion were both vice-presidents, Mr. Brion was kept waiting 20 minutes in Mr. Morley's outer office. A secretary explained, "Mr. Morley is in conference." Then a man from the accounting staff emerged. Finally came Mr. Morley, who greeted Mr. Brion and ushered him into the inner office with the remark, "That order of mine is some little bombshell, right?"

After some discussion, Mr. Morley summed up his reasons by saying, "It's a matter of factory cost. When we get behind and then speed up, everything costs more—overtime labor, machinery charges, maintenance, rejects, shipping. I'm convinced we'll have to catch up while on a normal manufacturing schedule. That, of course, means no new orders for a while. I can't say how long—maybe a month or two."

Mr. Brion suspected that he knew another reason for Mr. Morley's action. Recently, the manufacturing department had submitted to Majestic's board of directors a plan for factory expansion and new equipment. The plan had been disapproved because it was too costly. Mr. Brion believed that Mr. Morley might be refusing new orders as a forceful way of demonstrating the need for the factory and equipment he wanted.

Question

How should Clyde Brion respond to Mr. Morley's memo?

Sales ⟷ finance and accounting. These two groups can collaborate in controlling selling costs and in setting credit policies. In addition, the sales department can:

- Provide short-run sales forecasts as a basis for annual budgeting.
- Supply a long-range forecast for capital-expenditure planning.

The finance and accounting people can help by:

- Preparing marketing cost analyses as bases for pricing and discounts.
- Supplying credit information on a customer prior to a sales call.

Sales ⟷ personnel. These two departments can work together in selecting and training sales people. They can cooperate in preparing selection forms (job description, application blanks, interview forms). Together they can develop and conduct sales-training programs. Some companies rely heavily on the personnel department to do the selection and training. In other firms, most of this work is done by sales departments, perhaps using personnel's material.

Sales ⟷ legal. Coordination with the legal department is essential because so much legislation directly affects marketing and sales activities. The legal division can offer interpretation of laws. A sales executive may propose some policy and want an opinion of its legality before putting it into operation. In some firms the legal department and the sales-training department have joined forces to educate the field sales force regarding the Sherman, Clayton, Robinson-Patman, and other major laws related to sales-force activities.

Sales and other marketing activities. Advertising is the major marketing activity to be coordinated with personal selling. Together, they constitute the main parts of the selling function in a company. Sales-force executives also should work closely with the people in sales promotion and in the marketing information system (marketing research).

Sales ⟷ advertising. Even though this is an obvious area for a closely integrated effort, many firms have serious problems in coordinating their personal selling and advertising efforts. Often there is conflict between sales and advertising executives. Sales managers want such things as advertising campaigns designed to meet sales goals, more effective sales support, and advertisements that the sales people can talk about. Advertising executives want a major role in marketing planning and a more secure place on the team of marketing executives.[1]

Advertising and sales departments should collaborate, from the early stages of product planning all the way through to the final sale. Sales managers may discuss with advertising managers such topics as competition, problems in some territory, and selling points of various products. In this way, sales can help advertising direct its message more effectively at a given market. In return, advertising may help by informing sales about the advertising appeal, theme, and copy. In this way the sales force will be able to capitalize on the advertising by telling the same story.

Sales people in the field can help the advertising department by working with retailers to get the most effective use of cooperative advertising. The reps can report up-to-the-minute data regarding advertising done by competitors, especially at the local level.

At the same time, advertising can directly help the sales force in the field. It can pave the way for a call on a prospect by acquainting the prospect with the product. This service is particularly valuable when a sales person is calling on a prospect for the first time. Anything that helps open a customer's door and mind to a sales rep is bound to increase the rep's morale and effectiveness.

Basic Types of Organization

After looking at the sales organization charts in a large number of companies, you might get the idea that there are many different types of organizations. However, most organizations can essentially be classified in one of the following three basic categories:

1. The line organization.
2. The line-and-staff organization.
3. The functional organization.

Usually, most medium- and large-size firms find it advantageous to expand their basic organization in some specialized fashion to enable the sales force to perform more effectively. This specialization ordinarily is modeled on one or a combination of the following bases:

---

[1] One survey of large companies reported that the interface between the sales and advertising departments actually was quite limited. See Alan J. Dubinsky, Thomas E. Barry, and Roger A. Kerin, "The Sales-Advertising Interface in Promotion Planning." *Journal of Advertising* 10, no. 3 (1981), pp. 35–41.

1. Geographical territory.
2. Product line.
3. Type of customer.
4. Selling task.

Line Organization

Nature and use. A line organization is the simplest form of organizational structure. Authority flows directly from the chief executive to the first subordinate, from the first to the second subordinate, and so on down the line. In its pure form, a line organization has no specialists or advisers. Planning is not separated from operating, and authority is highly centralized. In the most rudimentary form of line structure, the chief executive does all the planning. He also is in charge of all the operations, whether they are in production, sales, finance, or any other area in the company.

This form of organization can well be used by a very small firm. For example, a person who owns and operates a small wholesaling company may have six employees, none of whom has any supervisory duties. This organization chart would look like the one in Figure 3–2.

As this firm grows, the owner-president probably will not be able to continue to run the whole show alone and still do an effective job. Therefore a line assistant is hired. There is no one best pattern for splitting the duties between these two. Usually the president still oversees all the functional areas of the business but handles only the broader aspects, such as establishing policies and planning the operation. The assistant sees that the plans are put into effect by the employees. The line of authority now flows from the president through the assistant to the employees, as shown in Figure 3–3.

A company of fairly large size can have a complex organizational structure for the entire firm, while at the same time, a simple line organization in the sales department.

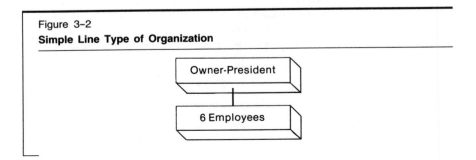

Figure 3–2
Simple Line Type of Organization

Owner-President

6 Employees

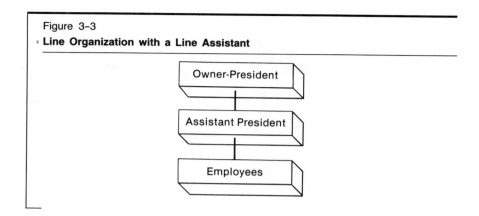

Figure 3–3
Line Organization with a Line Assistant

Relative merits. A line type of sales organization is a simple structure. It is usually a low-cost operation, because it has few executives. It should ensure quick decision making and speedy action in putting policies into operation. Because of its highly centralized authority and responsibility, there probably is less of buck-passing in the organization.

A line organization also has some severe limitations, especially if it is used in medium-size or large companies. One drawback is the lack of managerial specialization. A person cannot be an expert in all phases of a business. And, even if he were, there would not be enough hours in the day to do all the jobs well. Typically, a line organization, especially in a small company, lacks stability because it does not provide for replacement executives. Furthermore, the extreme centralization of authority generally retards the development of subordinate executives.

Line and Staff Organization

Nature and use. As the marketing operation in a company grows in size and complexity, it soon becomes apparent that a simple line type of organization is not sufficient for effective operation. The top marketing executive realizes a need for staff assistants who are specialists in various areas of marketing, such as advertising or marketing research. In addition, there is a need for an assistant executive who can manage the sales force. The result is a line-and-staff type of organization, as depicted in Figure 3–4.

In this type of organization, authority flows from the chief marketing executive through the general sales manager to the sales force. The middle vertical segment of Figure 3–4 is much like a line organization. The chief marketing executive is the line officer ultimately

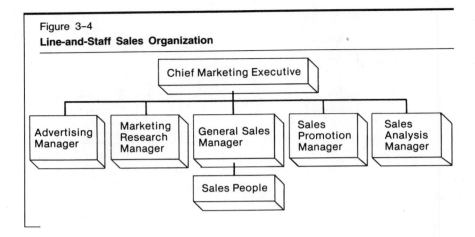

Figure 3–4
Line-and-Staff Sales Organization

responsible for developing all sales plans and for the success of sales operations. However, now this executive has staff assistants to aid in these tasks.

The job of a staff executive is to help the top marketing manager. Each staff manager is also responsible for all planning connected with his specialized activity. The staff executives have no authority over the sales force. These executives can only **advise** the sales reps' boss, the field sales manager.

The line and staff is probably the most widely used basic form of organization in sales departments today. It is likely to be used when any of the following conditions exists:

- The sales force is large in number.
- The market is regional or national.
- The line of products is varied.
- The number of customers is large.
- The company wants to put increased emphasis on sales planning in relation to sales operations.

Line authority and staff authority held by same executive.   In most firms the staff managers have some subexecutives or other employees under them. In this organizational structure, the head of the specialized activity is a line officer in some situations and a staff officer in others. The advertising manager, for example, has line authority over the people in his department. However, he still is in a staff capacity to the other staff executives and to the sales force.

Relative merits.   The line-and-staff form of organization enables a company to enjoy the benefits of division of labor. Planning and operating can be separated, and planning can be done by an expert in each field. This not only ensures better planning in each area but also reduces the chief sales executive's work load.

A line-and-staff organizational structure does have some limitations for a company, regardless of its size. The total executive cost can be high because additional specialists must be hired, and many of these staff executives have departments of their own. This form of organization also makes for slower operation. When a problem arises, a staff person is usually selected to study it and make recommendations. Of course, it is presumed that the more careful and expert consideration of problems is worth the price of a slower pace. Another potential limitation is in the responsibility-authority relationships. Strong staff executives may try to take on line authority instead of staying in the role of adviser.

Functional Organization

Nature and use.   The functional type of organization is a step beyond the line-and-staff form, even though at first glance the two may look alike. In both types, the activities of the marketing department are separated into groups, and a functional specialist is put in charge of each group. Thus a firm may have an advertising manager, a general sales manager, and a marketing research manager under either of the two forms. Here the similarity ends. In a functional organization, each of the specialized executives has *line* authority over his particular activity. In a line-and-staff structure these executives have only *advisory* authority.

In a functional organization, it is not at all unusual for a number of executives to be giving orders to the sales force. The sales promotion manager for a manufacturer may want the sales force to make a list of all the window displays secured by competitors. The credit manager might like the sales people to make collections on delinquent accounts. In a line-and-staff structure, these staff executives could only *recommend* to the general sales manager that the sales reps perform these duties. Under a functional plan, these staff executives would have line authority (1) to *order* the sales people to do the jobs or (2) to *order* the assistant sales manager to see that the jobs were done. In Figure 3–5, the functional authority is flowing directly to the sales force from these two managers.

A functional organization ordinarily is found in conjunction with a territorial or product type of structure. This type of authority is best fitted to a situation in which the number of executives who may use it is limited. The greater the number of executives with functional authority over the operating people, the greater the opportunity for trouble.

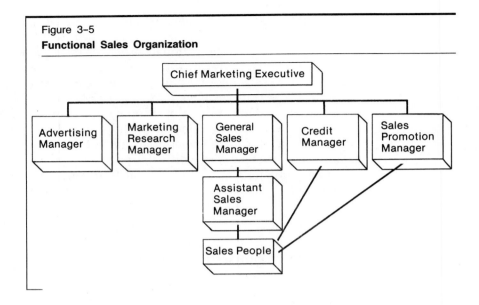

Figure 3–5
Functional Sales Organization

Relative merits. A major drawback to the functional plan obviously is that some of the line officers or sales people get orders from more than one person. The practice also involves the risk of overloading these people or of giving them conflicting orders. Furthermore, the line executives who are consistently bypassed may soon find their own influence and importance reduced. Theoretically, of course, some top manager coordinates this type of organization, but from a practical standpoint, effective coordination is very difficult.

A company that can successfully use a functional organization has all the advantages that result from specialization of labor. Each function gets expert supervision and control. Also, in contrast to a line-and-staff organization, there is little risk that plans formulated by functional executives will not be placed in operation. The functional officers can *order* that their plans be carried out. They are not in the position of having to *advise* that this be done, and then leaving it up to a line officer to determine *whether* it is done.

Specialization within the Sales Department

In the organizational examples considered earlier, the sales force has not been split on any basis. It has reported either directly (1) to the chief marketing executive (2) an assistant or (3) to the general sales manager. With a larger sales force, the job of the line executive charged with sales-force administration is more difficult. The number and complexity of a company's products and markets may also require some organizational division if the sales effort is to be effective.

The most common way to divide the responsibilities in a sales department is to split the sales force on some basis of sales specialization. The most frequently used bases are:

1. Geographical territories.
2. Types of products sold.
3. Classes of customers.
4. Selling tasks performed.
5. Some combination of these categories.

Geographical Specialization

Probably the most widely used system for dividing responsibility and line authority over sales operations is to organize the sales force on the basis of geographical territories. In this type of structure, each sales person is assigned a separate geographical area, called a **territory,** in which to sell. A reasonable number of sales people representing contiguous territories are placed under a territorial executive

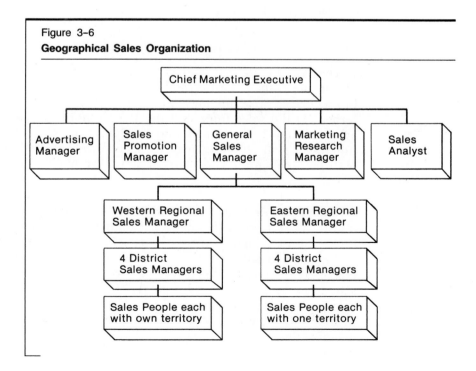

Figure 3–6
Geographical Sales Organization

Chief Marketing Executive

Advertising Manager | Sales Promotion Manager | General Sales Manager | Marketing Research Manager | Sales Analyst

Western Regional Sales Manager | Eastern Regional Sales Manager

4 District Sales Managers | 4 District Sales Managers

Sales People each with own territory | Sales People each with one territory who reports to the general sales manager. The territorial sales executive is typically called a regional, divisional, or district sales manager. Companies with large sales forces often have two or three levels of territorial sales executives (see Figure 3–6).

A firm can derive many benefits by dividing the line authority in its sales department on the basis of geographical territories. The plan usually ensures better coverage of the entire market, as well as better control over the sales force and sales operations. A second benefit is that the company is in a better position to meet local competition by having an executive responsible for a limited segment of the market. Local management also can act more rapidly in servicing customers and in handling problems. Line authority at the local level means there is no need to check with headquarters every time a decision must be made on some territorial issue. A territorial organization is also more flexible; it can adapt to individual regional needs and conditions.

Territorial specialization by function typically is lacking in an organization, and this is a drawback. Each district manager, for instance, may have to do a small amount of work in advertising, sales analysis, and credits and collections, in addition to managing a sales force. Another limiting factor is expense. As more levels of territorial executives are established, the company increases its overhead cost of management.

Product Specialization

The type of product sold is another frequently used basis for dividing the responsibilities and activities within a sales department. Product specialization may be employed in a number of different forms: (1) the sales force and the line authority in sales-force management may be separated into product groups, (2) the supporting functional staff activities may be specialized by product line, or (3) both the line selling and the staff activities may be divided by products.

Product-operating specialization. In the company whose organization chart is given in Figure 3–7, products have been separated into three lines. One group of sales reps sells only the products included in line A. All sales people in group A report directly to the sales manager of product line A, who in turn is responsible to the general sales manager. As far as sales operations are concerned, each product division is completely autonomous. To simplify this illustration, it is assumed that there is no territorial structure, otherwise the basis of organization would be a combination plan. The three product sales managers are strictly operating executives; they have no staff as-

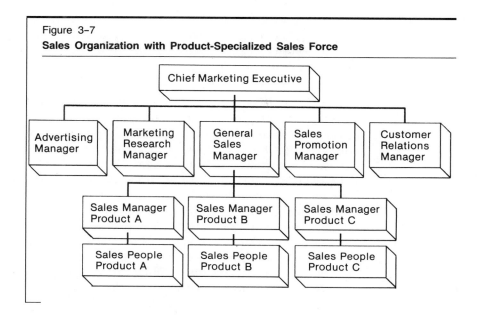

Figure 3–7

Sales Organization with Product-Specialized Sales Force

sistants. The staff executives in advertising, marketing research, sales promotion, and customer relations all are centralized in the home office and are not specialized by product line.

A product-operating type of organization is likely to be used when the company is selling:

- A variety of complex, technical products—as in the electronics field.
- Many thousands of products—a hardware wholesaler, for example. The products are not necessarily technical; there simply are too many items for one sales person to handle.
- Very dissimilar, unrelated products—a rubber company may use three sales forces to sell (*a*) truck and auto tires, (*b*) rubber footware, and (*c*) industrial rubber products, such as belts, bushings, and insulating materials.

The major advantage of this form of organization is the specialized attention each product line gets from the sales force. Also, each line gets more executive attention because one person is specifically responsible for a particular product group.

Probably the biggest drawback is that in many instances more than one sales person from a company calls on the same customer. Not only is this duplication of coverage expensive, it also can create ill will on the part of the customers. Another weakness is the increase in the cost of executive personnel that results from adding product sales managers, many of whom need an assistant or office staff. This structure has the same weakness as the territorial-operating type in that the product sales managers have no staff assistants. Therefore, functional specialization by product line is lacking at this executive level.

Functional-staff specialization by product—the product manager. Several different sales organizational structures are available to a company that intends to use staff assistants who specialize by product line. Figure 3–8 illustrates one of these alternatives. The company charted in Figure 3–8 has three staff executives, called **product managers.** They each bear the responsibility for planning and developing a marketing program for a separate group of products. These people have no line authority over the sales force or the sales-force managers. They can only advise and make recommendations to the line officers. The sales force is not specialized by products. Instead, each sales person sells the products of all three product managers. Each product manager works with other functional specialists in planning the advertising and personal-selling effort related to his or her group or products.

A company can use this structure when it wants some of the advantages of specialization by product line at the planning level, but does not need the specialization at the selling level. Thus, in one stroke the product-staff organization corrects two of the weaknesses

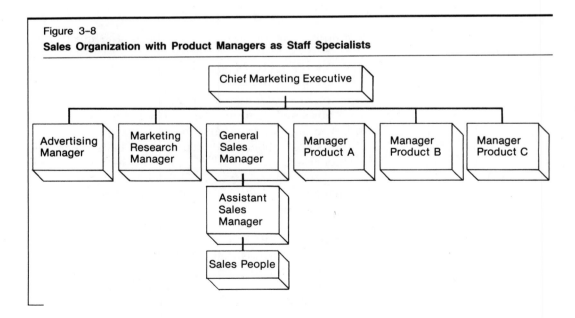

Figure 3–8
Sales Organization with Product Managers as Staff Specialists

in a product-operating structure—(1) the problems of duplicate calls on a customer and (2) the lack of specialization in planning the functional activities. Of course, a product-staff organization loses any advantage of having sales people specialize in a limited line of products.

The product-manager concept. The scope of activities performed by a product manager—also called a brand manager or a merchandise manager—varies widely among the adopters of this organizational concept. In many large firms—Procter & Gamble, Pillsbury, Kimberley-Clark (Kleenex), Clairol, General Foods, for example—the product manager's job is quite broad. This executive is responsible for *planning the complete marketing program* for one brand or for a group of products. This responsibility includes setting marketing goals and strategies, forecasting sales, preparing budgets, and developing plans for advertising and field-selling activities. At the other extreme, in some firms a product manager's activities are limited to the areas of advertising, personal selling, and sales promotion.

Probably the biggest problem in the product-manager system is that a company will saddle these executives with great responsibility yet not give them the corresponding authority. They must develop the field-selling plan, but they have no line authority over the sales force. They have a profit responsibility for their brands, yet they are often denied any control over product costs, selling prices, or advertising budgets. Their effectiveness depends largely on their ability to influence other executives to cooperate with their plans.

Actually, the product manager is not a new organizational concept. It has been used for years in department stores where there is a departmental-buyer system. Each merchandise manager has complete responsibilities for a limited line of products. In the manufacturing field, Procter & Gamble and Johnson & Johnson have used the brand-manager system for more than a half century with considerable success. It has only been in recent years, however, that increasing numbers of *industrial-product* manufacturers also have adopted this organizational structure.[2]

Because of its inherent problems, the product-manager concept has always been controversial. Moreover, there are some indications that this organizational structure may change considerably as we head into the 1990s. The product-manager system was widely adopted and thrived particularly during the period of economic growth and market expansion in the 1950s to the 1970s. In the 1980s, however, many industries experienced slow economic growth

[2] For a comparison of the position of consumer-goods and industrial-goods product managers, see Theodore Cummings, Donald W. Jackson, Jr., and Lonnie L. Ostrom, "Differences between Industrial and Consumer Product Managers," *Industrial Marketing Management,* August 1984, pp. 171–80.

in maturing markets coupled with a trend toward strategic planning that stresses centralized managerial control. Because of these environmental forces, one careful study concluded that the product-manager system will be greatly modified in many companies and eventually abolished in some firms.[3]

Combined functional and product specialization—the matrix organization.   The third and most complex organizational variation of product specialization involving sales departments is a *matrix organization.* Essentially, a matrix organization is a combination of functional specialization and product specialization (See Figure 3–9). In this structure, under the chief marketing executive are the usual managerial assistants in charge of activities such as advertising, sales promotion, and field selling. In addition, under the chief marketing executive there are separate product marketing managers, each with a separate sales force and a staff of functional assistants. These staff executives (advertising manager A, for example) are under the *line* authority of the product marketing manager (A, in our example). At the same time, these product staff executives are under the *functional* authority of the corresponding executive in the home office (the advertising manager, in our example). In Figure 3–9, under the line direction of each product marketing manager is a sales-force manager whose energies and sales people are devoted to one group of products. At the same time, a general sales manager in the home office coordinates all field-selling activities and has functional authority over each product sales-force manager. In effect, each product officer has two bosses. This, of course, is a major drawback to the matrix organizational structure.

This structure is especially adaptable to large firms that are dealing with complex product programs or total product systems. In fact, the concept of the matrix organization was developed by the aerospace industry in connection with its large, technologically complex projects in new-product development. In private industry this organizational concept has been adopted by some very large firms such as Xerox, IBM, General Foods, and DuPont.

Presumably, a matrix organization provides a company with a team of enthusiastic experts to develop and market a complex new-product system. However, because so many of those involved have two bosses, this structure requires very careful coordination to minimize personal conflicts. This structure is also very expensive.

---

[3] See Victor P. Buell, "Firms to Modify, Abolish Product Manager Jobs Due to Sluggish Economy, Centralized Planning," *Marketing News,* March 18, 1983, p. 8.

Figure 3–9

Matrix Sales Organization with Product-Functional Specialization

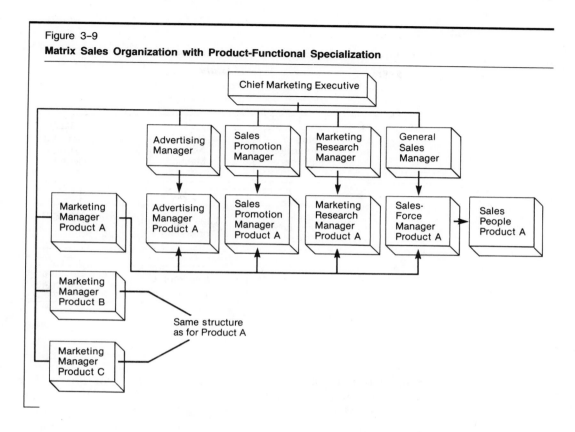

Customer or Market Specialization

Many companies have divided the line authority in their sales departments on the basis of type of customer, classed by either type of industry or channel of distribution. The customer basis of organization may be closely related to product specialization. In fact, some firms have split their sales forces by product line because each product goes to a different customer group. (You can see this similarity in Figure 3–10.) The sales managers in charge of each industry group are purely line operating executives with authority over one group of sales people. These executives have no staff assistants under them. Each sales rep sells the full line of products used by the customer group.

The use of customer-group specialization in the sales force is likely to increase as more companies fully implement the marketing concept. Certainly this basis of specialization is consistent with the customer-oriented philosophy that underlies the marketing concept.

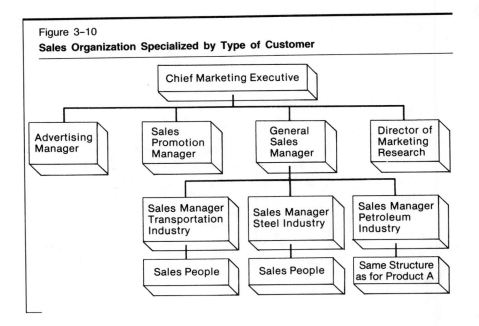

Figure 3–10
Sales Organization Specialized by Type of Customer

The emphasis is on markets rather than on products or production processes. Among the companies that already have made the market-specialization move in their sales organizations are such well-known names as Xerox, IBM, Gulf Oil, NCR, Hewlett-Packard, General Foods, and General Electric.

Xerox has embarked on an ambitious three- to five-year program that eventually will have all its 4,000 to 5,000 sales reps selling the company's full line of office-automation products. In effect, the company is switching from a product-oriented sales organization, consisting of several product sales forces, to a market-oriented structure. The company intends to spend $10 to 20 million a year in its training program to implement this organizational change.[4]

Although it overcomes some of the disadvantages of product specialization and conflict of interest between channels, the customer type of organization does have some limitations. It causes overlap in territorial coverage and, in this respect it is costly. Also, unless separating the sales force by markets also results in some product spe-

---

[4] For example, see Thayer C. Taylor, "Xerox's Sales Force Learns a New Game," *Sales & Marketing Management,* July 1, 1985, p. 48; Randall Smith, "IBM to Merge Two U.S. Sales Divisions That Serve Large and Smaller Customers," *The Wall Street Journal,* September 25, 1985, p. 6; and "Apple Computer's William Campbell (an interview)," *Sales & Marketing Management,* September 9, 1985, p. 60.

cialization, the customer-based organization is subject to the disadvantages of full-line selling.

Organization for selling to national accounts. One particular type of customer specialization that is getting managerial attention is the special organizational arrangements made for dealing with major accounts—that is, a company's large customers. These customers constitute a very important market segment for most firms.

Some companies label their major accounts as house accounts or corporate accounts, but perhaps the most widely used title is national accounts. However, a large customer—even though referred to as a national account—may well be a firm with only a regional or even a local market coverage.[5]

Some companies have made no changes in their sales organizational structure to accommodate national accounts. These customers are each serviced by the regular sales person in whose territory the national account is located. In this way the seller does not incur any additional organizational administrative costs in connection with selling through national accounts.

However, most firms derive the great bulk of their sales volume and profit from sales to large customers—the national accounts. Moreover, such customers often require experienced sales reps, specialized handling, and other services not needed by smaller customers. Many sales executives believe that national accounts are too important to be handled only by the average territorial sales rep. As a result, growing numbers of companies are modifying their sales organizations in order to provide more specialized treatment of national accounts.[6]

There is a variety of organizational arrangements from which to select for the handling of these accounts. Three of the more widely used approaches are as follows:[7]

[5] For a report on how industrial marketers determine which customers should be classified as national accounts, see Thomas H. Stevenson, "Classifying a Customer as a National Account," *Industrial Marketing Management,* April 1980, pp. 133–36.

[6] For a further discussion of the benefits and problems in national account marketing and the organizational arrangements for selling to these accounts, see John Barrett, "Why Major Account Selling Works," *Industrial Marketing Management,* February 1985, pp. 63–73; John F. O'Connor, "What Buying Pros See in National Account Deals," *Purchasing,* April 25, 1985, p. 47; Phillip Maher, "National Account Marketing: An Essential Strategy or Prima Donna Selling?" *Business Marketing,* December 1984, pp. 34 ff.; Thomas H. Stevenson, "Payoff from National Account Marketing," *Industrial Marketing Management,* April 1981, pp. 119–24; and Arthur J. Bragg, "National Account Managers to the Rescue," *Sales & Marketing Management,* August 16, 1982, pp. 31–34.

[7] Much of this discussion is drawn from Benson P. Shapiro, "Account Management and Sales Organization: New Developments in Practice," in *Sales Management: New Developments from Behavioral and Decision Model Research,* ed. Richard P. Bagozzi (Cambridge, Mass.: Marketing Science Institute, 1979), pp. 265–94, especially pp. 276–77.

1. A separate division to deal with national accounts. A company can establish a separate division to deal with its key accounts. This option has been used by some apparel manufacturers for producing and selling private-label clothing to the large general-merchandise chains such as Sears, Wards, and J. C. Penney.

This organizational structure has the advantage of integrating the manufacturing and marketing (including the sales) activities related to the major accounts. On the other hand, this structure is expensive because it duplicates other units in the selling firm. Also, the success of the key-accounts division (when marketing its products under the customers' brands) is totally dependent upon the major customers.

2. A separate sales force to deal with national accounts. A more widely used organizational approach is for a company to establish a separate sales force to service its key accounts. Under this option, the same production operations are used to service large or small customers alike.

The national-account sales force may be a separate unit with its own management hierarchy, or it may report through the same management structure used for the regular sales force. Some companies use the national-account sales people to call on the customers' home offices, while relying on the regular sales force to service the customers' branch and field offices.

A national-accounts sales force has generally the same merits and limitations that were discussed earlier in connection with sales forces specialized by type of customer. However, a key-account organization does provide management with one additional advantage. That is, a company can reward an outstanding sales rep by promoting that person to the national-account sales force, without having to promote that rep into a management position.

3. Use of executives for national-account selling. Many companies use their top sales and marketing executives, or their field sales executives, for key-account selling. This approach is an alternative for companies that cannot afford to establish a separate division or a separate sales force. A company that has only a few large customers may also find this a useful approach. By sending its top executives to call on key accounts, a company is using someone with the authority to make decisions regarding prices and allocation of manufacturing facilities. The customers should also be impressed that the seller thinks enough of that account to send a top executive to make the sale.

On the other hand, there is the risk that the selling executives will overrate the importance of their key accounts and fail to have a balanced view of their markets. Also, executive time spent on servicing key accounts is time taken away from planning and other management activities that the executive should be doing.

Selling-Task Specialization

Another basis for sales-force specialization is the selling tasks performed by the sales reps. One type of this specialization involves account development and maintenance activities. Another involves the use of inside and outside sales forces and telemarketing.

Account development and maintenance. In most firms and for most products, field sales reps have two very different jobs—*sales development* and *account maintenance.*[8] On the one hand, the reps must prospect for, generate, and develop a stream of new customers. At the same time, these reps must maintain and provide full service for existing accounts. The satisfactory performance of each of these jobs requires quite different techniques and personal qualifications.

One remedy for this situation is to organize the field sales force so that the sales people are assigned either development or maintenance work, but not both. Some marketers of industrial products commonly use development sales reps to work with customers in the early stages of marketing new products. Many consumer-products manufacturers use a missionary sales force to service and maintain existing accounts. These sales reps ordinarily do not close a sale or write up orders. Their primary job is to provide information, distribute promotional materials, and be sensitive to the customers' on-going needs.

There are some problems with this type of organizational specialization. Sometimes it is difficult to relieve sales reps from account-maintenance tasks so they can concentrate on development selling. Also, there is a scarcity of people who can qualify for the creative, developmental type of sales jobs. Sometimes customers object to having their account switched from one sales rep (development) to another (maintenance). In addition, management must constantly be alert to minimize the friction between the two groups of reps.

Inside and outside sales forces and telemarketing. An increasingly popular form of sales-force specialization by task is to set up both an inside and an outside sales force to go to customers. In Chapter 1, we said this book is about the management of a sales force that goes to the customer. Well, some firms have moved some of that outside selling effort to the inside of the company and are "going to the customers" by means of telephone and computer communications. Instead of the traditional in-person sales call, the sales reps are using

---

[8] George N. Kahn and Abraham Schuchman, "Specialize Your Salesmen!" *Harvard Business Review,* January–February 1961, pp. 90–98.

telephones and computers to talk with customers. In effect, outside selling is going electronic.[9]

Many companies have used telephone selling for decades. What is new today, however, is the innovative use of communication systems involving the telephone, television, and the computer to aid the selling effort and other marketing activities. The term *telemarketing* has been coined to describe these communication systems.

Two main reasons for the growing use of telemarketing as a form of sales-force specialization are: (1) many buyers prefer it over personal sales calls in certain selling situations, and (2) many marketers find that it increases the efficiency of their selling effort. For a buyer, placing routine reorders or new orders for standardized products by telephone or computer takes less time than in-person sales calls. Sellers are facing dramatic increases in the cost of keeping sales people on the road. So any selling done by telemarketing reduces that expense. Also, using telemarketing for routine selling tasks allows the field sales force to devote more time to developmental selling, major account selling, and other more profitable selling activities.

Obviously, not all selling activities lend themselves equally to telemarketing. But, there are several types of selling situations that are well adapted to this form of sales specialization. Some possible telemarketing situations are as follows:

- Order-taking for standardized products. For example, American Hospital Supply Corporation and some of its customers have a sophisticated mainframe computer capacity so that the buyer's computer can talk with American Hospital's computer. The buyer's computer can determine product availability and shipping dates, as well as place an order.
- Seeking and accepting reorders, especially routine ones.
- Dealing with small-order customers, where the seller would lose money if field sales calls were used.
- Servicing existing accounts.
- Prospecting for new accounts to generate leads for follow-up, in-person sales calls.[10]

Combination of Organization Bases

In the examples of organizational bases given earlier, it has been assumed that a company divides its sales force on only one basis,

---

[9] See "Rebirth of a Salesman: Willy Loman Goes Electronic," *Business Week*, February 27, 1984, pp. 103–4.

[10] For a further discussion of setting up a telemarketing system, see Thomas M. McCarthy, "The Transition from Field Sales to Telemarketing: Avoiding the Pitfalls," *Telemarketing*, August 1984, pp. 40–43; and John Quinn, "Preparation Is the Key to Telemarketing Profitability," *Telemarketing*, July 1983, pp. 16–19.

such as territory, product, or customer. Actually, many firms use some combination drawn from the several structures already discussed. The number of possible combinations is obviously quite large. For example, a firm may combine territorial specialization with product-staff specializations (through the use of product managers). Or a sales force may combine customer specialization with territorial specialization.

Summary

An organization is an arrangement of activities involving a group of people. The goal is to arrange the activities so that the people who are involved can work *together* better than they can *individually*. The sales-force organizational structure has a significant influence on the implementation of a company's strategic planning. Sales executives can better understand organizational relationships if they are familiar with three concepts in organization theory. The three are (1) the various treatments of human beings in organizations over the past century; (2) the trend toward marketing-oriented, *decentralized* organizational structures in sales and marketing; and (3) the role that the informal organization plays in maintaining a healthy organizational structure.

The six generalizations that characterize a good organization are: (1) an organizational structure should reflect a market orientation; (2) an organization should be built around activities and not around the people performing these activities; (3) responsibilities should be clearly spelled out, and sufficient authority should be granted to meet the responsibility; (4) the span of executive control should be reasonable; (5) an organization should be stable, but flexible, and (6) activities both *within* the sales department and *between* sales and nonmarketing departments should be balanced and coordinated.

Most sales organizations can be classified into one of three basic categories—a line organization, a line and staff organization, or a functional organization. A line organization is the simplest form of organization and is often well suited for small firms. A line and staff organization enables a company to use staff assistants who are specialists in various areas of marketing. A functional organization carries specialization a step further by giving more line authority to the executive specialists.

In most medium- and large-size companies, the sales forces are divided on some basis of sales specialization. The most frequently used bases for specializing a sales force are (1) geographical territories, (2) type of product sold, (3) classes of customers, (4) selling tasks performed, or (5) some combination of these categories. When organizing on the basis of selling tasks performed, a sales force may be divided into sales development and account maintenance groups, or into inside (telemarketing) and outside sales forces.

Giving each sales representative the responsibility for his or her own geographical territory is probably the most widely used form of sales force specialization. Specializing a sales force by type of product sold is often used when a company sells unrelated products, highly technical products, or several thousands of products. Product specialization may also involve the organizational concept of a product manager. Specialization by customers may be done on a channel-of-distribution basis or on an industry basis. Also, there is a trend toward handling very large customers (national accounts) on a separate basis.

Questions and Problems

1. In relation to management's treatment of workers, contrast the classical organization-theory approach and the human-relations approach. Which approach should be adopted in the organization of a sales force?

2. Explain the relationship between the degree of centralization and the span of executive control in a sales organization.

3. Some executives are hesitant to delegate authority and responsibility, even though they recognize that delegation is desirable. One writer offered the following reasons why these managers may be reluctant to delegate:

   a. They get trapped in the I-can-do-it-better-myself fallacy.
   b. They lack the ability to communicate what is to be done.
   c. They lack confidence in subordinates.
   d. They are handicapped by an aversion to taking a chance.

   What are some ways in which each of these obstacles may be overcome?

4. An authority in the field of management has stated the following reasons why subordinates avoid accepting responsibility:

   a. Subordinate finds it easier to ask the boss rather than deciding himself how to deal with the problem.
   b. Fear of criticism for mistakes.
   c. Subordinate already has more work than he can do.
   d. Subordinate feels he lacks necessary information and resources to do a good job.

   Suggest ways in which each of these points may be successfully counteracted by management.

5. Explain how coordination can be effectively secured between the sales department and each of the following departments:

production, engineering and design, personnel, finance, export sales.

6. *a.* What are the reasons for the lack of coordination that sometimes exists between advertising executives and field sales managers?

   b. What are some proposals for developing better coordination between these two groups?

7. The choice of organizational structure is influenced by factors such as:

   a. Size of the company.

   b. Nature of the products.

   c. Nature and density of the market.

   d. Ability of executives.

   e. Financial condition of the company.

   Explain how each of these conditions may affect the choice of structure.

8. In your opinion, what are the best policies or procedures for solving the following problems, which often are found in a line-and-staff organization?

   a. A strong-willed staff executive tries to take on line authority instead of remaining as an adviser.

   b. A line executive consistently bypasses or ignores advice from staff departments.

   c. The rate of executive decision making is slowed down.

9. What type of organizational specialization within the sales department do you recommend in each of the following companies?

   a. Manufacturer of high-quality women's ready-to-wear has 100 sales people selling to department stores and specialty stores throughout the nation.

   b. Hardware wholesaler covering the southeast quarter of the country with 50 sales people.

   c. Manufacturer of chemicals used in fertilizers has 35 sales people and sells to 500 accounts located throughout the country.

   d. Manufacturer of office machines with 1,000 sales people.

10. A regional hardware wholesaler located in Detroit, Michigan, employed 20 sales people, each of whom sold the full line of products. It became apparent that the list of products was simply too long for one person to sell effectively. The company felt it had a choice of (*a*) reorganizing the sales force by product lines or (*b*) adding more representatives, reducing each person's territory but still having each one carry the full line. What do you recommend?

11. What are the main problems that may occur when a company

adopts a matrix organization in its marketing department? What can management do to overcome these problems?

12. Sales development and sales maintenance were described in the text as two very different jobs. The satisfactory performance of each requires different qualifications. In what ways may the personnel requirements for these two jobs be different?

Case 3-1

Merrill Engineering Company*

Sales-Force Organization for New Products

The door division of the Merrill Engineering Company was planning to introduce a new product line in a new market—a steel entrance door designed for single-family homes. The general manager of this division, Ned Holloway, noted that the company's entire previous experience had involved technical products and services designed solely for industrial markets. Consequently, Holloway believed that the residential steel doors would have to be marketed quite differently from the way they generally had done business in the past. He was wondering particularly how his sales force should be organized to sell the new product line.

The Merrill Engineering Company was a large manufacturer of building products for the construction industry. The company also supplied extensive engineering services related to the products it sold. Merrill's home office was in Cleveland, Ohio, and the company maintained 35 sales offices and 15 warehouses that were strategically located throughout the country. Last year's sales were about $400 million. Both sales volume and net profit had increased about 20 percent last year over the preceding year, thus reflecting the major surge in the construction industry.

The Merrill Company was organized into four product divisions. One was the door division which, in the past, had produced steel doors for industrial users. A concrete products division manufactured reinforced concrete joists and other steel-reinforced concrete products for the construction industry. This division also provided engineering services to accompany these products. The third product division manufactured steel products such as reinforcing bars, joists, and other steel materials used in the concrete products. The fourth product division produced and marketed prefabricated steel buildings and the engineering services related to erecting those buildings.

* Adapted from case prepared by Creighton White under the direction of Prof. William J. Stanton.

The door division accounted for about one third of Merrill Company's total sales, and it was the most profitable of the four product groups. The door division also had shown the largest and most consistent growth over the past five years. It had outstripped the industry as a whole. Thus, Merrill had increased its market share in this product category. Holloway believed that his company's recent diversification into residential steel doors provided an opportunity for further growth and profitability.

Merrill faced two major competitors that had entered the residential steel door market some time ago. However, Holloway believed that his company could make up the lost ground caused by Merrill's late entry into the market. Holloway said that his company could capitalize on two factors. One was the company's dominant and established reputation in the industrial market for steel doors. The second was the product's superiority to those already on the market.

According to Ned Holloway, the residential steel door market was growing rapidly. He forecast that Merrill would sell 2 to 3 million units during the company's first five years. He further predicted that the sales would increase annually after that period.

He based his forecasts on the belief that people would increasingly adopt steel doors in preference to the customary wooden ones. This switch would occur as people became convinced of the advantages of steel doors. Holloway pointed out that the use of steel doors would result in significant energy savings. These new doors provided more insulation than did wood doors. He said that the steel door alone provided an insulation factor 2½ times greater than a solid-core wooden door with a storm door. Also, the steel door was more durable—it would not warp, crack, shrink, or swell. Moreover, it provided better security against burglary.

The steel doors were intended for use as exterior access doors, or as a fire door between a residence and an attached garage. They were not intended for use in the interior of a house.

All in all, Holloway believed that Merrill had a very competitive product that was technically superior to other doors on the market. "But what we don't have," Holloway said, "is a strategic marketing plan or a sales organization to enter this market successfully. All of our company's key personnel have engineering backgrounds. Typically our sales strategies have been based on an engineering orientation, not on a marketing one."

To reach the residential market, Merrill's major competitors were channeling their steel doors through local door companies and building materials suppliers. Holloway agreed that the most efficient way to market Merrill's residential doors was to sell through wholesalers. The company would not sell directly to home owners or contractors. That is, Merrill would sell to lumber companies, building materials supply houses, or local door wholesalers who, in turn, would sell to building contractors or directly to do-it-yourself home owners. Holloway said, "I have to figure out what is the best sales-force organizational structure to reach these middlemen."

Merrill's door division had a well-established sales force that operated out of the company's 35 sales offices and 15 warehouse locations. These sales people sold Merrill's industrial door product line directly to industrial users. The company did not use wholesaling middlemen in its channel of distribution for industrial doors. Because of their technical orientation, Holloway felt it probably would be more accurate to classify these sales reps as sales engineers. The sales force was paid on a straight-salary compensation plan.

Holloway discussed the sales organizational question with some of his fellow executives. The corporate vice president, Walter Craine, thought that the company should use its existing sales force to sell the new residential line.

He pointed out that the technical expertise needed to sell industrial steel doors was essentially the same as that needed to sell residential doors. He also thought that the sales force could sell the residential doors directly to building contractors without going through middlemen. Craine was concerned about the time, cost, and difficulty involved with recruiting and training a separate sales force. Craine reminded Holloway that the company had never developed a sales training program. In the past, Merrill had hired primarily engineers, and the company's production orientation did not suggest the need for sales or marketing training.

Ned Holloway was a little leery of Craine's proposal. Holloway believed that the company needed to hire more people with a marketing background in order to sell the new product line successfully. He believed that the marketing of residential steel doors would have to be done differently from the way the company had done business in the past. Selling prestressed or prefabricated concrete products, according to Holloway, had called for sales engineers to submit bids to prospective purchasers. Typically, a sale was made based on the engineering services provided, and little marketing was involved.

Holloway wondered whether the existing sales force could work out of its present sales offices and warehouses and still sell the new doors to local door companies and to building materials middlemen. He also wondered whether the present sales force would have the interest or incentive to sell this new, less technical product line aggressively. Furthermore, even if the existing sales force were used, Holloway saw the need to expand the size of this sales force.

Holloway anticipated selling the residential doors to two new markets—one was the market for new residential construction, and the other was the replacement market. He believed that—with effective distribution, advertising, and personal selling—there existed a great potential for replacing existing wooden residential doors. He questioned, however, whether the existing sales force could handle this replacement market. He also questioned whether the existing sales managers—in view of their engineering background and orientation—would have the ability or interest to manage the selling of this new product to a new market that called for marketing-oriented activities.

The president of the company, Terry Richardson, had been sitting in on the Craine-Holloway discussion. After listening to both points of view, Richardson wondered if a different alternative would not be better. He suggested that Craine and Holloway pursue the matter further and consider other alternatives.

Question

What sales-force organizational structure should the Merrill Company adopt in order to sell its new product line?

Case 3–2

Kennecott Supply Company*

Organizational Structure to Accommodate New Sales Person

"Man, I knew our past sins would catch up with us. A long time ago we should have paid some attention to our organizational structure, instead of just letting it grow in such a haphazard manner. Now we have a problem. Our business grows—that's the good news—so we hired another sales rep. But—and this is the bad news—what group of customers should this new guy sell to? In other words, what is his account base? What is his territory—you should excuse the expression, seeing as how we don't have any assigned territories." The moaning speaker was Eric Lampman, the vice president of sales and marketing at Kennecott Supply Company. He was talking with Tim Gould, the president of the company.

Kennecott Supply Company was like so many companies in that it started small, not needing any formal sales organization. Then it grew and prospered, and now the company had reached the point where the lack of a formal sales organization was creating some problems.

---

* Adapted from case prepared by Taylor Magnusson under the direction of Prof. William J. Stanton.

Kennecott Supply Company was started in a large southern city about 35 years ago as a wholesaler of paper products. About 25 years ago, the company added janitorial supplies to its line. Then 15 years ago, Kennecott expanded into restaurant and food service supplies. The company's sales volume in 1985 was $2.5 million. For the past several years the Company had reported a small annual net profit.

Kennecott's current president and chairman of the board of directors, Tim Gould, had been with the company for years. He started as a truck driver while he was still in college. In 1977, he bought out David Kennecott, the company's founder and majority stockholder. Currently, Eric Lampman and Grant Jacoby, the vice president of operations, were minority stockholders.

The line of industrial paper products distributed by Kennecott included paper bags, boxes, wrapping paper, and printing papers. The janitorial supply line included brooms, brushes, deodorants, soaps, and insecticides. In its restaurant supply line, Kennecott distributed kitchen cookware, china, glassware, and inexpensive tables and chairs. Restaurant supplies accounted for 50 percent of Kennecott's sales. The paper products represented 40 percent of the total volume, and according to Lampman, these products offered the greatest growth potential for the company. Janitorial supplies generated the remaining 10 percent of the company's volume. The sales and gross margins in this line were so small that Kennecott was considering dropping it.

About half of the company's sales volume came from special-order sales rather than in-stock inventory sales. Kennecott frequently offered "exclusive" specialty products that were not available through any other distributor in Kennecott's geographical market. Delivery time for these special orders ranged from a few days to two months.

Kennecott was unusual in that the company's product lines spanned several quite different industries. In contrast, most of its competitors were large regional wholesalers, each of whom specialized in one of Kennecott's three product lines. Several of these large distributors had increased their size and market share by buying out smaller wholesalers. In fact, Kennecott had received several takeover offers over the last few years.

The main competitive advantage of these large distributors was their ability to buy in larger quantities and thus to sell at lower prices than Kennecott. Kennecott countered by stressing its high-quality products, professional sales people, prompt delivery with its own fleet of delivery trucks, and better servicing of its accounts. Kennecott's competitive advantages were important because, in most cases, the customer's product knowledge was limited.

Kennecott had about a 5 percent market share for all three product lines combined in its regional market. But this overall figure was a little misleading. Actually, the company did not sell in the large central city in its market because the large competitors were too firmly entrenched there. However, in some of the outlying areas, Kennecott had as much as 30 percent of the market for paper products and 25 percent of the market for restaurant supplies and equipment.

Currently, Kennecott had four outside sales reps and one inside rep. Eric Lampman also did some selling of in-stock items. Even Tim Gould, the president, still maintained a few large, key accounts.

The inside sales person handled telephone orders and over-the-counter sales. The four outside sales reps were not organized in any formal fashion. They were not divided by product line or by geographic territory. One rep was assigned to the northern part of Kennecott's market. The other three reps tended to concentrate in a city of about 100,000 population located away from the central city in Kennecott's region. This city had a few large companies, many small industrial and service firms, a large university, and some government installations. Considering its population, this city also had an unusually large number of restaurants.

Lampman readily admitted that the sales organization was a "mish-mash," as he put it. "Yet everyone seems to have found a niche for himself. One guy concentrates mostly on restaurant and retail store accounts. Another rep tends to deal mainly with institutional and industrial markets. We have set up a system to prevent duplication of account coverage and to minimize competition for any given account. We provide the sales force with a list of each rep's accounts. We stress a family-style approach and discourage any unethical selling practices."

"I'll tell you—we must be doing something right. Sales cannibalism among our reps is virtually nonexistent, our reps have been with us for an average of 12 years, and we are making money."

But Eric Lampman also knew the sales organizational structure was living on borrowed time. Recently he had hired a new salesman, Paul Heyden. In fact, Lampman anticipated that Kennecott would be hiring about one new rep each year for the next few years. Lampman's immediate problem was that he did not know how to assign customers to the new sales people. The company wanted to provide a new rep with at least a minimal account (customer) base so that the rep would have a full opportunity to be successful.

Paul Heyden was expected to be ready for a field selling assignment after two months of in-house training under Lampman's guidance. Lampman realized that a decision regarding a new rep's customer base would have to be made soon.

The present sales people were paid a straight commission based on their gross margins. Each new rep, however, was to be paid a small salary plus a commission during the rep's first year of employment.

Lampman and Gould met to discuss the account-base situation for the new sales rep. Lampman started the conversation. "Tim, I've been giving this problem a lot of thought during the past few weeks, and I have decided one thing. We're too small to organize our sales force in any of the traditional ways such as by geographical territory, product line, or type of customer. One format I've considered, however, is simply to let the new guy call on any accounts that are not being served currently by one of our reps. These potential customers would include two groups. One would be any account we've never before called on. The other group is the accounts in our dead file. These are customers we once sold to but have not done business with for the past five years."

Gould responded, "I don't know, Eric. I'm not sure we should write off what you call the 'traditional' organizational structures. I'd like to discuss them further with you. In the meantime, I have another alternative for you to think about. How about stripping some current accounts from our present reps? We might pool those accounts where the rep is not realizing the account's potential, or where we feel the rep is somewhat ignoring the account. Let the new guy try to get more mileage out of those accounts. Sure, the present reps won't be too happy about this kind of a split. On the other hand, they have had their chance with these accounts. Why should a rep retain an account when he apparently isn't developing it successfully?"

"I'll tell you something else we might consider," countered Lampman. "How about a downward shift of accounts, starting with your own? You've told me that you would like to free up your time by unloading some of your accounts. OK, I'll take them. Then, in turn, I'll give up some of my accounts to our senior rep. He then transfers some accounts to the next rep in line—and so on down through the sales force. In this way the new guy will end up with an assortment of established accounts. This will give him a base to start from. Then he can add new accounts little by little."

"I don't know," Lampman commented, "maybe there is a better system we haven't thought of yet. All I do know is that I have only two or three months to come up with a plan and have it fully operational."

Question

What sales organizational structure should Lampman adopt in order to provide an effective customer base for his new sales person?

Case 3–3

Arnco Products Company*

Sales-Force Organization to Meet Customers' Needs

The president of Arnco Products Company, Paul Greenstone, believed that the company should study its sales-force organization to see if the structure was appropriate in the current market environment. About 5 months ago Greenstone became president of the company, replacing his uncle, Ron Joyce. Mr. Joyce was the company's founder and had been its only president. His background was that of an engineer and designer. He tended to concentrate his efforts on operations, particularly in the area of quality control. It was his belief that quality products would sell themselves.

Mr. Greenstone, on the other hand, had left a major consumer goods manufacturer where his position was that of national sales manager. His strong suit was in the development of key accounts and channel-of- distribution relationships. It was his firm belief that sales representatives should cultivate major accounts by providing the types of services that such accounts demanded.

Arnco was started 27 years ago as a manufacturer of glass containers for the beer and soft-drink beverage industries. Over the years, Arnco had expanded into supplying other industries with glass containers. The first new market had been dairies because of their home-delivery system which involved reusable glass bottles. Arnco then developed other forms of glass containers to allow it to expand into supplying food packers with jam and jelly glasses which were reused by consumers. Thus, Arnco became known as a specialist supplier of reusable glass containers. In all the industries to which it sold, Arnco maintained high quality levels and sold at prices higher than competitors. The company tended to rely on its quality reputation when selling.

What currently had triggered Paul Greenstone's interest in the sales-force organizational structure were some trends in his customers' industries. Two of these trends were (1) the increased use of plastic containers and cans in the beverage industry, and (2) virtually all milk producers had switched to plastic containers. Because of these trends, Arnco had experienced several years of flat sales volume.

One favorable factor, however, was beginning to have an impact on glass manufacturers. That was the increasing use of returnable bottles because of consumer demand for lower prices, environmental

* This case was prepared by Prof. Kenneth L. Jensen, East Tennessee State University. Reproduced with permission.

causes, and state legal requirements governing the sales of bottled drinks. Thus, Mr. Greenstone believed that there was a new opportunity for Arnco if the company could tap it. To do so required an analysis of Arnco's existing sales network and a study of customer buying patterns. Mr. Greenstone asked his staff to prepare the appropriate information.

Arnco's sales force consisted of 20 sales representatives organized on a geographic basis. There were two regional managers supervising the sales force (See Exhibit 1). Each representative was expected to service all accounts in his territory. Most of the accounts were in the beverage industry, although an increasing number were food packers. The dairy business had declined to almost nothing in terms of accounts. Each sales representative had, on average, 100 accounts, of which around two thirds were classified as beverage customers.

Because of the broad diversity of customer requirements, Arnco's product line was quite extensive. Each representative sold all items in the line. This required a great deal of knowledge on behalf of the sales force, for beer and soft drink customers had different product requirements from food packers. Beverage accounts were concerned more with the serviceability of the container. Food packers, on the other hand, tended to be more concerned with print requirements for reusable containers. Thus, different levels of technical knowledge were required by Arnco's representatives for various customers.

Once an order was placed, Arnco shipped directly to customers from one of two warehouses. One was located at company headquarters in Lancaster, Pennsylvania, and it served all accounts east of the Mississippi River. The other warehouse was in Denver, Colorado, and it handled the remaining domestic market. Orders were mailed in each day by sales reps, processed at the warehouse, and then filled and shipped by truck to the appropriate customer. The order

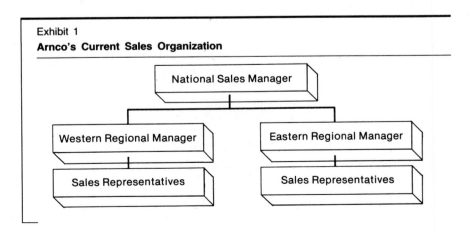

Exhibit 1
Arnco's Current Sales Organization

National Sales Manager

Western Regional Manager

Eastern Regional Manager

Sales Representatives

Sales Representatives

processing time varied from one to four days depending on the mail service, volume of orders received on any one day, etc. Truck delivery times varied from one to four days depending on the carrier and road conditions. Thus, total delivery time could vary from two to eight days, once a customer placed an order.

Promotional efforts were totally concentrated in direct selling to accounts. No advertising had ever been employed in the trade press nor had direct mail ever been used. When calling on an account, Arnco's representatives tended to stress their product quality and company reputation in order to generate an order.

Mr. Greenstone's staff conducted a mail survey to establish customer buying patterns and supplier selection factors. The staff used a random sampling plan, drawing customer names from their files. The results of the survey are shown in Exhibits 2 through 5.

When Mr. Greenstone looked at the results, several points came to mind. He called his staff and found out that 78 accounts (an 85 per-

---

Exhibit 2

Percentage of Time that Supplier Bids Were Requested for Component Parts by Customers

Percent of Time	Number of Responses
1–20%	4
21–40	4
41–60	12
61–80	14
81–90	25
100	19
Total	78

Exhibit 3

Percentage of Time that Customers Made Their Own Component Parts

Percent of Time*	Number of Responses
0%	40
1–20	27
21–40	5
41–60	4
61–80	2
Total	78

* No account made their own parts over 80 percent of the time.

Exhibit 4

Importance of Criteria Used to Select Suppliers

	Number of Responses			
Criterion	Very Important	Important	Little Importance	No Importance
Reputation of supplier	42	36	—	—
Price	38	40	—	—
Reciprocity	2	—	12	64
Supplier's services	48	26	4	—
Speed of delivery	52	24	2	—
Quality of goods	58	20	—	—
Gratuities	—	—	—	78
Supplier's financial condition	12	58	6	2

Exhibit 5

Size Distribution of Customer Respondents

Number of Employees	Number of Responses
100 or less	9
101–250	12
251–500	9
501–1,000	14
1,001–2,500	12
Over 2,500	16
Total	72*

* Does not add up to 78 because of some non-responses to this question.

cent return rate) had returned the survey form. The totals in each exhibit varied due to elimination of non-responses. Other points that Mr. Greenstone wanted examined were the relationships between variables. He, therefore, requested a cross-tabulation analysis utilizing a Chi-square test of independence. The results were given to Mr. Greenstone the next day. In order to eliminate zero-response cells, several of the cross-tabulations had to be collapsed. The variable reduced was "percentage of time bid." Four groups were decided on— low, moderate, extensive, and total. Low bidders were defined as customers who requested supplier bids for component parts 60 percent of the time or less. Moderate bidders requested bids from 61 to 80 percent of the time. Extensive bidders asked for bids in 81 to 99 percent of order situations. Total bidders were defined as those firms who always (100 percent of the time) asked for bids. Using these definitions, 20 accounts were classed as low bidders, 14 as moderate, 25 as extensive, and 19 as total bidders. Refer back to Exhibit 2.

At this point, Mr. Greenstone believed that he had enough basic data to examine his sales force regarding its structure. All that was left to do was to interpret the meaning of the data and to develop a sales plan for Arnco.

Question

What sales-force organizational structure should the Arnco Company use?

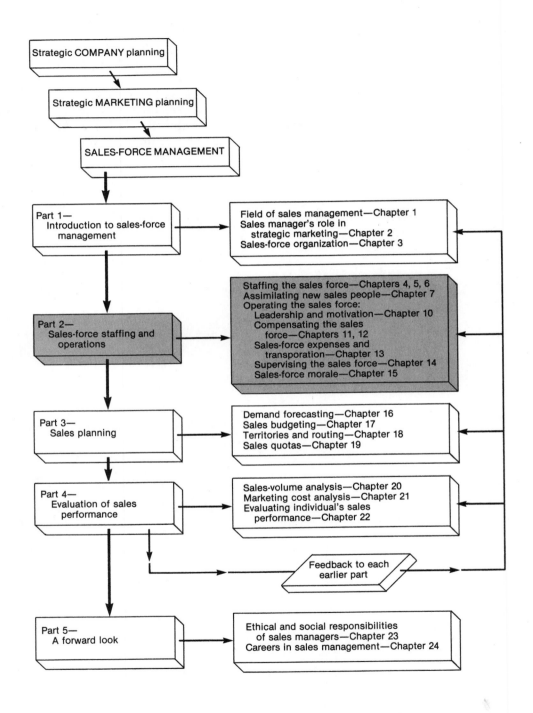

PART 2

Sales-Force Staffing and Operations

Most sales executives devote the bulk of their time to managing the many activities and people involved in operating a sales force. This is the stage in the management process when the sales organization actually implements the strategic planning designed to reach the company's sales goals.

Sales operations—the largest section of this book—includes staffing the sales force, training the sales people, motivating them, and directing their operations.

Staffing the sales force—selecting the right people—is the most important activity in the entire management process. Staffing involves determining the kind of people wanted (Chapter 4), recruiting applicants (Chapter 5), and processing these applicants (Chapter 6). The next step in sales operations is to assimilate the new sales people into the organization (Chapter 7).

Chapters 8 and 9 cover sales-training activities. Chapter 8 deals with developing and conducting the program—the planning, staffing, locating, timing, and methods of sales training. Chapter 9 discusses the content of a sales-training program.

Chapters 10 through 15 are devoted to motivating, compensating, and supervising a sales force. Some fundamentals and theories of motivation and leadership are introduced in Chapter 10. Then Chapters 11 and 12 deal with designing an effective compensation plan. The problems of expense plans and transportation of sales people are examined in Chapter 13. Chapter 14 covers sales-force supervision, sales meetings, and sales contests. Finally, various aspects of sales-force morale are discussed in Chapter 15.

4

Selecting the Sales Force— Determining the Kind of People Wanted

Eagles don't flock. You have to find them one at a time.
ROSS PEROT

A time-honored recipe for rabbit stew begins: "First catch a rabbit." Similarly, the first step in operating a sales force is to select the sales people. In the Preface and early in Chapter 2, we set forth a basic managerial philosophy that permeates this entire book. We believe that staffing—the selection of personnel at any level in an organization—is the most important activity in the management process. Consequently, the most important responsibility of administrators is to staff their organization with the right people for the various activities. Obviously, selection is not an administrator's *only* job, but it is the *most important* one. Selection of the right people is the key to success in any field of endeavor—athletics, politics, education, any area in business—even in marriage.

Sales-Force Selection and Strategic Planning

In most organizations the sales force is the one group that directly generates the revenues for the organization. Thus, the sales force is directly involved in carrying out the company's strategic planning. How well these plans are implemented depends to a great extent on who the company picks as sales people to do this implementing. Certainly the selection activities and the type of sales people hired should be consistent with the company's strategic planning.

Let's look at some practical applications of the relationship between sales-force selection and strategic planning. Assume that a company's goal is to maintain its leading market position and its market share. One major strategy may be to provide considerable service to existing accounts. The sales rep's job is primarily one of existing-account maintenance rather than new-account development. The selection activity is affected because the two tasks—maintenance and development—typically call for different types of sales people.

As another example, the company may adopt a strategy of promoting from within, as part of its strategic planning for the development of future executives. This strategy should influence management when it decides on its hiring qualifications and recruiting sources for sales people. Hiring older, experienced sales reps at high salaries probably would not be a sound way to implement this promoting-from-within strategy.

Importance of a Good Selection Program

At the beginning of this chapter we spoke in general terms about the importance of staffing in any organization. Now we want to consider the importance of *sales-force* selection especially in relation to a firm and its sales managers' various publics. Sales-force selection has *societal* implications, such as (1) the need for efficient utilization of manpower and (2) the waste of human resources that may result from poor selection. But it is also of vital importance to the continued well-being of the *individual firm.* After all, it is usually the sales force that directly generates the revenues for the firm.

Good Selection Improves Sales-Force Performance

In various departments of many—perhaps most—organizations, what we call the 80-20 principle is at work. That is, 80 percent of the results come from the efforts of 20 percent of the people. The 80-20 figure is used to describe this phenomenon of misdirected effort. Of course, the percentage varies from one situation to another.

This 80-20 situation certainly exists in most sales forces. Unfortunately, a small percentage of the sales force often accounts for a large share of the sales volume. Consequently, a carefully selected sales force can go a long way to bring that 80-20 split closer to 50-50.

A good selection job reduces the rate of turnover in a sales force. This can lead to long tenure in a territory which can help a rep build good customer relations. As a rep becomes better acquainted with the customers' needs and problems, customers become more likely to place their confidence in that sales person. The net result is a favorable impact on sales performance.

Cost Benefits from Good Selection

A good selection job can lead to both direct and indirect cost benefits. In the *direct-cost* category are the often substantial savings that accrue when the rate of sales-force turnover is reduced. A beginning sales person may cost a company well over $100,000 before reaching a productive status. These figures include recruiting and selection costs, the sales person's salary and travel expenses, and a share of the training and supervision costs.[1]

The *indirect costs* of poor selection are insidious because they don't show up as a separate item—like bad debts—in any accounting records. We are talking here about lost sales—the sales that would have been made if a rep had been better selected. We also are talking about the costs of dissatisfied or irritated customers.

Good Selection Job Eases Other Managerial Tasks

For any executive, doing a good job of selecting people to work for him or her simplifies the other administrative problems. Conversely, selection mistakes compound the problems in other areas. Sometimes, sales managers debate the relative importance of selection versus training, supervision, or some other managerial activity. Proper training, compensation, supervision, and motivation are all vitally important to the successful management of a sales force. However, if a company selects the right people for the sales job, then training them is easier, less supervision is required, and motivation is less difficult.

Sales Managers Are No Better Than Their Sales Forces

Within limits, a manager is no better than the people working under him or her, so it pays to select subordinates as wisely as possible. Generally, sales executives are judged on the basis of how their sales force performs. Under comparable product and market conditions, a slightly inferior sales force may outperform a better one, because the first one has a much more able manager. An executive with a very poor sales force, however, cannot surpass a competitor who has much better sales people, no matter how good the first executive may be.

---

[1] See John H. Dobbs, "Sales Force Turnover Can Make You—Or Break You," *Sales & Marketing Management*, May 14, 1979, pp. 53–59; and Gregory B. Salsbury, "Properly Recruit Salespeople to Reduce Training Cost," *Industrial Marketing Management*, April 1982, pp. 143–46.

Problem of Getting Good People

A sound selection program is essential because of the scarcity of qualified sales people. Many companies continue to recruit good sales reps even when there are predictions of an economic slowdown or production lines are shut down part-time. In fact, if some companies had an adequate number of qualified sales reps, production might not be curtailed.[2]

Qualified sales people are in short supply for several reasons. One is that selling as a career does not have the prestige attached to some other callings. This judgment is made even though a sales career offers opportunities for much greater financial rewards than generally are available in other fields. Another problem is that many young men and women are not aware of the excellent opportunities provided by sales jobs, especially in industrial sales. They often consider selling synonymous with clerking in a retail store.

But perhaps the biggest obstacle to finding good prospects is the fact that most people do not have the ability to be successful in selling. The jobs are hard work. They require considerable physical stamina and mental toughness. The results are easily measurable, and people fear proven failure.

Reasons for Poor Selection

Many of the reasons given for the poor job of hiring done by some sales managers can be grouped under one broad point—namely, the lack of a scientific attitude and method. A corollary factor has been management's refusal to take the necessary time for good selection and the reluctance to give the activity its proper recognition in administration.

Many executives have not prepared detailed descriptions of the sales job. As a result, they do not know what qualities to look for in a recruit. Failure to use an adequate number of tools can also cause poor selection. Firms may hire a person without doing enough interviewing, for example.

Often executives do not know what characteristics make a good sales person. Consequently, selection is made on the basis of a single outstanding physical or personality trait which the executive considers important. As a result of this basic weakness, many personal prejudices are found in selection. Some sales administrators have biases concerning certain physical or personality characteristics. Sales managers are apt to claim, "I know a good man when I see one." This is

---

[2] See Arthur Bragg, "Persistent Demand Keeps Sales Hires Steady," *Sales & Marketing Management*, August 12, 1985, pp. 70–72.

often the same sort of administrator who believes that "Salesmen are born, not made" and "A good salesman can sell anything."

Responsibility for Selection

In larger firms that have many sales people and sales branches, the responsibility for selection is delegated in various ways. The controlling factor is top management's philosophy regarding centralization versus decentralization of authority. In most large companies, a *sales executive* still retains the responsibility of final approval in hiring sales people. Very often, the *personnel department* helps the sales department by doing much of the recruiting or by preparing selection tools such as application blanks and interview forms. Personnel may even do the initial screening of applicants. However, the final authority for hiring usually rests in the sales department.

The question of who in the sales department will make the final decision regarding the applicant is apt to arise, particularly in companies that operate with a branch organization. In some concerns, territorial executives are given full authority to hire people in their regions. When selection is decentralized, the home office should do all it can to establish guides for the territorial executives to follow. Far more common than complete decentralization is for managers in territorial offices to do much of the preliminary work. Then the final hiring decision is left up to sales executives in the home office.

The Law and Sales-Force Selection

The legislation of the 1960s and 1970s providing for civil rights has had a major impact on the employment practices of business and nonbusiness organizations in the United States. This broad coverage includes the recruiting and selection of sales personnel. The particular laws and other regulations which are directly related to sales-force selection are:[3]

- *Title VII of the Civil Rights Act of 1964, as amended.* In any employment activity, an organization may not discriminate on the basis of race, color, religion, nationality, or sex. The Equal Em-

---

[3] For an excellent review of these laws and regulations designed to prevent discrimination in employment, see Ruth G. Shaeffer, *Nondiscrimination in Employment: Changing Perspectives, 1963–1972*, Report 589 (New York: The Conference Board, 1973), and Shaeffer, *Nondiscrimination in Employment, 1973–1975: A Broadening and Deepening National Effort*, Report 677 (New York: The Conference Board, 1975).

ployment Opportunity Commission (EEOC) was established under this law to administer its provisions.

- *Office of Federal Contract Compliance (OFCC) regulations.* This office in the Department of Labor has established affirmative action regulations and guidelines in employment practices which must be complied with by any organization holding a federal contract.
- *The Age Discrimination in Employment Act of 1967.* This law applies essentially to the 40–65 age group. An organization cannot discriminate in its hiring or termination practices because of a person's age.
- *Vocational Rehabilitation Act of 1973.* This law adds the physically or mentally handicapped people to the groups that employers cannot discriminate against in their hiring practices.
- *Uniform Guidelines on Employee Selection Procedures—1978.* In an unusual display of agreement and strength, the EEOC, the U.S. Civil Service, and the Departments of Justice and Labor jointly issued these guidelines.[4]

These laws and related regulatory guidelines emphasize two concepts in employment: **nondiscrimination** and **affirmative action.** *Nondiscrimination* requires elimination of all existing discriminatory conditions, whether purposeful or inadvertent. *Affirmative action* requires the employer to do more than ensure neutrality with regard to race, color, religion, sex, and national origin. It requires the employer to *make additional efforts* to recruit, employ, and promote qualified members of groups formerly excluded. These efforts must be made even if that exclusion cannot be traced to discriminatory actions of the employer.

In general, these laws and regulations prohibit a sales executive from discriminating on the basis of race, religion, color, age, sex, nationality, or handicapped status in the course of recruiting and selecting sales people. EEOC regulations apply to organizations with 25 or more employees. The OFCC requirements apply to firms with 50 or more workers. In addition, the OFCC requires companies to submit in writing their programs for complying with affirmative action guidelines. Either agency may conduct an audit of a firm to determine whether the company is in compliance with the regulations.

The guidelines set by both these agencies cover the full scope of sales-force selection activities—setting hiring specifications, recruiting applicants, and processing these applicants. Prescribed limits are set regarding the use of various tools in the selection procedure, such as application blanks, interviews, and tests.

---

[4] See *Federal Register,* August 25, 1978.

A day-to-day operating problem in the
Majestic Glass Company (B)

Adding Blacks to the Sales Force

There were seldom any vacancies on the Majestic Glass Company sales force, and Clyde Brion, general sales manager, was proud of that fact. He had several applications from available recruits on an informal waiting list, and he tried to keep the facts on these applicants up to date. Occasionally unsolicited applications were received, and some were from unusual types of applicants. For example, Brion had once been urged to hire an exconvict. On more than one occasion he had been asked to explain why there were no women on the force. When such requests were endorsed by other Majestic executives, by customers, or by public officials, Brion believed he could not ignore them.

One afternoon he was asked to come to the office of the company president, Boyd Russell. He found himself in a conference with Russell, several other department heads, and two black men who were introduced as representatives of the Affirmative Action Program in the Department of Health and Human Services.

The visitors explained that the Majestic Glass Company had been loyally served for many years by blacks who worked in the factory, on the custodial staff, and in a few cases in clerical jobs. However, there were no blacks holding supervisory, sales, or managerial jobs. There followed a direct request that the company place some blacks in each of these categories or suffer censure through national publicity. When asked if qualified blacks could be found, the visitors displayed well-prepared dossiers on several men. As nearly as Brion could judge during a quick examination of these files, the men easily met the minimum standards he had maintained in sales-force recruiting.

The meeting continued after the visitors had left. Brion said that a black man would find "rough sledding" on the sales force. There probably would be resentment toward him by some customers. And there was the uncertainty of getting hotel accommodations and service in restaurants, especially when entertaining customers and prospects. Brion also pointed out that there were no openings on the sales force now or in the near future. To accommodate a black, he would be forced either to discharge a salesman now at work or to create a new and unnecessary territory.

In closing the meeting, Russell said, "We'll have to look at this thing positively, men. Life could get mighty unpleasant for us if we don't!"

Question

What action should Clyde Brion take in this situation?

Note: See the introduction to this series of problems in Chapter 3 for the necessary background on the company, its market, and its competition.

Possibly the biggest problem these agencies pose for sales executives is that the burden of proof generally rests with the company to show that it is complying with the regulations. That is, the firm must be able to demonstrate that its recruiting and selection processes are *not* discriminatory. Management must be able to validate (if called on to do so) any of its selection requirements, sources, or tools. For example, assume that a firm uses a formal list of questions in an interview or in some kind of psychological test. Then the company must be able to demonstrate that these interview questions or the test scores are predictive of performance in a given sales job. And such validation is no easy task![5]

A company is very likely to be considered in noncompliance—at least on a prima facie basis—when:

1. Its work force does not include a significant number of women.
2. Its racial or ethnic composition is out of proportion to the ratios of the population in that part of the country.

Nature of the Sales Job

Not only does the sales job differ from nonselling jobs, as we noted in Chapter 1, but the sales job of today is quite different from that of yesteryear. The old type of salesman—the drummer, the Willy Loman of *Death of a Salesman*—is generally gone, and his talents are not especially sought after in the present economy. It is true that aggressive, hard-hitting sales people still exist and may always have a role in some fields, but they no longer are typical. Instead, with the acceptance of the marketing concept by firms, a new type of sales person is emerging—a territorial marketing manager. This new breed of sales people is concerned with relaying consumer wants back to the firm so that appropriate products may be developed. They engage in a *total* consultative, nonmanipulative selling job—missionary selling, servicing customers, selling the line of products, and training customers' sales people. They also serve as *territorial profit managers* and act as a mirror of the market by feeding back marketing intelligence.

In this new position, a sales person occupies many roles with many divergent role partners, and heavy emotional demands are

[5] For an example of an approach to sales-force selection that incorporates a validation procedure enabling management to determine whether it is complying with EEO legislation, see J. Michael Munson and W. Austin Spivey, "Salesforce Selection that Meets Federal Regulation and Management Needs," *Industrial Marketing Management*, February 1980, pp. 11–21.

placed on a rep.[6] Among the roles that sales people fill are persuader, service rep, information gatherer, expediter, coordinator, problem definer, traveler, display arranger, and customer-ego builder. They operate socially, psychologically, and physically independent of the usual worker-boss relationship. In their performances, sales representatives must cope with *role conflicts* of identification and advocacy. They must identify alternately with the company and with the customer. In so doing, there may be conflicts regarding whose position—the company's or the customer's—they are advocating. The several groups with whom they are interacting often have differing and conflicting expectations of the reps.

The sales person's job thus involves a wide range of behaviors. The emotional demands on sales people are great. This is (1) because of the high level of role conflict and (2) because they must handle the behavioral ambiguities pretty much on their own. If management can determine the emotional and interactional demands of a given sales job and then weave these into job descriptions and selection devices, the results of the selection effort should be successful.

Wide Variety of Sales Jobs

No two selling jobs are alike. The types of jobs and the requirements needed to fill them cover a very wide spectrum. Consider the job of a soft drink driver-sales person who calls in routine fashion on a group of retail stores. That job is in another world from that of the computer sales person who sells a system for managing information to an automobile manufacturer. Similarly, a sales person for a cosmetics manufacturer selling door-to-door has a job only remotely related to that of an airplane manufacturer selling a fleet of executive-type aircraft to large firms.

One useful way to classify the many different types of sales jobs is to array them on the basis of the creative skills required in the job, from the simple to the complex. One such classification developed by Robert McMurry, a noted industrial psychologist, is as follows:

1. Positions in which the sales job is primarily to deliver the product—for example, driver-sales person for soft drinks, milk, or fuel oil. The selling responsibilities are secondary. Good service

---

[6] This and the following paragraph are adapted from James A. Belasco, "The Salesman's Role Revisited," *Journal of Marketing*, April 1966, pp. 6–11. For a more complete discussion of role conflict and role ambiguity in a sales job, along with many excellent footnote references, see Gilbert A. Churchill, Jr., Neil M. Ford, and Orville C. Walker, Jr., *Sales Force Management*, 2nd ed. (Homewood, IL: Richard D. Irwin, 1985), Chap. 9.

and a pleasant personality may lead to more sales, but few of these people originate many sales.

2. Positions in which the sales person is primarily an *inside* order taker—for example, the retail clerk standing behind a counter. The customers come to the sales person. Most of them have already decided to buy; the sales person only serves them. The sales rep may use suggestion selling but ordinarily cannot do much more.

3. Positions in which the sales person is primarily an *outside* order taker, going to the customer in the field—for example, a packing house, soap, or spice sales person who calls on retail food stores. They do little creative selling. In contacts with chain store personnel, these reps actually may be discouraged from doing any hard selling. That task is left to executives higher in the organization.

4. Positions in which the sales person is not expected or permitted to solicit an order. The job is to build goodwill, perform promotional activities, or provide services for the customers. This is the missionary sales person for a distiller or the detail sales rep for an ethical pharmaceutical manufacturer.

5. Positions in which the major emphasis is placed on technical product knowledge—for example, the sales engineer.

6. Positions which demand creative selling of tangible products, such as vacuum cleaners, airplanes, encyclopedias, or oil-well drilling equipment. Here, the sales job often is more difficult because the customers may not be aware of their need for the product. Or they may not realize how new products can satisfy their wants better than those they are presently using. When the product is of a technical nature, this category may overlap that of the sales engineer.

7. Positions which require creative selling of intangibles, such as insurance, advertising services, consulting services, or communications systems. Intangibles typically are more difficult to sell because they are less readily demonstrated.

The above seven types of sales jobs may be regrouped into three categories—order-takers, sales-support personnel, and order-getters—depending on the activities that the reps perform (see Figure 4–1). People holding sales jobs in the first three of the above categories essentially are **order-takers**. Their work is fairly routine. The driver reps and outside order-takers usually have their pre-set travel routes where they call on existing accounts to seek repeat business.

People in the categories 4 and 5 are **sales-support** personnel. Their activities generally support the actual selling work done by the reps in the other categories. Support personnel are engaged in build-

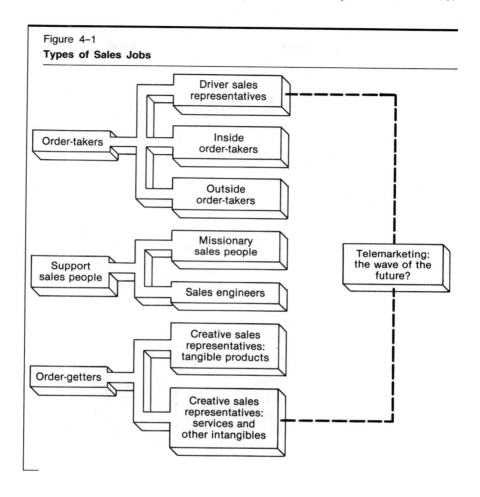

Figure 4–1
Types of Sales Jobs

ing good will, performing sales promotional activities, and working with customers' sales people in a training and educational capacity. The support people who are technical product specialists—sales engineers—work with customers to explain technical products. These reps may help a customer adapt its system to the seller's products or help the seller to design new products to fill the customer's particular needs.

The final two of the above seven groups are the ***order-getters.*** They are the ones who do the creative, developmental selling to existing accounts or to new markets. These are the most difficult types of sales jobs requiring considerable patience, perseverence, and persuasiveness, as well as product knowledge, and an understanding of the customers' needs.

In recent years, a new type of selling job has emerged that tends to cut across many of McMurry's seven categories. This new job is **telemarketing** selling. Several tasks in the order-taking, support work, and order getting categories can be done by means of telemarketing selling. We explained telemarketing in our discussion of sales organizational structures in Chapter 3. Telemarketing is a communications system that involves the innovative use of the telephone, television, and the computer to aid in the selling effort. Telemarketing is inside selling, but not in the traditional sense of the term.[7]

Scope of the Sales-Force Selection Program

The scope of sales-force selection includes three major activities, each of which may be further subdivided (see Figure 4–2).

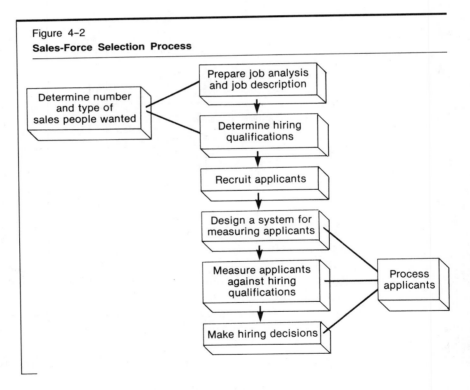

Figure 4–2
Sales-Force Selection Process

[7] For more on the selection of people for telemarketing sales jobs, see Michael Larson, "How to Recruit and Select Quality Telemarketers," *Telemarketing,* November 1984, pp. 36–39.

1. ***Determine the number and type of sales people wanted.*** This involves an analysis of the job and the preparation of a written job description. It also entails a determination of the qualifications necessary to fill the job.
2. ***Recruit a number of applicants.*** This step includes locating good sources of sales people, contacting the recruits, and maintaining a close relationship with the sources.
3. ***Process the recruits and select the qualified sales people.*** The final part of the selection function has two phases. First, it is necessary to establish a procedure for measuring the recruits (from Step 2) against the predetermined standards (from Step 1). Second, the system must be placed into actual operation in order to select the necessary number of people who have the proper qualifications.

The first step is the topic of the remainder of this chapter. Step 2, recruiting applicants, is discussed in Chapter 5, and Step 3, processing applicants, in Chapter 6.[8]

Determining the Number and Type of People Wanted

A good purchasing agent must determine both the quantitative and qualitative specifications for a product or service before ordering it. Even if the order is for nothing more complicated than lead pencils, the purchasing agent must state the quantity needed. Regarding quality, it may be essential to specify hardness of lead, color of lead, color of outer wood, diameter of pencil, type of eraser, and any printing that may be desired on the pencil.

In similar fashion, a sales manager needs detailed specifications when selecting sales people. Otherwise, he or she cannot know what to look for. Certainly, a company should be as careful in buying the services of men and women as it is in buying the products these people sell.

Number of Sales People Needed

A company should figure as closely as possible how many sales reps it needs and then hire only that number. It should not employ more than are needed with the intent of weeding out some as time goes by. This practice indicates that the firm has no faith in its selec-

[8] For a "Special Report" on sales-force recruiting and selection, including many practical suggestions, see *Finding and Hiring the Superior Salesperson* (New York: Research Institute of America, 1985).

tion system. Then management is using actual performance on the job as an additional selection tool.

Sales personnel needs should be forecast well in advance of the time the people will actually be employed. This policy forces the various sales units to plan systematically. It also allows better programming of recruiting, interviewing, and other steps in the selection procedure.

Management can estimate the number of sales people needed in a given future period by considering such factors as (1) expected losses from present sales force; (2) sales forecast for coming period; (3) proposed changes in product line, geographic scope of market, and intensity of market coverage; and (4) competition.

As an example, assume that a company with 100 sales people is selling in the eastern half of the country. The executives concerned with staffing the sales force can plan for the coming year along the following lines. Records show that 5 people will retire. Past experience indicates that an average turnover of 10 percent may be expected because of resignations and discharges; this is another 10 people. Plans call for 15 to be promoted out of the sales force. The total needs so far are 30 people. According to estimates, another 7 will be needed to enable the company to expand into the Oklahoma-Texas-Louisiana market. Thus, a total of 37 new sales representatives must be hired within the next year.

Some critics contend that most companies use highly unsophisticated methods to determine the number of sales reps needed. In fact, how did the above company decide that it needed seven more reps for expansion into the Southwest market? Many firms rely on their executives' judgment and past trial-and-error experience.

One method that the above company might use is to estimate the total workload involved and divide that figure by the estimated workload that one sales rep can handle effectively. To illustrate, let's say that a company manufactures small power tools that are sold to large hardware retailers, building-supply stores, and discount retailers such as K mart and Wal-Mart. The potential new accounts are divided into two categories—class A and class B depending on our estimated sales to each retailer. Class A accounts will be called on 10 times a year, and class B accounts called on 5 times a year. Then the total workload is as follows:

Customer Class	Number of Accounts	Calls per Year	Total Calls
A	400	10	4,000
B	600	5	3,000
			7,000

The manufacturer figures that its reps will be selling 5 days a week for 48 weeks in a year, making an average of 4 calls per day. Thus, each rep will make 960 calls a year (48 × 5 × 4 = 960). To summarize, each rep makes about 1,000 calls per year, and the company has a total workload of 7,000 calls. Consequently, this manufacturer needs to hire 7 additional sales people to expand into the Oklahoma-Texas-Louisiana market.

Job Analysis and Description

Conducting a job analysis is the first major step involved in finding out what type of person is wanted to fill the position. It is a detailed study made to clearly identify every aspect of the position. Three terms related to this topic are:

- *Job analysis*—the actual task of determining what constitutes a given job.
- *Job description*—the document that sets forth in writing the findings in the job analysis.
- *Job qualifications* (sometimes called hiring specifications)—the several specific, personal qualifications and characteristics that applicants should have in order to be selected for the given job.

We should not combine the analysis of a sales position with a determination of qualifications needed to fill the job. These are separate and distinct activities. It is true that some companies do include in their printed *job descriptions* a list of *job qualifications.* Certainly, no harm is done if a company wants to combine the two for publication purposes, just so it recognizes that the one printed statement is the result of two separate analyses.

Big differences are found among the many types of sales positions, and management should certainly conduct a separate analysis for each one. A firm ordinarily would not use the same analysis for the jobs of file clerk and typist just because they both are office jobs. By the same token, it should not accept the same analysis for missionary sales people and for senior product sales people, although both are sales jobs.

Once the job is analyzed, the resultant description should be put in writing. The job analysis and subsequent written description must be done in great detail. It is not enough to say that the sales person is supposed to sell the product, call on the customers, or build goodwill toward the company. Points such as these may make good section headings, but a complete job description will list many duties under each heading.

Figure 4–3
Job Description—Marketing Representative

Armstrong Cork Company, Floor Division

Job Function

Under general supervision of the District Manager or Assistant District Manager, this position is responsible for developing and achieving maximum profitable sales volume of Division products in an assigned territory.

Dimensions

Sales Volume—ranges from $____–$____ million.

Territory—the District is typically divided into geographic areas with this position responsible for one of those areas; additionally, the position will be given direct responsibility for 1–4 Armstrong wholesalers.

Product Line—consists of a wide range of resilient flooring products including: Corlon and Solarian sheet flooring; resilient tile; roto-vinyl sheet flooring; and adhesives and sundries.

Distribution—is achieved by sales to wholesalers who in turn sell to flooring specialty stores, flooring contractors, specialty stores, furniture stores, department stores and building supply dealers.

Major Emphasis—is directed toward developing and improving the wholesalers in all their functions through such means as training and assisting wholesaler salesmen, helping these people make specific sales, developing new business, and generally contributing to the effectiveness of their operations.

Organization Supervised

None

Principal Activities

1. Develops and achieves maximum sales volume consistent with realistic sales projections within assigned territory. Controls expenditures within approved expense budget.
2. Develops and maintains favorable wholesale distribution of entire Division line within assigned territory. Recommends the addition or termination of wholesalers. Develops thorough familiarity with wholesaler's business, sales activity, potentials and requirements.
3. Closely oversees operations of assigned wholesalers. Advises or assists them in such areas as inventory selection and control, service to customers, profit opportunities and ratios, etc. Investigates and corrects problem situations such as duplication of orders, receipt of poor quality goods, etc. Draws upon Armstrong staff services as special assistance is indicated.
4. Translates promotional goals into concrete plans and assignable responsibilities, determining what is to be done and achieved, and who is to achieve it.
5. Identifies the work which must be done to achieve intended results. Divides this work into parcels that can be performed by single individuals.
6. Maintains proper relationships and interrelationships to assure teamwork and a unified effort between wholesaler and retailer.
7. Promotes Armstrong product line and its features and sales points, and an understanding of Armstrong policies and procedures, among the entire wholesaler organization. Keeps personnel informed of new products, price changes, and related concerns. Adapts Lancaster promotional services to local needs and conducts sales meetings to explain same; follows through on all promotions.

Figure 4-3 *(concluded)*

---

8. Assists wholesalers sales personnel in concerned territory in their selling efforts, and trains same through promotional meetings, traveling with each person on a regular basis, helping in making specific sales, and developing new business.
9. Plans territory coverage. Regularly calls upon key retail accounts (current and prospective). Takes orders; promotes the marketing and display of Armstrong products; encourages dealer to capitalize on Armstrong's advertising and promotional efforts; introduces new materials; trains counter personnel; provides literature and samples.
10. Investigates and evaluates field complaints, recommends disposition of complaints accordingly.
11. Keeps District Manager's Office and Lancaster advised on matters of specific business interest such as market conditions, competitive situations, product needs, etc. Consults with District Manager's Office concerning matters of policy, unusual situations, pricing, etc.

Note: This description is written primarily for position-evaluation purposes. It describes duties and responsibilities which are representative of the nature and level of work assigned to the position. The principal activities are representative and not necessarily all-inclusive.

Figure 4–3 is an example of a job description for a sales job in the Floor Division of Armstrong World Industries (formerly the Armstrong Cork Company). This position—entitled marketing representative—involves selling to wholesalers a wide range of resilient flooring products, including sheet flooring, resilient tile, and adhesives.

Uses of job description. A job description is invaluable in all stages of the hiring process. Recruiters cannot talk intelligently to prospective applicants if they do not know in detail what the job involves. A firm cannot develop application blanks, psychological tests, and other selection tools if it has not first analyzed the job.

However, hiring is only one of the many uses for a job description. *It is probably the most important single tool used in the operation of a sales force.*

A job analysis can be the foundation of a sales-training program. By studying the description, the executive in charge of sales training knows in detail what the sales people's duties are, what they must learn, and possibly even the difficulty of the various tasks. Job descriptions are also used in developing compensation plans. If management does not have a clear idea of what the sales force is supposed to do, it is difficult to design a sound compensation structure. Sales supervision and motivation are other sales-management tasks in which the job analysis can be used extensively. By knowing the details of the job, supervisors are in a position to do a superior job of guiding sales people.

Often a job description is an official document that is part of the contract between management and a sales-force union. Also, a sales person's periodic performance ratings will be more meaningful if the company designs an evaluation form that includes many of the detailed aspects of the sales job. Finally, a good job description enables management to determine whether each sales person has a reasonable work load. In some cases, after an executive has had a chance to look at what a rep is being asked to do, duties may be reassigned to make the work load more realistic.

Scope of job description.   Most well-prepared job descriptions have similar items of information (see Figure 4–3). The following points are usually covered:

- *Title of job.* In sufficient description so there is no vagueness, especially in a company that has several different types of sales jobs.
- *Organizational relationship.* Who do the sales people report to?
- *Duties and responsibilities related to the job.* Planning activities, actual selling activities, customer servicing tasks, clerical duties, and self-management responsibilities.
- *Hiring specifications.* While job qualifications technically are not part of a job analysis, there is merit in presenting the job duties and the job qualifications in one document.

In addition, a good job description should include a minimum of two types of information.

1. The technical requirements of the job:
    a. What sales people must know about their products and services.
    b. What they must know in order to offer effective marketing and other business consulting services to customers.
2. The demands of the job—that is, the amount of autonomy given the sales people and the pressure they must work under.

Qualifications Needed to Fill the Job

Most difficult part of selection function.   The next step in a selection program—determining which qualifications are needed to fill the job—is probably the most difficult one in the entire selection process. One reason is that some of the qualifications that make a good sales person cannot be isolated from those needed in some other vocation. It is generally believed that a sales person should be in good health, but then so should a soldier, football player, or ditchdigger. The ability to meet people is a quality that good sales people share with good morticians, politicians, and bus drivers.

Another problem is that management must determine the *degree* to which each trait must be possessed. It is not enough to say that a sales person must be persuasive and ambitious. The question is *how* persuasive or *how* ambitious. Many degrees exist within the extremes. For numerous traits, particularly those dealing with personality, management has not been able to quantify the degree to which they are possessed by an individual.

A corollary requirement is to determine (1) how essential each quality is and (2) the extent to which a low score on one trait can be offset by a high score on another factor. A firm may state that a person must be a college graduate with three years' business experience before being hired as a sales rep. Are these two requirements absolutely essential or is some substitution permissible? Would the firm hire a person with only three years of college but five years of experience?

Further difficulty may arise in recognizing which of the desired traits are innate, and which may be acquired through good training. A firm may make a mistake in turning down potential sales reps because they speak too softly or lack experience in selling the company's product. These are traits that probably can be developed in a good training program. On the other hand, assume a person's history shows a lack of ambition, resourcefulness, and industriousness. It is probably a mistake to hire that applicant in the hope that these attributes can be acquired during training sessions.

Importance of individualized standards.   All types of sales work do not require the same characteristics. The traits found in successful sales engineers, for instance, are not the same as those possessed by missionary sales people. Consequently, the qualifications needed to fill each sales job should be determined on an individualized basis.

The standards of success used by one business are not necessarily valid for others, even in the same industry. Enterprises that sell virtually identical products may require different qualities in their sales forces, because of differences in the companies' methods of selling. A firm that sells vacuum cleaners or cosmetics by the in-home method probably looks for different traits in its sales force than does a company that sells the same products to wholesalers and large retailers.

A sales rep who fails in *one* company or territory may not necessarily fail in *all* companies or territories. Many people have become successful with one firm after being something of a failure in an earlier environment. Even within a given firm, sales people sometimes have performed poorly in one territory (because of social, religious, or other environmental factors) but have been successful after transfer to another region. Sometimes, these factors make it necessary for a company to establish different qualifications for two reps who hold the same type of job.

Are there generally desirable characteristics for sales people?   While the need for individualized hiring qualifications is recognized, there may be some basic characteristics that are generally desirable for all sales people. An appropriate answer to the question of *whether* there are such characteristics is a qualified yes. One reason for hesitancy is that such lists are extremely risky. Often sales executives adopt such a list to a far greater degree than was ever intended.

Another reason for the qualified answer is that lists of characteristics are often so vague and general as to be of little value for any given company or job. A typical list may include such requirements as good health, persuasiveness, self-confidence, enthusiasm, and emotional stability. Usually, no attempt is made to rate these traits in relative importance, nor is there any recognition of the degree of attainment desired for each characteristic. For example, it is impossible to generalize meaningfully on how much enthusiasm is needed in selling.

In identifying the mystique that distinguishes many outstanding sales reps, Robert McMurry observed that super-sales people have a "natural facility as 'wooers.' Some persons have an inherent flair for winning the acceptance of others."[9] At the same time, he noted, many of these "wooers" have a compulsive need to win—to gain the acceptance and affection of others. McMurry identified the following six attributes as being exhibited by successful sales people:

- A high level of energy.
- Abounding self-confidence.
- A chronic hunger for money, more status, and prestige.
- An established habit of working hard and without close supervision.
- A habit of perseverance.
- A natural tendency to be competitive.

[9] Robert N. McMurry and James S. Arnold, *How to Build a Dynamic Sales Organization* (New York: McGraw-Hill, 1968), p. 3; also see Bradley D. Lockerman and John H. Hallaq, "Who Are Your Successful Salespeople?" *Journal of the Academy of Marketing Science,* Fall 1982, pp. 457–72.

In an even shorter list, two industrial psychologists contended that to be successful, a sales person must possess at least two basic personality qualities:

- *Empathy*—the ability to identify with another person's wants, problems, and situation.
- *Ego Drive*—the desire to compete, to persuade, to convince, and to win in face-to-face sales situations.[10]

One of those industrial psychologists published a more recent study that identified the *job match* as a key factor influencing success on a sales job.[11] The job match is defined as how well the sales person's characteristics fit with the functional requirements of the job. As a generalization, the job match was found to be a more useful and valid hiring criterion than either work experience or a college education.

The concept of *matching* is found both in empathy and the job match—qualifications identified by the same researcher as being requirements for success in selling. Empathy involves matching your wants, problems, and so on with those of another person. The job match involves matching your characteristics (personality, abilities, and so on) with the requirements of the job.

For a sales manager to apply the concept of the job match in order to improve the chances of selecting successful sales people, two steps are involved. The first step is to determine (from the job description or other sources) what detailed requirements are called for in the job. For example, will the sales people be closely supervised, or will they be pretty much on their own? Will the sales rep have to handle much detail work? Does the rep need a high degree of conceptual ability? The second step is to determine whether the sales applicant has the personality and the empathy to meet each of these individual requirements.

We still have not *really* answered the question we posed as the heading for this section of the chapter. That is, are there generally desirable characteristics for sales people? Perhaps our best answer is that we do not know. Over the past several years, many research studies have been conducted to identify the personal characteristics

---

[10] David Mayer and Herbert M. Greenberg, "What Makes a Good Salesman" *Harvard Business Review,* July–August 1964, pp. 119–25.

[11] This discussion of the job match is based on Herbert M. Greenberg and Jeanne Greenberg, "Job Matching for Better Sales Performance," *Harvard Business Review,* September–October 1980, pp. 128–33. The study covered a sample size of 36,000 sales people in 14 industries. Half of those industries typically have a high turnover of sales people, and the other half have a low turnover rate.

What Makes a Super-Sales Person?

Here is another perspective on some common characteristics—

- Super-sales people are always taking risks and innovating. They stay out of the "comfort zone" and try to surpass their previous levels of performance.
- Super-sales people have a powerful sense of mission. Their personal goals are always higher than the quotas set by management, and they work well with their managers.
- Super-sales people are more interested in solving problems than in placing blame or bluffing their way out of a situation. They are always upgrading their skills.
- Super-sales people see themselves as partners with their customers, rather than as adversaries. They believe their task is to communicate with their customers as people, and not as objects.
- Super-sales people take rejection as a situation they can learn from, and they do not personalize a rejection.
- Super-sales people—like peak performers in sports and the arts—use mental rehearsal before every sale. They prepare a sales call in advance—from shaking the customer's hand when they walk in, to discussing his problems, and asking for the order.

Source: Charles Garfield, as cited in *Sales & Marketing Management*, August 13, 1984, p. 86. Professor Garfield, a clinical psychologist, over a period of 20 years has analyzed the common characteristics of more than 1,500 super-achievers in every field of endeavor. Garfield claims that the complexity and speed of change in the business world today means that a peak performer in sales requires a greater mastery of different fields than does a top performer in science, sports, or the arts.

---

needed for successful sales performance. The results of these studies simply have been inconsistent and inconclusive. In fact, in some instances, different studies covering the same industry came to opposite conclusions regarding whether a given personal characteristic was a valid requirement for sales success.

Our general conclusion from this wide range of research is the same point we stressed earlier in this section. That is, a company should establish its own individualized set of hiring requirements for each class of sales job in that firm. This is because the factors that determine successful sales performance essentially are job-specific.[12]

Rather than to try to develop a list of desirable traits, we suggest the following major categories of traits. The individual company can fill in the details to suit its own needs (see Figure 4–4).

1. Mental (intelligence, planning ability).

---

[12] For an excellent summary review of the research on determinants and predictors of sales performance, along with extensive bibliographies, see James M. Comer and Alan J. Dubinsky, *Managing the Successful Sales Force* (Lexington, Mass.: Lexington Books, 1985); and Gilbert A. Churchill, Jr., Neil M. Ford, Steven W. Hartley, and Orville C. Walker, Jr., "The Determinants of Salesperson Performance: A Meta-Analysis," *Journal of Marketing Research*, May 1985, pp. 103–18.

Figure 4-4
Predictors of Successful Sales Performance

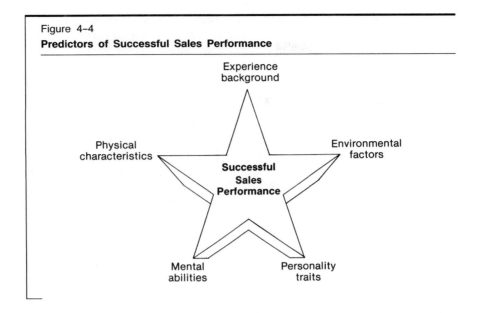

2. Physical (age, appearance, health, speaking abilities).
3. Experience (education, sales experience, other business experience).
4. Environmental (membership in organizations, amount of insurance owned, marital status, number of dependents, homeownership, length of residence in community, religion, race, family and social background).
5. Personality (ambition, interest, enthusiasm, tact, resourcefulness, emotional stability, persuasiveness, dominance, self-confidence, self-reliance, initiative).

When dealing with qualifications in any of these categories, care must be taken to comply with the laws regarding nondiscrimination in employment. In companies that are subject to EEOC and OFCC guidelines, many hiring qualifications that were traditionally used to screen sales-force applicants can no longer be used. That is, unless the company can show that these requirements are "bona fide occupational qualifications" (BFOQ). For example, an arrest (or even a conviction) cannot be used to screen out an applicant, unless the company can demonstrate the validity of the qualification. Otherwise, an interviewer cannot even ask, "Have you ever been arrested?" or "Have you ever been convicted of a felony?"

Methods of determining qualifications. There is no satisfactory method for every company to use in determining the qualifications needed in its sales force. Several different procedures currently are being used. Some are adaptable for companies that have large sales forces and have been in business for some time, so that recorded histories of background and performance are available. Other methods may be used by large or small, and old or new firms. Five methods are discussed in this section.

Study of job description. Many hiring specifications can be deduced from a carefully prepared job description. Job description statements about the degree of sales supervision, for instance, indicate to what extent the sales person should have the resourcefulness to work alone. Statements about the nature of the product, viewed in light of the company's training program, indicate something about the desired technical background or experience qualifications.

Analysis of personal histories. A company in business for several years and with a large sales force can determine its job qualifications by analyzing the personal histories of its present and past sales people. The age and size requirements for the data are necessary to get a sample of histories large enough so that the findings are reasonably reliable. The theory underlying this method is that, by analyzing various characteristics of good and poor sales reps, it is possible to discover certain traits present in the good reps and absent in the poor ones. These traits are then presumed to be some of the ones required for success, and they would be listed as essential qualifications.

In the past, the task of analyzing personal histories in a large or even medium-sized firm could be a time-consuming activity involving considerable clerical work. Today, management can use computer technology to store and retrieve the information in greater detail, faster, and at lower cost. Computerized information also enables management to conduct more types of analyses regarding job qualifications. The New England Mutual Life Insurance Company, for example, uses computer technology extensively to make personal-history analyses as part of the company's sales-force selection system. Through the use of lap-top portables and microcomputers, which are tied in to a central mainframe computer, the company analyses performance criteria and activities in relation to selection criteria and activities.[13]

The first step in this analysis is to get a list of all present and past sales people, along with (1) their *selection* records (application blanks, patterned interviews, and so on) and (2) their *performance* records (sales results, quotas, and job evaluations).

---

[13] See "New England Life Takes Steps to Insure Its Future: Computers Keep Quality Consistent," *Sales & Marketing Management,* August 12, 1985, p. 74.

The next step is to divide the sales force into two or three groups, depending on management's judgment of their sales effectiveness. In our example, the reps are divided into two groups, based on a good-poor classification. Obviously, sound executive judgment is needed in deciding to which group a particular sales person should be assigned. Some possible criteria are sales volume, percentage of sales quota attained, gross margin, ratio of expenses to sales, and performance in missionary selling jobs.

The third step is time-consuming and must be done in careful detail. A list is prepared of each characteristic that might have a bearing on success in selling. Then management must determine whether there is any significant difference in the extent to which the trait is possessed by the good sales people as contrasted to the poor ones. Some characteristics are much easier to determine than others. It is reasonably simple to ascertain differences between good and poor performers in such qualifications as age at time of hiring or previous sales experience. However, it is much more difficult to measure differences in personality traits possessed by the two groups.

Age at time of hiring and amount of education are two characteristics used here to illustrate how personal histories can be studied. Tables 4–1 and 4–2 show the results of the hypothetical case. Of 600 past and present sales people included in the sample, 360 were considered good—not a very high average, incidentally. Age brackets were established, and the 600 were placed in the bracket that represented each rep's age when hired. From an analysis of Table 4–1, it is apparent that the sales people most apt to succeed in company A were between 25 and 35 years of age when selected. Of those in that age group when hired, 90 percent turned out to be good sales reps. Under 25 or over 55 seem to be the poorest ages for hiring.

Table 4–2 shows that graduation from high school seems to be the ideal amount of education needed for future success in the job. A

Table 4–1

Sales People's Age at Time of Hiring *(Company A)*

Age Bracket	Number of Good Reps	Number of Poor Reps	Total Reps	Percent of Good Reps
Under 25	30	70	100	30
25–35	180	20	200	90
36–45	100	50	150	66⅔
46–55	40	60	100	40
Over 55	10	40	50	20
Total	360	240	600	

Table 4–2
Amount of Previous Education of Sales People (Company A)

Amount of Education	Number of Good Reps	Number of Poor Reps	Total Reps	Percent of Good Reps
Less than four years of high school	30	70	100	30
High school graduate	250	25	275	91
Some college	20	80	100	20
College graduate	55	45	100	55
Postgraduate study	5	20	25	20
Total	360	240	600	

person who started high school or college, but did not graduate, seems to be a particularly poor risk. From the findings on age and education, it is probable that some years of business experience are necessary in company A. If 18 is the average age of students graduating from high school and 25 to 35 is the best hiring age range, some years in between have to be accounted for.

Essentially similar analyses may be made for any other trait suspected of influencing success in selling in a given company. The firm could study environmental and experience factors in much the same manner as age and education. Mental abilities may be quantified by means of intelligence tests. General physical condition could be measured by giving a person the score on a physical examination, or a rating on general appearance and fluency of speech.

Personality traits are the one category that is extremely difficult to measure objectively or quantitatively. Many firms use personality tests for this purpose. In the final analysis, most firms probably must rely on executive judgment to determine which personality characteristics are present in good sales people and absent in poor ones.

After a complete analysis of personal-history records, a company should be able to describe the ideal qualifications for a specific job. The list will probably be quite long. However, a business must know how much less than the ideal it can take and still be reasonably assured of hiring a potentially successful sales representative. In Table 4–1, for example, 25 to 35 was found to be the ideal age range for hiring. The question is whether it is the *only* bracket to be considered. Or, could the firm hire someone in the 36 to 45 range if the applicant were outstanding in many other characteristics?

For quantitatively measurable traits, there is one possible solution to this problem. First, management would select what it considers to be the critical characteristics, say 10 to 20 of them. Then, gradations or subdivisions would be set up for each selected qualification. Examples are given at the left in Tables 4–1 and 4–2, where age brackets and varying amounts of education are established. After the personal-history analysis is completed, a score or rating may be attached to each subdivision.

This raises the problem of rating or scoring the relative importance of each characteristic and each gradation within the item. A careful study of the findings of the personal-history analysis usually shows that the various success factors are not of equal importance. Therefore, the company should assign different weights to each item and to the divisions within each one. For example, the maximum weight given to previous business experience may be 12, but the top possible score in educational background may be only 8. The scores assigned to grades within each qualification may be as follows:

Business Experience		Education	
None	0	Less than high school	2
Less than 1 year	2	High school graduate	8
1–2 years	6	Some college	3
3–4 years	8	College graduate	5
5–7 years	12	Postgraduate work	3
8–10 years	10	Graduate degree	2
Over 10 years	4		

The implication is that business experience as a qualification is about 50 percent more important than the educational background of a recruit (a maximum weight of 12 compared to one of 8). Also, five to seven years of business work is twice as valuable as one or two years (12 versus 6). Being a high school graduate with no additional schooling is worth about the same as three or four years of business experience (8 versus 8).

After points are assigned to each division of the selected qualifications, all the sales people studied in the personal-history analysis could be graded on these traits. Assume that 15 factors were selected, with the top possible score totaling 150. Probably no one would achieve a perfect score. However, the company can determine the minimum number of points that a person should get in order to have a reasonable chance for success. Company A (using Tables 4–1 and 4–2) may find, for example, that the minimum score achieved among the 360 good sales people was 110 out of the 150 points.

Some firms modify this procedure slightly to account for the age of the applicant. This is because the age at the time of hiring affects the score received on several other items. Compare two people, one hired at age 30 and the other at age 40. The older person probably belongs to more clubs, owns more insurance, and has more business experience. As a result, his total score is higher. In the long run, however, the younger person may turn out to be the more successful sales rep. To adjust for the age factor, some firms use it as the main control item rather than as an individual qualification to be scored along with the others. Each of the 360 sales reps in company A would be graded on the same basis, but the grades would be interpreted differently to account for the age at the time of hiring. The minimum score for those in the 25–35 age bracket might be 95. In the 36–45 group it could be 110, and in the 46-and-over division, 125 might be the lowest acceptable score.

There are some limitations in the personal-history analysis technique. One was implied earlier—relatively few companies have the data base needed to operate this analysis. Another is that the "good" and "poor" classifications refer only to the people actually hired by this firm. The good sales people were not necessarily the best that could have been hired. Furthermore, the analysis is historical. That is, it shows what qualifications were desirable in the past, but it does not allow for changing times and requirements.

Failure analysis: Knockout factors.   A by-product of a personal-history analysis is a list of the characteristics that a sales person should *not* have. That is, they are predictive of failure in the sales job. Although this is a negative approach to the problem of determining hiring specifications, it may be effective. One company, for example, identified the following knockout factors:

- Instability of residence.
- Failure in business within past two years.
- Divorce or separation within past two years. (For male applicants only. This did not constitute a knockout factor for women.)
- Excessive personal indebtedness—debts cannot be met within two years from earnings on the new job.
- A previous standard of living that was too high.
- Unexplained gaps in employment record.

An applicant who possessed any of these characteristics would *not* be hired. The company believed this applicant would *not* be successful in the sales job.

In view of current legal implications, a company has to be very careful in using the concept of failure analysis. Before the executives establish any knockout factor, they must be sure thay can validate that factor as a negative hiring qualification. That is, they must be able to prove that any given factor truly is indicative of failure in a particular sales job.

Analysis of exit interviews.   Many firms follow a practice of interviewing people who are leaving the sales force for any reason. An analysis of these exit interviews may tell the organization something about the qualifications needed for the job.

Theoretically, an exit interview would seem to be a good method of getting valuable information. When sales reps are about to leave a company, it might seem that they will be honest and forthright about their reasons for doing so. However, realistically, the exit interview is usually less than valuable and may even be misleading. Few give the real reason they are leaving, particularly if it reflects badly on the organization or any one in it. In the future these people may want a recommendation from the company, and they do not want to risk antagonizing anyone when they leave.

Sources of information outside the firm.   For companies too new or too small to get any value out of analyses of personal histories, an outside source may help in establishing job qualifications. One external source is a consulting firm that specializes in personnel selection. The use of outside sources seems to violate all generalization earlier stated that a firm should develop its own individualized job qualifications. From a practical standpoint, however, sometimes outside help is needed for a firm to get started in developing a good selection system.

Summary

In the Preface and again in Chapter 2, we stated one of our basic philosophies—namely, that selecting the right people (staffing the organization) is the most important step in the management process. Sales-force selection should be coordinated with an organization's strategic marketing and sales-force planning, because the sales force often plays a major role in implementing the plans. A good sales-force selection program is also important for other reasons. It will improve sales performance, reduce turnover, provide cost benefits, and make other managerial tasks easier to accomplish. It is difficult to get enough good sales people, and sales managers are no better than the people working under them.

The responsibility for selecting sales people usually rests in the sales department. These executives must understand the various civil rights laws and other government regulations that have a substantial impact on all phases of sales-force selection.

The sales-selection task is a three-step process. First, management determines how many and what kind of people are wanted. The second step is to recruit a number of applicants. The third step involves processing these applicants and selecting the most qualified ones.

Management can determine the *number* of sales people to be hired by conducting an analysis based on the company's past experiences and future expectations. To determine the *type* of person wanted, management should first conduct a job analysis and then write a job description for each different position to be filled. A good job description can be used in every stage of operating a sales force—in training, compensation, supervision, and so on.

Determining the qualifications needed to fill the job is the most difficult part of the sales-selection process. As yet, we simply have not been able to isolate the traits that make for success in selling. Nor can we measure the degree to which a given trait should be possessed by a sales person. Nor have we been able to identify basic characteristics that are found in all successful sales people.

However, we do know that it is important to develop *individualized* hiring specifications for a given job in a given firm. Management should set its own standards in qualification categories, such as mental, physical, experience, environmental, and personality traits.

To get some help in determining its hiring qualifications, a company can analyze the personal histories of its present and past sales people. Management also can (1) study its job description, (2) identify factors that are predictive of failure in the sales job (knockout factors), and (3) analyze its exit interviews.

Questions and Problems

1. "Careful selection is important, but not essential, in building an effective sales force. Improper selection of sales people can be overcome by a good training program, sound supervision, or an excellent compensation program." Do you agree? Discuss.

2. "Salesmen are born, not made." Do you agree? If so, why does a firm need a training program or sales supervisors? If you do not agree—that is, you believe sales reps are made, not born—then why is so much stress placed on the importance of good selection? Perhaps a firm should spend far less time and money on selection and, instead, place the effort in a thorough training program.

3. In the following companies, who should have the responsibility for selecting the sales force? Should it be the president, chief sales-force executive, district sales manager, or someone in the personnel department?
   a. Copier division of Xerox Corporation.
   b. Large distributor of home appliances.
   c. Automobile dealer in St. Louis, Missouri.
   d. Furniture manufacturer in Grand Rapids, Michigan.

4. Referring to the seven-way classification of sales jobs found early in this chapter, answer these questions:
   a. In which types of jobs is the sales rep most free from close supervision?
   b. Which types are likely to be the highest paid?

    c. Which groups are likely to involve the most traveling?

    d. For which groups is a high degree of motivation most necessary?

    Explain your reasoning in each case.

5. "A good salesman can sell anything." Do you agree? What evidence do you have to support your opinion?

6. If a person wants to be a top-notch professional career sales rep and has no interest in being a manager, is a college education necessary? Discuss. If your answer is yes, what courses should be required? If your answer is no, why do so many firms recruit sales people from colleges, and why is a college education so often listed in the qualifications for a sales job?

7. Assume that a company wants to hire a sales engineer—that is, fill a position where the major emphasis is placed on technical product knowledge. Should this firm recruit engineers and train them to sell, or recruit sales reps and teach them the necessary technical information and abilities?

8. When selecting a sales force, many companies have adopted the policy of hiring only experienced sales people, and preferably those who have had experience selling similar or directly competitive products. Under what conditions, if any, may this be a sound policy?

9. After interviewing some of the sales force and/or the appropriate executives, prepare a detailed job description for one of the following jobs.

    a. Automobile dealer sales person.

    b. Driver-sales person for local soft drink bottler.

    c. Missionary sales person for a manufacturer.

    d. Sales person for some type of wholesaler.

10. Prepare a list of qualifications needed to fill each job you analyzed and described in the preceding problem.

11. Prepare a list of the qualifications you feel are necessary to fill the sales job described in Figure 4–3.

Case 4-1

Banning Farms

Qualifications for a Telemarketing Sales Job

Jim Banning and his sister Susan were engaged in a lively discussion—some people might call it an argument—over who to hire as their telemarketing sales representative. The job involved promoting their new line of packaged gift fruit baskets. Jim and Susan had taken over the management of the family farms after their parents retired in 1986. Traditionally, Banning Farms had sold fruit baskets filled with citrus fruits from their own groves. The company's output was supplemented by other fruits, both fresh and dried, from neighboring farms. (See Exhibit 1.)

The major advertising media used previously had been selected magazines such as *Sunset, Sales & Marketing Management,* and the airlines' in-flight magazines. This magazine advertising campaign was supported by a large direct-mail operation. The results had been quite good. While sales and profit figures were confidential because the firm was privately held, sales were in the millions of dollars and the company was relatively profitable.

Susan had read about telemarketing techniques. She had attended a seminar on the subject and had spoken with several people who were doing it successfully. One person would be hired to work a telemarketing station built around an automatic dialing and message machine. This machine mechanically handled the burdensome task of dialing numbers and did the initial quick screening of prospects. After recruiting and interviewing eight people for the job, two dis-

Exhibit 1
Banning Packages Fruit Boxes Ready for Shipment

tinctly different candidates emerged for the position. Jim wanted to hire Fred, a 58-year-old man with considerable sales experience whose strong presence on the telephone was most impressive. The man really knew how to handle himself over the telephone.

On the other hand, Susan had been impressed with the argument advanced by some telemarketing experts that the best telephone sales people were not necessarily those who made a forceful personal impression. There was evidence that many meek and mild individuals, once provided with the psychological protection and anonymity of the telephone, become like tigers closing in on their prey. They used the telephone to redress their social inadequacies. Consequently, Susan was impressed with Anne Marie, a pleasant woman of 35 who needed the job to help support her family of four children and a construction-laborer husband. Tests had indicated that her telephone voice was both pleasant and persuasive. Susan argued that Anne Marie would not offer the initial threat to the respondent that Fred would. "After all," she added, "we're selling a food, and it seems to me that it's more appropriate for a woman to do it."

Jim countered, "As far as I'm concerned, there's no substitute for sales experience. Fred knows what he's doing and has the experience to prove it. I vote for going with the proven performer." Neither Jim nor Susan could persuade the other of their views. Thus, the selection of the new telemarketing representative was stalemated, since they were partners with equal authority.

Questions

1. What qualifications should be set for this telemarketing sales job?
2. What course of action should Jim and Susan follow in this situation?

Case 4–2

Gulf Coast Chemicals, Inc.*

Hiring Qualifications for Sales Representatives

Jim Hinson was well aware of the company rumors to the effect that he soon would be forced to change his policies for selecting sales people. In his position as director of sales operations for Gulf

* Case prepared by Professor Bruce D. Buskirk, Northwestern University. Used with permission.

Coast Chemicals, Inc., Jim Hinson reported to Andrew Witt, the new vice president of marketing. It was from Mr. Witt that the rumored selections pressure was coming. He had made several comments regarding the sales-force selection policies to various members of management, both above and below Hinson. Mr. Witt thought it was most unusual that the company's 22 sales reps all were more than six feet tall, weighed over 230 pounds, and didn't have any necks. People in the company snickered because they knew of Mr. Witt's dislike of football and its players. They also knew that this dislike would soon conflict with Hinson's policy of hiring only ex-college football linemen, preferably offensive guards, as sales reps.

At various times Jim Hinson had expounded on his beliefs that such men made the best sales reps for the company. He had said many times, "I am looking for people who know what it's like to work long hard hours doing a dirty job without much recognition or appreciation. I want people who are team players and want to win badly." When asked by a colleague if he was ever going to hire a woman sales rep, he replied, "I'm looking hard, but there are not too many of them playing guard yet."

The friend observed, "Better look harder, they're going to get you sooner or later. You are a sitting duck for any women's-movement agitator who wants to hang your scalp on her belt. I understand there are some women's football leagues around. Wonder what their guards look like?" He laughed. Jim didn't.

"You may think it's funny, but my job may be on the line with this Witt guy. Look at it from my point of view. I have a system that works. I know these guys. I know I am hiring in my own image, but I know how to motivate and talk to them. They respond to me because I am one of them. I've been there. I've spent my time in the pit and have scars to prove it. I've known defeat and I've known great victory, and I made up my mind a long time ago which one I liked best. My sales force relates to this type of thinking and our record proves it. We have built this company from almost nothing to a $140 million highly profitable firm. We're a hard-hitting sales force that doesn't quit."

Jim had joined a small firm (sales $5.4 million) fresh out of a well-known Southeastern university where he majored in football while minoring in marketing. He still cherished the role he had played in winning the Sugar Bowl game in his senior year. His outstanding sales performance during his first two years with the firm quickly earned him the sales managership. He quickly built the sales force into perhaps the best in the industry. He had not been offered a promotion into higher management for two reasons: first, he was making great contributions to the company as sales manager, and top management did not want to risk "killing the goose." Second, he knew little other than selling and sales management. He had made no effort to broaden his business skills. He was happy doing what he did best. As he put it many times, "I don't want to be quarterback. I want to knock people down. I love contact. Sales is where the business game is won or lost, and that's where I want to be. Not pushing paper around in the office upstairs."

While the turnover rate among the sales force was almost zero, the company did need several new sales reps to place in new territories. In particular, the company had expanded into Memphis, St. Louis, Little Rock, Nashville, and Knoxville with its line of janitorial chemicals, solvents, and metal finishing compounds. At least two new reps would be needed.

One of Jim's top producers, and close personal friend, urged him to hire a woman for one of the openings. "Be kind to yourself for a change, Jim. Hire one and get Witt off your back. She's not going to hurt us one little bit. Give her quotas the same way you give them to us. If she can't cut it, then you can't say you didn't try."

Jim protested, "That's tokenism. Just like a few years ago when you all wanted me to hire a black just to keep the wolves from baying at our door. Well, I wouldn't until I found some that would be successful for us. Now we have three blacks, but they fit our success formula."

"Yeah, they played guard for your old team."

Jim had been partial to hiring graduates from his alma mater. Over half of the reps had played football for the school. He defended his policy to one of his former professors by saying, "I think you professors now call it networking. We used to call it the 'good ole' boy' system. Sure, I believe in taking care of my own. Why not? They take care of me. The university was good to me. A lot of people went out of their way to help me through school. Now I feel that it's my obligation to help some others find their place in life. We're a family. I just know that if I bring in outsiders who don't understand our way of life, all these good things that I've built will start crumbling. I guess there are people who would say that I am just trying to hold on to my way of life. There is no way we could hold any of our sales meetings the way we do with women present. It just wouldn't be proper. Our language is worse than terrible, I am sorry to say. And the behavior of some of the boys is, well, let's say that if it were a movie it would be X-rated. You know I haven't been hiring them for their sainthood. I guess all of this sounds awful to you, but that's the way I really feel about it. What do you think I should do? Stand tough and slug it out on the basis of my record or throw 'em a morsel to keep them quiet?"

Questions:

1. Do you believe that a woman sales rep could be found who would fit into this sales force?
2. What advice should the professor give Jim?
3. If Jim insists on maintaining his selection policies, what advice would you give him for doing so?

5

Selecting the Sales Force— Recruiting Applicants

Leave no stone unturned.
EURIPIDES

After determining the number and type of sales people wanted, the next major step in selecting a sales force is to recruit several applicants for the position to be filled. *Recruiting* includes all activities involved in securing individuals who will apply for the job. The concept does not include the actual *processing* of the people by means of interviews, tests, or other hiring tools. This step is the topic of Chapter 6.

Recruiting and Strategic Planning

Management should effectively coordinate its sales-force recruiting program with its strategic marketing and sales-force planning. In a total selection program, recruiting activities can be an important element in implementing the strategic planning. A company's sales and marketing strategies should be a significant influence on management's choice of recruiting sources. If a company's sales plans require experienced reps, then sales-force recruiters should not bother interviewing graduating college seniors. A company whose cost-cutting plans call for substantial cutbacks in its training programs should recruit experienced sales people, not current college graduates. If a company has an executive-development policy of promoting from within the organization, then management can start to grow its own sales executives by recruiting sales people from nonselling departments within the company.

Importance of Planned Recruiting

A sound selection program cannot exist without a well-planned and well-operated system for recruiting applicants. If recruiting is done on a haphazard basis, a company runs the risk of entirely overlooking, or losing contact with, good sources of prospective sales people. Poor recruiting may also force an organization to hire unsuitable people simply because the firm must select immediately from the available applicants. An effective recruiting program is also needed because it is difficult to attract good prospects to the sales field. The demand for trained people in other occupations, coupled with the general lack of interest and prestige in selling, have done much to reduce potential sales personnel.

The high rate of turnover experienced in many sales forces means that firms should be recruiting continuously. The turnover factor is related in some respects to the tight labor market for sales people. When good people are in short supply, they receive and accept offers for employment more frequently, and turnover increases.[1]

The importance of recruiting grows in relation to increases in the costs of selecting sales people and maintaining them in the field. Certainly, the direct costs of recruiting are increasing—costs such as the expenses of maintaining recruiting teams and placing recruiting advertisements. But more important than the *direct* cost of recruiting is the effect that recruiting may have on the *total* costs of selection and training. For example, it may be desirable to *increase* the cost of the recruiting activity if it results in finding better-quality applicants. Management should view the selection process as a subsystem in sales-force management and use a *total* cost approach. Thus, recruiting activity should be optimized so as to reduce the total costs of selecting and developing new sales people to the point where their productivity is profitable.[2]

Need for Many Recruits

A philosophy to follow in recruiting is to get a sufficient number of qualified applicants in order to maximize the chances of finding the right person for a job. The laws of probability support this pol-

---

[1] Turnover $= \dfrac{\text{Number of people hired}}{\text{Average size of sales force}}$. A 100 percent turnover does not necessarily mean that the entire sales force has been replaced. In a staff of 500, half may have stayed the entire year, while the other 250 were replaced twice. All together 500 were hired in a year, so a 100 percent turnover is said to result.

[2] For a method of determining the amount to spend for recruiting and screening applicants for sales positions, see René Y. Darmon and Stanley J. Shapiro, "Sales Recruiting—A Major Area of Underinvestment," *Industrial Marketing Management,* February 1980, pp. 47–51. The authors concluded that many major corporations may be spending far less than they should on sales recruiting and selection.

icy. The shortage of qualified sales representatives makes it imperative for a business to screen several people for each opening. The following is a useful rule of thumb to determine the number of recruits needed to select one sales person:

- Recruit 20 people who are interested in the job.
- A review of application blanks will eliminate 10.
- The initial interview will eliminate another 6 or 7.
- The 3 or 4 finalists are screened further by interviews, tests, etc.
- One person is finally hired.

Recruiting Is a Screening Device

A recruiting program serves as an automatic screening device in sales selection. Therefore management must make sure it does not miss potentially successful sales people because of its recruiting procedures. Recruiters who interview college students, for example, should be careful not to screen out good prospects in the interviewing process. There is also a screening factor in the recruiting sources used, such as the choice of colleges visited or the selection of newspapers in which advertisements are placed. An advertisement in *The Wall Street Journal,* for instance, attracts a different type of recruit than does an ad in a metropolitan daily.

The Law and Sales-Force Recruiting

The civil rights laws and regulations referred to in the preceding chapter are applicable to a company's recruiting efforts. Management cannot discriminate on the basis of race, color, religion, nationality, age, or sex in its recruiting activities—in its choice of sources, for example. The affirmative action guidelines issued by the Office of Federal Contract Compliance (OFCC) state that management must take affirmative action to notify women and minority groups when there is a vacancy in the sales force. This means, for example, that the company must advertise in newspapers and magazines likely to be read by these groups. And the advertisements should state that the company is an "Equal Opportunity Employer M/F."

Find and Maintain Good Recruiting Sources

Most firms actively recruit sales reps from many sources. To determine the best sources, a recruiter should first find out where the company's best sales people came from in the past. This assumes that there has been no substantial change in the job description or job qualifications.

To determine these sources, an executive may use a method similar to that suggested in Chapter 4 for analyzing personal histories. All present and past sales people can be separated into two or three groups, according to their all-around sales ability. Then a study can be made to determine: (1) where the top performers came from; and (2) if there is any significant difference in these sources as contrasted to the sources of the people rated in the lower group.

An examination of the job description and hiring specifications will reveal other factors that affect a recruiter's choice of sources. The educational qualifications for the job, for example, may indicate whether colleges can produce desirable recruits.

Once satisfactory sources are located, management should maintain a continuing relationship with them, even during periods when the firm is not hiring. Firms that want college graduates should keep in touch with professors who have furnished assistance in the past. Customers who have supplied leads to good people should be reminded periodically of the company's gratitude and encouraged to suggest more prospects.

If a firm must do any significant amount of recruiting, it should be done continually. Even when no immediate need for new sales people exists, the firm should develop lists of future prospects and, if possible, contact and screen them. Of course, a company ordinarily cannot screen a group of applicants and then expect them to wait an indefinite period for a vacancy. However, the company at least can provide itself with lists of potential recruits so that a reservoir of leads is available when needed.

Sources of Sales Representatives

Some frequently used sources or leads to sources are as follows:

- Within the company.
- Other companies (competitors, customers, noncompetitors).
- Educational institutions.
- Advertisements.
- Employment agencies.
- Voluntary applicants.
- Women, minorities, and other underemployed groups.

Within the Company

Present sales force. A company's sales force is an excellent source of leads to new recruits. Present sales people should know what sort of person the firm is seeking. They know the job and company well, and, if they are satisfied, they can do much to sell the opportunities to prospective applicants.

A firm's sales people meet representatives from other companies and make contacts through social, athletic, fraternal, and business clubs. Thus the reps are in a good position to know when a person is interested in changing jobs. Often they are well acquainted with the general qualifications of some of the prospects.

Some companies offer a monetary incentive to encourage their employees (sales force and others) to provide names of people the company might recruit as sales reps. If an employee-referred recruit is hired, the employee who made the referral receives a cash award. Figure 5–1 illustrates the employee-incentive referral program used by the Business Systems Group in the Xerox Corporation in its sales-force recruiting program.

However, in using its own sales people, the firm may be encouraging them to spend time recruiting instead of selling. Also, the sales reps may recommend people on the basis of personal feelings rather than an impartial evaluation of the prospect's qualifications. The advantages of using the sales force for leads, however, far outweigh the drawbacks. Even if some unqualified people are recruited, the firm should be able to weed them out through its selection process.

Factory or office employees. Some companies recruit their sales force from among workers in their production plants or offices. Management has been able to observe these people and evaluate their potential as sales reps. These workers, particularly plant employees, are acquainted with the technical aspects of the product. They also have been indoctrinated in company policies and programs. Thus, the need for some of the training is eliminated. Hiring sales people from within the company can be a great morale booster, because most plant and office workers consider transfer to the sales department as a promotion.

Recruiting from within the organization has some limitations. It is risky to take workers who are excellent performers in the office or factory and transfer them to a sales job where they may not have the same success. In some cases, antagonism can build among plant or office supervisors who feel their workers are being pirated by the sales department.

Other Companies: Competitors, Customers, Noncompetitors

The controversial question of whether to hire competitors' sales people is argued from ethical and economic standpoints. The ethical aspects of the problem depend on who made the employment over-

Figure 5-1
Employee Incentive Referral Plan—Xerox Corporation, Business Systems Group

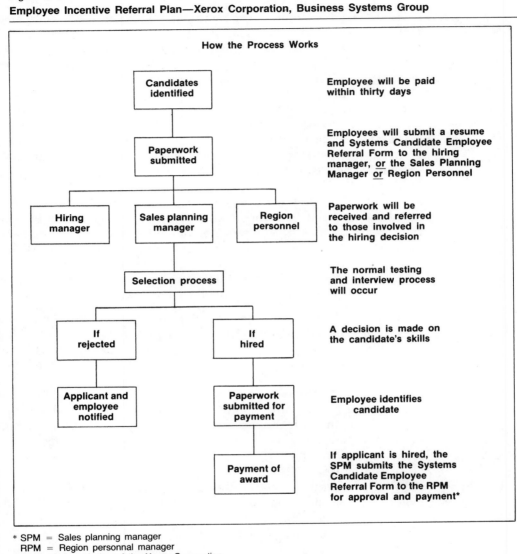

How the Process Works

Candidates identified	Employee will be paid within thirty days
Paperwork submitted	Employees will submit a resume and Systems Candidate Employee Referral Form to the hiring manager, <u>or</u> the Sales Planning Manager <u>or</u> Region Personnel
Hiring manager / **Sales planning manager** / **Region personnel**	Paperwork will be received and referred to those involved in the hiring decision
Selection process	The normal testing and interview process will occur
If rejected / **If hired**	A decision is made on the candidate's skills
Applicant and employee notified / **Paperwork submitted for payment**	Employee identifies candidate
Payment of award	If applicant is hired, the SPM submits the Systems Candidate Employee Referral Form to the RPM for approval and payment*

* SPM = Sales planning manager
RPM = Region personnal manager
Used with permission of the Xerox Corporation.

ture. If a sales person from company A seeks employment and is hired by company B, a competitor, probably no question of ethics is involved. The reason is that the sales person, not company B, made the overture.

On the other hand, some people feel it would be unethical for company B to raid A's sales force by actively recruiting its reps. One may wonder whether attempting to take a competitor's best sales people is any different from trying to take its best markets or customers. While the first practice is considered unethical, the second is called competition. Some companies refuse to hire competitors' sales people. Whether the policy stems from high ethical standards or fear of retaliation is an interesting point to consider.

From an economic point of view, there are mixed feelings regarding the recruiting of competitors' sales people. On one hand, they know the product and the market very well. They also are experienced sellers and therefore require less training. On the other hand, it may be harder for these people to unlearn old practices and make the adjustment to a new environment.

A firm may seek leads to prospects from its customers. Purchasing agents are often good sources of names. They know reasonably well the abilities of the sales reps who call on them. Customers' employees themselves may be a source of sales people. Often, retail clerks make good sales people for wholesalers and manufacturers. These clerks are acquainted with the product. They also know something of the behavior of the retailers—the market to which the hiring firm sells.

Sales reps working for noncompeting companies are another source—particularly if they (1) are selling products related to those sold by the recruiting firm or (2) are selling to the same market. Presumably recruits from this source have some sales ability and need less training. Sometimes, sales managers of other companies are willing to furnish names of applicants they have discovered but cannot use at the moment.

Recruiting from other firms raises some questions. Hiring the good employees of a customer obviously has drawbacks. The task must be handled very diplomatically to avoid losing the customer. People hired from other companies may not have the same degree of loyalty as recruits promoted from within. The outsiders are more mobile, as evidenced by their willingness to change employers. A firm that hires from the outside should determine (1) why the applicants are interested in changing jobs and (2) why they want to work for the hiring company. Applicants may figure that the quickest way to move up is to move from one company to another.

Educational Institutions

Colleges and universities are sometimes used as sources of recruits for *career* sales jobs. More often, however, companies using college recruiting are hiring graduating students for eventual management positions. The sales job is merely the first step on the career path.

Colleges are probably *not* a good recruiting source for *career* sales jobs. Unless the job involves creative selling, carries social prestige, and offers a great challenge, the better-than-average college graduate probably will not be attracted by it.

Graduates of high schools or vocational schools may be fine prospects for selling careers. This is true especially if the job is routine in nature and does not require much technical training or college-developed abilities. Junior college graduates may be a good recruiting source for the company that prefers its sales reps to have some college work, but does not require a four-year degree.

If the sales job is adequately demanding and carries enough compensation in dollars and other benefits, qualified college graduates may prove to be a fine source of applicants. Generally, these people are more easily adaptable than their experienced counterparts. They have developed no loyalties to a firm or industry and probably have not acquired many bad work habits. Usually, they have acquired certain social graces. They are often more poised and mature than a person of the same age without college training. Good students usually have developed their ability to think logically and to express themselves reasonably well. Graduation generally indicates a degree of perseverance. Finally, some students have had enough technical training so that they are well grounded in the principles applicable to a given field.

A major drawback to university graduates is that they are usually inexperienced in selling or in business generally. Another criticism is that they are jobhoppers and will not stay with one company very long. It is not known whether college graduates are significantly different from any other group of young people in this respect. However, many executives believe that college graduates today generally have unrealistic expectations regarding how far and how fast they can advance in a job.

The biggest single problem in recruiting college students is the extremely unfavorable impression that many students have regarding the field of selling. It is particularly distressing that many students sneer at selling, not from experience in the field, but because of gross misconceptions about what is involved in most sales jobs. Their understanding of selling is often limited to retail-store selling. However, students' attitudes toward selling are more favorable today than in the 1960s and 1970s.[3]

---

[3] For some suggestions for offsetting students' negativism toward personal selling jobs and for improving sales recruiting programs directed at college students, see Alan J. Dubinsky, "Recruiting College Students for the Salesforce," *Industrial Marketing Management,* February 1980, pp. 37–45.

Through Advertisements

Advertisements are both a *source* of leads to sales recruits and a *method* of reaching them. Newspapers and trade journals are the most widely used media, although others have also been used. Some companies use advertisements to recruit high-caliber sales people for particularly challenging jobs. However, most firms that use advertising—particularly in newspapers—are trying to fill the less attractive type of sales job, such as in-home selling or clerking in a retail store.

Advertisements ordinarily produce a large quantity of applicants, but the average quality of the applicants is questionable. The cost of reaching these recruits is low. However, an additional burden is placed on the subsequent phases of the selection system if little screening was done in the advertising copy.

The quality of prospects recruited by advertisements may be increased by careful selection of media and by proper statements of information placed in the copy. For example, by buying space in a trade journal rather than in a daily newspaper, a firm is automatically more selective in its search. The more information given in the notice, the more it serves as a qualitative screening device.

To be effective, a recruiting ad must **attract attention** and **have credibility.** An advertisement that does not get read, or one that is read but is not considered believable and sincere, is a waste of effort.

Now, what information should be included in a recruiting advertisement?

Here are some points to consider.

1. *Company name.* The answer is, it all depends. By placing their names in their ads, well-known firms may attract applicants who otherwise would not answer a blind ad. But companies with a poor public image (such as in-home sellers) often must hide their identities in an ad in order to attract prospects.
2. *Product.* Usually yes, unless it is a product (gravestones and cemetery lots, perhaps) that is likely to turn away prospects who otherwise might get interested once they learned more about the company and the job opportunities.
3. *Territory.* Yes, especially if it is *not* in the area where the ad is run.
4. *Hiring qualifications.* Include enough of them so the ad serves as a useful screening device. But keep in mind the legal guidelines when stating any hiring requirements. For example, specifying an age or sex requirement is illegal unless you can prove it is a bona fide occupational qualification. As a general rule, all ads should carry the "Equal Opportunity Employer M/F" line.

5. *Compensation plan, expense plan, and fringe benefits.* Include some information in these areas, especially if it is a strong point. A company paying straight salary is more likely to mention this point than is one that pays straight commission.
6. *How to contact the employer.* The ad must have a phone number, a mailing address, or a time and place for personal interviews.

Some organizations do no recruitment advertising. Instead they answer situation-wanted advertisements placed by people who are looking for sales jobs. These firms are interested in people who show enough initiative to seek out a job rather than waiting for one to come to them.

Voluntary Applicants

The counterpart of the person who places a situation-wanted ad in a newspaper is the one who walks in and says, "I want a job selling for your company." Voluntary applicants are an excellent source of sales recruits, although usually there are not enough of them. These applicants certainly are interested in the firm. Furthermore, it is likely that they have done some investigating to determine whether they would like the job. They probably possess a high degree of initiative, self-confidence, and self-reliance.

Employment Agencies

Agencies that place sales people are fine sources of retail sales clerks, part-time sales people, or in-home sellers. Agencies that specialize in placing executive personnel may also be a source of high-caliber, creative sales recruits. Federal and state employment services usually are not considered good sources because the better prospects probably do not register at these offices.

If the agency is carefully selected and good relations are established with it, the dividends can be satisfying. The agency can do some of the initial screening, because presumably it will abide by the job specifications given it. Ordinarily, a company should work with one or two agencies so that they get to know the company and its jobs. When a prospect sent by the agency does not measure up to the company's standards, the company should inform the agency. This feedback will help reduce misunderstandings of the company's needs.

The company, the recruit, and the agency should all have a clear understanding regarding the agency's fee—what it will be and who pays it. Fees usually range from 10 to 40 percent of the new employee's first year's compensation, and increase as the compensation goes up. Agencies where the fee is paid by the employer probably will attract a better quality of sales recruit. The cost to the employer for the agency's fee may be offset by the savings in the advertising and initial screening activities that the agency performs.

Women, Minorities, and Other Underemployed Groups

As sources of sales recruits, many companies rely heavily on groups available for part-time work—such as teachers, students, housewives, and members of the military. In-home selling firms in cosmetics or cooking utensils frequently use students or housewives as sales people. Firms that sell encyclopedias often bolster their sales force during the summer by hiring teachers. As a group, the underemployed lend themselves to sales work in many situations. They are easy to contact, readily available, and usually have flexible hours during which they can work. Some of the most difficult personnel problems faced by sales executives, however, are connected with the management of a part-time sales force. It offers real challenges in training, compensation, and supervision of personnel.

Minority groups. Nonwhites, particularly blacks, constitute a major underemployed labor force. In the past management did not aggressively recruit sales people from this labor pool, but today companies are paying increased attention to minority groups. The 1964 Civil Rights Act, of course, is one politico-legal impetus moving management in this direction. In fear of customer resistance, the sales force typically has the lowest percentage of black employees of any department in a company.

Looking ahead, the demographic situation is another stimulant to the hiring of blacks and other minorities. During the 1980s, the number of 16- to 24-year olds in the labor force will decline by about 1.3 million people. This is the age group that supplies most sales trainees. By 1990 the number of blacks in that same age group will double.[4]

Companies have experienced mixed results in their efforts to recruit sales and marketing employees from minority groups. Companies have reported good or excellent progress in recruiting for nonselling jobs in the marketing department or for inside sales work. Yet many executives have reported only limited success in attracting

[4] Arthur J. Bragg, "Recruiting and Hiring without Surprises: Higher Stakes—but Better Odds," *Sales & Marketing Management,* August 18, 1980, p. 51.

minority groups into outside sales jobs—that is, jobs where the sales people go to the customers. A company seriously interested in recruiting blacks, for example, is likely to encounter two problems— the shortage of experienced applicants, and lack of interest in industrial selling. Nevertheless, the need for good sales people is likely to increase rather than decline. Consequently, economic, political, and social pressures undoubtedly will continue to stimulate sales executives to intensify their recruiting efforts among minority groups.

Women. The same economic, social, and legal pressures are stimulating sales executives to recruit women for outside sales forces. For many years women have outnumbered men in retail, in-store sales jobs. Women have also played important roles in advertising and marketing research. Only during the past two decades, however, have businesses hired women for nonretail, outside sales jobs. In the 1970s, several major companies (Exxon, Republic Steel, IBM, Wang Laboratories, Xerox, Texaco, Honeywell, for example) for the first time either (1) recruited women for outside industrial selling jobs or (2) promoted female sales representatives into sales management positions.

Reports on the perceptions and experiences of sales executives concerning the problems and performance of women in outside selling jobs are both interesting and enlightening. Overall, these experiences and perceptions have been quite favorable toward women. Furthermore, this favorable reaction is not limited to consumer products companies or service industries. Women also are performing well as sales recruits in industrial sales jobs.[5]

Management's initial reluctance to hire women for outside selling jobs usually stems from some traditional points of concern. One is that women will encounter problems in traveling and in entertaining customers. Another is the fear of possible sexual involvements with customers or fellow salesmen. A third point is the belief that turnover rates may be increased because of marriage, pregnancy, or husbands being transferred to another city. In firms that have recruited and used women in outside selling, these problems apparently have not been significant. Turnover rates for saleswomen have not been appreciably different from those of salesmen.

---

[5] See, for example, Leslie Kanuk, "Women in Industrial Selling," *Journal of Marketing,* January 1978, pp. 87–91; and Richard H. Buskirk and Beverly Miles, *Beating Men at Their Own Game: A Woman's Guide to Successful Selling in Industry* (New York: John Wiley & Sons, 1980), pp. 4–8, 179–83. Also see Charles M. Futrell, "Salesmen and Saleswomen Job Satisfaction," *Industrial Marketing Management,* February 1980, pp. 27–30; and John E. Swan, Charles M. Futrell, and John T. Todd, "Same Job—Different Views: Women and Men in Industrial Sales," *Journal of Marketing,* January 1978, pp. 92–98.

There seems to be an increasing acceptance of saleswomen by customers, salesmen, and sales managers.[6] Sales executives generally report that, given the chance, qualified women typically have equaled their male peers in sales performance. Women often have lower rates of absenteeism than men.[7] Sales executives also note that saleswomen are easier to manage, and they typically incur lower selling expenses.[8] Another solid piece of evidence that women are performing well in outside selling jobs is the fact that increasing numbers of women are moving into sales-management positions.

When dealing with buyers, saleswomen may have some advantages over salesmen. For example,

- The buyer will nearly always see a saleswoman, even a buyer who has refused to see male reps from the same company.
- Because female sales reps are easily remembered, their companies and product lines tend to stick in a buyer's mind.
- Women tend to be better listeners, so buyers will openly discuss their problems. This gives the female sales rep a better chance to learn about the buyers' needs and then explain how her products can satisfy them.

Looking to the future, we can expect managers of outside sales forces to recruit women in increasing numbers. In one study, 88 percent of the responding executives said they would recommend industrial selling as a career for women college graduates.[9]

Factors Influencing Choice of Recruiting Sources

Throughout our discussion of recruiting sources, we cited examples showing when a given source might be used. In each instance, certain factors influenced management's decision.

[6] For a study of industrial purchasing agents' perceptions of female sales reps, see John E. Swan, David R. Rink, G. E. Kiser, and Warren S. Martin, "Industrial Buyer Image of the Saleswoman," *Journal of Marketing,* Winter 1984, pp. 110–16. For a report on the attitude of new-car buyers toward women sales reps, see William J. Lundstrom and D. Neil Ashworth, "Customers' Perceptions of the Saleswoman: A Study of Personality, Task and Evaluative Attributes by Respondent Location and Gender," *Journal of the Academy of Marketing Science,* Spring 1983, pp. 114–22.

[7] Kanuk, "Women in Industrial Selling," p. 9.

[8] Buskirk and Miles, *Beating Men at Their Own Game,* pp. 4–8.

[9] Kanuk, "Women in Industrial Selling," p. 91. Also see Rayna Skolnik, "A Woman's Place Is on the Sales Force," *Sales & Marketing Management,* April 1, 1985, pp. 35–37.

1. *Nature of the product.* If the product is highly technical, the firm will recruit sales people experienced in that field or prospects with appropriate technical background. The firm may look in its own production department.[10]
2. *Nature of the market.* To deal with knowledgeable purchasing agents, the firm may prefer to recruit experienced sales people. If long-standing buyer-seller relationships are important, it must recruit people experienced in that field. Ethnic customer groups may require sales people to speak a foreign language.
3. *Policy on promoting from within the company.* When this policy exists, recruiters know where to look first.

[10] For a further discussion of this topic, see Joseph A. Bellizzi and Paul A. Cline, "Technical or Nontechnical Salesmen?" *Industrial Marketing Management,* May 1985, pp. 69–74.

Figure 5–2
Recruiting Evaluation Matrix

Recruiting Sources	Evaluation Criteria					
	Consistent with Strategic Planning?	Number Recruits	Number Hired	Geographical Coverage	Cost	Frequency of Use

Within company:
  Sales force
  Other departments						

Other companies:
  Competitors
  Customers
  Noncompetitors						

Educational institutions						
Advertisements						
Employment agencies						
Voluntary applicants						
Women						
Minorities						

4. *Sales training provided by company.* A company that can train its new sales people can recruit from colleges and other sources of inexperienced people. Otherwise, it must recruit experienced sales representatives.
5. *Is the company hiring career sales people?* Is the job a stepping-stone to management positions? For career sales jobs, a firm probably will *not* recruit seniors in colleges and universities.
6. *Sources of successful recruits in the past.* Sources that supplied most successful recruits in the past can be consulted, provided there have been no substantial changes in the job.
7. *Money available for recruiting.* Limited recruiting funds force a firm to limit its recruiting sources and methods.
8. *Legal considerations.* Civil rights laws and federal agency regulations must be considered in deciding where to look for sales-force recruits.

Evaluation of Recruiting Program

A company should periodically evaluate the effectiveness of its recruiting program just as it evaluates the effectiveness of its total marketing program. To conduct this evaluation, management might use some form of matrix approach such as the one in Figure 5–2. This approach lends itself to computer technology, which can aid in the evaluation process.

Summary

After determining the number and kind of sales people wanted, the next major step in sales-force selection is to recruit several applicants for the job. Recruiting should be coordinated with a company's strategic planning, because recruiting can aid in implementing these plans.

A well-planned, well-operated recruiting system is essential for a successful selection program. A company must identify the sources that are likely to produce good recruits and maintain a continuing relationship with these sources, even during periods when the firm is not hiring.

Several sources are frequently used for recruiting sales reps. One major source is within the company doing the recruiting. Often the present sales force is an excellent source of leads to new recruits.

Also, some companies recruit new sales people from employees in their offices or factories.

Another major source of recruits is other companies—competitors, customers, or noncompetitors. A company may try to hire a competitor's sales people. Or a firm's customers may supply recruiting leads. Some companies will hire customer's employees, although this must be done very carefully. Another source is sales people who are working for noncompeting firms.

Many companies recruit sales people from educational institutions—universities, community colleges, high schools, or vocational/technical schools. Some firms rely on advertisements both as a *source* of leads to recruits and as a *method* of reaching prospective applicants. Voluntary (walk-in) applicants can be an excellent source, but usually there are not enough of these people. For some types of sales jobs, employment agencies can provide good prospects. Increasingly, companies are looking to women and members of minority groups as sources of applicants for sales jobs. This trend is expected to continue and to intensify.

Management's choice of recruiting sources will depend on several factors. These factors include the nature of the product, the nature of the market, the company's policy on promoting from within, the sales training provided by the firm, whether the company is hiring people for careers in selling or as a stepping-stone to management, and so on. Periodically a company should evaluate the effectiveness of its recruiting program.

Questions and Problems

1. Is it ethical for a sales manager to directly approach a competitor's sales person with an outright offer of a better job?
2. How would the sources and methods of recruiting sales people *differ* among the following firms?
   a. A company selling precision instruments to the petroleum industry.
   b. A coffee roaster and canner in Denver selling to wholesalers and retailers in the Southwest and the Rocky Mountain regions.
   c. A national firm selling kitchenware by the party-plan method.
   d. A luggage manufacturer selling a high-grade product nationally through selected retail outlets.

3. The following firms want to hire sales people. As recruiting sources, the executives are considering (*a*) other divisions of the company, (*b*) competitors' sales forces, and (*c*) colleges and universities. Evaluate each of these three as sources of sales people for each company.
   a. Manufacturer of paper and paper products.
   b. Manufacturer of breakfast cereals.
   c. Manufacturer of computer software.

4. One manufacturer of dictating machines recruits only experienced people and does no recruiting among graduating college students. A competitor recruits extensively among colleges in its search for sales people. How do you account for the difference in sources used by virtually identical firms?

5. How do you account for the fact that many college students have a very low regard for selling, even though the job of sales person can offer tremendous challenge and can be one of the highest-paying jobs in the country?

6. What methods and sources should a firm use to recruit women for its sales force?

7. Should the salary or probable amount of commission be stated in a recruiting advertisement?

8. The following companies are looking for product sales people and decide to use advertising to recruit applicants. For each firm, you are asked to select the specific advertising media and to write a recruiting advertisement for one of those media. You may supply whatever additional facts you need.
   a. Manufacturers' agent handling lighting fixtures for both the industrial and consumer markets.
   b. Manufacturer of outboard motors.
   c. Wholesaler of lumber and building materials.

9. What sources should be used to recruit sales reps to fill the job described in Figure 4–3?

10. Evaluate the following five recruiting advertisements for sales people.

a.

Sales

FIELD SALES REPRESENTATIVE

*HIGHLY VISIBLE POSITION
PLENTY OF GROWTH
POTENTIAL*

The Valspar Corporation, a rapidly growing national paint manufacturer, is seeking an experienced Sales Representative (2 to 3 years experience) for its Consumer Specialty Division which markets through hard-line distributors. Paint sales background is not necessary, but we do require a successful sales track record, along with program marketing skills. We offer a competitive starting salary (high 20s), bonus potential, excellent benefits package which includes profit sharing, automobile and expenses. If you are a highly motivated SELF-STARTER, you are urged to send us your detailed resume in confidence to:

THE VALSPAR CORPORATION

Mr. A. R. Patanella
Regional Personnel Manager
4000 E. Cottage Place
Carpentersville, IL 60110

An Equal Opportunity Employer

b.

SALES REPRESENTATIVE

Denver Area

A nationally renowned leader in the transportation industry has an immediate career opportunity for an aggressive sales professional to sell our relocation services to businesses and corporations.

The individual we seek will identify and develop existing and new accounts, meet or exceed sales revenue goals and develop product lines on a national and international level.

The outstanding candidate will have a successful track record of direct sales experience, preferably in the transportation industry, effective communication skills, and a high level of professionalism.

In return for your talents, we offer a highly competitive compensation/benefits package and an exceptional future within a growing and innovative organization. For immediate consideration, forward your resume with salary history in complete confidence to:

Box 166Q – Denver Post
An Equal Opportunity Employer
M/F/H

c.

**SALES AND
OPPORTUNITY
KNOCKS ONCE
IN A LIFE TIME
DON'T LET IT
PASS YOU BY**

Just one hour of your time to look into a career of a lifetime with a well-established Denver company. We offer above average income, complete training, advancement as fast as your ability lets you.
TAKE ONE MINUTE RIGHT NOW AND CALL FOR COMPLETE INFORMATION.
777–3097
MONDAY-FRIDAY

d.

Sales

**A CAREER
OPPORTUNITY**

If you are a career oriented individual who is seeking to make a change, we have an immediate opening in the greater Chicago area.

We are a national firm who is seeking a professional salesperson. YOU MUST BE ABLE TO START IMMEDIATELY AND HAVE A MINIMUM OF 2 YEARS HIGHLY SUCCESSFUL OUTSIDE DIRECT SALES EXPERIENCE.

This position offers a base salary plus bonus for a 1st year minimum income in excess of $31,150.

We also offer a complete benefit package that includes hospitalization and dental care.

The individual we select will be placed through a comprehensive training program and offers early management opportunities. Please call.

MR. CLAY
MONDAY ONLY
9 AM TO 5 PM
312/790–4135

e.

Case 5–1

Celestial Seasonings Herb Teas, Inc.

Recruiting Source for Sales Manager's Position

The peak selling season was approaching for the Celestial Seasonings Herb Teas company, but the firm lacked a vice president of marketing and a sales manager. Celestial Seasoning's president, Mo Siegel, decided that the company temporarily could do without a marketing vice president. The duties of the position currently were being handled by John Hay, the senior vice president. At the same time, Mr. Siegel very much wanted to hire a sales manager. However, he was not certain which recruiting sources he should use.

In the eyes of many people, Celestial Seasonings was quite an unusual company. It was the largest producer of herbal teas in the United States. Its home office and most of its production facilities were located in Boulder, Colorado. The company also had a manufacturing plant in San Francisco.

The company was started in 1971 by five young people—Mo and Peggy Siegel, John and Wyck Hay, and Cindy Ziesing—who were in their early or mid-20s. They started with an $800 loan and a common interest in environmental and ecological matters. The two men spent the summer and fall of 1971 picking herbs in the Colorado mountains, while the women sewed muslin sacks in which to package the herbs. During the first year the company produced 10,000 individual-serving bags of "Mo's 24 Herb Tea." (Since then the original formula for this particular blend of tea was modified to include some herbs from tropical jungles.)

From its early years, the company experienced a phenomenal growth in sales, reaching an annual volume of $10.5 million in 1979. One of Mr Siegel's goals was to surpass $35 million in annual sales by 1985. Throughout the 1970s the company continued to expand its plant capacity. Even then, the market demand for Celestial Seasonings products typically outpaced the company's production capacity.

From its inception, Celestial Seasonings was built around young people. Even in 1980 most of the employees were between 25 and 35 years of age. Another feature of the company was its managerial philosophy and goals regarding its employees. Top management felt a deep commitment and involvement with its workers. Mr. Siegel thought of his company as a family operation where all were encouraged to contribute. He often opened a business meeting with a prayer for guidance, and he encouraged the employees to care for one another. His goal was to provide many meaningful jobs for a group of "alive and creative people." He wanted his company to demonstrate the concepts of truth, beauty, and goodness in its business transactions and employee relationships. He hoped to continue the personal correspondence with customers that he had built up over the years.

Mr. Siegel did worry that some of these unusual personal employee relationships might be lost as the company continued its phenomenal growth rate. He was hopeful, however, that the company could achieve the transition to bigness while at the same time successfully maintaining close and warm employee relationships.

Celestial Seasoning's main product line was herbal teas—both single-herb teas and blends of several herbs. The blends were the largest sellers. Teas were packaged in tea bags and also in bulk (loose) form. Several of the teas were also available in tablet form. Most of the teas contained no caffeine. The company acquired some of its herbs from farms in the United States, but many of the herbs were imported from places in Asia, South America, and Africa. Whenever possible, Celestial Seasonings purchased its herbs directly from farmers.

Regarding the company's packaging and branding, as one executive put it, "We try to be catchy, creative, and tie in with our environmental and ecological image." The company selected such brand names as Red Zinger (the largest selling brand), Mo's 24 Herb Tea, Sleepy Time, Mandarin Orange Spice, Pelican Punch, Winterberry, and Morning Thunder. The boxes containing the tea were decorated with artwork and carried philosophical sayings. The tea bags were packaged one kind of tea to a box and also in a sample pack containing six different teas.

Competition for Celestial Seasonings teas came from several sources which included: (1) about 30 other producers of herbal teas; (2) large producers of regular teas, such as Lipton, Tetley, and Bigelow; (3) major coffee producers, and (4) producers of other mealtime or snack beverages, such as milk, cocoa, and soft drinks.

Celestial's products were carried in supermarkets, tea and coffee specialty shops, and natural (health) food stores. About 60 percent of the annual sales were made from January through April. The products were sold through food brokers who contacted the large supermarket chains and wholesalers. The wholesalers, in turn, reached the health food stores and the tea and coffee specialty shops.

Celestial Seasonings had no outside sales force. The company did have a sales manager who filled the important role of working closely with the food brokers.

About a year ago, Warren Bellows was vice president of marketing at Celestial Seasonings and his brother, Bob, was the sales manager. At that time—that is, a year ago—Warren decided he wanted more out of life than he was getting in Boulder, Colorado, so he resigned and went to live in Finland.

In selecting his replacement, the company executives decided that they needed a person with some professional marketing experience. They went outside the company and hired a man who had been the sales manager for a large candy and gum manufacturer. Within a few months, it became evident that the business philosophy and selling techniques which he had brought with him from his former company were not compatible with Celestial Seasonings. Consequently, about three months ago, he resigned at the request of the company's president. Since then, the duties of the marketing vice president had been handled by Mr. Hay, the company's top vice president.

About six months ago, Bob Bellows, the sales manager, also decided he was looking for something else in life. So he resigned and went to live with his brother in Finland. Since then, the sales department has been run by two people who carry the title of "sales coordinators." These two young people had joined the company about three years ago—one as a secretary and the other as a truck driver.

The net result of these executive resignations was that Celestial Seasonings currently lacked both a marketing vice president and a sales manager. Mr. Siegel felt that the company temporarily could go without the marketing vice president. However, he believed that the company needed a sales manager very badly because the peak selling season was approaching.

As noted earlier, the sales manager was the company's contact with its food brokers throughout the country. Consequently, a lot of traveling was involved with the job. The sales manager was also responsible for coordinating all activities in the sales department—especially with regard to product deliveries. Because of the company's increasing sales volume and rapid growth, Mr. Siegel believed that the sales manager's job required some degree of knowledge and experience—especially in the health food market and grocery store market. According to Mr. Siegel, "The salary for the job is negotiable depending upon the person's qualifications. And, certainly the pay will be competitive. If the new sales manager performs satisfactorily, that person later may be a candidate for the position of vice president of marketing."

In Mr. Siegel's eyes, probably the most important—yet tough to measure—qualification for the job was that the sales manager's manner, attitude, and philosophies must be compatible with those of Celestial Seasonings. Mo Siegel wrote in a pamphlet given to all new employees, "We are dedicated to the fourth industrial revolution, the one that places people as the most valuable commodity business has. Therefore, all department leaders will be held accountable for their people development as well as business results. We do not and will not sell products that fail to aid the evolution of the planet. Idealism may be our inspiration, but reality is the clear measure of achievement."

Recently, Mr. Siegel started his search for a sales manager by placing a recruiting ad in both *The Wall Street Journal* and *Advertising Age.* He received hundreds of responses from all over the country, but no one as yet had been interviewed. The reason for not interviewing any applicants was that both Mo Siegel and John Hay were having second thoughts about their recruiting sources. That is, they were not sure their ads were being placed in the media that would reach the type of person they wanted. They both were wondering about what recruiting sources they should use to get the type of person they wanted for the sales manager's position.

For many years the executive positions were filled from within the company. As the company grew, however, both Mo and John realized that they might have to look outside the company when filling some executive positions in order to get the required degree of specialized executive expertise and professionalism.

In this current situation, however, both Mo and John were considering continuing their past policy of filling the sales manager's position from within the company. The two present sales coordinators were the top applicants within the company. They both had college degrees but not in business administration. Neither had any experience as a sales manager, but Mr. Siegel wondered if possibly they could learn through an on-the-job, do-it-yourself training program. Both of these people were in agreement with the company's goals and philosophies. And, of course, they did have considerable knowledge of the company, its products, and its market.

(An interesting side note here was the fact that applicants from outside the company would have to be interviewed by both of these sales coordinators. Those who met with the coordinator's approval would then be sent to talk to Mo Siegel and John Hay. All four had to agree on the final selection decision.)

Then Mo and John also considered the possibility of looking for a sales manager currently employed in another company—either a competitor or a noncompetitor firm. Another source considered by Mo was some employment agency that specialized in recruiting and placing executive personnel. Mo had talked with a couple of these agencies in the past. They claimed they could provide a good-size pool of top-notch candidates. Mo felt, however, that if a person was as good as the agency claimed, that person would not have to register with an agency in order to get a good executive position.

Finally, Mo said to John, "Let's go back to the drawing board. Maybe there are some other sources that we have overlooked."

Question

What recruiting sources should Celestial Seasonings use to find a sales manager?

Case 5-2

Miller Metals, Inc.

Recruiting Women for Industrial Sales Jobs

Hal Stoner, sales manager for Miller Metals, pondered the messages he had been hit with over the past few days. It started with a management development program he attended. A professor whose specialty was the management of a sales force had presented the results of his research on the effectiveness of women in industrial sales. The bottom line of the research was that women were widely employed as industrial sales reps and were generally successful at it. Then he attended a cocktail party given by his boss, Mr. Miller, at which the boss' wife cornered him and asked why he hadn't hired any women for the company's sales force. He muttered something about never having had a woman apply for a job and not having any openings. Both statements were true, but they failed to satisfy her. He was only saved by the merciful intervention of his boss who wanted Hal to meet some guests.

The next morning Hal was saddened to learn of the unexpected death of Fred Wall, the company's sales rep in New England. No one was in training to take over the territory, nor did Hal have anyone in mind for the job. No applications were in the file.

Miller Metals sold a wide line of rare and semirare metals to manufacturers and research labs directly through its nationwide system of branch operations. The sales reps, all technically trained in metallurgy, earned an average of $68,000 a year in 1986, paid on a combination of salary plus performance bonuses. The 15 sales reps had been with the company an average of 16 years. They were considered by the customers to be exceptionally able.

Upon learning of the opening in New England, Mrs. Miller called Hal to insist that he hire a woman for the area. Hal carefully approached Mr. Miller to inform him of the telephone calls. Indirectly he was asking Mr. Miller to stop Mrs. Miller's interfering in the sales department. Mr. Miller did not respond as Hal had hoped. The summation of their meeting was that perhaps Hal should look for a woman as a replacement for Mr. Wall. It was clear that Mr. and Mrs. Miller had spent more than a few idle hours discussing the matter. Mr. Miller did not look happy about the situation, but that was how it was to be.

Hal began his search by calling the sales reps to ask if they knew of any technical saleswoman they could recommend. They did not. The state university's metallurgy department had two women students, but neither had the slightest interest in selling according to the department chairman. Hal called every employment agency in the city, but none had anyone who would fit the job specifications. It was suggested that the company would have to provide the necessary technical training, but Hal thought that the company was not prepared to do that. Moreover, the cost for just one trainee would be prohibitive.

Hal returned to Mr. Miller's office and reported the results of his inquiries. He had given it his best shot but had come up empty. How could he forget about Mrs. Miller's urgings for women on the sales force? Hal had his answer the next day. Mrs. Miller called, "I cannot believe that somewhere in this world there isn't a woman who could do a good job for us in New England. You have just scratched the surface. Dig deeper!"

Hal looked at Mr. Miller, who looked away and upward as he said, "Hal, looks like you've got a problem." As he left the office he wondered if life might not be easier doing something else, like selling in New England. But he recalled his years on the road and all the nice things his $115,000 a year salary was providing. Consequently, he decided that if the boss wanted a woman sales rep, that was the way it would be. A good team player followed the coach's orders, and Hal prided himself on being a team player. Now he wondered where he should look next.

Question

What would you recommend that Hal do to satisfy Mrs. Miller's demands?

6

Selecting the Sales Force— Processing Applicants

If you hire in haste, you may have to fire at leisure.
MARILYN MACHLOWITZ

In our selection process, the number and type of sales people needed have been determined, and applicants for the job have been recruited. Now management is ready for the third and final stage in the sales-selection function. This step involves (1) the development of a system for matching the applicants against the predetermined requirements, and (2) the actual use of this system to select the sales people. The major selection tools are:

- Application blanks.
- Personal interviews.
- References and credit reports.

- Tests.
- Physical Examinations.
- Assessment centers.

Processing Applicants and Strategic Planning

As was true of the first two stages of selection, this third stage— processing applicants—is also an integral part of implementing the strategic sales-force planning. If this processing stage is handled effectively, it can go a long way toward assuring a successful sales performance. On the other hand, a poor job in processing applicants can hinder implementation, even though the determination of qualifications and the recruiting were done well. This matching of company needs and applicants' potential is truly important to the strategic and tactical aspects of sales-force management.

The key here—and the central theme of this chapter—is for management (1) to select the best processing tools and then (2) to use them effectively to match the applicant with the hiring specifications. In this chapter we will discuss and evaluate major selection tools. However, management in any given firm should design their own individualized processing system to hire people for a particular sales job.

The sequence in which selection tools are used varies among companies. Initial screening (beyond that done by the recruiting) may start with an application blank, an interview, or some form of test. The purpose of the initial screen is to eliminate undesirable recruits as quickly and as inexpensively as possible. Therefore, no matter which technique is used first, it is usually brief—a short application blank, an interview of only a few minutes, or a simple test that can be administered and interpreted easily and quickly. This procedure is in line with the general idea that the *least costly selection tools should be used first*.

Since no single selection tool is adequate by itself, a series should be used to carefully determine an applicant's qualifications. In many cases, one tool can be used to complement or to verify information derived from another. Some pertinent data ordinarily come only through an interview, while other traits may be discernible only by testing.

The tools a company uses to process its sales recruits should be designed to fit the particular needs of the firm. Standardized forms (application blanks, interview forms, and so on) prepared for general use are typically less effective than those a company develops on its own.

These tools and procedures are only *aids* to sound executive judgment and not *substitutes* for it. The performance of prevailing selection systems has been considerably less than ideal. They can eliminate obviously unqualified candidates and generally spot extremely capable individuals. However, for the mass of recruits who normally fall between these extremes, the tools currently used can only predict those who will be successful in the job. As a result, generous quantities of executive judgment still are essential in selecting sales representatives.

Legal Considerations

The traditional use of several of the hiring tools has been considerably limited by EEOC and OFCC rulings. For companies subject to Affirmative Action guidelines, it is essential to keep an "applicant flow chart," which lists the processed applicants by sex and ethnic group. If there is a disproportionately high rate of rejection of women or minority applicants, each step in the hiring process may be reviewed to determine which tool is producing this result. Once identified, the particular tool must undergo a validation procedure if management wants to continue using it. If there is no disproportionate rejection of women or minorities in the selection process, there is no validation requirement. Today the validation process, especially for tests used as selection tools, is less complicated and less expensive than in the past. This is because today's management can employ advanced statistical techniques using computer technology. However, it still is very difficult to validate personal interviews.

Many questions traditionally asked on application blanks and interviews either are no longer allowable or must be handled very carefully. Sometimes questions in sensitive areas are asked *after* the person is hired—as in the case of age and marital status for insurance purposes. Questions in sensitive areas may be asked *during* these interviews, however, if they relate to bona fide occupational qualifications (BFOQ). Age and sex may be BFOQs, for example, if the sales job calls for a woman to model the line of apparel she is selling. If a certain ethnic background and ability to speak a certain foreign language are BFOQs, then obviously questions pertaining to these factors are perfectly appropriate. To summarize, any question asked, or hiring qualification required, must be "job relevant"—that is, it must be important to the job.

Application Blanks

Reasons for Using Application Blanks

The application blank, or personal-history record, as it is sometimes called, is one of the two most widely used selection tools. (The other is the interview.) Sometimes a firm uses two blanks—a short one and a longer, more detailed one.

The short one ordinarily is used only as an initial screening device. No executive's time need be taken to administer or interpret this form. Instead, an office employee can give the applicant the short blank to fill out and then can do the initial interpreting.

A longer blank may be used as an initial screen or for other purposes. The facts stated on the form can be the basis for probing in an interview—for instance, asking several questions relating to the job experience as stated on the blank. In the future the data on the blank may be used to reevaluate the characteristics needed for the job. As discussed in Chapter 4, application blanks are one of the main sources of information used by a firm (1) to study the backgrounds of its good and poor sales people and (2) to establish scores or weights on specific requirements for sales positions. Figure 6–1 is a copy of the application blank used by Xerox in its employee-selection program.

Figure 6-1

Employment Application Blank—Xerox Company

Federal, State and Municipal Laws prohibit Discrimination
because of race, color, religion, sex, national origin, age,
handicap or Vietnam-era veteran status.

Instructions:

1. Type or print in black ink.
2. Answer each question.
3. Read declaration carefully —
   then sign and date form.

Employment Application   ● Applicant - please complete

Name – Last, First, Initial					Social Security No.		Date

Present Address	Street		City	State	Zip	Home Phone (Incl. Area Code)	Alternate Phone & Area Code

Permanent Address	Street		City	State	Zip	If not a U.S. Citizen, current Visa status	

What Type of Work do you Prefer?

Geographic Limitations	Geographic Preference	Give name of close relatives employed by Xerox
		(1) (2)

Have you ever been convicted of a felony?   If "Yes", please explain:
(Record of conviction does not disqualify the
applicant from employment consideration):

☐ Yes   ☐ No

May we contact your present employer? ☐ Yes ☐ No

Wage or Salary Required | Date Available

Have you ever worked at Xerox?   If yes, where and when: Have you ever applied for work at Xerox?   If yes, where and when:
☐ Yes   ☐ No   ☐ Yes   ☐ No

Who referred you to Xerox?

How were you referred to Xerox? (Circle one letter only):	A By Your College	B Advertisement	C Employment Agency	D By An Employee	E Military Service	F Walk-In	G Resume or Letter	H Career Ctr/ Open House	I State Employment Service	J Other

School Name & Location	Years Attended		Graduate? (Yes/No)	What Degree	Major Subject or Total Hours, if applicable
	From	To			
Elementary					
High School					
College/University					
College/University					

Highest Degree Earned   H. High School   1. Associate   2. Bachelor   3. Master   4. Doctorate   Overall College
(Circle one number only):   Scholastic Average

Employment & Military History:
List all employment (include U.S. Military Service).
Start with present or most recent position. Include all jobs since age 18 (or last 4 jobs, whichever is less).

Dates		Name and Address of Employers	Type of Position	Supervisor	Salary		Reason for Leaving
From	To				Start	Finish	
Mo. Yr.	Mo. Yr.						
Mo. Yr.	Mo. Yr.						
Mo. Yr.	Mo. Yr.						
Mo. Yr.	Mo. Yr.						

Describe briefly the nature of your last two most appropriate positions, including supervisory responsibility, if any.
If you have done research, include a brief description of its nature and scope.

(1)

(2)

(3)

What are your plans for continuing your education?

Will you perform shiftwork? ☐ Yes ☐ No

Will you work overtime? ☐ Yes ☐ No

FORM 59225 (3/83)

Xerox is an Equal Opportunity Employer (M/F)

Figure 6-1 *(concluded)*

Outside Activities

Professional memberships, certificates or licenses held. (Exclude those indicating race, color, religion, sex, national origin, age, handicap, or Vietnam-era veteran status)

Patents and/or Inventions	Principal hobbies

In what extra-curricular civic or cultural activities have you been or are you currently active? Include offices held. (Exclude those indicating race, color, religion, sex, national origin, age, handicap, or Vietnam-era veteran status)

Professional/Work References We May Contact: (Include Area Codes with Phone Numbers)

Name	Home Phone No.	Name	Home Phone No.
Employed By	Business Phone	Employed By	Business Phone
Employer Address		Employer Address	

Persons employed at Xerox have access to confidential information regarding various phases of Company business. Therefore, the Company follows the usual practice of requiring new employees, at the time of employment, to sign a proprietary information and conflict of interest agreement.

Information concerning competitor's operation, products, designs or other proprietary information will not be solicited from an applicant for employment, or from the Company's employees. Xerox will honor any valid post employment restrictions contained in an applicant's employment contract and fully respects the applicant's duty of loyalty and non-disclosure to an applicant's former employer.

I certify that the answers provided above are accurate to the best of my knowledge and belief. I am aware that failure to complete this application, intentional omissions or misstatements may result in refusal of employment or discharge. If employed, I understand that continued employment may be subject to issuance and continuance of bond by the bonding agent of Xerox Corporation.

► Signature of Applicant

Date:

The following information is for your use in completing the next section.

A. "Veteran of the Vietnam Era" means a person (1) who (a) served on active duty for a period of more than 180 days, any part of which occurred between August 5, 1964 and May 7, 1975, and was discharged or released therefrom with other than a dishonorable discharge, or (b) was discharged or released from active duty for a service-connected disability if any part of such active duty was performed between August 5, 1964 and May 7, 1975, and (2) who was so discharged or released within 48 months preceding the alleged violation of the Act, the affirmative action clause, and/or the regulations issued pursuant to the Act.

B. "Disabled Veteran" means a person entitled to disability compensation under laws administered by the Veterans Administration for disability rated at 30 percent or more, or a person whose discharge or release from active duty was for a disability incurred or aggravated in the line of duty.

C. "Handicapped Individual" means any person who (1) has a physical or mental impairment which substantially limits one or more of such person's major life activities, (2) has a record of such impairment or (3) is regarded as having such an impairment. For purposes of this part, a handicapped individual is 'substantially limited' if he or she is likely to experience difficulty in securing, retaining or advancing in employment because of a handicap.

D. Race/Ethnic Groups

1. Black, not of Hispanic Origin. Persons having origins in any of the Black racial groups of Africa.

2. Asian or Pacific Islander. Persons having origins in any of the original peoples of the Far East, Southeast Asia, the Indian Subcontinent, or the Pacific Islands. This area includes, for example, China, Japan, Korea, the Phillipine Islands and Samoa.

3. American Indian or Alaskan Native. Persons having origins in any of the original peoples of North America and who maintain cultural identification through tribal affiliation or community recognition.

4. Hispanic. Persons of Mexican, Puerto Rican, Cuban, Central or South American or other Spanish Culture or origin, regardless of race.

5. White, not of Hispanic Origin. Persons having origins in any of the original peoples of Europe, North Africa, or the Middle East.

Used with permission of the Xerox Corporation

Information Sought on Application Blanks

Seek pertinent information only. The company ordinarily should ask only for information it intends to use now or later. Unless a question relates to some standard or job qualification, its presence on the blank is debatable. However, the question may be needed to complete personal records of some sort. For instance, the causes of the parents' death may be required for company insurance programs. However, items of this nature may be recorded elsewhere.

A number of factors affect the type and amount of information requested on an application blank. One is the objective the company has in using the blank. If it serves as an initial screen, it probably is shorter than one that will serve as a complete personal-history record. The other selection tools and records used often influence the design of the application blank. The company may want to omit questions that are answered by other tools. On the other hand, a company may duplicate its questions to check on applicants' honesty by comparing the answers on the blank with those obtained from other sources.

Job qualifications usually influence the questions on application blanks. A firm trying to hire people with 5 to 10 years of sales experience, for example, is not so concerned about a recruit's activity in college organizations as is the company that is hiring recent college graduates. The longer a person has been out of school, the more a firm can look at things other than university activities as indicators of abilities.

Another factor is the degree to which selection is decentralized. If home-office executives take part in the hiring, the application blank is probably detailed. These executives may have to do much of the screening without having an opportunity to interview the applicants. But if territorial managers do the hiring, the blank may be shorter because other tools—especially the interview—can be used more extensively.

Information typically requested. A five-part classification of sales job qualifications—mental, physical, experience, environmental, and personality—is proposed in Chapter 4. An application blank is an excellent tool for getting significant information in three of these categories—physical, experience, and environmental. In addition, carefully phrased and interpreted questions often shed some light on recruits' mental abilities and personality traits.

Assuming that a certain physical condition is a bona fide occupational qualification, a company might ask such questions as:

- What is your height? Your weight?
- What is your general physical condition?

- What defects do you have in speech? Hearing? Sight? Have you ever had any trouble with your feet?
- Date of last physical examination? Reason for it?
- Have you ever been rejected for life insurance? Reason?
- What has been the total medical expense during the last three years for yourself?
- Are you willing to take a physical examination now at company expense?

On an application blank, experience requirements are usually divided into two groups—educational background and work experience. Questions about educational background are asked because companies believe that applicants' performance in school tells something about their mental abilities and personality traits. Anyone who was graduated from high school or college (depending on the firm's requirements) is presumed to have the necessary basic intelligence. A course of study indicates much about a person's interests. Students who concentrated in foreign languages or fine arts have different interests and aptitudes than accounting majors, for example. Having graduated suggests a degree of perseverance. Having worked one's way, at least partially, through school may indicate self-reliance and industry. Further, holding office in school organizations may provide some evidence of leadership qualities.

Most application blanks ask for information about the candidate's employment history, including an accounting for periods of unemployment. If a company has certain experience qualifications, the application blank is a good tool for determining whether a candidate fulfills these requirements. People's business backgrounds often tell much about their talents and interests. The hiring firm is probably interested in how the applicant has progressed over the years. For instance, has each move resulted in a better job with more pay, added responsibility, or greater opportunity? Companies also are usually interested in the reasons a person gives for leaving each job. If possible, a prospective employer should check on this point with someone other than the applicant in order to get as complete a story as possible.

Companies ordinarily are interested in the environmental qualifications of prospective employees. Usually the first part of an application blank seeks such factual information as name, address, date of birth, marital status, home and business phone numbers, and social security number. Then questions are asked on such significant topics as the following: (Once again we are reminded that questions on age, marital status, or any of the following points must be in compliance with equal employment-opportunity legislation.)

- Amount of life insurance carried.

- Financial condition—savings investments, and so on.
- Membership in social, service, and business organizations.
- Offices held in organizations.
- Outside interests—hobbies, athletic endeavors, and others.
- Length of residence at each address for past 5 to 10 years.

Information on the prospect's environment can be extremely helpful because it can indicate a good deal about the person's interests, capabilities, and personality. Active participation in organizations may be evidence of an ability to meet and mix with people. Holding office may imply leadership traits and administrative abilities. Carrying adequate life insurance suggests that the applicant is stable, interested in security, and responsible.

Another group of useful questions on a blank pertains directly to the job for which application is being made. These include:

- Why do you want this job?
- Why do you want to change jobs?
- What minimum income do you require?
- Are you willing to travel? To be transferred?
- Can you drive? Do you have a driver's license?
- Has your driver's license ever been revoked? Why?
- Do you own an automobile?
- Are you willing to use your own car for business?

Personal Interviews

Nature and Purpose

Virtually no sales person is ever hired without a personal interview, and there are no satisfactory substitutes for this procedure. Much has been written about the use of weighted application blanks, various kinds of tests, and other aids in hiring. But none of these tools completely takes the place of getting to know the applicants personally by talking to them. Sales managers generally agree that the interview is an extremely important tool for selecting sales people. Furthermore, the interview can be used by sales executives in any size of company.

Reliability as predictor of success in selling. While interviews are the most widely used selection tool, unfortunately they do not rate very high as a predictor of an applicant's success in a sales job. Two psychologists at Michigan State University reviewed hundreds of studies dealing with the validity of various hiring tools as predictors of job performance. One conclusion from this meta-analysis was that

Table 6–1
Mean Validities of Job-Performance Predictors*

Predictor	Mean Validity
Ability composite (tests)	.53
Job tryout	.44
Biographical inventory (applications-blank information)	.37
Reference check	.26
Experience	.18
Interview	.14
Academic achievement	.11
Education	.10
Interest	.10
Age	−.01

* For entry-level jobs for which training will occur after hiring.
Source: John E. Hunter and Ronda F. Hunter, "Validity and Utility of Alternative Predictors of Job Performance," *Psychological Bulletin* 96 (1984), p. 90.

tests are the most powerful predictor of an applicant's performance in a job. (See Table 6–1.) In fact, the validity of tests as a predictor of job performance was almost four times as high as the rating for interviews. Interviews were well down on the list, out-ranked by job tryouts, application blanks, and reference checks.[1]

At the same time, the authors of this book firmly believe that a series of interviews, *properly conducted,* is the most effective of all hiring tools. Now how do we justify our belief in the face of the research evidence to the contrary? The key to our position lies in the idea of *properly conducting* the interviews. Our contention is that most people do not know how to interview an applicant effectively, nor do they know how to interpret the applicant's statements. Consequently, most interviewers do not accomplish their intended goal of matching applicants with the hiring specifications, and thus predicting job performance.[2]

The inherent weakness in the interviewing process is that it is heavily dependent on the behavior of the interviewer, which is difficult to control. An interviewer's reactions, for example, can greatly

---

[1] John E. Hunter and Ronda F. Hunter, "Validity and Utility of Alternative Predictors of Job Performance," *Psychological Bulletin* 96 (1984), pp. 72–98. This report includes an exhaustive bibliography.

[2] For some practical suggestions on how to interview effectively, see Arthur Bragg, "Recruiting's Finest Hour: The Interview—Interviews That Rate a '10,' " *Sales & Marketing Management,* August 17, 1981, pp. 58–60; and Jack Bucalo, "The Balanced Approach to Successful Screening Interviews," *Personnel Journal,* August 1978, pp. 420–26.

affect an applicant's responses. One study reported that when the interviewer smiled and nodded yes, he got different answers to the same questions than when he frowned and shook his head no. It is so important, and yet so difficult, for an interviewer to remain completely neutral and consistent through a series of interviews with several applicants.[3]

Reasons for interviewing recruits.   In selection, the personal interview is basically used to help determine a person's fitness for the job. It may be employed as the initial screening device and often plays a part in some subsequent stage of the hiring process.

A series of personal interviews also serves to determine characteristics that are not always observable by other means. An interview is probably the best way to find out something about the recruits' conversational ability, speaking voice, and intelligence. By seeing the applicant in person, an executive can appraise physical characteristics such as general appearance and care given to clothes. Certain personality traits may also be observed to some degree. The applicant's poise under the strain of an interview may be noted, along with any ability to dominate or lead a conversation.

Another purpose in interviewing is to verify and interpret facts stated on the application blank. For example, the applicant may have stated that he was a district manager in some previous job. The prospective employer may ask what his responsibilities were and how many employees he supervised. It also is possible to check on a person's truthfulness by repeating some of the questions asked on the personal-history record.

The interview needs to serve as a two-way channel of communication. The interview not only is a means by which a company determines an applicant's fitness for a job. It also offers an employer an opportunity to answer the recruit's questions about the company and the position. The applicant can be told about such things as the nature of the job, the compensation, the type of training and supervision provided, and the opportunities for the future.

Information wanted.   Fundamentally, all the questions asked during an interview are aimed at finding out four points about an applicant:

1. Is this person qualified for the job?
2. How badly does this applicant want the job?
3. Will the job help this person to realize his or her goals?
4. Will this applicant work to his or her fullest ability?

[3] See Joseph Matarazzo and Arthur Wiens, *The Interview* (Chicago: Aldine Atherton, 1972), as cited in Richard S. Nelson and Cathleen Platt, "Psychological Testing: Is a Much Maligned Selection Tool Making a Comeback?" *San Francisco State University School of Business Journal* 2, (1985), p. 7.

A list of the detailed questions that could be asked on these four major points might run for pages. Even then, each firm would have to select the questions judiciously; different queries would be pertinent for different firms. In general, the inquiries are intended to examine the applicants past behavior, experiences, environment, and motivation. What a person has been and has done in the past is indicative of what that person probably will be and do in the future. Certain types of questions regarding the future ordinarily are also included: "What would you like to be doing five years from now? How much do you hope to be earning in three years?"

Bases for classifying personal interviews. Four bases may be used to categorize selection interviews:

1. *Degree to which interviews are preplanned.* The questioning may be done in a formally patterned, guided manner, or in an informal, nondirected fashion.
2. *Timing of interview.* There may be a brief interview as part of the initial screening, or there may be longer ones in subsequent stages of the selection process.
3. *Persons interviewed.* The company may also want to talk with the applicant's spouse and family.
4. *Applicant's awareness of being interviewed.* The firm may or may not want prospective employees to be conscious of the fact that they are being interviewed.

Patterned Versus Nondirected Interviews

Selection interviews can differ, depending on the extent to which the questions are detailed in advance and the conversation is guided by the interviewer. At one end of the scale is the totally patterned or guided interview, and at the other end is the informal, nondirected type.

Patterned interviews. In a patterned interview, the procedure is highly standardized. The interviewers for a firm all use the same guide sheet which contains a series of questions. Each person interviewed is asked these questions in the order listed on the sheet. The standard form also has a place for the interviewer to record the applicant's answer to each question. The notations may be made in the presence of the interviewer after making a proper explanatory statement. Or the replies may be noted immediately after the conversation is ended.

The patterned or guided interview is designed to overcome problems encountered in using personal interviews as a selection technique. Many sales executives engaged in selection activities do not know what questions to ask. They may know what qualifications are necessary for the job. But they do not know what questions will draw out information about the applicant's possession of these characteristics.

Another common problem is the interviewer's unfamiliarity with the job description or application blank. The interviewer who does not know in detail what the job entails and what the necessary qualifications are cannot do a good interviewing job.

A third problem is that most interviewers are unable to interpret the answers to many of their questions. Qualified personnel have no opportunity to help interpret answers to queries in the nonpatterned type of interview, because the applicant's comments are not recorded.

Persons more qualified than the interviewer may have a part in the appraisal. In a company where the final selection is made in the home office (after the preliminary screening is done in the branches), the guided interview records are especially useful.

Some people criticize the patterned interview as being inflexible. Actually, a patterned interview need not be as inflexible as these critics imply. Trained interviewers can use their own judgment and make slight modifications without detracting from the full value of the guided form.

Nondirected interviews.   At the other end of the directed-interview scale is the informal, nondirected one. Ordinarily, the interviewer asks a few questions to get the applicant talking on certain subjects, such as his business experiences, home life, or school activities. The interviewer does very little talking—just enough to keep the conversation rolling. The theory of this type of interview is that significant characteristics come to light if the applicant is encouraged to speak freely.

The major problem with the nondirected interview is that much time may be consumed in unearthing little information. Some of what an applicant says may be irrelevant or incapable of being appraised. This type of interview requires far more interpretive skill on the part of the interviewer than is true of the patterned form. There is no written record that can be passed on to someone else for appraisal. In some cases, a tape recording of the interview may be made without the recruit's knowledge. Also, the values of standardization are lost in the nondirected interview.

Most firms today use an interview format that falls somewhere between the two extremes of the patterned and the nondirected interview. Usually, the interviewers have in mind a few topics they want to cover in the talks. They probably do very little writing in the presence of the applicants. Even in the same firm, interviewers vary considerably in regard to the interview content and the techniques used in interviewing. There seems to be a definite trend, however, toward the use of a more patterned or guided form of interview.

Timing of the Interview

During initial screening.   Companies often use an interview instead of an application blank as the initial screening device. For example, when recruiting teams visit college campuses, one or more team members may interview a prospect very briefly to determine only whether that person should be considered further. Initial screening interviews should be short—possibly only 15 or 20 minutes. Figure 6–2 is a copy of the form that the Xerox Corporation uses to evaluate a campus interview.

Because interviewing takes up executives' valuable time, the interviewer should find out as soon as possible if the recruit is uninterested or unqualified. The necessary information may be determined, first, by giving a brief description of the job and, second, by asking a few questions to ascertain whether the recruit meets the minimum requirements. Figure 6–3 is the patterned interview form used by Xerox when it uses a telephone interview as the initial screening device.

At later stages.   Firms that do a thorough selection job ordinarily interview applicants several times before they are hired. After applicants pass through the initial screen, but before a final decision can be reached, much remains to be learned about them. In turn, they must be told many things about the job.

A sound generalization is that a company should not depend on a single interview, a single interviewer, or a single place for the interviewing. This idea is based on the feeling that the more time spent with prospective recruits and the more people who talk with them, the greater is the opportunity to get to know them well. It usually is a mistake to hire a person after only one interview.

Interviewing the Spouse and Family

For many years management has been aware of how important an executive's spouse is to that executive's progress in the company. Sales managers also recognize the influence a *sales person's* spouse can have on that rep's performance. Unless the spouse and family are satisfied and proud of the rep's job, the representative probably will not give his or her best performance.

Consequently, interviewing the recruit's spouse before making a hiring decision is becoming more common. These interviews may be

Figure 6-2

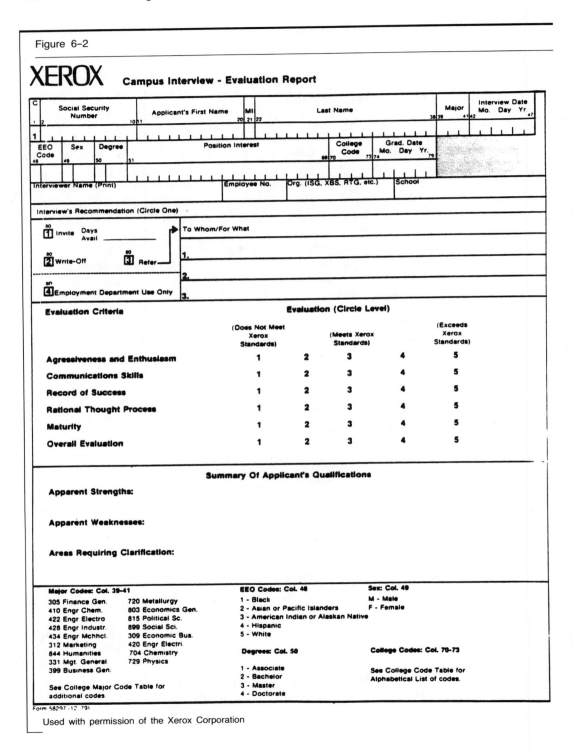

Used with permission of the Xerox Corporation

Figure 6-3

 Telephone Screen Evaluation

Applicant	Interviewer	Date

1. Would you tell me about your current job? (Determine whether the applicant has related experience, training, interest, etc.)

2. Why are you looking for a job at this time? (Determine whether reasons are acceptable.)

3. Why are you looking for this particular job at Xerox? (Determine whether the applicant's perceptions of the job are sufficiently accurate.)

4. What background, qualifications, and abilities do you feel you have which would enable you to be successful on this job? (Determine whether the applicant can sell him/herself and whether these qualifications are beneficial.)

5. What are your salary expectations? (Determine whether the applicant is realistic.)

6. Where do you expect to be five years from now? (Determine whether the applicant has sufficient ambition.)

7. When would you be able to start with Xerox? (Determine whether this fits into manpower needs.)

Summary Of Applicant's Qualifications

Apparent Strengths:

Apparent Weaknesses:

Interviewer's Recommendations

A. Recommended for testing: ☐ Yes ☐ No

B. Areas requiring clarification in additional interviews:

conducted with the couple in an office, during a social engagement, such as dinner, or preferably in the couple's home. By visiting the recruit's home, the interviewer also can appraise the home environment and meet the rest of the family.

To simplify this section, let's assume that the company is hiring a salesman. However, the points developed here are equally applicable when a firm is hiring a saleswoman. In that case, management should interview her husband to determine if he is supportive of her taking the selling job. In either hiring situation (man or woman), an interviewer also should try to talk with teenage children who are living at home.

During this interview, management can get the wife's opinion on specific topics, such as (1) the people her husband will meet, (2) the problem of being away from home so much, (3) the reputation of the company, (4) the nature of the product, and (5) the type of sales job. Many stories have been told about traveling salesmen, but they are not particularly funny to their wives. There may be a question of the prestige connected with the work. If a man is to sell a product about which there may be a social question (for example, ladies' lingerie or alcoholic beverages), a firm should know the wife's attitude toward it. Another purpose served by the interview is that it gives management a chance to sell the recruit's wife and family on the job and its opportunities.

Applicant's Awareness of Interview

In most interviews, the applicants are aware that they are being interviewed. Realizing this, companies sometimes wonder how much they are really finding out about applicants. People who are perceptive and want the job are very apt to give answers that they think will leave a favorable impression. These replies may not necessarily be the full truth, but then the full truth may not get them the job.

It is possible that a good interviewer can get honest answers to the questions asked. It is also possible to verify the answers given to some queries by resorting to other selection tools. However, applicants want to put their best foot forward, assuming that they want the job. Therefore, the main factor being measured is one aspect of a person's social intelligence—the ability to make the proper responses. Applicants know it is better to have left a former position for a better opportunity rather than because they thought the boss was incompetent and played favorites.

There is no questioning the importance of social intelligence in selling. It is also encouraging when a recruit has knowledge of the proper way to act in an interview. Probably, those lacking in these abilities should be eliminated. However, the prospective employer still must find out everything possible about the applicant.

An important type of interview is one during which the company hopes the applicants will forget, or not realize, that they are being interviewed. The purpose is to get them off guard or away from their interviewing manners and then talk with them when they are more at ease. Ordinarily an interview of this nature is not held on company premises. It may be possible to determine something about people's emotional stability by observing them under the stress of a golf match, a football or baseball game, or a cocktail party. Another reason is that people are apt to relax and say what they really think in such an informal setting.

In these situations, a leading statement in the form of a complaint from the interviewer may encourage a prospective recruit to speak more freely. During a golf game, for example, the interviewer may criticize the poor condition of the greens or complain about the way the club is operated. Recruits may start to speak their mind in these unguarded moments. Sometimes, chronic complainers just need someone to get them started, and they will be critical of many things. They may even tell what they really thought of their former job and employer. Care must be taken to differentiate between the person who is complaining just to agree with the interviewer, and the one who is a habitual complainer.

In interviews where the applicants do not realize they are being interviewed, the interviewer has a greater responsibility to interpret a person's behavior and remarks correctly. Notes may be made at the conclusion of the interview, but there is no standard list of questions. The interviewer's own judgment and ingenuity must be used during the encounter.

References and Other Outside Sources

When processing applicants for sales jobs, an administrator can get help from two general sources of information outside the company. In the first, the applicant furnishes the leads; this is typically called a *reference.* In the other, the company solicits information on its own initiative; this source includes credit or insurance reports.

A personal visit may take too much time and is not practical unless the reference is located near the prospective employer. A letter is probably used more frequently than the other two methods, but often it is of little real value. Firms hesitate to put in writing anything that is seriously derogatory. Using the telephone or a personal visit is advantageous in that any statements made by the reference are not in writing. However, some companies will not supply information to a stranger who calls on the telephone. The payoff from telephone reference checks can be increased if the caller talks to the applicant's former boss and not to someone in the personnel department.

When talking with an applicant's former employer, a key question to ask is: Would you rehire this person? Other questions may determine facts and opinions about dates of employment, attendance record, nature of duties, ability to get along with people, and the reason for leaving. One particular reference pitfall to watch out for is the "Boy Scout Oath" type of recommendation. That is, the applicant is said to be friendly, loyal, courteous, etc., and also is said to have lots of potential. This recommendation is sometimes given when the applicant is a "nice person" who everybody liked. But this person was discharged (allowed to resign) because of poor job performance.

Figure 6–4 illustrates the reference-check form used by the Xerox Corporation. Using a form such as this one provides the prospective employer with a written record of the reference-check conversation. Also, note topic number 13—is the applicant eligible for rehiring by the former employer.

Who is a valuable reference from the prospective employer's viewpoint? No simple generalization can be made about the value of former employers as references. In some cases, they can be excellent sources of information. They may know the applicant well and be willing to give an honest appraisal. If a present employer wants to get rid of or, for that matter, wants to keep the employee, it is doubtful whether such a reference can be of much help to the hiring firm. If the prospect has been a salesman, it may be a good idea to talk to some of his customers. They know something of his sales ability, personal habits, and personality traits.

On balance, the merit of the reference as a selection tool is questionable. Yet, management dare not bypass this tool. If only one significant fact is uncovered, it makes the effort worthwhile. Handled carefully and intelligently, references may be valuable, but unfortunately, most are worth very little. The use of references requires special caution in one respect. A person who is a success or failure in one job will not necessarily repeat the same performance in the next one. There may have been a good reason for doing poorly in one position, and this may well have been the fault of the employer.

A special source of outside information is the credit report, or a report from some other type of investigating agency. These agencies specialize in preemployment investigative interviews with former employers, co-workers, sales managers, neighbors, and creditors. Reports from local credit bureaus, through their affiliation with their national association, can provide a wealth of information on a prospective sales person. Often, former employers and other references give information to a credit bureau that they would not divulge to a prospective employer. These reports touch on many phases of a per-

Figure 6-4

 APPLICANT REFERENCE CHECK

ASK FOR THE FOLLOWING:

1. Title and Duties	7. Creativity
2. In what capacity and for how long applicant has been known	8. Quality and Quantity of work
3. Overall Performance	9. Ability to accept constructive criticism
4. Ability to get along with others	10. Supervisory ability (if applicable)
5. Personal Habits	11. Strengths and weaknesses
6. Work Habits	12. Reason for leaving
	13. Eligibility for rehire

NAME OF APPLICANT   POSITION

PERSON CONTACTED   FIRM

CONVERSATION:

RECRUITER   DATE

Form 52559 (1/70) Printed in U.S.A.   Xerographic Master - Reproduce Needs

Used with permission of the Xerox Corporation

A day-to-day operating problem in the
Majestic Glass Company (C)

Request to Rehire Former Salesman, Now in Penitentiary

Clyde Brion, general sales manager for Majestic Glass Company, was visited in his office by Mrs. Edgar Jenner, a pale, sick-looking woman. She was accompanied by a man who identified himself as parole officer of the Ohio State Department of Correction. As Brion knew, Mrs. Jenner was the wife of a former Majestic salesman based in Detroit. At this time Jenner was in the Ohio Penitentiary serving the third year of a seven-year sentence for manslaughter committed while driving a car under the influence of liquor. The case had attracted much newspaper attention because the victim was a pretty teenage daughter of a U.S. senator. She was struck down crossing a quiet street on her way to a church where she was to have been a bridesmaid at the wedding of another senator's daughter.

Except for an attempt to escape custody during his trial, Jenner had been a docile prisoner. The parole officer described him as remorseful, morose, and worried about his wife as well as about his own future. A doctor at the penitentiary had found him free of any addiction to alcohol. The doctor had recommended that Jenner be freed, if he could return to his regular work in familiar surroundings. Mrs. Jenner asked Brion to rehire her husband.

Until his conviction, Jenner had been a satisfactory, though not an outstanding, salesman for Majestic. In sales volume, his territory had never ranked higher than ninth among the 18 territories, despite his six years on the sales force. The Detroit area was believed to have considerably more potential than he was able to tap. Jenner had used his drawing account regularly, saying that he needed extra money to pay medical bills on his wife's long illness.

The Detroit territory had not been permanently filled since Jenner had left it. Because it was relatively close to the Majestic home offices, Brion had preferred to use it as a training territory for new salesmen, supervised by himself.

Question

Should Clyde Brion rehire Edgar Jenner?

Note: See the introduction to this series of problems in Chapter 3 for the necessary background on the company, its market, and its competition.

---

son's background, such as personal habits and financial condition, as well as the standard facts on educational and business background.

Psychological Testing

Psychological testing is another major tool often used in the sales-selection process. Typically a company uses a *battery* of these tests—that is, several different tests—rather than a *single* test. Over the years, psychological testing undoubtedly has been the most controversial of all the selection tools. Today the added burden of complying with legal guidelines has increased the complexity and controversy surrounding the use of testing in sales-force selection.

Validity and Use of Tests in Sales Selection

Nevertheless, there is no denying that tests are a better predictor of job performance than any of the other selection tools as currently used. Recall the Hunters' meta-analysis of validation studies which we referred to earlier in connection with personal interviews. The Hunters' study covered different types of occupations—not just sales jobs. Consequently, a sales manager might say that tests are okay if you are hiring for a clerical job or a production-line job. But selling is a far more complex, multi-dimensional job that is different in each firm and industry.

However, more recent studies of testing for sales jobs, using a new approach to validation, clearly show that tests can also be a powerful predictor of *sales* job performance. These studies support the concept of "validity generalization." That is, the test validity established for a particular job may be transferable to *similar* jobs in other companies or industries. Thus tests can predict performance across job lines and company lines.[4]

Civil rights legislation put a damper on the use of testing in selection procedures. Periodically for more than 20 years Richard Nelson of San Francisco State University has surveyed the members of the National Society of Sales Training Executives regarding their use of testing in the sales-force selection process. A summary of his findings since the passage of the Civil Rights Act of 1964 is as follows:

Year	Percent of Firms Using Tests
1964	83%
1969	59
1975	22
1984	26

Types of tests

The four main types of tests commonly used in the selection of sales people are:

1. *Mental intelligence tests.* Intended to measure a person's native intelligence (IQ—intelligence quotient) and general ability to learn. Some examples of these tests are (1) the Otis Self-Admin-

[4] See Nelson and Platt, "Psychological Testing: Is a Much Maligned Selection Tool Making a Comeback?"

istering Test of Mental Ability and (2) the Wonderlic Personnel Test.

2. *Aptitude tests.* Designed to measure a person's aptitude for selling. This category also includes tests that measure social aptitude (social intelligence). Some examples are (1) the Sales Aptitude Checklist, (2) the General Sales Aptitude Test, and (3) the Diplomacy Test of Empathy.

3. *Interest tests.* Designed to measure or compare a person's interests with the interests of successful people in specific occupations. Some examples are (1) the Strong-Campbell Interest Inventory and (2) the Kuder Occupational Interest Survey.

4. *Personality tests.* Intended to measure various personality traits in a person. These tests are the most risky and difficult to validate because of our inability to identify which traits are needed for a particular type of sales job. Some examples of these tasks are (1) the Bernreuter Personality Inventory, (2) the Edwards Personal Preference Schedule, (3) the Multiple Personal Inventory, and (4) the Gordon Personal Profile.

Legal Aspects of Testing

Some misunderstandings exist regarding the use of tests in the personnel-selection process. Some court cases and compliance agency rulings have left many executives with the belief that it is illegal to use testing in the selection process. *Testing is not illegal.* Many companies that are audited by compliance agencies are using tests. In fact, a testing and selection order issued by the OFCC (Office of Federal Contract Compliance) says that "Properly validated and standardized employee selection procedures can significantly contribute to the implementation of nondiscriminatory personnel policies" and that "Professionally developed tests . . . may significantly aid in the development and maintenance of an efficient work force."

The key phrases in this quotation are "properly validated" and "professionally developed." A firm should use either professional in-house psychologists or a competent outside consultant. The sales executives should *not* be the people who are selecting the tests to be used.

In our earlier discussion of application blanks and interviews, we observed that the questions asked must be relevant to the job being filled. Furthermore, if a compliance agency questions a company about relevance, the burden of proof is on the company to show that its questions and procedures are relevant. That same situation prevails regarding the use of tests. The test questions must be demonstrably relevant to the job. However, validation of tests is *not* required *unless* there is a disproportionately large rejection of women or minorities in the selection process.

To summarize the legal situation, testing is perfectly acceptable if done correctly. A company should use a battery of tests designed by a professional to meet the needs of the particular job. The company should keep records to show (1) that the tests are relevant and (2) that the tests do not screen out a disproportionately large number of women or minorities.

Problems in Testing

Most testing procedures generate the concept of an average or normal type of employee. The implication is that this person is the best type to hire for a given job. The danger is that a potentially successful sales representative may be screened out simply because he or she does not fit the stereotype. Testing may eliminate the truly creative person, who may not fall in the average or normal range in testing. At the same time, creativity may be the very trait that would make that person an outstanding sales representative.

Another problem with testing is that tests may be used as the sole deciding knockout factor. An applicant may look good based on interviews, the application blanks, and reference checks. But if the test scores are especially low, management may be scared off and not hire that person.

Tests are sometimes misused because executives fail to apply the concept of a *range* of scores. These managers believe that the highest score on a test indicates the best prospective sales person. For many kinds of tests, psychologists agree that a *range* of scores is acceptable. All who fall within that range should be judged as *equally qualified for the job.* Unfortunately, most people tend to feel that a person scoring near the high end of the acceptable range is a better prospect than one scoring in the lower part of that range.

Another factor to watch for in testing is that applicants can fake the answers on some tests, especially on some personality or interest tests. The reasonably intelligent applicants for a sales job realize that they should indicate a preference for mixing with people, in contrast to staying home and reading a good book.

Cultural bias is another situation that can creep into tests. A person may score poorly—not because of a lack of interest, aptitude, or native intelligence—but only because the test included questions which assumed a certain cultural background.

Finally, testing is affected by some of the problems we discussed in Chapter 4 in connection with determining hiring specifications. We cannot *isolate* the traits needed for success in a particular sales job. Some of the traits that make a good sales representative might also make a good lawyer, actor, or bus driver. A test may indicate that an applicant has these traits. But you don't know whether that person will turn out to be a good sales representative or a good bus driver. Furthermore, in sales selection we need to know (1) the *extent* to which each trait is needed for sales success and (2) the *extent* to which one trait can be substituted for another. So far, we have been largely unsuccessful in our attempts to quantitatively measure these traits by testing or by other means.

Conditions in Which Testing Is Most Effective

A program for testing in sales selection is more likely to be effective when any of the following conditions exist:

- The firm hires a relatively large number of sales people, and management realizes that its existing selection system is poor.
- The company is hiring young, inexperienced people about whom little is known. If experienced representatives are being selected, their performance records rather than test results should be the criterion.
- The personnel being selected are not likely to be "test-wise," so the danger of faking (intentionally answering incorrectly) is minimized.
- The executives responsible for interviewing the recruits are not adept at discovering personality traits and selling aptitudes. Normally, executives with a great deal of experience in hiring do a much better job of interviewing than an administrator who is new at the job.
- In companies where the cost of failure is high, the expense of testing may be considered a small insurance premium to make certain that no one slips through the selection screen. If the testing procedure catches just one failure a year who would otherwise have been hired, the costs of the testing may be justified.
- The executives are competent to interpret the psychologist's recommendations properly, and they feel free to act on their own judgment regardless of the tests.

Physical Examination

A physical examination is virtually a necessity when selecting sales people because of the physical activity and the mental and emotional stresses involved in a sales job. A person may be in poor physical condition and still be able to perform satisfactorily in some jobs, but not in a sales job. A sales recruit should appreciate the opportunity to get a complete physical checkup, and the company should insist on it. It is not enough merely to ask questions about the applicant's physical condition and medical history on an application blank or during an interview. The examination given during the course of the hiring process should be very thorough. Ordinarily, the results can be interpreted by a physician in consultation with the sales executives concerned.

Assessment Centers

The assessment-center technique is another hiring tool that a company can consider using as part of its sales-force selection process. Probably the main factor limiting the use of this technique is its high cost. The ***assessment-center*** technique is a centralized, comprehensive evaluation procedure involving tests, interviews, and simulation exercises such as business games, discussion groups, and individual presentations.[5] This technique is conducted by trained executive observers and usually takes from one to three days. These observers then take another one to three days to evaluate the applicant-participants and their performance. Assessment centers have been used primarily to evaluate people for promotion within a firm, to aid in an individual's professional development, and to evaluate training programs. This technique also has been used in selecting new sales people.[6]

Coming to a Conclusion about an Applicant

When all other steps have been completed in the selection process, one thing remains to be done. The company must make a decision on whether or not to hire each applicant. This involves a review of everything known about these people. What detailed impressions have they made? What are their qualifications from the past, and what is their potential? What do they want, and what can the firm offer them? This last point is far broader than just the monetary aspects of the job. It involves all the hopes and ambitions of each applicant as matched against the opportunities and rewards offered by the job and the company.

[5] Assessment centers was the topical theme of the entire February, 1980 issue of *Personnel Administrator;* especially see Cabot L. Jaffee and Joseph T. Sefcik, Jr., "What Is an Assessment Center?" pp. 40–43.

[6] See E. James Randall, Ernest F. Cooke, and Lois Smith, "A Successful Application of the Assessment Center Concept to the Salesperson Selection Process," *Journal of Personal Selling and Sales Management,* May 1985, pp. 53–61.

At this stage, it is important that the company not leave any applicant dangling. If the firm clearly has decided *not* to hire a certain applicant, an executive should gently, but clearly, tell this to the person. To those applicants who are still in contention for the job, an executive might say something like this at the close of an interview: "As you know we have several people applying for this position. My hope is that we will move along in the process and be able to notify you one way or another in two weeks."

If the decision is to hire a certain person, the next step is to make a formal offer. The conditions and details of the offer probably have been spelled out earlier. There should be no surprises in the formal offer. However, it is possible that some details of the job will not be known until after the induction training period. For example, the recruit may be told when hired that on completion of his training he will be assigned to one of three given branches. In all cases, the terms of the offer should be set down in writing for the protection of both the recruit and the firm. Many companies have contracts that must be signed by all new sales people. These documents spell out in considerable detail all the facts pertaining to territories, compensation, expenses, and other important information.

Summary

The last step in the sales-force selection process involves: (1) developing a system of tools and procedures to measure the applicants against the predetermined hiring specifications; and then (2) actually putting this system into operation to select the sales people. This processing of applicants is a key activity in implementing a company's strategic planning. When using any selection tool, management must make certain that they are complying with all pertinent laws and regulatory guidelines.

The application blank and the personal interview are the two most widely used selection tools. A short application blank may be used as an initial screening device. A longer application blank is a primary source of personal history information that can be used in hiring and in other phases of sales operations. An application blank is an excellent tool for getting information in three of the major categories of job qualifications—namely, the applicant's physical condition, experience background, and environmental information.

The personal interview is the most widely used of all selection tools, yet it ranks quite low as a predictor of job performance. This rating occurs, in the authors' opinion, simply because most people don't know how to interview. Basically, the interviewing process is designed to answer four questions regarding an applicant: (1) Is the person qualified for the job? (2) How badly does the person want the job? (3) Will the job help the person realize his or her goals? (4) Will the person work to his or her fullest ability?

Interviews may be classified on the following four bases: (1) to what degree is the interview patterned or nondirected; (2) at what stages in the selection process are the interviews made; (3) will the company also want to interview the applicant's spouse and children; and (4) to what extent are the applicants aware that they are being interviewed. A guiding principle in interviewing is to (1) have more than one interview before hiring a person, (2) use more than one interviewer, (3) interview the applicant's spouse, and (4) do some interviewing in social settings away from the office.

Reference checks are widely used in the sales-selection process. A personal visit or a phone call with a reference usually is a better method than letter writing. A key question to ask is whether the reference person would hire the applicant.

Psychological testing is another major selection tool, and researchers consider it the best tool for predicting job performance. The most commonly used tests cover four areas—mental intelligence, aptitudes, interests, and personality. There are some problems in using tests as part of the hiring process. Also, testing is more likely to be successful when certain conditions exist. Physical examinations and assessment centers were the final two hiring tools discussed briefly in this chapter.

Questions and Problems

1. One sales executive claims he "Knows a good man when he sees one," and therefore he does not like to be bothered by so-called scientific selection processes. What can you offer to refute this claim? Would your answer be any different if you knew that the sales manager who made the statement had a low rate of turnover in his sales force and was running a highly profitable operation?

2. In the "Application for Sales Position" form that an aptitude testing firm has prepared, the following questions are asked. In each case, what do you think the questions are designed to find out?

   a. What is the most monotonous task you ever did?

   b. In people you like, what do you like about them?

   c. What kind of a job do you think your spouse would like to see you have?

   d. What has been your outstanding disappointment in life?

   e. What is your spouse's (or family's) criticism of you?

    f. What type of selling do you think gives sales people the greatest satisfaction—frequent small successes or many turn-downs followed by one big success?

3. Many firms request interested applicants to send in a letter of application in their own handwriting. What is the purpose of this request? Is this selection method basically any different from using palmistry or astrology as selection aids? Under what conditions would a firm be wise to employ these tools?

4. How may the limitations of the interview be eliminated, reduced, or counterbalanced?

5. When interviewing an applicant for a sales job, management ordinarily should be vitally interested in complete answers to the following three points:

    a. How badly does the applicant want or need the job?

    b. Can the job furnish him with the success he wants or offer him the opportunity to realize his goals in life?

    c. Will he strive to achieve the level of work his capacity will allow?

Prepare a series of questions an interviewer might ask with respect to each of these three points.

6. What type of questions should an interviewer ask to determine if an applicant possesses the following traits:

    a. Ability to define a problem.

    b. Ability to make a decision.

    c. Dependability.

    d. Self-confidence.

    e. Resourcefulness and imagination.

7. Soon many of you will be interviewed by companies who recruit graduating students. The interviewer might ask the following questions. What is each question trying to determine, and how would you answer it?

    a. Why do you want to work for this company?

    b. Why should we hire you?

    c. How much do you hope to be earning in three years?

    d. If you come to work for us, what kind of a job do you expect to have with us in three years?

8. Can you eliminate the personal biases and prejudices of interviewers so they will conduct an interview impartially?

9. The following series of traits are generally considered undesirable in a sales person. What tools can management use to determine whether an applicant possesses any of these characteristics? If you feel that an interview or application blank can be used in this case, what questions should be asked?

    a. Failed in a business.

    b. Has a history of not staying in one job very long.

    c. Spouse or family is not sold on the job.

    d. Was not able to pass an insurance physical examination.

    e. Has financial problems.

    f. Does not get along well with other people; is the lone-wolf type.

10. The text rated the reference as a not very helpful selection tool. Do you agree with this appraisal? If so, why do you think it continues to be used by virtually every firm that is hiring sales people or other employees?

11. Under what conditions would you recommend that a company use a battery of tests as part of its procedures for selecting sales people?

12. What are some of the problems or dangers in using tests as part of the sales force selection process?

13. Many sales managers claim that the real factor that determines whether people will be a success in selling is their motivation to work hard. Where is this motivational factor measured in psychological testing? How should sales managers determine a person's motivation to do a good job?

Case 6–1

Hamilton Casualty and Surety Company

Selecting an Account Executive (Sales Representative)

Several months previously the founder and chief executive officer of the Hamilton Casualty and Surety Company died. At that time the company's board of directors promoted George Braman to the position of chief executive officer. Mr. Braman had been the account executive who handled surety bonds for construction contractors in the company's home state of Georgia. After his promotion, Mr. Braman tried to continue with some of his activities as an account executive. However, his promotion left a large void in the surety bond department of the company. Because this department was so important in the company's overall operation, it was imperative that Mr. Braman hire someone to fill his former position.

Located in Atlanta, Georgia, The Hamilton Casualty and Surety Company sold surety bonds and various forms of insurance (life, health, accident, casualty, property) to construction contractors in the state of Georgia. Hamilton was one of the major private insurance agencies in the state. A private insurance agency (also called an insurance broker) is a firm that represents several insurance companies in the sale of various kinds of insurance. In effect, Hamilton served as a sales force for the insurance companies. Premiums that Hamilton collected on the insurance policies and surety bonds it sold represented Hamilton's gross revenues (gross sales). Hamilton's gross revenues totaled $11.5 million in 1985.

Within the Hamilton Company the department that sold surety bonds was the most important department. Contractors are usually required to take out a surety bond on important jobs. A surety bond is the instrument which insures that a contractor will fulfill all obligations within the construction contract. Thus, if a contractor fails to perform, he may forfeit his surety bond. That is, the aggrieved party would collect damages from the surety company.

Hamilton's surety department, through its sale of surety bonds, generated nearly one third of the company's gross premiums. Furthermore, this department served as the basis for almost all of the other types of insurance sold by Hamilton. The philosophy of the company was that if Hamilton could not write surety bonds for a client, then Hamilton was not interested in that client's other insurance needs. Of the contractors who obtained surety bonds through Hamilton, 84 percent had purchased other forms of insurance. Thus, the surety department, either directly or indirectly, accounted for nearly all of Hamilton's sales volume and profit.

Because Hamilton concentrated its sales effort almost entirely in the surety bond field, the company's competitive position was imbalanced. In the sale of life, casualty, and other forms of insurance, Hamilton was not a strong competitor of other insurance agencies in the area. In the surety bond field, however, Hamilton was a major competitive force in the state of Georgia.

Hamilton had some very large accounts. Three customers represented 23 percent of the company's premium income, and 45 accounts generated 65 percent of the company's gross revenues. A great majority of the surety bond premiums were paid by a relatively few large contractors. This market concentration obviously meant that these large accounts were extremely important to any bonding agency.

The duties of the account executive included the development and maintenance of active accounts. In account development, his responsibilities were to find low-risk prospects who needed surety bonds, sell them on the Hamilton agency as a source of this surety underwriting, and then convince management that the prospect was a good risk. The account executive was supposed to generate more premiums from present and prospective customers in a profitable manner. This meant that the account executive had to be selective regarding prospects. Bad prospects—those who defaulted on their bonds—meant a decrease in bonus income from the companies that

Hamilton represented. Complaints were to be handled by the account executive in such a way as to develop long-range goodwill.

After the account-development process was completed, the account executive's duty to his contractor customers became one of maintaining the account. This activity required not only business know-how, but also a high level of social intelligence. The account executive had to handle the client's future surety needs, entertain the client periodically, and generally act as a public-relations officer for the Hamilton agency.

The account executive's position carried a salary of $32,000 plus bonuses. Additional benefits included a company car, full medical and dental insurance for the executive and his family, and other items. The total compensation package was worth close to $40,000 a year.

The person who filled the account executive's position would be taking over the accounts previously handled by Mr. Braman. Clients often preferred to maintain dealings with the same account executive. Consequently, there could be some potentially explosive situations when Mr. Braman turned over his accounts to the new sales representative. Some clients undoubtedly would insist on dealing only with Braman, and he would have to take the time to deal with these customers.

Braman also figured that most of his old clients would willingly switch to a new representative if that new person seemed to be competent and reliable. Consequently, Mr. Braman realized the new account executive had to have a genial personality and an excellent record of past performance. Optimally, the new rep should be between 28 and 35 years of age, and have previously proven himself in the surety bond field. He must be able to step right in and do a good job. There would be little or no time for fundamental training. The new sales rep also would have to be satisfied with the same job title for many years. He would receive compensation increases, but the company was small and there was little likelihood of promotion opportunities in the foreseeable future.

Mr. Braman felt that his best source for this type of account executive was a person now working for a casualty and surety insurance company such as Safeco, Travelers, or Fireman's Fund. Braman also realized that his agency now represented some of these firms. Hiring a person from those companies could have a potentially damaging effect on the Hamilton agency.

After consulting with several sources around the country, Mr. Braman had narrowed the list of prospects to three people. All three would require relocation. The Atlanta area would present a new life-style and a new climate for all of these applicants. Following is a summary of each person's qualifications:

Nicholas Hesston.   Mr. Hesston was 48 years old, married, with two children, and presently residing in a suburb of Chicago, Illinois. Hesston had an outstanding record in the surety field with Safeco Insurance Company. He had been a sales-volume leader in the company during his 12 years of service with Safeco, and he had shown a considerable ability in keeping his customers satisfied. His present salary was $35,000 a year. However, that salary would be increased to $40,000 a year if he was selected from a group of men for a promotion within Safeco. Hesston wanted that promotion badly, since it was a stepping stone to his ultimate goal of being company president.

Walter Laughlin.   Mr. Laughlin was 27 years old, married with one child, and lived in New Orleans, Louisiana. For the past four years he had been a sales representative for the Travelers Insurance Company. According to Mr. Braman's information, Laughlin liked his job immensely and enjoyed living in New Orleans. He had sales experience and a knowledge of accounting and financial controls. He also had a limited, but apparently successful, experience in the surety underwriting field. A source within the Travelers office in New Orleans had reported to Braman that Laughlin had a virtually unlimited sales potential within the surety field, once he had obtained a bit more experience. He possessed excellent customer relations abilities. His present salary was $32,000 a year. Although he enjoyed his job at this point, Laughlin believed that he was slated for a transfer to Connecticut in the near future. This prospect had soured Laughlin's view toward his present job. During the process of selecting an account executive, Braman learned that one of Hamilton's major competitors in Atlanta had offered Laughlin a position that would pay him an annual salary of $36,000.

Anthony Stark.   Mr. Stark was 31 years old, married with three children, and currently living in a suburb of Cleveland, Ohio. For the past seven years Stark had been employed as a sales representative for the Firemen's Fund Company. Much of his selling experience was in the surety bond field. Stark was the only one of Braman's three prospects who was not presently employed with a company represented by the Hamilton agency. Stark's sales record looked good in terms of volume, but he had not received a promotion during the past four years. Upon checking into this situation, Braman found that Stark, who was noted for his temper, had lost two accounts by exhibiting his anger toward customers. When threatened with dismissal, Stark had apparently changed his ways, however. Over the past two years Stark's customer relations had reportedly been excellent. Stark's present salary was $33,000 a year, but he wanted to increase his income in order to better support his growing family. Stark had become disenchanted with the Cleveland area. He had expressed a desire to move to Alabama where he had grown up and had gone to college.

Question

Who should Mr. Braman hire to fill the account executive position in the surety department of the Hamilton agency?

Case 6–2

Allied Food Distributors*

Selecting a Sales Representative

In April 1986, Elizabeth Ramsey, the district sales manager for the upper Midwest district of Allied Food Distributors, was preparing to hire a new sales representative for the southwest Indiana sales territory. The current sales representative in this territory was leaving the company at the end of June. Ms. Ramsey had narrowed the list of potential candidates to three. She wondered which of these applicants she should select.

Allied Food Distributors was one of the largest food wholesalers in the United States. The company carried hundreds of different packaged food items (fruits, vegetables, cake mixes, cookies, powdered soft drinks, and so on) for sales to supermarkets and grocery stores. Allied carried items in two different circumstances. First, some small food companies had Allied carry their entire line in all areas of the United States. Essentially, Allied was their sales force. Second, some large food companies had Allied carry their lines in less populated parts of the country. These areas were not large enough to sustain a sales representative for each food company.

Allied operated in all 50 states. The country was divided into 20 sales districts. Ms. Ramsey's sales district included Michigan, Indiana, and Illinois. Each district was divided into a number of sales territories. A sales representative was assigned to each territory.

The sales territory for which Ms. Ramsey was seeking a sales person was located in the southwest corner of Indiana. Exhibit 1 presents a map of the territory. It was bordered on the south by the Ohio River and the state of Kentucky, on the west by the Wabash River and the state of Illinois, and on the east by the Hoosier National Forest. The northern

---

* This case was prepared by Professor Thomas C. Kinnear, University of Michigan. Reproduced with permission.

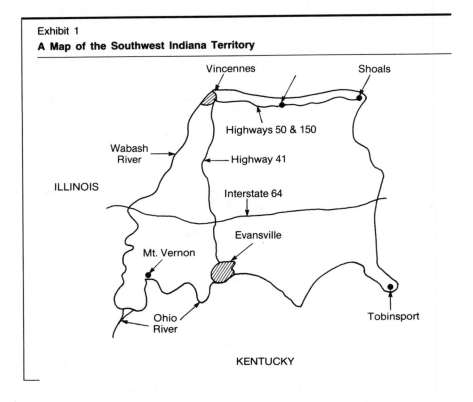

Exhibit 1
A Map of the Southwest Indiana Territory

Vincennes   Shoals

Highways 50 & 150

Wabash River   Highway 41

ILLINOIS

Interstate 64

Evansville

Mt. Vernon

Ohio River   Tobinsport

KENTUCKY

boundary ran a few miles north of Highways 50 and 150 that ran from Vincennes in the west through Washington to Shoals in the east. Evansville was the largest city in the area with a population of about 130,000. The sales person for the territory was expected to live in Evansville, but would spend about three nights a week on the road. The only other reasonably large population concentration was in Vincennes with a population of about 21,000. Vincennes was located about 55 miles straight north of Evansville on Highway 41. Interstate Highway 64 ran the 80 miles east-west through the territory about 15 miles north of Evansville. Evansville was 165 miles southwest of Indianapolis, 170 miles east of St. Louis, Missouri, and 115 miles southwest of Louisville, Kentucky. The territory was very rural in character with agriculture being the dominant industry. The terrain was quite hilly, with poor soil. As a result, the farms in the area tended to be economically weak. There were many small towns and villages located throughout this basically rural environment.

Allied maintained 75 active retail accounts in the southwest Indiana territory. About 10 of these accounts were medium- to large-sized independent supermarkets located in Evansville and Vincennes. The rest of the accounts were small, independent general food stores located throughout the territory.

The sales representative was expected to call on these accounts about every three weeks. The sales rep's duties included: checking displays and inventory levels for items already carried, obtaining orders on these items, informing retailers about new items, attempting to gain sales orders on these items, setting up special displays, and generally servicing the retailers' needs. Often, the sales rep would check the level of inventory on an item, make out an order, and present it to the retailer to be signed. The sales rep generally knew the store owner on a first name basis. The ordered goods were sent directly to the retailer from a warehouse located in Indianapolis.

The responsibility for recruiting sales people for the territories within a district was given to the district sales manager. The process consisted of the following steps:

1. An advertisement for the job was placed in newspapers in the state in question.
2. Those responding to the ad were sent job application forms.
3. The returned application forms were examined, and certain applicants were asked to come to the district sales office for a full day on interviews.
4. The selection was then made by the district sales manager, or all applicants were rejected and the process started again.

Allied did all its sales training on-the-job. The sales rep in the territory that a new person would be assigned to was given the task of training. Basically, this involved having the new person travel the territory to meet the retailers and to be shown how to obtain and send in orders. The district sales manager usually assisted in this process by traveling with the new sales rep for a few days.

The current sales rep in the southwest Indiana sales territory was earning a straight salary of about $24,000 per year plus fringe benefits. Ramsey indicated that she was willing to pay between $16,000 and $25,000 for a new person depending on the qualifications presented.

On the basis of application forms and personal interviews, Ms. Ramsey had narrowed the field of applicants down to three. A summary of the information on their application forms along with the comments she had written to herself are contained in Exhibits 2, 3, & 4.

Question

Who should Elizabeth Ramsey hire for the sales position in the southwest Indiana territory?

Exhibit 2

Information on Mr. Carley Tobias

Personal information:
  Born February 12, 1956; married; two children ages 1 and 4; height 6 feet, 2 inches; weight 170; excellent health; born in San Francisco; raised in Cleveland, Ohio.

Education:
  High school and Community College graduate in business administration; student council president at Community College; also belonged to a number of other clubs.

Employment record:
  1. Currently employed by The Drug Trading Company in Cincinnati as a sales person; job responsibility involves selling to retail drug stores; seven years with Drug Trading; current salary $1,600 per month.
  2. In 1978–79 U. S. Army private; did one tour of duty in Germany.

Applicant's statement:
  I am seeking a new position because of the limited earning potential at Drug Trading, plus my family's desire to live in a smaller town.

Other information:
  He is very active in civic and church organizations in Cincinnati; he is currently president of the Sales and Marketing Executives Club in Cincinnati.

Ms. Ramsey's comments:
  Very personable.
  Reasonably intelligent.
  Good appearance.
  He seems to like Cincinnati a lot.
  Good experience.

Exhibit 3

Information on Mr. Arthur Woodhead

Personal information:
  Born May 26, 1964; single; height 6 feet; weight 180; excellent health; born and raised in Chicago.

Education:
  Will graduate in May 1986 from the University of Illinois, Chicago Circle with a B.B.A. Active in intramural athletics and student government.

Employment record:
  Summer jobs only; did house painting and gardening work for his own company. Earned $1,000 per month in summer of 1985.

Applicant's statement:
  I really like to run my own affairs, and selling seems like a good position to reach this objective.

Ms. Ramsey's comments:
  Well dressed and groomed.
  Very intelligent.
  Management potential, not career sales person.
  Not very aggressive.

Exhibit 4

Information on Mr. Michael Gehringer

Personal information:
  Born July 15, 1944; married; three children ages 14, 16, and 19; height 5 feet, 10 inches; weight 205; excellent health; born and raised in Indianapolis.

Education:
  High school graduate; played football; no extracurricular activities of note.

Employment record:
  1. Currently employed by Allied Food Distributors in the warehouse in Indianapolis; two years with Allied; job responsibilities include processing orders from the field and expediting rush orders; current salary $1,200 per month.
  2. In 1983–84 employed by Hoosier Van Lines in Indianapolis as a sales agent; terminating salary was $900 per month; left due to limits placed on salary and lack of challenge in the job.
  3. In 1981–83 employed by Main Street Clothiers of Indianapolis as a retail sales person in the men's department; terminating salary $750 per month; left due to boring nature of this selling.
  4. Between 1964 and 1981 held six other clerical and sales-type jobs, all in Indianapolis.

Applicant's statement:
  I feel that my true employment interest lies in selling in a situation where I can be my own boss. This job seems just right.

Ms. Ramsey's comments:
  Seems very interested in job as a career.
  Well recommended by his current boss.
  Reasonably intelligent.
  Good appearance.
  Moderately aggressive.

Case 6–3

Sierra Ski Company

Selecting a Sales Representative

William Simpson, the regional sales manager for the Sierra Ski Company, was faced with the problem of adding a new sales representative in the growing Colorado market. In his selection process, he had narrowed his choice to three applicants, and now he was wondering which one of the three he should hire.

The Sierra Ski Company manufactured and marketed a wide line of skis as well as a line of boots, bindings, and goggles used in skiing. The company's home office and production facilities for skis and ski boots were located in a large western city. The ski bindings and ski goggles were manufactured in the company's European factory.

Sierra Ski's products were marketed throughout the United States and in some European cities. The company's annual sales volume in 1985 and 1986 was approximately $30 million. In each of these years, the company had reported a very small net profit. Sierra's top management attributed the company's very modest profit to several factors. The primary reason given was that inflation was pushing up Sierra's costs. However, these cost increases could not be passed on in the form of higher prices because of the intense competition and general overproduction which prevailed in the ski manufacturing industry.

The company produced a wide line of skis catering to all market segments ranging from beginning skiers to the world-class racers. Originally the company produced skis for downhill (Alpine) skiing. A few years ago, however, the company recognized the growing market for cross-country skiing (also called Nordic or touring skiing). At that time, Sierra started to manufacture a line of cross-country skis.

The market for ski boots was as intensely competitive as was the market for skis, according to Mr. Simpson. During the last two years, he believed that Nordica and Lange had run 1–2 in sales. He also felt that Sierra might soon challenge some of the leading brands for one of the top three or four market positions.

In 1984 the Sierra company introduced a new ski binding which generated some excitement and publicity in the industry. At this point Sierra had an extremely small share of the binding market, but again Bill Simpson expressed optimism. He believed that, as increasing numbers of skiers switched to Sierra bindings, the sale of Sierra skis and boots would increase also.

Skiers usually buy their equipment in one of two locations—in their home city or at the resort where they are skiing. The channels of distribution used by Sierra Ski company were designed to reach both of these locations. The company used its sales force to sell directly to retailers in all major ski markets in the United States. These retailers included ski specialty shops at ski resorts as well as department stores, sporting goods stores, and ski specialty shops in cities away from the resorts.

Up to the present time, Sierra had only one sales rep in Colorado to serve both the urban ski retailers and the ski resort shops. At this point, Bill Simpson realized that the demand and competitive situation were such that he should split the Colorado territory. Consequently, he was in the process of hiring an additional sales rep so as to develop the Colorado area more intensively. The new rep's territory would include the part of Colorado that was north of Denver and north of interstate highway 70, but not the Vail and Loveland ski areas which were on I-70.

In the course of selecting a new sales rep, Bill Simpson first reminded himself of the duties which were normally involved in that sales job. The rep would call on a variety of ski retailers located in the cities as well as at the ski resorts. The rep would be dealing with a wide variety of people in these stores. This variety ranged from workers in the ski repair department, through the ski equipment buyers, to the company presidents of smaller retailers. Some of these people (specialty ski shops) were often highly knowledgeable regarding ski equipment. Others (department stores and sporting goods retailers) were not necessarily ski specialists.

When selling ski equipment to a consumer, the equipment must be adjusted properly and must fit well. Consequently, the sales rep must be able to mount the bindings on the skis, adjust and fit the boots, and generally prepare the skis for use on the ski slopes. Furthermore, it is the rep's job to train the ski sales people and the repair shop workers so that they can perform these activities properly.

In addition to servicing all existing accounts, the new rep would be expected to open new accounts and to reopen old accounts that had become disenchanted with Sierra.

It was also the sales rep's job to train the retail sales people so that they were very knowledgeable about Sierra's products as well as those of the major competitors. Bill Simpson believed that ski buyers relied heavily on information and advice from the sales people in the retail stores. "Yet," he said, "most of these sales people don't know enough about what they are selling. When a customer asks what is the difference between two pairs of skis—one selling for $250 and one for $300 a pair—the sales person often cannot adequately answer the question. Or when a customer points to two different brands of skis each selling for $275 a pair and says. 'What's the difference between these two?' The sales person often cannot give a good answer. Other sales people talk about camber and edging and soft tips. Most beginning and intermediate skiers don't know what the sales rep is talking about." Consequently, Bill Simpson's goal for Sierra was to have a sales force that could service and instruct the retail sales people so they can answer the customers' questions directly and convincingly.

The job of sales rep involved much more than just the initial sale of the equipment. This individual must constantly be in contact with the retail outlets checking on their supply, reviewing their sales techniques, and briefing the store employees on the product. Service and quality were highly competitive in the ski industry. Obviously there was much missionary work involved in this job.

The new rep would work closely with Bill, but the rep was expected to make his own decisions when in the field. The high season for the ski industry in Colorado was from November to January. During those months, the sales rep might be working seven days a week from 8 in the morning until midnight.

The paperwork accompanying the job was essential in maintaining satisfied customers. Though the rep was expected to make decisions on his own, he also was expected to keep the company informed through a series of weekly reports which were supposed to be in the company's home office every Monday morning.

This job paid a base salary of $20,000 a year. In addition, a commission was paid on all new accounts. The company also paid a bonus based upon a general evaluation of the quality of service that the rep gave to his accounts. Bill Simpson, as regional sales manager, would confer with the ski shop managers regarding the sales rep's performance. The Sierra company paid all the business expenses incurred by the rep. The sales rep is given the option of leasing a car or of using his personal car. In either case, the company reimburses the rep for the use of the car on company business.

The Sierra company had no formal training program for its sales representatives. Consequently, one of the key hiring qualifications was that the sales people have considerable technical knowledge of skis, boots, and bindings. The reps did not necessarily need sales experience in the ski industry. But they did have to be able to explain their products to the ski retailers, and they had to be able to train the retailers in the proper mountings of the bindings on the skis and in the proper fitting of boots. A sales person must display professionalism in his sales presentations to generate credibility in Sierra's products. To do this, Bill Simpson believed that a sales person needed to have a large ego and a pleasantly aggressive nature. The sales person must be able to talk with, and be accepted by, a wide variety of people ranging from repair men to company presidents.

Two other hiring specifications were that the sales reps be able to manage their time effectively and to perform well under pressure. The peak season (November–January) would make heavy demands on the sales person's time. The rep must be able to wear well with customers under trying conditions and always be able to generate genuine enthusiasm. The sales person must be able to handle dissatisfied customers and not lose his cool.

Bill Simpson had always felt that it was good business to hire from within the company whenever possible. It gave the Sierra employees an incentive to work harder for the company when the possibility of promotion existed in the future. However, Bill also was aware that a hire-from-within policy well might exclude highly qualified individuals from outside the company. Consequently, Bill was also willing to look outside the firm for sales reps. Because of the need for technically experienced people, Bill felt it best to recruit from within the ski industry. He preferred to recruit qualified people now working for ski retailers. He was also willing to consider sales people now working for a competitor.

After screening a number of applicants, Bill Simpson had narrowed his choice down to three people. Following is a summary of the information on each of the three:

Leo Newhall. Leo was 29 years old, married, and had a baby daughter. He originally came from Denver. He currently was employed as a technician in Sierra's factory. He has worked for the Sierra company since he dropped out of college at age 20. Leo was considered a top-notch technician in the factory. His boss said that Leo was a perfectionist in what he produced, and he was always willing to work extra hours during the high season. Leo had a good rapport with management, and he was also well liked by his fellow workers in the factory. His boss reported that Leo was enthusiastic and seemed to be sure of himself and his abilities. He had been a dependable employee and now was earning the highest wage of all the technicians.

However, he was not satisfied with his present job. He was looking for something that had more challenge, greater opportunities for the future, and more pay. Leo had approached Bill Simpson as soon as he heard about the sales opening in the Colorado territory. Leo was very interested in the job and felt that he was well qualified. He admitted that he had no experience in sales but was familiar with Sierra's policies and was well acquainted with the product line. Bill and Leo had been good skiing buddies for about four years. Although Leo was an advanced skier, he had always done it strictly for recreation and had not engaged in any formal racing.

During the period when Bill Simpson was engaged in this selection process, Leo approached Bill several times expressing his (Leo's) interest in the position. He assured Bill that, given the opportunity, he would be a good sales representative.

Sam Taccone. Sam was 35 years old, married, and had three children in grade school. He currently was employed as a manager of a retail ski store in California—a store that specialized in Sierra equipment. He had been manager of this store for the past six years. He began working for this ski specialty store at age 24 in the ski installation and repair shop. Then over the years he had worked his way up to the management position.

For the past several months, Sam felt that he was not adequately challenged by his job as store manager, and he was looking for something new. Upon hearing of the opening in the Sierra sales force in Colorado, he applied for the job through the Sierra representative who called on his store. Both Sam and his wife were from Colorado originally and were anxious to move back closer to their families. They both graduated from UCLA and had been living in California since their graduation.

According to the Sierra sales rep in California, Sam was a very easy-going fellow who got along with his customers and his workers. He did a good job of running the shop, and it had been a profitable business. He was always well groomed and was not easily shaken. He seemed to have a positive self-image and would make a good salesman, according to the Sierra rep. The move to Colorado would mean a small salary raise for Sam. Bill Simpson thought that Sam was a good prospect because Sam had been doing business with Sierra for about 10 years. Bill had met Sam a few times over the years and was impressed with his enthusiasm for Sierra's products.

Bill was concerned, however, with the fact that Sam had been a professional racer on the "B" circuit for a number of years and was rather well known in racing circles. Bill had a somewhat negative image of professional ski racers. Ordinarily he hired them only to help promote a new product. He felt that they lacked the self-discipline and organization to handle a selling job and they could not handle responsibility.

Edward Brevel. Ed was 31 years old and single. Nine years ago he graduated from the University of Colorado, and since then he had become a well-recognized and highly successful salesman in the ski industry. During the first three years after his graduation, he worked as a sales rep for the clothing division of the Head Ski Company. In that job he covered the northern Colorado territory. Then six years ago he joined the Look/Nevada ski binding company where his sales territory was the state of Utah. For two of the past three years, he was the top salesman for Look/Nevada.

As a ski-binding sales rep, Ed was expected to train ski shop people in the proper mounting and fitting of the bindings. However, Ed was not technically familiar with the Sierra bindings. Also, he had limited experience with the technical aspects of skis and ski boots.

Although he was doing a good job for Look/Nevada, Ed had his eyes open for a new job opportunity that would offer him more responsibility and room for growth. He was also anxious to move back to Colorado. He had approached Bill Simpson twice, indicating his interest in the Sierra job. In the Sierra job he would be calling on some of the same customers he once had sold when he was with Head Ski Company. He was being paid a straight salary by Look/

Nevada, so he considered the Sierra job to be a promotion with more room for expansion and a higher income.

Question

Who should Bill Simpson hire as a sales representative for the northern Colorado territory?

7

Assimilating New Sales People into the Organization

The life of a rookie is no bed of roses.

Selection efforts made in the costly process of hiring people can be nullified completely if the new recruit is not properly integrated into the organization. This chapter covers the introduction of the new person into the work group. People often are motivated more by social than by economic forces. We will show how this affects their reactions to their initial relationships with superiors and fellow workers.

The infusion of a significant number of women into America's outside sales forces during the past decade has placed even more importance on assimilating the new sales person into the work group.

Initial Indoctrination

Most firms start indoctrinating the recruit the minute initial contact is made. Booklets describe the operations of the company and tell how distinctive the organization is. These publications are part of the recruiting process described in Chapter 5. Further introductory work is done in the selection interviews as shown in Chapter 6. The sales executive describes many aspects of the company's operations and answers questions the recruit may ask. If these activities are properly performed, trainees will know something about the organization before they start to work.

Some firms prepare detailed booklets about the company's history, the executives, the product line, and the various financial, health, and recreational programs available. If such a publication is given to the recruit upon hiring, the recruit can read and absorb its contents before coming to work. Immediately on reporting for work, the trainee should be encouraged to ask questions about the job and the company.

It is especially difficult to assimilate new sales reps when they are thrust into a sales territory with no home-office training. The new person has little opportunity to become integrated with the work group. In such situations, so-called lone wolves are born. While many sales managers complain that their sales people are not team players, little has been done to make them part of a team. For this reason, it is usually advisable to keep new sales people around the home office long enough so that they get to know the cast more than casually.

After an initial descriptive introduction to the business, the home-office trainee usually begins a program of familiarization with the actual operations of the firm. This is the initial stage of training, which is discussed in Chapter 8.

Details of the Job

In the employee introduction program, the details of the job, the company, and compensation are the little things that count (see Figure 7–1).

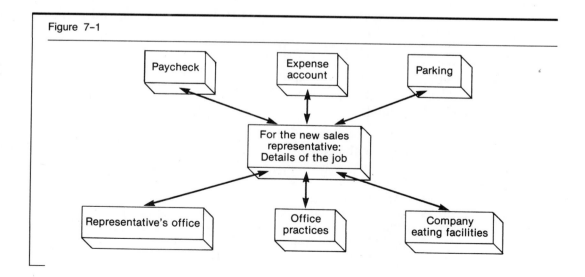

Figure 7–1

Parking

All employees are concerned with parking space. Many firms find it advisable to supervise the distribution of such status symbols closely, in order to avoid seeming inequities. Parking is of special interest to sales people who must come and go from the office or plant several times a day.

If sales people are unable to find convenient parking when on calls, considerable selling time may be lost. In metropolitan areas where downtown parking space is scarce, the sales manager may investigate the possibility of providing the sales force with commercial licenses, which allow parking in loading zones.

Eating

If the company maintains dining facilities, their use should be explained. New sales reps need to know if they can use the executive dining room to entertain customers. Some firms make arrangements with restaurants to accommodate the sales force and their customers, with the bill forwarded directly to the firm. These arrangements also need to be explained.

Office Practices

Office facilities and supplies should be checked to see that the new rep has everything needed and knows how to replenish supplies.

Some office practices and policies do not have official sanction but nevertheless have considerable force. Most groups have informal policies on such things as gift funds, betting, parties, and other activities incidental to the job. The new employee should be briefed on these by a fellow worker. If the manager did so, it might seem to give them official sanction. When the boss explains the football pool, for example, it is as if the employee is being told to participate.

The Paycheck

The pocketbook is a quick way to a good attitude. Misunderstandings concerning the paycheck can make anyone suspicious. It is most discouraging for a sales trainee who knows he is earning $1,800 per month to receive a check for $1,370. He realizes that some income tax and social security tax must come out of the $1,800, but he thinks, "There must be some error; taxes wouldn't be that much." A trainee should be told when and how he will be paid. All deductions should be itemized so that he will know exactly what to expect.

If a drawing account is provided, it is particularly important to explain it in detail. Some of the pertinent problems are:

- What happens if the rep gets too far in debt?
- What happens if the person leaves the company and still owes on the drawing account?
- Just how are commissions used to offset the advanced money?

The Expense Account

Many misunderstandings arise over expense accounts. The new sales rep must be told precisely what can and cannot be put on the expense sheet and in what manner the expense money will be paid. Can it be drawn prior to incurring the expenses or will it be paid after filing the report?

If certain tacit limitations are placed on various items, these should be made clear. The manager should tell the new person about any under-the-table arrangements rather than have the other sales people do it. For instance, one organization permits its employees to spend any amount necessary on entertainment. The total is left to the discretion of the sales person. However, if a considerable sum is spent on any one night, they want it distributed over several nights so as not to arouse antagonism in the accounting office. The sales manager unofficially tells the sales force of these practices.

The manager also should tell new employees how to recover money spent on selling expenses that do not clearly fall in allowable categories, but nevertheless were incurred working for the firm.

Meeting Fellow Workers

Both new and present employees are uncertain of the new person's status in the organization. This must be made clear to all, to avoid misunderstandings. Many firms distribute an information sheet on each new employee which tells what he or she will be doing with the company.

A new rep needs to know exactly from whom he takes orders. The entire organizational plan should be explained so he knows (1) his relationship to others, (2) who else reports to his immediate boss, and (3) who the boss's superiors are in the department and the company. Other employees need to know how the new employee fits into the organization. Secretaries must be informed of their relationship to the new person. Those who report to the same boss must be made acquainted with their workmate, and other employees also should be informed about the position he occupies.

Introductions are a two-way street—a new sales person is eager to meet fellow employees, and they want to meet him or her. However, short formal introductions do not fill the need. The introductory ceremony should be so arranged that the parties involved have enough time to do more than just say hello. A short chat with each person is a great aid. It allows individuals to get more than an instantaneous impression of one another, and it helps them to remember one another's names. Present employees should be given background information on the new sales person so that they will be able to converse on some common ground. The new rep should be briefed on the people to be met—who they are, what they do, and what their interests are.

The administrator must keep in mind that the manner in which the group treats the new worker will reflect management's treatment. If a sales manager does not show the person respect and consideration, probably the other employees will not do so either. In a sense, the manager's attitude establishes the individual's informal status in the group.

Consider the case of a new sales recruit who is young, just out of school, and who requires considerable training and experience. The sales manager's most idle remark, such as, "Oh, he will be okay in time, but right now he is just a green kid," can set the key for the rep's treatment by other employees: "He's just a green kid, that's what the boss said, and he should know." The individual is pegged as incompetent and from then on may have a difficult time with the group. For some, this person will never live down the initial unflattering stereotype.

If the manager should mention that a new sales rep is a top-notch prospect with a great potential, he will be looked on in a different light. Of course, such compliments must be handled judiciously so that other employees do not become jealous.

The initial introduction of the person to the work group is particularly critical in the hiring of women sales representatives. The reception, status, and initial relationships of the sales woman will depend to a large extent on how management regards her, and how the work group perceives management as regarding her. If she has been hired in token observance of equal rights laws, that attitude will probably be communicated to other members of the work group. This is a poor basis for good working relationships.

Need for Effective Communication

For some years now, the importance of effective communication has been stressed in management theory. It is especially relevant when new reps join a sales force.

Vertical Channels of Communication

The first weeks on the job are difficult for all. The new recruit has innumerable questions, uncertainties, and insecurities. The manager must do extra work to get the recruit started. Fellow employees may have to make some allowances for the new employee's lack of experience. These added tasks are necessary if the recruit is to be made part of the work group.

The first few days are particularly trying, since the new person has not had time to develop communications with the other members of the organization and must look to the manager for answers. The manager should give as much time as possible to getting the trainee started in the right direction. A good technique is to have a regular conference with the new employee at the beginning of each day, for a time, to answer questions and present new material.

New sales reps appreciate this attention. It makes them feel wanted and valued by the company—something most individuals earnestly seek. One of the quickest ways to affect a person's attitude adversely is to ignore him. New reps may interpret this lack of attention as meaning that the sales manager does not care about them. The truth probably is that the executive is just preoccupied with operational problems. It comes as quite a blow to new workers to encounter such apparent disinterest, since they were given so much attention while they were being interviewed. Suddenly the honeymoon is over. Now they think it was just sales talk, and they should have known better than to be taken in by it. The wise sales manager will try to prolong the honeymoon for awhile until the new people can take their place in the organization.

A classic example of the impact of the first few days on a new employee is this account by a college graduate who went to work for a large manufacturer of industrial products:

> On my first day at work I knew nobody except my boss and his assistant. I was given a little glass-enclosed office along the same line as some other such offices. People were working all over the place, but I didn't know who they were or what they were doing. I had been introduced to my boss's secretary and was told she would take care of me. I wasn't quite sure what he meant by that, and I discovered that she didn't either, for she was of no assistance. I could not get a letter typed by her. Later I made friends with another secretary who was new on the job and in the same position I was. She typed all my stuff and really looked after me. She would come in and dust off my desk and generally be my secretary. I am certain that she was supposed to be doing something else, but no one seemed to know what was going on, and I had no objection to having a secretary, so that was that. I guess we had been shoved together because of the complete indifference of everybody to our plight.
>
> I tried to look busy and kept reading all sorts of reports that were stacked around, but I had been given little direction. The boss had said

upon my reporting for work, "Here is a marketing consultant's report on a new product we are thinking of making. Read it and give me your impressions." That was the last I saw of him for three weeks, since he had to go out of town. I completed the report in two days. I really went over it and did some outside investigation on my own. But there was a limit to what I could do with it. So I quickly ran out of work to do.

Then I hit upon doing library research on the subject and started going down to the city library. It was a good place to loaf, and I enjoyed getting into a lot of books which I had never realized existed. It was quite an education, but it came to an end in time, and still I had no work to do or anyone to tell me to do something.

I started to go to the show in the afternoon, getting back just in time to punch out on the clock. Can you imagine that; all of us had to punch in and out on a time clock. It was ridiculous, since it accomplished nothing. I felt rather guilty about going to the show in the afternoons, but it was better than sitting around the office and having everyone look at you and wondering what you were supposed to be doing.

The secretary of my boss's boss was an old hen who thought she ran the place. She really gave me a bad time when she saw me goofing off. Boy, those icy stares of hers were enough to freeze the devil himself. I tried to get to see the top boss about my plight, but she would not let me near him. He was always in a conference or out of town or something like that. I knew that they were lies because I had seen him cutting it up a bit on several occasions in there, but what could I do? The old battleaxe controlled the door to his office, and we didn't meet anywhere. I had to eat in the cafeteria while he was in the big shot's dining room. We couldn't even use the same rest rooms. Boy, was he ever guarded!

Well, to make a long story short, it did not take me long to decide that I would quit at the end of summer and go back to graduate school. I made up my mind in late June and told them the first of August that I thought I needed more schooling. They gave me an exit interview and the personnel man asked me how I liked the company and all that stuff. I kept my tongue and told him that it was fine and that I had learned a lot. However, I felt incompetent and wanted to know more about marketing since I had majored in another subject in school. He said that he was sorry to see me go and that he thought I had a good future with the firm and all that bunk. Even my boss never tumbled to the real reason why I quit. It never dawned on him that he had not said over 100 words to me during the whole three months I was under him. To top it off, I had not moved to town yet but was commuting 100 miles a day to work, and they did not even know it. The boss was surprised when I told him the commuting problem was getting me down. Well, there were a lot more little things, but that is the basic story of what actually happened to me.

This actual case history is indicative of what happens when a sales manager is not aware of the needs of a new representative. If a new sales rep is not closely supervised and trained during the first few weeks on the job, he may become discouraged and quit. Although it might seem that new employees would enjoy "working" without supervision, such is not the case. They are eager to learn the profession and get into the field, so they can find a place in the organization.

Horizontal Channels of Communication

Sales managers should not force trainees to rely on the grapevine to find out what is going on in the organization and what is expected of them. However, they have no alternative if they are not provided with proper communication channels. Instead of being able to use vertical communication channels, they are forced to use horizontal ones. That is, they seek information from other people on their own level in the organization. In the example of the college graduate who went to work for the manufacturer, there was a lack of contact between subordinates and superiors. It had gone so far that the boss had surrounded himself with barriers to keep subordinates away.

When new people are forced to go to unofficial sources for instruction, the executive runs the risk that wrong or undesirable information will be given to them. Moreover, their allegiances become divided. The informant in effect assumes some managerial functions, and the recruit comes to rely on this source for information. For instance, in the earlier example, the secretary came to the new employee for work instructions; in fact, he became her manager. Her allegiance was transferred in part to her source of guidance.

The problem is further complicated because frequently those employees who actively solicit listeners may not be the ones with whom the recruit should be associated. Often, it is the malcontents, the office politicians, and the downright incompetents who are excessively interested in that type of activity. Information should come from management; moreover, it should be prompt and complete.

Meeting Social and Psychological Needs

An individual's assimilation into the organization involves considerably more than just getting started on the job. He or she should be socially integrated into the new environment. An administrator who forgets that people are essentially social animals is destined for disappointing results. For many people, their social and psychological needs overrule their economic requirements. Many employees could better themselves by changing positions or moving to another location. However, they are content to remain where they are, because they are happily integrated into the social structure around them. Individuals like to be among friends and familiar faces. It makes them feel as though they belong to something, and they feel more secure.

However, people often must pull up their roots and leave their home and friends. They are thrust into a strange city with a tired spouse, upset children, and a home in transition. It is a wonder that they can work with any degree of efficiency under such conditions. For this reason, many managers have a policy of hiring only local people for a territory. They do not want to force employees to move from their environment, feeling that people are far more effective if left among their friends and in their areas of acquaintance. However, this policy may be difficult to maintain. In many instances a firm may be forced to hire someone of a lower caliber than desired just to satisfy the location requirement.

The sales manager is in a position to cushion the shock of social uprooting. Some social activities and contacts should be provided in a new location. This means more than just inviting people to a party. Most college administrators, for example, are aware of this problem for new faculty members and have organized newcomers' clubs. The new faculty family is considered a newcomer for two years before it is expected to have formed its own social contacts. Even after the families leave the newcomers' club, they tend to stick together and do not really integrate into the major group. Hence, true assimilation of the family into the organization is not accomplished even by this plan. However, it is successful in that some social contacts are provided for a new family.

The manager should take positive steps to see that a family gets into activities in which they are interested. The golfer should be worked into a foursome, and the bridge player invited to join some group. However, this is not always easy to do. The foursomes are already set up. So until some break occurs, the new family may be left out, and it is not always possible to create a new foursome.

A vice president of marketing for a sizable consumer goods concern was elated when he persuaded a nationally prominent market research expert to join his staff. Two years later the boss was hurt and bewildered when the man resigned to go with a competitor. "They bought him from us," was his rationalization. The market researcher's version, however, was as follows:

> He was the weirdest boss I've ever had. When he hired me, you'd have thought we were really going to do some great things together. Then every time I tried to get approval for some project, he'd throw cold water on it. I had no social and precious little professional contact with the man during my two years with him. We had him and his wife over twice for some parties, but you know, I don't even know where he lives or what his home phone number is. I can't work for a guy like that. I need good, close relationships with my boss to do my job as I want to do it.

The researcher never really felt that he was a part of the team.

Importance of the Job

Aside from income, a job often plays an important social role. Fellow workers are an important reference group. People gain much satisfaction in life from personal relationships established on the job. Employees often spend more time with their co-workers than they do with their spouses. Thus mutual compatibility is important.

Much anguish can be avoided if recruits learn about the company and its people prior to employment. Some firms use summer internships to acquaint potential employees with the work situation. Other managers introduce recruits to the work group on a social occasion before they are formally considered for a job. It is not just happenstance that one of the best sources of new sales people is the present sales force. Sales reps have a good idea of who would be successful with the company.

Living Accommodations

A sales representative whose home life is in a state of confusion or who is unhappy about living accommodations cannot perform well. For that reason, sales executives in recent years have formalized company policies in aiding new employees in moving and getting established in a home.

Employee mobility has caused many businesses to provide allowances to alleviate some of the inconveniences of moving. Most have adopted plans for defraying the moving expenses of personnel, such as paying for a first-class carrier which furnishes all services. However, many firms do not compensate employees for the incidental and inescapable expenses of moving. It is usually necessary to buy new drapes, rugs, furniture, and other items to fit a new house. Many houses require a considerable investment for renovation. Thus moving is not a minor matter, economically or psychologically.

Most large companies usually pay for the following moving expenses when they transfer employees:

- Packing and moving of all household furnishings and equipment, with insurance to cover any damage.
- Meals, lodgings, and first-class transportation by land or air for the entire family and for family pets.
- Broker's commissions and legal fees for buying or selling homes.
- Entire expense of putting up the employee and family in a hotel for several weeks after arrival. Thereafter the company pays the difference between charges for hotel rooms and normal rental costs if other living space has not been found.
- Installation of appliances in the new home and allowances toward refitting draperies, carpeting, and blinds.

- A reasonable number of personal trips between the new and old location when the employee is separated from the family for a long time.
- A trip for the spouse to visit the new location to look for a new house and expenses while house hunting.

Many people arrive on the job financially embarrassed and in need of money to live on. They greatly appreciate receiving their expenses as promptly as possible. Some firms find that they must advance funds for support until payday. Some college graduates have not taken the jobs they wanted because they lacked the funds to get to the location. They had to accept positions with local firms. It is easy for an executive to forget that many families have no surplus funds. A proud person in this position—and there are quite a few of them—will not tell a prospective employer the real reason for rejecting a job offer.

Money is not the only factor involved in making a move. Time is also important. A manufacturer of heavy equipment for oil field, mining, and construction work has a policy for employee moves that seems to work well. First, it pays all moving expenses at the first-class tariff rate *in advance*. Many college graduates starting their first jobs with this concern move themselves in a trailer and keep the extra cash. Next, the firm pays all expenses for the family to live in a hotel or motel while looking for an apartment or house. No limit is set, but most people spend about two weeks under such an arrangement.

The purpose of this policy, from the company's point of view, is to allow new employees enough time to find suitable living accommodations. They do not want to force the family to move into anything that happens to be vacant. Such vacancies are usually marginal properties; that is why they are not occupied. It takes time for a family to find what it wants. By providing enough time, the company makes sure the employee will be satisfied and will not have to make a second move soon. People who have enjoyed the benefits of this policy say that it allows them to stay solvent. They are not forced to pay rent before receiving any salary, and company support keeps them from going into debt right at the start. Little money has to be spent before receiving the first paycheck.

A new trainee may need some assistance in locating a home, although this must be handled with tact and offered on a strictly voluntary basis. The sales manager is in a position to know the real estate market in the city considerably better than the newcomer. If new employees make a serious mistake in their purchase of a home, it can considerably injure their morale and effectiveness, in addition to damaging their financial status.

Experience indicates that people become better integrated into the community if they purchase a home rather than rent one. The renter always considers the home temporary, whereas the homeowner feels established and takes a more active part in civic activities. Because of its social responsibilities to its employees and the community, the company should do all in its power to encourage homeownership. Some firms loan their employees down payments for homes and otherwise assist them financially. Many have insuring devices by which they encourage their mobile employees to buy homes. They will guarantee the worker against loss on his house if he is forced to sell because of a move dictated by the company. With that guarantee, most employees do not hesitate to buy a house.

Assimilation of Minority Sales Trainees

Early in the Equal Opportunity-Affirmative Action movement, managers were greatly concerned about how well minority trainees would integrate into the sales force. Although those fears have subsided for the most part, companies still need positive programs for assimilating women and minority people into the work group. One study of industrial sales women indicated that, contrary to original worries, the women encountered little difficulty with their peers, who, by and large, were supportive.[1]

Another study put forth the following 10 guidelines for establishing a program for assimilating minority trainees into the sales force.[2]

1. Train your sales manager first.
2. Involve the sales team in the orientation and training.
3. Identify the trainee's needs and attitudes.
4. Pave the way by giving customers prior notice of the trainee's appointment to the territory. Avoid surprises.
5. Encourage questions from the trainee.
6. Openly discuss the issue of race in the selling situation. Don't ignore it or pretend it doesn't exist.
7. Demonstrate company commitment and support.
8. Convince the trainee that a customer contact marred by racial antagonism will not eliminate the possibility of a profitable business relationship.

---

[1] Richard H. Buskirk and Beverly Miles, *Beating Men at Their Own Game—A Woman's Guide to Successful Selling in Industry* (New York: John Wiley & Sons, 1980), p. 182.

[2] John W. Lee and Thomas Reuschling, "Orientation for Black Salesman in Predominantly White Sales Organizations," *Training and Development Journal*, ASTD., November 1973, pp. 16–19. Reprinted with permission. All rights reserved.

9. Stress that race should not be used as a selling tactic.
10. Monitor relationships between the trainee and fellow employees and customers.

Mentors and Networking

Not too many years ago, cynics were fond of saying, "It's not what you know but who you know that counts!" when they wanted to disaparage the study of business. Now management theorists have garnered support for such a claim. It's called networking and it is one of the "in" words of the late 1980s. Articles on networking theories abound in the academic journals.[3]

Networking is not new. It's a new word for the old concept that business is a matter of relationships. Notice we are back to the idea presented in Chapter 2 that the sales manager has six different relationships to nurture and tend. Well, so does everyone! Business is relationships, and, the better you are at developing them, the more successful you will be in business. Relationships begin when you are young and continue long after retirement. You may be surprised to discover that someone you developed a good relationship with when in grammar school will help you in your business life. College relationships can prove beneficial if you worked at developing them. The term "old school ties" is not used idly. Such forces are real and should be recognized.

A *mentor* is someone with knowledge, experience, position, or power who is willing to adopt you as a protege and help you advance in your career. A mentor is an important part of any network.

Mentors provide many advantages other than moral support. A well-placed mentor inside the company can protect your interests in the company's political arena as well as help you advance, if your talents warrant it. The mentor knows the cast of characters you must deal with and can provide valuable advice.

An experienced, successful mentor outside the firm can provide many meaningful insights into what it takes to be successful in business—a post-graduate professor, if you will!

However, you have to work at networking. Many people attend

---

[3] For a discussion of mentors in business see G. S. Odiorne, "Mentoring—An American Management Innovation," *Personal Administration*, May 1985, p. 63; and D. M. Hunt and C. Michael, "Mentorship: A Career Training and Development Tool," *Academy of Management Review*, July 1983, pp. 475–85. Also see A. Urbanski, "Networking for Sales," *Sales & Marketing Management*, May 16, 1983, p. 41.

prestigious business schools and spend two years with the very students who will be key players in their generation of business executives. Yet they fail to develop the networking relationships that will prove to be so helpful later.

Summary

Much of the sales recruit's long-run success with a company depends on how well he or she is assimilated into the work group during the first few months on the job. There is much to learn about the company, its people, and how things are done in the organization. The desire for social acceptance in the work group is so strong that the recruit who fails to gain it will probably quit. Moreover, the family's life in the community cannot be ignored. Even though a person may be happily situated on the job, if the family's life in the community is unsatisfactory, it is likely to affect the person's job performance. The sales manager should not just hire people then forget them. Successful assimilation of new sales reps requires some of the manager's time for the first few months.

Questions and Problems

1. The statement was made that a manager may find it advisable to supervise distribution of status symbols. What are some of these status symbols, and why should the manager be concerned with them?

2. In the story related by a college graduate about his first few days at work, one sales manager commented that the man was just a spoiled brat who simply was not capable of doing an honest day's work, and that the firm was fortunate in getting rid of him. He said that, after all, the sales manager cannot wet nurse each employee. A person must be able to come into a job and work without all the coddling sometimes recommended. Does this chapter distort the actual need for introductory activities out of proportion to the real problem in industry? Why not adopt a sink-or-swim philosophy on the matter? If a person is really good, why is all of this attention needed?

3. What are some of the actions a sales manager can take to provide new employees with social contacts and activities?

4. Why should sales managers encourage their people to own *nice* homes?

5. Should the sales manager warn the trainee about listening to or being influenced by other people in the organization for whom the manager has particularly low regard?
6. With the introduction of more women to sales positions, what special problems might arise in assimilating them into an all-male sales force?
7. To what extent can members of the peer group facilitate a trainee's assimilation into the work group? How could management encourage such efforts?
8. One manager maintained, "You can always spot the malcontents in our organization—just watch to see who runs to befriend the new person." Evaluate that statement. If it is true, of what significance is it to the person?
9. Many firms have a probationary period for new employees during which the new person can be terminated (fired) without being given a reason. How long should such a probationary period be for a sales trainee?
10. How long should it take for a new person to become well integrated into the work situation?

Case 7–1

Jasper Electronics Company

Assimilating First Woman into All-Male Sales Force

Cary Hartwell was the sales manager in the Dallas, Texas, sales branch of Jasper Electronics Company. Several things were running through his mind that day as his new sales representative, Anne Desmond, reported for her first day of work to enter the company's sales training program. There was no doubt in Cary's mind that, with good training and some on-the-job supervision, Anne would make a very fine contribution to the Jasper Company. Hartwell was wondering, however, just how he should go about assimilating Desmond into an all-male sales force. He was concerned that Anne might become discouraged during training and quit.

The Jasper Electronics Company was a western firm that manufactured and sold minicomputers. In comparison with the mainframe computers, the minicomputers were smaller, less expensive, and operated as a system of individual, decentralized computer terminal networks. Typically, the mainframe computers were concentrated in one large unit that processed data at a central location.

Jasper was established in 1958 and has enjoyed satisfactory growth in both sales and profits, especially during the past five years. The company provided both computer hardware and software and thus was able to supply a customer with a complete information-processing network. In fact, Jasper was considered to have one of the largest product lines in the industry. A customer could pay as little as $600 for an information processor or several million dollars for a large, complete system.

Technological advances in the minicomputer field enabled Jasper and other producers to offer both hardware and software at lower prices, but with increased product capabilities. As is true with most computer firms, Jasper was continually introducing new products. Just within the past year, for example, Jasper introduced several products including a new line of printers, video-display terminals, information-storage devices, software options, and central processors.

One competitive advantage Jasper enjoyed was that its software was compatible with its various generations of computers. That is, software designed for one generation of computers could be used on another generation. Thus, there was no software obsolescence, unlike the situation that generally prevailed in the computer industry.

Jasper faced competition from several well-known firms in the minicomputer market. Digital Equipment Corporation was the largest with an estimated 33 to 40 percent market share. Jasper's estimated market share was 15 percent. Other significant competitors were Hewlett-Packard, Data General, Honeywell, and Texas Instruments. While IBM leads the world in computer sales, its primary product line is the large mainframe computer, not minicomputers. However, IBM was committed to a minicomputer program for the 1980s.

Most computer firms, including Jasper, relied heavily on their own sales forces in their marketing programs. Since the minicomputer industry was relatively young, there was frequently a shortage of qualified sales people. Turnover in the industry ran about 20 percent, but could be much lower if the sales rep's location was desirable. Jasper's turnover averaged about 10 to 12 percent thoughout the company but was slightly less than that in the Dallas office. Industry sales reps typically generated large annual sales. Jasper's quotas for each sales rep averaged about $850,000 a year. Hewlett-Packard's quota ran around $750,000 per sales rep, and Honeywell's average was about $600,000.

Most firms in the industry compensated their sales reps partially (and in some cases entirely) by commission. In contrast, Jasper paid its reps a straight salary. Management believed that the straight-salary plan would raise the level of customer service. And this service factor was becoming increasingly important as competition intensified in the minicomputer market. Frequently, the lead time (time between writing and delivering an order) was fairly long for the Jasper Company, because its sales success created a large backlog of orders. Consequently, the sales reps had to keep in touch with those customers who were awaiting delivery.

Jasper's sales force was organized into two groups, each with a separate management structure. One group of sales people sold computer hardware, and the other, software. Frequently, there was a need for close coordination between the two groups since hardware and software packages were usually sold as a single system.

As he reviewed the industry and market in general, and his own company's sales-force structure in particular, Hartwell continued to think about Anne Desmond and her place in the organization. The computer industry was male-dominated. In the Dallas branch, for example, there was one woman who was two managerial levels above Anne Desmond. There were women in clerical positions, but Anne, as a field sales rep, did not really belong to this group. Instead, she would be a member of the Hartwell sales force which was comprised of 35 men in the Dallas office. In addition, virtually all of Anne's customers would be male.

Although Hartwell hired Desmond because he felt she could handle the job very well, he was a bit concerned about her age, inexperience, and educational background. In the past, Jasper had hired as sales representatives only those people who had (1) experience in the computer industry and (2) a technical degree in either engineering or computer science. Most of these representatives were around 30 years of age when they were hired. The majority of customers were also engineers.

Anne was 21 years old. She had a bachelor's degree in business with a major in marketing. She had no experience selling computers or any other technical products. The extent of her computer background was two computer courses that she had taken in business school.

The short supply of experienced, older recruits, however, had forced Jasper to change its hiring and training programs. Consequently, the company began to recruit graduating seniors from colleges and universities. Because these people were inexperienced, the company also started an intensive training program. The company tried to distribute these new sales people among as many branch offices as possible. Thus it was a rare occurrence when a sales office had more than one recruit such as Anne Desmond.

Hartwell was concerned that Anne would not find much in the way of common experiences with the other sales reps in the Dallas office. He also realized that the new training program would not help much in the assimilation process for Anne. The new training program for college graduates involved a combination of on-the-job training in the

Dallas region, plus thorough classroom instruction at the home office in California. The total program spanned a year.

The training started with a one-month orientation in which Anne would work out of the Dallas office. During much of this time, she would be making calls with an experienced sales rep to observe his sales techniques. During the second month, the trainees would be in the home office getting formal training in selling skills, computer applications, market development, and several other topics. Then Anne would go back to Dallas for almost three months to study market identification, problem analysis, resource management, and other topics.

And so the training program continued—a month at headquarters followed by two months in the branch office. After approximately eight months, the trainees began market area training at the home office. Market segments were identified, and the trainees studied product positions for each major market, the engineering needs in these markets, and specific market problems.

After completing the market-area training, Anne would be assigned to work with an experienced rep for three more months of on-the-job training. Upon the completion of this segment of the program, Anne would be assigned to handle certain accounts on her own. She would then be a full-fledged computer sales rep for Jasper Electronics.

Question

What should Cary Hartwell do to assimilate Anne Desmond into his male-dominated firm and industry?

8

Developing and Conducting a Sales-Training Program

Too much and too little education hinder the mind.
PASCAL

Selecting a sales force is costly. Money may be wasted if selection is not followed up with the proper training. The training program is a vital link in the process of converting the recruit into a full-fledged, productive member of the work group.

Each program must be tailor-made to accomplish the ends desired by management. Each firm's situation is unique, and the training plans of other firms are seldom applicable.

In this chapter we will discuss developing and conducting a sales-training program. The content of the program—what should be taught—will be covered in Chapter 9.

In developing a sales-training program, the administrator should consider the problem areas discussed in this chapter (see Figure 8–1). They pose such questions as:

- What are the objectives of the program?
- Who should be trained, and how much is needed?
- Who should do the training?
- When should the training take place?
- Where should it be done?
- What teaching methods should be used?

The four basic types of training programs are (1) initial or indoctrination training, (2) refresher courses, (3) continuous training programs, and (4) executive-development programs. The answers to the earlier questions vary with the type of program being considered.

Figure 8–1
Strategic Considerations in Sales-Force Training

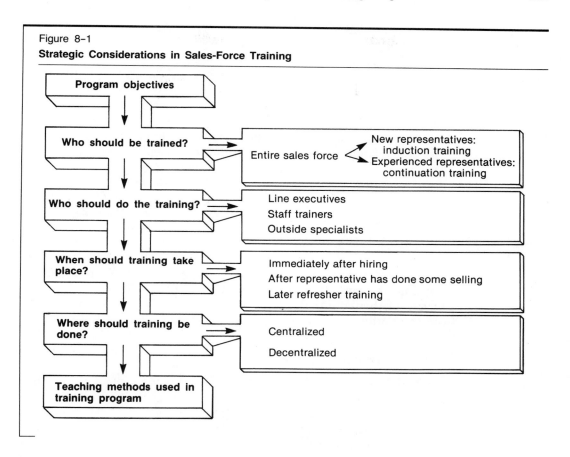

Program objectives

Who should be trained? → Entire sales force
  - New representatives: induction training
  - Experienced representatives: continuation training

Who should do the training? →
  - Line executives
  - Staff trainers
  - Outside specialists

When should training take place? →
  - Immediately after hiring
  - After representative has done some selling
  - Later refresher training

Where should training be done? →
  - Centralized
  - Decentralized

Teaching methods used in training program

Sales Training and Strategic Planning

In many aspects of sales training, the sales executives should take their lead from the company's strategic marketing plan. The organization's sales training program—when properly coordinated with its marketing objectives and strategies—can aid in implementing the company's strategic marketing plan. To illustrate, the objectives of a sales training program should be consistent with the firm's marketing objectives. In turn, the marketing objectives should also be considered when designing the content of the training program or when deciding who will be trained. An objective of increasing market share by 20 percent calls for a different training program than the objective of maintaining market share by providing better service to existing customers.

In another situation, assume that a company is adding a new line of products, which the existing sales force will sell. In this case, the content of the training program will be different than if the objective is to increase profits by cutting expenses.

If a company makes a major change in its sales organizational structure, an intensive training program for experienced sales reps may be needed. This sort of situation occurred when Xerox embarked on a three- to five-year program to have all 4,000 of its reps selling the full product line. In effect, the company changed from a sales organization built around products to a market-oriented organizational structure. To implement this major shift in market strategy, Xerox planned to spend $10 to 20 million a year on its sales training program.[1]

Objectives of Training

In addition to the obvious goal of increasing sales productivity, training programs have other objectives. They include a lower turnover rate, better morale, control of the sales force, improved customer relations, lower selling costs, and better use of time.

Lower Turnover

Good training programs lower job turnover because well-trained people are less likely to fail. Numerous firms push new employees into the field without adequate training, only to have them quit when they fail. They don't have a chance when they face customers without adequate product knowledge or sound selling techniques. New sales reps are apt to become discouraged when they fail to sell their first few customers. Once discouragement occurs, failure is not far behind.

A well-thought-out training program will prepare the trainee for the realities of a life in sales. One of these is that discouragement and disappointment are to be expected early in a sales career. Being forewarned of these mental hurdles is the first step toward overcoming them. The trainee who is able to handle the early problems is less likely to become discouraged and quit.

Better Morale

Closely tied to turnover is the matter of morale. People who are confident that they have been given the training they need have a much better attitude toward their job, the company, and life in gen-

---

[1] See Thayer C. Taylor, "Xerox's Sales Force Learns a New Game," *Sales & Marketing Management*, July 1, 1985, pp. 48–51.

eral. Those who are thrust into the business world without proper preparation are likely to suffer from poor morale.

Lack of purpose is one foundation of poor morale. Hence, one of the major objectives of a sales-training program should be to give trainees some idea about their purpose in the company and in society. Those who have a purpose in life can tolerate many inconveniences, disappointments, and adverse events to reach what they believe to be a worthwhile goal.

Control of the Sales Force

The training program should establish the behavior expected of the sales force. Sales people should know and understand the control mechanisms management uses to ensure that the selling job is being properly performed. An important section of any program should be a discussion of the importance of the reports the sales force submits and how management uses them.

Trainees should also be taught how to control their own activities. Instruction should be provided on routing, the use of personal records, the apportionment of selling effort, and other self-management techniques.

Improved Customer Relations

A good training program shows trainees how to render service to their customers. They should learn how to avoid overselling, how to determine which products are needed, and how to adjust complaints. Moreover, they should become aware of the importance of establishing and maintaining good customer relations. Well-trained sales personnel have acquired the skills necessary to please their customers.

Lower Selling Costs

Training programs should also instruct trainees in controlling and reducing expenses. Thus the program can result in direct savings. Moreover, selling expenses as a percent of sales are lowered as the sales reps become more proficient in their selling skills. Suppose that salary and expenses necessary to keep a representative in the field are $4,000 a month. If training increases the rep's productivity from $40,000 to $48,000 a month, for example, expenses would be lowered from 10 to 8.33 percent.

Better Use of Time

Management has become increasingly interested in how employees use their time. A growing realization that considerable time is wasted has led to the study of how to increase productivity. The goal is to learn how to produce more output from the relatively few hours available for working.

Need for Specific Objectives

After establishing the broad objectives of the program, such as those discussed earlier, the sales manager should set specific objectives for the training program. It is insufficient to say that the purpose of the program is to increase sales volume. This statement is so general that it serves only as a hazy guidepost for making decisions. The manager should break down the broad objectives into several specific goals, such as improving prospecting methods, handling objections, or strengthening closing techniques. Meeting these separate goals should result in achieving the broad objectives.

Naturally, the objectives of any segment of a sales training program will vary depending on the nature of the trainee. The program designed to convert an inexperienced recruit into a professional sales rep will be more comprehensive than a program intended to update the existing sales force on new products and refresh their selling skills. (Make no mistake, the existing sales people do need continual training because they develop sloppy work habits over time.) A newly hired, experienced sales rep may require much less training in selling skills than the raw recruit. Thus the objectives of a sales training program depend on the nature of the trainees.

Need for Training

All sales people need some training. Even accomplished professional sales people who have been with a firm for years need training on new products and a continual review and refinement of their selling techniques. New employees who have had a substantial amount of sales experience must be instructed in the company's products and its selling methods. Although their basic selling ability is transferable, they must be taught how to sell their new employer's products in the way the company desires. The recruit with little or no selling experience must be schooled completely in selling techniques, along with all other aspects of the job.

Overestimating the amount of training required is better than underestimating it. Many trainees exaggerate their experience and abilities in order to convince the prospective employer that they should be hired. Most recruits who have had some sales work still have an inadequate knowledge of selling techniques. Some may have considerable unlearning to do before they can get started properly, because they have acquired bad selling habits that need to be corrected.

To establish the amount of training needed, it is usually advisable to perform a ***difficulty analysis*** of the sales job. In making such a study, the sales manager attempts to discover what difficulties are encountered in the field. Then, proper training can be devised to help overcome those problems.

The difficulty analysis is usually made by going into the field and interviewing sales reps about their problems. Frequently the investigator goes over a series of calls in which the reps failed to get orders. In each instance, an attempt is made to discover just what caused the failure. If the analysis discloses that the rep is picking poor prospects, for example, additional training on prospecting would be required.

Who Should Do the Training

Three basic sources of trainers are regular line executives, staff personnel, or outside specialists. Any one or a combination of these can be used successfully. It is not uncommon to find firms that use all three, each for different purposes.

One investigation of more than 1,000 sales representatives and executives brought out the need for professional instructors. "Whether an internal or external trainer is employed, the professionalism of the teacher is a high priority . . . Basic teaching skills often are more important to the success of a training seminar than knowledge of the subject matter."[2]

Line Personnel

Training by line personnel consists of instruction by such executives as senior sales representatives, field supervisors, territorial managers, or sales managers who are in direct command of the sales force.[3]

Some firms have made effective use of peer training. They set up situations in which inexperienced people are partially trained by their peers on the sales force. It works well if the sales force is skilled and has a vested interest in developing the new person's selling ability. One small mens wear chain designated a few highly skilled sales people as senior sales reps. Their job descriptions each

---

[2] Dennis A. Miller, "Ten Ways to Improve Sales Training Programs," *Marketing News*, August 22, 1980, p. 4.

[3] Jack R. Snader, "Why Most Sales Training Doesn't Work and What You Can Do About It," *Business Marketing*, May 1984, pp. 86–90, urges management to use first line sales managers in much the same way athletic teams use coaches. Paul J. Kelly, "Coach the Coach," *Training and Development Journal*, November, 1985, p. 85, recognizes the need to teach the sales manager how to coach.

year specifically set forth that they were responsible for training new recruits. A percentage of their salary was designated as payment for such work. Moreover, their sales quotas took into account their training tasks. In this company, the sales people also received substantial bonuses at the end of the year if the store in which they worked achieved its sales projections for the year. A poorly performing colleague hurt everyone. There was considerable peer pressure on each sales person to perform. In several cases, sales trainees who were not applying themselves seriously were pressured out of their job. Hard working co-workers resented the trainees' casual attitudes toward "clerking" in a men's store. The sales people in this company were extremely well-paid for their work. Thus they did not take any threat to their bonuses lightly.

Advantages.   Line sales executives' words carry much more authority than those of staff people or outside specialists, since the trainees know that these people have had successful sales experience. When the boss does the training, a certain unity of action is achieved because there can be no mistaking what the supervisor expects. Further, recruits can be trained to sell the way the manager wants them to sell. Line executives who train their own sales people can evaluate each person's ability better than administrators who do not participate in the training program. Also, better rapport can be established between the executive and the sales force, since training affords a wonderful opportunity to become acquainted.

Disadvantages.   The disadvantages of using line personnel are lack of time and lack of teaching ability. The pressures of other activities force the manager to give, at best, only partial attention to the training program. This can be harmful to trainee morale. If a line executive is to do the training, adequate time must be available to do it properly.

A line executive may know a great deal about selling but be unable to teach others about it. As any college student can attest, many people who are experts in their fields are unable to communicate their knowledge to others. It is important to distinguish between the possession of knowledge and the ability to impart it to others.

Neither of these disadvantages is drastic, since both can be remedied by proper managerial action. Line administrators can be given the necessary time for training. And teachers are not necessarily born; they also can be trained.

Staff Trainers

Staff trainers can be hired specifically to conduct a training program. Or they can be staff people who hold other jobs in personnel, production, or office management. We will focus on the specially hired sales trainer, since use of other staff personnel ordinarily is not recommended. Members of the personnel department are seldom qualified to conduct a sales-training program. They may be involved in certain phases of the instruction, such as furnishing company information or handling the physical arrangements of the program. However, entrusting them with the technical details of the training program is generally unwise.

Advantages.   A trainer specifically hired to handle the training program can attend to all the details, prepare the many necessary materials, and give the trainee all the attention required. Frequently, it is less expensive to hire a specialized staff-training officer than it is to add the additional line executives needed to allow them more time for training activities.

A staff trainer can do far more than training the firm's sales force. The training department can conduct courses for distributors and dealers. It can also conduct training sessions in the field so field personnel lose less time.

Disadvantages.   In theory, the staff trainer lacks control over the trainees and does not speak with the authority of a line executive. However, in practice, this is an academic point, since the trainees know that the trainer has the backing of the boss.

Companies incur additional cost in maintaining a separate training department. The median salary of the trainer alone will be about $50,000 per year, depending on his or her qualifications. This limits the size of the firm that can afford to hire a sales trainer; smaller concerns cannot afford the cost. There is a danger that an ambitious staff trainer will institute far more training than is required. This is not an inherent disadvantage of staff training so much as it is an administrative weakness.

Outside Training Specialists

Practically every large city has firms that specialize in sales training. Their scope varies widely. Some will establish and administer an entire training program, while others specialize in teaching sales techniques. The latter leave the dissemination of product knowledge and company information to the firm's executives. Sometimes these training firms specialize in a very narrow field. Some organizations do nothing but train real estate brokers or insurance agents or retail sales clerks.

Individual experts also consult on training problems. One source of such consultants is college professors who are skilled in teaching salesmanship. These consultants are ideal for smaller firms that cannot use a full-time training specialist but do need someone with training talents. By retaining a consultant, they can buy as much training as they need, with minimum cost. Even large organizations find use for outside specialists, as in spot assignments, brief refresher courses, or training sessions at conventions. They are frequently the mainstay of executive-development programs.

When Training Should Take Place

There are two basic attitudes toward the timing of training. Some executives believe that no one should be placed in the field who is not fully trained, not only in product and company knowledge but also in selling techniques. Their training programs may last from a few weeks to as much as a year or more before sales people are sent into the field. They may have the trainee work for awhile in either production or service to acquire product knowledge.

Other managers want the recruit to exhibit a desire to sell before they invest in training that person. Some insurance companies require a new agent to sell a certain amount of life insurance before going to a sales school. The first training program is only a basic course. After that, the agent must again go into the field and sell successfully before attending the more advanced schools for underwriters.

This philosophy has considerable educational and managerial merit. From the educational point of view, it is much easier to train people who have had some field experience than those who have not faced a prospect. People who have experience in facing problems are eager to get answers to them. If many prospects have told them that the price is too high, for example, they will be eager to find out how to cope with that objection.

From a managerial point of view, weak prospective sales people are usually eliminated if they must sell before being trained. By putting new employees in the field first, the manager also has the opportunity to determine how much and what type of training they really need. The only trouble is that many people who might have been successful had they been given proper instruction may be eliminated by this push-them-off-the-dock method.

About the only time that delayed training should be used is in situations where product knowledge is easily acquired and the prospect does not require a polished selling approach. Delayed training is usually practiced by firms whose customers are sold only once, with each sale being of little importance to total volume. If a sales rep botches a particular sale, the company is not seriously injured.

The need for training does not end with completion of the initial program. Sales people continually need refresher courses, but this type of training can lower morale if it is not done properly. One question that arises is whether the refresher training will be done on company or employees' time. Some executives feel that later training should be done on the person's own time. Thus the individual loses no time on the job and is able to demonstrate sincerity about desiring better performance.

From this point of view, off-duty training has merit. However, the effect on morale can be bad. Sales people usually have little enough time at home and begrudge additional intrusion on their free time. Their attitude depends on the purpose of training. If it benefits only the firm, reps resent being forced to spend their own time. However, if the nature of the course is to encourage self-improvement, ambitious individuals may not mind attending it after working hours.

Where Training Should Take Place

The basic problem involved in the training program's location is determining the extent to which it should be centralized. Unless there is some reason for centralizing all training in one location, it should be decentralized. Centralized training is usually more expensive and requires more organizational effort than training in the field.

Decentralized Training

Decentralized training can take one form or a combination of several forms: (1) office instruction, (2) use of senior sales people, (3) on-the-job tutoring, or (4) traveling sales clinics. There are many advantages to decentralized training. It is usually cheaper than centralized training. The trainee remains in the field to work while learning, and the company avoids the substantial expense of supporting both the trainee and a central school staff.

There are also some definite educational advantages to decentralized training. Education is, to some degree, a matter of time. Studies prove that cram courses are inefficient, since students quickly forget much of what they learn. Centralized schools, of necessity, use intensified programs.

Considerable managerial benefits are realized in that the branch manager or an assistant usually is directly responsible for decentralized training. If the branch manager does a good job, trainees gain confidence in his leadership. At the same time, the manager has an excellent opportunity to evaluate the trainees.

The only weakness of decentralized training—and it is a big one— is that the branch manager may not be able to perform the training role properly.

Centralized Training

Centralized training may be presented in the form of organized schools with planned programs or periodic sales meetings held in some central location. Only companies that continually hire and process a large number of new sales people each year find it necessary to develop permanent training installations. Smaller concerns typically conduct one or two sales schools a year. Such programs last from two to four weeks and are usually conducted near the home office.

Strengths of centralized training. In centralized training, highly capable personnel, including skilled teachers, are usually readily available. Proximity to the plant or the home office allows the trainees to become acquainted with home-office personnel and manufacturing facilities. It is important for them to meet the top executives. Centralized training certainly saves executive time for instructing classes; there is no wasted travel time. Also, a centralized school normally has more formal facilities for training than are available in the field. Necessary equipment and materials are handy for the instructor's use. Another significant advantage is that the trainees can get to know one another. An esprit de corps can develop among the members of class, and this is conducive to good morale.

From an educational standpoint, removing trainees from the home setting, where they are not subject to the distractions of home life, has some merit. They can focus their attention on learning how to be better sales people.

Weaknesses of centralized training. Centralized training has two main weaknesses. First, as was noted, it is expensive to take people out of the field and support them while training.

Second, the amount of time a person can be kept at a central training location is limited. Moreover, trainees eventually become bored. When boredom sets in, education stops.[4] Married people, particularly, seldom want to be away from their families more than a few weeks at a time.

Techniques of Presentation

Several different teaching methods may be used to present material in a sales-training program (see Figure 8–2). All methods of presenting material are not equally effective. However, often the in-

---

[4] For a description of some ways that management can make centralized training more interesting, see Joseph A. Bellizzi and Lynn J. Loudenback, "Centralized Sessions Should Train Salespeople, Not Marathon Runners," *Marketing News*, August 22, 1980,
p. 5.

Figure 8–2

Presentation Techniques in Sales-Training Programs

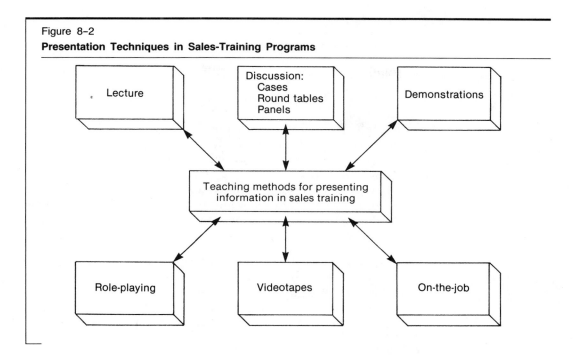

structor has little choice of methods because of the nature of the material. For instance, in teaching company information, it is impossible to use the role-playing technique. The lecture method supplemented with visual aids is about the only reasonable choice.

Lectures

The lecture method can present more information in a shorter period of time to a larger number of students than any of the other techniques. However, it is relatively ineffective for teaching salesmanship. Because lecture method is the easiest path to follow, trainers are often tempted to lecture excessively.

A *limited* amount of lecturing has a place in most sales-training programs. Although company information and some product knowledge can be presented in published material, some lecturing usually is necessary. Also, a lecture is frequently the best way to present a basic outline of a subject. It can stimulate, guide, and steer dicussion and other teaching methods into the channels desired. Although selling techniques are best taught by participation methods, short lectures introducing the students to the underlying problems and the principles can be extremely helpful. Just pushing the students into sales demonstrations without previous orientation to the subject can be quite confusing.

Discussion

Discussion should play a large role in any sales-training program, since it gives the students opportunity to discuss their own problems. It is the best method for making the experiences of competent sales people available to trainees. It also is the best method for providing experienced sales reps with a vehicle for exchanging thoughts and know-how.

Discussion can take several forms. Many are simply open talks on various topics between the teacher and the students, with the teacher controlling the discussion and stimulating it. However, some special devices have been developed to facilitate discussions.

Cases.   One widely used technique for stimulating discussion and for providing students with a realistic learning experience is the case history method. Each student is furnished with a written case similar to those at the ends of the chapters in this book. Each case should stimulate discussion in the specific areas the trainer wants to cover.

Round tables.   This form of discussion usually consists of dividing a large group into smaller ones so that each person can participate more fully. If the class has over 15 or 20 members, a few dominating individuals usually take far more than their share of time. If the class is divided into groups of 7 to 10 persons, each member may be forced to carry a share of the discussion. In small groups, any one trainee's silence is immediately noticeable, whereas in a larger group, this may not be true.

Round tables are most effective if experienced people are mixed in because inexperienced trainees usually have little background information to share with each other.

Panels.   The panel is basically a round-table discussion performed before an audience—the class. Usually, a moderator question various panel members and encourages their comments. Sometimes the panel answers questions submitted by members of the audience.

The panel should be staffed with individuals who have some standing in the student's eyes. Successful sales reps or executives of the firm often serve well in this capacity.

Demonstrations

Demonstrations can be used to great advantage in teaching both product knowledge and selling techniques. What better way to teach how a product operates than to actually demonstrate it? Instead of just telling about the different types of closes that can be used in getting an order, for example, it is better to demonstrate each before the class. Trainees can be shown how to handle innumerable selling situations that are difficult to describe.

The educational theory supporting the use of demonstrations in training programs is twofold. First, it has been proven many times that the eye is a better path to the brain than the ear. The visualization of any point increases the likelihood of its being learned. Second, many subjects are so complex and have so many interrelationships that they are clearer if the students actually observe these relationships.

Role Playing

In role playing, the trainee attempts to sell a product to a hypothetical prospect. If the role-playing method is to work effectively, care must be taken to make the prospect realistic.

This type of learning-by-doing education can be highly effective in teaching selling techniques, particularly in initial training programs. Trainees have to face many of the unforeseen developments that will arise in actual selling. Role playing also allows the instructor to work with the trainee on such important things as voice, poise, bearing, mannerisms, speech, and movement.

Role playing shows the student that *knowing* what to do is one thing, but *doing* it is another. One of the major weaknesses of most salesmanship courses is that they only teach the student *about* selling, not *how* to sell. Many students can recite all the various methods of approaching prospects, answering objections, and closing the sale. However, they are shocked to learn how much of this knowledge they can forget in an actual sales situation.

Many trainers prefer to have each sales presentation performed before the entire class so all students can benefit. While this reduces the number of presentations that can be made in a given time, it does have much to recommend it. First, students often see things that escape the teacher and can recommend actions that would otherwise go unmentioned. Second, possible resentment of criticism may be avoided by allowing the class to do the major criticizing. If all class members agree, the trainee is more likely to accept their opinions as the truth. Third, while the person doing the role playing is learning, the class learns by watching. Often class members are deeply impressed and see mistakes they resolve not to make.

Presentations invariably get better as each trainee takes a turn. The first few presentations are usually very poor. The teacher must inform the class and the person chosen to lead off that many mistakes will be made and things will not go smoothly. Instructors are wise to pick people with some skill in verbal expression and selling to make the first few presentations. This can get the sessions off to a good start and give inexperienced trainees some idea of the process.

In handling the role-playing sessions, the trainer must explain the importance of taking criticism the right way. Students must be convinced that the criticism will help them earn more money and is not meant personally. They must realize that many problems have no cut-and-dried answers. Criticisms on these points are only designed to give them some ideas about other ways to handle problems.

Frequently, the trainer is tempted to concentrate too much on small details at the expense of larger factors involved. One of the first questions the instructor should ask the class is: "Just why did Joan fail to make the sale?" or "Just why did Joe get the order?" Students must acquire an ability to see where a sale was made or lost. Frequently, one major reason or event decided the outcome. For instance, one trainee did a rather poor job in making her presentation and attempting to close, but she got the order anyway. It was easy to point out her many mistakes, but the class learned much more by finding out why she succeeded. In this case, the saleswoman had taken the trouble to locate an excellent prospect and allowed him to do the talking. She just let the man talk himself into the sale, which is good selling in many circumstances. This one factor overrode all the small errors she made.

Videotapes

Today role-playing sales presentations can be videotaped. Thus trainees can see themselves in action, and the instructor can comment at the proper moment. A great deal of instructional material can be videotaped so trainees can study at their convenience. All trainees would benefit by viewing a tape of the company's leading sales producer in action. All that is needed are a television camera, a video recorder, and some viewing sets. The cost of this equipment—approximately $2,500—is relatively small in relation to the benefits that can be derived.

On-the-Job Training

On-the-job sales training places the student in a more realistic situation than any of the other techniques previously discussed. Usually this method is used as the final stage of the trainee's sales education.

Actual supervision of on-the-job training can take several forms. The sales supervisor, the trainer, or a senior sales rep may go along with a new sales person on the first few calls to observe him or her in action. A few of these check rides are often included in a sales training program to determine how well the trainees have learned their lessons and to find out if additional training is required. If it is awkward for a second person to accompany the sales rep into the prospect's office, the trainer must discuss each presentation with the trainee afterward. Together they analyze the entire presentation to determine what was done right and what was done wrong.

Some companies allow the trainee to gain initial experience by selling to customers who come to the company's offices. In these cases it may be possible to set up facilities to observe the trainee in action.

The amount of on-the-job training that can be done economically is limited, since it is rather time-consuming for both the trainee and the trainer. The educational benefits of this type of training rapidly diminish after a few calls. Consequently, the trainer cannot make this method a major portion of the initial training program, but it is widely used in continuous programs.

Training Costs

Training costs are substantial. With such an investment in people management is quite concerned with the turnover in its sales force and in ways to reduce training costs. Most programs designed to reduce training costs focus on transferring the training from central (high cost) locations to on-the-job field training. Self-administered training systems, such as the video interactive system just described, hold promise for reducing instructional costs while improving the quality of the training.

Management's awareness of training costs is illusory. During a sales presentation of an educational system, the president of one large bank confessed that his organization did not know what it spent on training. Nor did he have any idea of what poor training was really costing the company in lost business, poor customer relations, and general employee inefficiency. He recognized that the costs of poor training may exceed direct training costs. The management of one company had computed its direct training costs. However, on close examination, it admitted that many of its training costs had been deliberately hidden in general administrative cost centers rather than charged directly to training expense. It is doubtful that management knows its training costs. Moreover, the full costs of training, both direct and indirect, are much larger than supposed. Probably the largest cost is incurred in improper training. The high cost of sales training is one reason new enterprises do little of it, preferring instead to hire experienced sales reps of proven ability who are ready to sell to the target customers.[5]

Summary

A good sales-training program can serve several purposes. It can lower the turnover of sales people while improving their morale and sales performance. It can provide better control over sales-force efforts, lower selling costs, and result in better use of the rep's time. While line personnel have distinctive advantages as sales trainers, they often lack the teaching skills essential to a training program. Thus training is often the responsibility of staff sales trainers.

Although initial training is often conducted centrally, most sales training is provided on-the-job. New reps need enough initial training to do a respectable job. However, there are advantages to delaying training until the new person has some experience that can be carried into the classroom.

Student participation in the training is essential to good sales training. Much use should be made of role-playing in which realistic buyers provide the trainee with some experiential learning experiences.

The advent of modern video interactive learning systems has great promise for making sales training more effective while lowering its costs.

Questions and Problems

1. "I don't have any training program. I just hire salesmen who have already proven successful for other companies and turn them loose. I let the big corporations do all my training for me and then just hire away their best people." This was the attitude expressed by the sales manager of one relatively small office machines agency. Is this a sound policy? What are some of the strengths and weaknesses of this position?

2. "Sales people are born, not made. It's futile to try to train a person to be a sales person, so I don't." How would you answer a sales manager who said this to you if you were trying to get him to hire you as a sales trainer?

---

[5] For an imaginative approach to measuring the value of a sales training program, see Michael A. Sheppeck and Stephen L. Cohen, "Put a Dollar Value on Your Training Programs," *Training and Development Journal*, November 1985, p. 59.

3. "The school of hard knocks is the best training school for sales people. I just shove them off the dock. Those that have it in them will learn selling on their own, and those who don't have it in them, well, we don't want them around the company anyway." How would you answer a manager who said this?

4. How can the sales manager keep top-notch sales reps interested in continual training programs?

5. You have been made sales trainer for a firm with 125 sales people. How would you determine their specific training needs?

6. How can the sales manager determine the excellence of the various instructors in the firm's training program?

7. You read an article about interactive video sales training and liked its message. You feel that it may be beneficial to you in your job as sales trainer to Large, Inc. Unfortunately, you know only what you read about it. You want to know much more. Exactly what would you have to learn about applying interactive video technology to your sales training programs?

8. Most of your sales reps own personal computers. How might you use those computers in your sales training program?

9. How should the sales trainer go about establishing the agenda or curriculum for a refresher course?

10. What are some of the pitfalls of on-the-job training?

Case 8–1

Drake Auto Parts Company

Proposal for Changes in Sales-Training Program

Randall Halper, the sales manager in the Cleveland, Ohio, region of the Drake Auto Parts Company, was wondering how he should respond to the president's request for a report on the company's sales-training program. Since Randy had been unhappy with some aspects of the present training program, he had suggested some changes. But Paul Blackwell, the general manager (and Randy's boss) in the Cleveland regional office, thought that Randy's plan would be too expensive. Eventually, the company president became aware of this discussion in Cleveland. As a result, he requested Randy to submit a report that would (1) review the present training program and (2) propose changes to increase the program's effectiveness.

Drake Auto Parts Company was a wholesale distributor of automotive parts. The company's product assortment was one of the largest in the industry—consisting of about 100,000 items. The company was divided into five regions with 25 warehouse distribution centers that served a nationwide market.

Drake bought from many manufacturers and put its own brand on several of these product lines. Drake sold its products to another level of wholesaler—called a jobber in the industry. These jobbers, in turn, sold to auto repair shops, service stations, car and truck fleet operators, and individual consumers who fixed their own cars on a do-it-yourself basis.

Throughout its national market, Drake was in competition with hundreds of local, regional, national distributors of auto parts. Probably the two largest national distributors were National Automotive Parts Association (NAPA) and the American Parts System (APS, better known in the industry as the Big-A). Both of these large distributors provided their customers with an extensive product assortment and a broad line of services. Most of Drake's competitors, however, only sold automotive parts and did not provide other services for their customers.

Randy Halper realized that the total market for automotive parts was very large and growing rapidly. The rising prices of new cars meant that people were keeping their old ones longer than in the past, thus spending more to keep them in good operating condition.

In spite of the growing market, Mr. Halper recognized the importance—the "vital necessity," as he put it—of having well-trained sales representatives to keep abreast of the competition.

Mr. Halper reviewed (1) the services that the company provided for its jobbers and (2) what the company expected in return from these firms. Drake sold *only* to its jobbers, but these jobbers were free to buy from any source. Each Drake jobber was assured, however, that it was the only jobber in its market area that was being sold Drake's products. Drake made this agreement under the assumption that the jobber was attempting to expand its market and thus the market for Drake's products.

In addition, Drake provided a line of managerial services for present and potential jobber customers. For example, Drake would analyze the market for a person who was thinking of opening a store. Drake helped in getting initial financing and in determining store location. Drake then helped train the new owner and his staff. Other services included designing a floor plan, stocking shelves with initial inventory, or replacing existing products with the Drake brand. Drake offered a guarantee against product obsolescence. If an item was not selling, Drake took it back and replaced it with a more popular item.

Drake also provided a modern inventory control system that the jobber could use. This system served the jobber's full product line. That is, it was not limited only to Drake's products.

As the sales manager in the Cleveland region, Randy Halper was responsible for selecting, training, and supervising the sales reps who operated out of the Cleveland office. According to Halper, a sales rep either should have certain qualifications before joining the company or else acquire them during the training program. These skills included a general knowledge of accounting and finance, inventory control, motivation techniques, time management, and ability to train others. The reps were paid on a straight-salary basis, and the pay level was above the industry average. Randy was convinced that he had recruited high-quality sales people. They were relatively young, and Randy felt that they were highly motivated, energetic people.

Each sales rep had about 15 jobber accounts, and the rep was expected to call on each jobber once a month. The reps were responsible for having product knowledge of the 100,000 automotive parts sold by Drake. The rep's selling job involved the following broad activity groups:

1. *Market analysis*—help the jobber identify its market potential; analyze this market in some detail so as to better tap into it; provide the jobber with market information regarding customers and competitors.
2. *Inventory control*—check the jobber's inventory movement; take out slow-moving items and replace them with more desirable ones; possess a working knowledge of how a warehouse distribution center operates. A sales rep rarely wrote out an order. This was because the jobber already had been provided with an inventory control and ordering system. The jobber ordered directly from a warehouse distribution center, and the order was delivered the next day.
3. *Training*—teach the jobber how to recruit and train his staff; explain Drake's system approach to selling; accompanied by a jobber's sales rep, the Drake rep makes sales presentations to some of the jobber's customers to show them how they can do more business in their own shops.

In summary, the success of a Drake sales representative was measured by his or her ability to help build the jobber's business year after year.

Drake's own sales-training program was conducted in the warehouse distribution centers and also in the field. New sales recruits spent from one to six months in the warehouse training stage. During this period, they learned the product assortment and the order-filling system. In this period, they were also taught Drake's selling system, methods, and philosophies. The reps attended the company's biweekly sales meetings. Various training methods (lecture, discussion, role playing, and so on) were used in the warehouse training.

After the initial period in the warehouse, a recruit was sent into the field to travel with an experienced sales person (called an account executive). The account executive's job was to train the recruit in the finer points that would be encountered in the field. The recruit continued to attend the biweekly sales meetings and received periodic feedback by telephone or personal visit from Mr. Halper. After six to eight weeks of riding with an account executive, the new recruit was given his or her own territory and several jobbers to call on.

In general, Mr. Halper was pleased with the performance of the sales force. But he did notice several specific performance weaknesses which he attributed to shortcomings in the training program. For example, Halper had noticed that the recruits were often unable to provide the jobbers with all of the information and assistance that the Drake system had to offer. He felt that the account executives should be able to handle all field situations on their own since they would be in the field alone for up to two weeks at a time. Often the questions that the account executives were asking in the sales meetings were in relation to information that they should have known. Halper also noticed that in the sales meetings many of the account executives were unable to answer questions on the basic Drake system. Halper also identified another problem—namely, if the sales recruits did not learn the Drake system while being trained, they, in turn, would be unable to teach it to the jobbers and their staffs.

Based on his analysis of the existing training program, Mr. Halper proposed some changes to his boss, Paul Blackwell. Halper wanted to make the training program more of an ongoing affair so that the account executives would get periodic refresher training.

Halper disliked what he considered to be a looseness in the program and wanted to see more structure. He envisioned a change to a six-month or one-year program where the recruit would be taught the product line as well as the system of services available to the jobber. Halper felt that this program would present information in a well-designed, structured manner that would be easier for the recruit to understand.

In response, Mr. Blackwell stated that the program should be maintained in its present form. He felt it was giving a recruit the needed experience in the warehouse and in the field. Even though the recruits did not know all of the information, at least they were starting to be productive earlier. With Halper's plan it could be a full year before a recruit began to be productive. Mr. Blackwell also believed that there was nothing that could replace the training that the recruit received in the warehouse. Even though the present training program was extremely expensive, Blackwell thought it was better than any alternative. Mr. Blackwell's main objection to Mr. Halper's idea was the time and cost of switching to a new plan.

The discussion between Blackwell and Halper escalated to the point where the company president finally became aware of the disagreement. Concerned that the disagreement might grow into a morale-destroying situation, the president intervened. His first step was to ask Randy Halper to submit a proposal for changes in the company's sales-training program. The proposal also was to include time, cost, and effectiveness considerations.

Question

What should Randy Halper say in his report concerning the Drake sales-training program? Identify, with supporting analysis, *(a) the feature of the present program that should be retained and (b) the changes that you think are needed.*

Case 8–2

Crescent Cleaner Company*

Developing a Sales Training Program

The Crescent Cleaner Company, a rapidly growing firm, manufactured and marketed carpet cleaning machines. Prior to 1985, the company had hired as sales reps only people experienced in some phase of the carpet care industry. Since that time, Crescent's business had expanded so much that it began to hire inexperienced people as sales reps. These new reps were sent into the field to sell without training. They were given a customer list, some selling aids, and demonstrator models of the products and told that the cream would rise to the top.

For several months, the vice president of sales, Thomas Decatur, had been receiving customer complaints regarding the work of these new reps. Decatur finally realized that he had a serious situation on his hands and he had better do something about it.

The Crescent Company was started in 1975 by a carpet cleaner sales rep. He had developed a cleaning machine which he then manufactured and sold one at a time. In 1979, the original owner sold the company to an investment group headed by Rembrandt (Rem)

---

* Adapted from a case prepared by Bruce Blincow, under the direction of Professor William J. Stanton.

Cowles who is the majority stock holder, president, and chairman of the board of directors. The company grew at a modest pace until 1983 when it developed a greatly improved line of carpet cleaning machines. Sales volume increased dramatically: $10 million dollars in 1986, more than twice the volume in 1984.

Mr. Cowles stated that the company's current financial condition was excellent. The company's target gross margin, after sales commissions were deducted, was 30 percent. The goal had been met regularly for the past several years. The company's goals, as stated by the president, were: (1) to be the primary manufacturer of carpet care equipment in the world; (2) to supply the carpet care industry profitably; and (3) to manufacture quality products marketed to develop a profitable relationship between the customer and the company.

In 1984, Cowles hired Thomas Decatur to replace the sales manager who had left the company. Decatur, with 22 years of sales experience with one of Crescent's major competitors, later was promoted to vice president of sales. Rem Cowles maintained close control of the company's finances. He had very little to do with day-to-day operations, a task left to Decatur, who might better have the title of executive vice president. The Crescent workers respected Decatur and considered him to be the most knowledgeable and dynamic executive in the firm.

Crescent's product mix was divided into four groups, each marketed under the same brand name—Steem Kleen. One product group consisted of nine models of carpet cleaning machines that used a steam process to extract soil from the carpet. Seven of these models were targeted at the professional carpet cleaner market and the franchised consumer-rental market. The other two models were high-pressure machines designed for heavy-duty use in industrial markets. This product group accounted for 60 percent of the company's sales volume and an even higher percentage of the net profit.

The second product group—floor tools and accessories—consisted of various models of high-pressure vacuum "shoes." These were the tools in the cleaning process that actually contacted the carpet. This product group accounted for 20 percent of the company's sales volume. The other two product groups—cleaning chemicals and replacement parts, respectively—together accounted for the remaining 20 percent of the sales volume.

In 1985, Crescent introduced a new extractor that Decatur referred to as a "revolutionary" development. The machine had no filter bags to clean and no tanks to empty. Vacuum dirt-laden air passed through a water bath where the air was washed and then discharged through an exhaust pipe.

Mr. Decatur believed that Crescent's steam-type of soil extracting machines had advantages over competitive models such as the rotary-brush, cylindrical brush, or vibrating-plate machines. The traditional method of carpet cleaning involved two steps—(1) applying wet detergent with one machine, and (2) retrieving the water and suds from the carpet with another machine. The amount of time between applying and retrieving the water enabled it to soak into the carpet backing causing shrinkage.

The stream extraction process used by the Crescent machines combined the two steps into one, thus eliminating shrinkage. Steam extraction, according to Decatur, did an excellent cleaning job without causing any distortion or flaring of carpet pile and without leaving any residue of shampoo to collect dirt. Furthermore, Crescent's machines were small, easy to carry, and easy to clean.

According to Tom Decatur, the Crescent Company faced five major competitors, one of which was a Canadian firm. In addition, there were some 80 smaller competitors located in the United States, Canada, and Western Europe. Decatur estimated that Chemko Company in Phoenix, Arizona, and Windsor Industries in Denver, Colorado, each had a market share of about 20 percent. Crescent's market share was estimated to be 10 percent.

Decatur pointed out that the nature of the product accounted for the large number of small firms in the industry. The relatively simple design and low production costs of carpet cleaning machines permitted easy entrance into the industry. No large initial capital investment was needed. Most businesses started (as Crescent did) with a model produced and sold from the inventor's basement or garage. Even as a firm expanded, a large capital investment still was not needed. Most of the parts needed in production could be subcontracted out until such time as the manufacturer was financially able to set up in-house production facilities.

The Crescent Company was efficiently established in its market so that the company no longer had to compete on a price basis. The company had the reputation of turning out well-performing, long-lived machines.

The end uses of Crescent's machines ranged from cleaning household carpeting to cleaning baseball and football playing fields covered with artificial turf. The many industrial users also included hotels, banks, retail chain stores, office buildings, apartment complexes, and convention centers.

Decatur stated that the prospects for growth in the industry were great. Demand stemmed from the high growth rate projected in the carpet industry. Decatur anticipated big increases in the use of carpeting in both the consumer and industrial markets. A small part of Crescent's sales volume went through export middlemen into foreign markets. Another small share was sold to retail chains under the store's private label.

The company's primary distribution channel, however, was through its own sales force to four customer groups. By far the largest of these four were janitorial supply houses. Crescent's sales reps spent 95 percent of their time servicing these accounts. The janitorial supply houses, in turn, sold (1) to industrial users who maintained their own cleaning facilities and (2) to maintenance contractors who cleaned large buildings for a contracted price.

The other three customer groups that occupied the remaining 5 percent of the sales reps' time were: (1) national accounts such as a national house cleaning service that franchised cleaning people and equipment; (2) professional carpet cleaners that serviced private homes and small businesses; and (3) franchised rental stores that rented all kinds of equipment to the do-it-yourself market.

Crescent sold to janitorial supply houses and national accounts at 40 percent of list price. Professional carpet cleaners and rental firms received only quantity discounts—no trade discounts. However, Decatur noted that the rental market had just recently been tapped. Currently it accounted for 5 percent of the company's sales volume. But Decatur anticipated that in the near future much more of the sales reps' time would be spent working with these accounts.

At the time that Tom Decatur was hired, the Crescent Company had three sales people. Soon thereafter these three reps either resigned or were promoted into managerial positions. So Decatur essentially had to build a new sales force. He did so by hiring seven new sales people each year in 1985 and 1986, thus bringing the sales force to its present level of 14 reps. Each sales person had a geographic territory, and the 14 territories covered the United States, excluding Hawaii and Alaska.

Before Decatur joined the company, the sales force was paid a straight salary. However, Decatur immediately changed the compensation plan to a straight commission. The sales people were responsible for providing their own transportation and paying their own expenses from their commissions.

The sales people were paid a commission of 10 percent on sales to janitorial supply houses and national accounts. The commission rates were 5 percent on sales to professional carpet cleaners and rental dealers. (Recall that the company sold to janitorial supply houses and national accounts at 40 percent off list price but charged full list price, less quantity discounts, to carpet cleaners and rental dealers.)

Private-label buyers, export middlemen, and house accounts were not called on by the Crescent sales force. However, each rep did receive a 5 percent commission on all sales to these accounts when the order was delivered in the rep's territory. In effect, a commission was paid on all orders delivered to a rep's territory, whether or not that sales person had contacted the purchaser.

To help the sales people generate a satisfactory level of sales volume, Decatur prepared the following list of job activities for each sales person.

1. Train the middlemen's (dealers' and distributors') sales forces, especially in product knowledge and effective selling techniques for the Crescent products.
2. Accompany the middlemen's sales people on some of their calls.
3. Help middlemen sell slow-moving items.
4. Be on call 24 hours a day, if needed, to provide repair service for end users.
5. Seek out new dealer and distributor accounts.
6. Encourage janitorial supply houses to conduct Crescent seminars for end users. Crescent reps should initiate and supervise these seminars.
7. Motivate middlemen to demonstrate Crescent products to end users. This relates to point 6. (Crescent products generally required a demonstration in order to be sold successfully. Often the best opportunity to demonstrate a machine to a purchasing agent or a head housekeeper was at a Crescent seminar. Otherwise the machines usually had to be demonstrated at night when buildings were closed and the cleaning was done. Often it was difficult to get the decision-makers to attend these night demonstration sessions.)

In the past, Crescent's policy had been to hire as sales reps only people with experience in the carpet care industry. The reasoning was that Crescent had neither the time nor the experienced trainers to instruct the new sales people. Also, management assumed that experienced people coming from the same industry: (1) knew a little about the products, and (2) had done some selling and therefore could sell Crescent products adequately.

During 1986, however, Crescent's business was expanding so rapidly that the company had to hire inexperienced people and send them immediately into the field. Management still felt that the company was too small and too busy to engage in formal sales training. If serious problems arose, Decatur would fly to the spot and work with the sales rep to solve the problem.

This new selection policy, coupled with a sink-or-swim philosophy regarding training, worked with the superior sales people. However, most of the new reps had no idea how to service broken equipment. Nor could they answer comparison questions involving competitive machines. Complaints from middlemen and end users piled up, and some middlemen dropped the Crescent line.

The customers were not the only ones complaining. Decatur had heard some grumbling among some of the sales people. They said the company was not giving them enough information and help. In fact, morale had declined to the point where two of the reps were discussing the possibility of leaving the company. Up to this point, sales-force turnover had been very low.

The situation came to a head when Mr. Decatur was persuaded to hire Roger Davenport. Roger was a recent college graduate whose father owned a janitorial supply house that was a good customer of the Crescent Company. Davenport did have some product knowledge as a result of working in his father's firm. However, he had no sales experience.

Tom Decatur realized he had to do something about: (1) the practice of hiring inexperienced sales people, or (2) the company's lack of sales training. He talked over these situations with some fellow executives in Crescent. They all agreed that there was little they could do about the selection situation. It was difficult to find and hire experienced sales people.

On the other hand, there was considerable disagreement over what to do about sales training. The production manager, Paul Flick, felt that the company's financial condition could support the hiring of an outside training consultant to come in and train all the current reps. The president, Rem Cowles, thought the company should continue on as in the past. "We got where we are now without any training program," said Cowles, "so why get all these fancy-Dan ideas now all of a sudden."

Decatur wondered how the consultant-trainer idea would work in an expanding market where the company was continuing to hire new reps. "Do we call in the guy every time we add a new rep or revise a territory?" asked Decatur. "If so, it'll cost a bundle. Furthermore, what do we do about continuous training for the reps after the initial indoctrination training is completed?"

One of the financial officers, Alex English, suggested that maybe the company could hold a training seminar similar to the ones that the sales people conducted for their middlemen's sales forces. This meeting could be held in some central geographic location for a few days. "We could explain the products to the reps and teach them some selling techniques," English said. "We might even use some of our experienced sales reps to lead the seminar."

Rem Cowles chimed in again, this time with another alternative. "How about letting a new rep travel with one of our top sales people for a week or two. For example, there's Sam Hardy in the Kansas City territory. He is a good salesman, does his paperwork well, and sends in honest expense accounts. I'm sure we could persuade Sam to take a new rep for a little while and show him the ropes."

"I don't know," pondered Tom Decatur. "Your ideas all sound fine in one respect or another, but maybe we should simply start from scratch and design an entirely new training program. It could cover both indoctrination training for new reps and continuation training for the sales people who have been with us for a while. If so, all I have to do is figure out who is going to do the training job, where it will be done, what will we teach them, what training techniques will be used, and how will we pay for the whole show. Thank you, gentlemen, for helping me."

Questions

1. What sort of arrangements, if any, should the Crescent company make to train its sales people?
2. Assume that the company wants to develop a formal indoctrination training program for new sales people and for the presently employed but inexperienced reps. Your assignment is to design such a program. In so doing, be sure to answer the questions raised by Mr. Decatur in the final paragraph of the case.
3. Should the company develop a continuation training program for its experienced sales people?

9

Content of Sales-Training Programs

Selling is the art of asking the right questions.

In the previous chapter, we examined the total training program. Now let's see what to put in it. Sales-training programs basically teach salesmanship. It would be difficult to plan and conduct a sales-training program without knowing how to sell. Thus, sales managers as trainers need to be competent persuaders.

Attitudes and Philosophies about Selling

Before beginning instruction on the techniques of salesmanship, trainees should be properly prepared psychologically. Several factors other than mastery of the persuasion process strongly affect success or failure in selling. The first is proper orientation of the trainees' attitudes and philosophies toward the job and the selling profession. Unless this is accomplished, the trainer is wasting time trying to perfect their sales techniques. They are largely unreceptive because certain myths block their learning. We will state the most prevalent of these myths and comment on why they have been proven false.

> *Myth no. 1.* Sales people are born—not made.

Probably nothing has so hindered the acceptance of sales training as this erroneous cliché. Even today many people, including some sales managers, still believe that great persuaders are born with sales ability and cannot be trained. This simply is not true. Such great sales forces as IBM, Xerox, and Procter & Gamble are based on excellent sales training programs. Each of these firms hires young people who are largely without sales experience or skills, and teaches them how to sell.

One of the first attitudes to instill in sales trainees is the value of sales training. They should accept the idea that, with proper training and the appropriate aptitudes and qualifications, a raw recruit can be developed into an excellent sales person. For trainees who do not accept this proposition the rest of the training program will be ineffective.

The idea that properly qualified people can be trained to sell is not an easy one to instill. To get the idea across, the trainer can use case histories of successful sales reps who entered a company's training program as anything but "born salesmen."

Myth no. 2.   Sales people must be good talkers.

Nonsense! Good sales people are good listeners. They know that the most useful talent is asking the right questions to get the prospect to talk. You never learn much while talking. The prospect has information you need. People like to talk and will tell you what you need to know to sell them. All you have to do is learn to ask the right questions, then listen to what they tell you.[1]

Myth no. 3.   Selling is a matter of knowing the right techniques or tricks.

People have always sought a magic way to solve their problems instantly. But history has yet to record anyone finding such a wondrous procedure. Neither have sales people discovered any "magic" selling techniques. Granted, there are certain methods that seem to work for some people, but sales success clearly does not depend on them. Successful sales people use a wide variety of selling techniques. Yet, many sales people who try to use the tactics that work for others fail in the process.

Success in selling is not merely a matter of mastering techniques. Rather it is a result of several potent factors, such as work habits, attitudes, products sold, and markets covered.

---

[1] See Jeremy Main, "How to Sell by Listening," *Fortune,* February 1985, pp. 52–54, for an excellent treatment of the art of listening.

Myth no. 4. A good sales rep can sell anything.

No so! Many successful sales people were failures earlier in their careers when they tried to sell a product not suited to their talents. A successful sales career results when the individual is joined with the "right" product made by the "right" company and sold to the "right" people. But this does not mean there is only one right situation for a person. Rather, there are a substantial number of sales jobs in which any one sales person can prosper. It will pay you handsomely to give considerable thought to how you and your talents match up with prospective jobs.

Myth no. 5. A good sales person can sell ice to an Eskimo.

A good sales person would never think of trying to sell ice to an Eskimo. Instead, the professional persuader would try to find someone who needed the ice and had the money to buy it. Selling is not a sport in which one tries to unload unwanted goods on an unwilling buyer who is unable to pay for them. Good selling starts by finding someone who needs the product and can afford it. This is called prospecting. Good sales people call on good prospects.

Myth no. 6. People don't want to buy.

Many sales managers think that people don't want to buy and that you must beat them over the head to get the order. If people really didn't want to buy merchandise, the majority of sales people would be starving. Most goods and services are not purchased because of the creative efforts of sales people. They are bought because people want them. People want new cars, nice houses, new dresses, shoes, or whatever. They want all sorts of things. Industrial buyers particularly must buy all the things their companies need for operations. They *must* buy! They are waiting for the sales person to show them how his or her proposition is going to benefit them.

The Purpose of Selling and the People Who Do It

A good training program should instill in trainees a thorough understanding of their role and importance in our socioeconomic system. People must appreciate the value of their contribution to enhance their self-esteem. In selling, morale is a key factor in determining success. An understanding of the social and economic purpose of selling should help trainees counter the critics of selling and the generally poor image of sales people in our society.

Introducing Innovation to Markets

Compared with the past or with many other nations, the rate of product innovation in this country today is staggering. The life cycle of products grows shorter. As soon as one new item reaches the market, two newer ones are developed in laboratories. But innovation is of little value until it is brought out of the laboratory. The task of introducing these new articles is the function of personal selling and advertising.

Without sales reps, the introduction of innovations would be impeded. People have neither the time nor the inclination to continually seek out the newest developments in their fields. See Figure 9–1.

Conveying Information

Professional sales representatives are experts in their fields. They should know more about their products and the problems they solve than any other person. This product-knowledge function is so important that a large segment of most training programs is devoted to it. The sales rep is a consultant to customers when they have technical problems. If the rep were not available, the customer would have to hire the same talent elsewhere.

Facilitating Consumption

People want all sorts of goods and services, but inertia may keep them from buying. Sales efforts stimulate the consumption process by reducing people's inherent reluctance to make purchase decisions. Persuasive activities encourage people to buy what they want and make it easier for them to do so.

Acting as Intelligence Agent and Communication Channel

One of the major problems in operating a complex society such as ours is maintaining communications between producers and their markets. At one time tailors were personally acquainted with their customers who told them exactly what to make. Today, various middlemen come between the producer and the consumer. Yet the basic problem of communicating the consumers' desires to the producer still exists.

Figure 9–1

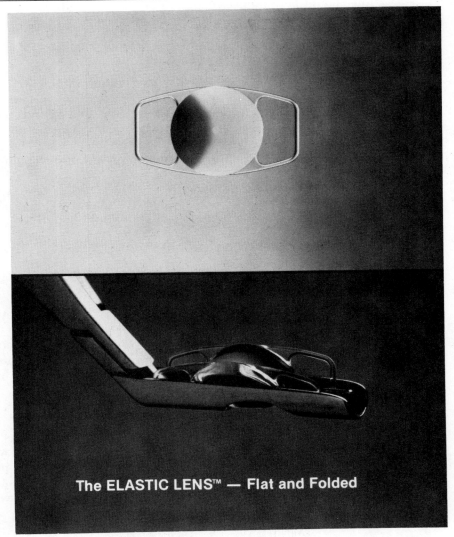

The ELASTIC LENS™ — Flat and Folded

The Staar Elastic Lens® (an intraocular lens for people undergoing cataract surgery) was introduced to the world's ophthalmologists by 16 experienced sales reps managed by John Wolf. The foldable silicon lens allows eye surgeons to replace the cataract patient's defective lens through a much smaller incision (3mm) thus reducing the surgical risks and enhancing the final results. The fortunes of Staar Surgical, a new venture, rest very much in the hands of its sales force.

The essential communication function is now performed largely by the sales force. Firms without sales reps may not know what is happening in the market. One firm selling supplies to floral wholesalers was being undercut by a competitor. He was giving an additional 10 percent free-goods deal under the table to key wholesalers who agreed to handle the line exclusively. Management in the first firm knew that its sales were dropping but did not know why. A good customer eventually told them of the competitor's practice, and they were able to counter it before losses became too large. However, this delay in meeting competition seriously injured the firm. A good sales rep would have quickly discovered the competitor's practice.

Helping Solve Customers' Problems

Good sales people know that when they get an order they have just started to work for the customer. They also perform many services for prospects before they get an order. If customers do not get service from a supplier, they will seek other sources of supply.

After selling a computer, for example, the sales engineer must make certain that it is operating properly, that the customer's personnel know how to operate it, and that the programming satisfactorily resolves the customer's problems. A sportswear saleswoman called on a small apparel dealer who had a serious overstock of outerwear, which reduced the store's open-to-buy budget. The saleswoman did not try to sell her line, but rather spent hours planning a promotion that would reduce the dealer's overstock. Thereby she created a loyal customer.

Product Knowledge and Applications

Sales people not only know about the products they sell but also must believe in their merits. A large part of most training programs is devoted to providing knowledge about the products and services to be sold and their applications. Ordinarily the amount of product training varies according to its technical complexity. One study indicated that 42 percent of the training time for newly hired sales people is devoted to product knowledge (see Table 9–1).

Often the task of learning about an extensive product line can be burdensome. Some product lines are so extensive and complex that no one can memorize them. Thus sales reps must become adept at using the company's catalogs and manuals to locate the information you need. Bear in mind that many sales result from a sales rep merely knowing what goods the company has to sell.

Table 9–1

Distribution of Sales-Training Time by Activity, for Newly Hired Sales People

Activity	Percent of Time
Product knowledge	42
Selling techniques	24
Market/industry orientation	17
Company orientation	13
Other	4
Total	100

* Percentages are the mean for 152 reporting sales units.
Source: David S. Hopkins, *Training the Sales Force* Report No. 737 (New York: The Conference Board, 1978), p. 6.

Methods of Teaching Product Knowledge

Several methods have been successfully used in teaching product knowledge. The key is to let trainees work with the products and learn how to operate them. Lectures are of little value by themselves. In the introductory phases, however, they are useful for familiarizing trainees with the product. Good visuals greatly increase the effectiveness of a lecture.

The South Wind Division of the Stewart-Warner Company started its trainees in the technical service department, where each person learned to tear down and repair the products. They became intimately familiar with the workings of the items and were able to perform any repair job that might arise. The trainee learned to take apart and reassemble each of the products and had to pass a written test on them.

Applications of Product Knowledge

Trainees who have learned about the product's technical aspects must also know how they can be applied to customers' problems. It is one thing to know products. It is another to be able to apply this information in the field. One of the big advantages of organizing a sales force along customer-class lines is that it greatly simplifies the teaching of product uses. A trainee who will call on only one type of customer needs to learn only the product-use problems in that industry.

Trainees should be taken into the field to study and observe the firm's product in actual use. There is, however, ample room for classroom study of product applications. Sometimes actual case problems can be used to project the trainee into commonly encountered situations. Laboratory exercises are useful in showing how the firm's product can be employed to solve a customer's problem. ***Application engineering*** is a term frequently applied to this aspect of selling. Xerox has prepared a large manual for its sales trainees which contains case histories of how its copying machines have been used in specific applications.

Knowledge of Competitive Products

Sales people should know their competitors' products almost as well as their own, because they must sell against them. A sales rep who is not familiar with competitors' goods cannot compare his line with theirs. He will also be unable to correct inaccurate statements a prospect may make about a competitor's product.

Detailed knowledge of competing products allows the sales rep to design a presentation to stress the advantages of his product over the competitor's. Every product has some competitive deficiencies. Once the sales rep determines what the major competition is, he can sell against it intelligently without actually mentioning the competitor's name. He merely stresses that his product does not have the deficiencies the competitors' item has.

Continuation of Product Training

Product training is a continuing function. Every time new models are brought out or new competitive developments appear, the sales force must be trained to handle them. Retraining on existing products is also frequently necessary, because sales people become forgetful or careless about technical knowledge. Much of this continuous training is done through product bulletins sent to the sales force to keep them abreast of product developments.

Knowledge about the Company

All trainees need a certain amount of information about the company's history and organization. The training program should also include an explanation of company policies and procedures, and the reasons for them. When a sales representative can answer a customer's complaint about a company policy, this not only may retain the customer, but it also boosts the rep's morale.

Company knowledge is not difficult to teach. The lecture method can be used extensively, combined with printed materials covering the information. A common weakness in training programs is that trainers spend too much time on company knowledge. A little bit goes a long way.

Trainees need to be shown how to work within the corporate system—who to contact to get things done and how the system operates. New employees of corporate giants, in particular, may be in awe of the organizational monster they are associated with.

The Selling Process

After trainees gain the requisite background information, they should be introduced to the selling process and the techniques that have proven effective in selling the company's products.

One of the first ideas trainees need to understand is that there are no magic sales techniques. No one method can be used to close every sale. The recommended techniques are simply those that experience has indicated seem to work better than others.

The actual selling process can be likened to a chain, each link of which must be closed successfully. If each of the steps in the process is not culminated successfully, the seller will fail to get the order. However, each step overlaps others, and their sequence may be altered to meet the situation at hand. For example, closing frequently is interwoven into the presentation. Many good sales reps like to try a close early in a presentation to see if the prospect is ready to buy.

The seven steps of the sales process are:

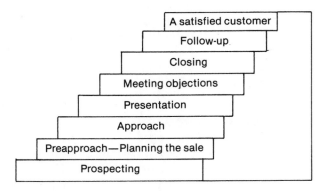

Prospecting

A prospect is defined as someone who needs the product and is able to buy it. Successful sales people do not waste their time calling on people who are not prospects.

Prospecting is the method or system by which sales people learn the names of people who need the product and can afford it.

Trainees must be shown how to develop a steady flow of good prospects. The trainer should focus on prospecting systems that have proven successful for the firm. Instruction on prospecting can be provided by a combination lecture and case-history method. Sales people for the firm who are particularly adept at prospecting may be brought in to discuss their systems.

Names and addresses of good prospects can be obtained in a number of ways. A sales manager may prepare a list for each sales representative. Customers can suggest new leads, and present users may want new or different models of the product. Many sales executives believe that a firm's best prospects are its present customers. They reason: These people know us and our wares. If they are satisfied customers, they will probably buy from us again in preference to a seller they have no experience with. A competitor's customers also can be good prospects. A saleswoman for a new copier sought out firms that were using Xerox copying machines. She reasoned that these concerns had already recognized a need for a copier, and her machine could offset the disadvantages of the Xerox model. Announcements of engagements, weddings, or births can furnish leads to the sale of many products.

When the sales rep first uncovers the name of a likely customer, it is merely a lead to a prospect—a "suspect." The person must be qualified as to needs and ability to buy before he can be considered a prospect. The qualification of suspects is one of the functions of the next step in the selling process—the preapproach.

The Preapproach—Planning the Sale

The preapproach step includes all of the information-gathering activities necessary to learn relevant facts about the prospect and his or her needs and situation.

Four functions of the preapproach should be made clear to trainees. First, it should qualify the lead or disclose the party's needs and ability to buy. Second, it should provide information that will enable the seller to tailor the presentation to the prospect. Third, it should provide information that may keep the sales rep from making serious tactical errors during the presentation. Finally, a good preapproach increases the sales rep's confidence and makes him feel able to handle whatever may arise during the sale.

If the prospect is an industrial firm, the sales rep should learn everything possible about that business—its size, its present purchasing practices, the location of its plants, the names of its executives, the names of people who influence the purchase, and other related data. If the prospective buyer has been having problems, the seller should become familiar with them.

A day-to-day operating problem in the—
Majestic Glass Company (D)

Poor Handwriting Causing Mistakes on Orders

Errors in handling a customer's orders could result in serious losses to Majestic. For example, Mardi Gras Toiletries, Inc., of New Orleans had notified Mr. Brion by collect telegram that it was returning, at vendor's expense, a shipment of jars which were not the type or quantity ordered. The jars were not a standard item maintained in warehouse stocks. The Majestic factory had produced them to what were thought to be the customer's specifications. Since they were unusual, Mr. Brion feared that no alternate customer could be found. The order had been billed at approximately $27,000.

Mr. Brion conducted a careful investigation lasting several days. He found that the error was caused initially by the poor handwriting of the Majestic salesman in New Orleans, Lester Jackson. Jackson had intended to write "8,660 each #776 Cosmetic Jar, annealed." Instead, the Order Processing Section at the home office had read his scrawled pencil entries on the order form as "8,000 gross #110 Cosmetic Jar, milled." Mr. Brion had examined the order form and agreed that he would have read it exactly as the Order Processing Section had done.

All orders were rewritten in the Order Processing Section. Then this Section routinely sent a typed copy of the new version to the salesman (1) if the order required special factory production, or (2) if it was expected to be billed at more than $1,000. The order was not filled until the salesman verified it by initialing each line item on the order, and returned it to the home office. In this case, Mr. Jackson had initialed the form in the proper place.

The order pads carried by Majestic salesmen had the words "PRINT— DON'T WRITE" in large black letters at the top. The words "ERRORS CAN BE COSTLY" were at the bottom. Careful order preparation was one of the topics covered in the salesmen's initial training, and had been often mentioned in sales meetings.

Mr. Jackson was a veteran salesman, age 50, with a wife and four children. In his 12 years with Majestic, he had somewhat improved the performance of the New Orleans territory, but he was not an outstanding rep. He had made errors before, but with only minor consequences. Mardi Gras Toiletries, Inc., was Majestic's best customer in the South.

Question

How should Clyde Brion handle the problem of order mistakes caused by poor handwriting?

Note: See the introduction to this series of problems in Chapter 3 for the necessary background on the company, its market, and its competition.

Before calling on anyone, the rep should know the correct spelling and pronunciation of the person's name and exact title in the firm. Knowledge of the prospect's educational background, experience in the company, fraternal affiliations, marital status, family, religion, and any other facts available concerning the person's personal habits and beliefs is also helpful. The purpose of obtaining such personal background material is twofold: (1) to keep from making serious social blunders and (2) to locate some common interests between the prospect and the sales person. For example, perhaps the sales person and the prospect went to the same university or were raised in the same hometown. Anything that the two have in common facilitates the presentation and makes the prospect more friendly.

Even to sales people who regularly call on the same accounts, pre-approach information is vital. Some companies make it a point to gather information about their customers. They store such information in a card system for easy review by their sales reps. Information such as birthdays and anniversary dates of customers is useful if it is acceptable to send token gifts on these occasions. While it might seem difficult to get such information, it is amazing what can be learned about customers. In industrial selling, the people inside the company who are interested in having the company buy the product will often provide a great deal of personal information about the firm's decision makers. Personal information also can be uncovered in directories and biographical publications such as *Who's Who in America.* Even such a simple tactic as driving by the prospect's home or place of business can disclose much about the person. When a sale is critically important, some firms order a credit investigation of the account. Why waste time getting an order the credit department will reject?

The Approach

When the sales representative has the name of a prospect and adequate preapproach information, the next step is the actual approach. The approach usually takes up the first minute or so of a sale. It frequently makes or breaks the entire presentation. If the approach fails, the sales person often does not get a chance to give a presentation.

Trainees should be informed that a good approach does three things. It gets the prospect's attention. It immediately inspires interest in hearing more about the proposition. And it makes an easy transition into the presentation. One textbook in the field of salesmanship lists 10 methods that can be used in approaching a prospect.[2] For a sales training program, only four basic approaches need to be considered: (1) the introductory approach, (2) the product approach, (3) the consumer-benefit approach, and (4) the referral approach.

Introductory approach.   In the introductory approach, the sales person introduces himself to the prospect and states what company he represents. While this approach is by far the most frequently used, it is also probably the weakest because it does little to further the sale. Often sales reps have to use another approach immediately after the introduction. Many prospects are apt to be thinking, "Ok, so you're Sally Gomez of the ABC Company. What are you going to do for me?"

Product approach.   The product approach consists of handing the product to the prospect, with little or no conversation. One salesman selling costume jewelry to department store buyers would walk up to the buyer and lay his leading designs on the desk, saying absolutely nothing. Almost inevitably, the buyer would look over the merchandise and say something like, "Ok, where is the rest of the line, and what's the story?" If the buyer had no use for this type and quality of merchandise, the salesman would know immediately, and little effort would be lost. The product approach can be used most effectively when the product is unique and creates interest on sight.

Consumer-benefit approach.   The sales person starts the sale in a consumer-benefit approach by informing the prospect of what the firm can provide in benefits. Then, he asks if the prospect would be interested in obtaining those benefits. The consumer-benefit approach directs the prospect's attention toward the benefits the firm has to deliver.

One life insurance agent would begin a conversation with a prospect by asking, "How would you like to receive $2,000 a month each month on retirement?" If the prospect admitted that such a sum would be attractive, the agent would reply, "If you will answer a few questions for me, I would like to draw up a plan that would give you just that. But, first, I must have some information about your personal circumstances."

Similarly, many industrial sales reps use the consumer-benefit approach. They start by asking the purchasing agent if the company would like to save a certain amount on a certain process during the coming year. The seller should use the preapproach to determine which benefit would be best to use as the opening for the sale.

---

[2] Frederic A. Russell, Frank Beach, and Richard H. Buskirk, *Selling—Principles and Practices*, 11th ed. (New York: McGraw-Hill, 1982), Chapter 9.

Referral approach. Often the referral approach is successful in getting an audience with a prospect who is difficult to see directly. It consists of obtaining the permission of a past or present customer to use his or her name as a reference in meeting a new prospect. A satisfied customer may even write a short note introducing the sales rep to a friend who is a prospect. This approach works well because the prospect has an immediate bond of friendship with the seller and, out of courtesy to the friend, will hear what the sales rep has to say. A referral will get a hearing, but some other approach must be used to make the transition into the presentation.

The Presentation

The presentation is the main body of the sale. The sales rep presents the product or proposition and shows the prospect its benefits. Trainees should know the characteristics of a good sales presentation. It is built around a forceful product demonstration. All selling points are visualized, and buying motives are dramatized to arouse the prospect's interest and desire. Trainees need to see the necessity of demonstrating everything possible during the presentation. If feasible, the prospect should participate actively in the demonstration. It is far better for a prospect to drive a new car than just be taken for a ride by the sales person, for example.

The advisability of using a prepared sales presentation, better known as a canned sales talk, is a matter of considerable controversy. Without doubt, a prepared presentation done poorly and without feeling is a dismal experience. However, many firms use them with successful results. The prepared presentation has several advantages:

- It gives new sales people confidence.
- It can utilize tested sales techniques that have proved effective.
- It gives some assurance that the complete story will be told.
- It greatly simplifies sales training.

The use of a prepared presentation does *not* mean that the sales person cannot use his or her own words. In many instances, individual thoughts are encouraged. Above all, the sales person's own feeling and personality should be evident in the presentation.

The heart of teaching salesmanship lies in the trainer's ability to provide trainees with the demonstration techniques and visual aids that have proven most effective for the firm. Trainees must be impressed with the importance of the presentation in order to make a successful sale.

In many circumstances, sales reps should not make a sales presentation until the prospect agrees that he needs the product or service and has the money to pay for it. They should establish the need and the money before giving their "show"!

Some claims made during the presentation are aimed at the prospect's likely buying motives. Then, by various techniques, the sales representative endeavors to prove the truth of those claims. If the prospect does not believe the claims made for the product, a sale is unlikely. Thus, the key to an effective presentation is believability.

Throughout the presentation, the sales rep makes *trial closes* in order to determine whether the customer is ready to buy. The customer may have shopped for the product for many months and already decided to purchase it. In such a case, all the sales rep has to do is make the transaction.

Some prospects know early in the sale that they want to buy, whereas others may remain unconvinced for some time. The trial close is used to ascertain just how favorable the prospect is toward the proposition. This can be done by asking such questions as:

- Which of these models do you think you would like best?
- Which color do you prefer?
- How would you like to pay for this—by cash or on terms?
- Now just exactly when would you need this article?

The person who is ready to buy answers such statements readily and positively. A prospect who is not convinced either avoids answering the questions or denies an interest in buying the item. If all goes well in the trial close, the sales representative goes right on into an assumptive close and wraps up the sale. If the sales rep encounters obstacles, however, and detects that the prospect is not convinced, the next phase of selling must be undertaken.

Meeting Objections

Objections are encountered in practically every presentation. They should be welcomed, because they indicate that the prospect has some interest in the proposition. A prospect who is not interested in buying seldom raises any objections. She or he will go along with the presentation silently, but say at the end, "I'm not interested in your deal."

Stated and hidden objections.   Objections can be classified as stated or hidden. Prospects may state their objections to a proposition openly and give the sales person a chance to answer them. This is an ideal circumstance, because everything is out in the open and the

sales person does not need to read the prospect's mind. Unfortunately, in many instances, prospects hide their real reasons for not
buying. Besides having hidden objections, their stated objections
may be phony. A woman may say she does not like the looks of your
product, when she really thinks your price is too high. Unless you
can determine the real barrier to the sale, you won't be able to overcome it.

Trainees should know the two major techniques for discovering
hidden objections. One is to keep the prospect talking by asking probing questions. The other is to use insights gained through experience in selling the product, combined with a knowledge of the
prospect's situation, to perceive the hidden objection.

However, some sales people have developed special methods for
getting the prospect to disclose what is blocking the sale. One saleswoman uses what she calls her "appeal for honesty" tactic. She says
to the reluctant prospect, "You expect me to be honest with you, as
you should. But haven't I the same right—to expect you to be honest
with me? Now honestly, what is bothering you about the proposition?"

Objections to price and product.   Objections to price come in two
categories. Either the prospect is saying that he cannot afford the
price. Or he is saying that the price is too high. Each requires a different approach in answering.

Product objections can be answered best when sales people have
extensive product knowledge of both their own products and competitors'. Without product knowledge, such as that provided for
trainees, the rep may be lost in answering such objections.

The prospect may be misinformed or may not understand some of
the technical aspects of the proposition. In this case, the sales rep
should provide additional information. Sometimes the prospect's objections can be met simply and effectively by altering the product to
suit the customer. A man looking at some long-sleeve dress shirts
with a neck size of 19 objected, "But I hate long sleeves, and these
shirts are always far too big around the body." The salesman replied,
"No problem. We'll cut off the sleeves and take in the body without
charge." The customer was so pleased he bought several shirts, and
the salesman made a $96 sale.

Procrastinating objections.   Procrastinating objections can be difficult to overcome. Some such objections are:

- Let me think about it awhile.
- I have to talk it over with my family.
- I have to wait until next month's paycheck.
- I want to look around some more.

Procrastinating prospects use such excuses to avoid acting on a proposition immediately.

The sales person who can be put off with procrastinating objections will lose far too many sales. In reality, the prospect is just vacillating. If the sale is not closed immediately, it will be lost to a competitor who is more perceptive. One real estate broker allowed a good prospect to think about a house over the weekend. When the broker called on Monday morning, he discovered that another agent had sold his prospect a house on Saturday night.

In door-to-door selling, a sale that cannot be closed on one call usually has little chance of completion. In many industrial sales, however, the prospect cannot be pushed into a sale without creating considerable ill will. Also, the amount of aggressiveness must be modified to fit the prospect and the situation. In some situations, the sales rep must be patient or lose the sale. Some people will not be pushed or rushed.

The general strategy in handling most objections is to avoid arguments at any cost. The trainee should be taught to ask questions that help the prospect clarify his thinking. This provides insights into the precise obstacles that are hindering the sale. Even if prospects are dead wrong, sales reps should never offend them. A sales rep can win an argument only to lose the sale.

The Closing

Up to this point in the selling process, the sales rep has had only one goal—to get the order. If the representative fails to close the presentation properly by asking for an order, all is for naught. Trainees may consider the close the easiest part of the sale to remember. In fact, however, many sales people do everything right until they get to the close, and then they fail to ask for the order. They seem to think the prospect will buy automatically. But often the prospect needs a little urging, and the close provides that impetus.

The assumptive close. Most sales people rely on what is known as the assumptive close, or some variation, as their basic closing technique. In using the assumptive close, they merely assume prospects are going to buy and begin taking orders by asking such questions as:

- Now what size do you want?
- Do you spell your name with an *e* or an *i?*
- What address do you want this delivered to?
- When can we deliver this—today or tomorrow morning?

- Will three dozen be enough, or should I send four?
- When can our engineers talk with your machine operators?

If the prospect answers such questions, the closing is underway.

The physical-action close. When the sales person finishes the presentation, certain physical actions may suggest to the prospect that it's time to sign. Such actions could be as minor as handing the prospect a pen. One carpet salesman had good success by pulling out a tape measure and starting to measure the premises. A saleswoman for a car dealer handed the keys to the prospect to signify "The car is yours now!" The assumptive close of starting to write up the order is a physical action. The physical-action close is merely a nonverbal extension.

Standing-room-only close. The prospect who believes the product is difficult to get may be encouraged to sign the order. If it is true that deliveries are delayed, or if supplies are scarce, the sales rep does the prospect a favor by describing the situation.

The rep might say: "In all honesty I cannot guarantee that we still have the model you want in stock. It is our most popular item and moves out rapidly. If you want it, I'll call the warehouse and see if we have it. OK?" Or, "We have a two-month waiting list for this machine, and it gets longer every day. If you want to get this equipment on line as soon as possible, let me phone in the order right now."

While this closing tactic involves some pressure, this is acceptable as long as it is the truth. The sales person often can't guarantee deliveries or doesn't have what the customer wants. Prospects should always be informed of the supply situation.

The standing-room-only close is a good one to use to overcome procrastinating prospects. The message to them is, "If you wait, you may not be able to buy it."

Trap close. The prospect's objection can sometimes be used to close the sale. The prospect says, "I wouldn't pay more than $10,000 for that car," though it carries a $10,600 ticket. Knowing that the boss will take the $10,000 and be happy, the sales person can say, "That's an awfully low price for that car. But we have nothing to lose by writing up the deal for that amount and seeing if the boss will accept it." Note that the prospect had to agree to buy for $10,000 before the seller accepted the deal.

The trap close can sometimes be used to answer product objections that can be met by altering the product rather than the price. If prospective homeowners do not like a house because it doesn't have a swimming pool, the contractor can quote a price that includes a pool and give the buyers what they want.

Special-offer close.   Some sales managers furnish their sales force with a special customer offer each time around the territory. The 3M Company's Scotch Tape division at one time used this closing tactic. If the special deal were a billfold, the sales rep might say, "If you put in this specially priced dealer display today, we will include this billfold."

Frequently the special offer is a particularly attractive price deal that is good only for a short time. Sears uses this tactic in selling appliances on its "One Day Only" sales. The basic idea is to forestall and overcome prospects' procrastinating objections.

Follow-Up

Trainees should be taught that the sale is not over once they get the order. Good sales representatives follow up in various ways. Immediately after obtaining the order, they reassure the buyer that he or she has made a wise decision. They make certain that they have answered all the buyer's questions and that the buyer understands the details of the contract. If the merchandise is delivered at a later date, they are present at the time of delivery or call soon after to ensure that everything is in order. At this time, they often obtain leads on other good prospects the customer knows.

Good follow-up is the key to building a loyal clientele, which ultimately results in a handsome income for the sales person. Satisfied customers voluntarily provide more business. People truly appreciate being served by good sales people. Once they locate a person who pleases them, they are not likely to forget that individual in the future.

One furniture sales person in a large department store built a tremendous following in his trading area through an excellent follow-up procedure. Immediately after obtaining an order, the salesman did everything possible to expedite delivery of the merchandise. He went to the warehouse and handpicked the customer's pieces to be sure the woods had beautiful grains and were not damaged. He made friends with the truck drivers, so they would see that his orders were delivered on time and in perfect condition. Shortly after the furniture was delivered, he called to see if everything was all right or if anything needed to be returned because it was damaged or defective. He claimed that on four out of five of these calls he sold additional merchandise with little or no effort. Customers simply wanted something else and were so pleased with their treatment that they gave him the order on the spot. The key to great selling lies in delivering satisfaction and making sure that customers are perfectly pleased with their acquisitions.

Summary

The content phase of the sales-training program should begin by stressing the importance of attitudes and work habits. Then the myths of selling should be debunked. Typically, sales-training programs stress product and company knowledge, which can be taught in a rather straight-forward manner. The teaching of selling techniques (the sales process) is a bit more involved. It begins with the critical aspect of prospecting for customers.

Once a prospect is located, preapproach information provides insights about how to develop an effective sales presentation. The presentation should focus on the proposition's benefits to the prospect. Sales reps must make sure that the prospect believes their claims.

Naturally, sales people encounter objections. Honestly stated objections about the product, its price, or the timing of the purchase should be welcomed because they give the sales rep an opportunity to provide answers. Unfortunately, the prospect's true objections are often hidden. Thus they must be discovered either by adroit questioning or insight.

Throughout the presentation, the adept sales rep asks questions such as, "Would this feature be of use to you?" or "When would you need delivery?" to discover if the prospect is ready to buy. If so, then the rep closes the sale. He or she starts writing up the order assuming the sale has been made. Once the customer signs the order, the rep should diligently follow up the sale to make certain that the customer is satisfied.

Questions and Problems

1. You want to improve your selling skills. How would you do so?
2. In what ways does lack of product knowledge hinder a sales rep?
3. Why should a training program cover philosophies and attitudes before actual selling techniques?

4. Develop a good prospecting system for a printing sales rep.
5. What preapproach information you would try to obtain on a prospect for a personal computer. Exactly where would you look for each bit of information?
6. You have accepted a sales job with a large company. After completion of its sales training program, you are assigned a territory on the northwest side of Chicago. After a few calls on both company accounts and new prospects, you realize that you need more training. You are not getting the job done to your satisfaction. What would you do?
7. Develop some good approaches to use in selling a personal computer.
8. What visuals would you develop for selling water softeners to homeowners?
9. What *trial* closes could you use to sell a personal computer?
10. What closes would you use to sell a personal computer?

Case 9-1

Adler Billiard Table Company

Visualizing Quality Construction

Mr. and Mrs. Adler owned and operated the Adler Billiard Table Company of Los Angeles for many years before their retirement in 1986. They manufactured and sold custom pool and billiard tables, most of which were replicas of classic antique tables. (See Exhibit 1.)

They sold the business to Mr. Vinton, who had been impressed by the many fine features of the Adler tables. Mrs. Adler had been the sales person in the front of the large factory, while Mr. Adler supervised production in the back factory (see Exhibit 2). Mrs. Adler had many excellent techniques for persuading prospects to pay premium prices ($2,000 to $7,500) for a custom pool table. The major sales points that she made to each customer were:

1. Adler used only ¾-inch slate from a special quarry in Pennsylvania. It was much more dense than the cheaper Italian slate used by almost all of Adler's competitors.
2. Adler used an especially dense rubber cushion around the table that provided truer caroms for a longer life.
3. The slate was covered with the finest English felt made specially for billiard tables.

Exhibit 1

Adler's celebrity customers are posted on the wall as a means to establish credibility.

4. The tables were made by woodcraftsmen who took particular pride in their work.
5. All bolts were drilled into the slate in such a way that the impact of balls on the rails did not place a shear load on the slate, but rather a lateral impact. Thus the rails would remain firm and true.
6. The tables were exact replicas of classic tables. Some of the tables were genuine antiques that were refurbished.
7. All assessories—cues, balls, leather pockets—were of the highest quality.

While Mrs. Adler had been most persuasive in her sales talk, Mr. Vinton wanted to develop some sales tactics for visualizing all of the firm's sales claims, including the long list of Hollywood celebrities who owned Adler tables.

Exhibit 2

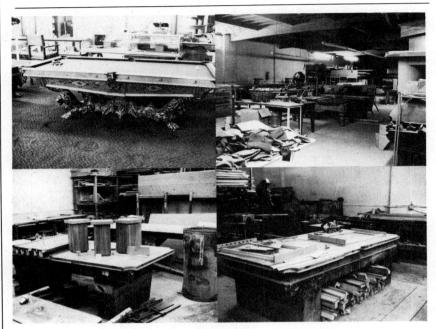

Customers are taken into the plant at the rear of the sales room to be shown the quality features that are built into the tables.

Question

Develop techniques for visualizing each of the company's sales claims.

10

Sales-Force Leadership and Motivation

People are as lazy as they dare to be and most of us are mighty daring.
MARK TWAIN

One hallmark of excellent leaders is their ability to motivate people to give their best efforts each day. It's not an easy task. Work can be boring, and distractions are everywhere. An organization bereft of leadership will accomplish little. Leaders have to develop ways to motivate the organization, particularly its sales force. But first, the sales manager must become a leader.

Leadership[1]

Is leadership essential for a sales manager to be effective? We think so! While management writers decry the lack of strong leadership in American industry today, a truly strong leader is not apt to survive long in large bureaucratic corporations. Such organizations tend to prize the talents of the compliant team player rather than the often disquieting behavior of leaders. Yet someone must be in charge of each organizational unit and provide the necessary leadership.

Leadership is neither easily nor clearly definable. It is a combination of many personal and managerial behaviors. An individual's leadership qualities can't always be judged by the performance of the person's administrative unit. The saving grace of many organizations is that their people get the job done in spite of poor leadership. But how often, how well, and at what cost? Leadership is the managerial ingredient that makes organizations more effective.

[1] For an excellent treatment of leadership, see Warren Bennis and Burt Nanus, *Leadership* (New York: Harper & Row, 1985).

But what is leadership? At least six major sets of personal traits affect leadership potential. For the sake of brevity, let's call them:

- Confidence.
- Energy.
- Creativity.
- Social skills.
- Physical characteristics.
- Persuasive skills.

Of course, managers also have leadership bestowed on them by their power position in the organizational hierarchy.[2] Until the manager proves otherwise, a certain amount of leadership capability—positional power—comes with the job. But we are interested in leadership factors not inherent in a position.

Confidence

The confidence a staff has in a manager's leadership capabilities is a function of three factors.

1. The manager's record of achievement.
2. The manager's knowledge.
3. The manager's behavior on the job.

Leaders act like leaders; they take charge.

Energy

Leaders are industrious. Some people blessed with high energy levels seem to rise to positions of leadership. They are the ones who step forward when something needs to be done. Naturally, such people are very healthy. It is difficult to have much energy when you are not feeling well. Generally, a leader is expected to take the initiative, and people with energy do.

Creativity

Leaders need some creativity and imagination. The organization looks to its leaders for solutions to its problems, and that often entails creativity and new approaches.

Social Skills

Social skills bear heavily on leadership capabilities. Leaders establish good working relationships with their people. That does not

[2] Paul Busch, "The Sales Manager's Bases of Social Power and Influence upon the Sales Force." *Journal of Marketing,* Summer 1980, pp. 91–101.

mean that they become good friends with them. Often they cannot and should not. Instead, they develop a good business relationship.

Physical Characteristics

Considerable evidence suggests that physical attributes bear significantly on a person's rise to leadership positions. Research indicates that large people tend to dominate small people merely by sheer size, and thus assume a position of leadership over them. It has been said of more than one college president that he "looks like what a college president ought to look like." Talents are not mentioned. It is as if the proper image were sufficient. While many physical attributes are beyond a person's control, grooming, appearance, and physical condition are not.

Persuasive Skills

Good leaders rely more on persuasion than power. They persuade people to do what they want them to do. Often that is not an easy task. Moreover, leaders are deal-makers. They make deals with all the people they do business with.

Motivation—What Is It?

Coaches want their athletes to do well in a game. Symphony orchestra directors want their musicians to play well. Parents want their children to reach certain performance levels in school, at home, and in society. The director of a play wants the actors to captivate the audience. And, sales-force managers want their sales people to reach assigned performance levels.

The question in each of these situations is—how do you get people to do what you want them to do? The answer is—you motivate them. Or, looking at these situations from the standpoint of the people involved—what makes workers exert the effort needed to reach the expected performance levels? The answer is—they are motivated.

To better understand the behavioral concept of motivation, let's first ask—why do people act as they do? Or, why does a person act at all? The answer is, because he or she is motivated. That is, all behavior starts with motivation. A *motive* is a stimulated need that an individual seeks to satisfy. Hunger, a need for security, or a desire for prestige are examples of motives.

Once a need is aroused (or stimulated) in a person, then the person's goal is to satisfy that aroused need. *The force that activates this goal-oriented behavior is what we call motivation.*

A motivating force may originate within a person, or it may be initiated by somebody or some thing external. For example, you may simply become hungry (internal motivation). Or you may see an ad for food, and your hunger is stimulated (external motivation).

Now let's apply these concepts in a sales-force setting. Various *internal* drives can motivate sales people. Their goal-oriented behavior may be activated by a strong personal pride or by a desire for self-respect. Or sales people can be motivated by *external* forces. Management may trigger effective goal-oriented behavior by providing a good compensation plan or opportunities for advancement.

Motivation and Strategic Planning

The role of motivation in implementing the strategic planning can influence the entire thrust of management's sales efforts. When Dave Hughes founded Herbalife, a highly successful direct seller of food supplements, he based his entire management philosophy on building a large, highly motivated, multilevel sales force. He relies on frequent and strongly motivational sales meetings. This strategy works . . . for Herbalife.

On the other hand, Bill Scarbourgh—owner of 16 Burger King franchise outlets in Northern California—does little to motivate his sales people. He pays minimum wages: the economics of the situation won't allow more. Turnover is 500 percent a year. He hires anyone who can come through the door to apply. And he is also highly successful. He relies on Burger King's operating system to make a profit.

In some selling situations, highly motivated sales people would be a detriment. They could alienate customers with undue sales pressure. However, such sales people require yet another type of motivation—a strong desire to succeed and do their job properly. Motivation does not mean that the reps must be pressured to push goods onto the customers. Consequently, in its strategic planning, management should consider how much and what kind of motivation its reps need.

Importance and Difficulty of Motivation

Sales executives generally agree that effective motivation of a sales force is essential to the success of any selling organization. It is probably obvious that strong and properly selected motivational forces are likely to lead to high levels of performance. Conversely, if the motivational forces are weak, or the wrong ones are used, then the performance level is likely to be lower.

The problem is that most sales executives usually have difficulty in determining what constitutes *effective* motivation in their own sales forces. That is, "Finding the right combination of motivators is extremely tough."[3] There are three fundamental reasons why it is so difficult to come up with the right combination of motivators.

Individuality of Sales People

The first of these three reasons lies in the individuality of each sales rep. Each rep has his or her own personal goals, problems, strengths, and weaknesses. Each rep may respond differently to a given motivating force. Yet management must develop one motivational mix that applies to a whole group. Ideally, the company should develop a separate motivational package for each sales rep. But obviously this tailor-made approach poses major practical problems.

A related point is that sales reps themselves may not know why they react as they do to a given motivator. Motivating forces may be grouped on three levels depending on (1) a sales person's awareness of them and (2) his or her willingness to divulge them. At one level, sales reps recognize, and are quite willing to talk about, what motivates them to perform a certain way. They may openly admit, for example, that they are working hard because they want to make a lot of money.

At a second level, the reps are aware of their reasons for performing certain selling tasks. But the reps will not admit to other people what these reasons are. A sales person may engage in certain selling tasks because it satisfies his ego. Rather than admit this, however, he will say that he is motivated by a desire to serve his customers.

The third level of motivation is the most difficult one to identify. At this level even the sales reps themselves do not know what motivating forces really account for their performance. For example, a sales engineer for a large semiconductor manufacturer was criticized by the sales manager for her inability to sell to, and her apparent

---

[3] Mary Lynn Miller, *Motivating the Sales Force,* Information Bulletin 64 (New York: The Conference Board, 1979), p. 2. Some of this section is adapted from this source.

unwillingness to call on, the buyers for very large companies. After much discussion of the problem, the manager finally concluded that she was avoiding those buyers because they were intimidating her in many subtle but effective ways. Early in her career, a series of uncomfortable calls on large firms produced nothing but failure. Results of these early calls conditioned her to avoid the discomfort of calling on such buyers.

Conflict in Company Goals

Often a company's sales goals conflict with each other. Under these circumstances, developing an effective combination of motivational methods is difficult. To correct an imbalanced inventory, management will need one combination of motivators. At the same time, management may want the sales people to do some missionary selling to strengthen long-term customer relations. This second goal is somewhat in conflict with the first one and consequently calls for a different set of motivating forces.

Changes in the Market Environment

Changes in the market environment can make it difficult for management to develop the right mix of sales-force motivational methods. What motivates the reps today may not work next month because of changes in market conditions. Conversely, sales executives can face motivational problems when market conditions remain stable for an extended period of time. In this situation, if management continues to use the same motivators, they may lose their effectiveness. The sales force may become bored with the "same old stimulators."

Behavioral Concepts in Motivation

Finding an effective combination of motivators may be easier if a sales executive understands some of the behavioral factors that affect sales-force motivation. In particular, these are (1) the unique nature of the sales job, (2) the ambiguity and conflict in a sales person's job, (3) the sales person's self-concept, and (4) job satisfaction.

Unique Nature of the Sales Job

The factors that make a sales job different from other jobs were discussed in the first chapter of this book. Since sales jobs frequently require a considerable amount of travel, sales people spend much time away from their homes and families. They deal with an apparently endless stream of customers who seem determined not to buy. Many of these customers are gracious, courteous, and thoughtful in their dealings with the sales people. But there are some customers who are rude, demanding, and even threatening. Selling is hard work, and the frustrations and discouragements can take their toll. Consequently, to reach the performance level management desires, sales people typically require more motivation than is needed in most jobs.

Role Ambiguity and Conflict

Sales people usually work with little or no direct supervision. Moreover, much of the job activity involves dealing with people outside the company—namely, the customers. As a result, there can be considerable ambiguity and conflict in the sales person's role. This role ambiguity and conflict, in turn, is a major influence on sales-force morale and motivation.

The fact that sales people generally operate without close supervision is probably the major contributor to role ambiguity. Often sales people are not sure what is expected of them. For example, reps may be uncertain of their authority to meet price competition or grant credit. They may have questions about expense account items, especially their use of company funds to entertain customers. Sales people may be unclear about their organizational relationships with staff executives. For example, a marketing research manager or a credit manager may ask the reps to perform some duties in the field.

Role conflict stems primarily from the fact that a sales rep is trying to serve two masters—the company and the customer. Because these two often have different and conflicting interests, a rep can get caught in the middle. For example, a customer wants lenient credit terms, but the credit manager wants to deal in short-term credit with stringent terms. Or a customer expects gifts and lavish entertainment, but the rep's management, fearful of accusations of bribery, wants to cut back on these items.

As sales reps travel through their territory, they may tend to identify with their customers. Then when the reps come back to their company office, they must identify with the company. They experience an advocacy conflict. They must represent their company when dealing with a customer, and represent their customers when dealing with the home office.[4]

[4] For more on role conflict and ambiguity, see James A. Belasco, "The Salesman's Role Revisited," *Journal of Marketing,* April 1966, pp. 6–11; Orville C. Walker, Jr., Gilbert A. Churchill, Jr., and Neil M. Ford, "Organizational Determinants of the Industrial Salesman's Role Conflict and Ambiguity," *Journal of Marketing,* January 1975, pp. 32–39; and Ford, Walker, and Churchill, "Expectation-Specific Measures of the Intersender Conflict and Role Ambiguity Experienced by Industrial Salesmen," *Journal of Business Research*, April 1975, pp. 95–112.

A Sales Person's Self-Concept

Another consideration affecting sales-force motivation is the sales person's self-concept or self-image. Your self-image is the way you see yourself. At the same time, it is the picture you think others have of you. Some psychologists distinguish between (1) the *actual* self-concept, (the way you really see yourself) and (2) the *ideal* self-concept (the way you want to be seen or would like to see yourself). A person's self-image is influenced by innate and learned physiological and psychological needs. It is also conditioned by economic factors, demographic factors, and social-group influences.

A sales person's self-image influences his or her goals, and those goals, in turn, influence that person's behavior. Therefore, to effectively motivate a sales person, an executive should identify that person's goals. In many situations, a sales manager can identify these goals *if* (and it is a big "if") the executive knows what that person's self-image is.

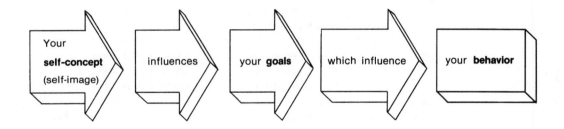

Your **self-concept** (self-image) → *influences* → your **goals** → *which influence* → your **behavior**

Job Satisfaction

Sales managers want the sales people to be satisfied with their jobs. Unhappy workers are not likely to be as productive as happy ones. Certainly job satisfaction is closely related to sales-force motivation. It is difficult to motivate dissatisfied people.

A circular relationship exists between job satisfaction and motivation because job satisfaction leads to effective motivation, and effective motivation leads to job satisfaction. Thus job satisfaction is both a cause and an effect of motivation. Sales reps must be satisfied with their jobs for motivational methods to be effective. That is, job satisfaction is a *cause* or basis of motivation. Likewise, effective motivation can contribute to job satisfaction. That is, job satisfaction is an *effect,* or result, of motivation.

In all of these relationships, note that we are referring to positive motivational methods. An organization can use negative motivational methods, such as fear or threats, and effectively motivate people who are dissatisfied with their jobs. Thus a teenager may do a household chore, albeit unhappily, if the alternative is to lose car privileges for the weekend.

There are some interesting generalizations regarding the relationship between job satisfaction and performance levels. Job satisfaction usually is a *prerequisite* for high performance, but it is not a *guarantee* of achieving high performance. Thus you usually cannot have high performance without job satisfaction. Sales people who are unhappy in their work are unlikely to reach the performance goals desired by management.

However, the opposite is not necessarily true. That is, having satisfied sales reps does not necessarily ensure high performance. Sometimes sales people are contented with their status quo. They are happy with their pay and work conditions and are not willing to put out the extra effort to reach higher performance levels.[5]

Again, note that these statements are generalizations. In some cases, people hate their jobs but work hard because they need the money. Here the positive motivator of money offsets the negative motivator of job dissatisfaction.

Throughout this discussion, we implicitly treated the concept of job satisfaction as a single factor related to sales-force motivation. Actually, the concept is a composite of several factors, each of which influences the degree of job satisfaction. Some of these factors that affect job satisfaction are as follows:

1. The nature of the job. Is it routine or challenging? Can you measure your accomplishment?
2. The pay. Does it provide security and incentive? Is the amount of pay competitive with other jobs and companies?
3. Opportunities for advancement.
4. The people you work with.
5. The nature of supervision and the supervisors. How closely are you supervised? How well do the supervisors communicate with you?

---

[5] See R. Kenneth Teas and James F. Horrell, "Salespeople Satisfaction and Performance Feedback," *Industrial Marketing Management,* February 1981, pp. 49–57; and Gilbert A. Churchill, Jr., Neil M. Ford, and Orville C. Walker, Jr., "Organizational Climate and Job Satisfaction in the Salesforce," *Journal of Marketing Research,* November 1976, pp. 323–32.

Two studies failed to find any relationship between job satisfaction and job performance as measured by annual sales. See Richard P. Bagozzi, "Sales Force Performance and Satisfaction as a Function of Individual Difference, Interpersonal, and Situational Factors," *Journal of Marketing Research,* November 1978, pp. 517–31; and John Hafer and Barbara A. McCuen, "Antecedents of Performance and Satisfaction in a Service Sales Force as Compared to an Industrial Sales Force," *Journal of Personal Selling and Sales Management,* November 1985, pp. 7–17. Also see James M. Corner and Alan Dubinsky, *Managing the Successful Sales Force* (Lexington, Mass.: Lexington Books, 1985), Chap. 7, for research on the role of job satisfaction in selling.

6. Nature of the sales training. This includes both induction and continuation training.
7. The physical environment of the job. Is it in a pleasant location? Are living conditions pleasant in the community?
8. The nature of customer relations. Do you like your customers? Do they respect you?
9. The social prestige or status of the sales job.

Psychological Theories of Motivation

Earlier we said that a motive is an aroused need that triggers behavior to satisfy that need. Stated another way—motivation is the force that triggers the goal-oriented behavior. The problem is that it is often very difficult to identify the need a person is trying to satisfy with his or her behavior. The behavior is usually an overt act that is easy to interpret. What we do not know is the motive behind the act.

To illustrate, three sales reps are engaging in the same behavior. They are striving to open new accounts or to push their sales of high-margin products. But each is doing so for a different reason. The first rep's motive (aroused need) is to impress her boss so she will be promoted. The second rep's need is to solidify his hold on the job, so he can provide financial security for his family. The third rep is new on the job and wants to be accepted by his fellow sales people.

In an alternative situation, three reps may have the same motivation but use different behavioral paths. They each want to get promoted or at least be recognized by management. One tries to satisfy this need by keeping his selling expenses low. Another tries to increase the average size of her orders. The third rep performs extra missionary selling activities. However, management may erroneously conclude that each is trying to satisfy a different need.

Management has to know what a sales person's needs are before the executives can determine how best to motivate that rep. Motivational programs often fail because they appeal to the wrong motives. What will motivate one company's sales force may fail in another simply because the two sales forces have different sets of needs.

Even psychologists can't agree on a theory to explain why people behave as they do. In fact, no single definition of motivation is generally accepted by psychologists. Thus, we have several psychological theories of motivation. Three of these may be particularly useful for sales managers: (1) Maslow's hierarchy of needs, (2) Herzberg's motivation-hygiene theory, and (3) the expectancy theory developed by Vroom and others.

Hierarchy-of-Needs Theory

A. H. Maslow formulated a theory of motivation based on the idea that humans seek to fulfill their personal needs in an orderly fashion.[6] He identified five levels of needs, arranged in the order in which a person seeks to satisfy them. This hierarchy is shown in Figure 10–1.

Maslow contended that people remain at one level until all their needs at that level are satisfied. Then new needs emerge on the next higher level. To illustrate, as long as a person is hungry or thirsty, the physiological needs dominate. Once they have been satisfied, the need for safety becomes important. When safety needs have been gratified, new and higher-level needs arise, and so on.

For the relatively few people who move through all five levels, Maslow identified two additional classes of cognitive needs:

- The need to know and understand.
- The need for aesthetic satisfaction (beauty).

Maslow recognized that there is more flexibility in real life than his model implies. Actually a normal person is most likely to be working toward need satisfaction on several levels at the same time. And rarely are all needs on a given level ever fully satisfied.

While the Maslow construct has much to offer, it still leaves unanswered questions and disagreements. There is no consideration of multiple motives for the same behavior. A sales person, for example, may strive to exceed his or her sales quota for several reasons—to make more money, to improve the chances of getting a promotion, or to get favorable recognition from top management. Other problems not fitting our model were noted earlier. For example, identical behavior by several people may result from quite different motives, and quite different behavior may result from identical motives.

However, Maslow's theory can still serve as a practical guide for sales managers in several ways. As an example, a sales executive can try to determine what need level a given sales rep is now on. Then the executive can develop a motivational package to satisfy those needs. Presumably these motivational tools will also channel the rep's behavior so it is in line with management's overall sales-force goals.

[6] A. H. Maslow, *Motivation and Personality*, 2d ed. (New York: Harper & Row, 1970), chapters 3–7.

Figure 10–1
Maslow's Hierarchy of Needs

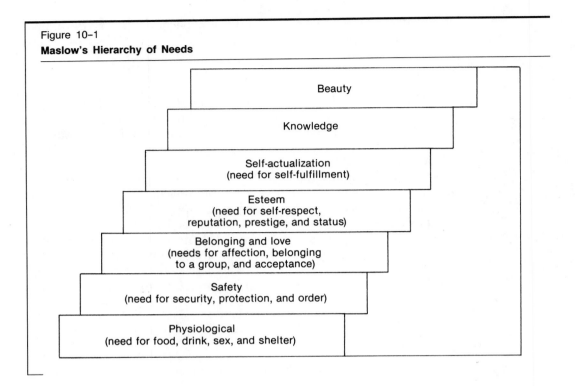

From Maslow's theory, management can learn that money's effectiveness as a motivator declines as we go up the need hierarchy. Money is important to satisfy physiological needs and safety-security needs. However, to satisfy higher-level needs such as self-esteem, management needs to offer something such as recognition awards or promotion to a higher-status position.

Motivation-Hygiene Theory

The motivation-hygiene theory, as developed by Frederick Herzberg is somewhat similar to Maslow's theory.[7] That is, both theories are based on the idea that people have needs that they will seek to satisfy with their behavior. However, the Herzberg model recognizes only two levels of needs—motivator needs (the higher level) and hygiene needs (the lower level). Examples of the needs included in each category are as follows:

[7] Frederick Herzberg, Bernard Mausner, and Barbara B. Snyderman, *The Motivation to Work,* 2d ed. (New York: John Wiley & Sons, 1959).

Motivator Needs	*Hygiene Needs*
The work itself	Salary and fringe benefits
Recognition	Work conditions
Achievement	Job security
Responsibility	Relations with peers, superiors, and subordinates
	Company policy

Herzberg's motivator needs are comparable to Maslow's higher-level needs such as self-actualization and self-esteem. The hygiene needs are more basic.

Herzberg develops a rather unusual relationship between his two levels of needs and the concepts of job satisfaction and dissatisfaction. He contends that job satisfaction is *not* the opposite of job dissatisfaction. Rather, these are quite separate concepts, each related to a different set of needs. Job *satisfaction* is associated primarily with motivator needs, and job *dissatisfaction* is related mainly to hygiene needs.

These relationships operate in a rather unusual fashion. If a worker's hygiene needs are not met, that person experiences job dissatisfaction. If the hygiene needs are fulfilled, however, the worker does not experience job satisfaction. Instead, the worker simply reaches a neutral zone—an average performance level. There is neither job satisfaction nor dissatisfaction.

In a similar vein, if the worker's motivator needs are fulfilled, the person experiences job satisfaction. If the motivator needs are not met, again we are in the neutral zone—there is neither job satisfaction nor dissatisfaction. The following diagram may explain these relationships more clearly.

Need Level	*Need Fulfilled*	*Worker's Reaction*
Motivator	Yes →	Job satisfaction
	No →	No satisfaction; but also no dissatisfaction
Hygiene	No →	Job dissatisfaction
	Yes →	No dissatisfaction; but also no satisfaction

Herzberg recognized that there may be some overlapping in these relationships. That is, fulfilling either level of needs can increase job satisfaction or decrease dissatisfaction. However, he contends that (1) the motivator needs–job satisfaction and (2) the hygiene needs–job dissatisfaction relationships are the ones that generally exist.

In a practical sense, what does all this mean to a sales manager? It suggests that executives should make certain that the hygiene needs are met, so that there is no job dissatisfaction. This means making certain that the compensation is satisfactory, the working conditions are good, and there are effective channels of communication between management and the sales force.

But the hygiene factors alone can only remove job dissatisfaction. They cannot generate job satisfaction. Therefore, executives should strive to fulfill a sales person's motivator needs. To get top performance, sales managers should provide the sales force with opportunities for recognition, advancement, personal growth, and increased responsibility.

Expectancy Theory

The so-called expectancy theory of sales-force motivation is perhaps more realistic and certainly more complex than the two need-oriented theories already discussed. Expectancy theory goes beyond a consideration of sales people's biological and sociopsychological needs.

In the expectancy theory, needs alone do not explain human behavior. Instead, a two-step sequence of expectations motivates people to work harder. In Step 1, people expect that if they work hard, they will accomplish a given task (i.e., achieve their goal). In Step 2, having achieved their goal, they expect that the rewards will be worth the effort.

Stated formally, expectancy theory involves a consideration of:

1. A sales person's goals.
2. The alternative performance paths to these goals.
3. The probability that each of these alternatives will achieve the desired performance level.
4. The rep's perception of how appropriate management's rewards are for the effort expended and results achieved.

The expectancy theory as used to explain the motivation and behavior of sales people is based on the work of Victor Vroom and others before him.[8] The title word "expectancy" relates to the notion that sales people have expectations of what they should get from management for their performance efforts and results. Procedurally, the theory explains why a sales person selects a certain behavioral path as he strives to reach his goal.

To illustrate expectancy theory in a sales-force setting, let's walk through the four points listed earlier. A sales person is mulling over

---

[8] Victor H. Vroom, *Work and Motivation* (New York: John Wiley & Sons, 1964); Edward C. Tolman, *Purposive Behavior in Animals and Men* (New York: Appleton-Century-Crofts, 1932); and Kurt Lewin, *The Conceptual Representation and the Measurement of Psychological Forces* (Durham, N.C.: Duke University Press, 1938).

the four points in the course of making personal decisions and value judgments. This entire expectancy process is often done very quickly and may even be a subconscious thought process.

1. What are my goals? Let's assume my goal during the next sales period is to reach a sales volume of 20 percent over my assigned quota. (I perceive that achieving this goal will satisfy my needs for self-esteem and recognition by management. Note the tie to the needs-oriented theories of Maslow and Herzberg.)

2. What are some alternative behavioral paths to this goal? There are several courses of action I can take to reach my goal. I can simply work more hours each week. I can spend more time calling on my large-order accounts. I can spend more time and effort developing business from new accounts. I can even try a little high-pressure selling, although this may boomerang on me in the long run. These are only a few of the behavioral choices that I might consider. My choice will depend largely on my answers to the next two questions— namely, what are my chances of success, and are the rewards worth the effort?

3. What are my chances of success? I now figure the probability of success for each of the alternative behavioral paths. My inclination to concentrate on large-order customers will be much stronger if I am convinced that this path has the greatest probability of success. Obviously, I want to channel my efforts where I think the results will be greatest.

4. Are the rewards worth the effort? Let's assume that whatever path I took, I did reach my sales goal. This fourth question has two parts: (1) Is there any reward from management and (2) if so, what value do I place on the reward?

Let's say the reward is a congratulatory pat on the back from management and a formal recognition award for the best sales performance of the period. I am working under a straight-salary compensation plan, so I get no financial reward. I might even have my quota increased for the next period.

This honor award is fine if I am bucking for a promotion or if I want to boost my status with management and my co-workers. On the other hand, such recognition will be a disappointment if what I really want is a nice bonus or a salary increase for my fine sales performance.

At the end of this expectancy-thought process, I may decide that the reward for reaching my goal is not worth the effort. So I might select a different goal and start another evaluation process.

Expectancy theory obviously has several managerial implications. Executives should try to understand their sales people's goals. A sales manager should discuss goals with each sales rep to see if they are realistically attainable. Managers can then point out the goal-seeking behavioral paths with the greatest probability of success. Improving the sales reps' performance in various behavioral paths can be incorporated into sales-training programs. Management should establish a reward structure likely to be attractive to a given group or level of sales people.[9]

Selecting Effective Combination of Motivational Tools

Management must determine the most effective combination of tools or methods to use in motivating the sales force. Motivational tools may be divided into two categories. The first are the general motivators that typically are essential for a successful program in any sales force. The second group contains the more specific types of motivators that management can use when developing a tailor-made program for a given company.

General Motivators for Any Sales Force

Three motivational elements must be included in any company's sales-force motivational program. The three are (1) an appropriate managerial attitude toward the sales force, (2) effective communication between management and the sales force, and (3) a clear understanding of the sales job. Without all three of these elements, it is highly unlikely that management can effectively motivate its sales force. That is, these elements must exist before other, more specific motivational tools will work. Motivators such as the contests or compensation plans are not worth much if the sales reps do not believe their executives, are not clear about the job, or feel they cannot communicate with management.

Appropriate managerial attitude toward sales people. The general attitude of management—the image that the executives project to the sales force—is extremely critical to the success of sales-force motivation. Management must be credible to the sales people. The reps must be thoroughly convinced that the executives are honest in their dealings with the sales force, and that they truly care about the well-being of the sales people.[10]

---

[9] For an excellent summary of expectancy-theory research, see Kenneth R. Evans, Loren Margheim, and John L. Schlacter, "A Review of Expectancy Theory Research in Selling," *Journal of Personal Selling & Sales Management,* November 1982, pp. 33–40.

[10] See Stephen X. Doyle, Charles Pignatelli, and Karen Florman, "The Hawthorne Legacy and the Motivation of Salespeople," *Personal Selling & Sales Management,* November 1985, pp. 1–6.

A day-to-day operating problem in the
Majestic Glass Company (E)

Motivating the Sales Force to Recapture Lost Business

Although Clyde Brion, the general sales manager, was not surprised, he was irritated at lunch one day when he was served milk in a paper container in Majestic's plant cafeteria. He went to the cafeteria manager and asked why milk was no longer obtained in bottles, since bottles were a product of Majestic. The cafeteria manager winced, then laughed and said, "Well, Clyde, the cat's out of the bag now! There hasn't been a milk bottle shipped into this cafeteria in over two years. No dairy in this part of the country uses bottles anymore. My girls have been pouring the milk out of the bulk cans or paper cartons into some bottles that I got from the factory. We kept using the same bottles over and over. I guess someone slipped up today and put some cartons on the serving line. Here, let me get you a bottle!"

Back at his office, Brion looked over some sales records that confirmed the cafeteria manager's statements. There had been a rapid drop in Majestic's sales of glass milk bottles in all territories.

Brion was also aware that many other products formerly packaged in glass were now being sold in containers made of other materials. Many beverage companies were primarily using metal cans. Many liquids used in house cleaning, laundry, personal care, and even food preparation were now packaged in something other than bottles. For these products, the producers were using aerosol cans, squeeze bottles made of plastic, or plastic film or aluminum foil.

On the other hand, many customers still preferred glass containers. They liked to be able to see the contents through the wall of the container. Also, glass carried an assurance of sterile-packaging methods. Glass containers were chemically inert against almost any product they might hold. This claim could not be made for any other packaging material. Reuse of the glass container was important in some product lines, especially milk bottles. Glass was also 100 percent recyclable, and hence was less objectionable to environmental conservation critics than other packaging. For bottlers, glass had a cost advantage, especially where there was a large investment in machinery to bottle products in glass.

Brion believed that the company must exert extra sales effort (1) to hold present customers for glass containers and (2) to win back those who had adopted nonglass packages for their products. He was planning how he could use his sales force in this extra effort.

Question

What action should Brion take with his sales force to recapture the accounts lost to competitive products?

Note: See the introduction to this series of problems in Chapter 3 for the necessary background on the company, its market, and its competition.

A pat on the back—the universal motivator
Everybody is motivated by a pat on the back. For each individual,
however, the effectiveness of this motivator is influenced by:
1. The tool the pat is applied with (a hand, foot, or something else);
2. How hard the pat is applied; and
3. How high or low on the back it is applied.

Effective communication between management and sales force. A fundamental prerequisite for sales-force motivation is an effective communication system between the executives and the sales people. The channels of communication must be open and clear both from management down to the sales force and from the sales force up to management. Nothing can destroy morale faster than a communications breakdown. This point is discussed further in Chapter 15.

Clear understanding of the sales job. Earlier in this chapter we noted that job ambiguity is a major reason why management's motivation task is so difficult. For any motivational program to be successful, the sales people must clearly understand all aspects of their job. The reps need a detailed job description and a careful explanation of what is expected from them. They need to understand how their accomplishments will be evaluated. The sooner they receive performance feedback, the more effective it will be.[11]

Specific Motivators

Given the general motivators just discussed, management then has a wide variety of more specific elements to select from when developing the motivational mix. Earlier in the chapter we noted the importance of developing an individualized motivational program for each company's situation. Sales people attach different values to the various motivational tools, depending on their age, marital status, length of service with the company, earnings level, and career stage. People in the early stage of their career typically have different psychological and social needs than people in mid-career or those nearing retirement. Consequently, the motivational tools management uses will vary depending on the person's career stage.[12]

Several specific motivators are outlined in Figure 10–2. For any of

[11] See Stephen X. Doyle and Benson P. Shapiro, "What Counts Most in Motivating Your Sales Force?" *Harvard Business Review,* May–June 1980, pp. 133–40.

[12] For an excellent review of the literature on sales-career stages and their relation to sales-force motivation and behavior, see William L. Cron, "Industrial Salesperson Development: A Career Stages Perspective," *Journal of Marketing,* Fall 1984, pp. 41–52.

Figure 10–2
Specific Elements in Motivation Mix

1. Basic compensation plan
   a. Salary
   b. Commissions
   c. Bonus payments
   d. Fringe benefits
2. Nonfinancial rewards
   a. Recognition awards, such as pins, trophies, certificates
   b. Praise and encouragement from management
3. Opportunity for promotion (this is both a financial and nonfinancial reward)
4. Sales contests
5. Sales meetings and conventions
6. Supervision—in person, by mail, by telephone
7. Sales-training programs—induction and continuation
8. Sales-planning elements
   a. Forecasts
   b. Budgets
   c. Quotas
   d. Territories
9. Evaluation of sales person's performance
10. General-management elements
   a. Organizational structure
   b. Management's leadership style

these specific elements to be effective as motivators, they must be accurately, realistically, and carefully set up. The wide variety and scope of these motivators cover most of the topics discussed in this book. Motivation permeates the entire field of sales-force management.

Negative Motivators—Fear

Except for one brief comment, this entire chapter has dealt with positive motivation. However, many people are motivated—and often very effectively—by the negative motivator that we call *fear.* For years, various companies have used fear appeals in marketing their products. Nonbusiness organizations such as the American Cancer Society and the American Heart Association try to scare people into stopping smoking. People are warned of the dangers of combining drinking and driving. A person is pictured as a social outcast for not using the advertised brand of toothpaste or deodorant.

When managing a sales force, fear also can be an effective motivator. A sales person may be motivated by the fear of losing his job or the fear of suffering a pay cut.

How effective is fear as a motivator in influencing sales people's performances? In our opinion, fear is more effective in the short run. With a smile and a gun, you can make a person do a job, but you cannot make him like it. People can run scared for a short time, but eventually they simply get tired and stop performing. Even the fear of losing your job can only carry your performance so far. At some point, management must stop relying on the negative motivator of fear and use more positive motivational tools.

Which Motivator Is Most Important?

No single answer to this question fits all companies or sales forces. However, we think the top motivator for most sales forces is money. We grant that this choice is a broad generalization with many exceptions.

In fact, perhaps the best answer to the question heading this section is—it all depends. As indicated earlier, the values placed on specific motivators can be influenced by personal factors such as a sales rep's age or marital status. Certainly the current earnings level of the sales people will influence their ranking of motivators. A rep earning $20,000 a year is likely to rate the compensation plan as a more important motivator than will the rep earning $50,000 a year.[13]

Status, prestige, and recognition awards are more likely to motivate the rep who has had high earnings for many years. This situation parallels society in general. Many people in the United States are concerned about environmental pollution and the quality of life. That is, they become concerned about these issues *after* they have acquired a supply of worldly goods—*after* they have plenty of money to feed, clothe, house, and educate their families. People in developing nations are too concerned with getting a job and avoiding starvation to worry much about air and water pollution.

Another factor influencing the rating of motivators is a sales person's career goals. A person who wants a career as a sales rep is probably more concerned with the compensation plan than is a rep who views the sales job as a stepping-stone to management.

Self-Motivators

Historically, management has sought to hire self-motivated sales people. Management wanted to put them into the field and have them do the job on their own. The sales rep was supposed to provide his or her own motivation.

---

[13] See Leon Winer and J. S. Schiff, "Industrial Salespeople's Views on Motivation," *Industrial Marketing Management,* October 1980, pp. 319–23.

Many people are self-motivated. They are able to achieve high levels of performance with little help from others. Their goals are internally generated and they will put forth considerable extra effort to achieve them.

Unfortunately for both management and the human race, self-motivators are in exceedingly short supply. Most managements find they not only have to supply their people with goals, but also show them what they will have to do to reach those goals. One sales manager believes in making his new sales recruits hungry for the good life. He reasons that most of the people he hires have not known much but poverty. They don't know what money will buy and what it can do. So he makes them want that lifestyle by treating them royally during the selection process and training. They stay at luxury hotels. He entertains them at his mansion several times so they can observe what can happen to successful sales people. "I want to make them thoroughly dissatisfied with the way they have been living. I want to deliver the message that if they will do as I tell them and work hard, they can live as well as I do."

Summary

Leadership is essential for sales managers to be effective. Six sets of personal traits that affect a person's leadership potential are confidence, energy, creativity, social skills, physical characteristics, and persuasive skills.

The reason that people act as they do is because they are motivated. That is, all human behavior starts with motivation. Motivation is the force that activates goal-oriented behavior as a person strives to satisfy an aroused need. This motivating force may originate *within* a person, or be stimulated *externally* by somebody or something.

Sales executives generally agree that effective motivation of a sales force is essential to the success of any sales organization. The problem lies in finding the right combination of motivators for any given group of sales people. Sales-force motivation is difficult because each rep is an individual who responds differently to a given motivator. Another motivational difficulty occurs when there is a conflict in management's sales goals. Finally, changes in the market or selling environment pose motivational problems.

The following four behavioral determinants affect sales-force motivation: (1) the unique nature of a sales job, (2) the factors of role ambiguity and role conflict, (3) a sales person's self-concept (self-image), and (4) the factor of job satisfaction, which can be both a cause and an effect of worker motivation.

An understanding of three psychological theories of motivation can guide a sales executive in setting up a motivational program. Two of these theories are directly related to a person's quest for need satisfaction. These are Maslow's hierarchy-of-needs theory and Herzberg's motivation-hygiene theory. The third theory—the expectancy theory—is based on the idea that sales people have expectations of what they should get from management as a reward for their performance. As a process, the theory explains why a sales person selects a certain behavioral path as he strives to reach his goal.

Management's task is to select the right combination of motivators—the right motivational mix—for a given sales force. Three broad, general motivators must be included in any sales-force motivation program. They are (1) an appropriate managerial attitude toward the sales people, (2) effective communication between management and the sales force, and (3) a clear understanding of the sales job and how the rep's performance will be evaluated.

Beyond these general motivators, management can use a wide variety of more specific motivational tools to build an effective motivational mix. No single motivator always ranks number 1 in effectiveness. However, the compensation plan (money) probably ranks highest for most sales forces over a period of years.

Questions and Problems

1. Define motivation and distinguish this concept from a motive and a motivator.
2. *a.* List several roles that a sales rep is likely to play.
    b. List several different role partners sales reps are typically involved with.
3. What types of role conflicts are sales reps likely to experience?
4. What can management do to reduce a sales person's:
    a. Role ambiguity?
    b. Role conflicts?
5. Explain how the factor of a person's self-concept might influence management's strategy for sales-force motivational.
6. As a sales manager, you perceive that your sales people have a strong need for security and protection. How is this factor likely to influence your planning regarding:
    a. Type of compensation plan.
    b. Personal supervision of sales people.
    c. Continuation of sales-training programs.
    d. Length of quota periods.
    e. Evaluation of a sales person's performance.

7. In terms of expectancy theory, explain with examples how a sales rep's expectations might influence that person's behavior on a sales job.

8. Explain how sales-force motivation is related to management's task of designing an effective sales-compensation plan. Use specific examples.

9. "If you pay a sales person enough, you will have a well-motivated salesman or saleswoman." Do you agree? Explain.

10. Explain how sales-force motivation is related to each of the following aspects of managing a sales force:
    a. Supervision of the sales force.
    b. Setting sales quotas.
    c. Recruiting and selecting sales people.
    d. Designing the expense-payment plan.

11. If you were a district sales manager, how would you motivate the following sales people?
    a. An older salesman who is satisfied with his present earnings level. He plans to remain as a career sales rep and retire in six years.
    b. A woman who has been one of your reps for two years and is discouraged with her acceptance and progress in the company. She is the only female rep in your district.
    c. An excellent sales rep whose morale is shot because he did not receive an expected promotion. He has been with the company five years.

12. A sales manager once said, "Motivating sales people is the same as babying them. I am careful to hire only motivated people. In this way I don't have to worry about motivating them. Good sales reps don't need any motivation from me—they motivate themselves." What do you think about this philosophy?

Case 10-1

Midwest Fixtures Company

Motivating a Lethargic Sales Force

Jim Ramsey, sales manager for the Midwest Fixtures Company, had just returned to his office from a meeting with Mr. Downs, the company president. Mr. Downs had clearly indicated that he was displeased with the performance of the company's sales force. While general business conditions had been good, and the company's competitors were turning in more than satisfactory performances, Midwest Fixtures had missed its sales projections for 1986 by 23 percent.

The sales forecast had been for the company's 34-person sales force to sell $71 million of fixtures. Actual sales were $54.7 million. This had resulted in a loss because management had been unable to curtail expenditures quickly enough to accommodate the unexpected shortage of sales volume.

Midwest Fixtures manufactured and sold a wide line of store fixtures such as wall hutches, hanging racks, counters, checkout stands, peg-board display racks, and just about every other type of fixture commonly found in retail stores. Though its home office was in Chicago, it maintained branch offices in Dallas and Atlanta. Mr. Ramsey directly managed 15 sales representatives working from the Chicago office. Bob Miller, the branch manager in Atlanta, had nine sales people reporting to him as did Joe Montez in the Dallas office.

The sales reps were paid on a combination salary-commission plan with a bonus for meeting individual sales quotas. In addition, there was a separate bonus if the rep's regional office met its quota. Salaries varied from $15,000 a year for the younger people on the sales force to as much as $30,000 a year for some old-timers who had been with the firm for more than 30 years. In addition, the reps were paid a 1 percent commission on their sales volume. Only three sales people had received bonuses in 1986, and only seven had received bonuses in 1985. The top producer was paid a total of $56,000 in 1986.

Midwest Fixtures was one of the lowest paying firms in the industry. The president felt that money was not nearly as important as employee benefits, recognition, and an overall one-big-happy-family corporate culture. The company furnished its sales reps with an attractive package of company-paid employee benefits such as medical insurance, life insurance, a dental plan, and a pension fund. Moreover, management planned company social events at every opportunity. The annual Christmas party was the highlight of the year. Not much productive work took place for a week afterwards. All the employees eagerly looked forward to such outings as the Labor Day picnic, the Fourth of July Big Bang, the Children's Easter Egg Hunt, and the Valentine's Day Dance. The president was firmly convinced that his policies were sound. Company labor turnover was the lowest in the industry. The company was known as a good place to work.

The company went to extreme lengths to recognize the performance of its sales reps. Any rep who closed a significant order was featured in the company's monthly newsletter. Outstanding sales people of the week were featured on the bulletin board at the entrance to the factory. The company gave an annual dinner to recognize the sales representative with the best performance in each region. The president wrote personal letters thanking reps who closed particularly large orders. The company's trade advertising often featured pictures of a sales representative describing a particular store application that he or she had designed for a client.

As the president often told his management team, "We cannot give our sales force too much recognition. They eat it up. They live on it. It's impossible to overfeed their egos, so heap the praise on and keep it coming." Unfortunately, the president was having more and more trouble finding praiseworthy performance.

Mr. Ramsey had called his two regional managers into the home office for a meeting about the problem. A plan had to be developed to motivate the sales force to meet the company's admittedly ambitious sales projections for 1987—$78 million. Mr. Ramsey opened the meeting by saying, "Gentlemen, we have a problem. We aren't selling enough goods. All our research tells us the market is there. We should have sold $72 million this year. We didn't! The evidence is that our sales reps simply are not sufficiently motivated to go after the business. We're missing too many sales. I've gone back over all of the call reports, and we're not closing a high enough percentage of the contracts we bid on. Ten years ago, we sold one out of every four contracts we bid. Last year, it was one out of six. We know our prices are competitive, and we know that our product line and our goods are equal to that of the competition. So I don't want to hear any garbage that our prices are too high or that our products aren't right for today's market. Our sales people just aren't working hard enough and I can prove it. I've seen it right here under my nose. The reps drift in late for one reason or another. They don't hit the streets until 10 or so. By four in the afternoon, they're history. I see them around the office too much. They aren't making us any money sitting around here talking to each other. The only time they should be in the office is to figure up a bid. And then there is the Wednesday afternoon golf tourney that most of them are in. So what are we going to do about it?"

Joe Montez spoke up while Bob Miller carefully examined a thread on his sleeve. "Jim, we haven't given them much reason to work very hard. It doesn't make much difference in their pay whether they sell their quota or not. Most of their pay comes from the salary and the benefit package they know they're going to get regardless of what they do. They know they aren't going to be fired. The old man wouldn't do it."

He continued, "I think we need to reconsider our whole motivational philosophy. We need to be able to offer some tangible rewards to the reps who produce. I heard a professor's speech the other day, and it made a whole lot of sense. He proved to me that the only reason people ever do anything is that they expect some benefit from it in the future. Now if we want our reps to get out and hustle, then we have to find some way to hang some tangible benefits in front of them. The present commissions and bonuses are too small to do the job."

Bob Miller spoke up, "I called my people together and talked about this situation. I must say it comes as no surprise. It was just a matter of time. From our talks, I've concluded that I have little power to change anything. My effectiveness as a manager is very limited because the reps know I can't fire them and that I don't control their salaries. Moreover, they know their performance doesn't really affect their salaries. We have a seniority system, and they know it."

"We're not being realistic if we expect the old man to change his managerial style. It just won't happen. We'll have to work within his framework. But we can do it if we're given the power to fire and the power to reward the performers. Let's get rid of the bums and pay the winners," Miller concluded.

Mr. Ramsey paused to ponder what he had heard, then he laid out his plan before his regional managers. "Gentlemen, I propose to go before Mr. Downs and suggest that we totally change our motivational philosophies. I agree with Joe. I propose to go to a straight commission compensation plan. If they don't sell, they don't get paid. Let's cut out this big-happy-family garbage and get these guys on the street selling. I'm tired of taking the rap for poor management when top management has created a situation in which there is little incentive to sell. Naturally, I want your reactions before I make this move."

Question:

What program would you develop to rectify this situation?

Case 10-2

Lincoln American Insurance Company

Motivating a Previously Successful Sales Agent

Upon his graduation from Arizona State University in 1984, Monte Geck became a full-time agent (sales person) for the Lincoln American Insurance Company. He worked in the company's district office in Tempe, Arizona, where the university is located. During his senior year at the university, Monte had first started selling life insurance as a college agent in Lincoln's college internship program. He had a successful selling record as a college agent, and this same high level of performance had continued throughout most of his first full-time year.

But during November 1985, Theodore Fraser, the sales manager, noted a drop in Geck's productivity. This performance decline continued, so Fraser talked with Geck about it during their monthly meetings in December and January. But Monte's performance did not improve, and Fraser's February meeting with Geck was coming up next week. Fraser realized he had to (1) do something to find out what was bothering Geck and then, (2) figure out how to motivate his formerly very successful agent.

The Lincoln American Insurance Company, established over 125 years ago in the midwest, was one of the 10 largest life insurance companies in the United States. The company received high marks from the Alfred M. Best Company—the most respected insurance-company rating agency in the industry. Lincoln's expenses were rated as "remarkably low," and its policy lapses and surrenders were well below the industry averages.

Lincoln sold insurance only through its 4,000 agents (sales representatives). The company did not use independent insurance brokers. Over half of its agents were college graduates, and about one third had qualified for membership in the professional association known as Chartered Life Underwriters (C.L.U.)

Lincoln marketed a wide variety of life insurance policies written primarily to cover individuals. However, the company also wrote a small amount of group life insurance. The individual life policies were purchased by individuals themselves or by trusts, business firms, or other organizations to cover individuals connected with the organization.

Lincoln's policies generally were some variation of the basic forms of life insurance—term insurance, whole life insurance (also called ordinary life insurance), endowment insurance, and annuities. The company also offered policyholders a variety of ways to pay their premiums.

Lincoln faced competition from approximately 2,000 other life insurance companies. In Arizona the Phoenix-Tempe market alone was covered directly or indirectly by one quarter to one half of these companies. In recent years Lincoln had also been facing competition from other types of financial institutions such as banks, mutual funds, and securities brokers. These organizations were beginning to market financial planning that provided for a person's retirement and financial protection for his dependents. Lincoln, along with other large insurance companies, met this competition by expanding the type of insurance and retirement programs they offered. They also were providing more flexible programs than in the past.

Theodore Fraser was the agency manager in Lincoln's district office in Tempe. He was very effective in motivating his agents, and he was well-respected by them. Over his many years in Tempe, Ted

Fraser had received several civic and state awards for community service. Fraser reported to Edward Dunham, the general manager in Lincoln's regional agency office in Phoenix, Arizona. Dunham also was well-respected by his district managers and was considered to be an effective administrator.

When Monte Geck was at Arizona State University, he was a finance major in the College of Business Administration. During his senior year he investigated various careers while interviewing with several companies. One of his interviews was with Edward Dunham. It was through this interview that he first became interested in Lincoln's internship program available to undergraduate students.

Subsequently, during his senior year, Geck entered this program as a college agent. At that time, he had no intention of becoming a full-time agent after graduation. He took the internship only to develop some sales skills and to earn a little extra money.

He began his internship talking with friends and classmates, explaining to them how life insurance worked and what they could get out of it. Before long he had sold several policies and had earned just over $4,500 in three months. He admitted that he was surprised at how well he had done. He seemed to be successful at persuading students to start their life insurance program before they graduated.

Near the end of his internship, he began to show interest in the life insurance industry as a career. He investigated the job of selling life insurance. He concluded that an agent essentially is in business for himself, working when he wants to and selling as much as he can. Basically, agents are paid on a straight commission basis, the job entails a lot of hard work, and the turnover rate is very high. Geck was told that only about 1 in 10 sales people who enter the business become successful agents. He learned the importance of prospecting for new customers and the various ways agents can generate leads to these prospects. He studied the various ways of making a sales presentation.

Based on this industry research and his successful internship experience, Monte Geck decided to become a full-time agent with the Lincoln company after his December graduation. He was assigned to the Tempe district office, working under Theodore Fraser. In his first six months as a full-time agent, Geck did very well, earning $15,000 in commissions. As he said, "not too many guys my age (22) have earned a five-figure income six months after graduation."

Monte's market primarily was the graduating seniors at Arizona State University. He also sold insurance to the graduate students in several departments on the campus. The more he established himself on campus, the more his position generated leads to new prospects. People on campus came to call him "Mr. Insurance." He was a likeable person the students believed in and listened to. He seemed to enjoy his work very much. He had developed an excellent sales presentation, explaining how his product would benefit the customer and how it would be tailored to fit an individual customer's needs.

Monte truly was enjoying his success. He purchased a new sports car and had a telephone installed in it. He moved into a luxury apartment and furnished it appropriately. He hired a secretary to do some of his paperwork and other jobs so he could concentrate on selling. Occasionally, he took off for a day or two to relax in the mountains. In fact, he was living so well that Mr. Fraser wondered whether Monte was living a little too high—perhaps beyond his means.

Mr. Fraser spent a considerable portion of his time personally supervising the activities of his agents. He talked with them frequently and was a good listener. He tried to spot developing problems and correct them before they got out of hand. Once a month he sat down with each agent individually to evaluate the past month's performance and to help the agent plan his or her next month's activities. These meetings covered a variety of topics such as prospecting activities, telephone-selling, in-person sales calls, new business, hours devoted to planning and preparation, and hours spent in telephone selling or in the presence of a prospect.

Fraser felt that, once this meeting was concluded, the agent had a pretty good idea of where he was going next month. The agent then could compare the goals and accomplishments throughout the month. At the same time, Fraser was always available to help guide an agent over rough spots during the month.

It was in the course of evaluating each agent's performance that Mr. Fraser first noted a decline in Geck's productivity. This was in November 1985—about 18 months after Monte Geck began selling full-time for Lincoln. Monte was not writing any new business, and he was falling behind in the number of phone calls he made each day. This led to a drop in the number of in-person sales calls. This decline continued into December. At their mid-December meeting, Fraser raised the issue directly with Geck. Monte agreed that a slump had occurred, and he assured Fraser that it was a temporary situation—that he simply had a bad month.

December passed by, and Monte continued to generate very little business or income for himself. His secretary spent most of her day reading books. Monte's prospecting and telephone calls still were not up to the prescribed level. Fraser thought at first that the situation could be explained by the fact that students were away during the Christmas break. Then Faser recalled that Geck had done very well during the previous summer when enrollment was low.

The same pattern continued through January, and Monte decided to let his secretary go. When other agents talked with Monte, he seemed depressed because he could not do things the way he had done six months earlier. The other agents got the impression that Monte did not care about the work any more. Instead of working harder to recover, he would take a day off now and then.

Fraser's February meeting with Geck was coming up next week. In preparation for that meeting, Fraser was wondering what he could do to get Monte Geck motivated again. "However, before I can get Monte to start up again," Fraser said, "I first have to find out why he has slowed down." Fraser also was wondering whether he should talk to Monte about the way he was spending his money and managing his financial affairs.

Fraser was considering a couple of options to propose to Geck. One was the idea of redefining Monte's target market. As Fraser said, "perhaps Monte is a little jaded from dealing with college students. Maybe he would like to join some new organizations, acquire some social mobility, and face the challenge of a new market."

Another idea that Fraser had was to move Geck to another agency in the Phoenix area. Perhaps Geck could be moved where he would be under the supervision of Mr. Dunham's, who recruited Geck in the first place.

Fraser continued, "maybe Monte feels that money is not enough. Maybe he feels that selling insurance does not carry enough prestige. Ed (Dunham) and I have talked about setting up a position of College Unit Director. This position would involve some managerial responsibilities as well as selling. The person in this position would be responsible for recruiting and supervising college agents in our internship program. Maybe we should put Monte in that new position. It could be the first step for him up the managerial ladder in our company."

The more Fraser sat and pondered the "Monte Geck situation," the more he became puzzled. He wondered if maybe there still was not a better answer than the ones he had come up with.

Questions

1. What should Theodore Fraser do to determine why Monte Geck's performance has declined?
2. What should Fraser do to motivate Geck?

11

Compensating the Sales Force

*How little you know about the age you live in if you
fancy that honey is sweeter than cash in hand.*
OVID

As we indicated in the preceding chapter, compensation is the most
widely used method of motivating a sales force. Yet over the years, a
stream of research studies, interviews with executives, and other reports have consistently stated that many companies are dissatisfied
with their sales-force compensation plan. Consequently, in this chapter and in the next one, we will study sales-force compensation.
Hopefully, we can suggest some ways that sales executives can reduce their frustrations in administering this very important element
in a sales-force management program.

The structure for sales-force compensation looks something like
this:

- *Financial compensation.*
  - *Direct* payment of money.
  - *Indirect* payment—paid vacations or company-financed insur-
    ance programs, for example.
- *Nonfinancial compensation.*
  - Opportunity to advance in the job.
  - Recognition inside and outside the firm.
  - Self-respect.
  - Other intangible benefits.

Most of our discussion in this and the next chapter will deal with
direct payments of **financial** compensation.

The compensation problem is twofold. A company must determine
both the *level* of earnings and the *method* of paying its sales force.
By **level of earnings** we mean the total dollar income paid to each

sales representative for a given period of time. The ***method of compensation*** is the plan by which the workers earn or reach the intended level. One company may use a straight salary method of payment, for instance, while another may choose to pay a commission.

Importance of Sales-Force Compensation

A sales force cannot be considered well-managed unless there is a well-developed and well-administered compensation plan. The pay plan is important because of its impact on the sales force, the company, and customer relations.

The sales force. A basic tenet of our economic system is that people should be justly compensated for their labors. A good compensation plan can do much to develop a highly productive sales force, because it will help to instill a high degree of morale and industriousness.

Part of management's problem with sales compensation stems from the sales reps' individuality and their attitudes toward various rewards. Each sales rep in a group may view a given reward differently. Furthermore, most sales reps seek a variety of rewards from their work. Consequently, from the sales rep's point of view, management should develop a tailor-made reward plan for each rep. Obviously, this is not practical from the organization's point of view. The solution then is to develop a compromise reward plan containing several components that will provide sufficient incentive for each sales person to achieve the management's objective.

The company. Management wants to keep its sales expenses as low as possible and at the same time encourage profitable operations by the sales force. The compensation plan can be used to control the activities of the sales force. When a company faces rising break-even points, it should increase sales volume, decrease expenses, or both. A properly designed compensation plan can often stimulate increased sales.

With regard to expenses, many firms feel, rightly or wrongly, that their production costs are already as low as practical. The only other major area for expense reduction is in the marketing department. And there, an easily noticed major item is the total cost of the sales force.

Customer relations and goodwill. If the compensation system encourages overselling customers, ill will can result. Sales compensation has social implications because selling is so important in our economic system. The extent to which marketing can deliver a high standard of living to consumers depends heavily on the methods used to pay one major group of deliverers—the sales people.

Most companies treat all personal-selling expenses—including sales-force compensation—as current operating expense items. However, what if the compensation expense is payment for efforts in *developing* a market, rather than payment for *maintaining* activities. Then the developmental compensation cost is better treated as a capital investment and amortized over a period of years. Kahn and Schuchman made some persuasive comments on the costs of a specialized development sales force:

> Maximum sales development simply cannot be obtained efficiently if management demands that income from it exceed its cost period by period. Development expenditure is not an operating cost, but a capital investment ranking among the most important that a firm can make. . . . The most valuable asset of a firm is its pool of customers, and if development is to succeed, it must be viewed as a capital investment in developing this pool.
>
> . . . Even more importantly, management must recognize that development selling cannot be expected to bear the immediate fruits of sales maintenance. It must come to recognize that expenditures for market development are the close and supporting kin to product development expenditures. Management must be ready to invest in the market in the same way as it invests in plant and equipment or research and development.[1]

If management uses the current period to evaluate compensation expenditures, it may decide to discontinue a seemingly unprofitable market venture. Yet, this same venture might have proved profitable if management had viewed it over a longer term, using the capital-investment concept of compensation costs.

Sales-Force Compensation and Strategic Planning

A close relationship exists between a company's strategic marketing planning and its sales-force compensation plan. The compensation plan has a direct bearing on successful *implementation* of the marketing plan. As an example of this relationship, assume that a manufacturer of industrial machinery is planning to introduce a new product or enter a new market in order to increase

[1] George N. Kahn and Abraham Schuchman, "Specialize Your Salesmen!" *Harvard Business Review*, January–February 1961, pp. 97–98.

the firm's market share. A straight-salary compensation plan probably would implement either of these strategies. On the other hand, a stronger incentive—perhaps a large commission—would be necessary when the strategy calls for aggressive selling to liquidate excess inventories. A company facing intensifying competition may decide on the strategy of providing extra service to hold existing accounts. In this situation, a pay plan of straight commission on sales volume would *not* be compatible.

For years, some retailers' marketing planning called for attracting top college graduates. Yet these stores never successfully implemented this strategy because they consistently offered starting salaries below those offered by manufacturers. Truly, the effective coordination of marketing planning and sales-force compensation has much to do with the successful implementation of this planning.

Determining Need for Revision of Present Plan

Most firms usually need to *revise* their present compensation plans rather than develop completely new ones. Before changing a plan, a company first should determine whether indications such as decreasing volume or increasing selling costs are evidence of weaknesses in the compensation system. Perhaps the fault lies elsewhere. If the results of this analysis indicate the compensation plan is at fault, the manager must determine *why* the present plan is not satisfactory. A list of key questions such as the following could be developed to help determine whether the plan needs to be changed:

- Are the sales people generally satisfied with the plan?
- Does it lead to the accomplishment of the objectives for which it was established?
- Does it encourage sales people to sell the profitable products and do the necessary missionary tasks?

If the answers are "no" to many questions of this nature, the compensation plan needs revision.

Considerations Preceding Actual Designing of Plan

Before designing a new pay plan, or revising an existing one, a sales executive should review a few fundamental points. These include some pertinent generalizations about pay plans, as well as the broad goals and the basic requirements of a good plan.

Some Useful Generalizations

There are inherent conflicts in the objectives of most compensation plans. Sales executives want a plan that will maximize the sales reps' income and at the same time minimize the company's outlay. Or they want one plan to give the sales force security and stability of income as well as incentive. In each situation, the desires are diametrically opposite. About all a manager can do is adjust the pay plan until a reasonably satisfactory compromise is reached.

Another point to recognize is that *no single plan fits all situations.* Consequently, a firm should have a plan tailor-made for its own specific objectives. There may be a marked similarity among the general features used by several firms, but the details should reflect the individual objectives of each company. Many companies also need more than one compensation plan because of differences in types of sales jobs, territories, or products.

Sales compensation should be related to the general compensation structure of the company. Sometimes office or factory workers feel they are underpaid compared with sales people. Other workers may envy a person who travels and has an expense account. Sales people, on the other hand, sometimes look longingly at the gains made by the blue-collar worker. Production employees have achieved benefits through the efforts of their unions. Similar benefits often were not given to the sales force or other white-collar workers in the same firm.

From a practical standpoint, however, *it is far more important to achieve external parity in sales people's earnings.* Management should pay its sales force at a level competitive with sales people in other firms, rather than attempting to equate the earnings of the sales force with those of office or factory personnel within the firm.

At frequent stages during the development of a compensation plan, *management should solicit suggestions from the sales force.* Soliciting their opinions may uncover facets of the compensation problem that never would have occurred to management. Sales people will also accept the new or revised plan more readily if they are consulted about it.

Broad Objectives of a Compensation Plan

The four broad, general goals of a good compensation plan are not mutually exclusive. In some situations, one goal may conflict with another. All four, however, are valuable guidelines for a sales executive to recognize and follow.

To correlate efforts, results, and rewards. One general objective is to correlate sales people's rewards with their efforts and results. This is an ideal that most companies constantly seek, yet seldom achieve. The key part of that equation (efforts = results = rewards), however, is results = rewards. Generally in the United States, in practically any situation—be it in business, politics, athletics, or social life—we pay off on *results* and not on *efforts*. It is nice, of course, if the results are commensurate with the efforts. But the key to rewards in most cases is results—also called performance or productivity.

This situation can be really frustrating. A person can work very hard (much effort) but get little reward, because the results of that effort are minimal. In the reverse, we all know of situations where seemingly little effort has brought big results and consequently big rewards. One student works very hard all during a course, yet gets a C on each examination. Another person studies very little but gets an A on each exam. One athlete trains long and hard (much effort), yet bats .185 in baseball or shoots way over par in golf. Another athlete with much natural ability can train or practice very little and still win gold medals.

The problem in sales management is that frequently it is hard to equate rewards with results. We often cannot accurately measure what a person is worth to a company. Sometimes it is also difficult even to measure results. For example, a given amount of effort on the part of salesman Bill Garner may result in $10,000 of sales. The same amount and quality of work put forth by Sue Anderson may not result in any sales. Instead, Sue is building the foundation for profitable future business with a customer. However, this relationship may not be reflected in sales until some months or even years later.

Sales managers undoubtedly would agree that a sales person's pay should be commensurate with performance—that is, with results. Yet, unfortunately in many sales compensation plans, pay is *not* correlated with the performance. This is especially true when salary is all, or part of, the total pay. Frequently a sales person's salary is related to age or length of service with the company. An older rep with many years of service in the firm is typically paid a higher salary than a younger person who was hired more recently. This occurs even though the younger rep is outperforming the older, more experienced person.

To control sales people's activities. A good pay plan should act as an unseen supervisor of a sales force by enabling management to control and direct the sales reps' activities. Today, this usually means motivating the reps to ensure a *fully balanced selling effort*. As a business implements the marketing concept, its sales people tend to become territorial marketing managers. This, in turn, means that they must be motivated to do a *total* selling job. That is, the compensation plan must offer incentive flexible enough to cover such varied tasks as full-line selling, missionary work, or controlling selling expenses.

In an ideal pay plan:

Efforts = Results = Rewards

But realistically we usually find that:

Results = Rewards

On the other hand, a business may not be interested in a fully balanced sales effort. Inventory problems may force a firm to put all its energies into selling a limited number of products. Or, entrance into new markets may call for short-run emphasis on customer development, even at the expense of immediate volume.

To ensure proper treatment of customers. A good compensation plan should encourage sales people to treat customers properly. This aim is, in some respects, a corollary of the goal of controlling and directing the sales force, because consideration of customer interests ordinarily is in line with company objectives. Improper treatment of customers is a sure way to lose them to competitors.

To attract and keep competent sales people. A good pay plan helps build the quality of a sales force that the company wants. A good compensation plan should assist in *attracting* the caliber of reps wanted by the company. Both the level and the method of compensation are important in reaching this goal. Either fact alone ordinarily is not enough. Many retail institutions, for example, have difficulty attracting qualified college graduates because the level of pay is too low. True, the company may offset a slightly lower level by providing greater future opportunity or by virtue of its desirable location. However, a business can only go so far in offering substitutes for a competitive level and an attractive method of compensation, and still attract the caliber of sales force it wants.

A sound plan should also help to *keep* desirable people and *eliminate* poor performers. Because no fool-proof hiring system has yet been devised, a firm with a reasonably good selection system may still make mistakes in hiring. Then the burden of discovering and eliminating these people falls to other managerial tools, one of which is the compensation plan. Evidence of incompetency usually appears soon after some incentive method is employed. Incompetent reps either cannot make their quotas or do not earn a large enough commission or bonus.

Basic Requirements of a Sound Plan

In order to have some chance of achieving general objectives such as the four just stated, the compensation plan needs to meet certain requirements (see Figure 11-1). There is no standard list of these points. In fact, there is no sharp dividing line between an *objective* and a *requirement* of a sound plan.

Provision for two types of income.   An ideal compensation plan for a sales force provides both a steady income and an incentive income. This represents another conflict in the goals of a compensation plan. It is not possible to design a workable system that offers the greatest degree of both security and incentive. The concepts are mutually incompatible. In practice, the company must develop a compromise structure.

Steady income.   Any plan should provide a regular income, at least at a minimum level. The principle behind this point is that sales reps should not have to worry about how to meet living expenses. If they have a bad month, if they are in seasonal doldrums, or if they are sick and cannot work for a period, they should have some income. However, the level of this steady income should not be so high that it lessens the desire for incentive pay.

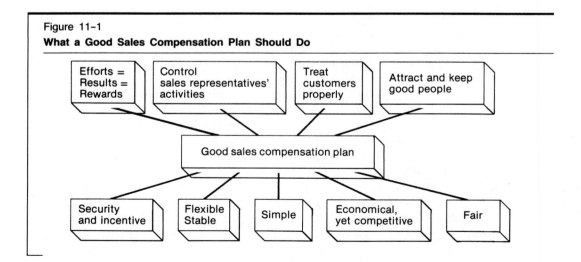

Figure 11-1
What a Good Sales Compensation Plan Should Do

Incentive income. Besides a regular income, a good pay plan should furnish an incentive to induce above-minimum performance. Most people do better when offered a reward for some specific action than when no incentive is involved.

Flexibility and stability. A good plan is sufficiently flexible to meet the needs of individual territories, products, and sales people. Not all *territories* present the same opportunity. A representative in a territory where the company is the leader ordinarily should not be compensated by the same method as a rep in a newly entered district. Flexibility is needed to adjust for differences in *products*. Some products are staples and can be sold on an ordertaking basis with frequent repeat sales. Others are sold one to a customer with no reorders. In this case, much creative selling is needed. Variations in a *sales person's performance* should be rapidly reflected in earnings. Few things ruin morale faster than failure to compensate a sales person for extra effort because the pay plan is inflexible.

At the same time, the basic plan should possess stability. Here again (as in our discussion of sales organization), we can use the analogy of a tree—stable below ground, but flexible above ground. The basic pay plan should contain features that enable a company to meet changing conditions without having to change the basic plan. For example, the basic plan may include three categories of commission rates—high, medium, and low percentages—to reflect the different profitability among products. However, a products category may be changed from time to time as competition and other external factors affect it's profitability. These category re-assignments can be made without changing the basic pay plan at all. In another situation, a company may use some other incentive—such as a contest—to stimulate sales of a given product or market over the short run, without having to change the basic pay plan.

Simplicity. Simplicity is a hallmark of a good compensation plan. However, sometimes simplicity and flexibility become conflicting goals. That is, a plan that is simple may not be sufficiently flexible, and a plan with adequate flexibility may achieve that goal at the expense of simplicity.

A plan should be simple enough that sales people have no trouble understanding it, and are able to figure out what their income will be. The plan also should provide for payment as soon as possible after income is earned. Delays in commission or bonus payments tend to destroy any simplicity in the plan, because reps have trouble keeping track of what they earned during the period. Delays also remove much of the incentive of such payments, since immediate rewards are more motivating than delayed ones.

Economy and competitiveness. From management's standpoint, a compensation plan should be economical to administer. Furthermore, a firm wants to keep its sales-force expenses in line with those of its competition. Otherwise, the firm will have to increase the price of its product or suffer decreased profit margins.

Fairness. A good compensation plan is fair to both the sales force and management. If sales people are paid on the basis of years of service rather than on how well they perform, younger reps will undoubtedly be dissatisfied. One way to ensure fairness in a plan is to base it on measurable factors that are controllable by the sales force. More is said on this point in the next section.

Steps in Designing a Plan[2]

Review Job Analysis and Description

The first step in the design of a new compensation plan or the revision of an established one is to carefully review the detailed job description. (See Figure 11–2.) This should disclose the exact nature, scope, and probable difficulty of the job. A separate description should be included for each selling position, such as sales engineer, missionary sales person, or sales trainee. The job descriptions indicate what services and abilities the business is paying for.

Determine Specific Objectives of Plan

Part of the job of designing a compensation plan is deciding *specifically* what it is intended to accomplish. It is not enough to say that the goal is to get an honest day's work for a day's pay or to attract good people. These are examples of the broad, general type of objective referred to earlier—objectives *every* plan should attempt to accomplish. The following are examples of specific objectives, along with suggestions for the compensation method that can best accomplish them.

1. *Increase volume of net sales.* Some form of incentive is usually necessary, such as a commission or a bonus.

---

[2] For a managerial guide to designing an effective sales force compensation plan, see John W. Barry and Porter Henry, *Effective Sales Incentive Compensation* (New York: McGraw-Hill, 1981). This book includes the general concepts as well as the practical details related to building or revising a sales-compensation plan.

Figure 11–2
Steps in Designing a Sales Compensation Plan

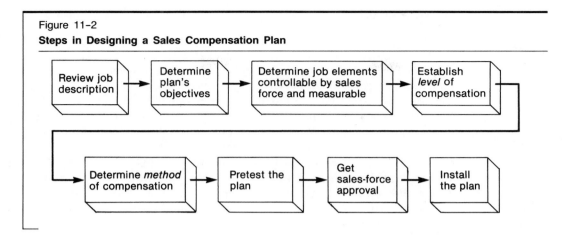

2. *Increase sales volume of a certain class of products or to certain classes of customers.* A higher rate of commission may be paid on sales of the high-margin items, or whichever line of goods the company is trying to push. A firm may pay a bonus or higher rate of commission on sales to desirable customer groups.
3. *Obtain new accounts.* A bonus may be paid for every new account brought in, or this activity may be reflected in a higher salary.
4. *Stimulate missionary work.* This includes such activities as training dealer sales people, making demonstrations, or building displays. Some of these efforts can be individually measured. If so, it is possible to pay some form of commission for their accomplishment. Efforts that cannot be measured easily may be rewarded by having salary form the bulk of the total compensation.
5. *Minimize expenses.* A bonus may be based on how much a sales rep's expenses run below an expense quota, or how much they decrease from one period to another.
6. *Develop a new territory.* Probably all income should be in the form of salary, at least in the earliest stages of development.

It is surprising how often a firm has a sales-force compensation system that is at odds with management's stated goals. Many firms typically say that they want a sales compensation plan that "emphasizes profitability." Yet most of these companies' plans will have a commission or bonus component based on sales volume. Other sales execs say that they want to "reward top performers," but their compensation plan fails to implement that goal.

Determine Job Elements Controllable by Sales Force and Objectively Measurable

Compensation should be based only on those items (1) that are controllable by sales people and (2) that can be measured. However meritorious, this ideal is virtually impossible to implement completely. Yet, effective management can move toward this ideal.

Most factors contributing to sales success are controllable by the sales force only partially or not at all. Sales people have some control over their sales volume, for instance, but this control is limited by product attributes and company pricing policies. The point is that a firm should base each sales person's compensation on factors over which the rep has a maximum of control. It should be based on the rep's own sales volume, for instance, rather than on total company volume. Or it should be based on the rep's profit after deducting his or her direct expenses, rather than on the net profit of the rep's branch.

The next step is to give as much consideration as possible to the elements that can be measured objectively. For instance, sales, selling expense, calls made, new accounts brought in, displays set up, or gross margin contributed are all quantitatively measurable. In contrast, such activities as building goodwill or training dealer sales people are not easily evaluated, even though they are largely controllable by the sales representatives. This is not to say that these factors should be ignored in compensation matters. However, executive judgment must be applied.

Establish the Level of Compensation

Importance of level. As noted at the beginning of this chapter, one of the two key tasks in designing a pay plan is to determine the *level* of compensation (the other is to develop the *method*). The level of pay means the average earnings of the sales people over a given period. Usually a firm establishes the level of pay before determining the method of compensation. In many respects, the level is more important than the method. To the sales reps, the level is their average gross income. People usually are more interested in *how much* they've earned, rather than *how* they earned it. To the company, the level of income is the direct sales cost.[3]

Management is interested in the compensation level because that is what attracts most sales people. If reps believe that they will not be able to earn enough, they probably won't be attracted to the job regardless of the method used. On the other hand, they may take a

---

[3] See Douglas J. Dalrymple, P. Ronald Stephenson, and William Cron, "Wage Levels and Sales Productivity," *Business Horizons,* December 1980, pp. 57–60.

job that pays a high income, even though the firm does not offer the combination of salary and commission they prefer. Even society should be concerned with the level of compensation. In the final analysis, it is the *amount* of the sales people's earnings, rather than the *method* of pay, that is reflected in the cost of a product.

In spite of the importance of the level of sales compensation, surprisingly little has been written on the subject. Most of the attention is usually devoted to *how* the sales force should be paid, rather than *what* that pay should be.

Unless a firm gives adequate attention to pay levels, it may be *overcompensating* its sales people relative to competitor's sales forces. This unduly raises selling costs and reduces profits. Overcompensation can have a dual affect on management personnel problems. First, the company may have difficulty filling management positions with sales reps, because they are reluctant to leave their higher paying sales jobs. Second, the morale of management personnel is undermined if sales people's earnings far exceed theirs.

It can be equally harmful to *underpay* the sales force in relation to competitive levels. Inevitably, underpayment results in attracting a lower quality of sales people, with attendant losses from poor performance.

When compensation levels are established on a company-wide basis, sales people may receive less than they would in competitive firms. Sometimes management underestimates the competitive level because of a lack of market knowledge. Underpayment also may occur when management judges the market level only on the basis of *direct* monetary compensation. That is, management does not consider the *indirect* monetary factors such as paid vacations, retirement plans, and insurance programs that other firms may offer.

Factors influencing level of compensation.   Over the years, the *Method* of compensation consistently has had a bearing on the *level* of compensation. Typically, sales people working under a straight salary plan earn less than reps who are paid under a straight commission or some form of combination plan. We see this situation in Figure 11–3, which is drawn from the Dartnell Corporation's *23rd Biennial Survey of Sales Force Compensation*. The median pay for all experienced sales people covered in this survey was $37,000 in 1985. Those reps on straight salary averaged $29,000, while the median straight-commission pay level was $36,000, and the combination-plan median level was $40,000. Apparently the incentive feature in a straight-commission or a combination plan stimulates the reps to perform better than they would do under a straight salary. Also, poor performers are likely to quit a job sooner under an incentive plan than if they were paid straight salary. Consequently, the reps remain-

Figure 11–3

Level of Pay for Experienced Sales People, by Method of Compensation, 1985: Median Range and Average of that Range*

Compensation Method	Level of Pay		
All plans	Average = $37,000		
Salary plan	$24,000	$29,000	$38,000
Commission plan	$27,000	$36,000	$45,000
Combination plan	$30,600	$40,000	$50,000

* Median range is the 25th–75th percentile.
Source: John P. Steinbrink, *Sales Force Compensation: 23rd Biennial Survey* (Chicago: Dartnell Corp., 1986), pp. 74–75.

ing under incentive plans tend to be above-average performers, thus earning more pay and raising the median level.

The going rate of pay for all sales reps—that is, the competitive level—is not a major determinant of compensation level. There is no clearly prevailing rate of pay for a given sales job as there is for certain office or factory jobs. Compensation levels for sales people vary considerably among different industries. Table 11–1 shows some examples of this spread. In the life insurance industry, the median earnings of experienced sales people were $55,000 in 1985. The median pay for reps in the electronics industry was $52,000. Some of the lower-paying industries were utilities ($23,500), petroleum products ($23,000), and paper products ($20,300).

The wide range of levels indicates that it is not clear just what constitutes a competitive earnings figure for sales people. So management must consider other guidelines, such as the experience requirements, the caliber of the job, or how well the company and its products are known. The pay level usually must be higher in a firm that spends less for advertising or is less well known than other companies. The firm with an effective sales-training program may pay at a lower level. The organization that has no such facilities must hire experienced sales people.

The amount the firm can *afford* to pay is an influencing factor in some cases, whether or not this level is competitive. A company in a weak financial position may have to tie sales representatives' earnings directly to their productivity by paying them straight commission.

Table 11–1

**Variations in Sales Compensation Levels in Selected Industries, 1985:
Median Pay for Experienced Sales People**

Industry	Compensation
All Industries	$37,000
Life insurance	55,000
Electronics	52,000
Radio and television	47,000
Computer products and services	45,300
Electrical equipment and supplies	43,000
Tobacco	42,136
Appliances (household)	42,000
Transportation equipment	39,000
Healthcare products and services	38,000
Iron and steel	36,000
Chemicals	35,000
Building materials	33,000
Airlines	31,000
Auto and truck	30,000
Banks and finance companies	28,083
Office machinery and equipment	28,000
Publishing	27,213
Food products	25,000
Utilities	23,500
Petroleum products	23,000
Paper products	20,300

Source: John P. Steinbrink, *Sales Force Compensation: 23rd Biennial Survey* (Chicago: Dartnell Corp., 1986), p. 86.

Some correlative relationships may be useful guides. The level of sales compensation seems to be closely related to the size of the company and the age of the sales people. Smaller firms in an industry tend to pay their sales forces more than larger firms. This seems to occur because the smaller firm usually is less known, spends less on advertising, and has yet to develop a reputation for its products. Management must rely heavily on personal selling and a competent sales force.

Sales people's earnings tend to be related to their age. This is understandable up to a point, because older representatives have more experience and have developed more skills, so their productivity should be higher. Some firms, however, tend to increase the pay level of older sales representatives even after their productivity has started to decline.

Placing limitations on earnings.   Should management place a ceiling or limit on the earnings of its sales people? The question is most likely to arise when part or all of the compensation plan is based on commission. Under a commission plan, in contrast to other types, a sales person is more likely to benefit from a *windfall sale.* This is defined as a single large order or a large new account for which the sales person gets a substantial boost in earnings. This boost comes even though the rep has put forth no special effort and has little or no control over the sale. The question of limitations may also arise when earnings are high because the rep is getting a good commission rate in a territory with a high market potential.

Executives responsible for managing sales compensation plans strongly believe that there should be a wide pay differential between a field sales manager and members of the sales force. The following are some of the reasons why a wide differential (in effect, a limitation on sales earnings) is favored:

- It reduces the chances that star sales representatives will earn more than their bosses, thus raising questions of the boss's managerial fitness and adversely affecting executive morale.
- It encourages field executives to think of themselves as managers and not just advanced sales people.
- A star sales person is not likely to turn down a promotion to manager if this means a raise in pay.
- In the case of windfall sales, the argument is that sales people should not receive financial benefit from circumstances over which they have no influence.
- A wide differential can facilitate many aspects of compensation administration. For example, a firm has some room to make regional cost-of-living adjustments in salaries without upsetting the entire sales person-executive salary chain.

The reasons for having no ceilings or limitations seem to outweigh the arguments favoring them. The more a sales person earns, the more the company makes, particularly if the earnings are in the form of a bonus or commission. The idea of a ceiling seems totally alien to the philosophy of selling. A firm ordinarily does not limit sales of its products to x dollars a year. It is ridiculous to discourage business beyond a certain figure, assuming plant capacity is available. Yet, placing limits on sales reps' incomes has the same effect. One recognized way to deter sales of low-margin items is to pay a very low rate of commission on these products. By the same token, one way to limit overall sales is to establish methods that slow down or stop a person's earnings after they reach a given point. Sales people do not earn incentive income unless they produce. And the more they produce, the better off the company usually is.

If management does decide to curb the earnings of its sales people, several methods are available. One direct attack is to establish a maximum amount—a ceiling—above which the company will not pay. Another approach is to reduce commissions or bonus payments on all sales. Or the firm may establish a system of regressive commission rates, whereby successively lower commission rates are paid as sales volume increases beyond a given level. Windfall accounts may be classified as house accounts. These accounts are turned over to the territorial sales manager, and the sales person receives no earnings credit for sales to them. Management may even change its basic compensation plan to place less emphasis on the incentive features and more on the fixed element of salary.

Summary

Compensation is the most widely used method for motivating a sales force. The structure for sales-force compensation includes: (1) *financial* compensation (direct payment of money and indirect payments such as paid vacations and other fringe benefits) and (2) *nonfinancial* compensation (recognition, self-respect, and opportunity for advancement). Most of our discussion involved *direct* payments of *financial* compensation. When building a compensation plan, management must determine both the *level* of earnings and the *method* of paying the sales force.

Sales-force compensation is important because of its impact on the sales force itself, as well as on the company and its customer relations. The sales-force compensation plan has a significant influence on the implementation of a company's strategic marketing plan. In most cases a company needs to revise an existing pay plan, rather than develop a completely new one. Thus management first must determine whether the existing plan needs revision.

Before actually revising an existing plan or designing a new one, management should review some basic points. For example, a plan should provide both security and incentive to the sales force. And the plan should be tailor-made for a given firm.

The four broad, general goals of a good compensation plan are (1) to correlate a person's efforts, results, and rewards, (2) to control the sales people's activities, (3) to ensure proper treatment of customers, and (4) to attract and keep competent sales people.

A sound pay plan will (1) provide both a steady income and an incentive income, (2) be flexible, (3) be simple and easy for the sales rep to understand and for the company to administer, (4) be fair to the sales rep, and (5) allow the company to keep its compensation expenses in line with those of its competition.

When designing a pay plan, a company first should review its job description to see what the reps are being paid to do. Then management should set specific goals for the pay plan. Compensation ideally should be based on items (1) that are controllable by the sales force and (2) that can be objectively measured.

A major step in building a compensation plan is to establish the *level* of pay for the sales people. The pay level is critically important for several reasons. Management also has to determine if it will limit its sales reps' earnings. This decision can have a significant effect on sales-force morale, the morale of lower-level management, and a sales person's interest in being promoted into management.

Questions and Problems

1. "The compensation plan is the most important influence on a sales person's morale, and it is the most effective of all managerial tools for controlling and motivating a sales force." Discuss all aspects of this statement.
2. Give several specific examples of evidence that may indicate that a sales-force compensation plan needs revision.
3. As stated in this chapter, two broad goals of a sound compensation plan are (a) to control and direct sales-force activities and (b) to ensure proper treatment of customers. Can these goals be reached by use of any managerial tool or activity other than a good pay plan?
4. When designing a compensation plan for sales people, of what use is the job description?
5. Study some companies located near your school to determine the extent to which their sales-compensation plans are actually aligned with management's stated goals for these plans.
6. "If a sales rep is entirely satisfied with the *level* of income, then the *method* of compensation is unimportant." Discuss.
7. Rank the following types of sales jobs by total earnings, showing which type you feel should have the highest level of compensation, which is second, and so on. Justify your rankings.
   a. Missionary sales for a large soap company.
   b. Sales for a steel manufacturer.
   c. Door-to-door cosmetics sales.
   d. Sales for appliance wholesalers.
   e. Life insurance sales.
   f. Sales for a manufacturer of office machines.
   g. Sales for a manufacturer of children's clothes, calling on retail department and other clothing stores.
   h. Sales for a firm selling conveyor systems.

8. "If the level and method of compensation are entirely satisfactory, management need not fear that the sales force will succumb to unionization." Discuss.

9. "The level and method of compensation vitally affect the program for selecting, training, and supervising a sales force. However, the selection systems or the training and supervision have no bearing on the level or method of compensation." Do you agree? Discuss.

10. Should the level of sales compensation in a firm with a national market be affected by regional variations in the general wage scale and the cost of living? Will your decision be influenced by the firm's policy regarding geographical differentials for its plant and office employees?

11. In 1983, a firm hired several college graduates for sales jobs at a salary of $18,500 a year plus expenses. By 1987, most of these people were making a salary of $22,000 to $22,500 a year plus expenses. In 1987, the same company hired more graduates and paid them $21,000 a year plus expenses. This was a competitive salary for qualified college graduates in 1987. Thus, the people with no experience received about the same pay as those with four years' experience. Discuss the problems involved in this situation and suggest remedies.

12. If management wants to reduce the *level* of earnings for its sales reps, what *method* will have the least harmful effect on morale?

13. Assume that sales people's earnings in a certain firm have no limit, and a good sales rep can earn more than some of the company's sales managers. What incentive do these sales people have to move into management? Especially consider those whose promotion means a decrease in income.

Case 11–1

Delta Truck Company*

Controlling the Level of Sales-Force Compensation

Last year Leon Halter earned $52,000 selling trucks for the Delta Truck Company. He was the top sales person in the company's Dallas, Texas, district. His earnings were higher than the total compensation received by Arnold Booth who was the Dallas district sales manager and thus Halter's boss. Some executives in the home office

* Adapted from case prepared by Rick D. Thode, under the supervision of Professor William J. Stanton.

were concerned about the potential morale problems among the district managers and the sales force in situations like this. Consequently, the home office suggested to Booth that he consider the idea of reallocating or redistributing the customers' accounts among the sales people. By this reallocation, Booth could then better control the level of sales force compensation.

The Delta Truck Company was a large manufacturer of heavy-duty trucks. The company headquarters were in the east, and it maintained about 50 branch sales offices throughout the country. The Dallas branch office, which had 10 sales people and sales last year of $7.3 million, was part of the southwestern region. The Dallas district covered north and west Texas and parts of Oklahoma and New Mexico.

The trucking industry classified motor trucks into eight categories according to their size. The Delta product line consisted of trucks in the number seven and eight categories. The largest over-the-road trucks comprised the eighth category, while smaller construction trucks made up the seventh category. Construction trucks include "low boy" tractors, ready-mix concrete trucks, dump trucks, and tank trucks.

In addition to the sales of new trucks, the Dallas branch was also responsible for the sale of a considerable number of trade-ins. About two thirds of all transactions for new trucks involved trade-ins. Selling prices were often considerably less than the list price for new trucks. Sales reps sought to achieve about the same margin on all of the trucks sold. The typical margin for a truck would be somewhere between $1,500 and $2,000.

In the southwest and Rocky Mountain regions, Delta's main competition came from International Harvester, Mack, and White trucks. Kenworth and Peterbilt trucks also were significant competitors in these markets. According to Mr. Booth, each major brand of truck had some competitive differential advantages. For example, he said that Mack trucks were considered to have one of the most economical diesel engines in the industry. Also Mack's transmission greatly enhanced the shifting capability of the truck. Kenworth and Peterbilt enjoyed a reputation for building large, comfortable, good-looking cabs, sometimes called the "Cadillac" of trucks. Many of the Ford and General Motors trucks had smaller engines and were more suitable to the flatter terrain and lighter load requirements in the eastern part of the country.

The market for Delta trucks in the Dallas district was segmented into four major types of buyers. The largest of these groups was the market for construction trucks, which accounted for about 50 percent of the sales in the Dallas district. This market was further subdivided into drilling exploration companies, oil companies, construction companies, and ready-mix concrete companies.

The second largest market segment (25 percent of the district sales) consisted of the independent over-the-road truckers. These independent truckers were called wildcatters. They would haul for hire under the label of the firms whose commodities they carried.

Fleet owners, accounting for 15 percent of the sales, made up the third market segment. Fleets were generally sold to individuals or trucking companies who would then lease these trucks for the transporting of general freight. The fourth group of buyers, accounting for 10 percent of the Dallas sales, were firms which owned and operated their own trucks.

About seven years ago Leon Halter, then age 29, was hired as a salesman by Ben Frey, who at that time was the branch manager in Dallas. Halter was a native of Dallas and had been a successful salesman for a Dallas automobile dealer for three years prior to coming with Delta. Prior to selling cars, Mr. Halter had been a long-haul truck driver for several trucking companies.

Within two years he became the top salesman in the Dallas branch. Mr. Frey had taken a personal liking to Halter and began grooming him for a managerial position. Mr. Halter continued to lead the Dallas branch in sales over the next two years. In his fifth year with Delta he became the top salesman in the entire southwestern region. That year he was asked to give a speech on salesmanship at a meeting of branch managers, which was held in the home office. At that meeting, the vice president of sales, Paul Dennison, was very impressed by Halter and openly discussed the possibility of promoting him to branch manager at the first opportunity.

Later that year, Mr. Frey was promoted to the position of regional sales manager, thus leaving open the job of branch manager in Dallas. Mr. Halter had hoped to get that job, but Mr. Dennison instead selected Arnold Booth as the new branch manager. Booth had been a salesman at the Dallas branch for about three years. He ranked third in sales, and his sales figures were considerably below Mr. Halter's. However, Mr. Booth had been with the company for 15 years and during that time had served as a branch manager for two years in Colorado. It was on the basis of this experience that Mr. Dennison decided to promote Mr. Booth instead of Mr. Halter. Halter was very disappointed at not getting the job, but his sales figures continued to improve.

In talking with Halter, Mr. Booth realized that Halter still hoped to become a branch manager. However, Halter enjoyed living in the west or southwest. Consequently, he was willing to wait for a branch manager's position to open in these regions, rather than taking a similar job in the east. It did not appear likely, however, that a branch manager's job would be open in the west or southwest during the next few years.

The branch manager was paid a straight salary of $36,000, plus a small bonus based on the profitability of the branch office. The sales reps were paid a straight commission based on their sales volume. The commission rate, however, was higher on sales with higher gross margins. During his first year under Mr. Booth, Leon Halter earned about $46,000.

Last year Mr. Halter again increased his sales to the point where he earned about $52,000. Early this year, Mr. Booth received a letter from the home office informing him that they had reviewed Mr. Halter's sales record. They were concerned about the implications of having a sales rep earn an income greatly exceeding that of a branch manager. The home office was afraid that Mr. Halter would be unhappy with a promotion to branch manager if it required a substantial cut in pay. The home office felt that the fact that Mr. Halter's sales were so much greater than any of the other sales people in the Dallas branch might be indicative of a need to reallocate accounts and territories.

Mr. Booth decided to review the situation to determine if such a reallocation was in order. He discovered that Halter's success was largely due to his ability to sell to customers in all four major market segments (construction, independent truckers, fleets, and manufactureers). Most of the other sales people focused their attention largely on only one of the major segments. Mr. Halter's greatest success had been in selling to independent truckers. Mr. Booth suspected that Halter's past experience as a truckdriver aided him considerably in developing a good rapport with these buyers.

Further analysis of the situation revealed some other advantages which Halter seemed to enjoy over the other sales reps. Halter generally made larger commissions because of his ability to negotiate larger margins on his sales. He also had a higher rate of obtaining reorders from his clients than any of the other sales reps. Halter had been with Delta for seven years. His high sales volume was largely the result of obtaining substantial reorders requiring little sales effort, while at the same time actively generating new accounts.

To further complicate matters, Mr. Booth had found it increasingly difficult to motivate the other sales people. Sales contests were often conducted at the branch office. However, these had failed to provide any substantial motivation for the sales reps in Dallas because Leon Halter almost inevitably won. Mr. Booth was looking for a way to give the other sales people a shot in the arm. He was considering redistributing some of Mr. Halter's older accounts among the sales force. Mr. Booth reasoned that he could give a sales rep an account that was in the particular market segment in which that rep was most proficient. Mr. Booth felt that such a plan would please the home office, while at the same time boost the morale and sales of the entire branch.

Mr. Booth also was considering specializing the sales people by market segments. This would involve the reshuffling of all the accounts. Such a move would radically affect Mr. Halter who would —retain only his independent trucker accounts. Inasmuch as most of the sales reps were effective in only one segment, Mr. Booth felt that such a plan might provide for greater efficiency of operations.

On the other hand, Mr. Booth was afraid that such a tactic could result in the loss of his star salesman. Halter's sales record was well known in the industry. And Booth had discovered earlier that Halter had recently turned down an offer to work as a salesman for the Dallas distributor of a major competitor. Booth also knew that Halter had a much better chance of becoming a branch manager for a competitor. What Booth did not know was whether or not Halter would be willing to suffer the loss of some of his accounts while waiting for a managerial post.

Questions

1. Should Mr. Booth redistribute the branch office accounts? If so, propose a plan for reallocation.
2. If not, how should Delta control the level of pay received by the sales people?

12

Compensating the Sales Force (continued)

There is nothing so degrading as the constant anxiety about one's means of livelihood.
MAUGHAM

Two steps will complete our job of designing a sales-compensation plan, which we began in the preceding chapter. One step is to determine the *method* of compensation. The other step is a series of final activities such as pretesting the plan, getting the approval of management and the sales force, and providing for the frequent evaluation of the plan.

The compensation *method* chosen by a firm should (1) enable the company to reach its specific objectives, (2) bring the average earnings of sales people to the desired level, and (3) meet as many of the requirements of a sound plan as possible.

The building blocks available to management when constructing a sales-compensation plan include:

- Salaries.
- Drawing accounts.
- Commissions.
- Bonuses.
- Expenses.
- Profit sharing.
- Indirect monetary benefits (vacation, insurance, pensions, and so on).

Some of these components act as an incentive for the sales force; others offer stability and security in earnings; still others may help the firm to control its sales costs. The more elements used in building a plan, the more complex it is (see Figure 12–1).

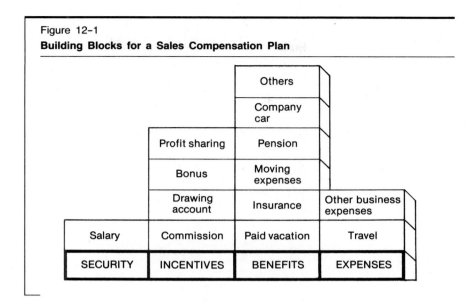

Figure 12–1
Building Blocks for a Sales Compensation Plan

Basic Types of Compensation Plans

Fundamentally, there are only three widely used methods of compensating a sales force:

1. *A straight salary*—a fixed element related to a unit of time during which the sales person is working.
2. *A straight commission*—a variable element related to the performance of a specific unit of work.
3. *Some combination of compensation elements.*

Over the past 30 to 40 years, there has been significant growth in plans that combine salary with an incentive feature. This trend has been primarily at the expense of salary-only and straight commission plans. Moreover, the incentive component of sales-force compensation is becoming a larger proportion of the total pay. (See Figure 12–2.)

These generalized statements do not reveal the wide variations among different industries. Aerospace firms and petroleum products companies, for example, tend to prefer straight salary plans. At the other extreme, companies manufacturing leather products, furniture, or apparel have traditionally favored straight commission plans.

Grouping companies into the categories of manufacturers, wholesalers, retailers, and service firms reveals some interesting differ-

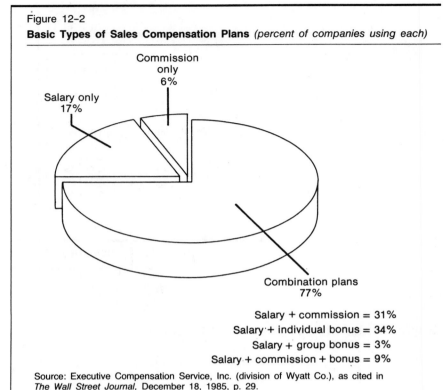

Figure 12–2

Basic Types of Sales Compensation Plans *(percent of companies using each)*

Commission
only
6%

Salary only
17%

Combination plans
77%

Salary + commission = 31%
Salary + individual bonus = 34%
Salary + group bonus = 3%
Salary + commission + bonus = 9%

Source: Executive Compensation Service, Inc. (division of Wyatt Co.), as cited in *The Wall Street Journal,* December 18, 1985, p. 29.

ences. Manufacturers and retailers strongly prefer some type of combination plan. Wholesalers prefer a straight commission plan. Service firms prefer a straight salary plan far more than any of the other three groups do. Interestingly, surveys of sales people report that the reps themselves strongly endorse some form of combination plan.

Emphasis Shifting from Volume to Profits

Traditionally, sales compensation plans in general and incentive features in particular have been geared to generate sales volume. For years, textbooks and business executives have recognized that gross margin and some form of net profit are sound bases on which to build incentives into pay plans. Yet, this recognition was largely lip service as far as sales executives were concerned. In recent years, however, there has been a modest shift in emphasis away from sales volume *alone* toward *profitable* sales volume.

The rise of profit consciousness probably coincides with increasing acceptance of the marketing concept and the profit squeeze faced by many firms. Executives have seen that an *increase* in company sales is often accompanied by a *decrease* in company profits. Consequently, they realize that sales volume alone is a poor indicator of a sales person's value to the firm.

The attention to profits does not mean that management has abandoned sales volume as a basis for incentive pay—far from it. Surveys show that a great majority of firms still base their commission payments on sales volume. These summary figures, however, sometimes hide a very important fact. While based on sales volume, these commission plans are often structured to achieve desirable goals, such as encouraging full-line selling or stressing profitable products.

When designing profit-stressing incentive plans, many firms adopt the gross-margin approach. That is, the commission or other incentive is based on the gross margin (net sales less cost of goods sold) resulting from a sales rep's total sales. Different rates of commission may be paid for different product lines in order to encourage greater sales-force efforts toward some products. An alternative approach is the contribution-to-overhead method. Under this method, incentive pay is based on the gross margin less all marketing costs that can be charged *directly* to a given sales person. The problem in most profit-based plans is to develop one that accomplishes management's goal, yet meets the "simplicity" requirement of a good plan.

Straight Salary Plans

A salary is a direct monetary reward paid for performing certain duties over a period of *time*. The amount of payment is related to a unit of time rather than to the work accomplished. A salary is a fixed element in a pay plan. That is, in each pay period, the same amount of money is paid to a sales rep, regardless of that person's sales, missionary efforts, or other measures of productivity.

Strengths of Straight Salary Plans

Assured regularity of income gives the sales person a considerable degree of security. A salary plan also provides stability of earnings, without the wide fluctuations often found in commission plans.

The assurance of a regular, stable income can do much to develop loyal, well-satisfied sales people. Sales forces on straight salary usually have lower rates of turnover than those on commission. Sales people on a salary are more likely to feel they are a part of the company, rather than being in business for themselves.

Management can direct the sales force into a variety of activities more easily under a salary plan than under any other method of compensation. As long as sales people are on a salary, it probably does not matter to them what job assignments they receive. This assumes that the performance evaluation they receive is correspondingly based on these assignments.

Because people on salary are less likely to be concerned with immediate sales volume, they can give proper consideration to the customers' interests. There is no need for high-pressure selling, and there is little danger of overstocking a customer. Customers often react more favorably to a sales person if they know he is on straight salary. They think the rep is more apt to consider their interests.

Limitations and Administrative Problems in the Plans

Often the limitations of a straight salary plan are really not *inherent* weaknesses but only a reflection of poor administration. One good example is the frequent objection that a salary plan provides no direct incentive to the sales force. True, a salary plan does not offer the strong, direct incentive that a commission or a bonus does. However, this drawback is usually accentuated out of proportion because of administrative weaknesses.

Part of the failure to furnish incentive usually can be traced to the *frequency* and *bases* of adjustment, which are administrative matters. Theoretically, salaries could be revised daily or weekly in relation to the sales person's performance, but from a practical standpoint this ordinarily is not done. Companies often go to the other extreme and seldom revise salaries. They do not make adjustments often enough to encourage extra effort or to keep the plan flexible.

Many salary plans fail to provide adequate incentive because the *bases* of adjustment are not sound. People should get pay raises periodically if their work is more than satisfactory. But often there is no clear-cut understanding of what constitutes satisfactory accomplishment. Salary administration often seems to be done on a basis of expediency or arbitrariness. A person who complains enough or threatens to quit may get a salary increase. Often, people with long service are paid too much in relation to their results, while high-producing younger reps are underpaid.

Another disadvantage of a straight salary is that it is a fixed cost. There is no direct relationship between salary expense and sales volume. When sales are down, the fixed cost of compensation can be a burden on the firm.

Another possible administrative problem is related to an advantage of a salary plan—namely, that management is able to direct the activities of the sales force. This presupposes (1) that the workers are adequately supervised and (2) that management gives proper credit for the types of activities it wants to encourage. A salary plan has no automatic feature that will stimulate a sales person to contact new prospects or sell high-margin items just because an executive says to do it. Suppose that management urges sales people to do nonselling missionary tasks, but then judges them on the basis of sales volume. They soon observe the inconsistency and respond only to direction that involves selling the product.

When a Straight Salary Plan Is Best

Generally speaking, a salary plan is best used when management (1) wants a well-balanced sales job and (2) is able to supervise and motivate the reps properly. Some of the specific situations for which a straight salary is better suited include:

- Sales recruits are in training, or they are still so new on the job that they cannot sell enough under a commission to make a decent income.
- The company wants to enter a new geographical territory or sell a new line of products.
- Several reps must work together for long periods in order to sell one account.
- Sales involve a technical product that requires lengthy presale and postsale service and negotiations.
- The job entails only missionary sales activities.

Straight Commission Plans

The straight commission plan involves a regular payment for the performance of a *unit* of work. A commission is related to a unit of accomplishment, in contrast to the salary method, which is a fixed payment for a unit of time. A commission is usually based on factors that are largely controllable by the sales people. A commission plan consists of the following three items:

1. A *base* on which performance is measured and payment is made—for example, net sales in dollars or units of the product.
2. A *rate*, which is the amount paid for each unit of accomplishment—for example, if a firm pays a nickel in commission for each dollar of sales, the rate is 5 percent.
3. A *starting point* for the commission payments.

The straight commission method may or may not include a provision for advances against future earnings (a drawing account). Also, the business may pay the sales people's travel expenses separately. Or the commission may be adjusted upward and the reps pay their own expenses.

The major advantages of a commission are usually the limitations of a salary plan, and the strong points of a salary are generally the weak ones of a commission. Essentially, the two methods diametrically opposed.

Advantages of Straight Commission Plans

Probably the major advantage of the straight commission method of sales compensation is the terrific incentive it gives the sales force. Many firms have no ceiling on sales reps' commission earnings, so their opportunities are unlimited. On the average, sales people on commission have a higher level of earnings than those on salary, except under very poor business conditions. In many types of commission selling, the sales reps are immediately rewarded for their efforts. They need not wait for the next salary review. Commission payments are a strong motivating factor to get the reps to work hard. Typically, a sales person on commission works more hours each week than one on salary does.

A corollary advantage from the sales-force point of view is the freedom of operation enjoyed by reps on straight commission. In many respects, they are almost independent business people. They often set their own hours and their own work schedule. Some sales managers believe that the combination of maximum incentive and freedom of operation attracts a better caliber of sales person. However, there are no acceptable statistics to support the claim that a commission plan, or any other pay plan, tends to attract superior sales people. It is probably true, however, that a commission plan does a better job of weeding out ineffective sales reps.

Sales representatives generally feel the commission plan is a fair one, assuming that the base and rate are fair, because their earnings are related to their own results. No one else's judgment affects their income, as is true under a salary plan. When incomes from *commissions* decline, not nearly so many complaints are apt to come from the sales force as when *salaries* must be decreased.

Another big advantage to the company is that selling costs are controllable in relation to sales or some other base. In some cases, a firm must resort to a commission because it cannot risk this lack of control over selling expenses, even though a salary plan might be better.

Disadvantages of the Plans

Several often-cited limitations of the commission method of sales compensation can be summed up under one point. It is difficult to supervise and direct the activities of sales people, because they tend to think they are in business for themselves.

Often, under the usual commission structure, the sales people's only concern is to sell more merchandise, without regard to the interests of the company or the customer. The reps may concentrate on easy-to-sell items and frequently ignore those that are slow moving. Customers may be overstocked or sold more expensive items than necessary. Sales reps often disregard any thought of a fully balanced sales job, and management cannot expect them to do missionary work.[1]

Another disadvantage of the commission method is that earnings may fluctuate widely for reasons beyond the sales reps' control. In boom times, they may have very high earnings through no particular effort of their own. On the other hand, when business is bad, sales people's earnings may drop sharply, even though they are working harder than ever.

Management is not totally helpless to combat some of these problems. In fact, it can exercise considerable control by judiciously modifying commission rates and bases. For example, to deter the sale of easy-to-sell, low-margin items, it can pay a commisson on gross profit. This use of the gross-profit base also may discourage price concessions. A lower commission rate on easy-to-sell products also reduces the attention they receive.

When a Straight Commission Plan Is Best

Conditions under which the straight commission method is best can be summarized as follows:

- A company is in a weak financial position and therefore selling costs must be related directly to sales.
- Great incentive is needed to get adequate sales.
- Very little nonselling, missionary work is needed.
- Adequate field supervision is not possible or feasible, so the firm must rely on a commission to accomplish the desired sales objectives.

[1] For an illustration of these potential problems drawn from the securities segment of the financial services industry, see Scott McMurray, "Brokerage Firms Push Salespeople to Produce More or Face Penalties," *The Wall Street Journal,* June 19, 1984, p. 33.

- Business conditions are good, and the sales force as a group prefers to go on straight commission.
- The firm uses part-time sales people or independent contractors.

Administrative Problems with the Commission Method

Several administrative problems are involved in the use of the commission method, whether it is the only element in a compensation plan or part of a combination plan.

Commission bases. Management must determine what *base* to use for paying commissions. Most bases are related to sales volume, gross margin, or, in some cases, nonselling activities. A commission may be paid on sales as measured in dollars or in units of the product.

A company can encourage attention to expense reduction or greater profit by basing commissions on gross margin or on gross margin minus direct sales expenses. In some firms, the commission ostensibly is based on sales volume. However, by establishing different rates for different product lines, the company, in effect, is stressing the profit feature. That is, higher commission rates are paid on the high-margin products to encourage their sales. Conversely, low rates are paid on sales of products that carry low margins.

Rates of commission. Management also must determine the *rate of commission*—that is, the amount paid for each unit of accomplishment. Rates vary among companies. Even within a given firm, there may be rate differentials among the products or territories. The choice of rates may be affected by factors such as (1) the level of income desired for the sales force, (2) the profitability of given products, (3) difficulty in selling a product, (4) classes of customers, or (5) territorial problems.

Rates may be constant throughout all stages of sales volume. Or they may be on a sliding scale, going up or down as sales volume increases. A **progressive rate** is one that increases as the volume increases. To illustrate, a business may pay 5 percent on sales up to $20,000 a quarter, 7 percent on the next $80,000 (sales from $20,000 to $100,000), and 10 percent on everything over $100,000. A sales person who had sales of $130,000 for the quarter would receive a commission of $9,600, computed as follows:

5% on first $20,000	$1,000
6% on $20,000 = $100,000	$5,600
10% on $30,000 (amount over $100,000)	$3,000
	$9,600

A progressive rate is intended to offer a great incentive to the reps in that the more they sell, the more they make on each sale. The company usually can afford to step up the rate because only the variable costs increase with each marginal dollar of sales. The larger the sales, the less the overhead charged to each unit of volume. A progressive rate is also justified if sales are increasingly difficult to make as volume goes up. A progressive rate requires careful administration to prevent reps from taking advantage of the system. They may postdate or predate orders so all fall in one period. Thus they artificially boost their volume during a given period and consequently qualify for a higher rate on the last orders turned in.

A **regressive rate** works in reverse. The concern may pay 7 percent on the first $20,000 of sales in a given period, 5 percent on the next $20,000, and 3 percent on all sales over $40,000. A regressive rate has some merit if it is hard to get the first order but reorders come frequently and automatically. A regressive rate also may be used to even out the earnings of all sales people or to reduce the effect of windfall sales. A regressive rate requires careful administration to discourage a sales person from (1) withholding orders at the end of a commission period when they would command a lower rate and then (2) turning them in at the start of the next period. (See Figure 12–3.)

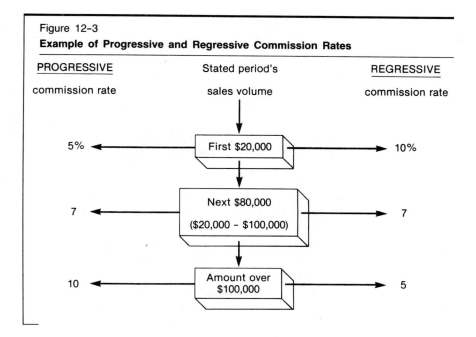

Figure 12–3

Example of Progressive and Regressive Commission Rates

PROGRESSIVE	Stated period's	REGRESSIVE
commission rate	sales volume	commission rate

PROGRESSIVE	Sales volume	REGRESSIVE
5%	First $20,000	10%
7	Next $80,000 ($20,000 – $100,000)	7
10	Amount over $100,000	5

Drawing accounts. Administrators must determine whether to use a drawing account. A drawing account may be a fixed sum advanced to a sales person at regular time intervals, such as weekly or monthly. Or it may be a limited amount that a rep can draw against as needed during the period. The amount drawn is paid back to the company out of the person's commission earnings during the same period.

A drawing account may or may not be guaranteed. Under a **nonguaranteed** plan, the advance is strictly a loan. Assume that a sales person does not earn enough in commissions to pay back the advanced funds in one period. Then the balance of the debt is carried over to the next period.

Let's illustrate the concept of a nonguaranteed drawing account with an example covering a three-month period. Our rep draws $1,800 at the beginning of each month, and she earns a commission of 10 percent on sales volume. Her monthly sales during this period are $40,000, then $15,000, and finally $30,000. The arithmetic in our example is as follows:

Month	Draw	Sales Volume	Commission Earned	End-of-Month Payment to Rep
January	$1,800	$40,000	$4,000	$2,200
February	$1,800	$15,000	$1,500	0 (rep owes $300)
March	$1,800	$30,000	$3,000	$900 (computed as follows)

Commission =	$3,000
Less draw =	−1,800
Less February debt.	− 300
Net	$ 900

A **guaranteed** drawing account is operated in much the same fashion, with one big exception. At the end of a stated period, if a sales rep's commissions total less than the draw, the debt is canceled. It is not carried forward, and the rep starts with a clean slate. Thus a guaranteed draw is much like a salary.

Drawing accounts are used to offset some of the drawbacks of the straight commission plan because they add a semblance of security and regularity of income. In businesses where sales fluctuate seasonally, an advance can be very helpful to sales people. In effect, the company is taking over some of their personal budgeting problems. For example, in one industry sales are high from October through December and April through June. Without a drawing account, the reps must make the high earnings of October to December stretch to cover the lean months of January to March.

When a firm hires a new sales person or opens a new territory, it may use a guaranteed drawing account for a period of time rather than change the compensation plan from commission to salary. This is particularly likely to happen if, in a relatively short time, the new sales people or those with new markets are likely to do well on a commission.

However, for many firms the operating and administrative problems far offset the possible advantages of drawing accounts. Clerical and bookkeeping work is increased to take care of the necessary computations. Unless a drawing account is carefully controlled, various abuses can arise. Sales people may come to think of the account as something that belongs to them—as a salary, rather than a loan. Some may run far in arrears until they see the situation is hopeless. Then, realizing they can never earn enough in commissions to pay back the debt, they quit their jobs. Because of the problems involved in drawing accounts relative to other methods, their use has declined. Today companies tend to supplement a commission with a base salary.

Many of these abuses are not inherent weaknesses of the system, but are simply evidence of poor management. Executives should be careful to point out to new reps that a drawing account is a loan and not a salary. Management should not allow a long period of time to elapse before settling the drawing accounts. A quarterly or semiannual settlement period is a reasonable length of time.

Split commissions. When two or more sales people work together on a sale, provision must be made to split any commission or other credit given. Various situations may call for a decision on the issue. It may take three people to complete a sale of some large, technical product. One may be the territorial sales rep, the second a sales engineer or service representative from the home office, and the third the district manager. If a commission or bonus is part of the compensation plan for each of these people, distribution of the credit is a problem.

Geographical location can also complicate the commission division. For example, a sales person in the Birmingham, Alabama, district may make a sale, but the order is placed through the buyer's home office in Atlanta. To further complicate matters, delivery may be made to plants in Nashville and New Orleans as well as to Birmingham. If each of the four cities is covered by separate sales reps, the sales manager has a real problem in splitting any commission involved. The Birmingham sales person may want to claim full credit, pointing out that the order basically originated in his territory and through his efforts. At the same time, the Atlanta rep may have been calling on the buyer's home office for some time. The problem

A day-to-day operating problem in the
Majestic Glass Company (F)

A Split-Commission Situation in Sales Compensation

Several of Majestic's largest customers were huge nationwide corporations having plants and offices in several cities. Some customers had numerous product divisions, and several executives in different cities might be involved in the purchasing. Such complexities made it difficult for Clyde Brion, general sales manager, to decide which Majestic sales representative should receive the commission for a particular order. Often these orders were very large.

For example, the Cincinnati sales representative, Elton Boggess, had turned in an order for more than $200,000 of cosmetic bottles. The order came from the Mi Charmé Products Company in Cincinnati. Furthermore, Boggess had written *New Customer* across the face of the order, thus claiming the additional 5 percent commission on orders from new customers. The order clearly stated that the bottles were to be shipped to the Mi Charmé plant in Baltimore, Maryland. Baltimore customers were called on by James Woodall, Majestic's sales rep based in Washington, D.C.

Brion remembered having read in a recent issue of *The Wall Street Journal* that the Mi Charmé Products Company had been purchased by Elaine Marhman, Inc., of New York City. This firm was best known for its foods line. It had been a regular buyer of Majestic salad oil bottles through Majestic's New York City salesman, Bradley Norton.

To complicate the incident, in the same mail that had brought Boggess's order, Brion found an identical order from Woodall. He also claimed the extra commission for having sold a new customer. Had the duplication not been noticed, Majestic might have delivered a double amount of merchandise.

Brion tried to resolve the situation by telephoning the director of purchasing for Elaine Marhman, Inc. This official offered little help, saying that the firm's buying procedures for the "cosmetics division" were not yet formalized. However, he was familiar with the order in question. He remembered having talked with Woodall about it while in Washington, D.C.

Brion then telephoned Norton, the New York City sales rep. Norton said that he was busily working on the Mi Charmé order but it had not yet been confirmed. He said that he did not intend to claim it as a new-customer order. Nor did he know to what extent Boggess or Woodall had participated in the sale.

Brion asked, "Who should get the commission, then?" Norton laughed and replied, "I guess that's what we have a sales manager for, sir!"

Questions

1. How should the regular 10 percent commission be split in this situation?
2. Should this order qualify for the additional 5 percent paid on new-customer orders?

Note: See the introduction to this series of problems in Chapter 3 for the necessary background on the company, its market, and its competition.

of split commissions can be particularly nasty when central buying offices are concerned. Often, the sales people in the outlying territories feel that their efforts avail them little.

No simple or generally accepted method exists for handling split credits. Instead, each firm must feel its own way, using executive judgment to arrive at a policy. As a rule of thumb, management should allow only a limited number of percentage splits, such as 50–50 or 75–25.

House accounts. House or no-commission accounts are customers who are serviced by the branch or home-office executives. Usually, no commission is given to sales people when sales are made to these accounts. Problems are minimized if management follows two policies. First, it must severely limit the number of house accounts. Second, it must clearly define all house or no-commission accounts in advance of solicitation. House accounts may be justified when windfall commissions would otherwise result without commensurate effort, as with reorders from large national accounts or the federal government. Abuses can creep into the system when management steps in too often, or takes the good accounts after they have been developed by the sales force.

Mail and telephone sales. An executive decision must be made on whether to pay a commission on an order mailed in or telephoned in by the customer. Most firms pay a commission on such orders because, presumably, they came as a result of selling effort made at some time by the territorial representative. In fact, many companies urge small accounts to mail or order by telephone in an attempt to reduce the sales expense connected with personal calls on such accounts.

Sales with trade-ins. A policy must be established for commission payments on sales made with a trade-in. Some firms pay the commission on the difference between the sales price of the product and the amount allowed on a trade-in. If the item sold for $1,000 and $300 was allowed on the used trade-in, the commission would be based on $700. Then, if the sales person later sells the item received on trade-in, the same procedure is followed. Another method is to pay on the "washout," or net profit made after both the new product and the traded-in items are sold. The following facts may be assumed in the sale of a new automobile, for example. The invoice cost plus freight on the new car is $7,200, and it is sold for $9,000. The amount allowed on the trade-in is $2,500; $500 is the cost to fix up the old car, and it is sold for $3,600. The company would pay a commission on the $2,400 it netted on the complete series.

Installment sales. On installment sales, some firms pay the full commission when the sale is made, even though it will be some time before full payment is received. Even if the buyer defaults and the product is repossessed, the sales person suffers no penalty. In other cases, the sales person receives the commission piecemeal, as the buyer pays the installments. Many life insurance companies use this system. A sales person may get 30 percent of the first year's premium and 10 percent of each subsequent annual premium. If the insured drops the policy, commission payments cease.

Bad debts. A policy must be set regarding who should bear the burden of loss from bad debts, particularly in sales when the merchandise cannot be repossessed. Usually this depends on how much authority the sales force has in determining whether a given customer should be granted credit. Probably the most widely used practice is to pay full commission to the sales person, even though the customer later defaults. This policy is usually adopted where the sales people have little or nothing to say about granting credit.

Combination Plans

Today, some form of combination pay plan is used in over 75 percent of all sales forces. Broadly speaking, the purpose of any combination plan is to overcome the weaknesses of a single method, while at the same time keeping its strong points. The various compensation elements may be grouped in countless ways to form a pay system. However, most of the combined plans fall within the following few categories:

- Salary plus and commission and/or bonus.
- Commission and guaranteed drawing account.
- Commission and bonus.

The additional compensation elements of profit sharing and expenses may be worked into any of these groupings. Or they may be combined with either straight salary or straight commission.

In a combination pay plan what portion should be incentive and what portion salary? The answer depends on the nature of the selling tasks and company's marketing goals. The incentive portion should be larger when a company is trying to increase its sales or gross margin, especially in the short run. The salary element is larger when management emphasizes customer servicing, a fully balanced selling effort, or team selling. The incentive portion in combination plans has been increasing over the past two decades.

Additional Components

Three components in combination plans have not yet been discussed. They are bonuses, profit sharing, and expenses.

Bonus.   Nature and purpose.   A bonus is probably the most loosely used word in the compensation vocabulary. As a result, it is sometimes difficult to assess accurately the extent to which it is used in pay plans. A *bonus* is a lump-sum payment for an above-normal performance. It is not related directly to the accomplishment of a *specific* unit of work as a commission is. Because of its nature, a bonus cannot be used alone, but instead, must always be combined with other methods such as a salary or commission.

Strictly speaking, management need not announce in advance either the amount of the bonus or the basis for distributing it. In fact, management theoretically has no obligation to pay a bonus in any given year, even though it has paid one in preceding years. Employees may know they will get a bonus, but they never know in advance how much it will be. Beyond these *narrowly defined* usages, however, a more realistic use of the term considerably broadens its meaning. Most sales bonuses are intended to stimulate the sales force to perform certain tasks by offering an incentive. Unless the plan is explained fully in advance, management will gain nothing for the bonus given.

The most commonly used basis for paying a bonus is the measure of a sales person's performance against a quota—typically, a sales volume quota or an expense quota. A sales rep may get a cash bonus for reaching a sales quota, or x dollars for going 10 percent over quota. Or, let's assume that the company's goal is to keep direct selling expenses within 8 percent of sales. Then at the end of the year the firm may pay each rep a bonus equal to half the amount by which his expenses are under the 8 percent ratio. If a rep's sales were $100,000 and expenses were $7,000 (7 percent), the bonus would be $500, or half the savings under the 8 percent ($8,000) expense quota.

Many other bonus-payment bases, while less commonly used, may serve management admirably in given situations. These bases include gross margin on sales, new accounts acquired, and profits earned by the entire company or by a geographical division.

Evaluation of bonuses.   Making a general evaluation of the bonus element in sales compensation is difficult because of the variety of payment bases and distribution methods used. The key to much of the success of a bonus lies in the method of its distribution. Unless sales people can see that the bonus they receive is related to their results, much of the incentive is lost. In some cases, a bonus is distributed equally among all sales people. In other instances, it may be spread in proportion to each person's total earnings. These two methods are questionable if a firm wants to stimulate its sales force effectively. One person may work much harder than another. But the first rep gets a much smaller bonus simply because his salary is lower than other sales rep's.

Profit sharing. Profit sharing is *not* widely used as a separate method of paying a sales force, nor is it a major part of a combination plan. It is a mistake to make profit sharing a significant part of a compensation plan for sales people, because they do not have sufficient control over profits. Inefficiencies in purchasing or production may raise costs to the point where profits are erased, even though the sales force does a better-than-average job. The reverse may also be true; production cost savings, plus a sellers' market, may result in huge profits with little effort on the part of the sales force. Profit sharing offers no direct incentive for increasing sales or performing any task ordered by management.

Expenses. *Ordinarily, reimbursement for travel and other sales expenses incurred by sales people should be kept separate from their compensation.* The two elements usually cause enough problems on their own without combining them. Even when handled separately, expense payments can result in a net addition or deduction from a person's earnings, so difficult is the problem of reimbursement. However, many companies do group the two by building a compensation plan under which the sales reps pay all their own expenses. Sales-force expenses are covered in the next chapter.

Salary-Plus Plans

Three commonly used combination plans involving salary are salary plus commission, salary plus bonus, and salary plus commission and bonus. In all three, sales reps are usually reimbursed separately for their expenses.

Salary plus commission. This plan is probably used more than any other type of compensation method. However, no generally agreed-on percentage division prevails between the fixed and the variable elements. The salary-commission plan tends to enjoy the advantages of a salary plus the incentive and flexibility features of a commission. But this plan is more complex and costly to operate because of the increased number of elements involved. Also, the addition of incentive features at the expense of the salary can reduce the element of managerial control over the sales force. In the final analysis, the success of this plan—or of any combination plan, for that matter—depends largely on the balance achieved among the elements.

Salary plus bonus. For the company that wants to control its sales force at all times and still offer some incentive, a salary plus bonus may be the answer. Usually, the salary element constitutes the major part of the total earnings—much more so than in a salary-commission plan. The salary-plus-bonus arrangement is excellent for the firm that wants some activity encouraged for a short time and then dropped. In general, this plan enables management to control and direct sales-force activities more than the straight salary plan does.

Salary plus commission and bonus. This plan is likely to be used by firms that use a salary-plus-commission plan, but occasionally would like to stimulate some specific, extra nonselling effort. Management may want to get some new accounts or push the missionary work behind one product line. In situations of this nature, the bonus feature is an ideal addition to the pay plan. Use of all three elements—salary, commission, and bonus—can result in an excellent structure if properly administered. The salary gives the control and income security advantages; the commission furnishes regular incentives; and the bonus is available to stimulate trouble-shooting assignments.

Commission-Plus Plans

Two additional typical combination plans involve a commission but no salary. In one, a commission is combined with is guaranteed drawing account, and in the other, with a bonus.

Commission plus guaranteed drawing account. As explained earlier, a guaranteed drawing account is an advance against commissions. It must be paid back if commissions are large enough in a given period. However, any indebtedness at the end of the period is canceled.

From a mechanical standpoint, a guaranteed draw is much like a salary. The draw plus a commission is similar to a salary plus commission over quota. In this case, the quota would be the amount of the drawing account. Assume that a rep was paid a guaranteed draw of $1,000 a month plus a commission of 5 percent on net sales. This rep would start receiving a commission when his sales reached $20,000 a month.

While this plan may be similar to salary plus commission from a computational viewpoint, it has significant psychological differences. First, management probably can adjust the level of the drawing account more easily than the level of salary. Second, under a commission-plus-guaranteed-drawing-account plan, the company has the fixed-cost weakness of the salary without the control advantages.

This is because most sales people probably link the plan more to straight commission.

Commission plus bonus. Sometimes an organization wants to alleviate the ills of a straight commission plan without having a fixed-cost element such as a salary or guaranteed draw. The addition of a bonus structure may be a happy solution, particularly when the commission is paid on net sales. When management wants to encourage sales of high-margin items, for example, a bonus may be paid for reaching a certain sales level for these products.

Point Systems in Compensation Plans

In a point system for compensation, credit for performance of a task is recorded in points. Then compensation is paid in proportion to the total points earned in a given period. *The point system is not a separate basic compensation method.* Instead, it is a distinct way of determining how much to pay a sales person under one of the plans discussed earlier. Under this system, management assigns point values to each task in relation to the emphasis attached to that activity.

The entire compensation plan, or only a part of it, may be related to a point system. For instance, under a straight commission plan a sales person may be paid $5 for every 10 points accumulated. These point values may be related to gross margin as follows:

1. Products with a margin of 10-18 percent: 1 point for each $25 of sales.
2. products with a margin of 19-30 percent: 3 points for each $25 of sales.
3. Products with a margin of over 30 percent: 5 points for each $25 of sales.

In addition, the firm may encourage that sales rep to pay attention to something other than sales volume by giving points for nonselling tasks, such as:

1. New prospect called on: 10 points.
2. Order from a new account: 25 points. (This is in addition to the points acquired in relation to the gross margin on the order.)
3. Display built: 20 points.

Probably the biggest advantage of a point system is its flexibility, which enables management to guide and control the sales-force activities. Management can change the emphasis on any given task simply by changing the point values for accomplishing it. A sales executive can broaden the base of a commission plan simply by assigning points to additional jobs. Furthermore, it usually is easier to change point values than to alter the base or rate for a commission.

A point system requires careful administration in establishing point values, if the system is to result in the desired degree of managerial control. The goal of a well-rounded sales job can be thwarted if sales people try to accumulate points through one or two jobs. They may do this because these tasks come easy for them. Or, it may be that a specific job carries more credit than the effort or results warrant.

Indirect Monetary Compensation

In the past, sales managers typically felt that their responsibility for compensation of the sales force ended when the paychecks were tendered. If there were any additional financial benefits, such as vacations or insurance, management usually reserved them for office and factory workers. The sales force was considered a unit apart, frequently not even a member of the family of employees. The salesman was a lone wolf, a rugged individualist, and a traveling man.

Today, however, young people going into selling are more security conscious, and management is acquiring a sense of social responsibility. Sales executives are realizing that rewards are due in two other general areas. One is *nonfinancial compensation* in the form of honors, recognition, and opportunity. These features help sales people develop a sense of self-worth and of belonging to a group. The other type of reward is *indirect monetary payment* of items that have the same effect as money, though payment is in a less direct form than salary or commission. These items, which are also referred to as fringe benefits, include such things as retirement plans, vacations, and insurance. Management's handling of these two broad types of rewards can have as much effect on sales people's morale as any policy relating to a salary level or commission rate.

Today most sales people enjoy the same employee benefits as other workers in comparable positions in a company. Indeed, what is referred to as "fringe" benefits today is better considered to be part of the whole cloth. These benefits averaged $7,330 per sales person in 1985, according to the Dartnell *Sales Force Compensation* study. This figure is in addition to the average earnings of $37,000 for experienced sales people and $29,500 for semi-experienced reps.[2] Figure 12–4 shows the most widely used sales-force benefits that are paid

---

[2] John P. Steinbrink, *Sales Force Compensation: 23rd Biennial Survey*, pp. 10, 18.

Figure 12–4
Company-Paid Fringe Benefits for Sales People *(benefit—percent of companies)*

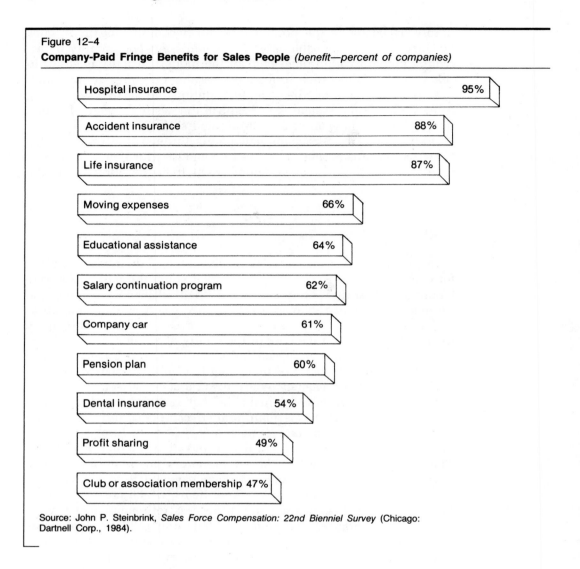

Benefit	Percent
Hospital insurance	95%
Accident insurance	88%
Life insurance	87%
Moving expenses	66%
Educational assistance	64%
Salary continuation program	62%
Company car	61%
Pension plan	60%
Dental insurance	54%
Profit sharing	49%
Club or association membership	47%

Source: John P. Steinbrink, *Sales Force Compensation: 22nd Bienniel Survey* (Chicago: Dartnell Corp., 1984).

for in part or in total by the company. Each of these benefit categories is more likely to be included in straight salary or combination plans than in straight commission plans. However, regarding fringe benefits, the commission plans are much closer to salary or combination plans today than was the case 10 or 20 years ago.

Firms give their sales people paid holidays and provide paid vacations of varying lengths, depending on the employees' length of service. Paid vacations present a managerial problem in connection with sales people who work partly or entirely on commission. They usually receive no vacation pay to represent the commission. Firms often give these reps their regular drawing accounts, which must be repaid from postvacation earnings. Also, many companies pay a commission to the reps on any sales that come in from their territories while they are on vacation. Most medium- and large-size firms provide various insurance programs (group life, medical, hospitalization) for their sales force. A significant number of firms have included their sales forces under a company retirement plan that supplements the federal social security program.

Indirect monetary benefits are proving to be important in attracting desirable sales applicants. Since these benefits are being given in so many competitive nonsales jobs, it has become almost a necessity to offer similar benefits in order to recruit qualified sales people. These benefits probably give sales people a greater degree of security and make them more loyal and cooperative. Such characteristics undoubtedly have some bearing on a reduction in the turnover rate. A good program of fringe benefits can be a strong deterrent to unionization of a sales force.

Factors Influencing Choice of Plan

Throughout our discussion of compensation plans, we cited examples of conditions under which a given plan would operate best. In each instance, one or more factors influenced the choice of a particular method of payment. Sales managers should consider these factors when selecting a compensation method. Some of the more important points to be taken into account are:

- Nature of the market and channels of distribution.
- Nature of the job.
- Caliber of the sales people.
- Financial condition of the company.
- General business conditions.
- Suggestions from the sales force.

Final Steps in Development of the Plan

Pretest the Plan

After management has tentatively selected the method of compensation to be used, the next step is to pretest the entire compensation plan. This involves determining how the proposed plan would have operated if it had been in effect during the previous few years. Management can estimate what the cost to the company would have been and what income would have been earned by the sales people. Pretesting a compensation plan is a simulation exercise that can easily be done on a computer.

No amount of pretesting will answer all questions. If the new plan had been in effect, sales might have been quite different. The commission features of a plan are easier to pretest than the salary element. If the base salary is increased 20 percent, it is hard to say how much more effective the missionary work will be or how much harder the sales force will work. However, several calculations can be made regarding the commission or bonus elements. By assuming various levels of sales for each line of products, management can compute what the compensation cost will be.

Regardless of its limitations, pretesting is a necessity. After spending untold hours in developing a compensation plan, it is unthinkable that management would not test its operation before installing it formally.

Introduce Plan to Sales Force

If the plan has been developed carefully, the sales people have already been asked for their suggestions and criticisms. When the plan is ready to be installed, the sales force should again be consulted. Often, sales people believe that management is only trying to cut sales costs. That is, any adjustment in compensation must be intended to lower their earnings. The final plan should be introduced in small conference groups. There the reps have a chance to ask questions, and management has the greatest possible opportunity to explain the system.

Install Plan and Evaluate It Periodically

A compensation plan may be installed throughout the entire sales force, or it may be tested in only one or two territories. If a company cannot conduct a realistic pretest, then it may field test the plan in a few districts under actual selling conditions.

The final step is to make certain the entire plan will be reappraised frequently to prevent it from becoming outmoded. A common mistake is to spend much time and money developing a good compensation system (or selection or training program) and then let the system become outdated. A person's job often changes over a period of time. Market and product conditions change. It is only sound management to keep a compensation plan in tune with the times.

Summary

A major step in designing a compensation plan is to determine the *method* of compensation. Fundamentally, there are only three methods for compensating a sales force: (1) a straight salary, (2) a straight commission, and (3) some combination of compensation elements (salary, commission, bonus, drawing account, expenses, and fringe benefits). Some form of a combination plan is used in over 75 percent of all sales forces. Today's sales-compensation plans tend to base compensation on the *profit* sales people produce rather than on the *sales volume* they generate.

A salary is a direct monetary reward for performing certain duties over a period of *time*. A straight salary plan assures a regular, stable income for the sales force. It enables management to direct the sales force into a variety of activities. The main drawback to a straight salary plan is that it does not provide any direct incentive to the sales force. It is also a fixed cost to the company. Generally speaking, a straight salary plan is best used (1) when management wants a fully balanced sales job and (2) when management can supervise the sales people so that they are properly motivated.

A straight commission plan involves a regular payment for the performance of a unit of *work*. The main advantage of a straight commission plan is the tremendous incentive it gives the sales force *to do what the commission is based on*. Sales reps enjoy much freedom of operation, and to management, a straight commission plan is a variable expense. Under a straight commission plan, it may be difficult to direct the activities of the sales people. There are several situations where a straight commission plan is best.

Several administrative problems occur in connection with a straight commission compensation plan. Management must decide on the bases and rates for paying the commission. Policies are needed regarding drawing accounts and split commissions. Commission-payment policies are also needed in situations involving trade-ins, installment sales, bad debts, sales returns, and mail or telephone sales.

In addition to the salary and/or commission elements, a company can consider using a bonus, profit sharing, or payment for sales people's business expenses. Many sales compensation plans also include fringe benefits. These may be *nonfinancial* rewards (honors, recognitions) as well as *indirect financial* rewards (such as paid vacations and company insurance plans). The final steps in designing a pay plan involve pretesting the plan, introducing it to the sales force, and actually installing the plan.

Questions and Problems

1. Following are three problems often faced by sales managers:
   a. Sales people tend to overemphasize the easy-to-sell parts of multiple product lines in an effort to build sales volume; other more profitable lines are forced into the background.
   b. Sales people need to spend more time developing new accounts.
   c. In order to improve a company's long-term position, sales people should be doing more missionary work and developing long-term customers to meet expected competition.
   In each case suggest a specific type of compensation plan that may be used to solve these problems.

2. What is the economic justification underlying the progressive commission rate? Is there any economic justification for a regressive rate? Which of the two rates is better for stimulating a sales force?

3. What factors determine the commission rate paid by a manufacturer of portable power tools? What conditions may influence a sales manager to reduce the established rates?

4. When sales reps are paid a straight commission and they sell merchandise on credit, should delinquent and defaulted accounts be charged to them? Would your decision be different if they were under a salary-commission plan?

5. What plan would you recommend for each of the following companies in handling split commissions?
   a. Manufacturer of sheets, pillowcases, towels, and related items sells to a department store chain. The order is placed through the chain's buying offices in New York. Delivery is made to stores throughout the country on an order from the department manager in each store. The manufacturer's sales people call on the units of the chain located in their territories.
   b. Manufacturer of oil well drilling equipment sells to main offices of drilling contractors, but delivery is made to field offices and drilling locations. Sales people in area where product is delivered must service the item.

6. What is the difference between a salary and a guaranteed drawing account?

7. If you were given a choice as a sales person, would you prefer an increase in earnings in the form of (a) some indirect monetary item, such as a company-financed annuity, or (b) an equivalent increase in salary or commissions?

8. All of a company's employees—sales and otherwise—receive paid vacations, except the sales people on straight commission. Should management establish a policy whereby these reps are given the same benefits? If so, how should management determine the amount to pay the commissioned reps during their vacations?

9. If a commission or a bonus is an element in the sales-compensation plan, explain how there may be seasonal fluctuations in earnings. How can management reduce or eliminate these fluctuations without changing the basic compensation plan?

10. In what respects would a compensation plan differ among sales people for the following firms?
    a. Manufacturer of small airplanes used by executives.
    b. Wholesaler of office equipment and supplies.
    c. Automobile dealer.

11. Give some specific examples of how each of the following factors can influence a company's choice of a compensation plan for its sales force.
    a. Caliber of the sales people.
    b. Nature of the job.
    c. Financial condition of the company.

Case 12–1

Bush-Jones Cleaning Systems, Inc.*

A Sales Compensation Plan in a Small Company

Bush-Jones Cleaning Systems was a small firm located in a large midwestern city, with just under 100 employees, including a sales manager and four sales people. The president, Mrs. Margaret Shondrick, felt that the personal selling portion of her promotional mix was not doing the job she expected. She identified the problem to a marketing consultant as an incentive problem involving the sales manager, Charles Cookson, who worked a four-day week.

The four-day work week had been instituted about 10 years ago as an experiment by the late Susan Kachmar, Mrs. Shondrick's mother, who had been president of the firm. It lasted about four years. When the firm switched back to the conventional work week, the entire sales force asked to stay on the four-day work week. The five

* This case was prepared by Professor Ernest F. Cooke of Loyola College (Maryland). Reproduced with permission.

claimed that they could do the job by working especially hard for four days a week. Each of the five had a different day off with Mr. Cookson taking Wednesday off to play golf. Mr. Cookson also played golf on the weekends, holidays, and during his vacation. Two of the sales people, Thomas Melendaz and his brother, Timothy, frequently worked on their day off.

The firm provided cleaning and janitorial services including supplies. Sales were about $1,500,000 per year. There were a number of house accounts, accounting for about $750,000 in annual sales, while the sales people were also responsible for annual sales of about $750,000. The house accounts were a few large customers who represented repeat sales. These accounts were covered by Mrs. Shondrick and her sister, Mrs. Mary Soeder, who was the firm's vice-president. Sales had increased almost every year since World War II. The rate of increase had approximated inflation, so there had been no real growth. The firm had been consistently profitable, had a good cash flow and sizable cash-equivalent assets.

The accounts covered by the sales people were smaller, with from 60 to 75 percent being repeat business that seemed to depend on how long the sales person had covered the territory. Except for supplies, new customers signed a contract for at least six months.

Sales people were paid straight commission, and they paid their own expenses. The rate of commission was 20 percent of the first $50,000 of sales, 10 percent of the second $50,000, and 5 percent of all sales over $100,000. Expenses consisted basically of travel with some money spent on lunches with customers. The company discouraged the use of business gifts but provided a wide variety of specialty advertising items. They ranged in price from 25 cents (ball point pen) to $5 (ceramic ash tray). The sales people paid half the cost of the specialty advertising items they used. Although he did not know for sure, Mr. Cookson estimated that all expenses (travel, lunch, specialty advertising) ranged from $2,500 to $5,000 for each sales person. Over half of that was travel, using the sales person's own automobile. Expenses seemed to be related to sales volume and ran about 17½ percent of commissions.

The Chicago area was divided into four territories with each sales rep covering one. An effort had been made to give each person an equal market potential over equal geographical areas. The sales people performed very little paperwork, but they were the major contact between Bush-Jones and their customers. The firm directed its efforts toward office buildings and some retail establishments. Customers were primarily businesses and institutions, with some government customers.

The sales people, their length of service as sales people, their educational background, age, and amount of sales last year were as follows:

Name	Sales Service	Education	Age	Sales
Thomas Melendaz	8 years	High school graduate	38	$247,000
Jack Armstrong	10 years	One year of college	52	202,000
Patricia Hollack	6 years	3 years of high school	42	174,000
Timothy Melendaz	1 year	One-half year of college	28	152,000

The Melendaz's were brothers. In fact, many members of management were related. All the sales people had started with the firm at relatively young ages and relatively low positions (i.e., with a mop and pail). There had been four sales people for many years. At one time there were no house accounts. But as sales people were promoted, retired, or left, certain of their larger more stable accounts became house accounts.

At one time, both Mrs. Shondrick and Mrs. Soeder had worked as sales people. In their teenage years, however, they had worked as cleaning women. Their mother, an immigrant from eastern Europe, had worked originally as a cleaning woman for Bush-Jones. She and some fellow workers took over the business in the 1930s in payment for back wages. Over a period of time she bought out her fellow workers.

Cookson was paid a straight salary of $24,000 in 1985. In 1984, his salary was $23,100. The president planned to increase his salary to $25,000 in 1986. She felt that Cookson could do more to increase sales. She was considering some sort of incentive plan. On occasion over the past few years, she had paid a bonus to certain key employees, including Cookson, but not to the sales people. This had been somewhat arbitrary and usually was not expected by the employees. It seemed to be related to how profitable business was and to her perceptions of how each employee had contributed to that success. The bonuses were approved by the board of directors. Employees were not informed who was to receive a bonus or how much each person received. Apparently the employees were "closed-mouth" about what they received. Cookson had not received a bonus for two years.

In discussing with Mr. Cookson what type of incentive should be arranged for him, the president asked him to suggest something. He proposed that he be paid a ½ percent override (commission) on all sales, including sales to house accounts. This would have added about $7,500 to his annual income. He was willing to take the override in place of next year's salary increase and any future bonus.

To help her in this problem situation, Mrs. Shondrick called in

Exhibit 1

Pay Plans for Cookson, as Suggested by Consultant

February 15, 1986

Mrs. Margaret Shondrick, President
Bush-Jones Cleaning Systems, Inc.
Chicago, Illinois

Dear Mrs. Shondrick:

Here are several pay plans you might want to discuss with your sales manager. These plans are based on sales by the four sales people and do not include sales to house accounts. Last year the sales made by your sales people amounted to $775,000, the year before $749,000, and this year are expected to amount to about $800,000.

Plan A.1: Salary—$23,200
           Commission—0.1 percent of sales

Plan A.2: Salary—$16,000
           Commission—1 percent of sales

Plan A.3: Salary—$ 8,000
           Commission—2 percent of sales

Plan B.1: Salary—$16,000
           Commission—2 ½ percent of all sales over $480,000

Plan C.1: Salary—None
           Commission—3.25 percent on first $400,000 in sales
                      2.75 percent on all sales over $400,000

Plan C.2: Salary—None
           Commission—3.0 percent of sales

Plan C.3: Salary—None
           Commission—2.75 percent on first $400,000 in sales
                      3.25 percent on all sales over $400,000

The effect of these plans is shown in the attached table (Exhibit 2). That table shows what Mr. Cookson would earn under each of the above plans, at different levels of assumed sales volume. Obviously many other combinations of salary, commission, and quota are possible in the above plans.

Yours truly,

Frank Gangale
Donald J. Cooke
Professor of Marketing

Frank Gangale, a university professor and consultant who specialized in areas of personal selling and sales management. They discussed the Cookson situation at quite some length, but Gangale was not told about Cookson's ½ percent override suggestion. Gangale then wrote a letter to Mrs. Shondrick in which he outlined several proposed pay

Exhibit 2
Cookson's Earnings under Each Plan, at Various Sales-Volume Levels

	Annual Sales Volume (not including house accounts)						
Plan	$400,000	$600,000	$700,000	$800,000	$900,000	$1,000,000	$1,200,000
A.1	$23,600	$23,800	$23,900	$24,000	$24,100	$24,200	$24,400
A.2	20,000	22,000	23,000	24,000	25,000	26,000	28,000
A.3	16,000	20,000	22,000	24,000	26,000	28,000	32,000
B.1	16,000	19,000	21,500	24,000	26,500	29,000	34,000
C.1	13,000	18,500	21,250	24,000	26,750	29,500	35,000
C.2	12,000	18,000	21,000	24,000	27,000	30,000	36,000
C.3	11,000	17,500	20,750	24,000	27,250	30,500	37,000

plans for Mr. Cookson (see Exhibits 1 and 2). Following Mrs. Shondrick's instructions, the letter was a brief summary of their conversations, but with no specific recommendations. Mrs. Shondrick wished to reserve that decision for herself.

In the course of analyzing Shondrick's compensation plan for her sales manager, Frank Gangale needed to examine the compensation plan for the four sales people. The more that Gangale studied the sales-force compensation plan, the more he wondered whether that plan was having a negative effect on sales-force motivation.

Questions

1. What changes, if any, should be made in the compensation plan for the sales force?
2. What incentive compensation plan should Mrs. Shondrick adopt for Charles Cookson?
3. If you were Mr. Cookson, which plan would you accept?

Case 12-2

Engineered Tools, Inc.*

Revising a Sales-Force Compensation Plan

Dave Decker, regional sales manager for Engineered Tools, Inc., of Cleveland, Ohio, had some serious doubts about the new compensation plan the company's top management had proposed for its sales

* This case was prepared by Professor Bruce D. Buskirk, Northwestern University. Used with permission.

force. Previously, the firm's sales engineers had received a salary plus a year-end bonus for reaching their sales quotas. The company reimbursed them for all expenses incurred in the field.

Engineered Tools, Inc., hired only college-graduate mechanical engineers for its sales force. About 60 percent of the sales were specially engineered for the customers' requirements. The production staff would develop the costs for such special customer jobs to which a standard markup would be added to cover overhead and profit. Such business would become quite profitable as customers were locked into the company for replacement parts and service. Such customers often became greatly dependent upon the technical skills of the sales engineer to provide the tooling they needed for their production processes.

The standard product line consisted of 3,000 different machine tools for which there was a standard list price. Upon the commencement of difficult competitive conditions, the sales reps were given the power to lower prices up to 10 percent with the approval of their regional sales manager. Dave had been so overwhelmed with requests for price rollbacks from his sales engineers that he gave up trying to evaluate the requests. He told his people to make their own decisions. Thus all prices had been effectively cut 10 percent. Management was unhappy with this development as it was duplicated in every other region. Management wanted the reps to be more discriminating in their cutting of price. The company needed larger margins, not smaller ones.

Unfortunately, for the past few years the market for machine tools had been declining. The sales engineers had received no bonuses for four years. Also, the company's financial condition had worsened because the gross margins had been declining, and the market kept slipping below sales projections. Top management felt that the sales force should try harder to make profitable sales under such difficult competitive conditions. Moreover, there was much appeal in top management to converting the fixed costs of sales salaries into the variable ones of sales commissions. Thus a straight commission plan based on the gross margin realized on the orders written by each rep was developed.

Under the new compensation plan, each sales engineer was provided with standard cost sheets for each item sold. The rep was then free to sell any item for any price over that cost. A commission of 20 percent of the difference between the price and the standard cost would be paid for the order. The firm would still pay all expenses. Thus management hoped to force the sales engineers to consider the gross margins obtained on a sale and push for higher margins. The same percentage would be paid for all custom machines—20 percent of the gross margin obtained.

The average sales engineer received about $54,000 a year in salary. The company's 25 sales engineers sold a total of about $28 million in 1986, down from $31 million in 1985. The gross margin in 1986 had been about $7 million.

Mr. Holtz, the president of Engineered Tools, had learned of this system for compensating sales reps from the Standard Tool Company. This competitor did not employ sales engineers, but rather used independent manufacturers' agents. The system worked well for Standard Tool.

Dave was fearful because the new plan had yet to be tested. He was afraid that some unforseen selling tactics might evolve which could hurt the company.

Question

Should the company adopt the proposed plan?

Case 12-3

Micro Measure

Compensating a New Sales Force

John Randall, founder of Micro Measure, was discussing his plans for compensating the 15-person sales force he was assembling that would pioneer the distribution of his new product, Micro Measure.

The Micro Measure was a small, hand-held, electronic device that provided instantaneous digital readouts, in either metric or imperial measures, of the distance between specified points. For example, if a distance was wanted from one end of a room to another, then the Micro Measure was placed at one end of the room and pointed at the other wall. When the button was pressed, an instant readout of the desired distance was obtained. The device worked on microwave principles. Randall planned to hire particularly outstanding sales representatives who were presently selling to his intended markets— the hardware and building materials trades. A special sales force was being developed to sell to large merchandisers such as Sears, J. C. Penney, K mart, and others.

Such sales representatives traditionally received 10 percent of sales as commissions for their efforts, and they paid their own expenses. Randall proposed paying them a 15 percent commission rate. He justified his plan to June North, his major financial backer, by explaining, "I want to attract the very best reps in the field, and to do so, I must give them a good reason for taking on our line. I need to pay them more than they are making on other products if I am to entice them into our venture."

North agreed that the firm's sales representatives should be top quality and that, to attract them, it would be necessary to offer them an exceptionally good deal. However, she wasn't sure that 15 percent would do the job. She reasoned, "I agree with you, Randy, but I'm not sure your 15 percent alone will get the job done. I think these people want a shot at a lot of money. Why don't we offer them stock options. Let's give them a piece of the rock if they perform. Set your quotas, tell them what you expect! If they reach quota, give them some options to buy our stock at a very low price."

Micro Measure had been capitalized for $1 million, which was represented by 1 million shares of authorized common stock. Mrs. North and Mr. Randall each owned 200,000 shares. Mrs. North had paid $200,000 for her shares, and Mr. Randall had been given his stock in exchange for his patents and technology on the Micro Measure device. Additional funding of $500,000 was going to be needed within the next year according to the company's cash flow projections. The company's business plan projected sales of $20 million for the coming year with a projected profit of $5 million. Both Mr. Randall and Mrs. North planned to sell the company to some established large hardware or tool manufacturer once profits reached the $5 million level. They hoped to receive a multiple of 10, which would make their company worth about $50 million.

Mrs. North continued, "Let's cut the sales force in on the loot if everything goes well. After all, if we achieve our sales goals, we're fairly well assured that we'll reach our target profits. If that's the case, we've created a very valuable company. Let's give the people who bring in the sales a portion of it. Let's say we set aside 15 percent of the stock for the sales reps. That's 1 percent for each rep who reaches the assigned sales goals. When we go to sell the company, that would be $500,000 for each of the successful reps. Now that's a lot of money. I think that there are a lot of reps out there who would work hard to make sure that they did the volume to get it. If they are as bright as we hope they are, they will see that this offers them an opportunity to become financially comfortable for life. They can take the half million, put it in municipal bonds, and live on the interest. It would be their retirement, their nest egg, their mad money."

Randall nodded but was doubtful. He demurred, "I don't know, June. It seems to me that giving these people $500,000 for doing what we are going to pay them well for doing in the first place is unnecessary. It's just too much money. That's $7.5 million right out of our pockets. And what about our future financing? Those potential stock options could queer whatever deal we try to put together. Investors in new ventures don't like options hanging over the company's head. We have 40 percent of the company, so if we give the reps 15 percent that will leave only 45 percent to give for future financing unless we water down our positions."

Question

What recommendations would you make for compensating the Micro Measure sales force?

Case 12-4

K-2 Distributors, Inc.

Revising a Compensation Plan for Driver Sales Force

K-2 Distributor, Inc., was a wholesale distributor for Dietz beer in a large western city. The distributorship was started in 1965 by two young men, Ralph Kennedy and Joseph Klein, who wanted to go into business for themselves. Through the years, the two founders and co-owners continued to actively manage the company. Currently Ralph Kennedy was the president, and Joseph Klein served as the general manager.

For some time now, Kennedy and Klein had been considering various methods that they might use to motivate their driver sales force to increase its sales of Dietz beer. Both men believed that a good sales compensation plan was the most effective motivator for driver sales people. However, the two men could not agree on what particular type of pay plan would be best for their sales force.

The Dietz Brewing Company was a regional brewer that marketed its products in several western states. In its market, Dietz faced competition from the large national brewers—Anheuser-Busch, Miller, and Stroh—as well as from two major regional brewers—Coors and Olympia.

Currently, Dietz produced and marketed four types of beer—the original regular Dietz beer, a light (low-calorie) beer, a premium beer, and a malt liquor. The company currently was in the process of developing a dark, heavy beer to add to the product mix.

The beer was packaged in several types and sizes of containers—barrels, half-barrels, small kegs (called pony kegs), cases of 24 12-ounce cans or bottles, and 12-packs and 6-packs in cans or bottles.

During the mid-1970s Dietz experienced a leveling off, and sometimes even a decline, in its sales even though total sales of beer were increasing in the United States. Three factors contributed to Dietz's loss of market share. First, some labor problems resulted in employee strikes and some public boycotts of Dietz beer. Second, the Miller Brewing Company, under its new Philip Morris ownership, was fabulously successful in the marketing of Miller Lite Beer. Consequently, Miller cut into the market share of all brewers. Third, in response to its market decline, Dietz changed formula for its regular beer, and the new formula was not well accepted. Later in the 1970s, Dietz revised its brewing formula, and the new brew was very well accepted.

By the mid-1980s, Dietz had recovered from its adversities of the 1970s. Currently its marketing performance was meeting management's expectations in spite of the continued intensive competition.

Over the past 10 to 15 years, the K-2 Distributors experienced the same pattern of ups and downs in sales volume in its local market as the Dietz Company had experienced in its total market. Throughout the years, Kennedy and Klein had been generally satisfied with the working relationship between their firm and the Dietz Brewing Company.

Nevertheless, Kennedy and Klein both believe that K-2 should be increasing its sales above the present level. Ralph Kennedy observed that the consumption of beer in the United States—in total volume and on a per-capita basis—had increased considerably over the past 10 years. He recognized that K-2 needed to improve its performance in several areas of marketing—for example, in the areas of promotion, point-of-purchase displays, and missionary selling techniques. However, both executives felt that the primary key to increased sales volume lay in the sales productivity of their driver sales people.

Currently the driver sales force consisted of five drivers. These five people call on a total of 350 accounts—classed as on-premise or off-premise accounts. On-premise accounts included all establishments where the beer was consumed in the customer's place of business—for example, restaurants, bars, hotels, or motels. Off-premise accounts included liquor stores, supermarkets, drugstores, convenience stores, and other establishments where the beer was purchased but consumed elsewhere.

The job responsibilities of the driver sales people primarily involved calling on existing and prospective accounts in order to sell Dietz beer. This sales activity included doing missionary selling, actively soliciting and writing up orders, calling on prospective new accounts, and making product deliveries. The drivers also were responsible for maintaining fresh supplies of beers, especially in their off-premise accounts. The drivers replaced outdated packages with fresh merchandise, and repaired or removed torn packaging. The drivers generally followed a prescribed route that had been set by the route manager in the office.

The task of managing a driver sales force was particularly difficult because of the relatively low occupational status of the sales job, and because the job was a hybrid of a truck driver and a sales representative.

K-2 executives also were concerned about the possibility of their sales force being unionized. The unionization of driver sales forces was especially prevalent on the West Coast. Some 50 years ago, the Teamsters Union started organizing driver sales forces in the soft drink, beer, and dairy industries.

In general, it was difficult to recruit high-caliber sales reps for the job of driver sales person. Then, once hired, it was difficult to keep the drivers sufficiently motivated so that they performed an effective selling job. Hence, Kennedy and Klein were quite concerned about their compensation plan—both as a managerial control tool and as a motivational device.

For the first 10 years of the company's existence, the K-2 sales force was paid on the basis of a straight commission plus a bonus. This was, and still is, the most widely used method for paying driver sales people in the beer industry. Then in the 1970s, when K-2 experienced a sales decline, the company switched to a salary-plus-bonus pay plan for its sales force.

This salary-plus-bonus plan was still in effect. The starting salary was $20,500 a year. However, because of their length of service with the company, the drivers were being paid $24,000 to $30,000 annual salaries. In addition, as a year-end incentive, a driver was paid a bonus of 1 percent of his salary for every 1 percent of his sales increase over the previous year. Thus, if a driver sales person's sales were up 4 percent this year over last year, then that driver received a bonus equal to 4 percent of his annual salary.

K-2 also provided what Mr. Klein referred to as a "substantial" benefits package for all its employees, including the sales force. This package included: insurance benefits (medical, term life, and a deductible dental plan), profit sharing, pension plan, free uniforms, hospitality bar with free beer, and a one-week paid vacation for every year you were employed with a maximum of four weeks' annual vacation. Finally, a bonus check equal to two weeks' salary was given by Mr. Kennedy to each employee at the company's annual summer picnic.

When K-2 switched from a commission to a salary during the period of declining sales in the 1970s, some people in the company said that K-2 was going counter to sound principles of sales-force compensation. These people felt that a salary plan would not provide the incentive needed to increase sales during those years. Mr. Kennedy believed, however, that the turmoil in Dietz's market situation created considerable uncertainty among Dietz's distributors. Consequently, Mr. Kennedy believed that the factors of job security and earnings stability engendered by a salary plan would be sufficient motivators for the sales force, especially during the period of uncertainty.

Moreover, he felt that by removing the pressures of commission selling, he would be encouraging the sales force to do more missionary sales work with their accounts. Kennedy and Klein both agreed on the importance of missionary selling by the distributors in the brewing industry. The Dietz Company advertised extensively in national media, including television, radio, newspapers, and magazines. However, this advertising was aimed at the ultimate consumer. Klein pointed out that it is up to the distributors to develop and hold their retailer accounts.

Currently, each Dietz distributor had an exclusive territory. So the competition came from distributors of other brands of beer. However, there were growing governmental pressures (either through legislation or administrative action of regulatory agencies) to abolish exclusive territorial protection. If this move should occur, then K-2 would also face competition from other Dietz distributors in that geographical area.

As a consequence of all of this, the K-2 management kept impressing on the sales force the importance of doing a good missionary selling job—a good job of servicing their accounts. This included such activities as setting up displays at retail locations, working with retailers in developing sales campaigns, maintaining beer coolers in good condition, and training retail sales people.

Mr. Klein agreed that the salary plan was working reasonably well. Under this plan K-2 could, and did, require extensive missionary selling work from its sales force. Yet he also felt that the sales force today needed additional incentive to tap the market's increased potential for sales. He also observed that most of the distributors of other major brands were relying heavily on a commission component in their pay plan. Klein felt that it was time for a change. The salary-plus plan might have been okay in the 1970s, but the 1980s called for a commission-plus type of plan.

He noted the difficulty of hiring high-caliber sales reps for driver sales jobs. Also, K-2 was a small business firm that provided very limited opportunities for sales people to advance into management. Consequently, he felt that the company had to offer better-than-average pay incentives for the drivers. He suggested to Mr. Kennedy that some type of commission, along with a small salary, might be best. He wanted to discuss with Kennedy various possibilities regarding the commission base and rate.

Kennedy felt the present plan should be retained in its existing form. Then Mr. Klein said that they should talk with the five drivers and get their ideas and suggestions. This would be more in line with the concept of participative management that was currently being discussed in business management circles. Kennedy was afraid to open that "Pandora's Box," as he put it. Yet he realized that something had to be done soon to increase the K-2 sales volume.

Question

What plan should K-2 use to compensate its sales force?

13

Sales-Force Expenses
and Transportation

Our men give their talent to the company and their genius to their expense accounts.
LIFE MAGAZINE

One sales manager observed that properly handled expense accounts are at best a nuisance, and improperly managed, they amount to grand larceny. This may have been an unusually sour view of the situation, but it points out the problem of controlling travel and business expenses incurred by the sales force.

Sales reps are among the few corporate employees who are allowed, even encouraged, to spend company funds. Furthermore, selling expenses are substantial. Some sales people spend more than $1,000 a week while in the field. If substantial travel is involved, expenses can be much higher. As a rule of thumb, it takes $20,000 to keep a rep in the field for a year.[1] A firm with 20 reps will incur a total cost of $400,000 a year. Such an amount deserves serious consideration.

Sales-Force Expenses and Strategic Planning

Expense-account policy is one element in a firm's strategic marketing plan. Often new enterprises are financially unable to bear the fixed costs of a rep's selling costs. The entrepreneur wants all costs to be as variable as possible—that is, related to sales volume. Thus, as a matter of strategy, the first reps will likely be offered a deal in which they pay all their own selling costs in exchange for a higher rate of commission. Higher commissions promise the hopeful reps

---

[1] Dartnell Corporation reported in its biennial survey that the average firm spent $16,781 in 1985. See *Sales Force Compensation* (Chicago: Dartnell Corp., 1986), p. 158.

that in the end they will make more money than they would if the company paid selling expenses. One fact can be counted on: if the reps pay their own expenses, there will be little waste.

On the other hand, some firms hope to woo customers by treating them generously. Through the adroit use of entertainment, the customer is lured into the company's fold and kept there. Other firms want to develop an image of prosperity. They require their reps to go "first class" in their travel and relationships with accounts.

Often firms use expense-account policy as a strategic tool for recruiting sales people. A generous expense account and a company car will attract many financially strapped college graduates.

Internal Revenue Service Regulations

Income tax laws significantly affect the travel, entertainment, and gift expenses of sales people. Congress and the IRS have progressively tightened the screws on the deductablity for income tax purposes of such expenses. Beginning with the Revenue Act of 1962 and continuing with the 1986 revision of the Internal Revenue Code, the government has taken a stringent stance on the deductability of business entertainment expenses. Beginning in 1987 only 80 percent of legitimate business entertainment expenses, including the business lunch, can be deducted as an allowable expense.

Legitimate Travel and Business Expenses

Management should identify in writing the expenses for which the company will pay—not only the broad expense categories, such as transportation or lodging, but also the details within each category. To say that transportation is a legitimate expense is not enough. For example, in the case of air travel, management may reimburse only for coach fare. Those who choose to travel first class pay the difference. Specific guidelines should let sales reps know whether they must lease the cheapest rental car available. If they take a taxi from the airport rather than the less expensive bus, will the company pick up the tab? Such matters need clarification.

When determining allowable items, a good general policy is that the sales person should be reimbursed (1) for business expenses incurred in connection with work and (2) for personal expenditures that would not have been necessary otherwise. The first part of the policy statement provides for expenditures for entertainment, telegrams, office supplies, and transportation. Many of these expenses may be incurred either on the road or while selling in the home-office city. The second part of the statement refers to such items as overnight lodging, meals, and possibly laundry or valet service away from home. Sometimes it is difficult to draw a line between what a person spends on the road and what would have been spent for the same thing at home. People must eat whether at home or traveling, but it usually costs more to eat out than to eat at home. Rather than trying to determine the difference in the cost of meals at home and on the road, most firms pay all meal expenses while the employee is traveling.

There is no unanimous agreement on what constitutes a legitimate expense for reimbursement, but we can generalize about major categories of expenses. In some cases, sales reps pay their own expenses so that reimbursement is not an issue.

Usually, companies cover all *transportation* costs incurred on the job and all *lodging* costs incurred while the rep is away from home overnight on business. Most firms require the overnight lodging to be in connection with an out-of-town trip. However, when sales people must stay in town late for meetings with customers, some companies permit them to stay at a downtown hotel at company expense. Some firms limit the amount allowed for a night's lodging. Companies usually cover the cost of *meals* while traveling out of town, but they frequently limit the amount.

Telephone, telegraph, and other *communication costs* are considered legitimate business expenses as are *office supplies*, including notebooks and briefcases, and *stenographic service*.

Generally, there is less agreement on reimbursement for such borderline items as laundry, valet expenses, or personal telephone calls to home. A common policy on laundry is to cover this expense only after the sales person has been away from home for some period, such as a week. Companies reason that such expense would be incurred whether or not the person were at home. However, management wants to encourage sales people to make a good appearance and realizes that laundry costs more on the road than at home. Therefore, a partial allowance is made by many organizations.

Undoubtedly, the most controversial of all expense categories is *entertainment* and *gifts*. A few firms allow no entertainment whatsoever, while others are at the opposite extreme. The prevailing practice seems to be to allow all necessary and reasonable entertainment expenses. There are limits in the form of per-person maximums on allowable items, such as meals and theater tickets. Or the entertainment may be restricted to lunches or dinners. If a luncheon can be used as a quiet interlude with a customer away from the distractions of the office or store, much can be gained by both the seller and buyer. Furthermore, allowing sales people to have entertainment expense accounts may mean they will work 14-hour days.

Giving business gifts is a practice of long standing. Now, however, many firms limit the practice to the Christmas season. Surveys show divided opinions on gift giving. Some firms do it because they like to; they don't care to stop. Other organizations prefer to halt the practice but feel they would suffer competitively, so they continue. Limiting the tax deductibility of business gifts to $25 per year per recipient has altered the gift-giving practices of many companies, but not all of them.

Characteristics of a Sound Expense Plan

A well-conceived and executed expense plan has certain general characteristics. Naturally, no perfect plan exists. Every plan has inherent limitations.

No Net Gain or Loss

The expense plan should be designed so that employees neither profit nor lose. A sales rep should net the same income working on the road as at home. Admittedly, this ideal is difficult to achieve in practice.

While expense allowances should not be used in lieu of compensation, some firms intentionally follow this practice, with the approval of the sales force. The employee often prefers an increase in a nontaxable expense account to a raise in taxable salary or commissions.

The practice of compensating people by way of the expense account is unwise for at least two reasons. First, it is poor management because it tends to nullify the control feature of a good compensation plan. Second, the practice encourages people to violate tax laws. An expense account is nontaxable only to the extent that it reimburses the employee for legitimate business expenses. If the total allowance exceeds total costs, the excess money is taxable.

Equitable Treatment

Sales reps should be able to maintain approximately the same standard of living on the road as at home. They should not have to sacrifice comfort to stay within expense limits. Sales managers should recognize differences in travel expenses among the different territories. Costs are higher in an Atlantic Seaboard territory than in the Great Plains, for example. A plan should be flexible enough to reflect expense differentials caused by variations in types of customers, the need for pioneering a territory, and seasonal factors.

No Curtailment of Beneficial Activities

A good expense plan should not hamper the performance of selling duties, nor should it curtail activities beneficial to the company. A plan that attempts to set selling expenses as a percentage of-sales may discourage a rep from developing a new territory. If expenses are limited to 1 percent of sales, for instance, no one would be anxious to go into a new territory where expenses are often abnormally high in relation to early volume. If a company wants a rep to train dealer sales people or build goodwill by working with the customers, it would be a mistake to limit expenses to a certain dollar amount.

Simple and Economical

A sound expense control plan should be simple and economical to administer. Clerical and administrative expenses should be minimized. Often expense reports require too much unnecessary detail. Some firms ask for information that could easily be placed on other reports. In fact, the information required on the expense account may be duplicated elsewhere.

Avoidance of Disputes

A good expense plan should prevent misunderstandings between management and the sales force. One way to reach this goal is to consult with the sales force when establishing or revising an expense-control plan. The plan should be explained to the sales force clearly, in detail, and in writing before it is put into effect. The company should pay promptly or, better yet, make an advance payment available to those who need it.

Company Control of Expenses and Elimination of Padding

A good plan keeps expenses in hand and curtails padding. However, control is not synonymous with stinginess. A sales executive should be able to get all the benefits of control without damaging sales-force morale by adopting a Scrooge-like approach.

Expense account padding is a problem most sales managers face at one time or another. Actually, it is more apt to be a *symptom* of a problem than a real problem. Often, good judgment in other areas will preclude sales reps' mistreatment of their expense accounts. Recognition of achievement, a good training program, and an adequate compensation plan are the sort of managerial practices that help eliminate expense-account padding. The problem is minimized when sales managers establish rapport with the sales people. Sales reps then understand the expense-account system and feel they are reimbursed fairly for all valid expenses.

Methods of Controlling Expenses

First, management must decide whether the company will pay for the sales rep's field selling costs or have the reps pay their own expenses out of their earnings.

The majority of firms pay for travel and business expenses incurred by their sales people. This practice is almost universally followed if salary is an element in the compensation plan. If the sales reps pay all their own expenses, the chances are that they are compensated by the straight commission method.

Sales People Pay Own Expenses

Several arguments may be advanced in favor of having sales representatives pay their own expenses. They often prefer the plan because it gives them more freedom of operation. They need not account for their expenditures. Some also feel that it enables them to get a better break on their income taxes. They are able to charge off a greater percentage of their total income as business expenses than they can if compensation and expense payments are carefully separated. From the company's standpoint, the plan is simple, and administrative costs are minimized.

When sales people pay their own expenses, however, management loses considerable control over their activities. People spending their own funds will do as they see fit, not as management directs. Also, sales reps paying their own expenses cannot be expected to travel considerable distance to take care of company business.

Sales people who are paid by a straight commission usually pay their own expenses for two reasons. First, management has decided that it is willing to pay a certain percentage of sales for the field sales function. It offers the total amount to the sales rep and says, in effect, "What's left over after you pay your costs is yours." Second, people being paid a straight commission might be tempted to cheat on an expense account during periods of lean sales.

Unlimited-Payment Plans

The most widely used method of expense control is to reimburse sales representatives for all the legitimate business and travel costs they incur while on company business. There is no limit on total expenses or individual items, but reps are required to submit itemized accounts of their expenditures.

One of the prime advantages of the unlimited method of expense control is its flexibility. Cost differentials caused by variations in territories, jobs, or products present no problems under this plan. Flexibility also makes the plan fair for both sales people and management, assuming reps report their expenditures honestly and accurately. Furthermore, this plan gives management some control over the sales reps' activities. If sales executives want a new territory developed or new accounts called on in out-of-the-way places, the expense plan is no deterrent.

On the other hand, the unlimited method of controlling expenses may not allow management to accurately forecast its direct selling costs. The unlimited feature is an open invitation for some people to be extravagant or pad their expense accounts with unjustifiable items. The plan offers no incentive for a sales person to economize.

It is questionable whether the unlimited-expense plan creates more or fewer disputes between management and the sales force than the other expense-control systems. The unlimited features should reduce the number of disagreements, but friction may arise if management questions items on the expense reports. Probably the major need in an unlimited-payment plan is to establish a successful method of controlling the expenses. The best general method may be to hire good people in the first place and then manage them so that they use expense accounts reasonably. More specifically, a good sales manager will analyze the reports to determine what is reasonable and practicable. When a rep's expenses get out of line, it will be apparent to the manager.

Limited-Payment Plans and Flat Allowances

There are two other general methods of controlling expenses that limit payment. One method limits the amount for each item. For example, management may say it will pay a maximum of $70 for a motel or hotel room, $7 for breakfast, $13 for lunch, and $25 for the evening meal (or $45 each day for food), 22 cents a mile for automobile transportation, and so on. The other method allows a flat sum for a period of time, such as a day or a week. One company may pay $100 a day; another firm may set its allowances at $600 a week. Companies may set similar limits throughout all territories or establish separate ones to account for territorial cost differentials.

Limited-payment plans may be suitable when sales reps' activities are sufficiently regular that expenses can be forecast. Some form of flat-allowance plan may be used when the sales job is routine and the travel plan repetitive.

Probably the major problem involved in administering the limited-payment plan is to establish the limits for each item or time period. A thorough job may require considerable managerial time and clerical expense. Management may study past reports to determine the mileage typically covered each day. It may examine hotel and motel directories to establish limits on lodging. A separate study must be conducted for each territory to ensure that regional differentials do not creep in unnoticed. Sales reps should be included in the deliberations to get their opinions.

Setting some limitations on expense payments has advantages. Management can budget its expenses more accurately because it can forecast a maximum for each person. One advantage claimed for limited allowances is that they reduce expense account padding, although it is doubtful that this claim can be validated. Friction and disputes between management and the sales force should be reduced, particularly if expense limits are fair.

A flat allowance has several drawbacks. First, high-caliber sales people may object to such a plan. They may feel that the company does not trust them. Second, the system is inflexible. A sales rep may have some unusual expense, such as an entertainment item he could not escape without losing the account. If entertainment is not an allowable expense, he may not be reimbursed. Some companies avoid such inflexibilty by allowing unusual expenses if they are reported separately with an explanatory note, and management approves the exception.

When management sets limits for each item, the plan may be hard to control. Reps may switch expenditures among expense items. They may attempt to recoup the money spent in excess of the limit for one item by padding the claim for some other item. When a rep spends over the limits for a day or a week, he or she may even file for expenses on days not actually worked.

Another potential drawback to any limited-payment plan is that it may not reflect a territory's changing cost structures. Moreover, the plan is good only if the sales force believes the limits are equitable. And it cannot prevent a cheater from economizing on expenses and then padding the account up to the allowable limits.

Combination Plans

The advantages of both the limited and unlimited plans can sometimes be realized by developing a control method that combines the two. Management may set limits on items such as food and lodging, for example, but place no ceiling on transportation.

Another combination method is an expense-quota plan. Under this system, management sets a limit on the total allowable expense, but the ceiling is related to some other item on the operating statement, such as net sales. For example, a quota of $2,000 may be set for a month because monthly sales are expected to be $40,000. Expenses can be tied to sales even more directly by allowing sales representatives a monthly expense account not to exceed 5 percent of their net sales. The compensation plan can play some part in this expense-control system by paying a bonus if the rep keeps expenses at some given amount under quota.

Expense-quota plans do have the advantage of enabling management to relate sales-force expenses to net sales. In this method, management has some control over this direct selling cost. Furthermore, the reps have some operating flexibility within the total expense budget. By making them expense conscious, they are not so apt to be wasteful.

Factors Affecting Expense-Control Plan

Various factors may affect the *level* of expense payment or the *method* of expense control a company decides to adopt.

Type of Compensation Plan

The method of compensation used has a bearing on the type of expense plan adopted. It is not uncommon for reps on a straight commission to pay their own expenses. When sales people are operating under a straight salary plan, almost invariably the company pays travel and business expenses.

Nature of Territories

The size, density, and location of territories can have a considerable effect on the type of expense plan a company adopts. A sales rep who covers the metropolitan Chicago district in a car should be reimbursed differently than a person who covers the upper New England area. Furthermore, the stage of business development in a given territory can affect a company's expense plan. Ordinarily, *new* territories require more expense money per dollar of sales than *established* districts.

Method of Transportation Used

When sales reps travel by car, the type of expense control plan must be different than when they use some other type of transportation. If sales people use their own cars, management must establish an equitable method for reimbursing them. Obviously, none of these problems arise if the rep travels by plane.

Nature of Job and Its Relation to Products and Customers

Three factors—job, product, and customers—may influence the type of expense-control plan used in an organization. To see the influence of the job alone, consider a soap manufacturer who sells to large retail chains. One group of sales people may sell the product to the home office of the chain and thus deal with high-level executives. These sales representatives probably require the flexibilty of an unlimited plan. However, the manufacturer's missionary sales reps who visit individual stores in the chain probably have a routine job with an established route list. Therefore some form of limited allowance plan is appropriate.

The nature of the product may call for differences in expense plans. A sales rep for a dress manufacturer calling on buyers for department and specialty stores probably would be under an unlimited plan. However, the representative of a chewing gum manufacturer calling on drug and grocery stores would be reimbursed for expenses by a fixed sum method. Some products require the sales person to spend extensive periods of time in servicing the account before the sale can be consummated. After the sale is made, an additional period of servicing may be required. In situations of this nature, it is more difficult to forecast expense requirements. Thus, the plan needs to be flexible.

Caliber of Sales People

An experienced, high-quality sales rep is more apt to be on an unlimited-payment plan than is a new recruit. Closely supervised sales people frequently are placed on some form of a flat allowance or limited-payment plan. The choice depends on management's regard for the integrity and good judgment of its sales people.

Control of Sales-Force Transportation

One significant expense with little room for discretion is the cost of transportation. Decisions regarding transportation expenses are usually rather clear-cut because they are based on the costs and the nature of the selling environment. The rep who covers Manhattan must use taxis, buses, and the subway; a car would be next to useless. Without a car in Los Angeles, the rep goes nowhere. The situation largely dictates the transportation requirement. Some aspects are open to managerial control, however.

Ownership of Automobiles

Since most sales travel is done by automobile, a car has become almost standard equipment. Management may provide company-owned cars, the vehicle may be leased, or sales people may use their own cars. While all three methods are widely used, today there is a trend toward leasing.

No one policy for car ownership is best under all conditions. The final decision rests on a consideration of the following factors.

1. Size of sales force. With a small sales force, simplicity and economy are achieved either by having sales people use their own cars or by leasing cars for them. Only with a large sales force does the company generally find it advantageous to own the cars.

2. Availability of centralized maintenance and storage facilities. If a company maintains centralized vehicle storage and repair facilities, it is in a good position to furnish the sales force with cars. A company that operates a fleet of trucks, for example, usually has garage and maintenance facilities available.

3. Unusual design required. Some companies require that the cars used by their sales people be a special color, have a specially constructed body, or carry some form of company advertising. Sometimes the vehicle must double as a sales car and a delivery truck. In these situations, the company should furnish the cars.

4. Control of car's operating condition. If the company furnishes the car, management is in a better position to demand that it be kept presentable. The company probably provides later-model cars than the sales person's own car, which may be old enough to embarass the company. However, a sales rep may take better care of his own car than a company-owned or leased vehicle.

5. Personal preferences. Some people are financially able and willing to furnish their own cars for work. When sales reps *must* provide the cars, however, management runs the risk of losing good applicants. Everyone will not want to drive their own cars for company business, or they may not have suitable cars.

6. Annual mileage. A rep's average annual mileage influences ownership of the automobile. The more miles driven, the more advantageous it becomes for the company to own the cars. The point of indifference varies depending on the cars used and the company's auto-expense allowances. Suppose the company pays a flat 30 cents per mile auto allowance. Management has calculated the cost of owning the preferred model to be $4,000 a year, plus 20 cents a mile. Under these circumstances, the point of indifference would be 40,000 miles. If the sales people covered less than this mileage, management would probably encourage them to own the cars.

7. Operating cost. It is hard to generalize on which of the three alternatives—employee-owned, company-owned, or leasing—offers the lowest operating cost to the company. The answer depends to a great extent on rental costs, number of miles driven, and method of reimbursing the sales force. It also is difficult to measure some of the indirect costs of company ownership, such as the administrative expense of operating the system.

8. Investments. If the company is not in a strong financial position or does not want to make the investment, it can lease cars or have the sales people provide their own. If firms hire people who do not own a car, these firms may prefer to arrange financing for the sales rep rather than buy the cars outright.

9. Administrative problems. One major administrative question that comes up when the company furnishes cars is whether they should be available for the reps' personal use and, if so, to what extent. Most companies allow reps to use company cars for personal transportation. Management may or may not suggest some limits. If a company adopts a no-limit policy, reps may not buy their own cars, or they may use the company car as a second family car. Use of a company car for private purposes can be an additional inducement to accept a particular sales job. Such a benefit is another indirect monetary payment, the same as group insurance or a paid vacation.

There is no general policy on the payment of operating expenses for a company car used for private purposes. Some businesses ask the rep to pay for the gas when driving the car for personal use. Others pay all expenses for both business and private use. Some ask that operating expenses be paid only on long personal trips such as vacations.

In 1985 the IRS began a crusade to have any personal use of a company-owned car declared as ordinary income on the employee's W-4 form and taxed as such. Thus, firms have been forced to develop systems so their people can report such personal use. Consequently, the attractiveness of company-owned cars has greatly diminished if reps use the vehicles a lot for personal reasons—and most of them do. Now many firms avoid the IRS edict by having reps use their own cars. Reps can then claim deductions for business use of the car, thus lowering their taxable income. Some companies even help with financing.

The strongest point in favor of leasing is not the economics of the situation but the convenience of management. Leasing is the easiest way to put the sales force on wheels. The marketing executive does not have to be a transportation expert, and the firm avoids the problems of buying the car, maintaining it, and later reselling it.

Reimbursement Plans

Sales people who must use their own cars on company business may be reimbursed for the cost. Three separate types of expenditures are involved in owning and operating a car. One is *variable costs*, which are generally related directly to the number of miles driven. Examples of these items are gasoline, oil, lubrication, tires, and normal service maintenance. A second class of expenditures is *fixed* costs, which tend to be related to time rather than miles driven. These costs include depreciation, license fees (state, city, driver), and insurance (public liability, property damage, comprehensive, collision). A third group of *miscellaneous expenses* is difficult to standardize or budget in detail in advance. Typical items in this group are tolls (bridge, highway), parking and storage charges, and major repairs. Usually the third type of costs is not incorporated into one of the ordinary automobile expense control plans. These items are listed separately on the expense account.

Sales people may be reimbursed for using their cars on company business by some kind of a fixed-allowance plan or by a flexible-payment method.

Fixed-allowance plans.   One general type of fixed-allowance plan is based on *mileage* and another, on a period of *time*. Under the first, the employee is paid the same amount for each mile driven on company business. The flat rate per mile is used by more companies than any other major plan, although there is a trend developing toward more flexible methods. Under the other type of fixed-allowance system, a flat sum is paid for each period of time, such as a week or a month, regardless of the number of miles driven. The reimbursements cover both fixed and variable automobile costs.

The fixed-allowance plans have several advantages. They are generally simple and economical to administer. Sales people know in advance what they will be paid. Also if payment is based on a flat allowance for a given period of time, the company can budget this expense in advance. People who drive many miles (20,000–30,000) prefer it because they can generally make money under such a plan.

The criticisms of fixed-allowance plans are so severe, however, that we wonder why they remain so popular. Generally speaking, the plans are inflexible and may be very unfair to some sales people.

Some may benefit financially while others lose. The fixed sum for a given time period can be reasonably good only if everyone travels in a routine fashion and costs are the same in each territory. Similarly, the flat-mileage allowance is equitable only if all reps travel about the same number of miles in the same type of cars under the same operating conditions. These conditions are highly unlikely and unrealistic.

Consider the inequities introduced, for example, by variations in the number of miles driven. In the operation of a car, some costs are fixed regardless of the number of miles driven. Therefore, the greater amount of driving, the more miles over which to amortize the fixed costs. So the fixed costs per mile decrease as the total mileage increases. Under a fixed allowance per mile, every additional mile works to the financial benefit of the sales reps. An example is outlined in Table 13-1. Assuming annual fixed costs of $3,000, variable costs of 12 cents per mile, and a mileage allowance of 25 cents, the results are shown for various annual mileages. If a sales representative drives 5,000 miles per year, he receives $1,250, when the real costs are $3,600. Thus earnings are reduced by $2,350. At the other extreme, a representative who drives 40,000 miles gets $10,000, which is a gain of $3,200 over actual costs. If the representative were paid a fixed sum per month, similar inequities would result but in reverse. That is, a payment of $400 a month would benefit the low-mileage traveler at the expense of the person who drove many miles in a year.

Flexible-allowance plans. To avoid the inherent weaknesses in a fixed-allowance system, companies have developed several flexible-control plans.

Graduated-mileage rates. One type of flexible plan pays a different allowance per mile depending on the total miles driven in a time

Table 13-1

Example of Results of Flat Rate per Mile Plan under Varying Annual Mileages

Annual Mileage	Fixed Cost	Variable Costs at 12 Cents per Mile	Total Costs	Per Mile Costs	Payment to Representatives at 25 Cents per Mile	Gain or Loss to Representatives
5,000	$3,000	$ 600	$3,600	$.72	$ 1,250	− $2,350
10,000	3,000	1,200	4,200	.42	2,500	1,700
20,000	3,000	2,400	5,400	.27	5,000	− 400
30,000	3,000	3,600	6,600	.22	7,500	+ 900
40,000	3,000	4,800	7,800	.195	10,000	+ 2,200

period. For example, one firm pays 25 cents a mile for the first 15,000 miles driven in a year and 15 cents a mile for those over 15,000. Mileage allowances are graduated downward to reflect the fact that total costs per mile decrease as mileage goes up. While a graduated plan corrects some of the faults of a flat-rate method, it usually does not consider differences in territorial costs and types of cars.

Combination of allowance per time period and mileage rate.   An improvement over the graduated-mileage method of expense control is the combination system under which management figures automobile allowances in two parts. Thus the differences between fixed and variable costs of owning and operating a car are reflected in the payment. To cover fixed costs, a flat payment is made for each given time period, such as a week or a month. In addition, variable costs are reimbursed by mileage allowances, which usually are flat rates although they could be graduated. For example, one company pays $200 a month plus 16 cents a mile; another pays $250 a month plus 20 cents a mile over 750 miles a month.

A widely recognized and respected plan was developed over 50 years ago by the founder of Runzheimer International, a management consulting firm for travel and living costs, headquartered in Rochester, Wisconsin. This company typically divides the United States into several geographic regions and then computes the total annual ownership and operating expenses for cars in each of these regions. As an example, Table 13-2 shows the 1986 cost allowances

Table 13–2

Ownership and Operating Costs For a 1986 Midsize Car in Selected Locations

Location	Operating Costs	Ownership Costs	Total Annual Costs
Los Angeles, Calif.	$1,110	$3,480	$4,590
Philadelphia, Pa.	915	3,367	4,282
Houston, Tex.	968	2,910	3,848
Washington, D.C.	1,088	2,700	3,788
Chicago, Ill.	1,065	2,705	3,770
Knoxville, Tenn.	982	2,589	3,571
Orlando, Fla.	968	2,572	3,540
Albuquerque, N.M.	923	2,459	3,382

Note: The above table is based on a 1986 model mid-size four-door sedan equipped with automatic transmission, power steering, power disc brakes, tinted glass, AM-FM stereo, cruise control, and air conditioning. Costs include operating or variable costs: fuel, oil, tires, maintenance; and ownership or fixed costs: insurance, depreciation, financing, taxes, license fees. Factors are based on a four-year, 60,000-mile retention cycle.
  Source: Runzheimer International. Reproduced with permission.

for mid-size cars in eight selected locations. In some respects, the Runzheimer plan gives the same results as the graduated mileage system in that the more miles driven, the smaller the per-mile allowance. However, the Runzheimer plan is much more accurate because payments reflect variations in types of cars, miles driven, and territorial operating costs. For an intermediate-size car in 1986, for instance, the annual fixed costs varied from almost $3,500 in the Los Angeles region to a little under $2,500 in Albuquerque, New Mexico. Annual operating costs ranged from $1,110 in Los Angeles down to $915 in the Philadelphia, Pennsylvania, area. In summary, a Runzheimer-type plan seems to be the most equitable and accurate method for paying sales people for the use of their cars.

Miscellaneous Methods of Expense Control

Credit Cards

Many firms use credit cards to control various expense items. A growing number of services and products may be purchased through a credit card system. When management encourages or even requires its sales people to use a credit card, they need to carry less money, and the risks of loss or theft are reduced. Credit cards are widely used for air travel and car rentals.

The Expense Bank Account

In some instances an undue burden is placed on representatives who have to pay for their expenses and then wait for reimbursement. They may have to finance three or four weeks' expenses—$600 to $1,200. To avoid this, some firms place a certain sum, say $600, in a checking account for each representative. The rep pays expenses by drawing on that account. When the account needs replenishment, or at regular intervals, the rep files an expense report. Upon approval of the report, the amount accounted for is deposited in the checking account to bring it back up to the initial sum.

Summary

The handling and control of expense accounts is one of the most sensitive areas in sales management. Expense accounts are strictly regulated by the Internal Revenue Service, which stipulates in rather minute detail what is and is not deductible. Corporate expense account policies largely reflect these government regulations. Management should identify in writing, and in detail, the expenses it will cover. Normally, sales reps are reimbursed for their business expenses plus some personal costs that would not have been necessary if the reps were at home. A sound expense plan should be simple to administer, neither enrich nor impoverish the reps, and control the level of selling expenses.

Management must decide if the company will pay for the sales force's field selling costs or if the reps should pay their own expenses. Sales people working on a straight commission usually pay their own expenses. Under any other compensation plan, however, the company should pay the rep's expenses as an item separate from the compensation plan.

In the most widely used expense-control plan, reps are reimbursed for all legitimate expenses, but must itemize expenses and document certain large expenditures. Under the other major plan, management either sets limits for certain items (such as food, lodging, and entertainment) or else provides a fixed total allowance for some time period. The type of plan selected is influenced by factors such as the nature of the job or territories, the compensation plan used, and the transportation method used.

A company must develop a plan for controlling the sales forces's transportation costs. When the reps travel by car, management must decide whether to own or lease the cars or else have the reps use their own cars. If the reps use their own vehicles, the company should formulate a program to reimburse them. Often some form of fixed allowance per mile or per time period is used. However, the preferred method is to develop some system of flexible allowances that considers the variation in the miles each rep drives and the costs of driving in the rep's area.

Questions and Problems

1. "The expense-control plan should enable our representatives to maintain (at no extra cost to them) the same standard of living while on the road that they enjoy at home," said the sales manager of a metal products manufacturer. Discuss the implications in this statement.

2. When recruiting sales people, some firms offer the opportunity for additional net income through the expense plan. Evaluate this policy on economic, human relations, and ethical bases.

3. A petroleum firm operating in the midwest with a sales force of 300 people planned to sell its fleet of company-owned auto-

mobiles and have the sales people furnish their own cars. What problems are involved in this change?

4. The oil company noted in question 3 was trying to decide which method should be used to reimburse the sales force for the use of their cars on business. Each rep traveled about 18,000 miles a year. The company was computing the costs on the assumption that they drove a mid-size car. The following payment methods were under consideration. What would be the total annual cost to the firm under each of the three proposals?

   a. A straight 25 cents a mile.

   b. $200 a month plus 15 cents a mile.

   c. The Runzheimer plan. Use Table 13-2 and assume that the 300-rep sales force was equally divided among territories based around Los Angeles and Houston.

5. In lieu of a salary increase last year, a television manufacturer granted its sales force the privilege of using company cars for any personal purposes, and the company paid all expenses. Previously, the firm had strictly prohibited any personal use of these cars. Discuss all aspects of this policy decision.

6. One publisher was considering leasing small Chevrolet or Dodge cars instead of paying its present 22 cents per mile to sales reps for using their personal cars. Several of the reps were driving economy cars and were willing to take less than 22 cents per mile in order to keep from changing cars. What should the firm do?

7. What should management do if a particularly good salesman is padding his expense account?

8. "I don't make any money when my reps are home. I want them on the road all the time. I want them to live in luxury. Our present gross margin allows us to spend a lot of money so we can make even more money. I don't care what the reps spend just so they are happy and keep selling. All I care about is how much they sell. Their only sin is not making sales." Comment on this entrepreneur's statement.

9. What are some of the cost factors and legal implications involved in selecting a state in which to license a company-owned car? Don't look in the text for the answer. It isn't there. Think!

10. A company was in dire need of a replacement part that had shut down its production line. A sales rep in the supplier's office was told to deliver it as quickly as possible. She did so in record time. She also received a ticket for speeding (85 miles per hour). On her expense account, she applied for reimbursement of the $150 fine. As sales manager with responsibility for the rep, what would you do?

Case 13–1

Baxter Company

Change in Expense Account Auditing

Donna Baxter was the new sales manager of The Baxter Company and the only child of the company's founder, Don Baxter. She had given much thought during the past few months to the firm's procedures for auditing its sales force expense accounts. She strongly felt some significant changes should be made, but she was not certain how they should be instituted.

Donna had worked for her father's company since she was seven years old. She would come into the office whenever possible to help out wherever she could. Sometimes she would do office work, such as licking envelopes or answering the telephone. Sometimes she would work in the warehouse putting labels on packages. When she was old enough to handle telephone sales inquiries, she began selling. It was her favorite thing to do and she was exceptionally good at it. After she graduated from a large West Coast private university, she took a tough sales territory in the South Bay area in Los Angeles calling on aerospace firms and their supporting subcontractors.

The Baxter Company manufactured and distributed all sorts of metal fasteners. Its sales volume in 1986 was $21 million with a profit of $4.6 million. Its major customers were aircraft manufacturers. Baxter employed 14 sales reps who were paid a salary plus a 1 percent commission on all sales. All expenses were reimbursed by the company: expenses in 1986 had been 1.9 percent of sales.

After six years of successful selling in the South Bay territory, Donna assumed the sales managership when the former sales manager retired. During her selling career she had become aware of the sales force's carefree attitudes toward the company expense account. Not only were the reps not careful with the expenditure of company funds, but many reps were less than truthful about their claims. When Donna mentioned this to her father in 1980, he shrugged his shoulders and said something about it being a cheap way to pay the sales force. He was not going to do anything about it. Padding the expense accounts had become a way of life at Baxter.

Upon becoming sales manager, Donna resolved to change how the expense accounts were audited. She detested liars, and the sales reps were lying about their expenses. She considered preparing a memo to all sales department personnel outlining her new policies on expense accounts. The last sentence read, "All expense account cheaters will be fired." She showed the memo to her father, who winced when he read it. He did not like it but would not interfere with

Donna's management of the sales department. He did suggest that it might be better to hold a face-to-face meeting with the reps to outline the new expense account procedures. However, he reiterated, "Why pry the lid off this can of worms? We can afford the expenses. The sales force is doing a good job. So they pad a little! So what? You're asking for trouble. But it's your operation and its going to be your company so go do what you will."

Questions

1. What should Donna do?
2. If she opts to change expense-account policy, how should she go about doing it?

Case 13-2

Formalens Company

To Pay or Not to Pay?

It was time to think about expense accounts. The two new company sales reps had to be told one way or the other how their selling expenses would be handled. Dr. Howard, founder and president of Formalens, had to set some compensation and expense account policies. The reps were to be paid a straight commission for selling the company's $50,000 machine to opticians and optical laboratories. The amount of this commission depended on the company's willingness to pay field selling expenses. The commission for selling the machines would be 5 percent of sales. Expenses were anticipated to be about $2,000 a month per rep. Each rep was expected to sell two machines a month. Thus Dr. Howard proposed paying the reps an extra 2 percent commission and have them pay their own expenses. He wanted to keep all costs variable: "If they don't sell, we don't pay."

The Formalens Company had been founded in 1985 to manufacture and market a new machine that allowed dispensers of eye glasses to make lenses overnight in their offices at exceptionally low cost. A lens that cost $18 from a lens manufacturer could be made for $1 by the Formalens machine. The patient's prescription would be punched into a built-in computer to get the needed mold formulation. Plastic would then be poured into the indicated molds and allowed to cure for 12 hours. The machine could process 100 lenses at a time.

Dr. Silver, executive vice president, demurred. "I think we are going to be paying more money than need be. You know our forecasts are too conservative. We'll probably sell 300 machines this year if we can produce them. The economics of our deal is so overwhelming that any sizable optician will have to buy. If so, we're going to be paying out $180,000 to cover field selling expenses. An expense account would be cheaper. Let's give them a fixed $2,000-a-month expense account. Then our costs will be known. $48,000 is sure a lot less than $180,000.''

"But what if we don't sell the 48 units forecasted. Things do go wrong. And cash is always tight." Dr. Howard continued, "Besides if we pay expenses as part of the sales commission, we won't have to pay the money out until after we get paid. It will do wonders for our cash flow."

Dr. Silver did not give in easily, "But how about the reps? What do they want? Do they have enough money to support themselves in the field until the commission checks come in? What if we fail to deliver promptly? They have their expense money out and will want it."

Dr. Howard quickly responded, "Listen, those two guys know a good deal when they see it. Figure it out. If they sell their quotas, they'll make $84,000 total. If things really explode like we all think they will, and they sell 100 units, they'll be paid $350,000. They're gambling on the future just like we are. They know a good deal when they see one. That's why they quit good jobs to come with us. That's why they demanded contracts to protect their deal. They don't want us to change the deal on them when things start rolling."

Questions

1. Should the reps be given contracts stipulating their pay and expenses? What advice would you give Dr. Howard concerning the contracts?
2. What recommendations would you make on the handling of the rep's selling expenses?

14

Supervising the Sales Force

Many receive advice, few profit by it.
SYRUS

A field sales supervisor for a large food products company described one of his workweeks as follows:

> On Monday I rode with a new saleswoman who needs a lot of help. She has a lot to learn, and I'll have to spend a good deal of time with her this year to develop her potential.
>
> Tuesday morning I spent with a man whose performance has fallen off to see what the trouble was. As I thought, he had been having problems with his wife. He'd been drinking, so she locked him out of the house. We talked about it at some length. Finally I had to tell him that if he could not get control of his personal life, I would have to recommend his termination.
>
> That afternoon I spent checking out the calls reportedly made by a salesman who isn't doing at all well. I am afraid he's through. He's been telling us some tales. He never made half of the calls he reported. I suspect his expense accounts won't stand much scrutiny either.
>
> Wednesday I spent with Bob Conner working on a very large potential account. He's a good man, but he needs help.
>
> Thursday I rode with two other reps just checking them out.
>
> Friday I spent on paperwork and planning next week. I also wrote letters to all of the people who report to me.

The word **supervision** is often used to refer to all the work of operating and controlling the sales force. More strictly, it refers only to *direct* working relationships between the sales person and superiors. The sales manager who checks with the sales people each morning to see what their plans are for the day is *directly* supervising their activities. Many other managerial actions constitute *indirect* supervision, such as auditing expense accounts or appraising sales performance.

Many large concerns employing hundreds, if not thousands, of sales reps often hire field supervisors whose sole assignment is to supervise the reps' field selling activities. More often, this supervisory function is performed by district or regional sales managers as one of their many responsibilities. Consequently, supervision is often neglected in favor of more pressing problems or more pleasant tasks.

Supervision and Strategic Planning

The amount and nature of the supervision given the sales force is part of the company's strategic marketing plan. Many firms, particularly smaller ones, decide to hire experienced proven performers and then turn them loose with little supervision. Other firms hire inexperienced reps and then supervise them closely.

An important factor in this strategic decision is the importance of any one sale to the firm's welfare. If each sale is vitally important to the firm (as it is for Boeing Aircraft), each rep will be closely supervised. If a sale or even a territory is not that important to total corporate well-being, then management is not apt to spend much money supervising the sale.

The supervision decision is a portion of the overall strategic decision as to how important the sales force is in accomplishing the firm's goals.

Reasons for Supervision

Training

One significant reason for supervising sales people is to give them more training. In many ways, the field supervisor is an on-the-job sales-training executive. The most effective sales training takes place over a period of time and is best done in the field while sales reps are actually facing day-to-day problems. Good supervision can do much to develop an inexperienced recruit into a productive sales rep.

Sales Assistance

In some selling situations, sales reps need technical help or other assistance in making sales. The supervisor must be prepared to provide it.

Enforcement

Supervision is often used as an enforcement tool to ensure that company policies are being followed. In this role, the supervisor is working in much the same capacity as a foreman in the plant—he or she makes sure that reps are doing their jobs properly. Jobs that call for little selling ability and consist mainly of repetitive, nonselling duties require rather close supervision to ensure that the tasks are actually carried out.

Better Performance

Some sales managers believe that direct supervision stimulates sales people to do better work. However, there is a limit to how much an employee can be prodded without becoming resentful. Just knowing that management is aware of one's efforts can be beneficial. Conversely, performance seem to suffer when sales reps know that management has no means of knowing what they are really doing.

Improved Morale

Supervision can develop good morale. It is important to some sales reps to know that someone in the organization cares about and recognizes the work they do. If the supervisor is adept, just the fact that he or she is in personal contact should have a good effect on morale. If not, morale can suffer.

Amount of Supervision Needed[1]

There are dangers in either over- or undersupervising the sales force. Supervision costs are significant, and management does not want to spend more on it than is necessary. Oversupervising hampers the performance of sales representatives. While some supervision can improve morale, too much has the opposite effect. Able, independent sales reps resent managers who hold too tight a rein on them. Many people go into selling to escape such direct control.

Oversupervision also means wasted time for both the rep and the supervisor. The major function of sales is to sell merchandise. This cannot be done if the sales people are overburdened with conferences and meetings with supervisors.

[1] For a conceptual approach to the essentially unanswerable question of how much supervision is needed in any given situation, see Frank E. Moriya and John C. Gockley, "Grid Analysis for Sales Supervision," *Industrial Marketing Management*, November 1985, pp. 235–238.

The dangers of undersupervision are much the same as those of oversupervision. Morale can suffer, and costs can rise. A sales rep who is not getting the attention or supervision needed to do the job properly is likely to develop a poor attitude. He or she may feel that the boss neither knows nor cares what is happening. Without proper supervision to improve performance, such a rep may eventually be fired or quit. Another type of sales person may be a potentially good persuader but have a few problems that are unknown to the home office. A good supervisor can identify and handle such problems.

Ignorance is another penalty for insufficient supervision. Without the information that supervision can provide, sales managers may not know what is happening in the field. Although they receive sales reports at regular intervals, they may have no way to determine their accuracy.

Factors Determining How Much Supervision Is Needed

The foremost factor in determining how much supervision is required in a given situation is the quality of the sales force. If a firm hires only top-notch recruits or sales people with proven talents, little supervision may be needed. The training, enforcement, and stimulation that supervision can provide are usually not needed for competent sales reps.

On the other end of the scale are the newly hired individuals with below-average ability and no selling experience. It would be difficult to give such reps too much supervision. They need the sales training and assistance that a supervisor can provide. They also need constant stimulation and must be watched closely to see that they abide by company policies.

In between these two extremes of sales-force quality is an almost unlimited number of variations. In determining the proper amount of supervision to be provided, the sales manager must consider several other factors. The first is the importance of the sales job in the overall achievement of the organization's objectives. If the importance of any one rep's performance is large in the firm's overall sales picture, management should make certain that this rep does the job well. One highly technical concern sold large projects to a few large companies through five sales engineers. A sales manager closely supervised their activities daily by telephone and worked closely with each rep on each project. Each sale was too important to do otherwise.

The geographical distribution and concentration of the sales force should be considered in determining the degree of supervision, because they affect its costs. Firms with a few sales people, each responsible for a territory of several states, may find the job of maintaining close contact too costly and difficult. Companies that sell in a small region, such as a metropolitan area or a small portion of a state, find close contact with their sales force relatively easy to maintain.

The size of the sales force also affects the amount and type of supervision management attempts. If the sales force is relatively small, many sales managers find that they can handle the job themselves, without supervisors. The larger the sales force, the more necessary it becomes to hire personnel who do nothing but direct sales people through formal supervisory activities.

The compensation plan used and the existence of other control mechanisms can affect the amount of personal supervision needed. In general, management usually finds close supervision more necessary when the reps are being paid largely by salary. A strong, *properly designed* incentive system can provide many of the benefits of supervision, as can a detailed method for evaluating sales performances.

Tools and Techniques of Supervision

The tools and techniques used in supervising the sales force include personal contact, correspondence and telephone contact, meetings and conventions, printed aids, and automatic supervisory aids provided by sales-management practices. Another tool, sales reps' reports, is discussed in a separate section.

Personal Contact

The topic of supervision usually conveys the idea of a field supervisor who is in personal contact with the reps. While this is an important method of supervision, it is only one of several that are used. Typically, the supervisor visits sales reps on the job and tries to help them with whatever problems are evident. The supervisor's range of activities varies from trying to help with personal problems to assisting in selling difficult customers or settling grievances.

Correspondence and Telephone Contact

Many sales executives try to supervise through the mails, but it is extremely difficult to communicate complex matters in a letter. Long-distance telephone rates have dropped to the point that sales managers can talk with reps everywhere for a reasonable cost, particularly at night. A great deal of telephone time can be purchased for the same price as the cost of a plane ticket to visit a single rep in the field.

Printed Aids

Sales manuals, bulletins, or company house organs help in supervising the sales force. A good sales manual tells sales people what to do in various circumstances. Their questions can be answered just as effectively in a publication as they can by personal contact.

Automatic Supervisory Aids

Several other managerial tools that provide help with supervision can be called automatic supervisory techniques. These sales-management techniques have inherent supervisory powers and work automatically toward company goals. Such techniques can be exceptionally effective. Unlike the field supervisor or other supervisory methods, these automatic techniques travel with the reps everywhere, every minute of the day, and on every call they make.

Compensation plan. By far the most important automatic supervisory tool is the compensation plan. The compensation plan encourages reps to do certain things to maximize their earnings. Assume that the job calls for an exceptionally high incentive to sell a large volume of goods. Then a compensation plan designed to achieve such a goal is far more effective in supervising the rep's activities than is any other method of supervision.

Territories. Establishment of specific sales territories automatically supervises reps to some degree. It tells them what areas they are responsible for and where to seek orders.

Quotas. Sales quotas can serve as a supervisory tool in addition to stimulating performance. By setting quotas for various product lines or for certain classes of customers, the sales manager can guide the activities of the sales force into desired channels.

Expense accounts. Policies on expenses automatically guide sales-force behavior as effectively as any personal supervision. For example, if the sales manager limits the amount spent to entertain prospects, the sales rep will have to curtail such activities.

Sales-analysis procedures. The sales-analysis procedure which are discussed in Part 4 are also an aid to supervision. Management can evaluate the performance of each sales person on the basis of (1) sales volume for each product or (2) various indexes of efficiency such as calls made and orders taken. With such an evaluation, the sales manager can spot those who need help on certain points.

Reports

Sales reports are used in supervision, but they serve other purposes too. As a supervisory tool, the report is a silent enforcer of company policy. Reps who know they must account for all their activities will feel more secure and comfortable if they stay within company policy.

Sales reports tell management what is happening in the field. Most managers expect sales people to report competitive activities, customers' reactions to company policies and products, and other information management should know.

Sales reports also provide records for evaluating sales reps' performance. Such information includes the number of calls made,

---

A day-to-day operating problem in the
Majestic Glass Company (G)

Falsified Reports from Sales People

One type of field report submitted monthly by all salesmen included a list of prospective new accounts. These were usually manufacturers, bottlers, food processors, dairies, or large stores. The salesmen often added comments about each firm on the list. These comments indicated the firm's size, business prospects, financial strength, estimated needs for the products Majestic sold, and its present sources of these products. One reason for requiring such reports was to justify the salesmen's expense statements.

In an effort to build new-account volume, Mr. Brion had mailed a sales letter and an illustrated leaflet about Majestic products. These were sent to 700 of the firms listed as prospective accounts on salesmen's reports in the preceding six months. To his amazement, Mr. Brion discovered that a large number of these firms were fictitious. The Postal Service returned many of the mailings marked "NO SUCH ADDRESS" or "ADDRESSEE UNKNOWN." Mr. Brion questioned one of his salesmen, Myron Schwartz of Atlanta, who was in the home offices at the time a bundle of these returned mailings arrived. Since he was leaving Majestic to attend college, Mr. Schwartz freely admitted that he had called on only 3 of the 22 firms he had listed. More than 10 of the others were completely imaginary, he said. Furthermore, according to Mr. Schwartz, all of Majestic's salesmen followed this practice. Not one sales rep had a clean record. An analysis of the returned mailings showed that some came from every one of the 18 territories.

Question

How should Mr. Brion handle this situation involving the falsified reports?

Note: See the introduction to this series of problems in Chapter 3 for the necessary background on the company, its market, and its competition.

number of orders taken, miles traveled, days worked, new prospects called on, and new accounts sold.

Sales reports help sales people plan their activities. When they know they will have to report what they did during the week, they have an incentive to organize their activities. A report that does not reflect sound, careful planning will not make a favorable impression. Reports should show, for example, that reps are routing themselves properly, calling on the various classes of customers in the right ratio, and so forth.

Management can use report forms as a basis to evaluate reps for management positions. Promptness in filing reports, accuracy and completeness of data, and reporting format can tell management many things about a rep's work habits and abilities.

A few sales managers try to minimize the time their reps spend on such nonselling tasks as report writing. As one sales manager put it, "I expect each rep to produce $5 million volume a year. That's $20,000 a day or about $4,000 an hour for the five hours a day they can work in this business. Now why in the world would I want them to spend two hours a week writing reports? That makes them $8,000 reports to my way of thinking."

Another manager protests, "But they can write their reports when they aren't selling."

"I don't want my people working on their own time," responds the first manager. "I want them fresh for the job the next day. Besides if they write reports, I'm obligated to read them carefully and I don't have time to do it."

Even on such a seemingly mundane topic as reports, there can be disagreement. Who is right? Both or neither depending on the situation. The answer depends on management's needs and the needs of the job. If management does not see any need for reports and does not use them, they are indeed pointless. If management needs such reports and makes good use of the information, then a system should be developed so the reports can be generated within a tolerable amount of the rep's time.[2]

Working with Sales People

The supervisor must first learn to evaluate the abilities of each sales person. One sales manager describes what he looks for when he rides with a sales rep:

[2] One study reported that sales persons were often found to be uncooperative and inadequate in reporting their activities, believing that such reports infringe on their main task—selling. See Thomas R. Wotruba and Richard Mangone, "More Effective Sales Force Reporting" *Industrial Marketing Management,* June 1979, pp. 236–45. See Hal Fahner, "Call Reports that Tell It All," *Sales & Marketing Management*, volume 12, 1984, pp. 50–52, for a practical call report program.

The first thing I look for is how well the rep knows his way around the territory. Right after I took this job, I rode with a man in Boston who had been in the territory for three years but couldn't find Boston University. It was obvious he hadn't been working the territory. I pinned him down, and he finally admitted that he was holding down two jobs. Swindling us! The real sales rep knows all the short cuts in his territory. He moves around fast.

Next, I look for how well he knows the people on whom we call. The good rep is on a personal basis with them. You can tell if he has been calling on them.

I always worry when the man climbs in the car, starts the motor, then asks me, "Where should I go?" He should have a plan. He should know where he is going, why he is going there, and what he is going to do when we get there. He should know what he wants to accomplish during each call. I fear for the man who makes courtesy calls. He's just making a nuisance of himself while wasting our money.

I like to see records of the call and see them used before making a call. He should study each call and refresh his memory of previous contacts by using the records.

When we get into the call, I like to see a person who knows how to dig in after a sale when the going gets rough. The guy who folds up when the customer says "no" needs a great deal of help. He may even need another line of work.

While we are riding between calls, I pump him for his philosophies of selling and his aspirations. I want to know his values. Above all, I am trying to get a good line on his intelligence, his wits.

Every now and then one of the more clever men will try to sandbag me by only calling on good friends. I guard against this by always dictating a few calls of my own.

Then there are those glib-tongued rascals who talk a good game but can't deliver the goods. They can fool you for awhile, but if you keep your eye on results and close your ears to alibis, you can quickly detect the feather merchants.

Finally, I like to see a person who loves the business and knows what it is all about. I fear for the rep who is not well wired into the industry. The guy who is working for us just because it's a job has no future. He's not much use to us nor even to himself.[3]

Common Problems Encountered

Certain supervisory problems are commonly encountered. These include conflict of values, role ambiguity, laziness, alcoholism, expense account abuse, and other personal problems.

Conflict of values. Supervisors and the reps they supervise often come from different generations and embrace different sets of values. Older hard-working supervisors become frustrated dealing with some

---

[3] From a speech by Thomas Horton, formerly vice president, Litton Industries, now president, Thomas Horton and Daughters.

younger reps who don't share such a hard-line belief in the work ethic. Older supervisors often have difficulty motivating younger reps; they simply don't understand each other. The bigger the gap, the bigger the problem.

Laziness.   The largest single reason people fail in selling is that they will not work hard enough. Many sales jobs attract people with easy-going personalities, because lack of close supervision allows them to work whenever they please. Unfortunately, they do not want to work often or hard enough to get the job done. The bill of particulars against the lazy sales rep is familiar to any experienced sales manager:

- Does not start making calls until late morning.
- Takes long lunch hours.
- Will not make late afternoon calls.
- Does not work at all when there is something else to do—golf, a ballgame, skiing.

It would be nice to be able to suggest some ways of dealing with the lazy sales person. However, there is little the manager can do but fire him. Some lazy people do change character when they discover a reason for working, but this must come from within the individual. They must develop goals that can only be achieved by hard work, and they must realize this fact. Otherwise no amount of nagging will build a fire under the lazy sales rep.

During initial sales training, it is important to tell the sales reps, in no uncertain terms, how much work is expected of them.

Alcoholism and drugs.   One of the most difficult personal problems sales managers encounter is the sales person with a drinking or drug problem. Unfortunately, some sales jobs are conducive to drinking by constantly putting the reps in social situations where drinking is expected. Such jobs are terrible risks for those who cannot handle alcohol or the temptations of drugs.

Alcoholic sales representatives cannot be tolerated. Their work habits suffer and so does the quality of their work. One problem is that the true alcoholic can disguise addiction for a long time, while it becomes increasingly harmful to work performance and other aspects of life. This book is not intended to instruct on the early detection of alcoholism. A great deal has been written about this, and the information is readily available.

Experience indicates that the sales manager dealing with an alcoholic or drug user should be firm and not coddle the person. The president of one outstanding company knowingly hired an alcoholic who possessed great talent when sober. "I told him when I hired him that if I ever so much as saw him with a drink in his hand or heard of him taking a drink, he was fired. It's the only way to deal with the problem. He's been sober ever since."

Expense accounts. The folklore of selling is full of tales of sales-expense accounts and their fictional contents. Expense accounts can be expensive problems. Expense-account policies should be clearly set forth when sales people are hired. Companies that expect the sales force to be honest make it clear that cheating on an expense account is grounds for dismissal. Then they back up that policy with action.

When the sales manager detects a rep's expense accounts are not factual but still wants to keep him, the manager should review the situation with the rep. Some managers simply disallow expenses they feel are not in order. Others will go over the expense report

---

A day-to-day operating problem in the
Majestic Glass Company (H)

Sales Person Receives Job Offer from Major Competitor

Bradley Norton had been Majestic's New York City salesman for more than a decade. Recently he sent a telegram to Mr. Brion's office announcing that he had received an offer of a job on the sales force of Corona Glass Company. He suggested that Mr. Brion choose between two alternatives. One was to match Corona's salary offer. The other was to pay Mr. Norton a "settlement" in return for his promise not to sell Corona containers to any of his present Majestic customers for a period of five years. The amount of the "settlement" was $50,000.

Mr. Norton was considered one of Majestic's three best salesmen. His New York City territory was a very lucrative one. However, Mr. Brion had noted earlier that more than 85 percent of sales in that territory were made to only a few very large accounts. These were customers with which Mr. Norton had developed a very close relationship.

The Corona Glass Company, Majestic's chief competitor throughout the nation, was especially strong in New York City. Its salesmen were paid a straight salary, plus a share of company profits. The offer that Mr. Norton asked Mr. Brion to match was about $5,000 per year more than the highest paid Majestic salesman was receiving. It also was above Mr. Brion's own salary.

Question

How should Mr. Brion respond to Bradley Norton's proposal?

Note: See the introduction to this series of problems in Chapter 3 for the necessary background on the company, its market, and its competition.

with the rep, thus letting him know that his expense reports are being watched. But such matters are sensitive.

Other personal problems.   Sales reps suffer all the personal problems people manage to get themselves involved with—financial, family, health, and so on. By their nature, many sales jobs are not conducive to good family relationships. If the rep must travel extensively or must work evenings, the family can be tested. Sometimes the manager can help by giving reps a territory that allows them to spend more time at home, but such instances are not common. More frequently, there is little the manager can do. A sales rep may ask the manager to talk with the spouse about the necessity to travel, but the manager must be careful to avoid becoming involved in other people's marital problems.

Many people find themselves in financial difficulty from time to time because of hospital bills, poor money management, bad investments, court suits, or other reasons. Some turn to their employers for help during such times. While the manager may be tempted to help out, such a policy can lead to other problems. It usually is a mistake to become an employee's creditor; it seldom works out well.

As a general rule, most firms expect their employees to be able to manage their personal lives. Most administrators do not want to become involved in their subordinates' personal situations.

Conventions and Meetings

Much of the manager's supervisory efforts focus around the meetings and conventions at which the sales force is assembled. Meetings and conventions are a vital part of the sales world. Some companies hold small meetings for local or regional sales forces, while others sponsor national conventions for the entire sales force. There are also industrywide conferences and trade shows. Meetings can be the bane of the manager's existence because, besides being costly, they take up so much time and effort.

Yet there must be good reasons for such meetings, despite the often-heard protests. Some meetings accomplish a great deal of work which can only be done in this manner.

Purpose

The three basic purposes of a convention are inspiration, training, and communication. Some meetings have no purpose other than to stimulate the sales force to work harder. However, many also include considerable training material, such as new product information or help on current sales problems. Several of the specific purposes that can be included under the basic training function of a convention are:

- To introduce new products or product modifications.
- To explain a forthcoming advertising campaign.
- To provide training in selling techniques.
- To make announcements of company policies on pricing, channels of distribution, organization, and personnel.
- To gain rapport between the sales force and management.

Planning and Conducting a Convention

Four basic aspects must be fully planned if a convention is to be a success:

- The time and place must be established
- The objective and theme or subjects must be determined
- The program must be developed in detail
- Arrangements must be made for space, meals, transportation, and other administrative details.

Make no mistake, it takes lots of time, effort, planning, and money to conduct a successful meeting. Often junior members of the sales department are awarded the honor of doing such work. Their future depends on how well they execute all of the details connected with the meeting. The key to most meetings is taking care of all the details and avoiding boring speakers. Before deciding to have a meeting, managers must make sure that one is really needed. Often other communication methods will do the job cheaper and better.[4]

Trade Shows

Often sales managers are able to combine their sales meetings with industry trade shows or conventions, which everyone should attend anyway. In many industries, trade shows or conventions are critically important sales events. An effective exhibit supported by the sales force is essential.

---

[4] See "Meetings!," *Sales & Marketing Management*, July 1, 1985, pp. 73–120, and November 11, 1985, pp. 87–140, for many ideas on conducting sales meetings.

Contests

Contests are frequently used to provide special incentives for the sales people. Despite their many faults and drawbacks, sales contests are widely used by sales managers. One student in a sales-management class complained that his firm, a large office equipment manufacturer, had three different contests going on simultaneously. In 1985, *Sales & Marketing Management* ran two large special sections on sales contests as they do each year. Its editors evidently feel that the topic of contests is that important to readers.[5]

Purpose of Contests

A contest should have a clear-cut definite purpose, such as something management wants the sales force to do that it isn't doing. It is senseless to hold one just for the sake of playing a game. Broad purposes such as increasing sales and/or profits should be avoided. Contests are best used to achieve such specific goals as getting new accounts, selling specific products, or relieving certain overstocked inventory positions.

The specific reasons for holding a contest should be placed in writing. This will help ensure that the design of the contest does not include factors that have no bearing on its original purpose. If the purpose of a contest is to gain new accounts, a sales manager may be tempted to insert an additional objective such as increased sales volume or lower expenses. However, each additional aim detracts attention from the major goal, thereby lessening the probability of achieving any objective.

Advantages of Contests

In some situations when sales people feel they are in competition with one another, a contest can serve to stimulate their interest in doing a good job. Many sales people obtain a great deal of psychological satisfaction from winning or placing high in a contest, regardless of the prizes offered.

Contests can be made as cheap or expensive as management desires. Many of the best ones may cost only a few dollars. The sales manager may promise to buy a steak dinner for the first person who meets a quota, for example. Contests can be used to cover short-run situations in which management does not want to make any permanent alterations in its other stimulation tools. It was pointed out that

[5] "Sales Incentives Get the Job Done," *Sales & Marketing Management,* April 6, 1985 and September 14, 1985.

it is a mistake to keep altering the compensation plan to meet every new situation. Hence the contest can frequently serve in place of such a change.

Objections to Contests

Many sales managers do not operate sales contests and can offer several valid objections. One of the major drawbacks is that once contests are initiated they cannot be easily discontinued. In fact, organizations that use contests seem to find it necessary to use them more and more.

Frequently, sales contests lead to undesirable selling methods, such as overstocking, overselling, and various pressure tactics. In the short run, such tactics may enable a sales person to win the contest, but in the long run they can cause trouble. Many executives object to contests on the grounds that they create morale problems. In any sizable sales force, inequities are bound to occur and must be negotiated. The mere fact that somebody must lose may create a morale problem regardless of what the sales manager does. Some administrators object to contests on the grounds that they are so time-consuming that other activities tend to be neglected. Also, the sales person is tempted to neglect activities not connected with the contest.

One of the biggest objections to sales contests is that, almost inevitably, a decline in sales occurs afterward. The sales force cannot keep up the high level of activity. Many questions have been raised about the long-run benefits of a contest. Obviously, if the contest has achieved wider distribution and new dealerships, a long-run benefit should occur. But if the contest has been focused mainly on sales volume, its long-range value is questionable. The absence of a permanent accomplishment is not necessarily bad. Many contests are designed for short-run purposes such as selling out an overstocked inventory.

Planning and Conducting Contests

If a contest is to be successful, it must be planned, and the following tasks must be completed in advance:

- A relevant theme must be developed.
- The opportunity to win should be equalized for all participants.
- The length of the contest must be established.
- The contest must be adequately promoted.
- A fair scoring system must be established.
- Proper awards must be selected.

Theme. A sales contest should have a theme even though it is strictly a sales theme. Many contests are built around a sport currently in season. Other examples of themes might be military campaigns, a search for gold, or something to do with earth satellites and outerspace.

Opportunity to win. Each person should have a chance to win a prize. If the average or poor reps learn that the top producers win all the prizes, they will silently withdraw from the competition.

Opportunity to win may be equalized in four ways. First, through the use of quotas, allowances can be made for differences in territories and selling abilities. The rep who makes the greatest improvement relative to the others is the winner. In this way, even the poorest sales person has a chance to win. One criticism of this technique is that the person who has been doing a poor job actually has a better chance of winning than the good sales rep does. This is because the poorer seller has more room for improvement. Quotas must be soundly and accurately established for this equalizing technique to work properly.

In the second method, sales reps are paired off so that they can compete against others of the same general ability. A third system is to have the reps compete against their own previous records. This is very similar to the quota technique and is subject to the same criticisms. Finally, the sales manager may assemble teams or groups in which good and poor sales people are combined. Then the groups compete against one another. In this way, an average or poor producer can be a member of a winning team.

Length of contest. Contests seldom run longer than three months; most often, the duration is one month. If a contest runs too long, the participants lose interest. This is especially apt to happen to those who see no chance of winning.

Scoring systems. An objective scoring system is important to the success of a contest. If the reps feel that it is not being fairly scored, considerable ill will can result. Sometimes it is difficult to be completely impartial. Even when quotas are established on a relatively unbiased basis, considerable dispute can arise. A bias existing in most market figures favors sales people who operate in rapidly growing territories and discriminates against those in other areas. Most scientifically established quotas are set on benchmark data that, at best, are a year or two old. These data provide the sales people in rapidly growing areas with a distinct edge, because their potential market is much greater than the sales manager realizes.

Prizes. Three types of prizes are commonly given in sales contests—cash, merchandise, or trips. Current managerial preferences lean away from giving cash. Its quickly spent and then forgotten. However, trips and merchandise are success symbols. Merchandise is kept and continually reminds the sales person and others of the accomplishment.

Another aspect of the award problem is that the manager must decide what percentage of the sales force is to win prizes. Some companies allow everyone to win but vary the value of the awards. This is sound managerial practice. Once a person has fallen so far behind that he cannot possibly win, he withdraws from competition, and the purpose of the contest is defeated. The more prizes that can be given, the more assurance the sales manager has of maximum participation.

Recognition and Honor Awards

One of the fundamental principles of good human relations is to give full recognition to individuals who deserve commendation. It is really difficult to give too much recognition to anyone. This is particularly true in reference to sales people, whose personalities often require considerable praise to keep up their morale.

The recognition method for stimulating the activities has much to recommend it. It can be used on a continual basis and is difficult to overdo. If the recognition system is properly administered, no ill will will be created. To ensure this, the manager must make certain that everyone gets recognized frequently. For example, one company published a monthly sales bulletin in which each sales rep in the United States had his sales reported in comparison with his quota. This allowed everyone to see just how he stood in comparison with all the other sales people.

Often clubs are developed for outstanding producers or those who meet certain goals. Membership in such clubs usually bestows upon the high achievers various recreational diversions in addition to the ego-gratifying recognition connected with just being in the select group. The life insurance industry has long had its Million Dollar Round Table to recognize those agents who sell that amount of life insurance each year. There are even more select groups to which even larger producers are admitted.[6]

---

[6] See "Three Cheers for Recognition!" *Sales & Marketing Management*, June 3, 1985, pp. 71–100.

Summary

Supervision entails a multitude of activities the sales manager undertakes daily to ensure that the sales force is operating effectively. While the ultimate goal of supervision is to increase sales while reducing costs, several secondary purposes are served in reaching that ultimate goal. Much supervision revolves around training and developing the individual's potentialities. Of course, the other side of supervision entails enforcement of the company's policies and monitoring the activities of the sales force to make certain they comply with management's wishes.

Most sales-management operations rely very heavily on automatic supervisory techniques such as: (1) the compensation plan, (2) sales territories, (3) quotas, (4) selling expense account policies, and (5) the reporting systems established by the company.

The amount of personal supervision instituted over a sales force is largely a function of the caliber of the sales people. Typically, highly talented sales people require very little supervision, whereas sales people in low-level sales jobs require far more.

Meetings and conventions take up more than their share of the manager's time and effort. Their costs are high. Thus it is essential that the company plan its meetings carefully lest the money be wasted.

Contests are widely used in spite of their deficiencies. Sales people seem to require something to add zest to their working life. Yet, care must be taken to maximize the participation of all the sales people in the contest. An everybody-a-winner attitude has much merit. It takes much planning and thought to design a meaningful contest that does not somehow backfire on the company.

Questions and Problems

1. How could a field supervisor determine why a certain rep was performing unsatisfactorily?
2. Bill Jolton, a salesman for a large national soap company, informs his immediate supervisor that he is quitting as of the end of the month. The supervisor is surprised to learn of this, since he had thought that Jolton was doing a good job and was happy with his work. He would like to keep Jolton with the firm, for he thinks Jolton shows exceptional promise. How should the supervisor handle the situation?

3. As sales management moves into the telecommunications age, you, as a recently hired marketing department trainee, have been assigned the task of preparing a report on how management can use the existing state-of-the-art communications equipment to improve its supervision of the sales force. What suggestions would you make?

4. As a supervisor of 10 sales people, what kind of relationship would you try to establish with them?

5. A sales manager of a large metropolitan automobile dealership required his sales force of eight people to meet each morning at 9 A.M. for about 30 minutes in order to plan their activities for the day. During this meeting, he would ask each rep to tell what he intended to accomplish that day. Were these meetings sound? What was the manager's thinking in establishing them?

6. One sales manager worked for a firm that sold on a nationwide basis with a sales force of 15 reps. The manager had a policy of spending one week each year with each sales person in the territory. What would this manager expect to accomplish during these visits? Is this a sound method for supervising these reps? Might there be a better way to accomplish the same tasks?

7. George Hermann, one of the top salesmen with the Mountain Machine Company, was continually arguing with his direct supervisor. He had complained many times to the sales manager and had asked to be left alone. One day, he stopped in the sales manager's office and declared: "If you don't get that clown you call a supervisor off my back, you can have my job. I'm not going to put up with any more of his suggestions, and that's final."

Hermann was consistently a top producer with the company. But the supervisor had told the sales manager that he could be doing an even better job if he would just listen to some advice. However, the supervisor maintained that Hermann was an arrogant, stubborn, conceited man who thought he knew everything about selling and was completely uncooperative. The sales manager knew that Hermann frequently did not obey orders in pushing certain items and doing certain things the home office requested. But overall his work was highly satisfactory. The sales manager felt that there was a personal antagonism between the two individuals, stemming from the time the supervisor had been promoted to his position over Hermann. The supervisor had been a successful salesman with the company before his promotion, but he had not been nearly so good a salesman as George Hermann. How should the sales manager handle the situation?

8. How can a sales manager design a sales contest that overcomes the tendency for activity to decline after its termination?

9. How can a manager design a contest to prevent overstocking of dealers or stealing of volume from future periods?

10. What is the best method for equalizing everyone's chances to win a contest?

Case 14–1

Stanley Equipment Company

Good Sales Rep Is "Moonlighting" on Job

Joseph Lorenz had been one of the best sales representatives in the Stanley Equipment Company ever since he joined the firm eight years ago. But about six months ago his sales volume started to decline—something that had never happened before. On several occasions, either George Peck, the company's owner-president, or Charles Molla, the general sales manager, had talked with Lorenz about his performance decline. It was only during the most recent of these talks that Mr. Peck finally learned that Joe Lorenz had been "moonlighting" on the job. He and a friend had started a small business on the side. Mr. Peck then asked Mr. Molla what he thought the company should do about this situation.

The Stanley Equipment Company was one of the oldest and largest distributors (wholesalers) of construction equipment in the west. The company was located in Salt Lake City, Utah, and served a broad geographical market that covered Utah, northern Arizona, southern Idaho, southwestern Wyoming, and eastern Nevada. Stanley represented 16 manufacturers of construction equipment. George Peck was especially proud of the long-term relationship that Stanley had maintained with both its supplier-manufacturers and its customers. The company had been in business for over 70 years. It had been representing two of its suppliers for over 60 years and three other suppliers for more than 50 years. Most of Stanley's suppliers had granted an exclusive distributorship to Stanley in that company's geographical market.

Mr. Peck attributed his company's long relationship with its suppliers to the company's ability to satisfy its customers so well. "This customer satisfaction," Mr. Peck said, "is built on three factors. First, we maintain a service department that is staffed with well-trained people who are experienced in solving equipment problems. Our field service staff resides in key locations throughout our market, so they can quickly handle on-site problems. And they are on call 24 hours a day."

"Second," Peck continued, "we recognize the critical importance of replacement parts in the heavy construction industry. We can supply these parts quickly and economically, because we have on hand at all times an inventory of over $3 million worth of replacement parts. Third, we provide flexible financing that can be tailored to an individual customer's needs."

Stanley carried several lines of construction equipment. The company intended to supply virtually all the heavy-construction needs of its customers, with the exception of dump trucks. These product lines included crawler tractors, excavator-shovels, motor graders, hydraulic cranes, backhoes, self-propelled scrapers, off-highway trucks, rubber-tire loaders, rollers and compactors, conveyors, and crushing, screening, and asphalt equipment.

The market for the products distributed by the Stanley company consisted of just about any organization doing large-scale construction. The large part of the market consisted of contractors who were building highways, sewer and water plants, housing subdivisions, or other large-scale building complexes. Other important parts of Stanley's market were asphalt producers, loggers, mining companies, and government agencies.

The Stanley Company faced competition in its geographic market from many independent construction-equipment distributors. The major competitors, however, were the distributors of such name brands as Caterpillar, Fiat-Allis, John Deere, and Case Power Equipment. Mr. Peck estimated that the Caterpillar distributor and the Fiat-Allis distributor together had close to a 50 percent market share. Peck said that Stanley's market share was about 20 percent.

The sales force in the Stanley Company consisted of 18 people, and each person was responsible for selling the company's entire product assortment. Because the construction equipment market included so many different types of customers and products, it was difficult to find sales reps who could handle the job effectively. However, the nature of the market in each rep's territory influenced the line of equipment that the rep was primarily involved with. For example, the sales person covering the northern Salt Lake City metropolitan area was heavily involved in selling asphalt equipment. In contrast, Joe Lorenz had a territory in eastern Utah where the market's major demand was for earth moving, excavation, and mining equipment.

Up until about six months ago, Joe Lorenz had been an excellent salesman. In fact, after his third year with the company, Lorenz was rated as Stanley's second best sales person. Through the years the general sales manager, Charles Molla, saw great potential in Lorenz. Molla told Peck on various occasions that Joe was one of the best sales reps that he (Molla) had seen in a long time.

Peck even felt that Lorenz might possibly be the next general sales manager if Molla should ever be promoted or leave the company. Peck's only concern was that Lorenz, while highly self-motivated, also seemed to have a strong desire to be independent—to be his own boss.

Currently Joe's territory accounted for 10 percent of the company's total sales. His sales last year were close to $1 million. For the four years previous to the current one, Joe's sales increased annually between 5 and 10 percent. During three of those years his volume had exceeded the company's projections by $200,000 a year. Mr. Peck admitted, "When there is such a large gap between our forecasted sales and Joe's actual results, either our forecasting procedures are lousy or Joe is just outstanding. Maybe the true situation is a little bit of both factors."

Management relied on a series of three reports as an aid in its supervision of the Stanley sales force. Two of these reports were submitted by the sales people themselves. The third report came from an outside service agency used by all firms in the construction-equipment industry.

Each sales rep was responsible for sending in a weekly call report showing (1) who the rep had called on, (2) the topics discussed, (3) any missionary worked performed for the customer, and (4) the type of product the sales person had tried to sell.

A lost-sale report was to be filed any time a rep did not get an order after (1) thinking he had a sure sale or (2) having contacted the customer enough times to expect a favorable buying decision. In this report the sales person was asked to state what other competitor got the order and why.

Once a month the Stanley company received a report from an industry service agency stating what piece of equipment was bought, on what day, and by who. This industry report then enabled Mr. Peck and Mr. Molla to verify the two reports sent in by the sales people.

Every six months each sales person had a performance-evaluation interview with Mr. Peck. In this interview with Joe Lorenz six months ago, Mr. Peck had observed that Joe's sales had declined 15 percent from the previous year's level. When asked why, Joe said it was just a slow period and that his volume would recover before the end of the year.

This decline worried both Mr. Peck and Mr. Molla, because Joe's sales volume had never declined before. Peck asked Molla to review Joe's call reports a little more closely for the next few months.

During these next few months, however, Joe Lorenz's sales were still down. In fact, Molla observed that Joe's sales were running 25 percent below the projected volume in his territory. This decline could perhaps have been understandable if the industry sales in that area also were down by 25 percent. But the monthly reports from the outside agency showed only 5 percent decline. "In effect," Molla said, "Caterpillar and John Deere are picking up orders that used to go to Joe."

Mr. Molla was particularly bothered by the industry sales reports involving an International Harvester loader that was carried by Stanley as well as by some other distributors. Competitors' sales of this product were at a high level. In Joe's call reports, he said he had been giving special emphasis to this particular piece of equipment. Yet he had not filed any lost-sales reports on it. When Molla reported this situation, Mr. Peck decided it was time for him to have a straight-forward talk with Joe.

When he was brought into Peck's office, Lorenz was asked in no uncertain terms for the real reason his sales were down. He was also asked why he had not been filing lost-sales reports on the International Harvester loader. Lorenz was told in plain language that if he did not "level" with Peck this time, it would leave Peck with no alternative but to discharge him.

Lorenz then told Mr. Peck that he (Joe) had entered into a partnership on the side with one of his old friends. They were selling home-construction equipment in Joe's territory. A lot of condominiums were being built in that area. So Joe thought it would be an opportunity to make some extra money, while at the same time help his friend. Joe intended to stop this extra activity as soon as his friend could handle the job himself or else could find a suitable replacement for Joe.

Peck was happy finally to clear up the mystery of Joe's sales decline. But Peck wondered if Joe was really telling the truth when he said this other work was only temporary. Peck feared that it might just be a good way for Lorenz to see how his new business worked out while still having financial support from Stanley. Then later if this new business did well, Lorenz would leave the Stanley company.

Peck ended the discussion by suspending Lorenz until Peck could discuss the matter with Molla and also with Ted Scovill, the company's executive vice president. The suspension shocked Lorenz, and soon management began to hear repercussions from customers and from others within the company. Many customers commented favorably on the service they had received from Lorenz. Within the firm, he was well liked and respected by his fellow workers.

Peck's discussion with Molla and Scovill did not help Peck much because there was such a difference of opinion. Ted Scovill believed there was no alternative than to fire Lorenz. Scovill pointed out that sales in Joe's territory were now down by a significant pecentage. Also, by not giving his customers the service they expected, Joe may have lost some of those customers for good. Scovill felt that Lorenz was simply using the company's money and time to his own advantage.

Charles Molla had a different feeling about the matter because he had been closer to Lorenz than either Peck or Scovill had. Molla did agree that Joe should not walk away free from this situation without some sort of disciplinary action. However, Molla reminded the other two executives of Joe's previously excellent sales performance during his many years with the company. Molla said, "I really believe Joe when he says this is only a temporary situation. Joe has everything going for him at Stanley and I believe that Joe knows this. Also, I believe that Joe knows that he has the potential for making a lot more money with Stanley than he can in this other business. I think that we should extend his suspension for a couple more months. And we should warn him that if he ever gets caught in anything like this again, he will be automatically terminated."

At the moment, Mr. Peck was undecided as to the course of action he should follow. He respected the opinions of Scovill and Molla, but he thought that perhaps there was a better choice than either of the two executives had suggested. Peck really believed that what Joe Lorenz did was wrong. Yet Peck reminded himself that only 18 months ago he had felt that Joe Lorenz would be the next general sales manager.

Question

What action should George Peck take regarding Joseph Lorenz?

Case 14–2

Republic Steel Corporation—Pipe Division*

Sales-Incentive Contest

The sales forecast for 1981 in the pipe division of the Republic Steel Corporation revealed that the sales volume would be no greater than in 1980. This estimate was based upon an estimate of the com-

* Case prepared by Professor Donald W. Scotton, Cleveland State University. Reproduced with permission. Some of the dates and figures in the original case have been changed.

petition, the state of the economy, and other variables outside the company's control. This forecast also was based on the assumption that the company's marketing program in 1981 would be similar to the one followed in 1980. At this point, the members of the sales advertising department considered the possibility of increasing sales by means of a sales-incentive contest for district sales representatives.

The Republic Steel Corporation was one of the largest steel producers in the United States. Through its pipe division, Republic produced and marketed a variety of standard and structural pipe products. Two of these lines were known as CSR (Continuous Stretch Run) and CW (Continuous Weld) pipe products. These products had a wide variety of uses and were marketed to a wide variety of industries.

Republic produced its CSR and CW pipe products in a wide variety of sizes and specifications. These products compared well with competing products in meeting the standards established by contractors, manufacturers, and other users. In fact, Republic's variety of sizes, lengths, wall thicknesses, and surface finishings made the products extremely competitive. Nevertheless, "Pipe is pipe, and steel is steel," as one major user said. So Republic's pipe products were characterized as standard nondifferentiated products, and therefore Republic was faced with strong competition for its market share.

Republic's distribution channels for these pipe products extended from the manufacturing plants to Republic Steel's 19 district sales offices throughout the United States. District sales representatives sold to industrial and mill supply houses. These wholesalers, in turn, sold to the multitude of contractors and fabricators who used these products.

The CSR and CW standard pipe products were an important product group from which Republic planned to obtain substantial sales volume and profit contributions. Consequently, a decision was made to run a sales-incentive contest during the last six months of 1981. The top sales executives were firmly convinced that sales could be increased by using such an incentive program.

The sales contest involved all sales people in the 19 districts. These sales reps sold a variety of Republic Steel products, including the pipe division products. However, only CSR and CW standard pipe were included in the contest. The contest was identified as the "CSR SELL-A-TON MARATHON," and the following objectives were established:

1. To increase sales of CSR standard and structural pipe.
2. To add new long-term pipe-buying customers to Republic's customer list and increase business with existing customers.

3. To increase enthusiasm of Republic sales people for CSR pipe during and beyond the program.
4. To provide Republic's management with a means of measuring the immediate and long-term effectiveness of sales-incentive programs.

The contest theme was borrowed from a very unusual and successful advertising campaign which Republic had been running in early 1981. This campaign was built around the advertising character of J. C. Frisbee, Sr. He was paternalistic, hard-hitting, and lovable. There was no doubt that he loved his life—that is, running a company, selling pipe, and social activity built around golf. But the message came through. J. C. was in business to sell a useful product, CSR Standard Pipe. Four monthly advertisements appeared in trade journals early in 1981. The reactions from customers and the sales force were very favorable.

For these reasons, it was determined that J. C. Frisbee, Sr., should be the theme of the sales-incentive campaign. To insure maximum impact, Frisbee was withdrawn from the advertising schedule and reassigned to the sales contest. It was anticipated that when he had completed the sales-incentive campaign, he would be recalled to spearhead future advertising programs.

Rules for participation were mailed to the sales offices and included the following:

1. The CSR Sell-A-Ton Marathon will start July 1 and end December 31, 1981. All CSR standard pipe shipments *invoiced* between these dates will be included in the program.
2. All district sales offices, except General Export, will participate.
3. *All* district office personnel who have responsibilities involving standard pipe orders or accounts are eligible to participate with the exception of district managers and assistants. Each district sales manager will determine who will participate in the Marathon and receive incentive awards. Individuals not eligible for the pipe Marathon will most likely be eligible for other incentive programs contemplated by the corporation at later dates.
4. Each district sales office has a tonnage goal which in most cases is equal to the standard pipe tonnage invoiced by each office in the last half of 1980. Some district goals have been adjusted to reflect unusual gains or losses in tonnage over which the district had little or no control. Should special circumstances warrant, goals may be adjusted during the six months of the Marathon pending approval of the Marathon Committee. Your district goal is _____ tons.
5. Goal tonnage includes CSR and CW standard and structural pipe

⅛ inch through 4 inch. It does *not* include API line pipe, rejects, ERW, or seamless pipe.

6. The Marathon incentive begins when a district's invoiced shipments exceed the district office goal. For each ton shipped over the goal figure, incentives will be earned as follows:

That portion over 100% of goal through
110% inclusive, $2 per ton
That portion over 110% of goal through
120% inclusive, $6 per ton
That portion over 120% of goal, $10 per ton

In addition to the incentive, special cash awards will be made to the two winning district sales offices. These cash awards will be added to the district's incentive fund for distribution to district office personnel.

a. $2,000 will be awarded to that office shipping the largest *tonnage* over its district goal. To be eligible to win, this tonnage must be at least 5 percent over goal.
b. $1,000 will be awarded to that office showing the largest *percentage* increase in tonnage shipped over its district goal. To be eligible to win, this percentage must be a minimum of 150 tons.
c. One district office cannot win both the tonnage and percentage special awards.
d. Recognition will be given to the district managers and assistant managers of the two winning offices.

7. The district manager will be informed of his district's total winnings at the end of the Marathon, upon completion of records. Each manager will then determine the distribution of the incentive funds to participating district personnel. Distribution should be based on his evaluation of their individual contribution to the total district performance.

In addition to the rules, instructions were mailed to the district managers to provide guidelines and suggestions for administering and interpreting the contest (see Exhibit 1).

Promotion and publicity. The contest was announced by letter to the district sales offices in June 1981 from the vice president of sales. Enclosed with that letter were materials explaining the contest. Objectives, rules for participation, and awards information were communicated. Of particular importance was a message to district managers (see Exhibit 2) which provided an outline of methods to be used for promotion and implementing the CSR Sell-A-Ton Marathon.

Exhibit 1

Guidelines and Suggestions for District Managers

The following information and suggestions are offered only as a guide as each district sales manager is most qualified to make Marathon decisions best suited to his particular district. It is important that district sales management be familiar with the details of the Marathon since your judgment will determine the success or failure of the contest within your district.

Computation of Incentive Award

Paragraph 6 of the rules describes the method of computing incentive. To avoid misunderstanding, we cite the following example:

District A's goal was 1,000 tons. Total Marathon tonnage invoiced from July 1 through December 31 was 1,250 -- 25 percent or 250 tons over goal.

The incentive award for district A is computed as follows:
That portion over 100% of goal to 110% inclusive -- 100 tons at $2 per ton or $ 200
That portion over 110% of goal to 120% inclusive -- 100 tons at $6 per ton or   600
That portion over 120% of goal   -- 50 tons at $10 per ton or   500
Total district incentive $1,300

Your first responsibility is to determine who within your district will participate in the Marathon. This includes inside and outside people. The only exclusions are district sales managers and assistant managers. The only suggested requisite for eligibility should be involvement or contribution to your district pipe sales effort. As previously requested, please forward names of your participating personnel as quickly as possible on the form provided.

Distribution of earned incentive will probably be your most difficult responsibility. It is suggested you first consider the division of incentive between outside and inside personnel -- this could be split 50-50 between outside and inside, 60-40, 70-30 or whatever. Next, these amounts could be split on a percentage based on your judgment of individual performance and contribution. With outside sales people, you might consider their percentage of Marathon sales to district goal or increase in tonnage during the period of the contest. For pipe specialists or sales engineers, consider their total contribution to the district effort. With inside personnel, it is suggested you consider the number of accounts each handles and the tonnage they represent, ability and willingness to accept responsibility, and over-all contribution to Marathon sales.

All participants must be employed by Republic Steel at the end of the program to be eligible for awards. Awards will be paid by check, with necessary deductions. The Marathon Committee may be consulted for guidance on any problems that arise during the course of the Marathon.

Republicsteel

Exhibit 2

Following is an outline of the methods that
will be used to promote and implement the CSR
Sell-A-Ton Marathon:

1. The program will be introduced by mailing an
announcement folder to all participating personnel. A copy of this announcement folder has
been enclosed in your kit. It explains what the
program is, rules and prizes, and introduces the
program's "Honorary Chairman." (See folder.)

2. In order to do this mailing, we must receive
your list of participating personnel before
June 26. You will find enclosed a participating
personnel list and a self-addressed, stamped
envelope for mailing. Please make every effort to return this list to us on or before
June 26 to allow everyone an early start in the Marathon.

3. A special letter head has been produced for this program and, henceforth, all communications to you and your participating personnel will be on this letterhead.

4. As you can see from the enclosed ad reprint, our Sell-A-Ton Marathon ties in with
our forthcoming CSR ad campaign. J. C. Frisbee (an imaginary character in this advertising) has been chosen to act as "Honorary Chairman" of the Sell-A-Ton Marathon.

    The J. C. Frisbee campaign is a humorous approach to advertising CSR pipe. This
approach will be carried into the Marathon. For further information on J. C. Frisbee,
read the back of the Marathon announcement folder.

5. In order to keep enthusiasm up for the duration of the Marathon, all participating
personnel will receive a "Monthly Memo From J. C. Frisbee." This memo will be printed
on a specially adapted piece of Marathon letterhead (sample enclosed) and will contain
"inspirational messages" from J. C., and also give monthly progress reports. This is
an inexpensive method of communication but one that we feel will be both entertaining
and informative.

6. Each District Manager will receive an "Official Sell-A-Ton Marathon Scoreboard" to
display in his office. This scoreboard will be delivered to you shortly with a complete
set of instructions on how to use it to its best advantage.

Republicsteel

The J. C. Frisbee theme was taken from the advertising program mentioned earlier, and Frisbee became the "honorary chairman" for the contest. The success of this theme in the earlier advertising campaign was seen as useful in arousing and maintaining the interest of the sales force throughout the incentive campaign. J. C. Frisbee was featured on scoreboards sent to each of the district sales offices. A "Monthly Memo from J C. Frisbee" was sent from the pipe division home office to the sales offices to give progress reports and sustain a high level of interest. The progress reports contained cumulative monthly rankings of the 19 sales districts according to the percentages of quotas achieved.

Exhibit 3 reveals pecentage of sales goals and cash awards achieved by each of the 19 sales districts. It was noted that 4 of the districts that did not achieve the sales quotas were operating under the disadvantage of construction trade unions' strikes. It was be-

Exhibit 3

CSR Sell-A-Ton Marathon
(results by sales districts, July–December 1981)

District	Percent of Sales Goal Achieved	Cash Awards
1	322	$9,174*
2	180	7,042
3	153	5,972
4	142	2,628
5	123	7,434†
6	114	1,214
7	111	1,184
8	107	884
9	103	138
10	102	58
11	99	—
12	89	—
13	84	—
14	84	—
15	79	—
16	75	—
17	59	—
18	38	—
19	27	—

* Includes largest over quota tonnage percentage award of $1,000.
† Includes largest actual tonnage sold of $2,000.

lieved that their sales goals would have been exceeded, if the strikes had not occurred.

An analysis of contest results by the market research division concerned itself with achievement of sales goals, cost of the contest, contribution of added sales to profit, share of market position, and possible generation of new customers. Findings in this analysis included:

1. The tonnage sales goal was exceeded by 6.5 percent.
2. There occurred a 2.8 percent increase in share of market, while industry shipments were declining by almost 9 percent.
3. There was an 8 percent increase in tonnage shipped during the last half of 1981 compared to the same period of 1980.
4. The cost of the contest was modest in relation to the contribution to profit generated by the increased sales volume.
5. During the contest, 77 new customers were added, and they contributed about 4 percent of the contest tonnage sold. This tonnage was important to the districts that exceeded sales goals. For example, Districts A, B, C, D, and E, achieved 37, 24, 23, 20, and 17 percent of their goals from new customers.

A final observation included the comment that sales during the early months of the contest were probably lessened by the effect of a price raise that occurred in May 1981. The effect of this action was stockpiling by buyers before the price raise went into effect. Also, the heavier inventory positions reduced purchases that would have normally occurred during the first months of the contest.

A final statement contained in the market research division's analysis of the CSR SELL-A-TON MARATHON summarized the outcome as follows:

> We conclude that the pipe contest was a substantial success. The Pipe Division increased tonnage, increased profit contribution, and generated new customers on which to build in the future. Even if the gains were temporary, the contest paid for itself many times over. But it is possible that many of these gains constitute the successful start of a continuing campaign which will see the Pipe Division maintain its new high share of butte-weld standard and structural pipe or even improve it. The contest has provided the launching pad for continued improved sales by the Pipe Division, provided the momentum can be continued.

Questions

1. Evaluate the sales incentive contest—its objectives, format, theme, rules, and so on.
2. Do you agree with the market research division's evaluation of the contest's results?

15

Sales-Force Morale

It takes two to speak the truth—one to speak and another to hear.
THOREAU

Leaders of all sorts of enterprises—sports, the military, and business—have long extolled the importance of morale in building effective organizations. Groups with only mediocre talent have achieved great results because their people had excellent morale. Conversely, great talent with poor morale seldom does much. Morale should be of great concern to every manager. But what is this intangible force we call morale?

The Nature of Morale

The word **morale** is commonly used to designate the mental and emotional attitudes of an individual toward his environment. Major elements of this environment include the family, business associates, the employer, neighbors, and the community. When the attitudes are positive, morale is said to be good, or high; when they are negative, morale is considered poor or low.

Group morale involves a sense of common purpose, while **individual** morale is concerned with one person's state of psychological well-being. The sales manager must be concerned with both. Group morale may be healthy, but individuals in the group can harbor poor attitudes for a number of reasons. Everyone does not prosper even in the best of situations, and everyone is not unhappy in the worst of them.

The group generally exerts a strong influence on the individual's morale. Good group morale can improve the attitudes of a member whose morale is sagging. In the same way, an individual with a positive outlook can affect the morale of the group.

One factor that limits the ability of the manager to work with the sales force as a whole is that, in many instances, no group actually exists. The sales people may be geographically distributed so that they have little contact with one another. Therefore, the sales executive generally must deal with sales people's attitudes on an individual basis.

Attitudes toward work are important for both economic and social reasons. From the economic standpoint, productivity is likely to be higher in groups whose members have relatively good morale. It does not always follow that high morale results in high productivity, however. A group may have a good attitude but poor results. Nevertheless, productivity is usually higher for employees who have good mental attitudes toward their jobs.

From a social point of view, people who develop negative attitudes toward work can make life miserable not only for themselves but for those around them. Life is too short to be spent working in an unpleasant environment. The proposition that good morale should be created in the work environment for its sake alone certainly has merit.

The factors of *satisfaction with pay, feelings of personal worth on the job*, and *general vigor* are also important components of morale. A person who has good job morale is apt to be more satisfied with the pay and have better feelings of self-worth. Thus morale is not only the overall result of a complex mixture of forces, it can have a reciprocal relationship with the forces that affect it. The effect is seen often in sales work. A sales person has good morale and is relatively satisfied with the job and what it pays. Then something happens; perhaps management changes, or there are problems at home. Suddenly morale sags. Now the same job and pay are unsatisfactory.

Morale and Strategic Planning

Managers in some firms are not concerned with morale. Their corporate climate is such that they are mainly concerned with group and individual output. Some managers think morale is unimportant. Others feel that there is little they can do to improve morale. Thus, building good organizational morale is not part of their marketing strategy. One owner of 16 units of a large fast-food franchise stated that his labor turnover was 500 percent a year. "We can only pay them minimum wage and they have to work fast and hard, so you can guess what our morale is. What can I do about it?"

On the other hand, some firms make high morale a keystone in their marketing strategy. They try to build a fiercely loyal, highly effective sales force that maintains good loyal customers. They call it giving better service than the competition. Such firms build relationships not only with their customers but with their own personnel.

The strategic role morale plays in an organization reflects top management's values—part of what modern management theorists call *corporate climate*.

Effects of Low Sales-Force Morale

A sales representative with a bad attitude toward the job and the company develops an antimanagement orientation. Such people fight suggestions made by the manager and are critical of the company's policies and practices. For real or imagined reasons, they regard the company as an adversary and attempt to retaliate against management suggestions. And when sales-force morale is low, a company can suffer in many areas.

Unsatisfactory Sales Performance

Probably no job in an entire company is so directly dependent on good morale as sales. No one with a poor attitude toward the job can sell effectively. Experienced sales managers know that when a sales rep's volume declines in relation to the rest of the sales force, the first place to look for trouble is in the individual. A rep's mental attitude is reflected throughout the sales presentation. A poor attitude can destroy the effectiveness of a sales presentation and result in lost sales. How can the customer have confidence in the product and the firm if the sales rep doesn't? While there may be no scientific proof that morale and sales performance are correlated, this is still a good working assumption for a sales manager to operate on.[1]

Excessive Turnover

One of the most widely recognized indexes for measuring morale in a firm is worker turnover. The theory is that most people with poor attitudes toward their jobs become so dissatisfied that they seek

---

[1] For an excellent discussion summarizing this complex problem of the relationship between morale, satisfaction, motivation, and job performance, see Robert Berl, Terry Powell, and Nicholas C. Williamson, "Industrial Salesforce Satisfaction and Performance with Herzberg's Theory," *Industrial Marketing Management*, February 1984, pp. 11–19.

employment elsewhere. Observation indicates that among sales people with high morale there is little turnover. Contented reps don't quit. The number of people quitting is a good measure of the state of morale in an organization.

Impact on Expenses

Sales people who do not have a good attitude toward their employers seldom control their expenses. Such reps may openly state that they intend to get everything they can from the company. When poor morale not only lowers sales volume, but also increases expenses, it puts a dual pressure on profits.

Effect on Fellow Employees

One person with a bad attitude can lower the morale of all those around him. There is no such thing as a perfect organization. People will always make mistakes, regardless of their standing in the firm. There is always some executive decision that a malcontent can use as a basis for complaint.

Magnification of Minor Complaints

Sales people who have poor morale are apt to magnify minor complaints. Things that normally would go unnoticed in an organization with good morale can become points of contention in other groups. For instance, inadequate office facilities might not be a cause of complaint in an organization with good morale. But they could be a source of annoyance in a firm where workers were generally dissatisfied.

Often the sales manager must handle a series of minor complaints instead of being able to deal with the real source of the irritations. Sales people who fail to perceive the real cause of their morale problems may seize on whatever is at hand to complain about. In sports, it has been observed that there are few problems on winning teams. But if the team starts to lose, complaints about all sorts of conditions are apt to be voiced.

Development of Outside Interests

People in a frustrating or unhappy situation may mentally withdraw. Such an employee refuses to become emotionally involved with the organization. Some hold two jobs simultaneously, others use company time to seek other work.

Unfortunately, however, many individuals with poor morale do not quit. For various economic and social reasons, they may go on working for years at a job they detest. Some of them cannot find as good a job elsewhere. Others do not want to leave the location. Or, they wait out the situation in hopes that it will improve or that the executives they blame for their dissatisfaction may move elsewhere. Usually in such situations, dissatisfied employees develop outside interests—they look elsewhere for their satisfaction in life. They spend as little time as possible on the job and do a minimum amount of work.

Disloyalty

Even more insidious than the disinterested employee is the disloyal one. Such people may provide competitors with confidential information, often in the hope of eliciting a job offer or other compensation.

Incentive for Unionization

One of the outgrowths of poor morale has been the development of labor unions. This was certainly the case in production, but it has also been true in some sales organizations. If a sales force comes to believe that management does not care about them, they will cease to care about management. Needing work, they do not quit, but they sometimes form their own organization—a union.

Causes of Low Sales-Force Morale

Any attempt to list the various reasons sales people may have for poor attitudes is bound to be incomplete. Like the effects of poor morale, the causes are numerous and varied. However, experience has shown that several common occurrences lead to poor morale. Through a study of these factors, the sales manager may gain insight into how workers are motivated. Poor morale in the sales force can be created in two broad areas—work relationships and personal affairs.

Work-Related Reasons for Poor Morale

The sales manager should become acquainted with the various work-related reasons for poor morale first. They are his direct concern and responsibility. Moreover, he has more control over them than over personal factors that affect morale.

A day-to-day operating problem in the
Majestic Glass Company (I)

Threat of Sales-Force Unionization

Clyde Brion received a telephone call one morning asking him to come to the office of G. L. Kendrick, Majestic's director of industrial relations. Mr. Kendrick's staff conducted all the formal training activities of the firm. Therefore, Mr. Brion supposed that the call concerned a refresher training course for salesmen, which he had been discussing with Mr. Kendrick.

He was surprised to find himself confronted by Kendrick and two other men. One was William Cline, who was a machine operator in Majestic's factory. The other man was introduced as Vittorio LaGono, business agent for the Amalgamated Glass and Vitreous Products Workers Union. Majestic's production workers had long been organized by the AFVPWU. Cline was an officer of the local organization.

"Clyde," said Mr. Kendrick, "Mr. LaGono tells me that he has cards signed by a majority of the members of our sales force. The cards authorize the union to represent the reps in negotiating a contract covering their wages, working conditions, and job security."

"The *salesmen*?" exploded Mr. Brion. "Why, the union can't—I mean, they're not glass workers! They aren't even employees, really."

"So?" said Mr. LaGono. "What else is new?"

"I guess some of the old distinctions we used to make don't matter any more," said Mr. Kendrick. "They've got the signatures, and they've notified us. I guess that's it."

"But how can I run a unionized sales force?" asked Mr. Brion. "I . . ."

"We'll be glad to help," said Mr. LaGono cheerfully. "It'll be a real pleasure to work with you."

Question

How should Clyde Brion respond to the possibility of his sales force being unionized?

Note: See the introduction to this series of problems in Chapter 3 for the necessary background on the company, its market, and its competition.

Inadequate channels of communication. The problem of communication is crucially important to many aspects of sales management. When channels of communication are absent or faulty, neither management nor the sales force knows what the other thinks.

Lack of communication is more than a lack of contact; it is also a lack of understanding. Although this seems absurdly simple, probably no greater problem exists in American industry today. How many sales people really know what management is trying to do and the reasons behind its actions? That is the essence of downward communication. How many executives really know what their employees think and feel? That is the essence of upward communication. Morale is affected by both.

Downward communication.   An important facet of communication involves relaying management's expectations to the sales force. A sales person may be placed in a territory to sell mechandise and do well. Only when he is passed over for a promotion does he find out that management was also interested in how well he performed other tasks, such as placing displays and doing sales-promotional work. He had been neglecting these tasks in favor of sales activity. Such a breakdown in the communications system may mean that a sales rep will never find out why he is not being promoted. Morale is bound to suffer in such circumstances.

Upward communication.   The sales rep in the field faces many problems that can result in grievances and troubles. The rep may be realistic enough to know that management can do nothing about many of these troubles, but still want management to know about them. Reps may not expect direct action on many complaints but they still value the opportunity to tell someone in authority. Some employees take drastic steps to gain upward communcation, such as deliberately violating company policy in order to gain a hearing. Others resign in order to communicate the fact that management is ignoring complaints.

Some sales managers form reps' grievance committees to ensure the sales people will have every opportunity to be heard. However, these committees alone are not the answer to communication problems. Upward communication consists of much more than hearing grievances. It is a matter of knowing what the sales people are doing, thinking, and feeling. This can be accomplished only through individual personal contact. Person-to-person communications is one of the major reasons morale is usually far better in a small sales force than in a large one.[2]

Communication is more than talking.   Although personal contact greatly facilitates good communications, it does not ensure them. Two people can hold a face-to-face conversation and yet fail to communicate with each other. This occurs when one, or both, of the parties is so intent on what he or she is saying that no attention is paid to the other's message. Good communication requires an understanding receiver as well as a good sender.

Understanding depends on how well a message is stated and explained and how earnestly the receiver attempts to comprehend it.

---

[2] See Don Waite, "Let Your Sales Force Speak Up!" *Sales & Marketing Management*, April 6, 1981, p. 50, for a study of upward communications.

An employee always understands management's policies and practices better when management gives a clear explanation. Communications are hindered when the parties are unable or unwilling to state their cases accurately and logically. Frequently, semantic problems hinder good comunications. Both the sales person and the manager may agree that the job requires incentive pay, but what each party actually means by *incentive* can vary tremendously. The sales manager may mean that the reps should be on a straight commission plan. However, the reps may mean that they should be given a relatively small bonus in addition to a substantial salary. To minimize misinterpretation, the administrator must be careful to use specific terms with exact meanings.

Unsatisfactory status in the organization.   Many people are motivated by high status. They cannot tolerate feeling inconsequential in an organization. Such individuals prefer to be big frogs in a little pond rather than little frogs in a big one.

Status is often measured by many seemingly trivial things. Some employees measure their status in the organization by the location and furnishings of their office. Others count the number of people under them or the various privileges they are allowed, such as eating in the executive lunchroom.

The sales manager informally determines the status of the various sales people in the organization by the way he treats them. If he consistently seeks out certain reps for advice in managerial matters, these reps are, in effect, elevated to higher positions in the organization. People who are not consulted can become dissatisfied with their apparently inferior status.

Unfair treatment.   Probably the quickest way to ruin sales people's morale is to give them good reason to feel that management is treating them unfairly. The rep may only be imagining it, but it will still affect morale adversely. Imagined grievances are usually the result of poor communications. The rep does not know the facts in the matter and has formed an opinion on the basis of rumor or just by guessing.

However, sales people often have real grievances against management for obviously unfair treatment. Such conditions must be remedied when discovered, but it is far better if they never arise in the first place. The sales manager must be careful to treat all reps fairly and not to discriminate against any of them. For instance, a salesman for a large business machines manufacturer learned that once the sales volume in his territory reached a certain level, the company would split the territory in half, thereby automatically reducing his volume. Since he was paid a straight commission, his earnings would be directly affected. In other words, his reward for a job well done was to have his income cut in half. Since the man was too old to get a comparable job, he did not quit. But his attitude was poor. The company was not realizing everything it could from his territory. He found a level of sales volume that the company was happy with, and that did not penalize him.

Poor working conditions.   The physical environment in which the sales rep is required to work can be a source of discontent. Many reps primarily work outside the home office. Consequently, their working conditions consist largely of the car they travel in and the style of living the company's expense account allows them to maintain. Usually this presents no problem, since most firms allow their sales people to drive good cars and provide satisfactory expense accounts.

Management also must consider the working conditions for inside sales people, such as automobile sales reps and those who sell out of an office. They need satisfactory desk space and a pleasant, clean place in which to talk with prospects.

Lack of confidence in ability of the manager or the organization.   A big cause of poor morale in the sales force, and one that is difficult to remedy, is lack of confidence in the manager's ability or in the organization. If the sales person does not feel the leaders are good managers, he or she will have a poor attitude. Most sales people realize that their productivity and welfare depend to some degree on the abilities of their superiors. If they lose confidence in management, they cannot avoid a poor attitude toward the company and the job.

This is the area that we will refer to in another section as the integration of interests. Building morale is basically a process of integrating the interests of the individual with those of the firm. Employees who lack confidence in the firm's leadership have found that their interests do not coincide with those of the firm or its executives.

One real estate organization had a manager who, in the opinion of all of its agents, simply did not have any ability to sell or to manage. The agents laughed at him behind his back, and they were all looking for other jobs. The owner of the firm recognized that the manager was ineffective and began investigating. The result was the employment of a new manager, who quickly captured the confidence of the sales force by his obvious grasp of the situation. The agents felt he really knew what he was talking about, and his plans were very practical. Morale was restored in a week.

At times sales reps lack confidence not in the sales manager but in the organization. Sales people may respect the manager but feel he is being hampered by inept leadership. Sometimes this lack of confidence stems from poor products or marketing policies.

One manufacturer of vacuum cleaners maintained a door-to-door sales force. The firm did not sell through retail stores or do any advertising. The reps were faced with the task of calling on customers cold. Not 1 out of 100 housewives called on recognized the brand name of the vacuum cleaner. They had not seen it advertised and had never seen such a unit in retail stores. This made a normally difficult sale even more difficult. The sales reps were distressed over the company's advertising policy. Every time two or more of them met, this was the first gripe they exchanged. Finally the firm was forced to alter its marketing policy and institute an advertising program just to get its brand name recognized.

Lack of recognition. Near the top of most lists of factors that cause poor morale is insufficient recognition for performance. When people have done a job well, they like to be recognized for it. Bestowing recognition on deserving individuals is one of the main tools a good sales manager can use to build better relations with the sales force. Recognition is important to the individual because it is tangible evidence that management appreciates his efforts. It expresses gratitude for the person's dedication to the company's affairs.

Poor compensation plans. The matter of pay level and method of compensation was discussed in Chapters 11 and 12. If sales people do not feel they are getting paid in proportion to the importance of the job they are doing, their attitude toward the company probably will be bad. Sales people are in continual contact with reps who work for other firms, and they are in a good position to know what other firms are paying. If the comparison is continually unfavorable, they may come to believe they are working for a low-paying concern and would do better elsewhere.

It is difficult for the sales manager to instill a good attitude among the sales force when their pay is not commensurate with their activities. The firm risks lowering morale if the compensation plan fails to be fair, offer some security and incentive, and otherwise meet the characteristics of a sound compensation plan as discussed earlier.

Nature of the job. In sales work, the job and the individual must be matched. Any employee who feels unproductive or noncreative will have poor morale. One major problem in managing a door-to-door selling organization is that many people do not feel right doing it. One organization selling encyclopedias door-to-door had worked up a prepared sales presentation that was largely untruthful. After a short period, many reps found they could not maintain their self-respect and dignity while delivering such a lie.

Additionally, the very nature of the selling job is frustrating. Reps can't get in to see the people they want to see. Good prospects seem to evade them. People who should be buying don't. They can't seem to close a particularly important sale. Selling is one long string of frustrating problems. Unless they learn to cope with such frustrating problems, their morale will most likely suffer.[3]

Lack of security.   An individual who is concerned with future employment possibilities cannot operate at anywhere near a normal level of productivity. People who have been afraid of losing a job can appreciate the fears and emotional stress that go with such a feeling. The manager who can alleviate these fears does much to establish good morale for the operation.

Ironically, people who do not care for security—and there are such individuals—may not make the best sales representatives. They usually believe that their best security is their own ability, and without doubt they are right. Since they have this ability, however, they often leave other sales organizations to form their own enterprises, such as manufacturers' representatives or brokers. These reps are usually too good for the typical sales organization to keep. If they do stay, they may be so independent that they present managerial problems. It takes a most skillful and understanding executive to manage such highly talented people.

Problems with sales quotas, report requirements, and restrictions.   Sales quotas cause their share of morale troubles. Reps who do not believe their quotas are fair or based on a logical analysis of their markets are apt to have poor attitudes toward their work. The sales quota often has a direct bearing on the rep's compensation.

Reports and paperwork can be troublesome if the sales manager refuses to be realistic about them. Paperwork should be kept to a minimum. If the sales people come to regard it merely as bureaucratic red tape, their morale will suffer.

Home-office restrictions on sales reps can be a source of considerable irritation. When the home office restricts reps' actions by credit regulations, for example, the reps must understand the reasons. Morale is better if they agreee with the restrictions or at least are willing to comply with them.

One women's apparel manufacturer was constantly urging its reps to open up new accounts. Yet, top management refused to accept new dealers unless they (1) had been in business for five years, (2)

---

[3] For excellent discussions of frustration in selling, see Alan J. Dubinsky and Mary E. Lippitt, "Managing Frustration in the Sales Force," *Industrial Marketing Management*, June 1979, pp. 200–6; and Alan J. Dubinsky and Mary E. Lippitt, "Techniques That Reduce Salesforce Frustration," *Industrial Marketing Management*, April 1980, pp. 159–65.

had a top credit rating, and (3) did not carry certain other lines of apparel. Few qualified new dealers could be found, yet management would not review its unrealistic restrictions. This was a frustrating situation for the reps.

Personal Reasons for Poor Morale

Sales managers have little, if any, responsibility for many conditions that cause poor morale in the sales force. Nevertheless, these nonbusiness factors can play an important part in determining the attitudes of the employees. The most effective control the manager has over these factors is the selection program. Most personal problems can be handled only by the individual. Therefore, the sales manager must pick a recruit who is likely to take care of his or her personal life in a satisfactory manner.

Domestic difficulties. An important factor in the selection decision frequently is the family situation. The right spouse can be important to success in selling. The wrong one can ruin an otherwise good sales rep. Support at home is important. People having troubles at home cannot devote proper attention to the job. It is usually unwise to enter directly into a domestic situation. Managers can only try to hire people who seem to have a domestic environment and life-style that does not impede the person's success on the job.

The sales manager of a large building products company that pioneered the hiring of women as marketing representatives related his experience with family matters:

> I now have a new problem. One of our women requested that she be given a new sales territory in San Francisco because her husband has been transferred there. We did not need anyone in San Francisco, but she made such a fuss that we made a job for her there. Now I have a man who has requested a transfer to Los Angeles because his wife has been transferred there. We don't need him in Los Angeles, but he means business. If we don't move him, I'm sure we've got a lawsuit on our hands.

In this age of two-career families, management must have some clearly stated policies on how to handle such problems.

Financial problems. Anyone in financial difficulty is worried and distracted and likely to acquire bad selling habits. The sales person with financial problems may push too hard to make extra income or may cheat on the expense account. Careful selection will not totally avoid the problem, however, since many financially sound people can encounter difficulties after they have been hired. Unexpected illness in the family, an accident, and other unforeseen events can cause major drains on a bank account. Sometimes it is necessary for the manager to offer financial help, but this can have unfortunate consequences.

Poor health. It is hard for someone in poor health to have a good attitude toward the job. Most employers hire only people in good health, but health is not a permanent condition. People do get sick. All the sales manager can do to protect the health of the sales force is to make certain that they live prudently while on the road and take good care of themselves. Much can be done to educate sales people on the importance of good health.

Special Problems in Morale

From time to time virtually every sales manager faces special morale problems that are difficult to handle.

Dissatisfaction with Promotions

Promotions can have serious repercussions on morale. For every opening in the executive hierarchy, there may be several people who feel they should get it. Many of them have valid cases. Administrators often face the dilemma that there are several equally qualified individuals for only one promotion. Such situations can create poor attitudes among previously good employees.

Individuals who are doing a good job are disappointed if they don't receive a promotion they feel entitled to. This problem has no easy solution. Often it has no solution. Some of these good people quit when a promotion is not forthcoming. Many times nothing can be done, since there simply is no room for them in the executive level.

The situation is even worse when the sales force generally believes the company has promoted the wrong candidate. Promotion of an individual that others consider undeserving has a bad effect on morale. The promotion of an undeserving person also creates problems when she or he attempts to exercise managerial authority over former peers.

Severance

Many administrators cannot face the task of firing someone. The sales manager who does not approach this problem correctly can ruin the morale of the entire organization. Others will easily identify with the discharged individual and regard the situation as unfair, even though ample cause may exist.

In some companies, sales reps are seldom fired but instead encouraged to quit. There is a distinct difference. A sales manager can take many actions to cause a person to want to resign. Indeed, when you hear some woeful tale of a sales rep who is being treated terribly, you may be hearing a story of how one manager has chosen to fire an unsatisfactory employee. If management is treating a rep badly, perhaps it is trying to tell him to resign.

Handling of Older Sales People

The handling of older sales people has plagued many managers and has a direct bearing on the morale of all sales representatives in the firm. Today, allowances are often made for older sales reps. Most of them do not expect to make the earnings they once did. Frequently they accept a reduction of territory or work load in exchange for the assurance that they will not be retired.

There is considerable evidence to support the older sales rep's place in most sales organizations. While he cannot cover the territory he once did, many times his selling efficiency and profitability can match those of any other person in the organization. One older salesman of women's apparel in the Southwest has been calling on his trade for so long that he has a large group of friends among retailers. As a result, he does not have to do the traveling that younger people in the same organization must do. When he wants to cover the state of Oklahoma, for example, he merely obtains a suite of rooms in a hotel in Oklahoma City and calls all his dealers by telephone. The dealers go to Oklahoma City to view his line, thereby eliminating the need for him to travel to all the small towns in the state. Younger reps in the same company have not been able to master this wonderful method of selling, since they do not have the necessary rapport with their customers.

Titles

What should we call the person who sells our product? Many management's ask that question today because of the changing realities of selling and its impact on morale. In the old days the answer was simple. You called the guy a salesman even if the "guy" was a woman. But as management has become more sensitive to the psychological side of business operations, it became aware that many potential sales people resented being called salesman. They wanted other titles, titles more reflective of their actual work. So organizations now try to give the person a title that accurately depicts the

A day-to-day operating problem in the
Majestic Glass Company (J)

Ownership of Invention Developed by Company Sales Rep

Elton Boggess, salesman in the Cincinnati territory, was not at his office when Mr. Brion visited unexpectedly one Wednesday morning. While waiting for him to return, Mr. Brion noticed that the desk was covered with drawings and literature about light-transmission devices. He remembered that Mr. Boggess held a college degree in physics. But he had not heard that Mr. Boggess was pursuing any interest in that field.

After a time Mr. Boggess arrived, struggling to carry a complicated apparatus. It consisted of glass rods, attached clamps, photoelectric meters, wiring, and other gear. He set up the apparratus on his desk and enthusiastically gave Mr. Brion a demonstration. He said that light could be transmitted around corners through glass rods without loss of intensity and without transmitting heat. He said he had been working on the idea with a small company in Cincinnati. Furthermore, he said that the posible applications for industrial and scientific—especially medical—uses of the principles were unlimited.

Mr. Brion asked what this work had to do with selling bottles. Mr. Boggess replied, "The glass, don't you see? It's another use for lots of glass, and it would be a high-margin item, too. And when you think about it," he chuckled, "I could really make a lot of money on it. I'll be at least part owner of some patents. If Majestic manufactures it, I could get an award from the employee suggestion system, plus my regular commission on every unit. And I'd even get a bonus, because it would be a sale to a new customer!"

Majestic had never entered into a formal agreement with its salesmen covering ownership of discoveries and inventions developed while in the firm's employ. Mr. Brion had occasionally warned his men against speculative ventures involving special products because of their high costs and doubtful profitability.

Question

What policy should Mr. Brion recommend to top management regarding ownership and/or compensation for inventions developed by company sales people?

Note: See the introduction to this series of problems in Chapter 3 for the necessary background on the company, its market, and its competition.

---

work done and at the same time bestows more status. A report by Dartnell Corporation stated that less than 20 percent of the firms surveyed still refer to their sales people as *salesmen*.[4]

[4] John P. Steinbrink, *Sales Force Compensation: 23rd Biennial Survey* (Chicago: Dartnell Corp., 1986), p. 113. For an excellent discussion of the prestige connected with job titles, see Robert T. Adkins and John E. Swan, "Increase Salespeople's Prestige with a New Title," *Industrial Marketing Management*, February 1980, pp. 1–9.

Some popular alternative titles for sales people are:

- Sales engineer.
- Sales consultant.
- Technical representative.
- Factory sales representative.
- District manager.
- Account representative.

- Management representative.
- Sales coordinator.
- Marketing representative.
- Sales associate.
- Area sales manager.
- Market specialist.

Four reasons were cited for the trend. First, there are more women in sales. Second, the new titles provide more status with the customers. Third, the new titles improve the person's self-image. And finally, the new titles are more descriptive of the selling job.

Determining the Cause of Poor Morale

The sales manager may know that morale is poor but not know the reasons for it. Four actions can help uncover the true cause of the discontent.[5]

An outlet for complaints. First, the sales manager must offer sales people an outlet for their complaints. From these complaints some common grievance may be discovered. Sometimes it is advisable to question reps informally at a social event. Often a sales rep will not complain while working but will say what is bothering him or her at a cocktail party or a ballgame.

Whatever a rep tells the manager it should never be belittled or dismissed as trivial. Although the complaint may seem silly, it is probably serious to the employee. If the sales manager does not listen understandingly and then do something about valid complaints, the reps will soon learn that talking gains them nothing.

Opinion and attitude surveys. A second method used to determine the facts about conditions that affect morale is to conduct opinion and attitude surveys among employees. Often a firm hires an independent consulting agency to conduct the studies. Such surveys do have *some* validity if properly done. However, employees often are reluctant to expose their real attitudes, even to a supposedly independent interviewer.

The exit interview. A widely heralded tool for uncovering trouble areas in an organization is the exit interview. Its proponents maintain that the departing employee will open up and tell the employer

---

[5] See Robard Yongue Hughes, "How to Get the Truth," *Business Horizons*, August 1980, pp. 15–16. Eleven ways for uncovering the truth from subordinates are presented in a most usuable format.

the real reason for leaving and his true attitudes toward the company.

This point of view is probably incorrect. Most employees know that they need a recommendation from past employers to get future jobs. Particularly, most sales people have enough social intelligence to know that it is never wise to tell an individual the truth about his own shortcomings. What sales rep in his right mind is going to tell the sales manager that the real reason for his leaving is that he thinks the manager is incompetent?

This does not mean that exit interviews should be discontinued, for if they are properly handled, they can provide some insight. If the interviewer does not accept the surface reason the employee gives for leaving, the real reasons may be discovered by proving. It depends on (1) the rapport the interviewer can establish with the departing employee and (2) how much confidence the worker has that any revelations made will not adversely affect future recommendations. One firm conducts exit interviews several months after the employee leaves. The theory is that this gives the employee time to evaluate what went wrong in the firm and also time to get whatever recommendations he needs from the firm. One practical difficulty is that frequently the people have moved to another area and are unavailable for interviewing.

Close relationships with subordinates.   Some sales executives cultivate close relationships with a few subordinates to learn what is going on in the ranks. The administrator who uses this technique must be careful not to ruin the informants' relationships with the other sales people. If the sales force learns that one of their number is being used in effect as a spy, his effectiveness is immediately curtailed.

In conclusion, a perceptive manager who is well aware of what is going on in the organization and who has a good grasp of human behavior in the oganization should have a fairly good idea of what might be causing morale problems in the sales force. If not, the manager has reason to fear for his own job.

The Morale-Building Process

This chapter has discussed the effects of poor morale and the factors that cause it. Little has been said of how the sales manager can constructively affect the morale of the sales force. It can be done by avoiding the situations discussed earlier. However, there are several other ways to help build a good attitude among sales people.

Integrating Interests

Building morale in the work environment depends on showing people that they can achieve their personal objectives in life by working for the organization. This is known as the *process of integrating interests*. It is founded on the principle that every person wants certain things out of life. Each has a set of goals. If the person is convinced he can achieve these goals through working for an organization, his morale in that group will be excellent. Should he become convinced that he cannot achieve his personal objectives, either his morale will be severely damaged or, in all probability, he will look for another job.

If the firm has no promotional opportunities for its sales reps, managers should not look for management-type individuals. Similarly, many firms have nothing but money to offer. Their jobs are not desirable and have little prestige or glamor. In such circumstances, managers should hire people who are primarily motivated by money, not those looking for prestige positions.

The process of integrating the interests of the person and the organization begins at the time of hiring. It is folly to hire anyone for whom the company cannot provide a work experience that will be considered *success* by the person. The sales manager must make a frank analysis of exactly what the firm is able to furnish its people.

Apply Self-Concept Theory

In the process of integrating the company's and the rep's interests, management should recognize the practical value of the self-concept theory and its influence on human behavior. The theory states that each person has a set of concepts of what he or she is and would like to be. The individual is constantly striving to come closer to these concepts. If an individual thinks some management action will have a favorable impact on him—that is, if he thinks it will allow him to move closer to one of his desired concepts—the influence on his morale is favorable. Should management make a decision that moves the person further from one of his goals, his morale will be adversely affected.

Suppose a firm's sales people generally regard themselves as extremely well off compared to most other members of society. If management furnishes them with low-priced, unequipped compact cars, they would be moved away from their self-concept. They would probably prefer to drive their own cars rather than have inferior transportation furnished. Yet, the same managerial decision about cars could have a beneficial effect on the morale of sales people who hold different self-concepts. Suppose your sales force consisted mainly of people who did not complete high school and were merely sales clerks. They would consider any car furnished by management an upgrading of their status, and their morale would thereby improve.

It is almost impossible for a manager to alter an individual's self-concepts to conform with what the company has to offer. This can be done only by the individual and it is an extremely painful process at best. Consequently, about the only control the administrator has over this aspect of morale is either (1) to hire individuals who conform with what the company has to offer or (2) to change what the company has to offer to conform with what the person wants.

Summary

Morale concerns people's attitudes toward their environment, both at home and at work. Morale is greatly affected not only by individual factors, but by the overall morale of the groups the person belongs to. Morale is important because it affects a person's happiness, and productivity. It is particularly important in sales work where it is difficult to operate effectively without a good attitude. People aren't apt to buy much from sales reps with a sour outlook on life.

Poor morale hurts sales, increases expenses, increases turnover among the sales force, and causes the sales people to magnify minor complaints into major ones.

The causes of poor morale are many and varied. They can be work-related or personal. Work-related reasons run the gamut from lack of communication with management to poor pay, lack of status, lack of advancement, unfair treatment, and poor working conditions. Financial and domestic problems are the main reasons for poor morale at home.

It is not always easy to discover the real reasons for poor morale, but the perceptive manager who has good communications with the sales force should have little trouble.

The morale-building process essentially provides the individuals with an opportunity to move closer to their personal goals. Morale is generally good when people feel they are making progress toward their personal goals. The essential management message is: You can best reach your goals by working for us as we direct you.

Questions and Problems

1. A branch manager of a large, nationally known appliance manufacturer said: "There's no problem in getting salesmen. Salesmen are things. You buy them like you buy merchandise.

You put them on straight commission, and they either cut the mustard or get out. After you've been through a few hundred of them, you will have your good sales force." Comment on this philosophy, bearing in mind that this manager's branch has been over quota each year he has managed it, whereas before it was a sick operation.

2. The Pittsburgh branch of a large plywood company had been having trouble keeping its managers. In the past year, there had been three managerial changes. The present manager, who had been on the job less than a week, said: "I really don't know what the troubles of the previous managers have been. I haven't had time to find out with all the work connected with moving in from Memphis. I understand the last man had some trouble adjusting to Pittsburgh. I believe he had been transferred up from the home office in Atlanta." Comment on this situation.

3. Under what conditions should the sales manager attempt to help a subordinate financially? When should help be refused?

4. How can the sales manager encourage a person to resign?

5. How can the manager integrate the interest of the individual and the organization?

6. Why would a sales rep be disloyal to the firm?

7. What things about the company and its plans would management not want its reps to know?

8. Managers are continually told to listen to their people and to be sensitive to the signals they emit. But managers continue to listen without hearing a thing. What does it mean to *listen*?

9. What are some of the methods the sales manager can use to determine the state of a recruit's morale before hiring him?

10. How can the manager give the sales force more status within the organization?

Case 15-1

The Staar Express

Proposal for Excursion Train to Convention

John Wolf, sales manager for the Staar Surgical Company, placed before the board of directors his proposal for an excursion train trip from Los Angeles to San Francisco. The 1985 meeting of the American Association of Ophthalmologists (AAO) was meeting the week of October 1 at the Mosconi Center in San Francisco. John planned to take the officers and directors, some key employees, the firm's 20 sales reps, and about 100 selected ophthalmologists who were either key customers or important prospects.

John thought that the trade show was a critical portion of the company's marketing program for the year. Staar was introducing two new products to the trade at the show. First, there was the XL-3, a state-of-the-art ultrasonic machine for removing eye cataracts. This machine used the phaeco emulsificaton technique in which the cataracts are pulverized with ultrasonic sound waves and the debris then irrigated from the eye. The XL-3 was designed for use in a doctor's office. As a result, cataract removal could be done without high-cost hospitalization. The machine cost $45,000.

The second product, Bac Stop, was an in-line bacteria filter that prevented contamination of the fluids that were pumped into and out of the eye during the phaeco emulsification procedure. The journals had reported several cases of eye infection resulting from contaminated fluids. Such infections were serious because they were difficult to treat. Staar had developed the Bac Stop filter to be used with any firm's surgical pack as well as its own. The price was $25 a unit.

John Wolf had high hopes for both products. He expected to sell 50 units of the XL-3. Ultimately, he envisioned that a Bac Stop would be used in every cataract operation, of which there about 1 million each year.

The Staar Company was formed in 1983 by Dr. Mazzocco, the ophthalmologist who developed the company's first product, the Elastilens, and Tom Waggoner, the company's president and driving force. An Elastilens was a foldable intraoccular lens that is inserted into the eye to replace the one destroyed during cataract surgery. It was currently proceeding nicely through FDA clinical trials before being given permission for unlimited marketing in the United States. The company was only marginally profitable in 1985.

The excursion train was to consist of three railroad cars provided by David Rohr, owner of the Golden Spike. The Golden Spike was a new venture formed by Mr. Rohr in which he rennovated old railroad cars. He then packaged excursions on a fixed-cost basis to organizations that desired to transport people anywhere in the nation by rail. The excursion cars were attached to an Amtrak train going to the desired destination.

The proposed price for the Staar Express was $20,000 for all food and services. This included bus transportation from the depot in Oakland to the downtown hotels in San Francisco. The excursion was billed as a wine-tasting trek through the California vineyards. Bottles of wine indigenous to the specific area being travelled were to be tasted as the train wended its way northward.

Mr. Wolf strongly recommended to the board that the expenditure be made because, in his words, "It will provide a marvelous opportunity for our executives and sales people to make an in-depth contact with our key customers and for them to become a part of the

Staar team. No one has ever done anything like this in the industry before, so I think it will help solidify our image in the industry as pioneers."

The board mused over Mr. Wolf's written proposal for a few moments before the company's accountant spoke up with some strong objections. "This is outrageous. We cannot afford to spend $20,000 on a 10-hour drinking spree to take a bunch of sales people and their customers to San Francisco. It is absolutely unconscionable at this stage of the company's development to squander this much money when we are not certain we'll be able to make the payroll Friday. As you know, we have yet to get our line of credit on our receivables from the bank, so we're really strapped for funds. I just don't understand why we are even considering John's proposal for a minute."

Tom Waggoner smiled and looked at John silently asking for a defense. John was quick to provide one. "The key to this company's survival is sales volume. We need $700,000 a month sales to break even. I'm not going to be able to deliver it without such strong promotions. Twenty thousand dollars invested in this promotion is not a lot of money when we consider the sales that can result from it. I think this cost is very reasonable in contrast to the stakes we're playing for. We've got to do something different and memorable to get the attention of these people. We have a whole lot of things to sell them, and we need time and exposure to do it."

The accountant kept shaking his head, mumbling about not knowing where the money was going to come from to pay the bills. He said, "The convention alone will cost us $20,000 and now adding this on to that, the entire week will cost more than $40,000. It's simply irresponsible of the board to spend this much money on sales expenses at a time when we ought to be cutting all costs to the absolute bone."

Question

Should the board accept John Wolf's proposal for the excursion train?

Case 15-2

Sporgan Container Company

Successful Sales Rep Bypassed for Promotion

Harry Dowell found himself in a very ticklish position. He recently had been promoted to the position of sales manager in the Cleveland, Ohio, branch of the plastic products division in the Sporgan Container Company. His main competitor for that position—in fact the only other person seriously considered—was Philip McBee who was a successful salesman in the same Cleveland office. After a few months on the job, Dowell felt that he was not getting a satisfactory performance from McBee. Dowell had also heard indirectly of some customer complaints regarding McBee's performance. Dowell knew he had to do something about Philip McBee, but he did not know what that "something" should be.

The Sporgan Container Company was a large manufacturer of glass, plastic, and corrugated cardboard containers. The company had manufacturing plants throughout the world. Within the United States, the company maintained a sales office in most of the areas where a manufacturing facility was located. The company's production and marketing facilities were organized into three divisions, corresponding to the major product lines. The glass container division manufactured and marketed a variety of bottles, jars, and other types of glass containers. The corrugated cardboard division produced a line of cardboard containers—most of which were used within the company to pack the glass and plastic containers.

The third division was the plastic products division which manufactured and marketed a wide variety of plastic container products. This division was started about 30 years ago when a major customer decided to switch from glass to plastic containers. This division continued to grow over the years as many other companies in a wide variety of industries discontinued using glass or metal containers in favor of plastic ones. Harry Dowell believed that plastic containers had an unlimited market potential, especially if brewers and soft-drink bottlers ever switched from glass and metal to plastic for their 12-ounce containers.

The plastic container industry was an extremely fragmented one with many small manufacturers. However, Sporgan recognized that its main competition came from the large firms such as Owens-Illinois, Continental Can Company, and IMCO. Another major group of competitors were manufacturers of other products who were vertically integrated to the point where they produced their own packaging containers.

Peter Torrance was the sales manager who preceded Harry Dowell in Sporgan's Cleveland sales office. In fact, it was Torrance's sudden death from a heart attack about six months ago that opened up that managerial position. Torrance had been the Cleveland sales manager for six years and had established a good rapport with his sales people. He was especially impressed with the abilities of Philip McBee. In fact, Torrance had recommended McBee for a promotion prior to the fatal heart attack.

Philip McBee was 51 years old and had worked in various capacities for the Sporgan Company for 23 years. He had been a sales representative in the Cleveland district for the past 12 years. Harry Dowell was 36 years old and had been working as a sales rep for Sporgan for the past five years.

McBee and Dowell both went through a series of interviews with various executives as the company worked to fill the sales manager's position in the Cleveland office. The managerial consensus was that both men were qualified for the job. Management's decision to select Harry Dowell for the job was based essentially on one factor—a recently-stated company marketing objective. This objective was to get a larger share of the container orders placed by one of the large manufacturers of soap and other cleaning products.

About eight years ago, McBee had been the Sporgan representative who called on that soap company. But he was moved off the account when disputes arose between him and some of the soap company's executives. The soap company then moved much of its Cleveland business to other container suppliers. The situation was not considered to be a significant negative mark on McBee's record. The soap company had a reputation throughout the industry of sometimes being hard on its suppliers of various products—not just containers.

One of Dowell's first actions as sales manager was to get to know the personnel in Sporgan's manufacturing plant in Cleveland. To get more soap company business, Dowell knew that he needed the full cooperation of the factory executives. This was because the soap company put such a high premium on suppliers' products meeting the company's exacting quality specifications.

During these visits, Dowell was surprised that the plant manager and the quality control manager had some negative things to say about Phil McBee. The essence of the complaint was that Phil simply was not doing his job in northern Ohio. Problems with customers in that area were being handled more and more by factory personnel. As far as visits with customers were concerned, the quality control manager complained that "Phil is around only when it is time to go for lunch or drinks."

After being in his new position for a few months, Harry Dowell felt that he was not getting the expected performance level from Phil McBee. Phil's reports were satisfactory, but in a one-on-one conversational situation, Dowell felt that Phil often was hostile and uncooperative. It also appeared to Dowell that McBee was drinking more than he should be.

Just yesterday, a situation arose that Harry Dowell considered to be the last straw. Louis Morgenstern, the sales manager of the glass container division, called Dowell and wanted to speak to him privately. One of the glass container sales people had made a call on a major account in southern Ohio and was intercepted by the account's plastic container buyer. The buyer wanted to know when or how he could get a hold of Phil McBee. He had not seen Phil in over three months and Phil did not return the buyer's calls. After further discussion about the situation, it came out that McBee was not well liked by the head buyer, and appeared to be avoiding this buyer.

Dowell went back to his office to think over this general situation involving Phil McBee. Phil obviously was not doing the job expected of him. However, only a few months ago he was being considered for the job of sales manager. Dowell tried to sort out in his mind what his options were in this situation. He realized that customer neglect was inexcusable. He also realized that if he were dealing with a less senior employee, the person would be discharged. Dowell even thought about transferring McBee to an inside sales job in the Cleveland office, or at least bringing him back into the Cleveland area where he could be watched more closely.

Dowell realized that these last two alternatives would be considered a demotion in McBee's eyes and also in the eyes of the other people in the Cleveland sales force. Dowell figured that the other sales people might view such a "demotion" as Dowell's way of "getting rid of his competition." Dowell was puzzled as to how he should handle Philip McBee.

Question

What should Harry Dowell do about Phillip McBee?

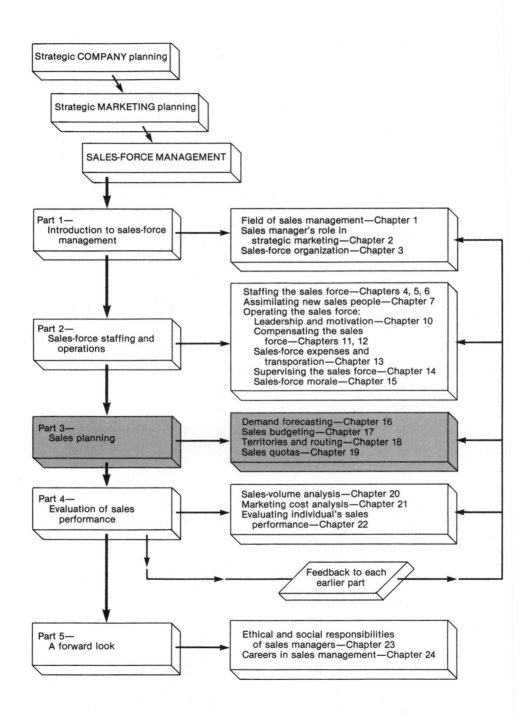

Strategic COMPANY planning

Strategic MARKETING planning

SALES-FORCE MANAGEMENT

Part 1—
Introduction to sales-force management

Field of sales management—Chapter 1
Sales manager's role in
    strategic marketing—Chapter 2
Sales-force organization—Chapter 3

Part 2—
Sales-force staffing and operations

Staffing the sales force—Chapters 4, 5, 6
Assimilating new sales people—Chapter 7
Operating the sales force:
    Leadership and motivation—Chapter 10
    Compensating the sales
        force—Chapters 11, 12
    Sales-force expenses and
        transporation—Chapter 13
    Supervising the sales force—Chapter 14
    Sales-force morale—Chapter 15

Part 3—
Sales planning

Demand forecasting—Chapter 16
Sales budgeting—Chapter 17
Territories and routing—Chapter 18
Sales quotas—Chapter 19

Part 4—
Evaluation of sales performance

Sales-volume analysis—Chapter 20
Marketing cost analysis—Chapter 21
Evaluating individual's sales
    performance—Chapter 22

Feedback to each
earlier part

Part 5—
A forward look

Ethical and social responsibilities
    of sales managers—Chapter 23
Careers in sales management—Chapter 24

PART 3

Sales Planning

The first stage in the sales-management process is planning, followed by implementing the plans through sales operations, and ending with an evaluation of the sales performance. Sales planning involves establishing sales goals and then deciding on the strategies and tactics used to reach these goals.

However, a company manages its sales force within the context of its total marketing program. Therefore, the path taken in *sales-force* planning depends on the company's strategic *marketing* planning. The strategic marketing planning, in turn, depends on the *overall company* planning. Sales executives, then, take their sales-planning cues from the firm's strategic marketing planning and corporate planning.

Our coverage of sales planning starts with sales forecasting and the determination of market potentials and sales potentials in Chapter 16. Sales budgeting is the topic of Chapter 17. Then in Chapter 18 we deal with designing sales territories, assigning sales reps to these territories, and routing the sales people. Various aspects of sales quotas are covered in Chapter 19.

16

Forecasting Market Demand

*We should all be concerned about the future because
we will have to spend the rest of our lives there.*
CHARLES KETTERING

Back in Chapter 2 we briefly covered sales-force planning. We presented the idea that strategic *sales-force* planning should be done within the broader context of strategic *marketing* planning and *total-company* strategic planning. That is, the sequence of strategic planning activities at various levels in an organization should be as follows:

1. Identify the organization's mission—that is, determine "what business are we in?" and "what business should we be in?"
2. Total company planning.
3. Strategic Business Unit planning. A large organization should identify its major divisions—called Strategic Business Units. Then management should determine each unit's mission and prepare a strategic plan for each unit. For planning purposes each unit is treated as a separate company.
4. Marketing planning.
5. Sales-force planning.

All of the above levels of organizational planning are affected by major environmental constraints. Some of these influences are external to the company, and some are internal. Thus, in sales-force planning, management must consider external factors such as market demographics, sociocultural influences, legal and political forces, economic conditions, and competition. Then within the firm, sales-force planning is influenced by the organization's financial resources, human resources, and production capabilities.

Market Opportunity Analysis

Early in the sales-force planning process, it is essential that management analyze the organization's market opportunity. Ideally any consumer want, as yet unsatisfied, provides a market opportunity for any firm. However, in a more practical sense, a company's market opportunity is obviously much more limited. Realistically, an organization's market opportunity must meet the following three conditions.

1. The potential market must be consistent with the company's mission, objectives, and image.
2. The potential market must be large enough in sales volume to meet the company's objectives.
3. The company must have the resources to generate a market share and net profit that will meet the firm's objectives.

The cornerstone of a successful market opportunity analysis is the quantitative measurement and forecasting of the market demand for the organization's product or service. This measurement of demand may be made at three different levels. The *first* measurement is an estimate of the total market potential for the product or service. The *second* measurement is an estimate of the share of this total market that the company can reasonably expect to capture. The *third* measurement is a forecast of the company's sales volume during a specified future time period and under a proposed marketing plan.

Explanation of Basic Terms

Before we discuss the methods used in forecasting, we need to define and explain some of the basic terminology in demand estimation. Some of these terms are closely related and often are confused with each other. Because the terms are used loosely in business, they frequently cause misunderstandings and inadequate communication.

Market Potential and Sales Potential

The definitional problems start with the term "market potential," because there is no generally accepted definition of this concept. The controversy centers on the word "potential" in reference to a market. What do we mean when we speak of a "potential" market for a product?

One point of view holds that the market potential is the *maximum possible* sales of the given product by the entire industry in a stated market over a specific time period. Under this broad interpretation we would include sales that potentially could have been made under ideal conditions, but actually were not made. Under another interpretation, market potential refers only to the *expected* industry-wide sales of the given product.

We prefer the second interpretation—that of *expected* sales rather than *maximum possible* sales. We believe that this perspective is more realistic and certainly more useful to any organization—business or nonbusiness—that is engaged in demand forecasting. Also, this interpretation is consistent with the one formally adopted by the American Marketing Association.[1] Therefore, our definition is as follows:

Market potential is the total expected sales of a given product or service for the entire industry in a specific market over a stated period of time.

As an example, the market potential for automatic clothes washing machines in the United States during 1988 is X dollars (or units). To be complete and meaningful, the definition must include these four elements:

1. The item being marketed (the product, service, idea, person, or location). In our example the product was automatic clothes washing machines.
2. Sales for the entire industry in dollars or product units.
3. A specific time period—in this case it was 1988.
4. A specific market delineated either geographically or by type of customer. In our example, the geographic market was the entire United States. The market potential also could be stated for laundromats, apartment houses, or some other customer group.

Sales potential refers to the share of a market potential that an individual company can reasonably expect to achieve. The term *sales potential* is synonymous with the term **market share.** When we speak of a company's sales potential, we must again specify the product, market, and time period.

---

[1] See Committee on Definitions, *Marketing Definitions: A Glossary of Marketing Terms* (Chicago: American Marketing Association, 1960), pp. 15, 20.

Relationship between Market Potential and Sales Potential

Market potential is a total-industry concept, while sales potential refers to an individual firm. Thus we may speak of the "market potential" for automatic washing machines, but the "sales potential" (or market share) for one company's brand of machine. In the case of either market potential or sales potential, the market may encompass the United States, or the entire world. It may be a small market segmented by income, by geographic area, or on some other basis. For example, we may speak of the *market potential* for washing machines on the Pacific Coast, or the *sales potential* for General Electric washers in homes with incomes of under $25,000. The market potential and market share (sales potential) are the same when a firm has a monopoly in its market, as is the case with some public utilities.

Sales Forecast

A **sales forecast** is an estimate of sales (in dollars or in product units) that an individual firm expects to make during a specified time period, in a stated market, and under a proposed marketing plan.

A forecast may be made for an entire product line or for individual items within the line. Sales may be forecasted for a company's total market or for individual market segments. A forecast is likely to be more accurate if a firm first estimates its market potential and/or its sales potential. However, many forecasters start their demand projections directly with a sales forecast.

The sales forecast and the marketing plan. The marketing goals and strategies—the core of a marketing plan—must be established before a sales forecast is made. That is, the sales forecast depends on these predetermined goals and strategies. Certainly, a different sales forecast will result, depending on whether the marketing goal is (1) to liquidate an excess inventory of a certain product or (2) to expand the firm's market share by aggressive advertising.

Once the sales forecast is prepared, it becomes the key controlling factor in all *operational* planning throughout the company. Forecasting is the basis of sound budgeting. Financial planning for working-capital requirements, plant utilization, and other needs is based on anticipated sales. The scheduling of all production resources and facilities, such as setting labor needs and purchasing raw materials, depends on the sales forecast.

The sales forecast and the sales potential. At first glance, the company's sales potential and sales forecast may appear to be the same. But usually that is not the case. The sales potential is what would be achieved under ideal conditions. The sales forecast depends heavily on the predetermined marketing plan—the marketing goals and strategies.

Typically a company's sales forecast is less than the sales potential for several reasons. The company's production facilities may be too limited to allow the firm to reach its full sales potential. Or, the company may not have a distribution system with which to reach all of its potential market. Or, the firm's financial resources may be inadequate to realize the full sales potential.

Market Factor and Market Index

A **market factor** is an item or element in a market (1) that causes the demand for a product or service or (2) that is related to the demand for it.

To illustrate, the "number of cars three years old and older" is a market factor underlying the demand for replacement tires. That is, this element is related to the number of replacement tires that can be sold. The market factor causing the demand is the miles traveled.

A **market index** is a market factor expressed as a percentage, or in some other quantitative form, relative to some base figure.

To illustrate, one market factor is "households owning appliance x"; in 1987, the market index for this factor was 132 (relative to 1975 equaling 100).

A market index may be based on two or more market factors. For example, the "buying power index" developed by *Sales & Marketing Management* magazine is based on three factors—population, effective buying income, and retail sales. In some mutli-factor indexes each factor is weighted equally, while in other indexes one factor may be weighted more heavily than another.

Frequently a market factor or market index is determined for a given geographical market segment. This enables a sales manager to establish territorial potentials, sales quotas, territorial boundaries, or some other market-segment measurement.

Need for Consumer Analysis

Determining the market factors underlying the demand for a product requires a penetrating analysis of consumers and their buying habits. A distinction must be made between the person who actually *buys* the product and the individual who *uses* the product. The market factor usually depends on the individual or firm *the product is intended for.* Although women buy a large portion of men's shirts, still the market potential for men's shirts is determined by the number of men, not by the number of women.

The starting point in any customer analysis is to determine who will use the product and to identify all possible characteristics of the users. Are they household consumers, industrial users, or both? If they are household consumers, for example, the seller wants to classify them further by age, sex, marital status, area of residence, income, occupation, religion, education, and possibly several other bases.

Another aspect of consumer analysis is to determine how rapidly the product in question is used. Many items are consumed daily or weekly, while others may be purchased only once every 10 or 20 years.

Determining exactly what causes the actual purchase is usually important. Many products are purchased as a result of some special event. When people get married, they usually buy furniture, appliances, dwelling units, clothes, and many other products. Manufacturers of these products frequently use the marriage rate as the basis for estimating the size of their markets. A manufacturer of baby furniture may base its entire market analysis on birth rates, for births are the events that cause demand for these products.

For certain products that are bought on several occasions or in various amounts during a given period, the analyst must determine the *quantities* the consumers buy. This is particularly important in such items as food, clothing, and most of the convenience goods on the market. Knowing who buys and how frequently is simply not enough. Management also must know how much they buy during the period.

Forecasting the market potential for the Staar intraoccular lens for cataract lens replacements is easy. There are about 1 million cataract operations a year, 80 percent of which will use a silicon intraoccular lens. Thus the market potential for the lens is 800,000 units a year.

Tom Watson, founder of IBM, estimated the market potential for his first computer at 12 units! At the beginning of the computer age, no one foresaw the demand for computers that would exist today. The product built its own market potential as it developed.

Determination and Use of Market Factors

No analysis of potentials is better than the validity of the market factors on which it is based. If the market factor is not really the cause of demand, or if it includes too many impurities that do not directly affect the demand for the product, then the resulting market potential cannot be accurate. Each product has its own characteristics. Many are relatively easy to work with, while others are extremely complex. Analyzing the potential market for an aluminum playpen for babies is easy compared to evaluating the market for an aluminum ingot producer. Market analysis is more complex if the product is sold to many markets and its demand is caused by numerous factors.

Basic Techniques for Deriving Potentials

The usual procedure is first to determine the market potential for the commodity and then estimate the portion of that amount that will go to a given brand. However, it is often more expedient to calculate the sales potential for an item directly. In some cases the market potential and the sales potential may be identical. If a product has no direct competition, the market potential and the sales potential are the same as long as the firm maintains its monopoly. The market potential for electric power in an area is usually identical with the sales potential of the firm that holds the franchise to sell in that region. In other cases, the sales potential may be such an insignificant portion of the market potential that it is useless to deal with the larger figure. The sales potential must be computed directly. One small manufacturer of cotton dresses determined its sales potential from the results of a few test markets. The total market potential for cotton dresses was so large that reference to it was useless.

The four fundamental techniques for determining market and sales potentials for a product are market factor derivation, correlation analysis, survey of buyer intentions, and test markets.

Market-Factor Derivation

The market-factor derivation method for determining the size of a potential market begins with the market factor. By eliminating various segments of the market, an estimate of the number of people who would purchase the product is finally derived.

A manufacturer of baby playpens discovered over the years that he sold 16 playpens for every 1,000 births in the United States.

Using births as a market factor, he directly computed his sales fore-cast as follows:

Estimated number of births, 1987: 4,000,000.
Rate of sale: 16 per 1,000.
Sales forecast for 1987: 64,000 playpens.

An independent supermarket operator in Nashville, Tennessee, computed his sales potential by using *Sales & Marketing Management's* estimate of food sales in that metropolitan area as his market factor.[2] He did not sell to the entire area but appealed only to a region in which about 15 percent of the population resided. So he estimated his market potential to be about $164 million. Since three other large supermarkets plus some smaller stores competed in that same area, he set 20 percent as his probable share of the market. Therefore, his sales potential was $32.8 million for the year.

Nashville food sales.	$1,092,263,000
Times: Percent of market covered.	× .15
Company market potential.	$ 163,839,450
Times: Market share.	× .20
Sales potential.	$ 32,767,890

This market factor derivation technique for determining market and sales potentials has several advantages. First, the face validity of the method is high. That is, individuals can follow the logic of it without a knowledge of statistics or marketing research. The method is usually founded on some valid statistics that have relatively little error. This is in direct contrast to two methods described later—the survey of buyer intentions and the test-market methods—in which the basic foundations of the process can be criticized. Another favorable aspect of this technique is that it is relatively simple, requires little statistical analysis, and is relatively inexpensive to use. The wise market analyst usually starts with this technique and goes to others only when forced to in order to get an acceptable figure.

The major weakness of the method is that frequently the bases on which segments of the total are eliminated are only estimates. No accurate data may exist for determining what portion of the total figures will be in the market for the product.

Correlation Analysis

The correlation-analysis method for deriving market potentials is closely related to the market-factor method except for the mathematical processes involved. In correlation analysis, the variation of

[2] "Survey of Buying Power," *Sales & Marketing Management,* July 28, 1986, p. c–170.

the market factor is correlated with variation in demand for the product under study, and a resulting mathematical relationship is derived. This method can only be used when a sales history of either the industry or the firm is available. This is because correlation is merely a mathematical analysis of the relationship between the variations in different series of data. If the sales history is for the industry, the resultant estimating equation will give the *market* potential. But, if the sales history is for the firm, the estimating equation will yield the *sales* potential.

One of the major virtues of this method is that its final result is a seemingly accurate estimating equation. The executive may insert an estimate of the market factor into this equation and obtain an apparently precise estimate of the product's demand. However, great care must be taken in using this technique. In many fields a correlation of ±.50 or ±.60 is considered highly significant. In market analysis, however, a coefficient of ±.90 or better is frequently needed to obtain a useful working estimate equation.

Probably the biggest drawback to correlation analysis is that the average sales manager does not understand what is being done and therefore tends to regard its results with a degree of suspicion. This is particularly true in cases that require multiple correlation and various curvilinear measures of relationship. Although the market analyst may thoroughly understand the procedure, other executives must accept the results strictly on faith.

Surveys of Buyer Intentions

The survey of buyer intentions technique for determining potentials consists of contacting potential customers and questioning them. The firm hopes to determine whether or not they would purchase the product at the price asked.

One businessman contemplating the production of an aluminum playpen for babies used this technique. The playpen was to be made exactly like the ordinary wooden playpens on the market, except that aluminum tubing would be used instead of the wooden bars. Since the cost of the unit would be higher than the wooden units, he wanted to know two things. First, how many people would buy such a product if it were placed on the market at the retail price of $59.95. Second, what customers thought such a product should sell for.

A survey was conducted through personal interviews with 240 mothers of infants. The results showed that 170 of the 240 (approximately 71 percent) would be interested in such a product. However, they indicated that the price would have to be $39.95 to capture that size of market. The average (mean) price quoted was $45. However, this price would eliminate half of the respondents who showed interest in the product. At the retail price of $59.95, only 10 women said they would be interested in purchasing the product. It is extremely doubtful that all 10 of these women would buy the product if it were placed on the market. Even if all 10 did buy at $59.95, that still represents only 4 percent of the market (4 percent of 240 = 9.6 mothers).

The survey indicated that only about one third of all childbearing families purchase playpens at all. This indicates that the total market potential for aluminum playpens would not be more than approximately 50,000 units at best. This figure was derived by dividing the total number of births per year, 4 million, by 3 and taking 4 percent of the result. Actually this rough calculation glosses over some of the other factors that exist in the situation. However, it showed the manufacturer that market interest in the playpen was sufficient to warrant further investigation. He had established previously that he would be satisfied if he sold only 5,000 units a year. This seemed possible on the basis of the survey.

Major disadvantages of this method lie in its cost and time-consuming execution. For the sales manager who must quickly get an idea of the market potential of a product, the survey method is not suitable. For the manufacturer who intends to distribute nationally, consumer surveys can easily run into the thousands of dollars and take three to six months for completion. Firms selling to relatively few concerns, as is often the case in industrial marketing, are usually able to survey their few customers to discover their customers buying plans. In planning the financial fortunes of many new ventures, the entrepreneur is often able to focus attention on a few target customers to determine their buying intentions.

Surveys of buying intentions are hazardous undertakings. It is easy for the respondent to say that he or she would buy a certain product. But the acid test is whether or not the person is willing to spend money to back up those intentions. However, if the customer has set aside funds for the item being bought, such information often is willingly shared with potential suppliers.

Test Markets

Although they take considerable time and money, test markets are probably the most accurate method available for estimating the sales potential for certain products. The reason is that a test market actually requires the buyers to spend their money, and this is the acid test of most marketing situations. All the other methods discussed require an *estimate* of what share of the market the product will achieve. Frequently, these estimates are merely guesses. The test market eliminates this guessing. Many factors are involved in the careful control of the test-market situation. However, it is not within the scope of this book to discuss the detailed administration of market testing. It is assumed that management has properly controlled the conditions surrounding the test market. However, this is no easy task.

The one obvious advantage of the test market technique is that it directly results in a sales potential for products under consideration. It is unfortunate, however, that the test market requires a considerable amount of effort and time before its results are known. Many products that require extensive investment in fixed assets before any output cannot be evaluated by this method. This is because most of the risks have been taken before the answers are known. The test market is used mainly when a relatively small number of units can be produced at a minimum cost. In this way the size of the market can be estimated before the firm invests any sizable amount of money in one venture. Test markets provide poor evaluations of products that require time to gain market acceptance or have a low rate of consumption.

In the world of new ventures, venture capitalists view the first stage of development in which the product or service is initially offered for sale as a test market. It proves whether there is a large enough market to warrant additional investments. Jerry Zimmer started ZDC, Inc., in Boulder, Colorado, with a $60,000 initial investment. He developed a computerized system for managing and measuring the energy used in master-metered apartment houses. He sold about $1 million worth of his systems in the Denver market area in the first year of operation. That was the test market. On the basis of that test, the company was able to raise an additional $500,000 to expand market coverage. The first few years of most new ventures are essentially test markets that prove that people will buy the product and that it is profitable.

Territorial Potentials

After the total sales potential has been determined, the sales manager usually wants to divide it among the various territorial divisions to allocate selling efforts properly and to evaluate the relative performance of each district. The usual method for accomplishing this is to use some pertinent market factor or index broken down by small areas. Data such as population, retail and wholesale sales, births, and industrial activity are available by counties. *Sales & Marketing Management's* annual "Survey of Buying Power" is primarily designed to aid the executive in allocating activities among areas. Data are furnished for each county and many cities in North Amer-

Table 16–1

Division of Sales Potential Among Territories Using Retail Sales as a Market Index

Territory	Percentage of Total Retail Sales	Territorial Sales Potential $25M × Col. 1 ÷ 100
New England	6.2	$ 1,300,000
Middle Atlantic	14.9	3,800,000
East North Central	16.8	4,800,000
West North Central.	7.6	2,000,000
South Atlantic.	16.6	3,950,000
East South Central	5.5	1,425,000
West South Central	11.3	2,675,000
Mountain	5.4	1,275,000
Pacific	15.7	3,775,000
	100.0	$25,000,000

* From "Survey of Buying Power," *Sales & Marketing Management,* July 23, 1984.

ica. Most managers find some appropriate figure that can be used to apportion the sales potentials.

One manufacturer of women's ready-to-wear whose total sales potential had been set at $25 million for 1987 divided it among territories as shown in Table 16–1. For convenience of illustration, the territories have been slightly regrouped to coincide with the census divisions.

Sales Forecasting

After the market or sales potential for a product is determined, then management can make a sales forecast. This is an essential step in sales planning.

Inportance of a Sales Forecast

The sales forecast is the foundation of all planning and budgeting. From it, production, personnel, finance, and all other departments plan their work and determine their requirements for the coming period. If the forecast is in error, so will the plans based on it. If it is unduly optimistic, the organization can suffer great losses because of overexpenditures of funds in anticipation of revenues that are not forthcoming. If the sales forecast is too low, the firm may not be prepared to sell what the market requires. This means the company will be foregoing profits and presenting its competitors with additional sales and market share.

A sales forecast is not equally important in all situations. When large amounts of money must be invested in advance of sales, investors want to see diligent sales forecasting. If little money has to be put up in advance of sales, then investors are not likely to be overly interested in spending a lot of money formulating a good sales forecast. Moreover, if production lead times are short, sales forecasting may be of little interest to management. In such cases a firm can quickly produce whatever sales are made, and management concludes that there is little need for advance planning.

Sales-Forecasting Periods

Sales forecasts are commonly made for periods of three months, six months, or one year. For purposes of this discussion, forecasts for periods of less than one year will be considered short-term. Those for a year will be treated as normal sales forecasts. Estimates for longer periods will be considered long-term. In actual practice, the traditional yearly forecast becomes a short-term one as it is modified every month or so as experience indicates. The sales-forecasting period usually coincides with the firm's fiscal period, since it is used as a basis for planning fiscal operations.

Some firms find that their conversion cycle of operations is considerably shorter than a year and prefer to forecast for that cycle. In the apparel trades, normally there are four conversion cycles per year. The firms produce goods for one season and then completely sell out those goods before starting the next season's work. They are concerned only with the coming season's activity, since they are buying goods and labor for that period only.

In operations where a high degree of accuracy is mandatory in the forecast, a short time period is often advisable, since greater accuracy can usually be obtained. It is usually easier to forecast for the coming month than for the coming year.

Firms usually undertake long-run sales estimates to plan capital expenditures. Top management often wants to know something about the long-run outlook for sales before it undertakes any plant expansion. While these composites are frequently called sales forecasts, in reality they more closely resemble sales potentials. That is, they usually measure only the market opportunity for the firm's products. They do not take into consideration the impact of the marketing programs.

Factors Influencing Probable Sales Volume

The sales forecast must take into consideration many factors other than quantitative statistics. The forecaster must analyze four major areas:

- Conditions within the company.
- Conditions within the industry.
- Conditions in the market for the seller's output.
- General business conditions.

These factors are visualized in the model shown in Figure 16–1.

Conditions within the company. Any changes in the price structure, channels of distribution, promotional plans, products, or other internal marketing policies may influence future sales. The forecaster must estimate the quantitative extent of these influences. It may be known, for example, that the firm will soon have to raise prices.

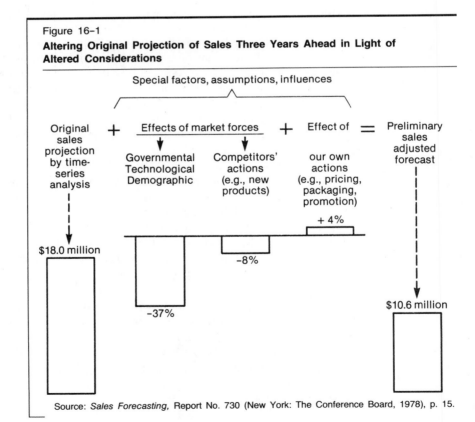

Figure 16–1

Altering Original Projection of Sales Three Years Ahead in Light of Altered Considerations

Source: *Sales Forecasting,* Report No. 730 (New York: The Conference Board, 1978), p. 15.

Although this action will reduce unit volume, total dollar volume might go up or down, depending on the product's price elasticity. Therefore, formulating a realistic sales forecast is impossible without taking price changes into consideration. If the firm had plans for altering its channels of distribution, such an action would influence future sales.

Conditions within the industry. A firm obtains its sales volume from total industry sales. Therefore, any change within the industry has a impact on the firm. New producers in an industry may mean that whatever volume they gain must come from existing companies. Thus, the sales forecast may have to be revised downward. If a competitor is planning to redesign its line of products, the firm must consider the possibility that the competitor may obtain a larger share of the market during the coming period.

Changed market conditions. If basic demand factors are in a slump, the future sales of the firm will be affected. The firm's manager must be aware of any basic changes in the primary demand for the industry's output. An analysis of future market conditions is particularly important if the concern sells to relatively few industries.

Mor Flo, a manufacturer of solar water heaters, saw its sales potential suddenly multiply several times when the nation suffered shortages of natural gas. And, as the price of gasoline soared, the sales potentials for the makers of compact cars expanded significantly. As gasoline prices dropped in 1986, sales of large cars increased.

General business conditions. A major influencing factor in future sales development is the general state of the economy. Basically, many of the methods of sales forecasting are simply reflections of overall opinion of what the general economy will be like during the coming period.

Methods of Sales Forecasting

Any of the following basic methods may be used to forecast the future sales of a product (see Figure 16–2):

- Executive opinion.
- Sales-force composite.
- Users' expectations.
- Projection of trends.
- Analysis of market factors.
- "Must-do" forecasts.

Executive opinion. The executive-opinion method of forecasting sales is the oldest and simplest technique known. It consists of ob-

Figure 16–2
Sales Forecasting Methods

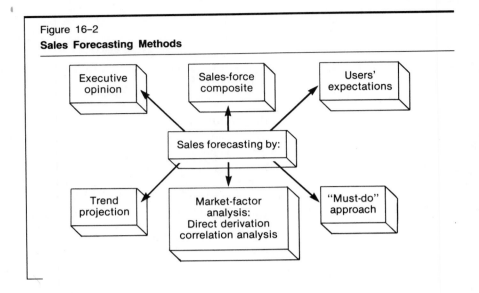

taining the views of top executives regarding future sales. These executive opinions may or may not be supported by facts. Some administrators may have used certain methods of forecasting to arrive at their opinions. Others may have formed their estimates largely by observation and intuition.

The major advantage cited for this technique is that it is quick and easy to do. The disadvantages are more numerous. First, many managers consider it highly unscientific, since it is little more than a premeditated group guessing. Most of the opinions brought into the conference are not based on fact but on personal feelings about future business conditions.

Nevertheless, executive opinion remains the method used by most small- and medium-sized companies. Usually the boss and the sales manager get together, study all the factors known to them, and come up with their guess as to what sales will be for the coming year.

The Delphi technique. A highly publicized technique developed at Rand Corporation for predicting the future, called the Delphi technique, is little more than a jury of expert opinion. In administering a Delphi forecast, a panel of "experts" is selected Then each expert is asked to make a prediction on some matter. The resulting range of forecasts is then fed back to the experts. Then they are asked once again to make another prediction on the same matter, with the knowledge of what all the other experts have reported. This process is repeated until the experts arrive at some consensus. This technique could be used in sales forecasting.

Sales-force composite. This approach begins by collecting from each sales person an estimate of the future sales of various products in his territory. Usually the sales reps are provided with appropriate forms to aid them in making their estimates. These estimates may be made in consultation with some sales executive or compiled without assistance.

The total sales forecast for the firm is a composite of the individual forecasts of each sales person. If all sales people do not forecast their sales accurately, their individual errors will not cancel out and allow an accurate forecast to evolve. It is more likely that some common bias will cause errors in one direction.

In certain situations, however, this method of forecasting sales can be accurate. It can be used most fruitfully when the sales force consists of high-caliber sales reps who are competent to do this type of work. The nature of the market also plays an important role in their forecasting ability. If the reps sell to relatively few accounts, they probably can furnish more reliable forecasts than if they sell to many small customers.

While this method places the responsibility for making the forecast in the hands of the people who have to make it happen and who are closest to the market, the sales people are often poor forecasters. They tend to be either overly optimistic or pessimistic. It does give them more confidence in the forecast. Moreover, it allows easy breakdowns of the forecast into products, territories, customers, or sales rep. Unfortunately, the sales reps not only may be motivated to understate the forecast if their goals are based on it, but they are often unaware of broader economic and company forces at work. Finally, the process does take much time from both management and the reps.

Users' expectations. Some industrial concerns forecast sales by asking their customers for information on expected purchases for the forthcoming period. This technique is limited to situations involving relatively few, well-identified potential customers. In such situations, the product being sold may be so unique that no other information is available on which to base a sales forecast. The advantages and disadvantages of this method are:

Obviously, the method cannot be used where users are numerous or cannot be easily located and contacted. Moreover, users may not be well informed or cooperative. However, this method does base the forecast on information from the people whose buying makes it happen. Users' expectations certainly give management a direct line on the thinking of the people in the market. Finally, it provides management with the opportunity to make a forecast for products for which there are no statistical data—i.e., new products.

Projection of trends.   The projection of past sales trends can be used for making both long-term and short-run forecasts. Throughout this discussion we have studiously avoided the word *cycle* since it connotes a regularity in future business activity that simply does not exist. Future business activity is determined by various economic and social factors and political decisions being made at present. It is illogical to forecast sales on the basis of cyclical trend analysis. The experience of our economy in the past 20 years should demonstrate the risks of predicting by a trend analysis.

There is a short-run forecasting technique based on adjusting present sales behavior by a seasonal index. However, it is little more than a mathematical formula to determine what the present sales picture means when projected into the future for a month or so. It is successful because over a period of a few months, few economic events can affect its accuracy to a significant degree. Unfortunately, such extremely short-run forecasts are not useful for the fiscal-planning activities that most firms find necessary. It is unwise to attempt a yearly sales forecast on the basis of seasonal behavior. However, for monthly or quarterly forecasts, it has proved to be accurate in most instances.

Analysis of market factors.   As noted previously, future sales depend on the future behavior of the factors that determine the product's demand. From a scientific point of view, the most valid method for approaching the problem of forecasting sales is by estimating the behavior of the market factors that underlie demand for the product. Once the forecast of market factors is made, it can be mathematically translated into sales volume. There are two basic procedures for making this translation, direct derivation and correlation analysis, both of which were discussed in the section on market potentials.

"Must-do" forecasts.   Often management forecasts the sales volume it needs to accomplish certain goals. In new ventures entrepreneurs trying to sell something for which a reasonably usable forecast cannot be developed often forecast the sales that must be made for the firm to reach its cash break-even point. In other words, the forecast is based on the sales volume needed to generate sufficient cash to pay the bills. Other times management may forecast a level of sales volume that will allow it to achieve some profit goal. Management makes a forecast, and then makes it happen.

Examples of Application of Forecasting Methods

In this section, the use of several methods for forecasting sales will be applied to various problems.

Long-Run Projection of Trend

The sales history for Connectors, Inc., from 1977 to 1986 and the calculations for extrapolating that trend to 1987 are shown in Table 16–2. The resulting trend line is shown in Figure 16–3. Note how well the line fits the past sales history. Using the least squares method for forecasting a sales trend, sales for the company for 1987 should be about $38.9 million.

The major fear that haunts the forecaster using such trend projections is that at some time in the future the trend will change—as it did in this case in 1982. A company can seldom maintain such a constant growth rate. Usually the firm's growth tapers off. But when? In this case, the growth rate changed in 1983. Using the five years 1982 through 1986 as the basis for projections, the forecast sales for 1987 would be $35.4 million.

Table 16-2

Sales Forecasting, Long-Run Extrapolation of Sales by Least Squares
(*$ millions*)

1977	−9	7.2
1978	−7	9.6
1979	−5	12.8
1980	−3	16.3
1981	−1	21.9
1982	1	26.0
1983	3	27.9
1984	5	30.0
1985	7	32.1
1986	9	33.3

$$N = 10$$
$$\Sigma y = 217.1$$
$$\Sigma xy = 517.3$$
$$\Sigma x^2 = 330$$

$$a = \frac{\Sigma y}{N} = \frac{217.1}{10} = 21.7$$

$$b = \frac{\Sigma xy}{\Sigma x^2} = \frac{517.3}{330} = 1.567$$

$$y = 21.7 + 1.567(x)$$

Forecast for 1987 (10-year base) would be: $21.7 + 1.567(11) = 38.9$

Forecast for 1987 (4-year base) would be: 35.4 (calculations not shown).

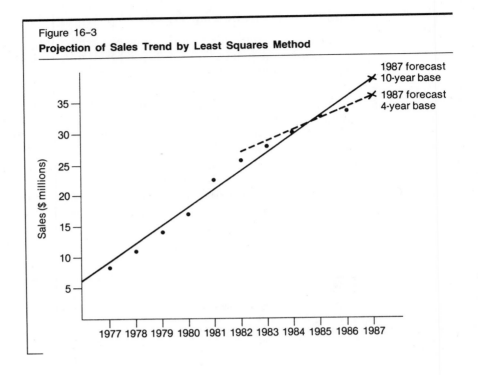

Figure 16–3
Projection of Sales Trend by Least Squares Method

Short-Run Projection of Trend

The monthly distribution of sales as a percentage of the total annual sales for a men's apparel retail store is shown in Table 16–3, along with the calculations for extrapolating sales for the next three months' operations.

The October sales of $74,000 indicate an annual rate of sales of $705,000 ($74,000/0.105); November sales indicate an annual rate of $711,000 ($86,000/0.121). The December rate of sales would be $729,000 a year ($102,000/0.14). If the sales for the last three months are totaled and divided by the sum of the percentages for those months ($262,000/0.37), we obtain an average annual rate of sales of $708,000. At this point the forecaster must do some subjective evaluation of those months' sales to select which base might be best to use to forecast the coming months' sales. There may be good reason to believe that the annual rate of sales is increasing as the data indicate. If so, the forecaster might decide that the most valid annual rate would be the one for December ($729,000). Perhaps a venturesome forecaster might even project an increasing annual rate of sales and base the January, or even the first-quarter forecast, on some annual rate even larger than the one for December. It is just a matter of judgment.

Table 16–3

Short-Run Extrapolation of Sales *(men's retail apparel store)*

Month's Sales as a Percentage of Annual Sales Based on 10 Years' Experience		1986 sales	1987 Forecast ($729,000 annual sales)
January....................	6.4%		$46,600
February...................	4.8		35,000
March	6.1		44,500
April......................	6.9		
May	7.1		
June......................	5.0		
July	5.7		
August....................	9.2		
September	12.2		
October...................	10.5	$ 74,000	
November.................	12.1	86,000	
December.................	14.0	102,000	
	100.0%		

Let's suppose, for some reason, the forecaster felt that the December rate of sales was not typical or not what could be expected in January or the first quarter of the year. He then might decide to use the average rate of sales for the last quarter of the year.

Assume that no irregular factors were seen in this instance. Using the December rate of sales of $729,000, the forecast for January would be about $46,600 ($729,000 × 0.064 = $46,656). The sales forecast for the first quarter would be about $126,000 ($729,000 × 0.173 = $126,117).

Understanding the premises on which such forecasting is based is important. First, it is assumed that a fairly reliable seasonal index is available. The method cannot be used if such an index cannot be developed. Second, the annual rate of sales is assumed not to change drastically in the short run. This is usually a fairly valid assumption, but there are times when it may prove to be false. Sudden turns in world events or domestic crises may jolt sales, but such developments may invalidate all forecasts.

Market Factor Derivation Method

Direct market factor derivations take many routes. Some are short and direct, while others are circuitous.

We will examine a short derivation first. A patio door manufacturer had determined that sales were directly related to the number of new dwelling units built. Research had shown that the firm sold

7.2 doors for every 1,000 dwelling units started each year. Thus, assume that the housing experts predicted 2 million units would be built in a coming year. Then the manufacturer multiplied its 7.2 market participation factor times 2,000 to estimate sales for that year as 14,400 doors. Such short derivations are common when a product's usage is a function of something that can be counted. The consumption of many products is proportional to such factors as the number of houses being built, the number of automobiles, or the number of people having some demand-affecting characteristics.

Let's use cars as the basis of a somewhat more complicated derivation. Suppose Mohawk Tire Company wants to forecast its sales volume for the coming year. It knows that in the areas in which it has distribution, it has a 3 percent share of the replacement market. While excellent data are available on the total number of tires sold in the United States by all tire manufacturers, they are not easily available for selected sections of the country. However, Mohawk could develop an estimate from the number of cars in each area, a statistic that is easily ascertained. Several approaches could be used to determine this, such as use of the following formulas:

$$\text{Sales forecast} = \frac{\substack{\text{No. of autos in} \\ \text{Mohawk territory}}}{\substack{\text{Total no. of autos} \\ \text{in U. S.}}} \times \substack{\text{Total no. of} \\ \text{replacement} \\ \text{tires sold} \\ \text{in U. S.}} \times 0.03$$

Or the forecaster might prefer to build up a forecast along the lines in Figure 16–4. Such derivations are simply a matter of logic. Start with the basic market factor, then operate on it with whatever other factors are relevant to the situation. Logic can be tricky. For example, the subtraction of new-car tire miles might be overlooked

---

Figure 16–4

Sales Forecast (Mohawk Tire Company)

Total autos in Mohawk distribution areas	40,000,000
Times: Average miles driven in year	× 10,000
Equals: Total auto miles driven in area	400,000,000,000
Times: Four	× 4
Equals: Tire miles driven in area	1,600,000,000,000
Minus: Tire miles by new cars	− 200,000,000,000
Equals: Replacement tire miles	1,400,000,000,000
Divided by: Average miles per tire	÷ 40,000
Equals: Number of replacement tires	35,000,000
Times: Percent of market share	× .03
Equals: Mohawk sales forecast	1,050,000

Note: All figures are hypothetical.

or mishandled. Mohawk does not sell tires to the car manufacturers, so this share of the market must be excluded from the company's forecast. However, new cars are on the road for an average of only six months rather than a full year, so that must be allowed for in their mileage. One bit of logic is missing from the above example, for the sake of simplicity—the spare tire. When new car owners have to replace the original set of tires, they need only three tires, not four. Such an adjustment to the figures could be made.

Correlation Analysis

Certainly correlation analysis ranks as the most powerful analytical tool available to the forecaster because it determines in a fairly precise way the mathematical relationships between series of data. In sales forecasting, one series, the dependent variable, is the sales of the product or firm being studied. The other series may be any one or several market factors the forecaster feels affect sales.

The widespread usage of the computer has caused a rather significant change in this section of the book. Previously a rather lengthy correlation analysis was illustrated, complete with the computations of the correlations and estimating equations. Such methods are now outdated by the computer. The packaged programs available for computer usage make the computation of complex multiple correlations simple. Moreover, business students are now being exposed to correlation and regression techniques in the quantitative courses they must take.

Some Guiding Principles for Forecasting

A number of principles on which to base market-demand forecasting are discussed in this section.

Minimize the Number of Market Factors

In market analysis, simplicity has great virtue. The more factors on which an analysis is based, the more difficult it is to determine exactly what it is that affects the demand for a product. Often the inclusion of many factors in a market index only results in the duplication of a few basic forces. One drug manufacturer computed a market index from the following factors: (1) number of drug stores, (2) population, (3) number of physicians, (4) income, (5) number of hospital beds, and (6) number of people older than 65. Actually, this market index essentially was based on two elements—population and income. Several of the supposed market factors were merely surface indicators of these two basic forces. The number of physicians in an area is a reflection of the population and income of that area. Similarly, the number of drugstores and the number of hospital beds usually depend on population.

Use Sound Logic

Sound logic is the basis of all good market analysis. In determining and using market factors, essentially all that is required of a market analyst is a keen, logical mind. To be logical, the analyst must have a fundamentally sound background in economics and marketing theory. Just being a competent statistician is insufficient. The true art is being able to discern what statistics to collect and use, and this requires marketing acumen.

Use More Than One Method

The experienced market analyst uses as many of the analysis techniques as possible in order to check one against another. The forecaster usually begins with the market factor derivation method, using several different factors as checks against one another. Then if a correlation analysis is possible, its results are compared with answers obtained previously. If consumer surveys are available, figures from them are used to check the previous results.

The market analyst can have more confidence in the results if all the estimates of the market potential reasonably agree with one another than if they vary widely. If wide variation occurs in the estimates, more research is needed to validate the work.

Use the Minimum-Maximum Technique

Sound research strategy dictates the use of both minimum and maximum estimates in all computations in order to obtain a range of possible variations. Analysts should work up one set of estimates that assumes the worst possible developments in each of the calculations. In doing this, they compute the lowest probable potential market for the product. At the same time, they should estimate what the market potential would be should all things be favorable. They also may prepare other estimates, each based on varying assumptions between the two extremes.

Understand Mathematics and Statistics

The determination of market and sales potentials is no work for the statistically and mathematically uninformed. Anyone who makes market analyses should be qualified to handle any statistical problems that may arise. A sales manager should be sufficiently acquainted with statistical techniques to recognize any serious errors in the material presented. The executive with little knowledge of statistics is at the mercy of a faulty statistician and often cannot perceive discrepancies or errors.

An example of this failure to understand statistical theory happened recently to a group of businessmen who planned to develop a large suburban shopping center. They wanted to know the average income of the families residing in the trading area of the proposed center. A consultant hired to undertake the survey determined that the average income per family was quite high. With a high average-income clientele, the stores in the shopping center catered to upper-income tastes. The development was a failure until the merchants became aware of the real situation. The average income quoted to the businessmen was meaningless. In statistical theory, an average is a symbol used to represent the central tendency of a group of figures. However, if no central tendency exists, the average is a meaningless figure. For instance, the average of a **U** distribution describes very little. In the shopping center case, the distribution of income was exceedingly bimodal. There was a very large group of low-income families with incomes of around $15,000 to $18,000 and relatively few families with exceedingly high incomes. These high incomes managed to offset the low incomes of most of the other families, so that on balance it appeared as if a rather substantial income existed throughout the area when really the opposite was so. The vast majority of the families in the area had modest living standards. In this case, the mode would have been the proper statistical measure of central tendency.

Summary

The sales forecast is the basis of most corporate planning. From that one figure, budgets are set, activities are planned, and production levels are determined. Should the forecast prove to be in serious error, management is faced with some serious problems.

Most forecasting techniques rely on historical data that are processed some way in order to anticipate the future. The real basis for forecasting rests on a careful analysis of market factors. In turn, the determination of market factors depends on a perceptive analysis of the consumer or user of the product.

The company sales forecast is closely related to the market potentials of the products or services it sells. Thus the forecasting process begins with understanding the firm's market and sales potentials.

The four basic techniques for determining market potentials are market-factor derivation, correlations analysis, surveys of buyer intentions, and test markets.

To determine territorial potentials, the total potential for the firm is apportioned among the territories by using some relevant market index.

There are several serious risks involved in forecasting. Growth elements are difficult to predict. How long will sales continue to grow for a new product or company? Sooner or later, and it is usually sooner, growth curves reach a plateau. Fashion is similarly difficult to predict as are various psychological factors that can enter into the picture.

The five basic sales forecasting methods are executive opinion, sales-force composite, users' expectations, projection of trends, and analysis of market factors.

Good forecasting requires time, money, and talent. Even so, it will still contain significant error at times. However, at best a sales forecast has the tendency to become a self-fulfilling prophecy. Management will do its best to make the forecast come true. Its failure to do so may be considered a mark of incompetence.

Questions and Problems

1. Indicate what market factor or factors you would use to estimate the market potentials for each of the following products.
   a. Jostin's class rings.
   b. Flintkote asphalt roof shingles.
   c. Tiger Shark golf clubs.
   d. Scott's grass seed.
   e. Kreepy Krawler automatic swimming pool cleaner.
   f. Mohawk carpeting.
   g. Head skis.
   h. Staar intraocular lens implants for cataract surgery.
2. After one year of market testing, the manufacturer of a new food product had sold 4,800 packages in the test city of Louisville, Kentucky. What would be the estimated national market for this product?
3. An automobile manufacturer expected to sell in the coming period 1.2 million new automobiles in the United States. What would be the expected sales for each state?
4. Under what conditions must price levels be forecasted before a sales forecast can be formulated? How can price be removed from the forecast?

5. How would a sales manager locate and hire a fully qualified marketing analyst?
6. What are some of the pitfalls in conducting test markets?
7. What market factors would a large lumber company use to predict construction activity?
8. A study was made of all the articles appearing in *Fortune* magazine that contained forecasts of future events. In most instances, these forecasts were far too conservative. Change and growth have been far more rapid than forecasters want to admit. Why is this so?
9. One major state university has developed a model for predicting the sales potential for any given restaurant location. It has programmed this model for a computer and offers the service to prospective restaurant owners. What factors do you think are in that model?
10. Why is the executive-opinion method for forecasting widely used, and why does it frequently give usable results?
11. Should sales reps be paid a substantial bonus for correctly forecasting their sales volume for a coming period?

Case 16–1

The Iron Factory

Forecasting Sales

Mike Bowers, sales manager for The Iron Factory, contemplated methods of forecasting sales for 1983, as he had been ordered to do by the company's new president. The firm's former forecasting procedure had been most informal. Previous management called it the "beat last year" system. They had increased the previous year's sales by 10 percent, and that had become the forecast for the next year's sales. That method was now history. The new president had handed Mike a book on sales forecasting and said, "Now we are going to do it the right way!" Mike always thought the other way had worked very well. The sales force had always been able to achieve each forecast.

The Iron Factory poured iron castings to the specifications of its manufacturing customers. Each job was bid to specifications. The company had no proprietary products. Sales for the last five years had been:

1978—$15,300,000
1979— 16,910,000

1980— 18,505,000
1981— 20,401,000
1982— 22,460,000

The plant had been operating at about 87 percent capacity. With some changes and an additional, modest investment, management felt it could expand capacity by 20 percent. But it was unsure of the market. Could the additional capacity be sold? Mike did not have the answer to this question and some hints were dropped that perhaps he should find one. Since the company's Chicago location had always furnished sufficient market potential, former management had not worried about such questions. The company was making good money and everyone was happy. But then the company had been sold, and the new management wanted to use more sophisticated forecasting methods.

The company's six sales engineers worked directly with the manufacturer in the Chicago area. Most of the firm's accounts had been with The Iron Factory for more than 10 years. Good working relationships had been built between the company and its customers. Each of the sales engineers tended to specialize in selling to certain types of companies. For example, one rep, who had been with the company for 16 years, only sold to manufacturers of farm equipment, trucks, and other types of industrial vehicles. Another rep handled most of the phoned-in requests for quotations from firms that did not already have a relationship with one of the other sales engineers. The sales force was paid by a salary. A generous expense account was furnished. A bonus of 20 percent of salary was paid to each sales engineer who achieved the sales quota assigned to him for the year. The quotas were set by dividing the sales forecast by six. The quotas were uniformly met each year. The level of earnings was considered above industry average. There had been no turnover in the sales force for 10 years.

Mike saw his task as twofold: to develop a sales forecast for 1983 and to determine the company's sales potential. He was unsure of how to go about these tasks.

Question

Mike has come to you for advice about how to accomplish these two jobs. What will you tell him?

Case 16–2

Sunset Hot Tubs Company

Sales Forecasting

Donald Stanford, president of the Sunset Hot Tubs Company, was developing some strategic marketing plans. He hoped that this would result in continuing his company's rate of growth. Central to this planning was Sanford's need for an accurate sales forecast for hot tubs. For five of the past six years, the firm's actual sales of hot tubs in both dollars and units were significantly below the forecast figures. Mr. Sanford wondered what forecasting method or methods he should use to generate more accurate sales forecasts.

Located in a city in central California, the Sunset Hot Tubs Company was both a retailer and wholesaler of hot tubs and other bathing products. Sunset's sales in 1986 were $5.5 million. Hot tubs and their accessories (heaters, fixtures, tile, and water chemicals) accounted for close to 90 percent of the company's sales and gross margin. The remaining 10 percent from sales of saunas, whirlpool bath tubs, small steam baths, and related accessories.

Sunset carried two lines of hot tubs, one made from acrylic and the other of wood. The acrylic tubs were generally less expensive and weighed less than the wooden ones. Acrylic tubs were available in sizes ranging from 180 to 600 gallons, and were marketed in a wide variety of shapes and colors. Sunset bought its acrylic tubs from a manufacturer in Los Angeles, California.

About two thirds of Sunset's hot-tub sales were in the wood models. "Perhaps I'm prejudiced" Sanford commented smilingly, "but I believe the real Aficionados—the real devotees—of hot-tub bathing prefer to bathe in genuine wood tubs,"

Compared with the acrylic models, the wood tubs used more expensive materials and required more labor, time, and skill to produce—hence their higher price.

Most people use a hot tub either for relaxation or for entertainment purposes. Only a small percentage of buyers use the tub for medical or physical therapy purposes. Generally, if a customer wanted a product for therapy purposes, that person would buy or use a whirlpool bath rather than a hot tub.

Most wooden hot tubs are made of California redwood, although other woods such as teak or cedar are used in some models. A heater is used to warm the tub water to anywhere from 95 to 106 degrees. Wooden tubs commonly are round or polygonal in shape. They range in size from four to six feet in diameter and from three to four feet in depth. They usually hold from 6 to 12 people.

A new wood tub may leak for a period of time. It usually takes from one day to two weeks for the tub staves to swell and seal tightly. After installation, very little maintenance is required. The algae level is controlled with chlorine. About every six months, the inside of the tub must be scrubbed and the filter cartridges cleaned or replaced. The tubs may be installed indoors or outdoors.

Sunset bought its wood tubs from two manufacturers in Washington state. Mr. Sanford had decided to be a dealer-distributor for only three manufacturers (two wood and one acrylic). In his opinion, "these manufacturers offer the best quality, and they will be around to support their product. This business is so volatile that I won't even talk to a hot-tub manufacturer who hasn't been in business for at least four years."

Sunset reached both the consumer and an industrial market. In its capacity as a retailer, Sunset sold directly to homeowners who arranged for their own installation or had Sunset do the job. The typical homeowner was in the upper-income bracket, athletically inclined, and married. The married buyers usually fell into one of two demographic categories: (1) between 25 and 30 years of age with no children, or (2) over 45 years old with teenagers.

As a wholesale distributor, the Sunset Company sold to small firms such as plumbing contractors, athletic clubs, health clubs, and resort hotels and motels. The plumbing contractors resold and installed hot tubs in new homes and in homes being remodeled.

The Sunset Company had a sales force of 20 people who sold to the homeowner market and to the small firms in the industrial market. These sales reps drove their own cars and were paid a straight commission. The sales people were not assigned to territories.

There were always at least five sales people in the Sunset store at any time. The procedure for handling prospective customers who stepped into the store was much like a system used by many automobile dealers. Under this system the sales people rotated with each new prospect. That is, one sales person would handle the first prospect, a second rep handled the second prospect, and so forth. Mr. Sanford estimated that 80 percent of the people who came into the store were definitely going to buy a hot tub. The only question was, which firm would they buy it from? Therefore, it was essential for Sunset's success that the sales reps be able to sell Sunset hot tubs to the prospects on the spot.

Mr. Sanford believed that hot tubs were in the growth stage of their life-cycle. He cited the following factors as encouraging market indicators: (1) the increased population in the 25–50 age bracket; (2) the good economic conditions in his geographic market; (3) the continuing interest in health and physical fitness; and (4) the increase in vacation travel.

Hot tubs first became popular in the 1970s in California. Since then they had caught on to some extent in other parts of the country. In his long-range strategic planning, Mr. Sanford was seriously considering the possibility of expanding his operations into the Denver, Colorado, area. He was looking at markets outside California because competition was intensifying in his home market.

Late in 1986, Donald Sanford was engaged in marketing planning as he contemplated various strategies that would enable his company to continue to grow. He fully realized that an accurate sales forecast was essential if plans were to be of any real value. He particularly wanted an accurate forecast for hot-tub sales, because that product, with its related accessories, accounted for 90 percent of the company's sales volume.

Sunset purchased its tubs from outside suppliers, so forecasting inaccuracies could cause serious inventory imbalances. These imbalances, in turn often had a negative impact on costs and sales. An oversupply of tubs raised warehousing costs above desirable levels. Sometimes excess supplies of tubs were stored outside where they got dirty and had to be cleaned at least once a week. Also, many customers wanted to pick out the actual tub they were going to buy. Thus, an undersupply of tubs could result in lost sales when Sunset did not have the particular model on hand that a prospective buyer wanted.

Mr. Sanford reviewed the history of Sunset's sales forecasting in the nine years since he joined the firm. When Sanford came to Sunset in 1977 the company was relatively small and did no formal fore-

---

Exhibit 1

Forecasted and Actual Sales of Sunset Hot Tubs, in Units and Dollars, 1978–1986

Year	Unit Sales		Sales ($000s)	
	Forecasted	Actual	Forecasted	Actual
1978	750	900 ·	$1,050	$1,260 ·
1979	1,075	1,090 ·	1,505	1,560 ·
1980	1,250	1,200	1,975	1,900
1981	1,400	960	2,275	1,505
1982	1,550	1,275	3,300	2,740
1983	1,750	1,530	4,200	3,670
1984	1,950	1,350	5,040	3,575
1985	1,725	1,800 ·	4,760	5,165 ·
1986	2,000	1,750	5,600	4,900
(estimated)				

casting. For the first three years that Sanford forecasted Sunset's sales (1978–1980), his estimates were reasonably close to the actual sales results. See the table in Exhibit 1 and the graphs in Exhibits 2 and 3.

However, for five of the past six years (1981–1986) actual sales were slightly below the forecasted figures. This six-year pattern disturbed Mr. Sanford very much. He realized that he had to select a forecasting method that would generate much more accurate estimates.

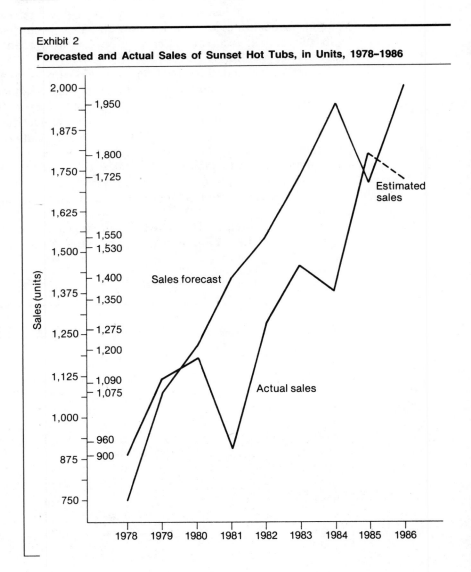

Exhibit 2
Forecasted and Actual Sales of Sunset Hot Tubs, in Units, 1978–1986

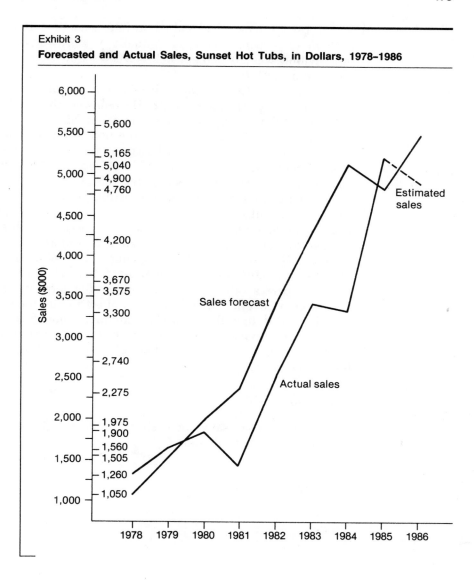

Exhibit 3

Forecasted and Actual Sales, Sunset Hot Tubs, in Dollars, 1978–1986

Sanford said that essentially what he had been doing these nine years was to base his forecast on past sales coupled with his own (executive) judgment of other market factors. He recently admitted that maybe he had been a bit lucky the first three years (1978–1980).

In preparing his 1981 forecast, Mr. Sanford once again (1) looked at Sunset's past sales record, (2) considered the growing popularity of hot tubs, and also (3) informally factored in the prospects of good economic conditions. "But my luck ran out that year," he said.

His 1981 forecast had called for the sale of 1,400 tubs, up 150 units or 12 percent over 1980. Actually in 1981 Sunset sold only 960 tubs, which was 20 percent below 1980's unit sales and 31 percent below the 1981 forecast.

Continuing with essentially the same forecasting methods, Sanford prepared his estimates for 1982. He believed that 1981 was simply not a typical year. So he again increased his unit forecast by 150 tubs—the same unit increase over the preceding year as he had done for 1981. At the end of 1982, however, that forecast grew to be 275 tubs (22 percent) above actual sales. Except for 1985, the same pattern of forecast exceeding actual results had continued to exist.

Mr. Sanford talked over his forecasting problems with some of the company executives and also with some of the sales people. There was a general agreement that Sunset was large enough and had been in business long enough to use a better, and more formal, forecasting method. The company's top salesman, Fred Williamson, proposed that the company establish formal territories. Then each sales person could prepare a sales forecast for his or her territory. Another sales rep, Angelo Covelli, resisted the idea of setting up territories. He proposed instead that the company conduct some form of survey of buyers' intentions, or users' expectations. The company's financial manager suggested that Sanford should use some form of market-factor derivation method or a similar mathematically-based method.

Question

What method of sales forecasting should the Sunset Company use to estimate its hot-tub sales?

17

Sales-Department Budgeting

Happiness is meeting budgets.
A SUCCESSFUL SALES MANAGER

Sales managers are inclined to lament the paperwork in which they are immersed. They long for simpler days, but such is not to be. In modern business, paperwork is mandatory, and much of it is connected with budgets.

Once a sales forecast has been prepared, the next step in sales planning is to prepare budgets for the sales department and all other segments of the enterprise. As noted in Chapter 16, the sales forecast provides the basis of budgeting.

A *budget* is simply a tool, a financial plan, that an administrator uses to plan for profits by anticipating the revenues and expenditure of funds. By adopting various budgetary procedures, management hopes to guide the operations of the organization to a predetermined end—a given level of profit on a certain volume of operations. Without a budget, management could never be certain whether operations were going successfully. Executives would not know if the firm's goals were being met until the final accounting for the fiscal period. Then it would be too late to revise the plan or provide remedies.

Budgeting and Strategic Planning

Just how does budgeting fit into strategic planning? The answer is that the budget reflects the dollar manifestation of the plan. It is all too easy to sit at a desk and dream up grandiose schemes to capture a market. It is quite difficult to put dollar costs to those schemes and make them all result in a profit. The budget is the strategic planner's governor. It forces a reality on the planner that is mandatory for profitable operation. Ultimately all plans must be quantified into dollars and checked against reality. Can the plan be realized or are we dreaming?[1]

Management by Percentage

Many business people plan and control their enterprises by percentages. They have learned from experience what portion of the sales dollar can or must be spent on each function of the business to achieve the desired profit. Such managers are prone to think and talk in terms of percentages. "I can pay only 6 percent (of sales) for rent . . . if I don't hold wage costs to 19 percent, I'm in trouble . . . I've got to hold my cost of goods sold to 34 percent to get the gross margin I need . . . Telephone costs of 1.2 percent? Outrageous! Check the bill! Who's calling home?" Percentages are used in planning and controlling sales and their costs.

The manager knows that if expenses are kept within their percentage budgets, final operations will come out as planned. Predictability is management's goal. Managers want to manage the organization to the planned end result—they hate surprises.

Benefits of Budgeting

Budgeting has numerous functions, some of which are discussed in this section.

Controls Expense-Revenue Ratio

Maintaining the desired relationship between expenditures and revenues is important in operating a business. The objective of a business is to buy revenues at a reasonable cost, and a budget establishes what this cost should be. If sales of $5 million are forecast, management can establish how much it can afford to pay for that revenue. If the company wants a profit of 10 percent on sales, then $4.5 million can be paid to "buy" the $5 million in revenue. Part of the $4.5 million would go to the production and administrative departments, and another portion would be available to operate the sales department. Thus the sales executive has a definite sum to use in selling the merchandise. In this way, the budget restricts the sales

---

[1] For an excellent discussion of budgeting in sales management, see Douglas J. Dalrymple and Hans B. Thorelli, "Sales Force Budgeting," *Business Horizons,* July–August 1984, pp. 31–36.

executives from spending more than their share of the funds available for the purchase of revenues. Hence, the budget helps to prevent expenses from getting out of control. It keeps them in proper alignment with sales.

Acts as a Coordinating Mechanism

Budgeting is the best way to coordinate the activities of the various segments of an enterprise. Production must be coordinated with sales. It is folly to produce more or less merchandise than can be sold. A budget serves quite well as a coordinating tool. With a budget based on a sales forecast, the production manager can plan output so that the necessary goods will be available when required. But until the sales department tells production its anticipated needs, there is no way of knowing how much to produce.

Budgeting also allows the financial executive to plan for upcoming expenses. He needs some established forecast of what the organization will be selling and what it will be spending for materials, labor, and marketing expenses. Otherwise, the financial executive has no way of knowing how much money will be required during periods of the conversion cycle. The sales budget allows the controller to judge how much money the firm will require to finance accounts receivable, inventory, and various overhead expenses. The production budget allows him to predict the expenditures for purchases of raw materials and labor.

Provides a Standard of Performance

The budget serves not only as a plan of action but also as a standard of performance for the various departments. Once the budget is established, the department can begin organizing to realize that plan. If the budget has been based on a sound analysis of potential markets and competition, the organization will be encouraged to realize its full potential. Otherwise, the departments might not know what they could or should be achieving. This is of special importance to sales people. It is through a detailed breakdown of the sales budget among products, territories, and customers that they learn what management expects of them.

Serves as an Evaluation Tool

Any goal, once established, becomes a tool for evaluation of performance. If the organization meets its goals, management can consider the performance successful. Hence, the sales department budgets become tools to evaluate the department's performance. If the sales manager is able to meet the sales and cost goals set forth in the budget, it is strong evidence to demonstrate his success as an executive. The manager who is unable to meet budgetary requirements is usually less well regarded.

Budgets for Sales Department Activities

Sales executives have the responsibility for formulating four basic budgets: the sales budget, the selling-expense budget, the advertising budget, and the sales department administrative budget.

The Sales Budget

The sales budget is the revenue or unit volume anticipated from sales of the various products. This is the key budget. It is the basis of all operating activities not only in the sales department but also in the production and finance areas. The validity of the entire budgetary process depends on the accuracy of this one sales budget. If it is in error, all others will also be in error.

An example of a sales budget is presented in Figure 17–1. Management must estimate the sales of each product, and many times makes separate forecasts for each class of customer and each territorial division. Budgets for territories and classes of customers usually are of interest only to sales executives. Other departments typically need only the sales budget for product divisions.

The sales budget calls for extreme detail. Every single product sold by the firm must be accounted for, since it must be either purchased from outside or produced within the organization. It does little good to tell production planners that $100,000 worth of small parts will be needed. They must be told specifically what small parts will be sold in what quantities and at what time.

To some extent a sales budget can become a self-fulfilling prophecy. You predict that 100 units of Model 101 will be sold in January so 100 units are produced to be sold in January. While sales of that item might fall short of the goal, they cannot exceed it for that's all there is to sell. Moreover, there is considerable pressure to make the planned sales figure a reality. Thus once the sales budget is set, management digs in to make it become fact.

This is a difficult task. Almost all sales managers complain about not having enough of the right goods to sell and too much of the wrong goods. At a meeting of the Staar Surgical Company board of directors, the sales manager was unhappy. He was unable to sell about $350,000 of a certain lens solely because production had not made them. But production had made a lot of some lenses that the sales manager hadn't sold. Staar had a sales budget problem, and the board ordered its new chief financial officer to solve it. Production had to be matched to sales department needs, but in order to do so, production needed an accurate sales budget.

The Selling-Expense Budget

The selling-expense budget anticipates the various expenditures for personal-selling activities. These are the salaries, commissions, and expenses for the sales force. This is not a difficult budget to develop. If the sales people are on a straight commission, the amount of the revenue allotted for compensation expense will be determined by the commission rate. Experience clearly indicates how much money must be set aside for expenses. If sales reps are paid a salary, the process is merely compiling the amounts, taking into consideration any raises or promotions to be made during the coming period. Any plans for sales force expansion also should be anticipated in this budget.

The Advertising Budget

Several methods are widely used to determine the funds appropriated for advertising. Many firms allocate a certain percentage of anticipated sales for advertising. The advertising budget may be established by the amount of funds available or by the task advertising is supposed to accomplish. The decision on the method to be used is ordinarily a matter of executive judgment.

Once the total amount of advertising money has been agreed on, the funds must be allocated to time periods, media to be used, products to be promoted, areas where the promotions will occur, markets to be stimulated, or any other important marketing areas.

The Administrative Budget

Besides having direct control over management of the sales force, the typical sales executive is also an office manager. Ordinarily, there are sales department secretaries and office workers; the total staff can be large. Under the sales manager may be several assistant sales managers, several sales supervisors, and sales trainers. Budgetary provisions must be made for the salaries of these individuals and their staffs. Management also must budget for such sales office operating expenses as suppliers, rent, heat, power and light, office equipment, and general overhead burden.

Figure 17–1

Sales Budget, 1987, Colorado Ski Company *(all figures in units except last column)*

| | JOE | | | GUS | |
PRODUCTS / SALES REP	CUSTOMER A*	CUSTOMER B†	TOTAL	CUSTOMER A	CUSTOMER B
Skis:					
Ski #45	1 400	1 140	2 540	1 360	1 120
Ski #60	390	260	650	240	210
Ski #80	210	420	630	190	290
Total Skis	2 000	1 820	3 820	1 790	1 620
Ski Accessories:					
Ski Poles #100	400	600	1 000	300	400
Ski Poles #200	300	400	700	200	300
Boots #30	80	180	260	10	40
Boots #50	50	140	190	20	50
Boots #70	30	100	130	20	70
Laces	1 200	3 200	4 400	1 750	2 000
Bindings	250	300	550	200	270
Safety Straps	300	900	1 200	100	500
Wax	4 800	7 500	12 300	4 600	5 600
Mittens #3	1 200	2 400	3 600	800	1 400
Mittens #5	1 400	1 800	3 200	900	1 000
Goggles #1	1 500	2 800	4 300	750	1 500
Ski Pants:					
Pants #10 Men's	1 100	800	1 900	800	600
Pants #10 Women's	1 400	1 500	2 900	950	800
Pants #20 Men's	900	1 100	2 000	610	750
Pants #20 Women's	1 500	1 100	2 600	800	970
Total Pants	4 900	4 500	9 400	3 160	3 120
Parkas:					
Parkas #8	2 500	1 700	4 200	1 800	1 200
Parkas #15	3 200	2 200	5 400	900	1 000
Total Parkas	5 700	3 900	9 600	2 700	2 200

Figure 17-1 *(concluded)*

TOTAL	PAULA CUSTOMER A	PAULA CUSTOMER B	TOTAL	TOTALS CUSTOMER A	TOTALS CUSTOMER B	TOTAL	DOLLAR VOLUME $
2 480	1 290	1 080	2 370	4 050	3 340	7 390	339 940
450	260	140	400	890	610	1 500	90 000
480	220	180	400	620	890	1 510	121 200
3 410	1 770	1 400	3 170	5 560	4 840	10 400	551 140
700	150	250	400	850	1 250	2 100	816 800
500	100	200	300	600	900	1 500	15 000
50	20	30	50	110	250	360	10 800
70	20	50	70	90	240	330	16 500
90	20	50	70	70	220	290	20 300
3 750	800	1 200	2 000	3 750	6 400	10 150	6 280
470	75	110	185	525	680	1 205	19 280
600	50	300	350	450	1 700	2 150	1 400
10 200	3 000	3 700	6 700	12 400	16 800	29 200	29 880
2 200	700	1 300	2 000	2 700	5 100	7 800	23 400
1 900	600	800	1 400	2 900	3 600	6 500	32 500
2 250	650	1 500	2 150	2 900	5 800	8 700	34 800
							226 940
1 400	500	400	900	2 400	1 800	4 200	84 000
1 750	700	600	1 300	3 050	2 900	5 950	119 000
1 360	450	500	950	1 960	2 350	4 310	172 400
1 770	540	600	1 140	2 840	2 670	5 510	220 400
6 280	2 190	2 100	4 290	10 250	9 720	19 970	595 800
3 000	1 200	800	2 000	5 500	3 700	9 200	147 200
3 750	1 600	1 000	2 600	7 100	4 650	11 750	352 500
6 750	2 800	1 800	4 600	12 600	8 350	20 950	499 700
						TOTAL DOLLAR VOLUME	1 873 580

The Budgeting Process for the Firm

For convenience in discussion here, budgets are grouped as follows: sales department budgets, financial planning budgets (such as cash and profit and loss budgets), production budgets, and general administrative and overhead expense budgets. Figure 17–2 shows the flow of information from one budget to another.

Everything starts with the sales budget described earlier. From it, data flow in five directions. The sales budget provides the basis for establishing the various sales department budgets, such as advertising, selling expenses, and sales office expenses. Sales budget figures also flow directly to the production department. Here the total production budget is established, and from that the various materials and labor budgets are determined.

Anticipated-sales figures from the sales budget also are given to the financial officer for preparation of the cash and the profit and loss budgets. The cash budget is a tool by which the financial officer determines how many dollars will be flowing into and out of the firm each month. This budget is necessary because of the time between expenditure and receipt of funds. It is necessary to lay out money for materials, labor, advertising, and selling expenses many months prior to selling the merchandise. Then after sales of the goods, it may be several months before the firm receives cash. The financial officer must ensure that the firm has sufficient cash to en-

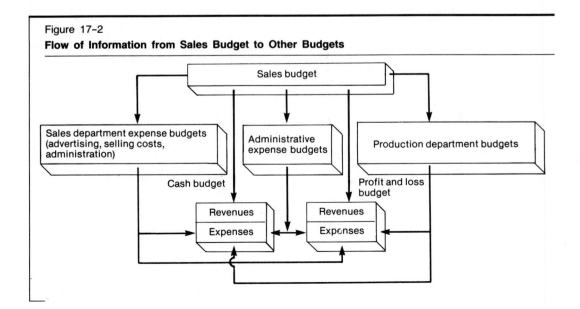

Figure 17–2
Flow of Information from Sales Budget to Other Budgets

able it to finance the lag between the expenditure and receipt of funds.

The financial officer also uses the anticipated net sales figure as the beginning of profit and loss budget. The budgets for sales department expenses, production, and general administrative expenses all flow into the profit and loss and cash budgets to determine the expected costs of operation. Thus, all budgets are summarized in the profit and loss and cash budgets. Errors in the sales department budgets have a twofold effect on the financial plan. First, the revenues will not be correct. Second, expenses will be out of line because the sales budget determined the production and administrative expenses.

Budget Periods

The three major periods for which budgets are commonly created are yearly, semiannually, and quarterly. Some firms prepare budgets for all three periods; others prefer to operate on an annual basis, thereby reducing the amount of paperwork required. The length of the budget period is closely associated with its flexibility. Firms that use a three-month period have a much more flexible system than those that use an annual budget.

The quarterly budget forces an executive to reappraise the firm's position four times a year, thereby decreasing the likelihood that operations will get out of control. Many companies find a quarterly system advisable because that is roughly their conversion cycle of operations. Garment makers usually have four conversion cycles per year. That is, they put out four different lines of goods, one for each season, and find it convenient to budget for each selling season. The main advantage of a short planning period is that it is more likely to be accurate. The shorter the forecasting period, the less likelihood there is that the estimate will be disturbed by unforeseen developments.

In deciding which period to use, a firm must balance the degree of control with the costs of compiling the budgets. All departments need not use the same period. The advertising budget may be on a quarterly basis, even though the selling-expense and sales office budgets are on an annual basis. However, any alterations in one budget will force changes in all others affected by the first one.

The Budget-Making Procedure

The first step in establishing a budget is to determine the sales forecast. Then each administrative unit must estimate the funds it will require to operate at the projected rate of activity. This is usually done by (1) surveying each of the activities the unit must perform, (2) determining just how many individuals will be required to accomplish the job, and (3) figuring what materials and supplies will be required for them to do it properly.

In a large organization, the chief sales executive, for example, may request that separate budgets be prepared by the managers of each administrative unit in the sales department. The executive then audits these budgets to determine if any changes are needed to fit into the overall sales program. Any necessary modifications should be made only after a conference between the sales manager and the department head involved. Factors unknown to the sales manager may justify the original figure. Once the sales department budgets are compiled into one major budget, it is forwarded to the financial executive, who disseminates the information to the other departments.

The due dates on various budgets must be staggered if the budgeting program is to be a success. The budget from the marketing research department, for example, must be completed before the due date of the total sales department budget. This is so that the sales executive will have sufficient time to study the figures. In a similar manner, the sales department budget must be in the hands of the financial officer before final preparation of the production budget, since the production budget is completely dependent on the sales budget. The job of compiling all the budgets into the overall cash and profit and loss budgets can be done only after all other work on the plans of the organization has been completed.

Line-Item Budgeting versus Program Budgeting

There are two basic approaches to apportioning funds among the organizational units. The first, and oldest, is the *line-item budget,* in which funds are allocated in considerable detail to each identifiable cost center. Under such a line-item system, the sales department might have budget amounts for such items as:

- Office supplies
- Postage
- Taxes
- Wages
- Insurance
- Travel
- Entertainment
- Research

- Legal expenses
- Telephone
- Recruiting costs
- Consulting fees
- Equipment
- Power
- Automobile costs

Each item would have to be forecast and accounted for in minute detail.

Program budgeting was developed to avoid some of the problems with line-item budgeting. In this plan, the administrative head of each program is budgeted a lump sum sufficient to carry out the unit's mission. Then the manager uses this amount in whatever way seems most advantageous. Thus program budgeting provides for considerable flexibility. Moreover, it eliminates the need to play games to get money for items that are needed but for which there are no funds left in the budget. A scant recruiting budget, for example, may be bolstered by calling such costs entertainment and paying for them from the budget. Such diversions negate the purpose of line-item budgeting.

Zero-Based Budgeting

A few organizations have adopted a recent development called *zero-based budgeting* an answer to one problem posed by traditional budgeting procedures. Traditionally, a firm budgets for the coming period by adjusting the previous period's budgeting amounts. This history-based approach can perpetuate practices that are no longer appropriate.

Under zero-based budgeting, each period starts from scratch. The administrator must justify each dollar requested. Thus each existing program must prove its requirements before new funding is provided. In theory this sounds wise and prudent, but in practice it is a terrible waste of administrative time. The manager must spend too much time proving to other people the department's need for funds. One sales manager said of the plan, "If I have to prove to my boss each year that the sales department needs funds to operate on, I'm going to get a new boss, a smarter one."

Reasons Some Firms Do Not Use Budgets

Budgeting is by no means a universal business practice. A number of firms operate without any formal budgeting process. Some of these are successful in their activities and feel no real need to adopt a budget system. They give various reasons for not wanting to use a budgeting system. A few are quite valid, and others are actually the result of unwise budgeting procedures.

Unreliable Sales Forecasts

Some executives believe that a good budget system depends on an accurate sales forecast. They ask, "If we really don't know what to expect in sales, how can we budget expenses?" It's a lame excuse—the sign of an inept manager who is too lazy to do his or her homework. Right or wrong, the firm *must* operate on some assumption of expected sales volume no matter how uncertain it may be. Under such conditions, some type of budget system must be devised to budget for essential expenses.

Time Requirements

Some executives feel that the budget procedure takes more time than it is worth. They point out that a budget makes no money in itself, but it costs money to create. They usually operate on the idea that the company can fill whatever sales orders are received, and they always try to keep their costs at a minimum. Assume that a firm (1) can immediately meet any new demand for its goods, and (2) its incidence of expenses is regular and unaffected by sales volume. Then probably the executive is basically right in contending that the budget takes more time than it is worth. However, this describes a relatively small segment of the business world.

Revenue Lag

One of the problems of budgets is that they may commit the firm to expenditures before the actual revenue develops. Thus losses will result if sales drop substantially during the period. The longer the budgetary period, the greater the chances that this will happen. Suppose a firm forecasts $10 million in sales volume for the coming year. It then decides to spend $2 million to advertise its products. If some unforeseen situation occurs—such as a strike, stronger competition, or a sudden economic reversal—the sales forecast will prove to be too high. If the firm already has contracted to spend $2 million, the operations for the period probably will result in a loss.

Inflexibility

Budgets are capable of inserting a considerable degree of inflexibility into the sales picture. This is particularly true if the sales executive is not in continual contact with developments in the field and has not provided for unanticipated occurrences. An inflexible budget can prevent a firm from taking advantage of market opportunities that may come its way. Suppose that after a budget is established, the sales manager discovers a considerable market opportunity for a certain new product. If he did not anticipate such developments, he may have difficulty locating funds to develop it.

Reduced Incentives

In some cases, the budget tends to become a goal that, once reached, reduces the incentive of the organization to improve its performance. Once a firm establishes a sales budget and focuses its activities on achieving that performance, it may have difficulty going beyond that goal.

The argument that budgets reduce incentive is basically not an objection to budgeting in itself. Instead, it is an indication that the firm is unable to forecast sales goals accurately or to motivate its people effectively.

Waste

Another criticism leveled against budgets is that they lead to waste because various departments think it is necessary to spend budgeted funds regardless of need. This criticism essentially reflects a weakness caused by inflexibility in budgeting. Frequently administrative officers plead with their departments to spend all the funds in a certain budget before the end of the period. Otherwise the surplus will revert to a general fund, and the amount will be reduced in the next budget.

Sometimes budgeting can lead to constant attempts to increase the funds each period. A budget discussion might go as follows. "Last year we were given $500 for supplies. Let's ask for $800 this year, and maybe they will give us $600." The budget should be established on a basis of need but it can degenerate into a competition to get more money.

Waste can also occur when funds are allotted to one budget and then allowed to be transferred to others at the whim of a department head. Executives often find it easier to get funds for one budget than for another. Therefore, they ask for more than they need in the easy-to-get areas and then later transfer the surplus to other uses.

Many of these problems are caused by dividing the budgets into too many categories. The more classifications made, the more chances that excess funds will be granted in any one. The real solution to this problem is not in the mechanics of the budget, but in indoctrinating the organization with the correct philosophy. It can be disastrous if department heads regard a budget as something to be beaten rather than as a tool designed to help them do their jobs better.

Conservatism

Critics of budgeting sometimes argue that budgets almost inevitably tend to be ultraconservative, thereby preventing the organization from reaching its full potential. These critics claim that the people who prepare the budget are influenced by the belief that they are going to be judged by the plan. Therefore, they understate their department's capabilities so that the actual performance will make them appear in a favorable light. Few people set their goals higher than they believe they can reach because the results could make them appear incompetent.

The charge of conservatism has enough truth to make it difficult to refute. This criticism reveals the administrator's basic philosophy: Is he a businessman or a gambler? The gambler will be antagonistic toward all budgets, since they restrict his freedom of operation. The true businessman does not want to assume the risks the gambler willingly incurs. He prefers to work steadily, making a planned profit and minimizing all the risks society forces him to underwrite. He grants the critics of budgeting many points, but he answers them by saying that a slightly faulty plan is better than no plan at all.

Summary of Criticisms

The criticisms levied against budgets can be condensed into two main categories. First, some sincerely think that they cannot make reliable forecasts on which a meaningful budget could be based. Often what these administrators really mean is that they are unwilling to do the research necessary to form accurate forecasts. Under many conditions a workable sales forecast is difficult to derive, but not impossible.

Second, and more important, the use of the budget is usually a matter of business philosophy. Many administrators cannot use a budget. They would be unwilling to abide by it even if some of their staff members were to convince them that the organization requires one. Many executives who operate successfully without the benefits of a budget would rebel at being forced to adopt it as a planning tool. In many cases, they receive a high degree of psychological satisfaction from being able to operate their businesses successfully through their ingenuity and insight.

Many of the criticisms of the budgeting procedure are not faults of budgeting, but instead indicate administrative weaknesses. Evidence is provided by the executive who (1) allows the budget to become his master or to restrict him, (2) budgets in too much detail and spends too much time doing it, (3) is unable to forecast sales volume accurately, or (4) is too conservative in establishing goals and too generous in alloting funds. In essence, executives who either refuse to budget or who claim that budgets are not adaptable are saying that as business administrators, they are incapable of planning their activities.

Managing with Budgets

Once prepared and in operation, the budget becomes one of the manager's regularly used tools. The previous month's actual sales and expenses come back from the accounting department by the middle of the present month. Hopefully the manager's assistant has already carefully examined each figure and compared it with the budgeted amount. All figures that are over budget are marked for attention. Some of the accounts that are over budget are understandable; the manager knows the reason and either accepts it or knows that the matter will be corrected in the near future. Then an account pops up that is significantly over budget and the manager does not know why.

"Pull all the documents on this account! Let's find out why it is over budget," the manager instructs the assistant. The process continues until all the overbudget accounts have been considered.

Shortly thereafter, the documentation on each questioned over-budget account is in front of the manager. Now some actions may be forthcoming if the manager sees some things that are unacceptable. Perhaps some branch office telephone bill is way out of line, indicating that the calls are not being made to customers. Perhaps the postage account is way over budget; examination shows that the people in the mail room are sending all packages by overnight delivery without thinking about it.

Not only does the manager stay on top of the operation with this monthly drill, but the people in the department quickly realize that they will be held accountable for their foolishness. They start to think about the money they spend for the firm. Employees see that the company is serious about its money and wants to know what happens to it.

Summary

Budgets are an inescapable reality for managers in modern enterprises. People who are inept at budget work won't rise far in most organizations. The budgetary process begins in the sales department with the formulation of a sales forecast. From that figure, a detailed sales budget is developed which contains the expected sales of each item in the product line. The production budgets and the selling expense budgets are developed from the sales budget. Finally, the financial officer compiles the various financial plans from a distillation of all budgets.

The purpose of the budget system is to keep expenses in line with revenues so the firm can realize its anticipated profit. But the budget process is replete with problems. There is waste. There are administrative costs. There are game players who waste managerial time and patience. However, most of these problems lie not with the budget process per se, but rather with its administration.

Questions and Problems

1. Can a very small firm use budgets?
2. How can a manager build flexibility into the budgeting process in order to provide for unexpected events?
3. How can an executive keep subordinates from wasting funds in overly generous budgets?
4. How can an executive avoid having subordinates ask for more funds than are needed?
5. Can budgets be developed without an accurate sales forecast?
6. If total expenses must be reduced by 10 percent, should an across-the-board cut or a selective reduction be used? If selective, how should the selection be made?
7. One executive claimed that if the department failed to spend its funds during one budget period it should be allowed to keep them and still get its regular allotments. Do you agree?
8. One sales manager commented, "Zero-based budgeting is a fraud . . . a gimmick dreamed up by some accountant to get attention. There is no way in the world management can ignore the past costs of operation. If it cost us $500,000 last year to produce $5 million in sales, and we want $6 million in sales this coming year, then the past budget has to affect the future budget." Comment.
9. A sales executive observed, "Perhaps line-item budgeting is overly detailed and leads to many inflexibilities, but if you think I am about to turn over a lump sum of money to a project manager to spend as he or she desires, you're badly mistaken. If they go off the deep end and blow the dough, all I can do is fire them, even though the company has been badly damaged." Comment on this thought.
10. "Budgeting is a bunch of bureaucratic baloney dreamed up and supported by administrators who prefer to shuffle papers rather than go out into the streets to sell something." Comment on this statement by a highly successful saleswoman.

Case 17-1

Biomedics, Inc.

Use of Budgets for Start-Up Ventures

"I've tried budgets, but they just don't work for us," George Thompson insisted. "The problem is that we simply can't forecast our sales with any degree of accuracy. We may sell $200,000 one month and $500,000 the next. Our expenses are all over the place. One month I may have to spend a lot of money on a piece of equipment and the next month our legal bills may go through the roof because somebody sues us. I've got to have some predictability of sales and expenses to develop a useable budget system here at Biomedics. After all, it does take a lot of time and effort to develop budgets, and right now we're fighting for our lives. I just don't have the time to do it considering the usefulness of the end result."

George Thompson was founder and chief executive officer of Biomedics, Inc.—a company that specialized in developing blood serum products. The company had "gone public" two years previously. The $5 million dollars that investors had supplied was gone, and the firm was being forced by financial realities to operate on its cash flow. This had placed severe strains on Biomedics management because they tenaciously resisted laying off workers. The common refrain was, "We can't. We need everybody we have. We can't lay off anybody. Besides, it really wouldn't do any good because the amount of money we need is so large."

Nevertheless, George had been pruning his staff rather carefully and was being forced to watch cash expenditures with an eagle eye. While the company had been able to meet all its payrolls, the feat had not been accomplished without leaving many scars. There were suppliers who had not been paid for 120 days. Two months previously, George had to borrow money on his stock to loan to the company in order to meet payroll.

Dr. Cunningham was an outside director whose expertise in both business and medicine had made him a valuable consultant. He had periodically urged George to adopt a rigid budget system and establish better financial controls. He was particularly incensed that George refused to develop cash flow projections. The board of directors had yet to see any meaningful financial planning and control. George's excuse was usually that the accounting department was too shorthanded to get the work done. The company's part-time financial officer, Mr. Marshall, C.P.A., was too busy to develop a budget system for the company.

Question

What recommendations would you make if you were retained as an outside consultant to the company in this matter?

Case 17–2

Oil Well Supply Company

Reducing Budgets

In late 1985 it became painfully apparent that the revenues for the Oil Well Supply Company for 1986 would fall far below projections. The industry was in a severe slump. Red Moore, sales manager, had been invited to attend a top management meeting that had been called to deal with the serious problem of too little revenue and too many bills.

Mr. Henry, president, opened the meeting by summarizing the situation. Anticipated 1986 revenues would be $75 million, down from 1985 revenues of $122 million. Budgeted expenditures for 1986 would have to be $70 million, down from $110 million in 1985.

The Oil Well Supply Company, located in Houston, Texas, sold a wide line of supplies and equipment to drilling contractors and oil producers throughout the western hemisphere. Its 175 sales reps and sales engineers worked from 11 branch offices.

The sales department budgets had been set traditionally at 20 percent of sales as a matter of policy. Red Moore glanced at his budget breakdowns for 1985.

Sales force costs	$17.1 million
Advertising	5.0
Sales office administration	2.1
Total	$24.2 million

He knew he had some tough decisions to make to get the total down to $15 million. But first he wanted to fight for a bigger share of total revenues. When Mr. Henry finished his opening speech, he asked each department head for a statement of what was going to be done to achieve the targeted expense reductions.

When it was Red's turn to talk, he first put on the paper easel his rough 1986 budget targets. They were:

Sales force costs	$13.5 million
Advertising	.5
Sales office administration	1.0
Total	$15.0 million

He explained. "I've tried to give as much money as posible to the sales force. That's the key to revenues. I've cut advertising as far as I can and still have any presence in the market. It's mainly trade-show money. I've cut the office staff to the bare bone. It means laying off a lot of people who have been with us for some time. It means stopping all research. But there it is. I do think that under these circumstances it would be wise if we could put a bit more of our revenue dollar into marketing. Twenty-two percent would loosen the noose around our neck somewhat."

Mr. Henry asked, "How are you going to reduce selling costs by that much?"

"I am laying off some of our weaker producers and giving their key accounts to nearby reps. Some of the sales engineers will not be needed because the work load is down. We'll absorb their territories into other territories. And we'll just stop calling on some smaller customers."

Mr. Henry replied, "I think you're cutting advertising back too much just to protect your sales people. It's easier to let the advertising media take the loss than our people. But is now the time to stop advertising when we're cutting back our field coverage?"

Red argued, "I think that right now it is more important to keep in personal touch with our customers just when all our competition is cutting back on theirs. We're all in the same boat. Advertising doesn't play a big part in the buying decisions of drilling contractors and the oil well supply house buyers. Personal relationships are what count most. I want to keep every dollar I can in the sales force."

Mr. Henry countered, "Can we keep all our sales force and just cut their earnings? Pay them by commission! We've been paying them generously and heaven knows that our expense accounts are out of sight. Let's bring them back into this world."

The company had loosely considered that it took about $100,000 a year to keep a sales rep or engineer in the field. The reps made an average of about $60,000 a year. The firm spent a total of about $35,000 per rep on expenses. The rep spent about $20,000 of the amount, and the remaining $15,000 was spent on various customer entertainment activities such as tickets to ball games, fishing and hunting facilities, and other company-sponsored customer activities. The company used entertainment extensively as a selling tool. They treated their customers quite nicely.

Mr. Henry continued, "And if the customers aren't buying from us, then why are we entertaining them so much. Cut back on all entertainment."

Red Moore defended, "But this downturn is temporary. Things go up and things go down. Now we're down. Tomorrow we'll be up. But our customers will remember who was around when things were bad and who wasn't. The last thing we want to be are fair weather friends. Sure we'll be careful about who we entertain, but I think it would be a mistake to pull in our horns now. It would tell the industry that we're in trouble. And who wants to buy from trouble? As for the advertising, I've yet to meet a customer that ever enjoyed one of our ads. Right now we've got to get out and dig for business. Ads won't do that job for us."

"I'm not certain that the board of directors would agree with you, Red. I think you'd better be ready for some stern questioning of your budget next month."

Questions

1. Should the advertising budget be slashed so severely?
2. Should entertainment be curtailed?
3. If you agree with Mr. Henry, prepare his case for the board of directors meeting. If you agree with Red, prepare the defense of his budget.

18

Sales Territories and Routing

It is a bad plan that admits of no modification.
SYRUS

Establishing sales territories is another part of sales management's strategic planning job, along with determining market and sales potentials, making sales forecasts, and preparing budgets. Territories make it possible to bring the other aspects of planning down to a regional basis. Ordinarily, it is not practical to plan, direct, and control sales people's activities without establishing sales districts. A company's total market is usually too large to be managed efficiently without them.

> A **sales territory** is
>   a number of present and potential customers,
>   located within a geographical area,
>   and assigned to a sales person, branch, or middleman
>   (retailer or wholesaler).

In this definition, the key word is **customer** rather than **geographical.** To understand the concept of a sales territory, we must recognize that a market is made up of people, not places—people with money to spend and the willingness to spend it. A market is measured by people times their purchasing power rather than in square miles. Geographical factors should be considered only to the following extent:

- The customers who constitute a territory should be located in the same general area to facilitate effective coverage by the sales force.

497

- Geographical boundary lines should be drawn around the groups of customers to facilitate quantitative identification of a territory and control by management.

Reasons for Establishing Sales Territories

To ensure proper coverage of potential market. Sales people are likely to cover their market more thoroughly if they are each assigned to a specific geographical area rather than if they are allowed to sell in any area. The areas should not be so large that anyone must spend an undue amount of time traveling. Also, the sales potential should not be so great that the rep only skims the cream off the market.

To improve customer relations. Carefully established territories can improve the quality of service the sales people give to their accounts. Routed properly, a sales person can call on accounts regularly, and they learn to look forward to the visit. Regularity in sales calls is especially important if a staple, repeat-order type of product is being sold. If the regular sales person is not there, the order can just as easily be given to a competitor.

To increase sales people's morale and effectiveness. The delineation of territories is likely to encourage responsible managerial attitudes in the sales force. When sales representatives have their own territories, they are virtually in business for themselves. They realize that they alone are responsible for the results in their districts.

Setting territories defines a sales job more concretely. It is more effective to say, "You are assigned the seven counties that constitute this trading area," than it is to say, "Your job is to go out and sell." Furthermore, restricting sales representatives geographically may sharpen their sales abilities. They may route themselves more carefully and plan the frequency of their calls better.

To control and evaluate sales-force activities. Restricting a sales representative to a given territory gives management an effective control device. A list of customers can be given to a rep, along with instructions on the frequency of calls for each account. A territorial structure also can be a great help to management in its evaluation of sales people's effectiveness. Management can measure their actual performance against a territorial potential or territorial quotas.

To facilitate performance of other sales and marketing activities. Analyzing sales and cost data can be more meaningful if the task is done on a territorial basis rather than for the market as a whole. Management can use marketing research more effectively to set realistic quotas and to prepare sales and expense budgets.

To reduce selling costs. If management is careful in designing the territories and in routing the sales force, it can reduce selling costs considerably. No overlapping territories, with the waste of duplication, will occur. When reps are restricted to one area, they probably spend less time and money traveling than if they are allowed to sell anywhere in the total market. If they spend less time traveling, an increase in effective selling time should result.

Reasons for Not Establishing Sales Territories

Formal territories may not be needed in a small company with a few people selling only in a local market. In this case, management can undoubtedly plan and control sales operations without the aid of districts and still achieve many of the specific objectives discussed in the preceding section. Territories generally become more necessary as a company's markets and sales force increase in size.

New territories may not be needed *immediately* in a company that has an established territorial structure in one part of the nation, but that wants to expand geographically. Management should wait until it has more information about realistic sales expectations in the new market.

The absence of territories may be justified when personal friendships play a large part in the market transaction. This is one reason automobile dealers and commodity and security brokers usually do not district their sales forces. Highly specialized sales engineers also are not often confined within territorial boundaries. Instead, they may serve in troubleshooting assignments or be called in to help close an important sale anywhere.

Use of Computers in Territory Design and Management

In sales-force management, one area in which computer technology is being widely used is in the design, revision, and day-to-day management of sales territories. Over the past two decades sophisticated computer-based mathematical models have been developed to aid companies in designing their sales territories. Unfortunately, because of their complexity and limiting assumptions, these models are still not widely used in business.[1] Computer-based

---

[1] For a series of computer-based decision models pertaining to sales-territory alignment, see *Sales Management: New Developments from Behavioral and Decision Model Research,* ed. Richard P. Bagozzi (Cambridge, Mass.: Marketing Science Institute, 1979), pp. 325–76, which includes the following papers: Thomas A. Glaze and Charles B. Weinberg, "A Sales Territory Alignment Program and Account Planning System (TAPS)," pp. 325–43) and Andris A. Zoltners, "A Unified Approach to Sales Territory Alignment," pp. 360–76. Each of these papers includes an extensive bibliography with references to several other models of sales-terroitory alignment.

models have also been developed to aid companies in deploying their sales forces and in allocating selling effort to customers and products. Some of these models carry suggestive names such as CALLPLAN, SCHEDULE, and ALLOCATE.[2] Some companies have found these models to be quite useful in such tasks as allocating sales calls and determining call frequencies, travel time, length of call, etc., for various classes of customers and products. For the most part, however, these models have enjoyed only modest success in terms of the numbers of companies using them—again, because of their complexity. Later models of sales-force deployment have been developed that are less sophisticated, but potentially more acceptable because of their operational, practical nature.[3]

Sales reps and their managers are using computer technology more and more in the day-to-day management of their territories. These people are especially making effective use of microcomputers, personal computers, and lap-top portable models. Let's look at just a few examples. One area that can be computerized is the planning of the reps' call patterns and their account coverage. Computer-based ratings of accounts by size and likelihood of closing a sale enable the reps to focus on the best prospects. Computer information also helps in determining call frequencies.

Sales reps are using computer-based information to analyze and re- apportion their work loads so as to get more selling time. Computers are helping to reduce the sales reps' paperwork. Daily call reports, weekly reports, and monthly reports are done quickly with a computer. Orders are sent in by computer, thus avoiding the tediousness of writing orders by hand and the mistakes caused by poor handwriting. The reps and managers are using computers to plan daily and weekly routing schedules for calling on customers.

Another situation in which the computer is being used is *during* sales calls. The sales people can call in (via computer) for up-to-the-minute information on inventory and delivery conditions. Price quotations can be made, and altered if necessary, during a sales call.

---

[2] See Leonard M. Lodish, "CALLPLAN: An Interactive Salesman's Call Planning System," *Management Science*, December 1971, pp. 25–40; for some later modifications of the CALLPLAN model, see by the same author, " 'Vaguely Right' Approach to Sales Force Allocations," *Harvard Business Review*, January–February 1974, pp. 119–24, and "Assigning Salesmen to Accounts to Maximize Profits," *Journal of Marketing Research*, November 1976, pp. 440–44. Also see Gary M. Armstrong, "The SCHEDULE Model and the Salesman's Effort Allocations," *California Management Review*, Summer 1976, pp. 43–51; and James H. Comer, "ALLOCATE: A Computer Model for Sales Territory Planning," *Decision Sciences*, July 1974, pp. 323–38.

[3] See, for example, Raymond W. La Forge, Clifford E. Young, and B. Curtis Hamm, "Increasing Sales Productivity through Improved Sales Call Strategies," *Journal of Personal Selling & Sales Management*, November 1983, pp. 53–59; and Raymond W. La Forge, David W. Cravens, and Clifford E. Young, "Improving Salesforce Productivity," *Business Horizons*, September–October 1985, pp. 50–59.

Computer graphics can aid in sales presentations. Various proposals can be shown during a sales call. Finally, computers are implementing the sales people's use of electronic mail. Sending one message to 10 people back at the office takes one computer call, not 10 phone calls. The reps also can send letters, greeting cards, and other communications to their customers.[4]

Procedure for Establishing Territories

The ideal goal in territorial design is to have all districts equal in both sales potential and the sales representatives' work load. When sales potentials are equal, it is easier to evaluate and compare sales reps' performances. Equal opportunities also reduce disputes between management and the sales force and tend generally to improve workers' morale. To achieve both objectives is an ideal, usually unattainable, goal, but this should not deter an executive from constantly striving to reach it.

In many organizations where territories have existed for some time, management has made no planned approach to their establishment. Usually they were established arbitrarily by assigning each person a few states or cities. Management paid little attention to market potential, flow of trade, or competition. Then, the districts were allowed to grow indiscriminately. Frequently new ones were added and old ones revised unsatisfactorily, often on the basis of expediency.

Changing market conditions put continuing pressure on companies to adjust their territories. Different procedures may be used to design the districts. However, a company's territorial structure is influenced (1) by the potential business in the firm's market and (2) by the work load required of its sales force. One plan for establishing territories includes the following six steps. See Figure 18–1.

1. Select a control unit for territorial boundaries.
2. Analyze sales people's work load.
3. Determine basic territories, considering sales potential and call patterns.
4. Assign sales people to territories.

---

[4] For additional case examples of company experiences using personal computers and microcomputers to aid in day-to-day territorial planning and operations, see Thayer C. Taylor, "The Computer in Sales & Marketing," a special section in *Sales & Marketing Management,* October 7, 1985, pp. 59–62; December 9, 1985, pp. 65 ff.; December 3, 1984, pp. 61 ff. Also see G. David Hughes, "Computerized Sales Management," *Harvard Business Review,* March–April 1983, pp. 102–112; and William M. Bulkeley, "Better Than a Smile: Salespeople Begin to Use Computers on the Job," *The Wall Street Journal,* Sept. 13, 1985, p. 25.

Figure 18-1
Procedure for Designing Sales Territories

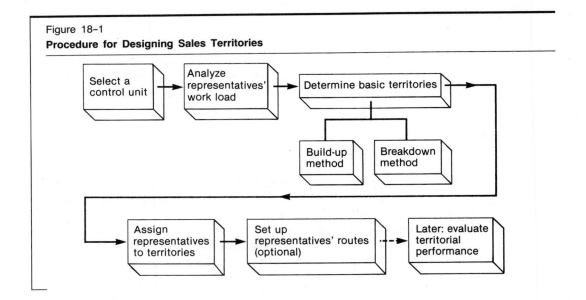

5. Establish a route plan for the sales force. (This step is optional.)
6. Conduct territorial sales and cost studies on a continuing basis. (This step is discussed in Chapters 20 and 21.)

Determine Basic Control Unit for Territorial Boundaries

When establishing territories, the first step is to select a geographical control unit to serve as a territorial base. Commonly used units are states, counties, cities, ZIP-code areas, metropolitan areas, and trading areas. A typical territory may comprise several individual units. One person's district may consist of four metropolitan areas; another's may be three states. The unit should be small for at least two reasons. First, a small unit will aid management in realizing one of the basic values of territories—the geographic pinpointing of potential. Second, the use of small control units makes it easier for management to adjust the territories. If an organization wants to add a little to one person's district and reduce another's, a county unit facilitates the adjustment better than a state unit.

In the past it was customary for firms to use some political unit (state, county, or city) as a base and to draw territorial lines to coincide with political boundaries. These units afforded a base that was easily understood by both management and the sales force. Furthermore, much government census data and other market information are available for political units.

Today, political units, particularly counties, are still used extensively as a basis for territorial boundaries. This is simply because of the availability of market data by counties. However, a marked change has occurred in their manner of use. Other market factors are recognized, such as customer buying habits and normal patterns of trade flow. Counties are grouped into metropolitan areas as a basis for territories, even though the metro area may cross a state's borders.

States. Many companies still use a *state* as their control unit in establishing territorial boundaries. For some conditions, this unit may be satisfactory. Territories may be built around states if a firm has a small sales force covering a national market and is using a selective distribution policy. A luggage manufacturer on the West Coast who sells directly to a limited number of selected retail accounts has used the state unit with apparent success.

Territorial systems built around states are simple, inexpensive, and convenient. However, for most companies, states do not serve well as bases for territories, because customers often are oblivious to a state line in their buying habits. An Oregon-Washington boundary ignores the fact that many consumers and retailers in southern Washington buy in Portland. Trade from Alton and East St. Louis, Illinois, gravitates to St. Louis, Missouri, rather than to any city in Illinois.

Counties. For companies that realize the drawbacks to the state unit, but prefer to use a political subdivision as a territorial base, the *county* may be the answer. There are almost 3,100 counties, and only 50 states. Working with smaller control units helps management to design territories that are equal in potential and pinpoint problem areas. Many kinds of statistical market data (population, retail and wholesale sales, income, employment, and manufacturing information) are available from several sources on a county basis.

The only serious drawback to the county unit is that for some companies it is still too large. A manufacturer or a wholesaler may want to assign several reps to cover one county because the potential is far too much for one person to handle. This situation may prevail in such counties as Los Angeles, Cook (Chicago), Wayne (Detroit), or Cuyahoga (Cleveland). It then becomes necessary to divide the city into a series of territories, and some control unit smaller than a county is needed.

Cities and ZIP-code areas. In the past, such firms as wholesalers of food, drugs, and tobacco often used a *city* as a control unit, because most of the market lay within urban limits. In fact, in many instances even the city was too large, and firms used several sales reps within a single city. Then some subcity unit was needed, and business made use of precincts, wards, or census tracts.

Postal ZIP-code areas are one particular subcity unit that is widely used when an entire city is too large to use as a basic control unit. (ZIP- code areas are also used extensively in other market measurement activities such as (1) segmenting markets, (2) targeting advertising expenditures, and (3) calculating territorial market and sales potentials.)

By using ZIP-code areas, a company is working with geographical areas that typically have a high degree of economic, social, and cultural homogeneity. Management can establish territories with reasonably comparable potentials and workloads. However, it is difficult to get much statistical market data for geographical units smaller than a county or city.

Metropolitan statistical areas. Many companies have found that a significant share of their market has shifted to suburban and satellite cities outside the major central city. These firms have been aided tremendously by the delineation of *Metropolitan Statistical Areas.* The federal government has identified, and established the boundaries for, about 325 of these areas. A Metropolitan Statistical Area is an economically and socially integrated unit with a large population center. An urban area can qualify in one of two ways to be classed officially as a Metropolitan Statistical Area (MSA). An MSA is a county or group of contiguous counties (1) that has a central city with a population of at least 50,000, or (2) that has a general urban area of 50,000 with a total metropolitan area of at least 100,000 population. The bulk of the workers in an MSA must be nonagricultural employees, and an MSA may cross state lines.

Because an MSA is defined in terms of counties, a vast amount of market data is available. Although small in total land area, the metropolitan statistical areas account for 75 to 80 percent of the nation's population, effective buying income, and retail sales.[5] Thus, they constitute lush, concentrated markets for many consumer and industrial products. Because of this market potential, some firms assign territories that consist of a number of metropolitan areas. They encourage their sales people to work only in the metropolitan area and to skip the region outside or between the areas.

Trading areas. A popular territorial base, especially for firms that sell to or through wholesalers or retailers, is the *trading* area. This control unit is a geographical region that consists of a central city, which dominates the market, plus the surrounding area whose trade

[5] For a wealth of market information on the metropolitan statistical areas, see "Survey of Buying Power," *Sales & Marketing Management,* July 28, 1986.

Figure 18–2
Territorial Control Units

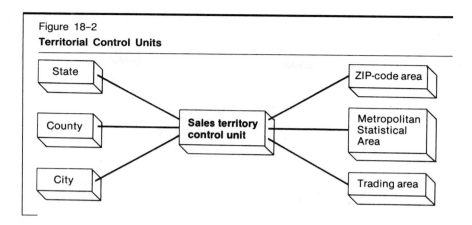

normally flows to the hub city. Thus, a trading area is based on consumer buying habits and normal trading patterns. A trading area usually ignores all political boundaries. However, its boundaries are drawn arbitrarily to coincide with county lines so that the census and other market data may be used.

The concept of a trading area is used in general terms as a base for territories. Actually, however, a trading area must be thought of in terms of a specific product. A retail trading area exists for drugs or furniture, or a wholesale trading area may exist for groceries or dry goods. There is no such thing as a Denver trading area. Rather, there is a Denver wholesale trading area for jewelry or furniture.

Use of a trading area as a territorial base for the sale of a given product has several advantages. These areas are based on economic considerations, not political ones. They are realistic in that they represent patterns of trade; they are based on customer buying habits. They should facilitate sales planning and control. For instance, there is little danger that after a manufacturer's sales rep does considerable missionary work with retailers, they will buy the product from a wholesaler in another rep's territory.

Probably the major drawback to using trading areas is the difficulty in defining them for a given product. Areas differ considerably in size and shape, depending on such factors as (1) the nature of the product, (2) topographical conditions, (3) the highway network, (4) the number and size of potential customers, (5) the channel of distribution used, and (6) the level of distribution (wholesale or retail).

A company may have to develop its own trading area map at considerable expense. However, several organizations have prepared trading area maps covering various types of products. Rand McNally, for example, publishes a trading-area map of the United States showing 494 basic trading areas and 50 major trading areas. In most large cities major newspapers and other private firms prepare market information maps from which trading areas may be delineated.

Analyze Sales People's Work Loads

Territorial design depends basically on the company's sales potential and the work load of its sales force. Consequently, it is important that management identify and measure the factors that influence these work loads. Two companies, each selling in markets of comparable potential and geographical size, may have quite different territorial structures simply because of a difference in the sales reps' work loads.

Nature of the job.   A sales rep's call patterns are influenced by the nature of the job. A rep who only sells can make more calls per day than the rep who must do a considerable amount of missionary work along with selling. In strongly competitive markets with a concentration of large accounts, management may have two sales people cover each account. One may call periodically to do straight selling, while the other takes care of any necessary missionary work. If the total job is split between two people, they each can cover a larger territory.

Nature of the product.   The nature of the product can also affect a sales person's call pattern. A staple, convenience good with a rapid rate of turnover may require more frequent calls than would an industrial product with a very limited repeat-sale business. Therefore, a representative who sells this industrial product can handle more accounts than the person who sells the convenience good. Often, the nature of the product influences the number of outlets or the number of customers. A rep who sells a specialty good purchased by one or two outlets in a city can cover a larger territory than the rep who sells a convenience good purchased by every grocery store and drugstore.

Stage of market development.   When entering a new market, a company's territories typically are larger than in markets where the firm is well entrenched. This situation occurs even though the market potential is comparable in the old and new regions. A large geographical district is needed initially to yield an adequate volume of business.

Intensity of market coverage.   If a firm wants mass distribution, it will need smaller territories than if it follows a selective or exclusive distribution policy. A firm can also eliminate a number of its unprofitable accounts without reducing the size of its territories. The sales reps are encouraged to devote more time to the remaining accounts, in an attempt to develop additional business.

Competition. No general statement can be made about the net effect competition has on the size of the territory. If management decides to make an all-out effort to meet competition, then territorial borders will probably be contracted. Sales people will be instructed to intensify their efforts by increasing the frequency of call and the length of time spent with each account. On the other hand, competition may be so fierce, or the territorial markets so overdeveloped, that the company is not going to make much profit in the district. Therefore, it may decide to expand the geographical limits of the district and have the sales rep call only on selected accounts.

Ethnic factors. A company may adjust its territorial boundaries in large cities because of the market concentration of certain racial, national, or religious groups. One part of a city may have a heavy ethnic concentration. Retailers may also be predominantly of the ethnic group, and use of the group's native (foreign) language may be widespread in the area. A firm that sells to these retailers may alter its territorial boundaries so that the particular nationality group comprises one district. In the city of Chicago, a concern that sells to retail businesses may establish separate territories in some parts of the city to cater to the black, Hispanic, Italian, Polish, or Jewish markets. The person who covers each of those districts is from the corresponding ethnic group and can speak the foreign language.

Determine Basic Territories

The third general step in designing sales districts is to establish a fundamental territory based on statistical measures. This step can be accomplished by using either the buildup or the breakdown method. Under the *buildup* procedure, territories are formed by combining small geographical areas based on the control unit selected. The *breakdown* system involves division of the whole market into segments. The buildup method is particularly adapted for manufacturers of consumer products or for companies that want intensive distribution. The breakdown method is more popular among manufacturers of industrial products or organizations that want selective distribution.

Buildup method. Several variations are possible in establishing territories by building up from the basic control unit. Usually, however, these variations all depend on some type of customer analysis, as well as study of the sales people's call patterns. A suggested procedure is outlined in the following paragraphs.

1. **Determine number, location, and size of customers.** Management should determine the number, location, and size of both present and prospective customers within each selected control unit. Size is measured in terms of potential purchases of the seller's product. An

analysis of sales records, should establish the location of *present* customers in each trading area or other control unit. *Prospective* customers can be identified with the aid of company sales reps plus outside sources such as (1) trade directories (for example, Thomas' Register), (2) publishers of mailing lists (for example, R. H. Donnelley Corporation), (3) subscription lists from trade journals, (4) trade association offices, (5) classified telephone directories, or (6) credit rating firms (for example, Dun & Bradstreet, Inc.).

Once the customers are identified, management should assess the potential business it expects from each account. For these estimates, a company may refer to some of the same sources used to build customers lists.

Management then can classify these accounts into several categories, based on their potential profitability to the seller. This step furnishes some of the necessary background for a determination of the sales people's call patterns.

2. Determine desirable call patterns. Following the customer analysis, management should establish desirable call patterns in each territorial control unit. This means determining (1) the number of calls to be made in a day and (2) the frequency with which each account should be visited.[6]

The *number of calls* that can be made effectively in one day depends on several factors. One is the average length of time required for a call. This is influenced by the number of people to be seen in each account, the amount of missionary work to be done, and the number of interruptions. Quantitative data about the average length of time for each call may be gathered from sales people, a time and duty analysis, or an analysis of call reports. Another factor that influences the number of daily calls is the amount of travel time between customers.

The *call frequency* is affected by the nature of the product, customer buying habits, the nature of competition, potential business done with an account, and the cost of calling on a customer.

3. Determine number of accounts to assign each sales person. By relating (1) the average *number* of daily calls and (2) the average *frequency* of calls for each class of accounts, management can tentatively determine the number of customers for each sales rep. This step of determining the number of accounts to assign ordinarily must be done on an individual territorial basis because of the differences among territories.

To illustrate the process of assigning accounts to the sales force,

---

[6] For a conceptual model of the call-planning process in commercial and industrial sales, see John M. Gwin and William D. Perreault, Jr., "Industrial Sales Call Planning," *Industrial Marketing Management,* July 1981, pp. 225–34. This article includes several bibliographical references to models of the sales-call planning process.

we assume that one person can average 6 calls a day (30 a week) and his average frequency of call is monthly. We also assume that each customer is called on with the same frequency. In this example, each sales rep can call on approximately 120 customers.

In a second situation, management may want to refine its analysis by classifying customers in three divisions, A, B, and C, based on a profit analysis of accounts. Class A accounts are the most profitable and are called on semimonthly. Class B accounts are visited monthly, and class C accounts bimonthly. Table 18–1 shows the number of calls per year for each class of account, assuming a certain number of accounts in each of two trading areas. If a sales person can average 6 calls a day, this equals 30 calls per week, or 1,500 per year, in trading areas X and Y. Consequently, either trading area will take slightly over 40 percent of a rep's time (40 percent of 1,500 calls per year = 600 calls). Both areas require about the same number of calls, even though Y has 50 percent more accounts than X. The reason for this is that Y has far more small, unprofitable accounts that require a call only every other month.

As shown in Table 18–1, a sales person could cover trading areas X and Y and still have room for accounts that called for a total of about 210 calls a year (1,500 − [630 + 660] = 210). A sales person could cover any number of customers who, in total, required 1,500 calls a year. For example, one rep could cover 125 accounts if they were divided this way: A, 25; B, 50; C, 50. Or a rep could call on only 80 if 50 were good accounts (class A), 20 were B accounts, and 10 were in class C.

4. Draw territorial boundary lines. The final step is to accumulate enough contiguous territorial control units so that the number of accounts included constitutes an adequate potential and a reasonable work load for one sales person. A company has a choice of places from which to start this grouping. On a national scale, a firm that groups contiguous trading areas into territories may start in Maine

Table 18–1

Example of Call Frequency for Different Customer Classes

Customer Class	Call Frequency	Trading Area X		Trading Area Y	
		No. of Accounts	No. of Calls per Year	No. of Accounts	No. of Calls per Year
A.....	2 per month	10	240	5	120
B.....	1 per month	25	300	15	180
C	1 every 2 months	15	90	60	360
		50	630	75	660

and work south to Florida, then go back to Ohio and again work south to the Gulf of Mexico. Another firm, using county control units, may start each territory with a county that includes a major city and then complete a given territory by fanning out in all directions until the necessary number of contiguous counties are included. Other organizations group counties or trading areas around a branch office or plant.

Let's illustrate the grouping of territorial control units into sales districts. We use the example of the sales person who averages 6 calls a day, with a monthly call frequency and thus is able to cover 120 accounts. For simplicity's sake, assume that each control unit has 24 customers. To give this person a full work load, the territory assigned would be composed of five control units ($120 \div 24 = 5$). In another situation, there may not be a perfectly even distribution of customers among the control units. The rep who can call on 120 customers may have them divided among five control units, as follows: area A, 15; area B, 30; area C, 25; area D, 40; area E, 10.

When a company does not use the same call frequency for all customers, a slightly different approach must be taken. Management cannot work merely on the basis of *number* of accounts, as in the preceding examples. Rather, the *importance* of the accounts must be considered. Quantitatively, the importance is reflected in the number of *calls* needed to cover the trading area. In a previous example, it was assumed that a rep can make 1,500 calls a year. Trading area X requires 630 calls for adequate coverage, and trading area Y takes 660. Trading area Z is contiguous to X and Y. If Z can be covered with approximately 210 calls, then these three trading areas can constitute one person's territory ($630 + 660 + 210 = 1,500$). This territory may have a total of 140 customers. An adjacent territory may include four trading areas and 190 customers. But because they are not such large accounts, they still can be adequately covered with 1,500 calls and are assigned to one person.

Often, unless a company splits a trading area, it is unable to group contiguous trading areas or other control units into statistically reasonable territories. In the earlier case, trading areas X and Y together required 1,290 calls. However, no trading area may be contiguous to X and Y that can be covered with approximately 210 calls. That is the number needed to give the sales rep a normal load of 1,500 visits per year.

A good rule of thumb in these cases is not to split the control unit. Statistical data may not be available for partial units, so territorial planning and control would be more difficult. Rather than split a control unit, the call frequency for some accounts may be increased or the number of daily calls reduced. In this way the sales person can intensify efforts in a smaller geographic region. In the opposite situation, the size of the total territory may be *increased* by cutting the call frequency or raising the number of daily calls.

In these examples, the selected territorial control unit is assumed to be small enough so that a sales person's district includes at least one of these control units. However, in some part of the market, the basic unit may be too large in sales potential for one person to cover. If two or more reps are needed to cover a control unit, in those areas management should use a smaller basic unit. For example, a firm that uses the county unit may find it adequate in all but 8 or 10 counties in the nation. In those 8 or 10, it needs a smaller unit. But the procedure for determining the number of customers, call pattern, and so on is essentially the same as outlined earlier.

Breakdown method.   The other major method used to establish the basic statistical territories is the breakdown method. As noted earlier, it is often used by firms that want exclusive distribution or that sell some types of industrial products.

1.   **Determine sales potential.**   The first step is to determine what sales volume the company can expect in its entire market and in each territorial control unit. To obtain regional potentials, the firm first estimates the *industrywide* potentials in the total market it operates in. Then the firm can calculate its sales potential in its total market and in each territorial control unit.

2.   **Determine volume expected from each sales person.**   Next, management must establish how much each sales representative must sell in order to have a profitable business. A study of past sales experience and a cost analysis are often used to help in this matter.

3.   **Determine number of territories needed.**   The third step is to divide the total sales potential by the volume needed from each person. The answer is the number of territories a company must establish. For instance, if the total potential is $20 million and the average volume per person is $500,000, then the business needs 40 sales reps.

4.   **Tentatively establish territories.**   The final stage in the statistical phase of the breakdown method is to divide the entire market so that each sales rep has about the same potential. In the company with 40 sales people, each would be assigned an area comprising about 2.5 percent of the company's total sales potential. The potential has already been established for each of the basic territorial control units. Therefore management needs to assign a sales person enough contiguous units so that he has 2.5 percent of the total potential. The boundaries of each territory should coincide with the borders of the control units. As in the buildup method, control units should not be split between two people, even if that means a slightly different potential for each one.

5. **Modify basic territories.**   Up to this point in the breakdown procedure, the company's sales potential has been the controlling factor
in designing the territories. Now, management should modify these
tentatively established districts according to the work-load requirements set for the sales people. As mentioned before, such factors as
the nature of the product or the stage of market development, may
influence the work loads and call patterns and, consequently, the
territorial boundaries.

Assigning Sales People to Territories

After the sales territories have been established, management is in
a position to assign individual sales people to each district. Up to
this point, we have implicitly assumed that the sales people are
equal in their selling abilities, and that each person would perform
equally well in any territory. Obviously, this is not a realistic assumption.

In any given sales force, the sales people may differ in their selling effectiveness. Representatives also vary in experience, age, physical condition, initiative, and creativity. A sales representative may
succeed in one territory and fail in another, even though the sales
potential and work load are the same in both districts. Sales performance may be influenced by differences in local customs, religion, ethnic background, or other cultural factors.

When assigning sales people to territories, management's goal is
simple. It tries to place each sales person in the district where he or
she will contribute the most to the company's profit over the long
run. Obviously this goal is somewhat of an ideal. It is easier to state
it than to accomplish it.

Broadly speaking, there are two approaches to measuring a sales
person's ability in relation to territorial potential and work load. Essentially, one approach relies considerably on executive judgment. A
rep can be evaluated on such judgmental factors as selling ability,
age, physical condition, ability to work without direct supervision,
creativity, and willingness to travel. The other approach to assigning
sales people to territories uses computer-based assignment models.
At the present time, these complex mathematical tools are not
widely used in business, but they do have the potential to be of considerable value.[7]

---

[7] For some examples of these models, see A. Parasuraman and Ralph L. Day, "A
Management-Oriented Model for Allocating Sales Effort," *Journal of Marketing Re-
search,* February 1977, pp. 22–33; Roy J. Shanker, Ronald E. Turner, and Andris A.
Zoltners, "Sales Territory Design: An Integrated Approach," *Management Science,*
November 1975, pp. 309–320.

Routing the Sales Force

After management assigns territories, it can consider the possibility of routing the sales people within their respective districts. **Routing** is the managerial activity that establishes a formal pattern for sales reps to follow as they go through their territories. This pattern is usually reflected on a map or list that shows the order in which each segment of the territory is to be covered. Although routing is referred to as a managerial activity, this does not imply that it is done only at some executive level. Often a firm asks its sales people to prepare their own route schedules as part of their job.

Routing is an optional step in sales planning. For reasons discussed later, many firms omit the activity entirely. However, other companies believe that the job of districting the sales force is not complete until a route plan is designed to ensure systematic coverage of the territories.

Reasons for Routing by Management

Managerial routing of the sales force can be expected to reduce travel expenses by ensuring an orderly, thorough coverage of the market. Studies indicate that it is not at all unusual for reps to spend one third of their daily working hours traveling. At that rate, for four months out of a year the sales representative is not even inside a customer's office.

Proponents of management's handling of the routing activity believe the typical sales person is unable to do the job satisfactorily. They feel that sales people will look for the easiest, most pleasant way to do their job, although this may not be the most effective way. Left to their own routing devices, they will backtrack and crisscross in a territory in order to be home several nights a week.

Some companies have pinpointed this problem by showing the percentage of potential sales realized from each account. Around a rep's home base can be drawn a circle whose radius is about the distance he can travel in one day and still get home at night. On either side of the circle's edge is an area bounded by several minutes of travel time. Within this area, actual sales are far below potential. This is the marginal area that a rep can cover and still get home at night. Beyond this marginal region, the rep is resigned to being gone overnight, so he concentrates on selling and turns in a creditable performance.

Objections to Routing

Many sales executives feel that routing reduces people's initiative and straitjackets them in an inflexible plan of territorial coverage. They believe the sales rep in the field is in the best position to decide in what order the accounts should be visited. Market conditions often are very fluid. Therefore, it would be a mistake to set up a route plan and prevent a sales person from making expedient changes to meet some situation. High-caliber representatives usually do not need to be routed, and they may resent it if a plan is forced on them.

Factors Conducive to Routing

Before deciding to route its sales force, management should consider the nature of the product and the job. If the call frequencies are regular and if the job activities are reasonably routine, planning a person's route is easier than if the visits are irregular. Sales people for drug, grocery, tobacco, or hardware wholesalers can be routed without serious difficulty. In fact, to attempt an *irregular* call pattern with a given customer can result in loss of the account. A drug retailer, for instance, plans his buying on the basis of a sales rep's call, say, every Tuesday morning. If this retailer cannot depend on the sales rep's call regularity, the buyer may seek another source of supply.

Procedure for Establishing a Routing Plan

If management has done a thorough job in designing its territories, most of the research needed to set a routing plan has been completed. The present and prospective accounts can be spotted on a map of the territory. The daily call rate has been determined, along with the desired call frequency for each account. With all this information available, the actual establishment of routes is reasonably mechanical. Some of the most commonly used route patterns are circular, straight line, cloverleaf, and hopscotch.[8] When call frequencies differ among the accounts, management may employ a skip-stop routing pattern. On one trip, the sales person may visit every account, but on the next trip he may call on only a third of the accounts—the most profitable third.

The problem of routing sales people effectively is another sales operational area that is ideal for computer application. In a given sales person's territory, management knows the number of cities, the number of accounts, and the location of these accounts. Call frequencies can be set for each account. A number of computer models have

---

[8] In a hopscotch pattern, a sales rep starts one trip at the furthest point, say north, of his home and works back toward home. Then on the next trip, he goes to the most distant point in another direction and works toward home. See Theodore H. Biggs, "Salesmen's Routing Plans," in The Conference Board, *Allocating Field Sales Resources*, Experiences in Marketing Management, No. 23 (New York, 1970), pp. 68–72.

been designed to help management determine the one route through a territory that will minimize either total travel time or travel cost.[9]

Revising Sales Territories

As companies and markets change over the years, the territorial structures may become outdated and need revision.

Problems in Territorial Design

Revising territorial boundaries is a very difficult job. It should be done infrequently, and then only after a thorough study. Before making boundary adjustments, management should be certain that the danger signals are the result of poor territorial design, and not of poor administration in other areas. The fault may lie in the compensation plan, inadequate supervision, or a poor quota system.

Indications of Need for Adjustment

Frequently, sales potential outgrows a territory, and as a result the sales person is skimming rather than intensively covering the district. When out-of-date measures of potential are used, a territory can become too large for one person to cover effectively. Also, the performance results from this district can be quite misleading. In a fast-growing region, for instance, one sales person's volume may have increased 100 percent over a four-year period—the largest increase of any rep in the firm. Management praises him highly and holds him up as the model of a good sales rep. Actually, he may have been doing a very poor job because the territorial potential increased 200 or 300 percent during that time. The company really was losing its former share of market, because the districts were not small enough to encourage thorough coverage.

On the other end of the scale, territories may need revising because they are too small. They may have been set up that way, or changing market conditions may have caused the situation.

Overlapping territories are a structural weakness that should be corrected. This problem generally stems from previous boundary revisions. To illustrate, salesman Carter originally had as his territory the three West Coast states—California, Oregon, and Washington. As the potential grew in this territory, it was divided into two districts.

---

[9] See Wade Ferguson, "A New Method for Routing Salespersons," *Industrial Marketing Management,* April 1980, pp. 171–78. This article includes several references to other computer-based routing models.

Carter kept California, and a new rep, McNeil, was assigned Washington and Oregon. However, Carter was also allowed to keep certain preferred accounts in what is now McNeil's territory. The reason given for this decision was that Carter had spent much time developing the accounts. The customers liked him, and they might switch to a competitor if Carter did not call on them. Rather than create a possibly serious morale problem with a good sales rep (Carter), management allowed the overlap to develop in the territories. By avoiding a morale problem, which probably could have been handled easily by a good administrator, the company planted the seeds for even greater morale problems later. Eventually, McNeil will chafe under the arrangement. Also, higher cost and selling inefficiencies generally result from overlapping territories.

Territorial adjustments are necessary when claim-jumping is practiced. It may be that the company has established territories with definite boundaries. However, management has tolerated having a person in one district go outside its borders and sell in another's district. On the face of it, the practice seems unsound. If each territory has an adequate potential, and one sales rep jumps another's claim, then the first one obviously is not satisfactorily developing his own area. On the other hand, let's assume that one person has done a thorough job in his own region and still has the time or need to go into the next district. Then some adjustment is needed because the first territory is too small. The increasing costs, inefficiencies, and friction among the reps that can develop when one cuts into another's region should be obvious.

Effect of Revision on Sales Force

Most people dislike change, partially because they cannot predict the consequences. Management may hesitate to make needed adjustments in territorial boundaries for fear of hurting sales-force morale. In fact, many of the territorial problems—overlapping districts, for instance—are a result of management's trying to avoid friction in the past.

Morale problems are particularly apt to arise when territories are reduced in size. The reps may suspect that management is trying to curtail their earnings. In addition, the reps are reluctant to lose accounts that they have cultivated over a period of time. It is helpful to get the sales people's suggestions during the revision process.

When management cuts a territory, it is inevitable that the rep's income (along with morale) will initially drop unless management makes some compensation adjustments. If the job of redistricting has been done properly, the reduced territory ultimately offers a better volume opportunity and the chance to cover the area more inten-

---

A day-to-day operating problem in the
Majestic Glass Company (K)

Splitting a High-Potential Territory

Majestic's Milwaukee territory was one of the smallest in area, because of the concentration in that city of a substantial segment of the brewing industry, an important user of bottles. Herman Millard, who perhaps was Majestic's best salesman, was awarded this territory after a long apprenticeship in territories with smaller potential.

Recently, increased competition for the beer container business had been felt, particularly from manufacturers of metal cans, which Majestic did not produce. To keep the brewers' business, Clyde Brion, general sales manager, believed it necessary to intensify sales efforts in Milwaukee. He wanted to maintain almost continuous contact with customers' executives at several levels of management. As a temporary measure, Mr. Brion went to Milwaukee to assist Millard, but he allowed Millard full commissions on all sales that either of them made.

Because he had other duties, Mr. Brion could not stay in Milwaukee indefinitely. He believed that his assistance to Millard was resented by Majestic sales people in other territories. Therefore he proposed to Millard that another sales person be hired and given a fraction—perhaps one third—of the Milwaukee territory.

To this proposal Millard objected strenuously, saying, "I earned my right to this territory, and now you want to take it away from me!"

Question

Should the Milwaukee territory be split? If so, how should Clyde Brion handle Herman Millard's objections?

Note: See the introduction to this series of problems in Chapter 3 for the necessary background on the company, its market, and its competition.

---

sively. Until the sales rep can fully develop the smaller territory, however, that person probably will need some compensation help during the transition period. It is a practice among many firms to make *no* adjustment whatsoever in a person's pay. Instead, management tries to sell the reps on the idea that the intensive development of their remaining territory will quickly bring their income to its former level, or higher. Understandably, it is usually quite difficult to get a rep to accept this line of reasoning.

Another procedure frequently employed is to guarantee the sales people their previous level of income during a stated adjustment period. While this approach may allay the reps' immediate fears, it may also lull them into a false sense of security. They may continue to put off the time when they must exert the necessary effort to reach their former level of sales in the new, smaller region. Then, when the guarantee period expires, they are suddenly jolted by the sharp decrease in their earnings level.

Summary

A sales territory is a number of present and potential customers located within a geographical area. This area is assigned to a sales person or to a middleman. There are several good reasons for establishing sales territories. However, formal territories may not be needed in a small company with a few sales people selling in a local market. Also, territories may not be established when a company first enters a new geographical market.

Different procedures are available for designing sales territories, and some of these approaches involve sophisticated mathematical models. Basically, however, a company's territorial structure depends on (1) the potential business in the company's market and (2) the work load required from the sales force. The plan we proposed included three broad steps.

The first step is to select a geographical control unit to serve as a territorial base. Commonly used control units are Metropolitan Statistical Areas, trading areas, states, counties, cities, and ZIP-code areas.

The next step is to analyze the work loads of the sales people. This involves considering the nature of the job and the product, the stage of market development, the competition, the intensity of market coverage, and other factors.

The third step is to determine the basic territories. This is done by considering the company's sales potential and the desirable call patterns. This step can be accomplished by using either the buildup or the breakdown method.

The *buildup* method involves forming territories by combining small geographical areas based on the control units selected. Under this method, management first determines the number, location, and size of customers. Then the desirable call patterns are set—considering both the daily call rate for the sales rep and the frequency of call for each account. The next decision is how many accounts to assign to each rep. Finally, the territorial boundary lines are drawn.

Under the *breakdown* method, we start with the total market and divide it into segments. This involves determining the company's total sales potential and the sales volume expected from each sales person. With this input, management then can set its basic territories. These areas then may have to be modified in light of individual work-load requirements.

After the sales territories have been established, management must assign individual sales people to each district. Management can then decide whether or not to formally route the sales people within their districts.

As companies and markets change over the years, the territorial structures may become outdated and need to be revised. Revising boundaries is usually a very difficult job. A key principle to follow is that management should avoid overlapping territories.

Questions and Problems

1. What companies might logically use states as control units for territorial boundaries?
2. For the following industries, in which trading area is your school located?
   a. Wholesale food.
   b. Wholesale sporting goods.
   c. Wholesale jewelry.
   d. Retail furs.
   e. Retail high-fashion women's ready-to-wear.
3. What control unit would you recommend in establishing sales territories for the following companies? Support your recommendation.
   a. Manufacturer of men's shoes.
   b. Food broker.
   c. Appliance wholesaler.
   d. Manufacturer of textile machinery.
   e. Manufacturer of outboard motors.
   f. Lumber wholesaler.
4. The text discussed several qualitative factors that may affect a territory's sales potential and thus necessitate a change in the statistically determined boundaries. How can variations in competition, or ability of the sales force, each be reflected in square miles, trading areas, or other geographical measurements of territories?
5. What are some of the signals indicating that a company's territorial structure may need revising?
6. Assume that a territory's potential has increased to the point where the district should be realigned to form two territories. Properly developed, each of the two new units should bring an income equal to what was previously earned in the one large

district. Should management assign to one of the new districts the same sales person who formerly had the combined territory? Or should the rep be transferred to an entirely different area before the division is attempted?

7. Sales people typically are prohibited from going outside their territorial boundaries in search of business. Sometimes, however, a customer located in one district will voluntarily seek out a sales rep or branch office located in another district. Perhaps this customer can realize a price advantage by buying outside his home area. What should be the position of the seller in these situations? Should it reject such business? Should it insist the order be placed in the territory where the customer is located? If the order is placed in the foreign territory, should the sales person in the customer's home territory be given any commission or other credit?

8. If a company has several branches and insists that each of its suppliers send the same sales person to all branches, what problems are involved in such a situation? What course of action do you recommend for firms that sell to the company in question?

9. In the process of redistricting, many firms do not allow a sales person to keep any of his former accounts if they are outside his new district. One hardware wholesaler realigned its territories. Then the company found that it faced the loss of some good customers, because they said they would do business only with the wholesaler's salesman who had been calling on them for years. Should the wholesaler make an exception and allow this salesman to keep these accounts outside his new district, and thus have overlapping territories? Is the loss of these good accounts the only other alternative?

10. Since it is impossible to equate territories perfectly, should the manager use them to provide promotions for good people? For example, should the best reps be given the choice areas?

11. "Routing is a managerial device for planning and controlling the activities of the sales force." Explain the function of routing in relation to each of these concepts.

12. *a.* Under what conditions is a firm most likely to establish route plans for its sales force?

   b. What type of sales job lends itself *least* to formal routing patterns for the sales force?

Case 18-1

Foster Tire Company*

Territorial Assignments for New Sales People

In the spring of 1986, Cam Dolan, midwestern regional sales manager for the Foster Tire Company, received a memorandum from the director of training at the firm's headquarters in Akron, Ohio. The memo stated that 5 of the 48 people who would complete the sales-training course in April would be allocated to the midwestern region. This was in accordance with a request for new sales representatives which Mr. Dolan had filed in December 1985. The memo also asked Mr. Dolan to designate which of his territories would be assigned to each of the five people. Then each rep could make a territory study as one of the last phases of the sales-training course. Enclosed with the memo was an information sheet on each of the five reps, prepared by the director of training. These sheets (see Exhibits 1–5) were the only source of information Mr. Dolan had about the reps. He had not interviewed them but would do so before they began work in their assigned territories.

The Foster Tire Company was a large manufacturer of high-grade tires for automobiles, trucks, aircraft, farm implements, and other vehicles. The firm had international distribution through a system of warehouse branches, company-owned retail stores, and some independent dealers. It also made direct sales to vehicle manufacturers, fleet owners, government agencies, and other large-volume buyers of tires. Other products, such as batteries and auto accessories, were purchased for resale through the Foster retail stores and dealers. However, these other products were handled by a separate sales force. Tire sales people were not directly concerned.

The sales-training course for tire sales representatives was 12 weeks long. It was conducted at the Akron headquarters by an experienced staff of marketing and sales promotion personnel. The trainers used lectures, discussions, films, factory tours, model-store training, assigned reading, and workbook exercises in the program. Management believed that the trainees were given the finest indoctrination into the tire business available anywhere in the world. Each phase of the training course included a written examination. The scores on this exam became a part of the trainee's permanent record. Trainees were housed and fed in a company dormitory during the

* Case prepared by Professor Phillip McVey, then at the University of Nebraska-Lincoln. Reproduced with permission.

```
┌─────────────────────────────────────────────────────────────────────────┐
│ Exhibit 1                                                                 │
│ Foster Tire Company, Training Department—Evaluation of Trainee            │
│ ─────────────────────────────────────────────────────────────────────    │
│ Evaluation of: TOM ANDERSON                 Date: March 14, 1986          │
│ Home address: Greenville, N.C.              Course: Tire Sales            │
│ Date of birth: 1964                         Supervisor: K. Salgren        │
│ Marital status: Single                                                    │
│ Health: Suffers occasionally from sinus trouble. Not disabling.           │
│ Previous experience: Graduated from Wofford College (bachelor's degree    │
│                      in arts and sciences). No work experience.           │
│ Employment by Foster: Recruited from college.                             │
│ Performance in training course:                                           │
│    Test scores:  1. Company information and procedures ..... 72           │
│                  2. Tire manufacture and specifications ...... 41 (failed. retake 60) │
│                  3. Tire markets .......................... 63            │
│                  4. Dealer profit planning .................. 70          │
│                  5. Techniques of promotion .............. 77             │
│                  6. Customer relations ..................... 81           │
│                  7. Reports and records ................. 70             │
│                  8. Self-management ..................... 75             │
│                  9. Territory analysis .................... to be taken   │
│                 10. Final examination .................... to be taken    │
│ Trainers' comments: Passing the course has been an uphill battle for him. Tries │
│                     hard but needs much supervision. Lacks an understanding of │
│                     the importance of objectives, either for himself or for Foster │
│                     Tire Company.                                         │
│ Trainee's assignment preference: None stated.                             │
└─────────────────────────────────────────────────────────────────────────┘
```

first 12 weeks. Their necessary travel expenditures were reimbursed, and they were paid a salary.

The company hoped that sales trainees would pursue lifetime careers within the marketing division of Foster. Management wanted them to advance upward from (1) the less-demanding sales positions (such as selling to company-owned retail stores) into (2) the higher-paid positions (such as fleet-owner sales, aircraft tire sales, auto manufacturer sales, government sales, and so on). Many of the territories contained a composite of these different types of tire business. Consequently, the training program did not attempt to produce specialized sales people for each type. However, when regional sales managers chose territories for new reps, they tried to match up (1) the types of business that were dominant in a territory with (2) the personality, past experience, test scores, and preferences of the reps.

Mr. Dolan's midwestern region comprised 10 states, including all of the East North Central states except Michigan and Ohio and all of the West North Central states. There were territories for 55 sales people in this region.

Exhibit 2

Foster Tire Company, Training Department—Evaluation of Trainee

---

Evaluation of: WILLIAM BRILL   Date: March 14, 1986

Home address: Akron, Ohio   Course: Tire Sales

Date of birth: 1946   Supervisor: K. Salgren

Marital status: Married, 4 children. Wife invalid.

Health: Fair. Has a limp resulting from polio. Cannot lift heavy weights.

Previous experience: Did not attend college. Worked in Akron machine shop before
  coming to Foster.

Employment by Foster: Transferred from Foster tire factory, where he worked for
  six years in materials estimating.

Performance in training course:

Test scores: 1. Company information and procedures ... 85
              2. Tire manufacture and specifications 98
              3. Tire markets 84
              4. Dealer profit planning 82
              5. Techniques of promotion 70
              6. Customer relations 81
              7. Reports and records .... 50 (failed. retake 69)
              8. Self-management 62
              9. Territory analysis .... to be taken
             10. Final examination .... to be taken

Trainers' comments: Very hard worker. Well-liked by other trainees, who call him
  "Uncle Bill," and seek him out for advice. On the other hand,
  he lacks emotional stability and feels the pressure of personal
  problems. Frequently stayed up all night studying training manuals and requested many extra counselling sessions.

Trainee's assignment preference: (1) Akron, Ohio area; (2) Arizona or Southwest.

Mr. Dolan's office was in Minneapolis. Each sales person resided in his or her territory and maintained contact with one of seven assistant regional sales managers, who reported to Mr. Dolan. Each sales person was responsible (1) for soliciting all available tire sales in his or her territory; (2) for planning tire promotions; (3) for helping retailers merchandise tires; and (4) for collecting and forwarding important information about market conditions in that territory. For this work the reps were paid a salary plus a small commission on all sales while traveling. They traveled in company-owned cars and were reimbursed for out-of-pocket expenses incurred.

Six territories were expected to be vacant in April 1986. Earlier Mr. Dolan had expected only five vacancies, but late in January the Foster sales rep in central Iowa had resigned suddenly, saying he wished to return to college for an MBA degree. The following information is available about each of the vacant territories:

Exhibit 3
Foster Tire Company, Training Department—Evaluation of Trainee

Evaluation of: GEORGE HAYES
Home address: Des Moines, Iowa
Date of birth: 1960

Date: March 15, 1986
Course: Tire Sales
Supervisor: M. Johns

Marital Status: Divorced. Responsible for support of child.

Health: Excellent

Previous experience: U.S. Air Force (discharged in 1985 after serving in West Germany). Had worked part-time for Foster company store in Peoria, Ill., while attending Bradley University. Completed 2 years college before military service. Science major.

Employment by Foster: See above.

Performance in training course:
  Test scores: 1. Company information and procedures 88
                 2. Tire manufacture and specifications 90
                 3. Tire markets 73
                 4. Dealer profit and planning 68
                 5. Techniques of promotion 65
                 6. Customer relations 70
                 7. Reports and records 95
                 8. Self management 91
                 9. Territory analysis .... to be taken
                10. Final examination .... to be taken

Trainers' comments: Has some weak spots. Likes routine, well-organized work in which he can be sure of himself. Pleasant personality. Eager to please.

Trainee's assignment preference: (1) Europe (England, France, West Germany)
                                 (2) Midwest U.S.

Territory 18.   Southeastern Wisconsin, including the cities of Milwaukee, Racine, and Madison. Contained a good number of heavy industry accounts, including manufacturers of trucks, tractors, and machinery, who purchased tires for use as original equipment. Trucking industry also had many firms based in this area. Hotly competitive target of all tire manufacturers.

Territory 26.   Eastern Nebraska and western Iowa, including the cities of Omaha, Council Bluffs, and Sioux City. A profitable territory for Foster, but Firestone and Goodyear were far ahead in dealerships and total sales.

Territory 55.   Southern portion of Missouri not including St. Louis. A very large, predominantly rural area in which Foster had never yet placed a resident sales person. Some good small-town independent dealers were selling Foster tires in this territory, having been signed up a few years ago by the Foster representative in St. Louis. Competing tire makers were beginning strong efforts here.

Exhibit 4

Foster Tire Company, Training Department—Evaluation of Trainee

---

Evaluation of: SALLY LEIGHTON   Date: March 15, 1986

Home address: Wichita, Kansas   Course: Tire Sales

Date of birth: 1962   Supervisor: M. Johns

Marital status: Married, no children

Health: No defects.

Previous experience: Part-time work for construction company while attending college.

Employment by Foster: Recruited at University of Kansas where she completed
MBA degree.

Performance in training course:

Test scores:
1. Company information and procedures 80
2. Tire manufacture and specifications 73
3. Tire markets 70
4. Dealer profit planning 90
5. Techniques of promotion 88
6. Customer relations 95
7. Reports and records 75
8. Self-management 81
9. Territory analysis .... to be taken
10. Final examination .... to be taken

Trainers' comments: Tends to be a "sharpie," who is very intelligent, but skips
details that appear unimportant to her. Has a mind of her own
and may have difficulty following company rules.

Trainee's assignment preference: None. Says she wants an early chance at a
management position in the company. Does not
intend to remain a sales rep very long.

Territory 10.   Kansas City, Missouri, and Kansas City, Kansas. Foster had four territories in Greater Kansas City. Within this area the territories were divided by class of customer, rather than geographically. The vacant territory consisted of all company-owned stores and independent tire dealers in the area. The person assigned here must be able to work closely with the other Kansas City sales people, one of whom was Foster's oldest and most successful representative. He was a domineering man, who considered the other sales people in the area as his assistants. He believed he could cover all four territories without their aid. A highly profitable territory.

Territory 45.   Northern Indiana not including Indianapolis. Contained a mixture of industrial, agricultural, trucking, and dealer business. The previous sales rep in this territory retires on April 30, after having represented Foster there for more than 20 years. His customers were close friends, and the accounts belonged to him more than

Exhibit 5
Foster Tire Company, Training Department—Evaluation of Trainee

Evaluation of: RICHARD SCHOFIELD

Home address: Skokie, Illinois

Date of birth: 1964

Marital status: Married, 2 small children

Health: Excellent

Previous experience: Worked as part-time sales clerk in competitor's store while attending college.

Employment by Foster: Recruited on graduation from DePaul University (bachelor's degree in business; marketing major)

Date: March 14, 1986

Course: Tire Sales

Supervisor: K. Salgren

Performance in training course:

Test scores:		
1. Company information and procedures	91	
2. Tire manufacture and specifications	90	
3. Tire markets	93	
4. Dealer profit planning	85	(score disputed)
5. Techniques of promotion	94	
6. Customer relations	90	
7. Reports and records	82	(score disputed)
8. Self-management	90	
9. Territory analysis	to be taken	
10. Final examination	to be taken	

Trainers' comments: Top student in class. Strongly disputed the only two test scores in which he did not score 90 or higher. Not well-liked by instructors or other trainees. Monopolized training sessions by talking. Missed class frequently; never appeared for counseling. May be overconfident.

Trainee's assignment preference: Chicago, Illinois (says this is his first and only choice)

to Foster. His records were sketchy and mostly in his memory. A fairly profitable territory.

Territory 20. Central Iowa. Foster's market share in this territory was well above its national average, thanks to the hard work of the young salesman who resigned in January. He had worked tirelessly to build a reputation for fast, helpful service to key dealers and industrial accounts. He was personally well-liked.

Question

What territorial assignments should Mr. Dolan make for the five trainees?

Case 18–2

Fairmont Office Systems*

Revising Sales Territories

"Tom, when you guys cut my territory twice during the past two years, I didn't like it, but I figured, okay, that's strike one. Then not long ago you tell us that we have a new pay plan that goes into effect at the beginning of next year. That still bugs me because as I read it, the new plan may mean a cut in pay for me. I figured that's strike two. Now you tell me that you may have to revise my territory. 'Revise'—that's a fancy word for 'cut.' Well, I'm here to tell you, Tom, that if you cut my territory again that will be three strikes and I'm out—out of the company, that is—I'll quit."

With that said, Teresa Dacco stormed out of Thomas Huffman's office, closing the door not too gently on her way out. Tom had figured that Terry Dacco would not be too pleased at the prospect of another cut in her territory, but he was stunned by the intensity of her reaction.

Teresa Dacco was a very successful sales person in the Fairmont Office Systems company, working out of the company's district sales office in Seattle, Washington. Tom Huffman was the district sales manager in that office. The Seattle-based sales district was one of the company's largest districts geographically.

Recently Huffman had received a strong directive from the head office to the effect that he should seriously consider adding another sales person in his district. This would mean restructuring the existing sales territories in that district. It was this possibility of another revision of territorial boundaries that had triggered Dacco's outburst.

Fairmont Office Systems was founded in the early 1970s as a manufacturer and marketer of word processors. The company was located in a small city south of San Francisco, California, in the area popularly known as Silicon Valley. The founder and current president, Lawrence Corby, was a young engineer who had a dream of ultimately developing a line of automated office systems. Like other entrepreneurs in computer-based industries, Corby had honed his managerial skills by working for the companies he now considers to be his competition. In fact, it was during this previous work experience that Corby first recognized potential in the office-automation market.

---

* Adapted from a case prepared by Marline McClay, University of Colorado student, under the supervision of Professor William J. Stanton.

Improvements in computer technology—particularly in small computers and personal computers—enabled Corby to bring the concept of a systems approach into the field of office equipment. Corby's earlier dreams had materialized sufficiently so that his company's current goal was "to be a major world-wide supplier of high-performance office automation systems" and "to make a profit while reaching that goal."

Fairmont's performance record suggested that Corby was on the right track. Sales went from $8 million in 1978 to $90 million in 1982 to $160 million in 1986. The company currently had 400 sales people operating out of 38 branch offices in the United States, plus offices in Canada and Western Europe. During the past two years alone, there had been a 30 percent increase in the number of Fairmont sales people.

Word processing—that is the concept of "computer writing"—consists of a cathode-ray tube (CRT) display screen, a keyboard (like a typewriter), and a printer. The operator types on the keyboard, views and edits from the screen, and then stores the information on a disk and/or prints out the material.

Fairmont's product line included both hardware components and software systems specifically designed to do repetitive tasks that do not require programming techniques. These tasks ranged from functions as basic as correspondence and document creation, to pre-designed software programs that enabled management to do financial modeling or to execute payroll records, accounts payable, and other complicated tasks.

The individual hardware units ranged from an entry-level stand-alone word processor to large clustered systems that supported a series of work stations with shared mass storage and printers.

These products could communicate with each other and with computers by way of software systems developed at Fairmont. A key advantage of Fairmont's product was that they could be merged into larger systems, thus minimizing the risk of obsolescence.

Like most producers of office automation systems, Fairmont purchased the majority of its parts from vendors rather than manufacturing them inhouse. Most of these vendors also sold to Fairmont's competitors. Fairmont handled its own design, testing, and assembly operations.

The hardware components in office automation systems are quite similar among major competitors. Thus, it is the software, developed by each competitor for its own system, that is a firm's major distinction in primary marketing emphasis.

Mr. Corby stated that there were hundreds of firms competing in one or more aspects of the automated office systems market. He estimated, however, that two large firms—IBM and Wang—accounted for about two thirds of the sales in this market. Other major competitors facing Fairmont were Lanier, NBI, and Xerox. All of Fairmont's major competitors were well-established firms, having moved into word-processing equipment as a natural extension of their experience in data-processing equipment.

From its inception, however, the Fairmont company had concentrated on the word-processing market. Mr. Corby intentionally had stayed away from data-processing equipment, and a broad assortment of products ranging from electronic typewriters to main-frame computers. Instead, he had positioned his firm as a specialist in what he called the "middle range of computer-based office products." "We are not trying to be all things to all office people," he said. "We simply want to be the best in automated word-processing systems."

Mr. Corby was well aware of how rapidly situations could, and did, change in his industry. He had seen companies have a string of successful years and then two years later go out of business. He was enough of a realist to know that Fairmont's specialist position and rapid growth rate would not go unchallenged by competitors. Technological advances, new companies, and product-line extensions in existing firms threatened to erode Fairmont's market position. During the past couple of years, for example, he noted a significant increase in aggressive marketing effort by firms whose previous marketing activity had been relatively limited.

"To maintain our position, we must be constantly vigilant," Corby asserted in an executive committee meeting. "This means we must maintain our technological superiority and back it up strongly with a competitive pricing strategy and an aggressive, professional marketing effort."

The one thing that Mr. Corby knew he had going for him was the virtually unlimited market potential for word-processing systems. Almost every organization—business or nonbusiness, large or small—that had an office operation was a potential customer. Corby projected an industry growth rate of 30 percent a year for the next several years.

Users were also in the market continually. They tended to buy the newest technological developments, with the associated software, to replace older equipment. First-time buyers tended to upgrade their equipment and also to buy peripheral equipment. Consequently, market penetration had two aspects—new-account aquisition and current-account maintenance.

Corby was not satisfied with simply maintaining Fairmont's market share and letting an expanding market account for the annual increase in his company's sales. Instead, he placed a high priority on increasing Fairmont's market share. But during the past six months sales slacked off. This was largely because of a backlog of orders for some newly-developed systems that were not yet ready for delivery. Furthermore, for the first time in the company's history, management was projecting a net loss for the coming three-month period.

To stimulate sales, and especially to generate new customers in order to increase Fairmont's market share, management decided to revise its sales compensation plan. Previously sales reps had been paid a fixed amount for every word-processor work station that the rep sold. In addition, the sales people also were paid a straight commission on their sales of software, printers, and other peripherals. The reps had made good money under the previous plan. However, that plan encouraged the sales people to call on established accounts to sell them more peripheral equipment and supplies. In effect, the reps were not sufficiently stimulated to generate new business.

The new pay plan, to go into effect in three months, was designed to curtail some of this repetition and at the same time encourage more new-account selling. Management significantly raised the rate of pay for selling word-processing hardware, hoping that more total automated office systems would be set up. At the same time, management eliminated the commission on 6 out of 10 of the company's peripheral packages, and reduced the commission rate on the other four packages.

Mr. Corby was pretty sure that the reps, at least initially, would not like the new pay plan. He left it up to the district sales managers to explain the new plan to the reps and to promote the long-term advantages of the plan.

Tom Huffman did not look forward to explaining the new plan to his sales people. He was right—they were not pleased. However, he was encouraged that no one threatened to leave the company.

Huffman had been in his current position as district sales manager for three years. Previously he had been a very successful sales rep for the company in the midwest. In fact, Tom took a cut in pay when he was promoted to district manager. He liked his job. He had established good working relationships with his 12 sales people, half of whom were women.

Shortly after explaining the new pay plan to his people, Tom Huffman got a strongly worded directive from the home office. The message stated that he should seriously consider adding another sales person in the Seattle district and again revise (reduce) the territories of some of the present sales people. This situation was not new to Huffman. He had received a similar directive each year since he became district manager. The Seattle district had experienced the same rapid growth as was the case generally throughout the company. In fact, during Huffman's three years the districts sales force had grown from 3 to 12 people.

Tom held another meeting with his sales force to discuss the new directive. It was after this meeting that Teresa Dacco marched into

Tom's office and initiated the confrontation described at the start of this case.

Terry Dacco was the top sales rep in the Seattle district, and one of the top 10 in the entire company. Last year her sales were about $1.3 million, on which she earned commissions of just over $100,000. Now 30 years of age, she had joined Fairmont three years ago as one of the first reps in the Seattle district. Previously she had worked three years as a sales person for IBM.

Originally Dacco's territory had consisted of the entire central business district in Seattle, plus an area on the fringe of that central section. Twice since then her territory had been reduced in size. Under the currently proposed realignment, her new territory would consist of an area within a three-block radius in the core of downtown Seattle. This would be a reduction from her present 10-block territory.

The increase in numbers of territories and sales people, with corresponding reductions in the size of existing territories, reflected the growing market for Fairmont's products. Management maintained that with each reduction in territorial size, the potential sales volume would be approximately the same, and indeed Dacco's commissions seemed to substantiate this claim. Consequently, Huffman had hoped that Dacco would accept the proposed reduction, although perhaps grudgingly, as she had done before.

But such was not to be Huffman's good fortune. Dacco said that a cut in her territory would be the last straw, especially coming on the heels of the new unpopular compensation plan. She made it clear that any further reduction in the size of her territory would mean her resignation.

Tom Huffman liked to think that he treated all his reps equally. His relationship as Dacco's manager had not been so easy to establish. He felt that she was a tough person to deal with at times.

At the same time, Huffman recognized that her "aggressively persistent style," as he put it, seemed to work very well for her when selling. In fact, Fairmont's head office recognized her success and several times offered her a promotion into management. Each time she had turned down the offer because she wanted to stay in sales.

Huffman certainly did not want Dacco to leave the company. Consequently he was considering some alternatives, looking for one that he thought Dacco might accept. In this respect, he realized that his options were limited.

As a district manager, it was within his authority to recommend that this was not the time to add a new sales person—the factor leading to a reduction in Dacco's territory. He had not previously ever rejected a head-office recommendation to add a new rep in his district. If he did not follow the current directive, he wondered what the implications might be for him as a manager.

He also considered offering Dacco a management position. There were several possibilities in this option—a position as district sales manager in another district, a marketing-related management position in the home office, or something in product management. He thought perhaps he could get her to look ahead to the day when she would not want to continue selling.

He thought about asking her to help him redesign the territories—hoping that she might be more amenable to the change if she took part in formulating it. He also considered offering her the choice of three to six key accounts that she could keep, even though they soon would be located in somebody else's territory.

As Tom Huffman gazed out his office window overlooking Puget Sound, he wondered how to handle the territorial redesign situation and still keep Terry and the home office happy. He wondered if there might still be a better alternative that he had not yet thought of. In any event, he knew he had to make a decision and make it soon.

Question

How should Thomas Huffman deal with Teresa Dacco and the problem of redesigning her territory?

19

Sales Quotas

You cannot put the same shoe on every foot.
SYRUS

Up to this point in our sales-planning activities, we have prepared a sales forecast and a sales budget. We also have established the sales territories. Now it is time to translate the results of these planning activities into work assignments in the form of sales quotas for our sales force or other marketing units.

Nature of Sales Quotas

A **sales quota** is a performance goal assigned to a marketing unit for a specific period of time. The marketing unit may be a sales person, a branch office, a district or region, or a dealer or distributor.

For example, each sales rep in a firm might be assigned a sales-volume goal or a gross-margin goal for the coming three-month period. This quota-goal may be stated in dollars, product units, or selling activities, depending on the type of quota. The specified time period usually is a month, a quarter, six months, or a year. A marketing unit's quotas also may be established for individual products and/or types of customers.

Relation to Sales Potential and Sales Forecast

A sales quota—especially a *sales volume* quota—is related to a company's sales potential and sales forecast. The sales potential influences the sales forecast, and the forecast helps to shape the

533

quotas. However, a sales quota is *not* the same as *either* of these planning tools. Recall from Chapter 16 that a sales potential is the share of total industry sales that a company expects to sell. But often certain territorial conditions or the characteristics of the sales rep— experience, physical condition, etc.—are such that a particular territory cannot reach its full sales potential. Consequently, in that territory the sales-volume quota may very well be *less* than the district's sales potential.

The sales forecast for a territory—what the company actually expects to sell under a given marketing plan—often is a little less than the sales quota. This is because management wants to give the sales people a psychological incentive by setting the sales quotas slightly above the forecast sales figures.

Sales Quotas and a Sales Manager's Publics

Sales quotas can have a considerable effect on a sales manager's relationship with several of his or her publics—especially the sales reps, customers, and higher management. Quotas are performance standards assigned to sales reps. Consequently, quotas can have a big impact on a sales person's morale. Sales executives manage their sales people, at least in part, through the use of quotas. Sales reps often view quotas as a menace or threat to their well-being. Because of these behavioral considerations, it is important that management do the best job possible when setting quotas.

Sales managers can also improve customer relations with carefully and accurately established quotas. Quotas that are too high can cause sales reps to high pressure and overload the customers. Finally, when sales quotas are properly set and achieved by the sales force, the sales manager looks good in the eyes of upper-level executives.

Sales Quotas and Strategic Management

Sales quotas help in planning and evaluating sales-force activities. When setting sales quotas, the sales managers should consider the goals and strategies developed in the marketing planning. If the marketing goal is to increase market share, then a sales *volume* quota may be appropriate. However, if the goal is to increase a company's return on investment or net profit as a percentage of sales, then a sales *volume* quota probably is *not* appropriate. Instead, some form of quota based on gross margin, or even an expense quota, is more in line with a profit-oriented goal.

Accurately established sales quotas can guide the sales reps' activities and boost their morale. Thus good sales quotas can help effectively implement the strategic plans. Finally, sales quotas are a widely used basis for evaluating sales-force performance. Sales people who meet their quota are judged to be performing adequately in the activity the quota concerns.

Purposes of Sales Quotas

To indicate strong or weak spots in the selling structure. When accurate quotas are established for each territory, management can determine the extent of territorial development by whether or not the quota is being reached. If the actual sales are under the quota, management is immediately warned that something may be amiss in that district. By the same token, if the sales total significantly exceeds the predetermined standards, management should also analyze the reasons for this type of variance. Failure to meet a quota tells management that something has gone wrong. Of course, it does not tell *why* the failure occurred. It may be that competition is stronger than expected, the sales people have not done a good selling job, or the potential was overestimated. Any one of a legion of factors may account for failure to reach a quota.

To furnish a goal and incentive for the sales force. In business, as in any other walk of life, individuals usually perform better if their activities are guided by standards and goals. It is not enough to say to a sales person, "We expect you to do a good selling job." It is much more meaningful to express this expectation in the concrete form of a quota, consisting of a given dollar sales volume or number of new accounts to be acquired during the next month. Without a standard of measurement, a football team cannot tell whether it made a first down, golfers cannot tell whether they shot par, and sales reps cannot be certain their performance is satisfactory.

To control sales people's activities. A corollary to the preceding point is that quotas enable management to direct the activities of the sales force more effectively than would otherwise be possible. Through the use of the appropriate type of quota, executives can encourage a given activity such as selling high-margin items or getting orders from new customers. The sales reps are not in a position to know which area of activity should be stressed unless management informs them. Left to their own devices, they may do a fine job, but in some area that does not interest management.

To evaluate productivity of sales people. Quotas provide management with a yardstick for measuring the general effectiveness of sales representatives. By comparing a rep's actual results with his quota, management can evaluate that person's performance. Quota performance also provides guidance for field supervisors by indicating areas of activity where the sales force needs help. Decisions on whether to give sales people promotions or raises in salary are often based in large part on their performance in relation to their quota.

To improve effectiveness of compensation plans.   A quota structure can play a significant role in a sales-compensation system. Quotas can be used to furnish incentives to sales people who are paid on a straight salary. A sales rep knows, too, that a creditable performance in meeting assigned quotas will reflect favorably on him or her when it is time for a salary review. Quotas also are fundamental to many plans involving commission payments. For instance, a company may pay a salary plus a commission after a sales quota is reached.

Inequities in territorial potential may cause inequities in compensation unless a firm establishes a quota system. In one territory, a person may get a $1,500 monthly salary plus a 5 percent commission on sales over a quota of $10,000. In a district that presents a small potential and a more difficult selling job, the sales rep may have the same arrangement, except that the commission starts when the rep reaches a quota of only $7,000 each month.

To control selling expense.   Management can often stimulate expense control by the use of expense quotas alone, without tying them to the compensation plan. Some companies gear payments for the sales people's expenses to a quota. For instance, a business may pay all the expenses of a sales rep up to 8 percent of sales. Other companies may set an expense quota and let the sales people know their effectiveness is being judged in part by how well they meet it.

To evaluate sales contest results.   Sales quotas are used frequently in conjunction with sales contests. Sales people rarely have equal opportunities in a contest unless management makes some adjustment to compensate for variation in territorial potentials and work loads. By employing the common denominator of a quota, management can assure each participant a reasonably equal chance of winning, provided the quota has been set accurately.

Types of Quotas

The most frequently used types of sales quotas are those based on:

1. Sales volume.
2. Gross margin or net profit.
3. Expenses.
4. Activities.
5. Some combination of these four.

The type of quota that management selects depends on several considerations, including the nature of the product and the market. Let's assume a company wants to correct an unbalanced inventory situation, for instance. Then a volume quota set by product lines may be used to move the surplus stocks of the given items. A firm that sells to a few large accounts can set a volume quota *for each customer* more easily than an organization that sells to many outlets. If management wants to develop a new territory, it should probably set an activity quota in preference to a volume or expense quota. See Figure 19–1.

Sales Volume Quotas

Undoubtedly the most widely used type of sales quota is one based on sales volume. A volume quota may be established for a geographical area, a product line, a customer, a time period, or for any combination of these bases. If management uses a volume quota, the smaller the marketing unit for which the goal is set, the more effective the quota is as a tool for managerial control. Instead of setting a quota for an entire region, it is better to have one for each territory. Ordinarily, it is more effective to set a monthly or quarterly quota than an annual one.

Management uses volume goals because they are simple to understand and easy to calculate. Many sales managers are still volume conscious. They regard sales people's sales volume as the only real measure of their worth to the company. However, sales volume alone does not tell the full story of a rep's productivity and effectiveness. It does not indicate the profit generated by the person's efforts. Nor does it measure the extent to which the rep has done a fully balanced sales job. In fact, volume quotas discourage balanced activities by the sales force because they stress volume to the detriment of nonselling activities.

Figure 19–1
Types of Sales Quotas

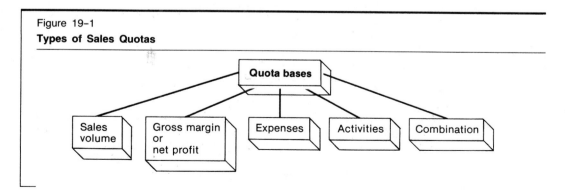

When using volume quotas, management must decide whether to express them in dollars or units of product sold. The dollar base is probably the more frequently used of the two. It is particularly good if the firm sells a wide variety of items, as does a wholesale hardware or drug company. Using dollars as the base also enables management to relate volume quotas to other measures, such as expenses or compensation, by means of ratios.

If a product line consists of relatively few items that carry high unit prices, a quota may be expressed in units. Even when a company sells a large number of products, it may be feasible to group them into a few broad lines and then set unit quotas for each line. For example, an appliance wholesaler may set unit goals for small appliances in one group, white goods (refrigerators, ranges, washers) as a second group, and electronic products (radio, television) as a third line.

Profit Quotas

Many companies set quotas based on gross margin or net profit. These goals may be established on many of the same bases as a volume quota. For instance, a gross margin quota may be set for a sales person, a branch, or a group of products. The preference some companies show for profit instead of volume quotas reflects management's recognition of the importance of profit as compared with volume.

High-volume operators are not necessarily the best sales reps for company interests. Easy-to-sell items may be low-margin items. Unless the firm controls these reps, they may decrease company profits every time they increase their volume. They are emphasizing the sales of profitless items or sales to profitless customers.

Note, however, that a volume quota may work essentially toward the same end as a gross margin quota. This happens when management properly sets a volume quota for each product line to encourage the sales of high-margin items and give little credit for low-margin goods.

One significant drawback to gross margin or net profit quotas is the possibility that friction may arise between management and the reps. The sales-force members may not (1) understand the derivation of their quotas or (2) be able to compute their progress. Another limitation— particularly of a net profit quota—is that the goal is based on factors over which the sales representatives do not have complete control. A compromise approach is to base the quota on a sales rep's contribution to profit. Contribution to profit (or contribution margin) is the amount left after deducting a sales person's direct expenses (the ones he has control over) from his gross margin. The remainder is the amount the rep is contributing to cover the overhead (fixed) costs.

Expense Quotas

Some companies attempt to encourage a profit consciousness by establishing a quota based on the rep's travel and other expenses. Often, the expense quota is related to sales volume or to the compensation plan. A sales representative may be given an expense quota equal to 4 percent of his sales. That is, his direct expenses, such as travel, entertainment, food, and lodging, must not exceed 4 percent of his net sales volume. In another example, a person may get a $500 bonus if his monthly expenses drop to a given level.

Granted, expense quotas probably encourage a sales person to be more aware of costs and profits than do volume goals. Nevertheless, it seems that an expense quota is a negative approach to the problem. A rep's attention is devoted to cutting expenses rather than to boosting the sales of profitable products.

Activity Quotas

One way to decrease the overemphasis on sales volume is to establish a quota based on activities. Management may select from such tasks as (1) daily calls, (2) new customers called on, (3) orders from new accounts, (4) product demonstrations made, and (5) displays built. An activity quota properly established and controlled can do much toward stimulating a fully balanced sales job. This type of quota is particularly valuable for use with missionary sales people. Probably the principal difficulties in administering an activity quota are, first, to determine whether the activity actually was performed and, second, to find out how effectively it was done.

Combination Quotas

Companies that are not satisfied with any single type of quota may combine two or more types. As an example, a firm may want to establish a quota based on three activities, plus gross margin in one product line and sales volume in another. The results for one rep may come out as follows for the January–March quarter:

	Quota	Actual	Percent of Quota Attained
Sales volume, product line A	$20,000	$22,000	110
Gross margin, product line B	$30,000	$25,000	83
Product demonstrations made	120	135	117
Orders from new accounts	15	17	113
Window displays obtained	20	19	95
		Average =	103.6%

The sales person in this example reached a little over 103 percent of her combined quota. The five components were weighted equally, but management may want to assign more value to some elements than others.

A combination quota is an attempt to use the strong points of several individual types of quotas, but frequently such a plan is limited by its complexity. Moreover, a sales rep may overemphasize one element in the quota plan. In this illustration, for example, the rep may reach 200 percent of the quota for product demonstrations and do virtually nothing to secure orders from new accounts.

Procedure for Setting a Sales Volume Quota

The sales-volume quota is selected to illustrate the quota-setting procedures because it is the most commonly used type. However, the same procedure can be used for the other types. Fundamentally, three general approaches may be used to set volume quotas:

1. Quotas are set in conjunction with the determination of territorial potentials.
2. Quotas are set in relation to the company's sales forecast or market potential estimate for the total market. Territorial estimates have not been prepared.
3. Quotas are set independently of any consideration of sales or market potentials.

Once again we are dealing with a topic—quota setting—that lends itself to the use of computer technology. In the past, companies often steered clear of quotas based on gross margin or net profit. One big reason for this was the heavy clerical and administrative costs involved in establishing these types of quotas. With computers, these problems no longer exist. Computerized quota settings, based on computerized sales forecasting, enable a company to set fair and equitable quotas to a degree that was not possible in the precomputer era.[1]

When Territorial Potentials Have Been Determined

Quotas related directly to potentials. One common practice in quota setting is to relate quotas directly to the territorial sales potentials. These potentials are the share of the estimated total industry

---

[1] See, for example, "Haworth Pegs Quotas to Local Markets," *Sales & Marketing Management*, December 9, 1985, p. 68.

sales that the company expects to realize in a given territory. The companywide sales forecast for many firms is often built by piecing together estimates calculated for each territory. In the course of computing territorial forecasts, management considers several factors, such as past sales, competition, and changing market conditions. It also takes into consideration any projected changes in pricing, product policies, or promotional policies.

Thus if the territorial sales potentials or forecasts have already been determined, and the quotas are to be related to these measures, the job of quota setting is largely completed. For instance, let's assume that the sales potential in territory A is $300,000, or 4 percent of the total company potential. Then management may assign this amount as a quota for the sales person who covers that territory. The total of all territorial quotas then would equal the company sales potential. The general reasoning in support of this practice is that the territorial potentials were accurately determined.

Reasons for adjusting potential-based quotas. Companies frequently prefer to use the estimate of territorial potentials only as a starting point to determine the volume quota. These figures are then adjusted in order to arrive at a quota for the person who covers the territory.

Human factors. Several of the reasons for adjusting territorial potentials are based on the human factor in quota setting. In one instance, a quota may have to be adjusted downward from the potential figure because an older salesman is covering the district. He may have been with the company for years and have done a fine job. But as he approaches retirement age, his physical limitations prevent him from performing as he once did. Obviously, it is not good human relations to discharge him. Nor will it help his morale to give him a quota that is impossible for him to reach, however realistic it may be in relation to sales potential. In part, the problem may be solved by reducing the size of his territory and then equating his quota to the potential in the curtailed area.

Another territory may be covered by a weak sales person. In one case, the regional potential was $600,000 in a year, but the sales were only $400,000. This had been the pattern for the previous several years. Executives had studied the problem and were convinced that failure to meet the quota was due to the sales person's poor performance and no other reason. However, management ordinarily should not try to remove a large deficit in one quota period. In fact, it may take two or more quota periods for weak producers to reach the point where their quota can be set at the territorial potential.

A situation requiring careful handling occurs when management has not used up-to-date figures for its sales potential. The goal may have been set at $400,000 for several years, for example, because five years previously a study indicated this was a reasonable estimate of potential. Since then, the potential has grown, until today it is $700,000. Management finally updates the figures, and realizes the sales person's quota should be increased 75 percent to make it accurate. Management may have a morale problem if the new quota is set at $700,000. It may be better to use two or three quota periods to raise the goal to the desired level. From then on, management should keep its estimates of potential up to date so the problem does not recur.

Psychological factors. Management understands that it is human nature to relax after a goal has been reached. Therefore, some sales executives set their quotas a little higher than the expected potential just in case some reps can do better than expected. Other managers set all quotas a shade above potential as a precautionary measure. As an illustration, assume that the quotas are equal to potentials. One person may have reached only 90 percent of his goal, while another sold 102 percent—an average of 96 percent between them. The second person did what was required, and had no adequate incentive to strain further. However, if all quotas had been set at 110 percent of potential, the first person still would have attained only 90 percent, but the other might have hit 110 percent or more. The average then would have been at least the desired 100 percent.

Management must not set the goal unrealistically high. A quota that is too far above potential can discourage the sales force. They soon will see that it is unattainable, and their morale and sales performance may suffer. The ideal psychological quota is a bit above the potential but can still be met and even exceeded by working effectively.

Compensation. Some companies relate their quotas basically to the sales potential, but adjust them to allow for the compensation plan. In such a case the company is really using both the quota and the compensation systems to stimulate the sales force. As an example, one organization may set its quotas at 90 percent of potential. It pays one bonus if the quota is met. It pays an additional bonus if the sales reach 100 percent of the quota, at which point the sales would approximate the potential.

When Only Total Market Estimates Are Available

Some companies prepare a total sales forecast for their entire market. Or they estimate the market and sales potential for the market as a whole. In either case, no territorial breakdown is available. If these firms want to set volume quotas for sales people or branches, the first step is to estimate the sales that can reasonably be expected in each territory. For instance, the total sales forecast may be allocated among districts in the same proportion as past territorial sales were to total sales in the company. Or the territorial divisions of market potentials (industrywide sales) may be adopted by the individual company. However, usually the best method for apportioning the total sales estimate among territories is to employ some market index that is related to sales of the company's product.

Once the territorial potentials are established, the procedure for quota setting follows a pattern similar to the one discussed in the preceding section. The same qualitative factors that influence a company to adjust a quota based on territorial potentials are present in this case.

When Potentials Are Not Directly Considered

A company that does not wish to set its sales quotas in relation to territorial potentials has these alternatives:

- Quotas may be set strictly on the basis of past sales.
- Quotas may be determined by executive judgment alone.
- Quotas may be related to the compensation plan.
- The sales people may set their own quotas.

Past sales alone.   In some organizations, the byword is "Beat last year's figures." As a result, sales volume quotas are based strictly on the preceding year's sales or on an average of sales over a period of several years. Management sets each sales person's quota at an arbitrary percentage increase over sales in some past period. About the only merits in this method of quota setting are simplicity of computation and low cost of administration. If a firm follows this procedure, it should at least use as a base an average sales figure for the past several years, not just the previous year's sales.

However, a quota-setting method based on past performance *alone* is subject to severe limitations. This method ignores possible changes in a territory's sales potential. General business conditions this year may be depressed in a district, thus cutting the sales potential. Or new potential customers may have moved into the district, thus boosting the potential volume.

Basing quotas on previous year's sales may not uncover poor performance in a given territory. A person may have had sales of $100,000 last year, and his quota is increased 5 percent for this year. He may even reach the goal of $105,000. However, the potential in the district may be $200,000. The representative may perform poorly for years without management recognizing that a problem exists. Quotas set on past sales also ignore the percentage of sales potential already achieved. Assume the sales potential in each of two territories is $200,000, and one person's volume was $150,000 last year while the other's was $210,000. It is not realistic to expect each to increase his sales the same percentage over last year's figures.

Executive judgment. In setting quotas for sales reps, some companies rely entirely on what they refer to as executive judgment, but is more precisely called guesswork. Executive judgment is usually an indispensable ingredient in a sound procedure for setting quotas, but to use it *alone* is certainly not recommended. Even though the administrator may be very experienced, too many risks are involved in relying solely on this factor without heed to quantitative market measures.

Quotas related to compensation. Earlier in this chapter we discussed the idea of relating compensation to volume quotas based on potential. Quotas may also be used in compensation plans but without any relation to potential. As a case in point, a company may prefer to pay its sales representatives by straight commission. However, management realizes that the reps prefer a salary-plus-commission plan. Therefore, the company adopts a combination plan, with a salary of $1,200 per month and a commission of 6 percent on all sales over $20,000 a month. By using the quota, management in effect achieves its preference for a straight commission, because no commission is paid until the salary is recouped (6 percent of $20,000 equals $1,200).

Sales people set own quotas. Some companies place the quota problem in the laps of the sales representatives by letting them set their own performance goals. The rationale for this move is that the sales people are closer to their territories than management is and thus can do a better job. Also, setting their own quotas allows the reps to reflect their individual abilities. Finally, if sales reps make the decisions about their own goals, they will have higher morale and strive more to attain the quota.

From a practical standpoint, however, this method leaves much to be desired. Sales people do not have access to the necessary information. Also sales people often tend to be optimistic about their capabilities and the opportunities in their districts. Therefore, they may set unrealistically high quotas. Then as the period goes on and it becomes evident that they cannot reach the goal, a serious morale problem may develop.

Administration of Sales Quotas

Usually the sales department is responsible for establishing the sales quota, and no approval of a higher executive is needed. Within the sales organization, the task may rest with any of several executives. The chief sales executive may be responsible for setting the total company quota. But the individual breakdown may be delegated down through the regional and district managers. Or territorial sales potentials may be given to the district managers, and they set the sales people's quotas.

Characteristics of a Good Quota Plan

Several characteristics of a well-designed quota structure have been alluded to earlier in the chapter. Many are the same attributes found in good compensation plans, territorial designs, and other aspects of sales management.

Realistic attainability. If a quota is to spur the sales force to the efforts management wants, the goal must be realistically attainable. If it is too far out of reach, the sales people will lose their incentive as soon as they realize the cause is hopeless.

Objective accuracy. Regardless of what type of quota management uses, it should be related to potentials. Executive judgment is also required, but it should not be the sole factor in the decision. If the sales force is to have faith in the performance goal, they must be convinced it was set impartially and was based on market research.

Ease of understanding and administering. A quota must be easy for both management and the sales force to understand. A complex plan probably will make the sales force resentful and suspicious. Also, from management's point of view, the system should be economical to administer.

Flexibility. All quota systems need adequate flexibility. Particularly if the quota period is as long as a year, management may have to make adjustments because of changes in market conditions. At the same time, management should avoid unlimited flexibility, since this may result in confusion and destroy the ease with which the system is understood.

Fairness. A good quota plan is fair to the people involved. The work load imposed by quotas should be the same for all sales reps. However, this does not mean that quotas must be equal for all people. Differences in potential, competition, and sales representatives' abilities do exist.

Typical Administrative Weaknesses

Companies that do not use sales quotas may justify their position by citing various limitations in a sales-quota system. Generally speaking, however, these are not limitations that are *inherent* in the system. Instead they are *administrative* weaknesses that reflect management's failure to put into practice the characteristics of a good quota plan.

Probably the major criticism against quotas is that it is difficult or even impossible to set them accurately. This point may be justified in some cases. Perhaps a company is selling a new type of product for which very little marketing information is available. Or a firm is selling a product that requires several quota periods to elapse before the sale is consummated. However, just because a company cannot set a goal that is 100 percent statistically correct is no reason for management to abandon the entire project. The company may have an expense control system, a compensation plan, and a territorial structure—all founded on something less than perfection. The executives cannot say they will have no compensation plan because they cannot establish one that is entirely accurate.

In other instances quotas are not used because management claims they lead to high-pressure selling and generally emphasize some activities at the expense of others. These criticisms may well be justified if a sales volume quota is used alone. Or the compensation and quota plans may be linked to encourage a high volume of sales, irrespective of the gross margin. A quota also may overstress a given selling or nonselling activity. However, these are indications of planning or operating weaknesses. They are not inherent disadvantages of quotas.

Obtaining the Sales Force's Acceptance of a Quota Plan

A final essential ingredient in a well-planned and well-operated quota system is its wholehearted acceptance by the sales force. Sales people often are suspicious of quotas, either because the purposes are not apparent or because there are questions about the factors underlying the plan. They must be convinced that the quota is intelligently computed and that it possesses the attributes of a good quota plan. The purposes of the quota should be explained to the sales force. The bases on which the quota are set and the methods used in the process can also be discussed. When the final product is ready for formal installation, the sales force will probably be more inclined to accept it if they have had a hand in its development. Management also stands to gain by soliciting ideas from sales people because they may introduce considerations that escaped management's notice.

Sales reps should be kept informed about their progress toward meeting the performance goal. Conferences and correspondence with the reps often are necessary. The sales force also needs some incentive to reach the goal. This may come from a bonus for achieving the quota or from some other direct link with the compensation plan.

Management can make it clear that quota performance is reflected in periodic merit rating, salary review, or considerations for promotion.

Summary

A sales quota is a sales-performance goal. It is assigned to a marketing unit—a sales person, branch, middleman, or customer. Sales quotas aid in the planning, control, and evaluation of sales activities. More specifically, sales quotas serve such purposes as (1) indicating strong and weak spots in a company's selling structure; (2) furnishing a goal and an incentive for the sales force; (3) improving the effectiveness of compensation plans; (4) controlling selling expenses; and 5) evaluating sales contest results.

Sales volume (in dollars and in product units) is the most frequently used basis for setting sales quotas. Other commonly used bases are gross margin or net profit, selling expenses, selling activities, or some combination of these elements.

Basically, three general approaches may be used to set sales volume quotas. In the first situation, quotas are set after territorial potentials have been determined. In some cases here, the quotas are related directly to the territorial sales potentials. In other instances, management starts with the potential-based quotas and then adjusts them in light of human factors.

In the second general approach, the quotas are set in relation to a company's total sales forecast or an estimate of the market potential in the total market. That is, territorial potentials have not been determined or are not used.

In the third general situation, quotas are set independently of any consideration of sales or market potentials. For example, the quota may be based strictly on past sales. Or they may be determined by executive judgment alone. In some firms, the sales people set their own quotas.

Management should recognize the characteristics of a good quota plan. Management also should realize that some of the limitations often attributed to quota plans are not *inherent* weaknesses in quotas. Instead, they are *administrative* weaknesses that reflect management's inability to set up a good quota plan.

Questions and Problems

1. What types of quotas do you recommend for the sales job described in Figure 4–3?
2. Is it necessary to establish territories before setting quotas? Can

sales quotas be set without a sales forecast, sales budget, or determination of territorial sales potentials?

3. Cite some specific instances when management may have good reasons for not using sales quotas. What are the reasons in each case?

4. What factors influence the type of quota used?

5. Should branch managers be assigned a quota? If so, what type should be used? Answer the same two questions for a sales supervisor.

6. "The use of quotas, or need for them, is an indication of an administrative weakness in some other area of sales-force management. For instance, if the firm had a well-designed compensation plan which offered adequate incentive to the sales force, there would be no need for quotas." Comment on this opinion.

7. "The higher the caliber of a sales force, the less there is a need for a quota system." Do you agree?

8. Should quotas be used in each of the following cases? If so, what type do you recommend, and what should be the length of the quota period?

    a. Missionary or promotional sales rep for a manufacturer of candy bars.

    b. Sales person selling computers.

    c. Sales person for manufacturer of industrial central heating and air-conditioning units.

    d. Sales person for manufacturer of room air-conditioners for home or industry.

    e. In-home selling of cosmetics.

9. When establishing volume quotas for the sales force, many executives believe in setting the individual goals so that they total something *more* than the company's sales forecast. That is, they add an extra amount for psychological purposes. Yet, when these same executives prepare various budgets, they often tend to be conservative. They base their estimates on a total sales volume that is somewhat *less* than the firm's sales forecast. How do you account for this apparent inconsistency in executive reasoning?

10. A luggage manufacturer uses volume quotas for its sales force.

    a. What effective measures may this firm take to encourage its sales people to do nonselling tasks such as prospecting for new accounts or setting up dealer displays?

    b. How can the customers be protected against overstocking, high-pressure selling, and other similar activities by this manufacturer's sales force?

11. Should quotas be tied in with the compensation plan?

12. One wearing-apparel manufacturer established volume quotas for its sales representatives. The 1986 quota was 20 percent

higher than in 1985. The sales force seemed perfectly happy with the new quota and generally was meeting it. Reps were paid a straight 5 percent commission on net sales. Under what conditions would this type of quota work?

Case 19–1

Some Quota Incidents

Incident 1

John Wolf, sales manager for Staar Surgical, was building his sales force by recruiting experienced sales reps from competing firms. These reps were paid a 15 percent straight commission on sales volume, from which they paid their own expenses. Twenty-six reps had been attracted into the fold, even though the company had yet to receive full Food and Drug Administration (FDA) clearance on its key innovations. However, the company did develop "me too" products to sell. Consequently, the company could operate at a cash break-even point until the FDA clinical investigations were completed and accepted.

The company forecast sales of $15 million for 1986. The sales potential of the various territories varied tremendously. Florida was the prime territory because the major market factor that determined the number of cataract operations was the number of elderly people in an area.

John wanted to set sales quotas for the new reps, but he was uncertain how to go about it. One group of reps wanted to divide up the $15 million evenly. Reps who exceeded their quotas would get a bonus. However, the reps in the poor territories objected, "We would be shut off from the bonuses. Let's negotiate a fair quota for each rep."

One of John's co-workers asked, "Where is it written that we must have sales quotas? Forget them, John! You don't have anything to base them on."

Question

What would you suggest?

Incident 2:

"I've had it! That's enough! No more! I won't bust my back for that ridiculous quota you just gave me. You know it can't be done. The farm belt is dead. We're in big trouble out there and you eastern bozos don't want to see it. If you won't get real, I'll move on. I just don't want to go through another year like '85."

The complainer: Joe Morgan, sales rep in Iowa for a furniture manufacturer.

The audience: Hal Beckett, sales manager for the High Point Furniture Company.

The complaint: Joe had not been able to meet his sales quota for three years. This had reduced his total earnings significantly. A 20 percent bonus was paid to all reps who achieved their sales quota.

Facts: Sales quotas were set by dividing the company's sales forecast by the percentage of the nation's population residing in the rep's territory. Joe had been with the company for 20 years and had been regarded as a good sales person.

Question

How would you answer Joe?

Incident 3:

"The reps should be given some reward for meeting their quotas. Now we give them nothing but a pat on the back and a larger quota for the next year. So why should they work hard to make quota?" asked a district manager of his boss.

"I can think of two immediate reasons. First, they will be allowed to continue to work for us if they make quota. Second, their salary increases depend on it." The sales manager continued, "They are rewarded for meeting or beating quota. Their pay the following year is affected by it. Why pay for the same thing twice?"

Question

What could you say to the sales manager?

Case 19–2

Wilson Tile Company

Establishing a Quota System

Morris Carson had been in his new position for only a week when it became apparent that the performance of the company's sales force was something less than inspiring. It didn't seem to him that sales of $310,000 per rep was very good. He was going to tell the five regional managers who supervised the firm's 35 sales reps that he couldn't understand why the company's performance was so much lower than other firms in the industry. The industry trade association study of sales force performance had indicated that sales per sales rep averaged $533,000. And Morris always considered average to be a high grade of poor.

One month previously, Morris Carson had been appointed sales manager of the Wilson Tile Company when it was acquired by the General Company, a huge conglomerate. Morris had been in sales for one of General's other companies. His boss at General had given him the stern directive, "Clean up their sales act!"

The Wilson Company sold a wide line of imported ceramic tile to the building-materials trade throughout the nation. Wilson had been marginally profitable, but was sold when Dan Wilson, its founder, retired.

Morris called a meeting of the five regional managers. Matters were sticky from the beginning. The five seemed to resist everything Morris was saying. When the subject of quotas came up on the agenda, Morris said, "I understand that this company has never had any sales quotas. Is that right?"

The managers nodded in agreement.

"Well, that's over. We will now have sales quotas. They will be meaningful quotas and will play an important role in the reps' lives. Their pay and jobs will depend on their meeting quotas with some degree of reasonableness," Morris stated with some sternness. He wanted to let the managers know that he was not happy with matters as they had been and that if things did not change, people would be changed.

The managers did not miss the point. One of them said, "If they have quotas, then we all will have quotas."

"You catch on real quick," Morris said. He continued, "For starters, until we can get some good research on the problem, let's start out giving the reps a quota based on what the average company in this industry sells. We are at least that good aren't we?" Not waiting for an answer, he continued, "We have a wider line and a better competitive package, or so I'm told. So here are your quotas. Every rep will sell $533,000 for the year. We will break that down by month by a seasonal index and mail it to you. But that's it. Any person who doesn't meet quota won't receive any bonuses and will have his or her record reviewed for termination. Now let me say this one thing so you will know where I'm coming from. My career with General is on the line here. I turn this operation around or I'm history. That will not happen."

The regional managers were outraged. "We just don't do things this way here at Wilson. We don't have quotas for good reasons. There is no need for them. We are on top of the situation in the field. There are good reasons why we don't sell up to industry average. You haven't asked us our opinion on this," the manager from Dallas said.

Another manager chimed in, "Let's come up with a program to stimulate sales. After all, this does affect all bonuses and that is about 25 percent of our take-home pay."

Morris asked, "When can I have that program?"

The manager replied, "I think we can develop a sound program in the next three months."

Morris exploded, "In three months this sales force will be up to projected performances or some changes will be made. If you can't go along with this program, then I'll find people who can."

Questions:

1. Is Morris being irrational in his demands on the Wilson sales force?
2. How would you have handled the matter?

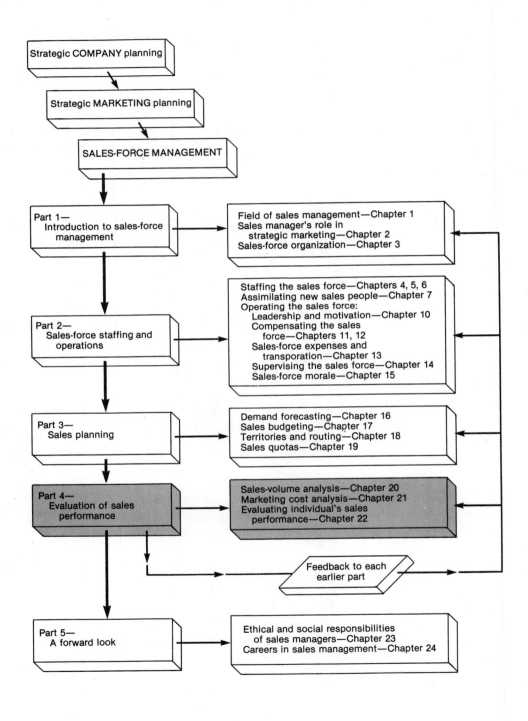

Strategic COMPANY planning

Strategic MARKETING planning

SALES-FORCE MANAGEMENT

Part 1—
Introduction to sales-force management

Field of sales management—Chapter 1
Sales manager's role in
strategic marketing—Chapter 2
Sales-force organization—Chapter 3

Part 2—
Sales-force staffing and operations

Staffing the sales force—Chapters 4, 5, 6
Assimilating new sales people—Chapter 7
Operating the sales force:
Leadership and motivation—Chapter 10
Compensating the sales
force—Chapters 11, 12
Sales-force expenses and
transporation—Chapter 13
Supervising the sales force—Chapter 14
Sales-force morale—Chapter 15

Part 3—
Sales planning

Demand forecasting—Chapter 16
Sales budgeting—Chapter 17
Territories and routing—Chapter 18
Sales quotas—Chapter 19

Part 4—
Evaluation of sales performance

Sales-volume analysis—Chapter 20
Marketing cost analysis—Chapter 21
Evaluating individual's sales
performance—Chapter 22

Feedback to each earlier part

Part 5—
A forward look

Ethical and social responsibilities
of sales managers—Chapter 23
Careers in sales management—Chapter 24

Evaluation of Sales Performance

Up to this point, the major parts of this book (after the introductory section) have been devoted to sales planning and sales operations. Part 4 deals with the final major stage in the sales-management process—namely, evaluating the performance results of the field-selling effort.

Performance evaluation is both a look backwards and a look ahead. Looking backwards, management analyzes its operating results in relation to its objectives and strategic plans. These findings then can be used in forward planning for the next operating period. To illustrate, looking back, management finds that too much sales volume is in low-margin products. This evaluation result then can influence management's future plans for sales-force training, supervision, and compensation.

In the first part of Chapter 20, we introduce some general concepts in performance evaluation and misdirected marketing effort. The balance of that chapter is devoted to the analysis of sales volume. Chapter 21 is a survey of marketing cost analysis. Chapters 20 and 21 together constitute a marketing profitability analysis. The evaluation of the performance of individual sales people is discussed in Chapter 22.

20

Analysis of Sales Volume

*Economic distress will teach men . . . that fact-finding is
more effective than fault-finding.*
CARL BECKER

The managerial functions of planning, implementing, and evaluating
are related in a continuous fashion, as shown in Figure 20–1. Plans
are made; they are put into operation by the organization; the results
are evaluated. Then new plans are prepared, based on the evaluation
findings.

Planning and evaluation are especially interdependent activities.

Figure 20–1

Interrelationship of Planning, Implementation, and Evaluation

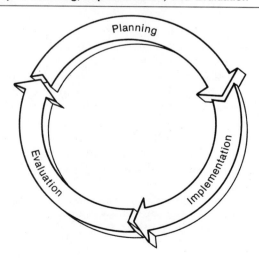

Evaluation both follows and precedes planning. Evaluation *follows* the planning and operations of the current period of company activity. Planning sets forth what *should be* done, and evaluation shows what *really* was done. Without an evaluation, management cannot tell (1) whether its plan has worked, (2) to what degree it has been successful, or (3) what the reasons are for its success or failure. Then evaluation *precedes* the planning for the next period's operations.

Introduction to Performance Evaluation

Performance evaluation is a broad term that covers the (1) analysis of sales volume—the topic of this chapter, (2) marketing cost analysis and profitability analysis—the topics of Chapter 21, and (3) various analytical measures used to evaluate a sales person's performance—the topic of Chapter 22.

The Marketing Audit: A Total Evaluation Program

The essence of a total evaluation program is embodied in the concept of a marketing audit.[1] An audit is a review and evaluation of some activity. Therefore, a **marketing audit** is a systematic, comprehensive, periodic review and evaluation of the marketing function in an organization—its marketing goals, policies, and performance. This audit includes an appraisal of the organization, personnel, and procedures employed to implement the policies and reach the goals.

To qualify as a complete marketing audit, any appraisal must include *all* the marketing areas referred to in the definition—goals, policies, performance, organization, personnel, and procedure. A fragmented evaluation of some marketing activities may be useful, but it is not a marketing audit. It is only one part of such an audit.

A complete marketing audit is a very extensive project which provides something of an ideal for management to work toward. It is expensive, time-consuming, and difficult. But the rewards from a marketing audit can be great. Management can identify its problem areas in marketing. By reviewing its policies and strategies, the firm is likely to keep abreast of its changing marketing environment. Suc-

---

[1] See *Analyzing and Improving Marketing Performance: "Marketing Audits" in Theory and Practice,* Management Report 32 (New York: American Management Association, 1959), especially Abraham Schuchman, "The Marketing Audit: Its Nature, Purposes, and Problems," pp. 11–19, and Alfred R. Oxenfeldt, "The Marketing Audit as a Total Evaluation Program," pp. 25–36.

cess also can be analyzed, so the company can capitalize on its strong points.

Traditionally, an audit is an after-the-fact review. In marketing, the use of an audit is broadened to include an evaluation of the effects of alternatives *before* a decision is reached. Thus the audit becomes an aid in decision making. Further, an audit should anticipate further situations as well as review past ones. In this way, an audit is intended for "prognosis as well as diagnosis. . . . It is the practice of preventive as well as curative marketing medicine."[2]

The Sales Management Audit

A marketing audit covers an organization's entire marketing system. A company can also apply the audit concept to the major divisions *within* the marketing system. Thus, for example, a company might conduct a physical-distribution audit, an advertising audit, or a product-development audit. Or, as is pertinent to this book, management can audit the personal selling and sales management activities in a company's marketing system. Thus, like a marketing audit, a sales-program audit evaluates a firm's *sales* objectives, strategies, and tactics. The *sales* organization and its policies, personnel, and performance are appraised.[3]

The Evaluation Process

The evaluation process—whether it is a complete marketing audit or only an appraisal of individual components of the marketing program—is essentially a three-stage task. Management's job is to:

1. Find out *what* happened—get the facts; compare actual results with budgeted goals to determine the variations.
2. Find out *why* it happened—determine what specific factors in the marketing program accounted for the variations.

---

[2] Schuchman, "Marketing Audit," p. 14. For more recent reports on the subject of a marketing audit, see Philip Kotler, William Gregor, and William Rodgers, "The Marketing Audit Comes of Age," *Sloan Management Review,* Winter 1977, pp. 25–43; Philip Kotler, "From Sales Obsession to Marketing Effectiveness," *Harvard Business Review,* November–December 1977, pp. 67–75; and Louis M. Capella and William S. Sekely, "The Marketing Audit: Methods, Problems, and Perspectives," *Akron Business & Economic Review,* Fall 1978, pp. 37–41.

[3] For an excellent explanation of a sales management audit, including a detailed outline of its elements, see Alan J. Dubinsky and Richard W. Hansen, "The Sales Force Management Audit," *California Management Review,* Winter 1981, pp. 86–95.

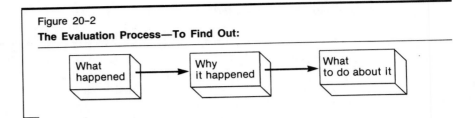

Figure 20-2
The Evaluation Process—To Find Out:

What happened → Why it happened → What to do about it

3. Decide *what to do* about it—plan the next period's activities to improve on unsatisfactory conditions and capitalize on favorable ones. See Figure 20-2.

Components of Performance Evaluation

Because of the time, cost, and difficulty involved in a full marketing audit, sometimes it is more reasonable to evaluate the separate components of the marketing mix. An evaluation of field-selling efforts involves an appraisal of sales-volume results, related marketing expenses, and the performance of individual sales people. These components are sufficiently independent so that management can conduct one or two evaluations without the need to do all of them. One company may decide to analyze its sales volume, but not its marketing costs. Another firm may study various ratios involving sales-force activities without making any detailed sales or cost analyses.

An *analysis of sales volume* is a careful study of a company's records as summarized in the net sales section of its profit and loss statement. It is a detailed study of the dollar or the unit sales volume by product lines, territories, key accounts, and general classes of customers. An analysis of sales volume may be expanded to include a corresponding study of cost of goods sold. The result is an analysis of its gross margin, also broken down into such segments as products or territories. A *marketing cost analysis* continues from the analysis of sales volume. It is a study of the marketing expenses to determine the profitability of various marketing segments in the organization.

In a general sense, the two types of analyses are component parts of a detailed study of a company's operating statement. A sales volume analysis is a review of the statement through the net sales and possibly through the gross margin section. A marketing cost analysis starts where the analysis of sales ends and continues to the end of the operating statement. In effect, a sales volume analysis (SVA) and a marketing cost analysis (MCA) together constitute a marketing profitability analysis (MPA). Or, look at it this way:

$$SVA + MCA = MPA$$

Relation of Performance Evaluation to Sales Control

Many writers and business executives refer to the subject of this chapter as *sales control* or *control of sales operations.* We do not use any such label because we believe it is a misleading and unrealistic use of the term *control.* Control is not an isolated managerial function. It permeates virtually all other managerial activities. For example, management controls its sales force by means of the compensation plan, quota system, territorial structure, and expense-payment plan. Control is also exercised through the training program, sales contests, supervision, and other devices.

Performance Evaluation and Misdirected Marketing Effort

A marketing profitability analysis is one step that may be taken to correct the misdirected marketing effort that exists in many companies today.

Nature of Misdirected Marketing Effort: The 80–20 Principle

A company does not enjoy the same rate of net profit on every sale. In most firms a large proportion of the orders (or customers or territories or products) account for a small share of the profits. This relationship between selling units and profits has been characterized as the 80–20 principle. That is, 80 percent of the orders, customers, territories, or products contributes only 20 percent of the sales or profit. Conversely, the other 20 percent of these marketing units accounts for 80 percent of the volume or profit. The 80–20 figure is used to epitomize the misplacement of marketing efforts. Actually, of course, the percentage split varies from one situation to another.

The 80–20 situation is caused by the misdirected efforts that are found in most marketing programs.

Marketing efforts and costs follow the number of territories, customers, or products rather than their actual or potential sales volume or profit.

A firm may have one sales person and one branch office in each territory, with all the attendant expense, regardless of the volume obtained from these districts. For every order received, the seller must process a purchase order, invoice, and a payment check. Approximately the same order-filling and shipping expense is involved whether the order is for $10 or $1,000. In most companies, if marketing efforts were to be matched with results, much of the marketing cost would be credited with only a small part of the total sales and profits.[4]

Reasons for Misdirected Effort: The Iceberg Principle

Many executives are unaware of the misdirected marketing effort in their firms. They do not know what percentage of total sales and profits comes from a given product line or customer group. Frequently, executives cannot uncover their misdirection of effort because they lack sufficiently detailed information. The analogy of an iceberg in an open sea has been used to illustrate this situation. Only a small part of an iceberg is visible above the surface of the water— the submerged 90 percent is the dangerous part. The figures representing total sales or total costs on an operating statement are like the visible part of an iceberg. The details on sales, costs, and other performance measures for each territory or product correspond to the large, but submerged, segment.

Total sales or costs on an operating statement are too general for a marketing executive interested in sales analysis. In fact, the total figures are often inconclusive and misleading. More than one company has shown satisfactory overall sales and profit figures, but when these totals were subdivided by territory or products, serious weaknesses were discovered. A manufacturer of rubber products showed an overall annual increase of 12 percent in sales and 9 percent in net profit on one of its product lines one year. But when management analyzed these figures, the sales change within each territory was found to range from an increase of 19 percent to a decrease of 3 percent. In some territories, profits increased as much as 14 percent, and in others they were down 20 percent. This is a practical example of the iceberg principle.

The reason for the imbalance of marketing efforts and results is that, historically, management has measured the success of a marketing program by the criterion of sales volume. This attitude is typified

---

[4] For some ideas about how to correct an 80–20 situation of misdirected marketing effort, see Alan J. Dubinsky and Richard W. Hansen, "Improving Marketing Productivity: The 80–20 Principle Revisited," *California Management Review,* Fall 1982, pp. 96–105.

in the countless companies that use sales-volume quotas and compensate their sales people by a commission on sales volume.

There is a more fundamental reason for misplaced marketing effort. Sales executives must make decisions even though their knowledge of the exact nature of marketing costs is inadequate. In other words, management lacks:

1. Knowledge of the disproportionate spread of marketing effort.
2. Standards for determining:
   a. What should have been spent on marketing.
   b. What results should have been obtained from these expenditures.

As an example, a sales executive really does not know exactly how much to spend on sales training, marketing research, or sales supervision. What is even more troublesome is that after some money has been spent, management has no yardstick to determine whether the results of these expenditures are satisfactory. If a firm adds 10 missionary sales people or employs field supervisors where none existed before, the executives ordinarily cannot say how much the volume or profit should increase. Nor can they compare the value of two expenditures. Assume that a company spends $200,000 on a contest for the sales force. No one can say how much additional volume this expenditure will bring, as compared with spending the same amount on advertising or on sales training, for example.

Problems Involved in Analysis of Sales Volume

Lack of Adequately Detailed Information

Sales administrators who want to analyze sales volume may find that adequately detailed data are lacking. The sales department works largely with figures supplied by the accounting department. But these records are rarely sufficiently itemized for the needs of sales managers. Often, a company will have one account for gross sales and another one for sales returns and allowances with no further breakdown. Facts on net sales by product line, groups of customers, or other classifications usually are not readily available. Before a worthwhile analysis can be made in most companies, a system must be established to supply the sales department with the necessary facts.

The possible classifications of sales data and the combinations of these breakdowns have almost no limit. Some of the more widely used subdivisions for reporting and analyzing sales are the following:

1. *Sales territories.*
2. *Sales people.* If each representative has a district, an analysis of sales volume by territories also serves for individual sales reps.
3. *Products.* Reports may be in dollars and/or physical units for individual products or lines of products.
4. *Customers.* Management may classify the volume by the individual customers, key accounts, industrial groups of customers, or channels of distribution.
5. *Size of order.*

Any of this information may be reported monthly, quarterly, or for some other period of time.

Sales Volume Analysis Usually Insufficient

An analysis of a company's sales volume alone usually does not furnish enough information to the sales department. Furthermore, the data produced may be misleading. A study may show, for example, that the dollar *volume* of product A is 20 percent greater than the sales of product B. Yet, if the company were to determine the gross margin or net profit of the two products, management would find that B's dollar *profit* is 10 percent higher than A's. Granted that a full-scale sales and cost study—a marketing profitability analysis—is ideal, a good marketing cost analysis usually is difficult and costly. Further, while an analysis of volume alone has its limitations, it is far better than no analysis at all. In spite of the acknowledged value of a marketing cost and profitability analysis, the most widely used measure of sales performance continues to be sales volume.[5] See Figure 20–3.

A compromise between a volume analysis and a full-scale distribution cost study is to expand the volume analysis to include the cost of the merchandise sold. Thus management ends up with a gross-margin analysis by territories, products, or customer groups with relatively little additional expense.

Bases for Analyzing Sales Volume

Total Sales Volume

A reasonable place to begin an analysis of sales is with the total volume—the combined sales of all products in all territories for all

---

[5] See Donald W. Jackson, Jr., Lonnie L. Ostrom, and Kenneth R. Evans, "Measures Used to Evaluate Industrial Marketing Activities," *Industrial Marketing Management,* October 1982, pp. 269–74.

Figure 20-3

The Iceberg Principle *(This company may be headed for real trouble. The impressive totals may be hiding some problems that ultimately can destroy the company.)*

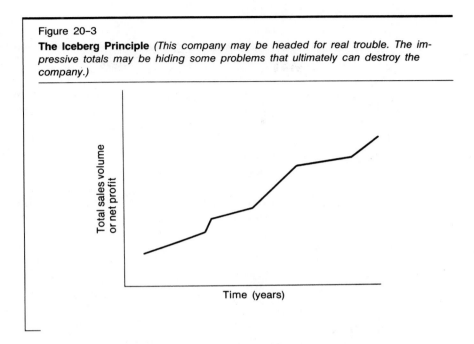

customers. This is the most readily available figure and the one that will give an overall picture of how the company is faring. However, the *trend* in sales is usually far more important to administrators than the volume for any given year. They are interested in two trends—the trend of the company's sales over a period of years and the trend of the company's share of the total industry market.

A study of total sales volume is probably the easiest to make of all types of analyses. The only data needed are (1) the annual sales figures for the company over the past several years and (2) the annual industry sales in the geographic market covered by the firm. Then the company's share of the market can be determined.

Table 20-1 shows the sort of information developed in a total volume analysis for a hypothetical firm, the Colorado Ski Company. This concern carries two basic product lines—ski equipment (skis and accessories) and a limted line of ski clothes (ski pants and parkas). The company manufactures some of these items. Others are purchased from outside sources, but are sold under Colorado Ski's brand. The firm sells to two classes of customers—sporting goods stores and specialty ski shops—in some of the major ski markets in the nation. Annual sales in 1986 were $9.0 million.

An analysis of the company's volume shows that its sales have generally increased each year since 1977, with the exception of 1981

Table 20–1

Information Used in Analysis of Total Sales Volume, Colorado Ski Company

Year	Company Volume (in millions)	Industry Volume (in millions)	Company's Share of Market
1986	$9.0	$120	7.5%
1985	8.4	130	6.4
1984	7.8	120	6.5
1983	6.8	104	7.0
1982	7.0	100	8.2
1981	6.4	78	8.3
1980	6.6	80	8.9
1979	6.4	72	8.9
1978	6.0	60	10.0
1977	5.0	50	10.0

and 1983. So far, the picture is encouraging. However, industry figures shed a different light on the situation. The industry's sales also have increased since 1977, but at a more rapid rate than Colorado's volume. As a result, the company's share of the market has steadily declined. Looking at the 10-year picture, management finds that its sales have increased 80 percent, but its share of the market has declined 25 percent.

After management has uncovered the facts as shown in Table 20–1, the next step is to determine the reasons for the decline in the company's market position. Obviously, competition has outdistanced Colorado Ski. The administration must ascertain whether this result stems from weaknesses in the firm's operations or from strengths in the competitors'.

The possible weaknesses in Colorado Ski's operation are almost limitless. Something may be wrong with the product itself such as its styling, construction, or color. Some aspects of the pricing structure may be the problem. The weakness may lie in some phase of advertising, such as the choice of media or the advertisements themselves. Then the entire area of sales-force management can be examined.

On the other hand, it may be that all of Colorado Ski's operations are as good as they ever were, but the competitors have shown marked improvement. Possibly there are more competitors. Or some of these firms may have made significant improvements in their product, distribution, or promotional effectiveness.

If a company's total sales are *declining*, management must determine the trend of the industry's sales. If the industry's volume is *increasing*, then, again, there are (1) weaknesses in the company's operations, (2) strengths in the competition, or (3) a combination of both factors. However, if the industry's volume is also *decreasing,* apparently the demand for the given line of products is declining. Different strategies will be needed if the reason for the decline in sales lies in company weaknesses or competitor's strengths, rather than in a shift in consumer demand for the product.

Sales by Territories

Companies can usually do an analysis of total sales volume easily and inexpensively. However, its value to management is limited because it tells so little about the details of a firm's marketing progress. The iceberg principle is at work; only the aggregate picture emerges and the separate parts remain submerged. As a step toward uncovering these parts, it is a common practice to analyze sales by territories. Frequently, some version of the 80–20 principle is operating in that the bulk of the volume comes from a small percentage of the sales regions. Management is ordinarily interested in identifying which districts are strong or weak in relation to potential. This is a step toward determining whether the company is receiving sufficient value for its investment in its branches, advertising, and other territorial items. Also, an administrator must find out *which* territories are weak before he can determine *why* they are weak.

One reasonably simple, inexpensive procedure for analyzing sales volume by territories follows these four steps:

1. Select a market index that indicates with reasonable accuracy what percentage of total sales should be obtained from each sales territory. For example, one firm may find it can establish standards for territorial sales performance by using retail sales as an index. If 10 percent of the total national retail sales were in the midwestern district, then 10 percent of the company's sales should also come from that district. Or if the firm sells in only eight southeastern states, then the total retail sales in the eight-state area would be equated to 100 percent. If 22 percent of the eight-state retail sales were tallied in Alabama, then 22 percent of the sales in the company should also come from Alabama. Other firms may find that a market index, such as wired homes, automobile registrations, or *Sales & Marketing Management's* "Buying Power Index," is related to their sales. (Market indexes and their use in determining territorial sales and market potentials were explained in Chapter 16.)
2. Determine the company's actual total sales in dollars or units during the period being studied.
3. Multiply the territorial index by the total sales figure to determine the goal in each district.

4. Compare actual regional sales with the regional goals to see how much variation has occurred.

An example of this procedure is developed in Table 20–2. The five territories that comprise the western division of the Colorado Ski Company are being analyzed. Incidentally, it makes no difference whether this firm sells in a national or in a regional market. Nor does it matter whether these five territories represent all or only part of Colorado Ski's total market. The approach used in Table 20–2 would serve any of these conditions.

In the western division, Colorado Ski's total sales were $4 million distributed among five territories as shown in the column headed Actual Sales. Sales were $900,000 in territory A, $1 million in territory B, and so forth. Next we apply a pertinent market index to the western division's total sales. We find that 26.7 percent, or $1 million of the total sales in the five-territory market *should* have been made in territory A. The goal in territory B was 22.7 percent, or $1,020,000. In C, the goal was 15 percent, or $676,000, and so on.

A performance percentage is computed by dividing actual sales by the territorial goal. A rating of 100 percent in the district means that the area turned in its predetermined share of the company's business. Table 20–2 shows that territories B and C did much better than expected. Districts E and D were a shade below par, and A fell considerably short of expectations. In terms of dollars, A was $300,000 under what it should have been. B's sales were $132,000 over the goal.

It is not enough to study the *percentage* by which an area's sales are over or under the goals. The more important measure usually is the *dollar volume.* It is possible that the district may be only a few

Table 20–2

Analysis of Territorial Sales Volume in Five-Territory Western Division, Colorado Ski Company

Territory	Market Index (percent)	Sales Goals	Actual Sales	Performance Percentage	Dollar Variation
A	26.7	$1,200,000	$ 900,000	75	−$300,000
B	22.7	1,020,000	1,230,000	121	+ 210,000
C	15.0	676,000	828,000	122	+ 152,000
D	19.8	890,000	852,000	96	− 38,000
E	15.8	714,000	690,000	97	− 24,000
Total	100.0	$4,500,000	$4,500,000		

percentage points under par. However, because the territorial potential is very large, these few percentage points may represent a significant sum of money. This may be many more dollars than in a small territory that is far below par percentagewise.

A market segment that is below par—its actual performance does not reach its goal—may be called a *soft spot.* In sales management, the **soft-spot principle** is that an administrator reaps the largest possible gain by working with the weakest segments of the organization. In line with this principle, a sales manager in the Colorado Ski Company should devote most of his attention to territory A, because it has the greatest room for improvement. By the same token, it is doubtful that even considerable executive attention could improve B and C very much. Already they are far above their goals. Probably the main benefits from a study of B and C would be determination of (1) why they apparently are so successful and (2) whether this information can be used to improve A.

Once the administrator has ascertained which territories are strong and which are weak, the next problem is to determine the reasons for the relative performances. Territory A may be doing poorly because competition is particularly effective or because some aspects of Colorado Ski's operation are especially weak. Management also may want to find why such variation in territorial potential exists. Territory E is supposed to bring in only 15 percent of the total, while A's goal is 26.7 percent. If all five districts were equal in potential, each should contribute 20 percent of the total volume.

Assuming that *industry* volume figures for each territory are obtainable with reasonable effort, another procedure may be used for a territorial-sales analysis. Industry's sales can be distributed on a percentage basis among a company's territories by dividing the dollar sales of a district by the industry's total sales. Thus industry percentages are established in each district. Then, the percentage of the company's sales in each district is compared with these industry percentages. A sales manager may find, for example, that 15 percent of the *industry's* sales are made in territory A and 10 percent in B. In comparison, 12 percent of the *company's* sales are in A and 20 percent in B. Thus, the company is doing far better than the industry average in B, but the firm is below average in A.

Sales by Products

The 80–20 and the iceberg principles apply to products as well as to territories in many companies. Very often, most of the products in a company's line account for a small percentage of total volume or profit. Conversely, a few products may bring most of the volume. Also, there is no relation between volume and profit. Products that account for a large proportion of the volume may or may not contribute a corresponding percentage of the net profits.

Several types of volume analyses by product lines may be very helpful to management. The first is simply a summary of present and past total sales divided into individual products or groups of products. An appliance manufacturer may want to study the sales trend for each individual product. A hardware wholesaler, however, would be content to group thousands of products into divisions such as housewares, plumbing goods, sporting goods, electrical equipment, and so on. This type of examination shows the percentage of total volume contributed by each product or product group.

If *industry* figures are available for each product line, they may provide a yardstick with which a company can measure its own sales performance by products. For example, assume that the sales of product A are decreasing in one firm. Its management need not be so concerned if over the same period the industry's sales have decreased at about the same rate. In another situation, let's assume that product A accounts for only 5 percent of a company's volume while the remainder is divided equally among three other products. Management can appraise this situation better if industry figures are used as a comparison. It may be that product A accounts for only 3 percent of the industry's sales. Therefore it is doubtful that the company will expend much promotional effort to increase the sales of A, unless A is an extremely high-profit item.

A further refinement of volume analysis by products is to study the sales of each product line in each territory. In this way, management can find out in which geographical market each product is strong or weak in sales. Product A's total sales may be up 10 percent over last year, but in the southwestern region, A's volume is down 14 percent. Another example is a company with four product lines. About 20 percent of the volume in each of three lines is sold in the Pacific Coast division. But this area accounts for only 5 percent of the volume in the fourth line. Once these facts are known, an administrator can try to determine the reasons for the variations and then take necessary corrective steps. In this example, it may be that the fourth line faces strong regional competition on the Pacific Coast. Or perhaps the product is just generally underconsumed, and the industry as a whole does poorly in that area.

An analysis of sales by product lines also can be used to refine the territorial analysis discussed in the preceeding section. Thus we can better pinpoint the problem areas. A study of Table 20–2 shows that territory A was 25 percent *under* par. B and C were 21 percent and 22 percent *above* par, respectively. By investigating the product sales in these districts, management can better isolate the reason for the variations from the expected norms.

Table 20-3

Analysis of Product Sales Performance in Two Territories, Colorado Ski Company

Product	Territory A (in thousands)			Territory B (in thousands)		
	Goal	Actual	Variation	Goal	Actual	Variation
Skis	$ 528	$570	+$ 42	$ 436	$ 540	+$104
Accessories	90	78	−12	74	120	+46
Pants	300	120	−180	270	360	+90
Parkas	282	132	−150	240	210	−30
Total	$1,200	$900	−$300	$1,020	$1,230	+$210

Table 20–3 gives an example for the Colorado Ski Company. Market indexes were applied to the company's actual volume of $4 million in the western division to establish targets for products in each of the five western territories.[6] For instance, let's assume that the western division's sales had been distributed in relation to potential. Then sales in territory A would have been $1.2 million with skis contributing $528,000, ski accessories accounting for $90,000, and so forth.

In Table 20–2, we found that the company was short of its sales goal in territory A by $300,000, or 25 percent. However, this shortage was not distributed equally among all four products. Further analysis by product lines exposes more of the submerged part of the iceberg. We now can see that the sales of ski pants and parkas were the primary sources of the shortages. The company failed to reach its target by $180,000 and $150,000, respectively, for those two products. Sales of skis actually were $42,000 over the performance standard.

In territory B, the district as a whole was $210,000 over par. However, the product-sales analysis shows considerable variations from the target figures. Volume in skis, ski accessories, and ski pants was satisfactory. But sales of parkas fell $30,000 (about 12.5 percent) short of the goal.

Let's assume that the sales volume has now been analyzed by products, and the soft spots have been identified. The next problem

---

[6] Ideally, a separate index should be used for each product or line of products. To use the same index on all items means that the percentage share of the national market set as a target in the territory is the same for all products. In Table 20–2, 26.7 percent of the company's total western division sales should have been contributed by territory A. If the same index is used for all four products, then 26.7 percent of the sales of each product should be obtained from territory A. Such situations are unusual. Ordinarily, a company selling many different products should not expect that a given territory would contribute for each product the same percentage of the total sales of that product.

is to determine what policies should be adopted by the company. This is particularly needed with respect to low-volume products and goods whose sales have fallen short of the expected goal. Based on the findings in Table 20–3, ski pants and parkas in territory A and parkas in territory B seem to be soft spots. Thus they should offer the best opportunity for improvement.

A different situation prevails for low-volume products. Management's initial thought may be to drop these products. But before taking such a drastic step, other considerations should be taken into account. A cost analysis will aid in these decisions. If the product is a losing proposition for the company, this would be a strong point in favor of dropping the item. In some cases, however, a low-volume product must be kept whether or not it is profitable. It may be needed to round out a line, or customers may expect the company to carry the item.

A significant factor here is the industrywide situation for low-volume product. If the item accounts for a very small percentage of the total industry's volume, the company would not seem to be in a weak position. However, if a low-volume product enjoyed high-volume sales in the industry, the company obviously is in difficulty. Management must determine *why* the firm's product is doing so poorly. After uncovering the reason, management must then decide whether to make a competitive fight, go along with present sales, or simply drop the item from the line. Several factors influence this decision.

Sales by Customer Classifications

A company is even more apt to find the 80–20 principle in operation when sales are analyzed by customer groups. It is not at all unusual to find that a small percentage of customers account for a major share of total volume. Typically, a firm sells to many accounts on a marginal or even unprofitable basis.

A firm can analyze its volume by customer groups in several possible ways. It may classify accounts on an **industry** basis. An oil company may group its customers into industry divisions, such as service stations, marine, farm, transportation, industrial, and governmental agencies. Another basis of classification is by **channels of distribution.** A sporting goods manufacturer may group its accounts by sporting goods wholesalers, department stores, and discount houses. A third classification is on the basis of **accounts** or just the key accounts. Any of these three groups may be cross-classified. An oil company may want to analyze its sales to key accounts in the service-station industry groups, for example.

Any of these customer classifications may and usually should be analyzed for each territory and for each line of products. In one company, it may be that sales to wholesalers are satisfactory on an overall basis. However, in line with the iceberg principle, sales to wholesalers may be particularly poor in one territory. An oil company may assume that a given industry market that accounts for 10 percent of total sales also contributes about 10 percent of the volume of each product line. However, an analysis may disclose that this industry accounts for 18 percent of the volume in product A, but only 5 percent in product B.

Use of Computers in Sales Analysis

Surveys indicate that the most meaningful application of the computer in sales-force management is in the area of sales analysis. This is understandable. Companies typically are faced with iceberg and 80–20 situations in their total sales volume. Marketing effort is likely to be misdirected if management is unaware of the sales performance of specific product lines or individual territories in relation to potentials. Detailed sales analyses are needed as a basis of planning, operating, and evaluating. The computer can process swiftly and economically the masses of data used in a sales analysis. As a marketing executive in the Sperry-Rand Corporation put it, "You no longer have to wait for the present to become past history to learn from its lessons. With the computer, you're on to your mistakes much faster."[7]

Done by hand, a sales analysis in a large firm ordinarily cannot be done (1) quickly enough to be of much use or (2) at a low enough cost to be of much economic value. With a computer, sales can be analyzed in just about any detail management desires.

In the air freight division of American Airlines, for example, early in the day the vice president can tell (1) which sales people in Boston are behind quota, (2) that the volume of electronic parts shipped out of Dallas is declining, and (3) that a sudden spurt in shipments of TV sets from San Francisco to Cincinnati has put that air route 20 percent ahead of forecast. With these fresh facts, the vice president can act immediately: (1) the Boston sales manager is asked whether the sales territories are too large or the sales reps are having other problems, (2) Dallas is asked whether other industries' shipments can take up the slack, and (3) San Francisco is queried as to

[7] Thayer C. Taylor, *The Computer in Marketing,* rev. ed. (New York: Sales Management, 1970), p. 95.

whether the TV business is a one-shot deal or is likely to be a recurring situation.[8]

Another air freight marketing executive at American Airlines explained that sales analysis has a prominent role in the company's computer operations because "Air freight is a time-perishable product. If a plane takes off with unsold space, we never get another crack at the sale." As this executive sees it: "The computer lets you focus the analysis where you want—by salesman, product, account, type of business. As a result, you're giving the salesman meaningful, accurate, up-to-date information. This helps him to deliver a consistently improving level of sales performance."[9]

In the Grocery Products Division of General Mills, every territorial sales executive receives, at the start of the day, a detailed teletype report on what happened in his area the day before. This report includes orders placed, sales volume, cumulative totals by brand, percentage of estimated sales achieved to date in the period, and comparable progress percentages at the same time last year.[10]

One problem sometimes occurs as a result of the computer's data-processing capacities. Sales people and sales managers often are inundated with computer printouts to the point where these reports are not used optimally. Management needs to do two things in these cases—(1) condense and highlight the data and (2) show the sales force and field sales executives how to use the data in the reports.

Summary

A marketing audit is a *total* evaluation program. As such, it is a comprehensive, periodic review and evaluation of the marketing system in an organization. A marketing audit does not only appraise past performance in light of a company's objectives and plans. This audit also helps to determine *future* goals, strategies, and tactics.

The evaluation process essentially is a three-stage task. First, find out *what* happened—actual results are compared with budgeted goals. Second, find out *why* it happened—what factors accounted for the variation between goals and results. Third, decide *what to do* about the situation—that is, plan next period's activities.

Because of the time and cost needed for a full-scale marketing audit, many companies evaluate only the major components of their marketing programs. One such performance evaluation includes an

[8] Ibid., p. 92.
[9] Ibid., p. 94.
[10] Ibid., p. 97.

analysis of (1) sales volume, (2) marketing costs, and (3) sales people's performance. A sales volume analysis combined with a marketing cost analysis constitutes a marketing profitability analysis.

Performance evaluation is a key tool in reducing the misdirected marketing effort in an organization. Misdirected marketing effort means that a company is expending much effort, but getting relatively few results. The 80–20 principle and the iceberg principle illustrate misdirected marketing effort. That is, marketing efforts (costs) follow the *number* of marketing units (territories, products, customers), rather than the *sales volume or profit* derived from these marketing units.

The basic reasons for misdirected marketing effort are management lacks (1) knowledge of the disproportionate spread of marketing effort and (2) reliable standards for determining (*a*) what should be spent on marketing and (*b*) what results should be derived from these expenditures.

A sales-volume analysis is a study of a company's actual sales volume as compared with the budgeted sales goals. This volume analysis should be done in great detail. That is, the company's sales should be analyzed in total and also by territory, products, customer groups, sales people, and order size. In each of these subdivisions, the company's performance should be compared with industry figures. In this way, management can measure its performance against that of the competition.

Detailed sales-performance analysis has been improved immeasurably by the use of computers and other electronic data processing equipment.

Questions and Problems

1. Explain the relationship between planning and evaluation in the management process.
2. What is the relationship between a marketing audit and each of the following?
   a. Sales volume analysis.
   b. Job analysis.
   c. Sales forecasting and setting sales quotas.
3. Explain the concept of a marketing profitability analysis.
4. How do the iceberg and 80–20 principles work together?
5. If the sales volume in a firm is increasing each year by a satisfactory percentage, is there any purpose in the firm's going to the expense of a volume analysis?
6. As a result of a sales-volume analysis, many firms have elimi-

nated some of their products or customers. Yet in several of these cases the sales volume has *increased* after the market cutback. How do you account for this result?

7. A territorial-volume analysis indicated that a firm's sales had increased at about a 10 percent rate for the past three years in a given district. Is this conclusive evidence that the company's performance is satisfactory as far as sales volume is concerned in the given territory?

8. A company with 15 territories found that product A accounted for 40 to 50 percent of the sales in 13 of the districts. But this product brought in only about 20 percent of the volume in the remaining 2 territories. What factors might account for the relatively low standing of product A in the two territories?

9. Is it possible for a product, territory, or class of customer to be far below par, but still not deserve much executive attention? Give examples.

10. Should sales people be furnished with complete statistics, not only on their own performances but on the performance of other sales people as well?

11. If a company made a *territorial*-volume analysis and found some subpar territories, how might these facts affect the following activities as related to sales people?
    a. Supervision.   *c.* Training.
    b. Compensation.   *d.* Stimulation.

12. If a firm analyzed its sales volume by *customer classes,* how might the results affect the supervision, compensation, training, and stimulation of the sales force?

Case 20–1

Sturdi-Wear Clothing Company*

Analysis of Sales Volumes

The Sturdi-Wear Company was founded in January 1971. The owners of the firm were experienced in the manufacture and sale of men's and boys' clothing. Sam Smith, president, had been the production manager for an old-line clothing company prior to his present venture. His partner and vice president, John Adams, had been an outstanding salesman and was associated with the same firm as Smith. Sturdi-Wear was successful primarily for two reasons. First,

* Case prepared by Professor Donald W. Scotton, Cleveland State University. Reproduced with permission.

Mr. Smith was able to produce quality clothing at competitive prices. Second, Mr. Adams was successful in transferring the business of his old customers to the new firm. Particularly pertinent was a contract negotiated in 1984 with two of the leading chain department stores headquartered in Chicago. The firm had been selling to these chain organizations for the past three years.

The firm manufactured and sold men's and boys' suits, sport coats, and slacks. These items were manufactured for the low-price market but were of good quality and style. Mr. Adams had an unusual ability to select the styles and patterns most desired by the market.

This firm had restricted distribution to the states of Indiana, Illinois, Iowa, and Missouri. The owners believed that there was sufficient opportunity for sales within that four-state area to absorb the maximum output of the plant. In addition, the plant was located centrally so that close contact with the accounts was possible. Reorder shipments could be received by the accounts within four days from the date of order, and transportation costs were relatively low.

The firm employed six sales people who were assigned as follows: (1) two people covered the Chicago area, which consisted of Cook, Du Page, and Kane counties; (2) one rep traveled the remaining portion of Illinois; and (3) the other three reps were assigned one state each consisting of Indiana, Iowa, and Missouri. The three-county Chicago area was divided between the two sales reps working there so that one was responsible for all activity within the Chicago city limits. The other sales person traveled the other sections of Cook County and all of Du Page and Kane counties.

The sales people sold directly to large retail accounts and to wholesalers to obtain coverage of smaller retail outlets. The Chicago sales rep was also responsible for servicing the two chain organizations mentioned earlier. Although chain accounts were solicited, the reps had not been successful in obtaining others.

Sturdi-Wear sales for the year 1971 were $2 million and increased at the rate of almost $2 million per year until 1981. The 1981 sales were $20 million. Sales from 1982 through 1984 were:

Year	Chain Sales	Nonchain Sales	Total Sales
1982	$1,000,000	$21,000,000	$22,000,000
1983	2,000,000	22,000,000	24,000,000
1984	2,600,000	17,400,000	20,000,000

The management was concerned about the decline in sales between 1983 and 1984 and decided that an analysis of sales might be helpful. Although the owners knew a great deal about their customers, they recognized that continuous study of sales segments might be necessary.

Mr. William Brown was hired in January 1985 to fill the newly created position of marketing analyst. The owners were aware that it would take some time to install a satisfactory system of market analysis and control. So they suggested that Mr. Brown review 1980 sales first. They hoped that this analysis would serve as a beginning point in understanding the problem and possibly reveal some areas for further study.

Mr. Brown selected counties as geographical-control units. He experimented with various general indexes. Then he found that a coefficient of correlation of .95 existed between his firm's *total* sales and the *Sales & Marketing Management* magazine's Buying Power Index. He believed that some geographic-segment analysis within each of the states would be valuable. Thirty counties were selected at random to discover the correlation between county sales of his firm and the Buying Power Index. This testing demonstrated that the general index was not sufficiently correlated to the firm's sales at the *county* level. So he made a statistical study of market factors affecting the sales of the firm's products. It was found that an index consisting of population (weighted 1), effective buying income (weighted 2), and total retail sales (weighted 3) had a coefficient of correlation of .92 when related to county sales of Sturdi-Wear products. On the basis of these findings, it was decided (1) that the sales analysis of the four states would be made using the *Sales & Marketing Management's* general index and (2) that the *specific index* would be employed in the analysis of county sales.

In preparing 1984 sales for analysis, it was noted that billings were:

Illinois	$12,600,000
Indiana	2,000,000
Iowa	1,600,000
Missouri	3,800,000
Total	$20,000,000

Because the Illinois sales were large, it was decided that this area should be analyzed further. In addition, it was believed that the sales to the chain store organizations should be examined as a possible influence on the other states. Finally, Mr. Adams suggested that Chicago area sales were large enough that they should be examined separately from the Illinois state totals.

To facilitate the analysis, the following information was gathered:

1. Chain-store sales were made at Chicago in the amount of $2.6 million. The chains reported that the goods represented by these sales were shipped and sold in their stores as follows: Illinois, 40

percent; Indiana, 30 percent; Iowa, 20 percent; and Missouri, 10 percent.

2. The chain groups indicated that all the Illinois sales of Sturdi-Wear clothes were made as follows:

> Cook County 70%
> Du Page County 20
> Kane County 10
> Total 100%

3. Other sales in the Chicago area (Cook, Du Page, and Kane counties) consisted of $6 million to large independent retail stores in Cook County and $4 million to wholesalers.

4. The Chicago area wholesalers reported that the Sturdi-Wear sales to retailers were distributed (at manufacturer's sale price) as follows:

> Cook County $2,400,000
> Du Page County 1,000,000
> Kane County 600,000
> Total $4,000,000

The sales-analysis computations were presented in Exhibits 1 through 5 by Mr. Brown. Mr. Adams and Mr. Smith were interested in the findings, but they expressed doubt as to the adequacy of the analysis. Specifically, they suggested that a more comprehensive analysis follow this first effort. In addition, they requested that a plan be drawn for interpreting the results and taking corrective action.

Exhibit 1

Buying Power Index and Related Variables, by State, 1984

State	Population (000)	Effective Buying Income ($ million)	Retail Sales ($ million)	Buying Power Index	State Percent of Index total
Illinois	11,553	$134,759	$ 58,872	4.95	48
Indiana	5,557	54,591	30,095	2.22	21
Iowa	2,941	30,325	14,638	1.17	11
Missouri	5,047	51,813	28,598	2.09	20
Totals	25,098	$271,488	$132,203	10.43	100

Source: "Survey of Buying Power," *Sales & Marketing Management,* annual issue, July 22, 1985.

Exhibit 2

Efficiency Index by States, 1984

Outlets by State	Buying Power Index	Sales Actual (000s)	Sales Par (000s)	Excess or Deficit (000s)	Efficiency Index
Illinois:					
Chain		$ 1,040			
Wholesale and retail		10,000			
Total	47.5	11,040	$9,500	1,540	116
Indiana:					
Chain		780			
Wholesale and retail		2,000			
Total	21.3	2,780	4,260	−1,480	65
Iowa:					
Chain		520			
Wholesale and retail		1,600			
Total	11.2	2,120	2,240	−120	95
Missouri:					
Chain		260			
Wholesale and retail		3,800			
Total	20.0	4,060	4,000	60	102
Total	100.0	$20,000	$20,000	0	

Exhibit 3

Specific Index Variables for Illinois Counties, 1984

Illinois County	Population 000s	Population Percent of Four-State Total	Effective Buying Income $ Millions	Effective Buying Income Percent of Four-State Total	Retail Sales $ Millions	Retail Sales Percent of Four-State Total
Cook	5,164	21%	$ 61,341	23%	$27,151	21%
Du Page	728	3	11,622	4	5,380	4
Kane	299	1	3,682	1	1,517	1
All others	5,362	21	58,114	22	24,824	19
Total	11,553	46%	$134,759	50%	$58,872	45%

Source: "Survey of Buying Power," *Sales & Marketing Management,* annual issue, July 22, 1985.

Exhibit 4

Specific Index Computation for Illinois Counties, 1984

Illinois County	Population*	Effective Buying + Income†	Retail + Sales‡	÷6 =	Specific Index
Cook	1 × 21	+ 2 × 23	+ 3 × 21	÷6 =	22
Du Page	1 × 3	+ 2 × 4	+ 3 × 4	÷6 =	4
Kane	1 × 1	+ 2 × 1	+ 3 × 1	÷6 =	1
All others	1 × 21	+ 2 × 22	+ 3 × 19	÷6 =	21

* Population weighted 1.
† EBI weighted 2.
‡ Retail sales weighted 3.

Exhibit 5

Efficiency Index of Illinois Counties, 1984 (based on the specific index)

Outlets by County	Specific Index	County Percent of Index Total	Sales Actual (000s)	Sales Par (000s) (% index total × total sales)	Excess or Deficit (000s)	Efficiency Index (actual ÷ par)
Cook:						
Chain			$ 728			
Wholesale			2,400			
Retail			4,000			
Total	22	46%	7,128	$ 5,078	+ $2,050	140
Du Page:						
Chain			208			
Wholesale			1,000			
Total	4	8	1,208	883	+ 325	137
Kane:						
Chain			104			
Wholesale			600			
Total	1	2	704	221	+ 483	319
All others	21	44	2,000	4,858	− 2,858	41
Total	48	100%	$11,040	$11,040	0	—

Questions

1. Appraise the job of sales-volume analysis performed by William Brown.
2. What conclusions can be drawn from the results of the sales-volume analysis?

21

Marketing Cost and Profitability Analysis

While an analysis of sales volume is useful, it tells us nothing about the *profitability* of territories, products, or customer groups. To determine the profitability of any of these sales control units, we need a marketing or distribution cost analysis. (The terms **marketing cost analysis** and **distribution cost analysis** are used synonymously in this chapter.) Sales executives are particularly interested in a marketing cost analysis because this information can significantly affect the management of a sales force. The discovery of an unprofitable territory may suggest the need for a shift in territorial boundaries or a different call schedule. The discovery of unprofitable products may result in a change in the commission rate paid for sales of those items.

Nature and Scope of Marketing Cost Analysis

A marketing cost analysis is a detailed analysis of a firm's distribution costs. It is made in order to discover unprofitable segments and inefficiently performed functions of the company's marketing program. It goes beyond a sales volume analysis to determine the profitability of various aspects of the marketing operation. Thus it becomes an important part of an overall sales performance analysis.

Various sales-department budgets frequently are an integral part of cost analyses. Management often wants to establish standards of performance (budgets) for some selling expenses, and then study the causes of variation between the actual and budgeted expense. Once the facts of the situation are known, management is in a better position to improve the situation.

Relation between Marketing Cost Analysis and the Accounting System

Marketing cost analysis is somewhat different in purpose and scope from the usual accounting system in a firm. Accounting is concerned largely with maintaining a complete *historical* record of those company events that in any way have a financial flavor. Thus the system feeds to management a story of merchandise sales, materials purchased, equipment depreciation, salaries paid, and all other activities involving financial considerations. Marketing cost analysis is a managerial tool designed more for use in the planning and control of *future* operations in a firm. Of course, an analysis of past financial events often serves as a guide for future operations.

A marketing cost study is *not* usually a part of a company's regular accounting system. It takes up where the accounting system stops. A study of costs is largely analytical and statistical in nature. It is not concerned with the routine accounting practices. The accounting system is operated perpetually, and each transaction is recorded. The cost analysis is often performed on a sporadic or sampling basis. The profitability of certain products may be studied in 25 percent of the territories for six months out of a year.

In a marketing cost study, regular accounting records provide virtually all the data. Therefore, to do a thorough cost analysis, it is imperative that there be a detailed system of account classification. For instance, one account for sales commissions is not at all sufficient to analyze the commissions paid (1) on sales of a given product (2) to selected customers (3) in a territory.

Marketing Cost Analysis Compared with Production Cost Accounting

Marketing cost analysis and production cost accounting serve as tools for controlling costs in their respective areas. Beyond this general similarity, the two concepts have marked differences.

First, in production cost accounting, the costs ordinarily are computed only for the units of the *product.* Knowledge of this single relationship is usually adequate for managerial control of production expenses. For marketing costs, the situation is quite different. Sales administrators are not satisfied with knowing only the costs of selling each product. They also want to know the distribution expenses for territories, customer groups and order sizes, or for any combination of these control units.

Marketing cost analysis is less exact than production cost accounting. This is because the bulk of production costs can usually be attributed to machines or people whose work can be closely supervised. On the other hand, many marketing costs are incurred by sales people who are not under constant direct supervision and whose jobs are *not* totally routine. It is usually not feasible to conduct a time and motion study of a sales person's activities in order to determine the exact time and cost of various phases of the sales job.

There is another significant difference. In controlling production costs, management is concerned with the effect of volume on costs. In the control of distribution costs, management's attention is directed toward the effect of costs on volume.

Cost-volume relationship in production and in marketing:
In production: Costs are a function of volume.
In marketing: Volume is a function of costs.

Production managers are striving to reach the optimum point of output. So they study what happens to unit production costs when the volume of output increases or decreases by some given percentage. If the company is operating in the decreasing stage of its production cost curve, production managers know that their unit costs can be cut by increasing output. Also, they usually know the exact quantitative relationship between an increase in output and a decrease in costs.

The sales administrator, on the other hand, wants to know what the effect on volume will be if a given cost is changed. For example, what change in volume would occur if two sales people were added to the eight now operating in the Dallas district? Or what would the effect be on sales volume if one field supervisor were added to the staff of each branch? Sales executives typically cannot determine answers to these questions with nearly the degree of accuracy that production managers can. In other words, management is much less certain about the effects of marketing costs on volume, than about the effects that volume changes have on production costs.

Problems Involved in Marketing Cost Analysis

Marketing cost analysis projects can be expensive in time, money, and manpower. To minimize this expense and still retain the benefits of such analyses, a company may conduct a cost analysis on a time-sampling basis. Thus, costs may be analyzed by sales territories for the July–September quarter, or a customer-group analysis may be conducted from October through December.

Another major problem is to get adequately detailed data in a form that is useful to management. Some of the aspects of this problem are discussed in this section.

Bases for Cost Classification

Accounting-ledger costs versus activity-category costs. In typical accounting records, the expenses are classified according to the immediate object of the expenditure. Ledger accounts may be found for such marketing expenses as sales salaries, sales commissions, branch office rent, office supplies, and cost of advertising space or time. For purposes of a marketing cost analysis, sales executives usually must regroup these expenses into various activity classifications. All the expenses related to a given marketing function, such as warehousing or advertising, are grouped together.

The problem in separating costs into activity categories is twofold. First, management must decide on the categories to be established. Second, many expenses listed in accounting records cut across several activity groups. Consequently it is necessary to *allocate* a given ledger account among the appropriate activities. For instance, the ledger account for office supplies must be allocated to each activity group (such as direct selling, advertising, and shipping) that incurs this expense.

Each firm should decide on a list of the major activities that are relevant to its marketing program. A retail chain ordinarily performs activities that are different from those carried on by a manufacturer of electric generators. A typical list, however, usually includes many of the following categories of expenses:

1. Personal selling expenses: sales-force compensation and travel expenses, and all costs connected with branch sales offices.
2. Advertising and sales-promotion expenses.
3. Transportation and shipping expenses.
4. Warehousing expenses.
5. Credit and collections expenses: losses from bad debts, and expenses related to the credit office.
6. Financial, clerical, and handling expenses: costs of processing purchase orders, billing, receiving payment, interest on investment in accounts receivable and finished goods inventories.
7. Marketing administrative expenses: all costs of central sales offices and sales and marketing executives.
8. Marketing's share of general administrative expenses: compensation and travel expense of the president and other general execu-

tives in the company, and the expense of maintaining executive offices.

Direct (or separable) versus indirect (or common) expenses. Direct (also called separable) costs are those incurred in connection with a single unit of sales operations. Therefore they can readily be apportioned in total to a specific marketing unit, whether it is a territory, product, or customer group. If the company were to drop a given territory or product, all direct expenses tied to that marketing unit would, by definition, be eliminated. Indirect (also called common) costs are those that cannot be related *only* to specific products, territories, or other market segments. That is, a given cost item is shared by more than one segment. In general, most distribution costs are totally or partially indirect.

Whether a given cost is classed as common or separable depends on the market segment being analyzed. The cost never remains permanently in one or the other category. Assume that each sales person in a company has a separate territory, is paid a straight salary, and sells the entire line of products. Sales-force salaries would be a direct (separable) expense if the cost analysis were being made by territories. But the salary expense would be an indirect (common) cost if the cost were being studied for each product. Sales-force travel expenses would be a *direct* territorial cost, but an *indirect* product cost.

The term **overhead costs** frequently is used to describe a body of expenses that cannot be identified solely with individual product lines, territories, or other market segments. Sometimes, overhead costs are referred to as fixed costs. However, it is preferable to think of these items as *indirect* rather than fixed expenses. They are not fixed in the sense that management is unable to influence them. Instead, they are fixed only in the sense that they are not directly allocable among territories, product lines, or some other group of market segments. The point is that these costs cannot be attached solely to individual market units.

Difficulty of Allocating Costs

A major problem in a marketing cost analysis is that of allocating distribution costs to individual territories, products, or whatever segment of the market is being studied. Actually, the problem of prorating arises at two levels—(1) when accounting-ledger expenses are being allocated to activity groups, and (2) when the resultant activity costs are apportioned to the separate territories, products, or markets.

A direct cost can be apportioned in its entirety to the marketing segment being analyzed. This phase of allocation is reasonably simple. For example, assume that a territorial cost analysis is being made and each sales person has his own territory. Then all his expenses—salary, commission, travel, supplies, and so on—can be prorated directly to his district. Some of the advertising expense, such as the cost of advertisements in local newspapers and the expense of point-of-purchase advertising materials, can also be charged directly to a given territory.

However, the majority of costs are common (indirect) rather than separable, and the real allocation problems occur in connection with these expenses. For some costs, the basis of allocation may be the same regardless of the type of analysis made. Billing expenses are often allocated on the basis of number of "invoice lines," whether the cost analysis is by territory, product, or customer group. An invoice line is one item (6 dozen widgets, model 1412, for example) listed on the bill (invoice) that we send to a customer. Let's assume that 22 percent of all our invoice lines last year related to orders billed to customers in territory A. Then 22 percent of our total billing costs would be allocated to that territory. In a cost analysis by product line or customer group, we would use this same allocation basis—number of invoice lines—when apportioning our billing costs.

For other costs, however, the basis of allocation will vary according to whether we are analyzing our costs by territory, product, or customer group. Consider sales-force salaries as an example. In a territorial cost study, these salaries may be allocated directly to the district where the people work. In a product cost analysis, the expense probably is prorated on the basis of the proportionate amount of working hours that a rep spends with each product. In a cost analysis by customer classes, the salaries may be apportioned in relation to the number of sales calls on each customer group.

Cost allocation is also difficult because often it is not possible to use the same allocation basis for all component parts of a given activity- cost category. In a product cost analysis, let's consider sales-force commissions, sales-force salaries, and sales-force travel expenses. Each of these costs may require a separate allocation basis, even though all three items are part of the direct-selling activity category. Commissions on net sales may be apportioned directly to each product line. Salaries may be prorated according to the sales people's time spent with each line. And some other basis may be used to apportion the travel expenses.

The last big allocation problem discussed here concerns costs that are *totally* indirect. Within the broad category of indirect expenses, some costs are *partially* indirect (common), and some are *totally* indirect. Many expenses do carry some degree of direct relationship to the territory, product, or other marketing unit being analyzed. Order-filling and shipping expenses, for example, are partially indirect costs. They would *decrease* to some extent if a territory or product were eliminated. They would *increase* if new products or territories were added.

However, other cost items, such as sales administrative or general administrative expenses, are totally indirect costs. They have no direct relationship whatsoever to the marketing unit being analyzed. The cost of maintaining the chief sales executive (salary, staff, office, and so on) will remain about the same, regardless of whether or not the number of territories or products is changed.

Many administrators question whether it is reasonably possible to allocate totally indirect costs. Consider the problem of allocating the general sales manager's expense to territories. Part of the year he travels in these districts. The costs of his transportation, food, and lodging while he is on the road probably can be allocated directly to the territory involved. However, how should his salary and the expenses of his office be apportioned among sales districts? If he spends a month in territory A and two months in B, then presumably one twelfth of these expenses may be allocated to A and one sixth to B. At the same time, this method may be unfair to territory A. During his month's stay in A, he spent much time on telephone calls involving unforeseen difficulties in territory F. Moreover, how would the company apportion the expenses incurred while he is in the home office and not dealing with the affairs of any one particular territory?

In another example, consider the problem of allocating sales people's salaries and travel expenses among the products they sell. To allocate in proportion to the volume sold ignores the fact that all products are not equally easy to sell. Short of a time-and-duty analysis, it may be impossible for management to get an accurate basis for apportioning sales-force salaries and other expenses.

The following three methods are frequently used to allocate indirect costs. Each reflects a different philosophy, and each has obvious drawbacks.

1. Divide the costs equally among all territories, products, or whatever market segments are being analyzed. This method is often applied to administrative expenses. The method is easy, but at the same time it is patently inaccurate and usually unfair to some segments.
2. Allocate the costs in proportion to the sales volume obtained from each territory (or product or customer group). This method is often used for many costs such as billing and order filling as well as for the sales and general administrative costs. The underlying philosophy is that the burden should be applied where it

can best be borne. A high-volume territory would be charged with a larger share of the indirect expenses than would a small-volume district. Again, this system is simple, but it also can be highly inaccurate. It tells management very little about the profitability of the market segment. What is even worse, the results of such a method of allocation can be very misleading.

3. Prorate (allocate) the common (indirect) costs in the same proportion as the total separable (direct) costs. If product A had been charged with $200,000 out of a total of $800,000 *direct* expenses, this product would also be charged with 25 percent of the total *indirect* costs.

The Contribution-Margin versus Full-Cost Controversy

In a marketing-cost analysis, two ways of handling the allocation of indirect expenses are the contribution-margin (also called contribution-to-overhead) method, and the full-cost method. A real controversy exists regarding which of these two approaches is the better one for managerial control purposes.

In the **contribution-margin** approach, only the direct expenses are allocated to each marketing unit (territory, product) being analyzed. These are the costs that presumably would be eliminated if the corresponding marketing unit were eliminated. After deducting these direct costs from the gross margin, the remainder is the amount that unit is contributing to cover total overhead (indirect expenses).

In the **full-cost** approach, all expenses—direct and indirect—are allocated among the marketing units under study. By allocating all costs, management is trying to determine the net profit of each territory, product, or other marketing unit.

For any given marketing unit, these two methods may be summarized as follows:

Contribution-Margin Approach		*Full-Cost Approach*	
	$ Sales		$ Sales
less	Cost of goods sold	*less*	Cost of goods sold
equals	Gross margin	*equals*	Gross margin
less	Direct expenses	*less*	Direct expenses
equals	Contribution-margin	*less*	Indirect expenses
	(the amount available to cover overhead expenses plus a profit)	*equals*	Net profit

An example of the contribution-margin approach is shown in Table 21–1. The net sales, cost of goods sold, and gross margin are shown for each of the three geographical divisions in the Colorado

Table 21-1

Colorado Ski Company: Income and Expense Statement by Geographic Divisions, 1986, in $000 (using contribution-margin approach)

	Total	Eastern	Mid-western	Western
Net sales	$9,000	$3,000	$1,500	$4,500
Less cost of goods sold	6,300	2,200	1,100	3,000
Gross margin	$2,700	$ 800	$ 400	$1,500
Less *direct* operating expenses:				
Personal selling	1,029	300	189	540
Advertising	250	84	36	130
Warehousing and shipping	44	14	11	19
Financial and clerical	51	17	8	26
Total *direct* expenses	$1,374	$ 415	$ 244	$ 715
Contribution margin	$1,326	$ 385	$ 156	$ 785
Less *indirect* operating expenses:				
Personal selling	$ 240			
Advertising	146			
Warehousing and shipping	79			
Financial and clerical	69			
General administrative	192			
Total *indirect* expenses	$ 726			
Net profit	$ 600			

Ski Company. (This is the hypothetical firm introduced in Chapter 20.) The direct operating costs of the Colorado Ski Company are allocated among the three divisions. These expenses are then deducted from the division's gross margin. The result is each division's contribution to the remaining $726,000 of indirect (overhead) costs. The eastern division, for instance, incurred $415,000 in direct costs and contributed $385,000 to the overhead expenses and net profit. If the company eliminated the midwestern division, presumably management would save $244,000 in direct expenses. However, the division's $156,000 contribution to overhead would then have to be absorbed by the remaining two regions, assuming the indirect costs still totaled $726,000.

Table 21-2 illustrates the full-cost approach to cost allocation. An alternative procedure is shown in Table 21-3, where the contribution-margin and the full-cost approaches are combined. First, the direct expenses are allocated to determine each division's contribution to overhead. Then the allocation of indirect costs is shown separately, to arrive finally at a net profit figure for each region.

Table 21-2

Colorado Ski Company: Income and Expense Statement by Geographic Divisions, 1986, in $000 *(using full-cost approach)*

	Total	Eastern	Mid-western	Western
Net sales	$9,000	$3,000	$1,500	$4,500
Less cost of goods sold	6,300	2,200	1,100	3,000
Gross margin	2,700	800	400	1,500
Less operating expenses:				
Personal selling	$1,269	$ 370	$ 229	$ 670
Advertising	396	144	60	192
Warehousing and shipping	123	49	31	43
Financial and clerical	120	38	29	53
General administrative	192	64	32	96
Total operating expenses	$2,100	$ 665	$ 381	$1,054
Net profit	$ 600	$ 135	$ 19	$ 446

Table 21-3

Colorado Ski Company: Income and Expense Statement by Geographic Divisions, 1986, in $000 *(combining the contribution-margin and full-cost approaches)*

	Total	Eastern	Mid-western	Western
Net sales	$9,000	$3,000	$1,500	$4,500
Less cost of goods sold	6,300	2,200	1,100	3,000
Gross margin	$2,700	$ 800	$ 400	$1,500
Less *direct* operating expenses:				
Personal selling	$1,029	$ 300	$ 189	$ 540
Advertising	250	84	36	130
Warehousing and shipping	44	14	11	19
Financial and clerical	51	17	8	26
Total *direct* expenses	$1,374	$ 415	$ 244	$ 715
Contribution margin	$1,326	$ 385	$ 156	$ 785
Less *indirect* operating expenses:				
Personal selling	$ 240	$ 70	$ 40	$ 130
Advertising	146	60	24	62
Warehousing and selling	79	35	20	24
Financial and clerical	69	21	21	27
General administrative	192	64	32	96
Total *indirect* expenses	$ 726	$ 250	$ 137	$ 339
Net profit	$ 600	$ 135	$ 19	$ 446

There is considerable argument over the relative merits of the contribution-margin and full-cost methods. Proponents of the full-cost approach contend that the purpose of a marketing-cost study is to determine the net profitability of the units being studied. They feel that the contribution-margin approach does not fulfill this purpose. Furthermore, the full-cost advocates believe that a contribution-margin analysis may be misleading. The iceberg principle is in action. A given territory or product may be showing a contribution to overhead—this is the visible tip of the iceberg. Yet, after the indirect costs are allocated, this product or territory may actually have a net loss—this is the submerged part of the iceberg.

Contribution-margin supporters contend that it is not possible to accurately apportion the indirect costs among market segments. Furthermore, items such as administrative costs are not related at all to any single territory or product. Therefore the unit should not bear any of these costs. These advocates also point out that a full-cost analysis may show that a product or territory has a net loss, whereas this unit may be contributing something to overhead. Some executives might recommend that the losing department be eliminated. But they are overlooking the fact that the unit's contribution to overhead would then have to be borne by other units. Under the contribution-margin approach, the company would keep this unit, at least until a better alternative could be found.

Actually, both approaches have a place in marketing cost analysis. The full-cost method is especially suited for the systematic reporting of historical costs as a basis for future marketing planning. A full-cost analysis is useful when making long-range studies of the profitability of various market segments. This type of analysis also can be helpful when establishing *long-range* policies on product lines, distribution channels, pricing structures, or promotional programs.

The contribution-margin approach is especially useful as an aid to decision making in *short-run* marketing situations. Also, when cost responsibility is directly assignable to particular market segments, management has an effective tool for controlling and evaluating the sales force.

Types of Marketing Cost Analysis

A company's marketing costs may be analyzed in three ways:

1. As they appear in the ledger accounts and on the income and expense statement.
2. After they are grouped into functional (also called activity) categories.

3. After they have been allocated to territories, products, or other marketing units.

Analysis of Ledger Expenses

The simplest and least expensive marketing cost analysis is to study object-of-expenditure costs as they are recorded in the company's accounting ledgers. The procedure is simply to take from the ledger accounts the totals for each cost item (sales-force salaries, branch-office rent, office supplies), and then analyze these figures in some detail. Totals for this period can be compared with similar figures for past periods to determine trends. We can compare actual expenses with budgeted expense goals. When trade associations disseminate cost information, a company can compare its figures with the industry's averages. In some cases, the trade association data are classified by geographic region or by size of firm as measured by annual sales volume. Then, management in one firm can compare its totals with those for other companies of similar size and geographic location.

An analysis of ledger-cost items is of limited value because it provides only general information. A study may show that telephone expense last year was up absolutely, and as a percentage of sales, over the average of the preceding three-years. Or a company may note that sales compensation costs are 4.7 percent of sales, whereas the industry's average for firms of similar size is 6.1 percent. Findings of this nature are of some help in guiding management and controlling the sales force. However, a more detailed analysis is needed to pinpoint the reasons for (1) the trends observed in the company's costs and (2) the variations from industry norms.

Analysis of Activity Expenses

For more effective cost control, management should analyze its marketing costs after the ledger expenses have been allocated into categories representing the company's major marketing activities. An activity-expense analysis is a two-stage procedure. The first part is to select the appropriate activity categories. Some typical categories were listed earlier in the chapter and are also used in Table 21–4.

The second step is to take each ledger expense and allocate its total among the activity categories. A useful tool here is an expense distribution sheet such as the one pictured in Table 21–4. All the ledger costs are listed vertically in the left-hand column, and the activity categories are listed at the top of the columns going across the sheet. Some ledger expenses are easy to apportion because they are direct expenses. That is, the entire amount can be allocated to

Table 21–4

Colorado Ski Company: Expense Distribution Sheet, 1986

(showing distribution of ledger expense items to activity categories)

		Activity-Cost Categories				
Ledger Expenses	*Totals*	*Personal Selling*	*Advertising*	*Warehousing and Shipping*	*Financial and Clerical*	*General Administrative*
Sales-force commissions	$ 780,000	$ 780,000	—	—	—	—
Sales-force salaries	300,000	300,000	—	—	—	—
Sales-force travel...................	114,000	114,000	—	—	—	—
Office supplies	36,000	6,000	$ 5,100	$ 6,900	$ 13,500	$ 4,500
Media space and time	290,000	—	290,000	—	—	—
Advertising salaries	75,000	—	75,000	—	—	—
Administrative salaries	310,000	48,000	10,000	42,000	60,000	150,000
Property taxes	48,000	—	4,500	21,600	11,400	10,500
Heat and light	58,500	5,100	4,800	21,000	11,400	16,200
Insurance..................	27,600	4,050	1,350	15,000	4,650	2,550
Telephone	21,000	8,400	1,350	1,350	6,000	3,900
Depreciation	27,000	2,400	1,500	11,700	9,000	2,400
Miscellaneous	12,900	1,050	2,400	3,450	4,050	1,950
Totals	$2,100,000	$1,269,000	$396,000	$123,000	$120,000	$192,000

one activity. In Table 21–4, advertising salaries of $75,000 were allocated entirely to the advertising activity. Sales-force travel expenses of $114,000 were apportioned entirely to the personal-selling category.

Other expenses are indirect. Thus they must be apportioned among several activity groups. The main problem for each indirect expense is to select a basis for its allocation. For example, property taxes may be distributed on the basis of square feet used for each activity. In the Colorado Ski Company example, about 45 percent of the total floor space was in the warehousing and shipping department. Consequently, $21,600 of the property tax expense (45 percent of $480,00) was allocated to this physical distribution activity.

After all individual ledger expenses are allocated, the columns are totaled, and the resultant figures are the activity expenses. In Table 21–4 the expenses totaled $2 million. The total for personal selling alone was $1,269,000.

From this type of analysis, the total cost of each activity can be determined rather accurately. Moreover, a study of an expense distribution sheet each year shows not only which *ledger* costs have increased or decreased, but which *activities* were responsible for these changes. An analysis of activity expenses also provides an excellent starting point for analyzing marketing costs by territories, products, or other marketing units.

Analysis of Activity Costs by Marketing Units

The third and most beneficial type of marketing cost analysis is a study of the costs and profitability of each segment of the market. Common practice in this type of analysis is to divide the market by territories, products, customer groups, or order sizes.[1] A cost analysis by market segment enables management to pinpoint trouble spots or areas of satisfactory performance. This can be done much more effectively than with an analysis of either ledger expenses or total activity costs. Neither of the latter two types of analyses will shed much light on the *profitability of various segments* of the marketing system in a company.

A complete marketing-cost analysis by sales territories or some other marketing unit involves the same three-step evaluation procedure outlined in the preceding chapter. That is, we determine what happened, why it happened, and what we are going to do about the situation.

To determine *what happened,* the procedure in a cost analysis by marketing units is quite similar to the method used to analyze activity expenses. Each component of each activity cost is allocated to each territory or whatever marketing units are being studied. By combining a sales-volume analysis with a marketing-analysis, a profit and loss statement may be prepared for each territory, product, or class of customer.

To determine what happened in the geographic divisions of the Colorado Ski Company, as an example, we would go through the following four steps:

1. Determine the gross margin for each region. The net sales and the cost of sales in each area should be reasonably easy to uncover in the regular accounting records. Possibly the company regularly conducts an analysis of sales volume or gross profit. If so, this step has already been completed in a cost analysis.

---

[1] For a report on the groupings of marketing units that are useful for profitability analyses, see Donald W. Jackson, Jr., and Lonnie L. Ostrom, "Grouping Segments for Profitability Analyses," *MSU Business Topics,* Spring 1980, pp. 39–44.

2. List all the activity expenses and their component parts. For example, list personal selling and its parts—sales-force salaries, travel expenses, telephone charges, office supplies, and so on.

3. Allocate each part of each activity cost among the three geographic divisions. Table 21–5 lists examples of some reasonable bases for allocating groups of activity costs among sales territories and among product groups. (Remember that some component parts of a given activity cost total may require separate allocation bases. Also, some of these components may be direct expenses, while others are indirect costs.) Management may allocate only *direct* costs to each district (contribution-margin approach). Or *all* costs may be apportioned (full-cost approach), as was explained earlier and as was illustrated in Tables 21–1, 21–2, and 21–3.

4. Assume that the contribution-margin approach is employed. Then we subtract the total direct expenses for each region from the gross margin to obtain the region's contribution to overhead. If the full-cost approach is used, the total operating expenses for each division can be subtracted from its gross margin to arrive at the net profit for that division.

Use of Findings from Profitability Analysis

So far in our discussion of marketing cost analysis, we have been dealing generally with the first stage in the evaluation process. That is, we have been finding out *what happened*. Now let's look at some examples of how management might use the combined findings from both sales volume and marketing cost analyses—the profitability analysis.

Territorial Decisions

Once management has completed its volume and cost analyses, then the executives may decide to adjust territorial boundaries to match their current potential. Possibly the district is too small. That is, the potential volume is not adequate to support the expense of covering the territory. Or it may be too large, so that the sales person may be spending too much time and expense in traveling.

Management also may consider a change in selling methods or channels in an unprofitable area. Possibly mail or telephone selling should be used instead of incurring the expense of personal-selling visits. A company that sells directly to retailers or industrial users may consider using wholesaling middlemen instead.

A weak territory sometimes can be made profitable by an increase

Table 21–5

Bases of Allocating Activity Costs to Sales Territories and to Product Groups

Functional Cost Group	Basis of Allocation	
	To Sales Territories	To Product Group
Selling—direct costs: sales salaries, incentive compensation, travel, and other expenses	Direct	Selling time devoted to each product, as shown by special sales call reports or other special studies
Selling—indirect costs: field sales office expense, sales administration expense, sales personnel training, marketing research, new product development, sales statistics	Equal charge for each sales person	In proportion to direct selling time or time records by projects
Advertising: media costs such as TV, radio, billboards, newspaper, magazine; advertising production costs; advertising department salaries	Direct; or analysis of media circulation records	Direct; or analysis of space and time by media; other costs in proportion to media costs
Sales promotion: consumer promotions such as coupons, premiums, and so on; trade promotions such as price allowances, point-of-purchase displays, cooperative advertising	Direct; or analysis of source records	Direct; or analysis of source records
Transportation: railroad, truck, barge, and so on; payments to carriers for delivery of finished goods from plants to warehouses and from warehouses to customers; traffic department costs	Applicable rates times tonnages	Applicable rates times tonnages
Storage and shipping: rent or equivalent costs for storage of inventories in warehouses; insurance and taxes on finished goods inventories; labor and equipment for physical handling, loading, and so on	Number of shipping units	Warehouse space occupied by average inventory; number of shipping units
Order processing: preparation of customer invoices; freight accounting; credit and collection; handling cash receipts; provision for bad debts; salaries, supplies, space, and equipment costs	Number of order lines	Number of order lines

Source: Adapted from Charles H. Sevin, *Marketing Productivity Analysis* (New York: McGraw-Hill, 1965), pp. 13–15.

in the appropriation for advertising and sales promotion. Possibly, the sales people are not getting adequate support in this respect. Or competition may have strengthened so much that management must be resigned to a smaller market share than formerly. The problems in poor territories may lie with the activities of the sales people. They may need closer supervision, or too large a percentage of their sales may be in low-margin items. There is also the possibility that they are simply poor sales reps.

As a last resort, it may be necessary to abandon a territory entirely, not even using the facilities provided by mail, telephone, or middlemen. Possibly the potential once present no longer exists. However, before dropping a territory from its market, a company should consider the cost repercussions. The territory presumably has been carrying some share of indirect, inescapable expenses, such as marketing and general administrative costs. If the district is abandoned, these expenses must be absorbed by the remaining areas.

Products

When a cost analysis by products shows significant differences in the profitability of each line of products, the executives should determine the reasons for the differences. It may be that these profit-variations stem from factors (typical order size or packaging requirements, for example) that are rather firmly set. That is, they provide management with very little opportunity for profit improvement. On the other hand, many low-profit items often do present opportunities for administrative action. A firm may be able to simplify its line by eliminating some models or colors for which there is little demand. This will reduce the costs of storage and inventory. Also, simplification makes it possible for the sales force to concentrate on fewer items and probably increases the sales of the remaining products.

Sometimes the profitability of a product can be increased by redesigning or repackaging the item. Packaging the product in multiple rather than single units may increase the average order size. This will cut the unit costs of order filling, shipping, and packaging. Another possibility is to alter (increase or decrease, as the case may be) the amount of advertising and other promotional help appropriated for the product. Possibly, a change in the sales-force compensation plan is needed (1) to increase the sales of profitable items or (2) to discourage the sales of low-margin goods.

A low-volume item cannot always be dropped from the line. Nor can a company always drop an item even though it shows an irreducible net loss. The product may be necessary to round out a line, and the customers may expect the seller to carry it.

Classes of Customers and Size of Order

Another major type of cost study is based on some classification of customers. They may be grouped by **channels of distribution.** For example, a manufacturer who sells to wholesalers, large retailers, and other manufacturers may use those three categories to group its accounts for a cost analysis. Another possible classification is based on the **major industry groupings of customers.** A glass-container manufacturer may sell to food processors, breweries, and soft drink bottlers. This producer can classify each account in one of those three categories and then make a distribution cost analysis of each of the classes.

Marketing costs can then be allocated to each of the customer groups. Following the 80–20 principle, ordinarily the bulk of the volume and profit comes from a small percentage of customers who constitute the large purchasers. The majority of customers ordinarily account for a small percentage of the total volume and profits.[2]

Small-order problem. Management should also consider a cost analysis by **size of order.** A common situation plaguing many companies is the **small-order problem.** That is, often a significant percentage of orders are so small that they result in a loss to the company. Many costs such as direct selling or billing are often the same for each order, whether it is for $10 or $10,000.

A cost analysis by customer groups is closely related to an analysis by order size. Frequently, a customer class that generates a below-average profit also presents a small-order problem. Also, large-volume purchasers sometimes build up their volume by giving the seller many small individual orders. Management should review both their customer and order-size analyses before making policy decisions in these areas.

Accounts that are small-order problems or are otherwise losing propositions require careful consideration. At first blush, it might seem that customers who are sold at a loss should be eliminated, and orders below the break-even point should not be accepted. Actually this is a hasty conclusion. An administrator first should determine *why* the accounts are unprofitable and *why* the average orders are small. Then, he should consider the many possible ways these situations could be improved.

---

[2] For an analytical approach that encourages sales people to adopt a profit perspective, instead of emphasizing only sales volume, see Alan J. Dubinsky and Thomas N. Ingram, "A Portfolio Approach to Account Profitability," *Industrial Marketing Management,* February 1984, pp. 33–41. This approach involves applying the portfolio concept to customers. That is, present customers are grouped into categories according to the customers' present and potential contribution margin.

Any of several reasons may account for the small orders or the unprofitableness of a customer. An account may buy a large amount in total over a period of a year, but it buys the products from several suppliers. Thus, it represents only a small customer to each of these suppliers. Or take the case of a company that buys a large amount in total and buys it all from one supplier. This firm still can present a small-order problem if it purchases frequently on a hand-to-mouth basis, so that the average order is small. In other situations accounts may be small but growing, and the seller caters to them in hope of future benefits. A small-order problem is also caused by a customer who is now small and, as far as can be projected into the future, will remain small.

Sometimes the accounting method used in figuring marketing costs can be the difference between a profitable or unprofitable small-order customer. If costs are computed on an average basis, a given account may show up as a loss for the seller. But if only marginal costs were allocated to this account, it would be a profitable one. As an illustration, assume that there is a small store located across the street from a large department store. A manufacturer's sales rep calls on the large, profitable account. Then this sales person makes a brief call on the small store across the street. Now let's further assume that only the additional (or marginal) costs of making that brief call are assigned to that small account. A different profit figure will result for that small customer than when an average cost is applied to all accounts.

There are many practical suggestions for increasing the average size of an order or for reducing the distribution costs of small orders. For example:

1. Educate the customer who is buying from several different suppliers. The seller should point out to this account the obvious advantages of concentrating its purchases with one supplier.
2. For the customer who purchases a large total quantity, but does it with frequent small orders, management again faces an educational task. Its sales people should point out the advantages of ordering, say, once a month instead of once a week. The buyer will eliminate all its handling, billing, and accounting expenses connected with three of the four orders. The buyer will write one check and one purchase order instead of four. There will be one bill to process and one shipment to put into inventory instead of four.
3. The seller may have to educate its sales force as well as its customers. In fact, it may be necessary to change the compensation plan to discourage acceptance of smaller orders.

4. Direct mail or telephone selling may be substituted for sales calls on unprofitable or small-order accounts. Or the sales reps may continue to call on these accounts, but on a less frequent basis.
5. An account may be shifted entirely to a wholesaler or some other type of middleman, rather than dealing directly, even on a mail or telephone basis.
6. A firm may drop its mass-distribution policy and adopt a selective one. Several firms that have adopted this policy have found that their total sales actually increased. The sales people were able to spend more time with the profitable accounts and thus were able to do a better selling job.
7. A seller may establish a minimum-size order.
8. In pricing, the seller may establish a minimum charge or a service charge to combat small orders. Or the freight charge may be shifted to the buyer. However, the seller must make certain that the new policies do not violate the Robinson-Patman Act (restricting price discrimination) or any other pricing legislation.

Return on Investment—An Evaluation Tool

The concept of return on investment (ROI) is another useful managerial aid in evaluating sales performance and in making marketing decisions. The following formula can be used to calculate return on investment:

$$\text{ROI} = \frac{\text{Net profit}}{\text{Sales}} \times \frac{\text{Sales}}{\text{Investment}}$$

The first fraction expresses the rate of profit on sales. The second fraction indicates the number of times the total investment (assets employed) was turned over. By multiplying the rate of profit on sales times the investment turnover, the ROI is determined.

Two questions may quickly come to mind. First, what do we mean by "investment?" Second, why do we need two fractions? It would seem that the sales component in each fraction would cancel out, leaving net profit ÷ investment as the meaningful ratio.

To answer the first query, consider a firm whose operating standards shows annual sales of $1 million and a net profit of $50,000. At the end of the year, the balance sheet reports:

Assets	$600,000	Liabilities		$200,000
		Capital stock	$300,000	
		Retained earnings	100,000	400,000
	$600,000			$600,000

Now, is the investment $400,000 or $600,000? Certainly the ROI will depend upon which figure we use. The answer depends on whether we are talking to the stockholders or to the company executives. The stockholders are more interested in the return on what they have invested—in this case, $400,000. The ROI calculation then is:

$$\text{ROI} = \frac{\text{Net profit } \$50,000}{\text{Sales } \$1,000,000} \times \frac{\text{Sales } \$1,000,000}{\text{Investment } \$400,000} = 12\frac{1}{2}\%$$

Management, on the other hand, is more concerned with the total investment, as represented by the total assets ($600,000). This is the amount that the executives must manage, regardless of whether the assets were acquired by stockholders' investment, retained earnings, or loans from outside sources.[3] Within this context, the ROI computation becomes:

$$\text{ROI} = \frac{\text{Net profit } \$50,000}{\text{Sales } \$1,000,000} \times \frac{\text{Sales } \$1,000,000}{\text{Investment } \$600,000} = 8\frac{1}{3}\%$$

Regarding the second question, we use two fractions because we are dealing with two separate elements—the rate of profit on sales and the rate of capital turnover. Management really should determine each rate separately and then multiply the two. The rate of profit on sales is influenced by marketing considerations—sales volume, price, product mix, advertising effort. The capital turnover is a financial consideration not directly involved with costs or profits—only sales volume and assets managed.

To illustrate, assume that our company's profits doubled with the same sales volume and investment, because management operated an excellent marketing program this year. In effect, we doubled our profit rate with the same capital turnover:

$$\text{ROI} = \frac{\text{Net profit } \$100,000}{\text{Sales } \$1,000,000} \times \frac{\text{Sales } \$1,000,000}{\text{Investment } \$600,000} = 16\frac{2}{3}\%$$

$$10\% \quad \times \quad 1.67 \quad = 16\frac{2}{3}\%$$

As expected, this 16⅔ percent is twice the ROI calculated earlier.

Now assume that we earned our original profit of $50,000 but that we did it with an investment reduced to $500,000. We cut the size of our average inventory and closed some branch offices. By increasing our capital turnover from 1.67 to 2, we raise the ROI from 8⅓ to 10 percent, even though sales volume and profits remain unchanged:

---

[3] In fact, it has been suggested that the term *assets employed* or *assets managed* be used in the formula instead of *investment* when using the ROI concept as a measure of managerial performance in marketing. See Michael Schiff, "The Use of ROI in Sales Management," *Journal of Marketing*, July 1963, pp. 70–73; and J. S. Schiff and Michael Schiff, "New Sales Management Tool: ROAM (Return on Assets Managed)," *Harvard Business Review*, August 1967, pp. 59–66.

$$ROI = \frac{\$50,000}{\$1,000,000} \times \frac{\$1,000,000}{\$500,000} = 10\%$$

$$5\% \quad \times \quad 2 \quad = 10\%$$

Assume now that we increase our sales volume—let us say we double it—but do not increase our product or investment. That is, the cost-profit squeeze is bringing us profitless prosperity. The following interesting results occur:

$$\frac{\$50,000}{\$2,000,000} \times \frac{\$2,000,000}{\$600,000} = 8\tfrac{1}{3}\%$$

$$2\tfrac{1}{2}\% \quad \times \quad 3.3 \quad = 8\tfrac{1}{3}\%$$

The profit rate was cut in half, but this was offset by a doubling of the capital-turnover rate, leaving the ROI unchanged.

Use of ROI to Evaluate Field Sales Managers

The ROI concept is particularly useful for evaluating the performance of a territorial sales manager or some other segment of the field sales organization. The factors in the equation would be modified to make them appropriate for the organizational segments being analyzed. If management is evaluating territorial performance, for instance, sales volume in each district presumably is readily available. For the profit figure, management can determine the contribution margin in each territory. That is, from a given territory's sales, we deduct the cost of goods sold and all operating expenses directly chargeable to (that is, controllable by) that district. The investment (assets employed) in the territory consists of the average accounts receivable and inventory carried to serve that district. In equation form, this is:

$$ROI = \frac{\text{Contribution margin}}{\text{Territorial sales}} \times \frac{\text{Territorial sales}}{\text{Average accounts receivable} + \text{Inventory}}$$

Territorial managers can improve their return on investment by influencing sales volume, contribution margin, or district investment. Thus, field sales managers can use the ROI concept when they are considering the addition of new customers or products in their regions. In effect, return on investment is an analytical tool that facilitates the delegation of profit responsibility to territorial sales managers.[4]

[4] For a program to improve a sales person's ability to manage his or her territory, see J. S. Schiff, "Evaluate the Sales Force as a Business," *Industrial Marketing Management,* April 1983, pp. 131–37. Schiff designed a seven-topic sales training program dealing with (1) evaluating territorial profitability and (2) developing an annual territorial marketing plan. See also Jack S. Schiff and Michael Schiff, *Strategic Management of the Sales Territory,* New York Sales and Marketing Executives, 1980.

Summary

A marketing cost analysis is a detailed analysis of a company's distribution costs. It is made in order to discover which segments (territories, products, customers) of the company's marketing program are profitable and which are not. A marketing cost analysis is a part of a company's evaluation of its marketing performance.

In marketing cost analysis, we need to understand the differences between accounting-ledger costs and activity-category costs. Another useful distinction is the one between direct and indirect expenses. In a marketing cost analysis, one of the major problems is the difficulty of allocating costs. Management must allocate ledger accounts into activity categories. Then each total activity cost must be allocated to the marketing segment (territory, product, customer group) being analyzed. Cost allocation is especially difficult in the case of indirect expenses.

The difficulty of allocating indirect costs leads to the contribution-margin versus full-cost controversy. In the contribution-margin approach to marketing cost analysis, only the direct cost incurred by the marketing unit (territory, product, and so on) are allocated to that unit. The unit's gross margin minus its direct cost equal the amount the unit contributes to pay the company's overhead (indirect expense). In the full-cost approach, all costs (direct and indirect) are allocated to the various marketing units being studied. In this way, management is trying to determine the unit's net profit.

The company's marketing costs can be analyzed in three ways. One way is to analyze the costs as they appear in the accounting ledgers and on the company's income and expense (profit and loss) statement. A second approach is to analyze the marketing costs after they have been allocated to activity categories. The third type occurs after each activity cost has been allocated to the sales territories, products, or other marketing units being studied.

The types of analyses we have summarized here tell management *what* happened. Then the executives must try to determine *why* these results occurred. Finally, management must decide *what changes* are needed in the marketing program to correct the misdirected effort.

A marketing cost analysis can be especially useful first in the identifying, and in remedying, the small-order problem that occurs in so many firms.

Return on investment (ROI) is another tool that management can use in evaluating sales performance and in making market decisions. This concept is especially useful for evaluating the performance of field sales managers.

Questions and Problems

1. Explain the similarities and differences between marketing cost analysis and production cost accounting.

2. Is an analysis of expenses as recorded in a company's accounting ledgers better than no cost analysis at all? What specific policies or operating plans may stem from an analysis of ledger expenses alone?

3. A national manufacturer of roofing and siding materials has 40 sales people. They each have their own territory and sell all three of the firm's product lines. They sell primarily to wholesalers and large retailers in the lumber and building materials field. The company wants to make a *territorial analysis* of marketing costs. What bases do you recommend it should use to allocate each of the following costs?

   a. Sales-force salaries.
   b. Sales-force travel expenses.
   c. Sales-force commissions paid on gross margin.
   d. Salaries and expenses of three regional sales managers.
   e. Sales-training expenses.
   f. Television advertising (local and national).
   g. Newspaper advertising.
   h. Billing.
   i. Shipping from three regional factories.
   j. Marketing research.
   k. General sales manager's salary and office expenses.
   l. Advertising overhead.
   m. Credit losses and markdowns on returned goods.

4. The company in the proceding problem wants to analyze its marketing cost by *product lines.* Suggest appropriate bases for allocating the above-listed cost items to the three product groups.

5. What is meant by "unprofitable business" or an "unprofitable sale"? Explain in detail. Should a company accept unprofitable business? If so, under what possible conditions?

6. What supporting points could be brought out by the proponents of each side in the full-cost versus contribution-margin controversy over allocation of indirect marketing costs? Which of the two concepts do you advocate? Why?

7. In an analysis of expenses grouped by activities, a manufacturer noted that last year the firm's direct selling expenses (sales-force compensation, travel expenses, branch office expenses, and so on) increased significantly over the preceding year. Is this trend necessarily an indication of weaknesses or inefficiencies in the management of the sales force?

8. Each of the following firms made a territorial cost analysis and discovered it had some districts that were showing net loss. What actions involving the sales force do you recommend that each company might take to improve its situation?
   - *a.* Hardware wholesaler, covering six southeastern states.
   - *b.* Regional manufacturer of cereals and dog food.
   - *c.* Paint and varnish manufacturer.
   - *d.* National business machines manufacturer.

9. What actions involving its sales force can each of the following firms take if they discover unprofitable products in their lines?
   - *a.* Distributor of electrical goods.
   - *b.* Flower seed producer.
   - *c.* Manufacturer of small power tools.

10. "Large-annual-volume customers never present a small-order problem, while low-annual-volume customers always create small-order problems." Do you agree?

11. Under what conditions should a firm completely discontinue selling to a small-order account?

12. To determine return on investment, we multiply two fractions: net profit/sales and sales/investment. Why can't we cancel out the sales factor in each fraction and simply divide net profit by investment?

13. Explain how the ROI concept may be used to evaluate the profit performance of a territorial sales manager.

Case 21–1

Hanover–Bates Chemical Corporation*

Sales Volume Analysis and Marketing Cost Analysis

James Sprague, newly appointed North East district sales manager for the Hanover–Bates Chemical Corporation, leaned back in his chair as the door to his office slammed shut. "Great beginning," he thought. "Three days in my new job, and the district's most experienced sales representative is threatening to quit."

On the previous night, James Sprague, Hank Carver (the district's most experienced sales representative), and John Follet, another senior member of the district sales staff, had met for dinner at Jim's suggestion. During dinner, Jim had mentioned that one of his top priorities would be to conduct a sales and profit analysis of the dis-

---

* This case was prepared by Professor Robert E. Witt, University of Texas at Austin. Reproduced with permission.

trict's business in order to identify opportunities to improve the district's profit performance. Jim had stated that he was confident that the analysis would indicate opportunities to reallocate district sales efforts in a manner that would increase profits. As Jim had indicated during the conversation, "My experience in analyzing district sales performance data for the national sales manager has convinced me that any district's allocation of sales effort to products and customer categories can be improved." Both Carver and Follet had nodded as Jim discussed his plans.

Hank Carver was waiting when Jim arrived at the district sales office the next morning. It soon became apparent that Carver was very upset by what he perceived as Jim's criticism of how he and the other district sales representatives were doing their jobs—and more particularly, how they were allocating their time in terms of customers and products. As he concluded his heated comments, Carver said, "This company has made it darned clear that 34 years of experience don't count for anything . . . and now someone with not much more than two years of selling experience and two years of pushing paper for the national sales manager at corporate headquarters tells me I'm not doing my job . . . Maybe it's time for me to look for a new job . . . and since Trumbull Chemical [Hanover–Bate's major competitor] is hiring, maybe that's where I should start looking . . . and I'm not the only one who feels this way."

As Jim reflected on the scene that had just occurred, he wondered what he should do. It had been made clear to him when he had been promoted to manager of the North East sales district that one of his top priorities should be improvement of the district's profit performance. As the national sales manager had said, "The North East sales district may rank third in dollar sales, but it's our worst district in terms of profit performance."

Prior to assuming his new position, Jim had assembled the data presented in Tables 1 through 6 to assist him in analyzing district sales and profits. The data had been compiled from records maintained in the national sales manager's office. Jim believed that the data would provide a sound basis for a preliminary analysis of district sales and profit performance. He also had recognized that additional data probably would have to be collected when he arrived in the North East district (District 3).

In response to the national sales manager's comment about the North East district's poor profit performance, Jim had been particularly interested in how the district had performed on its gross profit quota. He knew that district gross profit quotas were assigned in a manner that took into account variation in price competition. Thus, he felt that poor performance in the gross profit quota area reflected misallocated sales efforts either in terms of customers or the

Table 1

Hanover-Bates Chemical Corporation—Summary Income Statements, 1982–1986

	1982	1983	1984	1985	1986
Sales.....................	$19,890,000	$21,710,000	$19,060,000	$21,980,000	$23,890,000
Production expenses	11,934,000	13,497,000	12,198,000	13,612,000	14,563,000
Gross profit..............	7,956,000	8,213,000	6,862,000	8,368,000	9,327,000
Administrative expenses	2,606,000	2,887,000	2,792,000	2,295,000	3,106,000
Selling expenses	2,024,000	2,241,000	2,134,000	2,274,000	2,399,000
Pretax profit	3,326,000	3,085,000	1,936,000	3,169,000	3,822,000
Taxes	1,512,000	1,388,000	790,000	1,426,000	1,718,000
Net profit	$ 1,814,000	$ 1,697,000	$ 1,146,000	$ 1,743,000	$ 2,104,000

mix of products sold. To provide himself with a frame of reference, Jim had also requested data on the North Central district (District 7). This district was generally considered to be one of the best, if not the best, in the company. Furthermore, the North Central district sales manager, who was only three years older than Jim, was highly regarded by the national sales manager.

The Hanover–Bates Chemical Corporation was a leading producer of processing chemicals for the chemical plating industry. The company's products were produced in four plants located in Los Angeles, Houston, Chicago, and Newark, New Jersey. The company's

Table 2

District Sales Quota and Gross Profit Quota Performance, 1986

District	Number of Sales Reps	Sales Quota	Sales Actual	Gross Profit Quota*	Gross Profit Actual
1 7		$ 3,880,000	$ 3,906,000	$1,552,000	$1,589,000
2 6		3,750,000	3,740,000	1,500,000	1,529,000
3 6		3,650,000	3,406,000	1,460,000	1,239,000
4 6		3,370,000	3,318,000	1,348,000	1,295,000
5 5		3,300,000	3,210,000	1,320,000	1,186,000
6 5		3,130,000	3,205,000	1,252,000	1,179,000
7 5		2,720,000	3,105,000	1,088,000	1,310,000
Totals		$23,800,000	$23,890,000	$9,520,000	$9,327,000

* District gross profit quotas were developed by the national sales manager in consultation with the district managers and took into account price competition in the respective districts.

Table 3

District Selling Expenses, 1986

District	Sales Reps' Salaries*	Sales Commission	Sales Reps' Expenses	District Office	District Manager's Salary	District Manager's Expenses	Sales Support	Total Selling Expenses
1 ...	$177,100	$19,426	$56,280	$21,150	$33,500	$11,460	$68,500	$ 388,416
2 ...	143,220	18,700	50,760	21,312	34,000	12,034	71,320	351,346
3 ...	157,380	17,030	54,436	22,123	35,000†	12,382	70,010	368,529
4 ...	150,480	16,590	49,104	22,004	32,500	11,005	66,470	348,153
5 ...	125,950	16,050	42,720	21,115	33,000	11,123	76,600	326,558
6 ...	124,850	16,265	41,520	20,992	33,500	11,428	67,100	315,655
7 ...	114,830	17,530	44,700	24,485	31,500	11,643	58,750	300,258
								$2,398,915

* Includes cost of fringe benefit program, which was 10 percent of base salary.
† Salary of Jim Sprague's predecessor.

Table 4

District Contribution to Corporate Administrative Expense and Profit, 1986

District	Sales	Gross Profit	Selling Expenses	Contribution to Administrative Expense and Profit
1	$ 3,906,000	$1,589,000	$ 388,416	$1,200,544
2	3,740,000	1,529,000	351,346	1,177,654
3	3,406,000	1,239,000	369,529	870,471
4	3,318,000	1,295,000	348,153	946,847
5	3,210,000	1,186,000	326,558	859,442
6	3,205,000	1,179,000	315,376	863,624
7	3,105,000	1,310,000	300,258	1,009,742
	$23,890,000	$9,327,000	$2,398,636	$6,928,324

Table 5

North East (District 3) and North Central (District 7) Sales and Gross Profit Performance by Account Category, 1986

District	A Account	B Account	C Account	Total
Sales by account category:				
North East..................................	$915,000	$1,681,000	$810,000	$3,406,000
North Central	751,000	1,702,000	652,000	3,105,000
Gross profit by account category:				
North East..................................	$356,000	$ 623,000	$260,000	$1,239,000
North Central	330,000	725,000	255,000	1,310,000

Table 6

Potential Accounts, Active Accounts, and Account Call Coverage: North East and North Central Districts, 1986

District	Potential Accounts			Active Accounts			Account Coverage (total calls)		
	(A)	(B)	(C)	(A)	(B)	(C)	(A)	(B)	(C)
North East	90	381	635	53	210	313	1,297	3,051	2,118
North Central	60	286	499	42	182	218	1,030	2,618	1,299

production process was, in essence, a mixing operation. Chemicals purchased from a broad range of suppliers were mixed according to a variety of user-brand formulas. Company sales in 1986 had reached a new high of $23,890,000, up from $21,980,000 in 1985. Net pretax profit in 1986 had been $3,822,000, up from $3,169,000 in 1985. Hanover–Bates had a strong balance sheet, and the company enjoyed a favorable price-earning ratio on its stock, which traded on the OTC market.

Although Hanover-Bates did not produce commodity-type chemicals (e.g., sulfuric acid and others), industry customers tended to perceive minimal quality differences among the products produced by Hanover-Bates and its competitors. Given the lack of variation in product quality and the industry-wide practice of limited advertising expenditures, field sales efforts were of major importance in the marketing programs of all firms in the industry.

Hanover-Bates's market consisted of several thousand job shop and captive (i.e., in-house) plating operations. Chemical platers process a wide variety of materials, including industrial fasteners (e.g., screws, rivets, bolts, washers, and others), industrial components (e.g., clamps, casings, couplings, and others), and miscellaneous items (e.g., umbrella frames, eyelets, decorative items, and others). The chemical plating process involves the electrolytic application of metallic coatings such as zinc, cadmium, nickel, brass, and so forth. The degree of required plating precision varies substantially, with some work being primarily decorative. Some involves relatively loose standards (e.g., 0.0002 zinc, which means that anything over two ten-thousandths of an inch of plate is acceptable), and some involves relatively precise standards (e.g., 0.0003–0.0004 zinc).

Regardless of the degree of plating precision involved, quality control is of critical concern to all chemical platers. Extensive variation in the condition of materials received for plating requires a high level of service from the firms supplying chemicals to platers. This service is normally provided by the sales representatives of the firm(s) supplying the plater with processing chemicals.

Hanover-Bates and the majority of the firms in its industry produced the same line of basic processing chemicals for the chemical plating industry. The line consisted of the following products: a trisodium phosphate cleaner (SBX); anesic aldehyde brightening agents for zinc plating (ZBX), cadmium plating (CBX), and nickel plating (NBX); a protective postplating chromate dip (CHX); and a protective burnishing compound (BUX). The company's product line is detailed in the accompanying Table 7.

Hanover-Bates's sales organization consisted of 40 sales representatives operating in seven sales districts. Sales representatives' salaries ranged from $20,000 to $33,000, with fringe-benefit costs amounting to an additional 10 percent of salary. In addition to their salaries, Hanover-Bates's sales representatives received commissions of one half of 1 percent of their dollar sales volume on all sales up to their sales quotas. The commission on sales in excess of quota was 1 percent.

In 1984, the national sales manager of Hanover-Bates had developed a sales program based on selling the full line of Hanover-Bates products. He believed that if the sales representatives could successfully carry out his program, benefits would accrue to both Hanover-Bates and its customers: (1) sales volume per account would be greater, and selling costs as a percentage of sales would decrease; (2) a Hanover-Bates sales representative could justify spending more time with such an account, thus becoming more knowledgeable about the account's business and better able to provide technical assistance and identify selling opportunities; and (3) full-line sales would strengthen Hanover-Bates's competitive position by reducing the likelihood of account loss to other plating chemical suppliers (a problem that existed in multiple-supplier situations).

The national sales manager's 1984 sales program had also in-

Table 7

Product Line Date

Product	Container Size	List Price	Gross Margin
SBX	400 lb. drum	$ 80	$28
ZBX	50 lb. drum	76	34
CBX	50 lb. drum	76	34
NBX	50 lb. drum	80	35
CHX	100 lb. drum	220	90
BUX	400 lb. drum	120	44

cluded the following account call frequency guidelines: A accounts (major accounts generating $12,000 or more in yearly sales)—two calls per month; B accounts (medium-sized accounts generating $6,000 to $11,999 in yearly sales)—one call per month; C accounts (small accounts generating less than $6,000 yearly in sales)—one call every two months. The account call-frequency guidelines were developed by the national sales manager after discussions with the district managers. The national sales manager had been concerned about the optimum allocation of sales effort to accounts. He felt that the guidelines would increase the efficiency of the company's sales force, although not all of the district sales managers agreed with this conclusion.

It was common knowledge in Hanover-Bates's corporate sales office that Jim Sprague's predecessor as North East district sales manager had not been one of the company's better district sales managers. His attitude toward the sales plans and programs of the national sales manager had been one of reluctant compliance rather than acceptance and support. When the national sales manager succeeded in persuading Jim Sprague's predecessor to take early retirement, he had been faced with the lack of an available qualified replacement.

Hank Carver, who most of the sales representatives had assumed would get the district manager job, had been passed over in part because he would be 65 in three years. The national sales manager had not wanted to face the same replacement problem again in three years. He also had wanted someone in the position who would be more likely to be responsive to the company's sales plans and policies. The appointment of Jim Sprague as district manager had caused considerable talk, not only in the district but also at corporate headquarters. In fact, the national sales manager had warned Jim that "a lot of people are expecting you to fall on your face. They don't think you have the experience to handle the job or to manage and motivate a group of sales representatives most of whom are considerably older and more experienced than you." The national sales manager had concluded by saying, "I think you can handle the job, Jim. I think you can manage those sales reps and improve the district's profit performance, and I'm depending on you to do both."

Questions

1. Evaluate the performance of the North East district in comparison with the other Hanover-Bates sales districts. Consider such performance bases as sales volume, gross margin, and contribution to profit.

2. Where are the weak spots in the North East district's performance?
3. What should management do to improve areas of poor performance in the North East district?

Case 21-2

Vaudio Music Box/Learning System*

Marketing Cost Analysis

The O.K. International Corporation had successfully introduced the "Vaudiosette" in the United States market. The Vaudiosette was a technologically advanced music box/learning system designed for the preschool and grade school market. The system involved a combination of audio and video technology of an advanced, as well as low-cost, nature. Through the use of disks, this product provided a combination of entertainment and learning. This system had caught on like wildfire in the United States market.

At this time, the introduction of Vaudiosette was being considered in several overseas markets. In the case of Northern Latasia, the following assumptions for the *initial screening* of the product introduction had been made.

1. All Vaudiosettes and disks will be produced domestically in O.K.'s New York plant.
2. Vaudiosettes and disks will have a landed cost in Northern Latasia of $42.00 and $2.20 respectively.
3. Market research costs total $400,000. Twenty-five percent of this total will be spent during the year before the product sales start, 50 percent during the first year of sales, and the remainder will be spent during the second year.
4. Advertising and promotion costs are expected to be $300,000 during each of the first two years of Vaudiosette sales and $200,000 during each of years three and four. During the final year of sales, management does not expect to do any advertising or promotion of Vaudiosettes.
5. Vaudiosettes are expected to have a five-year product life cycle with unit sales of 50,000, 200,000, 200,000, 150,000 and 100,000 respectively. Toward the end of year 5 we expect to be

* This case was prepared by Professor William L. Ferrara, Pennsylvania State University. Reproduced with permission.

getting ready to launch a technologically superior product in year 6.

6. Disk sales are expected to average 10 per year per *cumulative* Vaudiosettes sold through year 5 and 2 per year thereafter through year 10. No disk sales are expected after year 10.

7. Vaudiosettes will have a retail selling price of $49.00 each while disks will sell for $2.99 each.

8. Variable selling and distribution costs in Northern Latasia are expected to be $.30 per Vaudiosette and $.02 per disk.

9. We assume that our existing sales and administrative force in Northern Latasia will be able to handle almost all incremental activities due to the added Vaudiosette volume. Consequently, our incremental fixed selling, distribution, and administrative costs will average only $100,000 per year while Vaudiosettes are sold and $20,000 per year thereafter.

10. Corporate headquarters in the United States has a policy of levying a charge of 20 percent of sales dollar volume to cover corporate selling, advertising, distribution, and administrative activities.

11. Assume that any net income will be taxed at a 50 percent rate.

12. To simplify your calculations you may ignore the cost of money—that is, the interest rate.

Questions

1. In light of the above assumptions, would it be profitable to introduce the Vaudiosette into the Northern Latasia market?

2. Would Vaudiosette be a profitable product if sales volume could be increased 50,000 units per year (years 1 thru 5) by increasing advertising and promotion $50,000 per year (years 1 thru 5)?

3. Given the increased sales volume of question 2, what would happen if the landed costs of Vaudiosettes and disks were $40 and $2 respectively?

4. Considering only the original 12 assumptions used for question 1, suppose that the life cycle of Vaudiosettes could be extended to a sixth year by delaying the introduction of the anticipated technologically superior product. What impact would this have on cash flows? Answer only in terms of concepts.

5. Assume that the government of Northern Latasia insisted that Vaudiosettes should be assembled at least partially in that country. Then what factors must be assessed in order to decide whether that product should be introduced into Northern Latasia?

22

Evaluating an Individual's Sales Performance

The yardstick for measuring people is other people.
ANONYMOUS

Throughout the chapters on motivation, morale, and supervision, we stressed the importance of treating each sales rep fairly. Unfair treatment triggers trouble. But how is the manager to know which reps deserve rewards and which do not? Usually such judgments are based on personal observation, managers' attitudes, and superficial and obvious performance data. This chapter discusses more sophisticated tools with which to evaluate the sales reps.

In considering the evaluation of a firm's selling effort, the preceding two chapters have emphasized the performance of the *total* sales force. This chapter focuses on appraising the productivity and effectiveness of *individual sales people.* After examining the nature and purposes of this managerial activity, we will outline a complete program for evaluating sales performance. The last section of the chapter is a case example of how one firm interpreted the performance data it assembled.

Nature and Importance of Performance Evaluation

Appraising the performance of a sales person is a part of the managerial function of evaluation. It is part of a marketing audit. Management is comparing the results of a person's efforts against the goals set for that person. The purpose, of course, is to determine what happened in the past and then to use this information for taking corrective actions and making plans.

Concept of Evaluation and Development

Evaluation has an added dimension when viewed from the perspective of evaluation *and development* of individual sales people. Within this richer context, management is engaged in a counseling activity rather than a cold statistical analysis. Certainly management wants to measure past performance against standards to identify strengths and weaknesses in the firm's marketing system, particularly as a basis for future planning. But this activity is optimized only if it also is brought to the personal level of the sales person. It should serve as a basis for the person's self-development and as a basis for a sound company program for the guidance and development of sales personnel.

Importance of Performance Evaluation

A statistical evaluation of sales-force performance is a major tool for improving sales performance and for lowering marketing costs. Management can identify the outstanding sales producers and then study their sales techniques with an eye toward having the other sales people adopt them. It also can show high-cost performers how to reduce their selling costs.

Thus a good performance review can be a major aid in other sales-force management tasks. Promotions and pay increases can be based on objective performance data rather than on favoritism, subjective observations, or opinions. Weaknesses in field selling efforts, once identified, may be forestalled in the future by incorporating corrective measures in training programs. Performance evaluations may uncover the need for improvements in the compensation plan. The existing plan may be resulting in too much effort on low-margin items or inadequate attention to nonselling (missionary) activities.

Performance analysis especially helps in sales supervision. It is difficult to effectively supervise someone unless the supervisor knows *what* the person is doing correctly or incorrectly and *why* he is doing it. If a rep's sales volume is unsatisfactory, for instance, a performance review will show it. Moreover, the evaluation probably will identify the cause—whether the rep has a low daily call rate, is not working enough days per month, is calling on the wrong prospects, is having trouble with the sales presentation, and so on.

An effective procedure for appraising the work of an individual could be called morale insurance. Any person who knows what he is expected to do, and has some benchmarks for measuring accomplishments, feels more secure. A performance evaluation should ensure that those reps who deserve favorable recognition receive it, and those who deserve criticism are handled appropriately. The sales person with the highest sales volume is not necessarily the best one and may not even be doing a good all-around job. To reward this person on the basis of sales volume alone, without knowing the full story, can hurt morale of others in the sales force. Similarly, morale suffers if management criticizes a rep for low volume, when the contributing factor was low territorial potential or unusually stiff competition. A performance-appraisal system should forestall such situations.

By evaluating the sales people's achievements, management helps them discover their own strengths and weaknesses. This should motivate them to raise their levels of performance. Like most people, sales people seldom can make an effective self-evaluation. A sales rep may know he is doing something wrong from his output. But he is unable to determine the reasons for his poor productivity.

Difficulties Involved in Evaluating Performance

Many firms seem to lack an effective procedure for evaluating the performance of their sales people. Undoubtedly, the time, people, and expense necessary to do a satisfactory job are contributing factors. However, firms encounter other difficulties in the evaluation task. Most managers rely on *qualitative* rather than quantitative measures of performance when evaluating their reps.[1] Many of the bases used in evaluations are approximations at best. The measure of a sales person's effectiveness in training his customers' sales reps or his ability to prospect for new accounts can only be estimated.

Many of the duties assigned to sales people cannot be measured objectively, and some tasks are difficult to evaluate even on a subjective basis. A manufacturer's representative is supposed to service the firm's accounts with dealers and distributors; a wholesaler's sales rep is told to avoid high-pressure selling; all sales people are supposed to build goodwill with customers. Even if the company has close field supervision of the sales force, these tasks can be evaluated only subjectively. And, if management does not closely supervise the sales people in the field, it may be virtually impossible to measure results from some of these duties.

By the same token, however, management sometimes does not recognize that many tasks of a seemingly subjective nature can actually be quantified. A sales person's tendency to high-pressure or oversell customers, for instance, can be measured by tallying his canceled orders, the number of lost accounts, and the rate of reorders.

---

[1] For an excellent discussion of this propensity to rely on qualitative standards, see Donald W. Jackson, Janet E. Keith, and John Schlacter, "Evaluation of Selling Performance: A Study of Current Practices," *Journal of Personal Selling & Sales Management,* November 1983, pp. 43–51.

The wide variety of conditions under which sales reps work makes it difficult for management to compare the productivity of the people involved. There is no satisfactory method for equating territorial differences in potential, competition, or working conditions. It is difficult to compare the performance of city sales people with country sales people, for example. Even if the districts are equal in potential, they are not comparable in area, customer size, or on other bases.

Sometimes performance evaluation is difficult because the results of a sales person's efforts may not be evident for some time. A district's improved position may show up only after a rep has been working there for a year or more.

When two or more people are involved in making a sale or in servicing a customer, it usually is difficult to give individual credit for results. Whether two sales people are involved, or a sales person plus an executive (supervisor, branch manager, product manager), individual contributions are hard to measure.

Importance of a Good Job Description

In the task of sales-force evaluation, as we have observed so many other sales-force management activities, a good job description is critically important. Evaluators must work from the reference point of a statement about *what* a sales person is supposed to do. Otherwise, they are not in a good position to determine *whether* he did the job or *how effectively* he did it.

Program for Evaluating Performance

This section suggests a procedural system for evaluating sales-force performance. The program is a complete one; but it is also expensive and time-consuming. A firm probably would not participate in the entire program unless it is using electronic data processing equipment.

Establish Some Basic Policies

Preliminary to the actual evaluation, management should set some ground rules. One question that calls for a decision is: Who is to participate in the evaluation? Several executives normally are involved. The most likely one is the sales person's immediate superior. Perhaps this is a field supervisor, a district manager, or a branch manager. The boss of the immediate supervisor is also likely to be involved. Certainly, the sales person being evaluated should participate actively, usually with some form of self-evaluation. The personnel department may take part in the appraisal procedure. However, its role is probably one of staff support—preparing forms, gathering data to help set performance standards, and so on.

Another needed policy decision concerns the frequency of evaluation. For a *complete* evaluation of a sales person's total performance, probably once a year (or twice, at the outside) is enough, in light of the time and costs required. Many firms combine annual performance evaluation with a compensation review. Some form of appraisal is usually being conducted continuously as an inherent part of sales training or sales supervision.

The role of self-evaluation by sales reps should be clearly understood by the sales reps as well as by the executives involved in the appraisal system. What evaluation data will be given to the sales people? What evaluation forms will they be asked to fill out? What appeal procedures are available?

Select Bases for Evaluation

One key to a successful evaluation program is to appraise a sales rep's performance on as many different bases as possible. To do otherwise is to run the risk of being misled. Let's assume that we are rating a sales rep on the basis of the ratio of his selling expenses to his sales volume. If this percentage is very low compared to the average for the entire sales force, he probably will be commended. Yet, he actually may have achieved that low expense ratio by failing to prospect for new accounts or by otherwise covering his territory inadequately. Knowing the average number of daily calls he made, even in relation to the average call rate for the entire sales force, does not help us very much. By measuring his ratio of orders per call (his batting average) we learn a little more, but we still can be misled. Each additional piece of information—his sales volume, plus his average order size, plus his gross margin, and so on—helps to give a clearer picture of the person's performance. Both quantitative and qualitative factors should be used as bases for a performance appraisal.

Quantitative bases. The quantitative factors that can be used as evaluation bases fall into two categories—input (or effort) factors and output (or results) factors. Productivity is a concept that involves the relationship between the two—(1) ***output results*** as measured by sales volume, gross margin, and so on and (2) ***input effort*** as indicated by call rate, expenses incurred, nonselling activities, and others.

In a performance evaluation, the importance of output factors is readily recognized. Sometimes, however, the value of input effort factors is underestimated. They usually are critical in locating trouble spots. Assume a sales person's output performance (average order size, gross margin, and so on) is unsatisfactory. Very often the cause lies in the handling of the various input factors over which the rep has control.

A list of some *output* factors that ordinarily are useful as evaluation bases would include:

1. Sales volume.
   a. In dollars and in units.
   b. By products and customers (or customer groups).
   c. By mail, telephone, and personal sales calls.
2. Sales volume as a percentage of:
   a. Quota.
   b. Market potential (that is, market share).
3. Gross margin by product line, customer group, and order size.
4. Orders.
   a. Number of orders.
   b. Average size (dollar volume) of order.
   c. Batting average (orders ÷ calls).
   d. Number of canceled orders.
5. Accounts.
   a. Percentage of accounts sold.
   b. Number of new accounts.
   c. Number of lost accounts.
   d. Number of accounts with overdue payment.

Some *input* factors that may be used as bases for evaluation are:

1. Calls per day (call rate).
2. Days worked.
3. Selling time versus nonselling time.
4. Direct selling expense:
   a. In total.
   b. As percentage of sales volume.
   c. As percentage of quota.
5. Nonselling activities:
   a. Advertising displays set up.
   b. Letters written to prospects.
   c. Telephone calls made to prospects.
   d. Number of meetings held with dealers and/or distributors.
   e. Number of service calls made.
   f. Collections made.
   g. Number of customer complaints received.

As evaluation bases, these output and input factors fall into two categories. One group consists of factors measured individually—sales volume, number of orders, daily call rate, or displays set up, for example. The other category includes ratios involving almost any two of the individual variables—such as expenses/sales, orders/call, or average order size.

Qualitative bases. It would be nice if the entire evaluation could be based only on quantitative factors. This would minimize the subjectivity and personal biases of the evaluators. Unfortunately, this cannot be done. Too many factors—all of a qualitative nature—must be reckoned with because they directly influence a sales person's performance. These qualitative factors can cover a wide gamut.

1. Personal efforts of the sales reps.
    a. Management of their time.
    b. Planning and preparation for calls.
    c. Quality of sales presentations.
    d. Ability to handle objections and to close sales.
2. Knowledge of:
    a. Product.
    b. Company and company policies.
    c. Competitor's products and strategies.
    d. Customers.
3. Customer relations.
4. Personal appearance and health.
5. Personality and attitudinal factors. Some examples are:
    a. Cooperativeness.
    b. Resourcefulness.
    c. Acceptance of responsibility.
    d. Ability to analyze logically and make decisions.

Sources of information. When deciding on which factors to use as bases for a performance evaluation, management should select only those for which data are available, at a reasonable cost. The four main sources of information are company records, the sales reps themselves, field sales managers, and customers.

Company records are the main source for data on most of the quantitative *output* factors. By studying sales invoices, customers' orders, and accounting records, management can discover much about sales peoples' volume, gross margin, average order size, and so on. Most firms fall far short of making optimum use of their records for evaluation purposes. One reason for this shortcoming is that the information is not recorded in usable form for a performance evaluation. Firms may find that it is too expensive and time-consuming to tabulate and present the data in usable form. However, companies today are using data processing equipment as an aid in collecting, analyzing, and reporting data in a form useful for evaluation purposes.

Reports submitted by the sales force are an important source, particularly for performance *input* factors. The regular use of call reports, activity reports, and expense reports can provide the necessary data on the sales people's work. Call reports can furnish the details of each visit to each customer. Daily or weekly activity reports summarize the rep's work with present and potential accounts. These reports can also furnish territorial market information on competitors' advertising and pricing, customers' credit standings, and so on. Expense-account reports tell management something about the number of miles traveled, days worked, and customers entertained. Analyses of the expense data may indicate to management the reasons for the performance level of a given sales rep. Perhaps he is not entertaining the appropriate customers or is not spending enough time with customers in the far reaches of his district.

The Achilles' heel in using sales people's reports as a source of evaluation data is that the information is only as good as the accuracy, completeness, and punctuality of the reps' reporting efforts. This is a serious problem.

As a rule, sales supervisors and other sales executives regularly spend some time in traveling with the sales reps in the field. The managers observe the reps during sales calls on customers. These executives, then, can make an eyewitness appraisal of a sales person's performance with customers. They also can evaluate the individual's self-management abilities—his ability, for instance, to plan his work and work his plan.

As a source of evaluation information, the customers can be used in one of two ways. The more common method is to gather information submitted by customers on a voluntary, informal basis. Unfortunately, this usually takes the form of complaints, because customers rarely take the time to report commendatory performance by salesmen. A less widely used approach is to actively solicit opinions from customers on a regular basis. However, both the sales force and the customers are quite likely to resent this approach. It can be a dangerous tactic.

Set Performance Standards

Management's next step is to set standards for the evaluation bases. Standards usually can be set for any of the quantitative factors. Qualitative factors, by their nature, present a different problem. The standards serve as a benchmark, or a par for the course, against which a sales rep's performance can be measured. Also, they let a sales person know what is expected, and serve as a guide in planning work.

Setting standards is one of the most difficult phases of performance evaluation. Standards must be equitable and reasonable, or the sales people may lose interest in their work and confidence in management. As a result, their morale may decline. If the standards are too high or too low, the resulting interpretations will be worthless or even harmful in that management can be misled.

Standards for many of the output (results) factors can be tied to company goals for territories, product lines, or customer groups. Such performance measures as sales volume, gross margin, or market share probably have already been set.

It is more difficult to set performance standards for the effort (input) factors. A careful time-and-duty analysis of sales jobs should give management some basis for knowing what is satisfactory performance for daily-call rates, displays arranged, and other factors. Another approach is to use executive judgment based on the personal observations made by those who work with the sales people in the field.

To measure the efficiency of a company's selling effort, management must balance the output against the input. Consequently, a firm should develop standards for such output/input ratios as sales volume/call, orders/call, gross margin/order, and sales volume/expenses.

Compare Performance with Standards

The next step in the performance evaluation procedure is to interpret the accumulated information. This step involves comparison of an individual's performance—both efforts and results—with the predetermined standards.

Problem of data comparability.   A key point to consider is the problem of comparability of the various data on performance. Ideally, a sales person should be judged only on factors over which he has control. Consequently, management should identify the uncontrollable factors that affect sales performance and then take these factors into consideration when appraising an individual's performance.

The sales potential in a territory, especially in relation to its size and the number of customers, is a good example of these factors. In a large territory with many small, scattered customers, a sales person's expenses are likely to be higher than in a smaller district with fewer but larger volume accounts. Differences in competitive activity or physical conditions among territories must be considered when comparing performances. Usually, there are territorial variations in the amount of advertising, sales-promotional support, or home-office technical service available to customers. These and several other factors tend to impair the comparability of performance data.

Interpreting quantitative data.   A few of the factors ordinarily used as bases for performance appraisal, and how they can be used by management, are discussed in the following sections.

Sales volume and market share.   The first criterion most sales managers use for judging the relative performance of sales people is their sales volume. Some executives believe that the rep who sells the most merchandise is the best sales person, regardless of other considerations. Unfortunately, sales volume alone may be a poor indicator of a rep's worth to the company. Total volume alone tells the firm nothing about the rep's contribution to profit or customer relations. It does little good to move huge volumes of merchandise at no profit.

Sales volume can be a useful indicator of performance, however, if it is analyzed in sufficient detail and with discretion. For evaluation purposes, a rep's total volume may be studied by product line, by some form of customer grouping, or by order size. Even then, the volume figures are not very meaningful unless they can be related to some predetermined standard of acceptable performance—a volume quota for each product line or customer group, for example.

Another important evaluation factor is the share of market each sales person obtains. Firms compute this figure by dividing the rep's sales volume by the territorial market potential. Here again the data are more useful if share of market can be determined for each product line or customer group.

Management must be cautious when comparing market-share performance of one person with another, because these figures may have limited comparability. Sales rep A may get 20 percent of the market in his district, while sales rep B captures only 10 percent of his market. Yet B may be doing a better job. Competition may be far more severe in B's district. Or the company may be furnishing A with considerably more advertising support.

Gross profit.   In most firms, a sales manager is (or should be) more concerned with the amount of gross profit the sales people generate than with their dollar sales volume. Gross margin in dollars is a much better measure of a sales person's effectiveness because it gives some indication of his ability to sell the high-margin items. Since the prime objective of most businesses is to maximize profits, a person's direct contribution to profit is a logical yardstick for evaluating his performance.

Management can reflect its gross margin goals by setting volume quotas for each product line. In this way, the company can motivate the sales force to achieve a desirable balance of sales among the various lines. Then, even though the reps are later evaluated on the basis of sales volume, this evaluation will automatically include gross margin considerations.

As an evaluative yardstick, gross margin has some limitations. When management ignores selling expenses, there is no way of knowing how much it costs to generate gross margin. Thus, sales rep A may have a higher dollar gross margin than sales rep B. But A's selling expenses may be proportionately so much higher than B's that A actually shows a lower contribution margin. Furthermore, a sales person does not fully control the product mix represented in his total sales volume. Territorial market potential and intensity of competition vary from one district to another. These factors can influence the sales of the various product lines.

Number and size of orders. Another measure of performance effectiveness is the number of orders and the average size of orders obtained by each sales rep. The average sale is computed by dividing a rep's total number of orders into his total sales volume. This calculation may be made for each class of customer to determine how the rep's average order varies among them. This analysis discloses which reps are getting too many small, unprofitable orders, even though their total volume appears satisfactory because of a few large orders. The analysis also may show that some reps find it difficult to obtain orders from certain classes of customers. However, in total they make up for this deficiency by superior performance with the other accounts.

Calls per day—call rate. A key factor in sales performance is the number of calls made. A sales person ordinarily cannot sell merchandise without calling on customers; generally, the more calls, the more sales. Sales rep A makes three calls a day, but the company average is four for sales reps who work under reasonably comparable conditions. If management can raise A's call rate up to the company average of four, his sales *should* increase about 33 percent.

For evaluation purposes, a sales person's daily (or weekly) call rate can be measured against the company average or some other predetermined standard for this activity. However, discretion must be exercised in interpreting a rep's call rate. Its significance is limited by the comparability of conditions under which the various sales people work. Call rates are influenced by the number of miles reps must travel and by the number of customers per square mile in the territory.

Usually, in a given business a certain desired call rate yields the best results. If the rep falls below this rate, his sales decline because he is not seeing enough prospects. If he calls on too many prospects, his sales may also decline, since he probably does not spend sufficient time with each one to get the job done.

Batting average. A sales person's batting average is calculated by dividing the number of orders he gets by the number of calls he makes (O/C). The number of calls made is equivalent to times at bat; the number of orders written is equivalent to the hits made. As a performance index, the batting average discloses ability to locate and call on good prospects and ability to close a sale. A sales person's batting average should be computed for each class of customers called on. Often, a rep varies in ability to close a sale with different types of customers.

Analysis of a sales rep's call rate in relation to his order rate can be quite meaningful. If the call rate is above average but the number of orders is below normal, perhaps the rep is not spending enough time with each customer. Or suppose the call rate and batting average are both above standard but the average order is small. Then a field supervisor may work with the sales person to show him how to make fewer but more productive calls. The idea is to raise the size of the average order by spending more time and talking about more products with each account.

Direct-selling expenses. Direct-selling expense is the sum of travel expenses, other business expenses, and compensation (salary, commission, bonus) for each sales person. These total expenses may be expressed as a percentage of sales. Also the expense-to-sales ratios for the various sales people can be compared. Or for each sales person management can compute the cost per call by dividing total expenses by the number of calls made.

In a performance evaluation, these various cost indexes may indicate the relative efficiency of the sales people in the field. However, management must interpret these ratios carefully and in detail. An expense- to-sales ratio, for instance, may be *above* average because the sales person: (1) is doing a poor job; (2) is working in a marginal territory; (3) is working in a new territory doing a lot of prospecting and building a solid base for the future; or (3) is working a territory that covers far more square miles than the average district. A rep with a low batting average usually has a high cost per order. Similarly, the one who makes few calls per day has a high ratio of costs per call.

Routing efficiency. Dividing the miles traveled by the number of calls made gives the average miles per call. This figure either indicates the density of the sales rep's territory or measures his routing efficiency. If a group of sales people all have approximately the same size and density of territories, then miles per call is a significant figure for indicating each one's routing efficiency. Suppose five sales people selling for an office machines firm in a metropolitan area vary considerably in the number of miles traveled per call. Then the sales manager may have reason to control the routing of those who are out of line.

Basic performance equations. The quantitative evaluation of a sales rep's performance can utilize either of the following equations:

$$\text{Sales} = \text{Days worked} \times \frac{\text{Calls}}{\text{Days worked}} \times \frac{\text{Orders}}{\text{Calls}} \times \frac{\text{Sales}}{\text{Orders}}$$

$$\text{Sales} = \text{Days worked} \times \text{Call rate} \times \text{Batting average} \times \text{Average order}$$

If the sales volume for a representative is unsatisfactory, the basic cause must rest in one or more of these four factors. An analysis (such as done in Figure 22–2) can help direct the manager's attention to the trouble spot so additional detailed investigation can pinpoint the rep's exact difficulties.

Evaluating qualitative factors. Lack of objectivity in evaluations is largely minimized when *quantitative* factors are used as bases in a performance evaluation. However, when the evaluation is based on *qualitative* factors, the personal, subjective element comes into full play. The evaluator assumes a key role at this point. The success of a qualitative evaluation depends in great measure on the evaluator's ability to be objective and completely impartial.

Merit-rating forms are a helpful tool in this evaluation procedure. These forms permit several evaluators' judgments to appear in a generally standardized manner. Such uniformity aids in comparing one person with another. Rating forms also provide a written report for company records. More important, however, they make an evaluator more thorough because his appraisals will be on record.

There is an almost limitless variety of evaluation forms. Each manager develops whatever form seems appropriate for the situation. Most such subjective forms suffer from three major defects.

First is the halo effect. Evaluators are biased by a generalized, overall impression or image of the person they are evaluating. If the manager does not like the way a rep dresses, that attitude will bias all aspects of the manager's evaluation. Similarly, the manager who is impressed with a person's sales ability is likely to rate other aspects of the person's performance highly.

Second, such rating forms generally overvalue inconsequential factors and undervalue truly important ones. Teacher-rating forms commonly used in colleges are an example. The important aspect of a teacher's performance is whether or not the students learned what they were supposed to learn from the course. However, few rating forms probe that aspect of the classroom situation. Instead, they ask how organized the professor seemed to be or other questions that have little to do with learning.

In a sales context, the manager should be interested in the sales person's ability to make money for the firm, not whether the individual is socially adept or impressively dressed. It is essential in evaluation for the manager to keep in mind what is important and what is not. If something is not important, it should not be evaluated. The charge of evaluating what is *not* important is often a key point in legal cases involving discrimination in hiring and promotion.

Third, most subjective evaluation forms force the evaluator to make judgments on some factors even though he or she has no valid basis for doing so. Lacking valid information on the factor, the evaluator allows the halo effect to take over.

In addition to the halo effect, firms face two even more serious problems. First, many raters refuse to give bad ratings to those who deserve them because of fear of reprisal. As one executive put it, "Who knows what the future holds. The person I downgrade today may be my boss tomorrow." Such managers fail to see any personal advantage in giving accurate ratings. Yet, in any good management evaluation program, a manager's ability and willingness to accurately appraise people is a key factor in that executive's rise in management. Second, some people just don't get along. In these cases, evaluators have difficulty being fair.

Management writers have extolled the virtues of "Behaviorally Anchored Rating Scales," better known as BARS, as superior instruments for subjectively evaluating people. A BARS instrument contains detailed descriptions of the subject's behavior to guide the evaluator's numerical rating of that person. A sample of one question is shown in Figure 22–1. However, one study of BARS for sales-force evaluations concluded, "It is not possible at present to claim the superiority of behaviorally anchored scales over more traditional rating systems."[2] No amount of instrument sophistication can overcome the basic weaknesses inherent in subjective rating systems.

Discuss the Evaluation with the Sales Person

After each sales person's performance has been evaluated, the results should be reviewed in a conference with the sales manager. This important discussion should be viewed as a counseling interview. The sales manager should explain the person's achievements on each evaluation factor and point out how the results compared with the standards. Then, the manager and the sales person together may try to determine the reasons for the performance variations above or below the standards. It is essential to discuss the managerial ratings on the qualitative factors and to compare them with the sales person's self-evaluation on these points. Based on their review of all the evaluation factors, the manager and the sales person then can establish goals and an operating plan for the coming period.

The performance-evaluation interview can be a very sensitive oc-

---

[2] Benton Cocanougher and John M. Ivancevich, "BARS Performance Rating for Sales Force Personnel," *Journal of Marketing,* July 1978, p. 94.

Figure 22–1

A Performance Dimension and Seven Behavioral Anchors for a Sales Position: Promptness in Meeting Deadlines

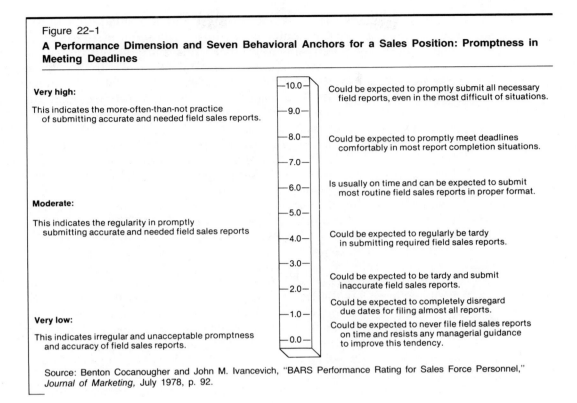

Very high:

This indicates the more-often-than-not practice of submitting accurate and needed field sales reports.

Moderate:

This indicates the regularity in promptly submitting accurate and needed field sales reports

Very low:

This indicates irregular and unacceptable promptness and accuracy of field sales reports.

10.0 — Could be expected to promptly submit all necessary field reports, even in the most difficult of situations.

9.0 —

8.0 — Could be expected to promptly meet deadlines comfortably in most report completion situations.

7.0 —

6.0 — Is usually on time and can be expected to submit most routine field sales reports in proper format.

5.0 —

4.0 — Could be expected to regularly be tardy in submitting required field sales reports.

3.0 —

2.0 — Could be expected to be tardy and submit inaccurate field sales reports.

Could be expected to completely disregard due dates for filing almost all reports.

1.0 — Could be expected to never file field sales reports on time and resists any managerial guidance to improve this tendency.

0.0 —

Source: Benton Cocanougher and John M. Ivancevich, "BARS Performance Rating for Sales Force Personnel," *Journal of Marketing*, July 1978, p. 92.

casion. It is not easy to point out a person's shortcomings face to face. If the sales manager is not extremely tactful, the rep may resent this kind of interview. People dislike being criticized and may become quite defensive in this situation. Some sales executives resist evaluation interviews because they feel these discussions can only injure morale. The concern is real and valid. They reason, "Why stir up trouble when you are basically happy with the person's performance." Unperceptive managers often lose sight of subordinates' virtues and strengths and criticize unimportant factors. One key in management is learning to use people's virtues to best advantage, while not allowing their weaknesses to hurt the firm.

Using Evaluation Data: An Example

The case example in this section illustrates the computations, interpretation, and use of several quantitative evaluation factors, both input (efforts) and output (results).

The Colorado Ski Company distributes on a national basis four lines of products—skis, ski accessories, and a limited line of ski pants and parkas. The company manufactures some of these products. Others are purchased from other firms, but are sold under the Colorado Ski Company's brand name. The firm sells to two basic classes of customers—sporting goods stores and specialty ski shops. The company uses its own sales force to reach these customers directly. Sales people are paid travel expenses plus a straight commission of 5 percent on sales volume.

For purposes of a performance evaluation, the sales manager of the Colorado Ski Company has divided the products into two basic lines: skis and ski accessories (equipment) and (2) ski pants and parkas (clothing). The retailers' usual initial markup on all these products is 50 percent of the retail selling price. There are no significant variations among products in the gross margin percentages realized by the Colorado Ski Company.

The sales manager is especially interested in the performance of three of the sales reps: Joe, who sells in the Rocky Mountain region (a huge territory); Gus, who is selling in the Pacific Northwest; and Paula, who covers the New England market. Much of the quantitative performance data for these three sales reps is summarized in Figure 22–2. Based on an analysis of these data, the sales manager is trying to decide: (1) which of the three did the best job and (2) which particular points should be discussed with each person in an effort to improve performance.

If the sales manager of the Colorado Ski Company were to look just at the sales production of these three people, he would have to conclude that Joe was best by far. He might even consider replacing Paula, since her volume looks weak in comparison. However, after comparing each rep's volume against the market potential, it is evident that Paula sold a larger share of her market than either Joe or Gus did.

Joe's Sales Performance

Concentrating on evaluating Joe's performance, the sales manager could see that Joe had worked the fewest numbers of days (220), made the fewest calls (700), and took the fewest orders (500). He also spent more money than the others ($48,000) and traveled far more miles (60,000). The sales manager can make some allowance for this because Joe's territory is the Rocky Mountain region, which is more sparsely settled than either Gus's or Paula's territory.

Joe's batting average (.714) is certainly adequate, and his average order ($2,400) is more than satisfactory. In fact, it is astonishingly high in comparison with the others ($1,133 and $612). The sales manager can justify this. The tremendous market potential ($6 million) in Joe's territory, in comparison with number of customers evidently located there, would naturally result in a high average sale. We assume that Joe has done a satisfactory job of covering potential prospects. Evidently the market potential per dealer in the Rocky Mountain region is far higher than in the other areas in the country. This would explain why he was able to take such large orders. Joe makes a little over three calls per day, which is relatively low in comparison to the others (3.55 and 4.8). However, it is not sufficiently out of line to cause any action to be taken, in light of his territory. The large number of miles per call is again indicative of the territory.

Considering expense per sales dollar, it *appears* that Joe is the most efficient sales rep, since he is spending only 4 percent of sales for expenses. The reps are being paid a straight commission of 5 percent of sales, which brings Joe's total cost of selling to 9 percent. However, the sales manager can see that this low expense ratio is simply a function of his abnormally high sales, which, in turn, are a result of his large market potential.

Joe's cost per call ($68.57) and cost per order ($96) seemed exceedingly high in comparison with those for the other reps. He worked 20 fewer days than Gus and 10 fewer than Paula. Granted that he traveled 15,000 miles more than Gus, the cost of those miles at 20 cents a mile would be about $3,000, which leaves something to be explained. The sales manager probably should investigate Joe's expense accounts. Expenses are usually related to the number of days worked and miles traveled. They are not related directly to sales volume; it costs as much to take an order for $100 as one for $600. A large market potential that results in large sales can cause the expense-to-sales ratio to be misleading. Thus, Joe's high sales volume caused his expense ratio to appear low, when in reality he was spending too much money making calls.

Let's analyze Joe's selling effort with regard to products and customers. He has a more difficult time getting orders from a sporting goods store (.500) than from a ski shop (.875). This is so even though his average sale to sporting goods stores ($5,067) is fantastically high. The sales manager may wonder if this is part of Joe's trouble on his batting average. Possibly in attempting to sell sporting goods stores so much merchandise he is simply scaring some of them away. However, the sales manager should be cautious here. In total, it is better that Joe continue to sell a high average order to sporting goods stores and settle for fewer orders than to bring both figures to average.

The sales manager may want to investigate the high average order to sporting goods stores. It may be that a few large discount sporting goods stores in the territory are placing huge orders with Joe. This may be no reflection at all on his ability to build up an order. There-

Figure 22–2

Evaluation of Sales Representatives' Performance

Sales representative:	Joe Jackson			Gus Dean	
Product line:	Equipment	Clothing	Total	Equipment	Clothing
Total sales (000s)	480	720	1200	220	460
Sporting goods stores	320	440	760	160	320
Ski shops	160	280	440	60	140
Calls made—Total			700		
Sporting goods stores			300		
Ski shops			400		
Orders taken—Total			500		
Sporting goods stores			150		
Ski shops			350		
Days worked			220		
Expenses			48000		
Miles traveled			60000		
Market potential—Total (millions)	$2	$4	$6	$1.2	$2.4
Sporting goods stores	1.6	2.4	4	.8	1.6
Ski shops	.4	1.6	2	.4	.8

	Sporting gds. stores	Ski shops	Total	Sporting gds. stores	Ski shops
Average order	$50.67	$12.57	$24.00	$10.67	$13.33
Batting average	.500	.875	.714	.900	.375
Calls per day			3.18		
Miles per call			86		
Expense per sales $ dollar			4%		
Cost per call, excluding commission			$68.57		
Cost per order, excluding commission			$96.00		

	Equipment	Clothing	Total	Equipment	Clothing
Percent of market—Total	24	18	20	18.3	19
Sporting goods stores	20	18	19	20	20
Ski shops	40	17.5	22	15	17.5

Figure 22-2 *(concluded)*

| | Paula Burns | | | | Total | |
Total	Equipment	Clothing	Total	Equipment	Clothing	Total
680	240	280	520	940	1460	2400
480	100	160	260	580	920	1500
200	140	120	260	360	540	900
900			1100			2700
500			500			1300
400			600			1400
600			850			1950
450			400			1000
150			450			950
240			230			690
40000			36000			124000
45000			35000			140000
$3.6	$1.2	$1.2	$2.4	$4.4	$7.6	$12
2.4	.72	.64	1.36	3.12	4.64	7.76
1.2	.48	.56	1.04	1.28	2.96	4.24

Total	Sporting gds. stores	Ski shops	Total	Sporting gds. stores	Ski shops	Total
$11.33	$6.50	$5.78	$6.12	$15.00	$9.47	$12.31
.666	.800	.750	.773	.679	.769	.722
3.75			4.8			3.9
50			32			52
5.9%			6.9%			5.2%
$44.44			$32.72			$45.92
$60.57			$42.35			$63.59

Total	Equipment	Clothing	Total	Equipment	Clothing	Total
19	20	23.3	21.7	21.4	19.2	20
20	13.9	25	19.1	18.6	19.8	19.3
16.7	29.2	21.4	25	28.1	18.2	21.2

fore, if his batting average could be raised in the sporting goods field, possibly no loss would occur at all to the average order. Then the result would be higher sales volume. It is something to investigate.

Another thing the sales manager may notice about Joe's performance is that he seems able to sell equipment (24 percent of potential) better than he sells clothing (18 percent of potential). He is well above average in his ability to sell skis, particularly to ski specialty shops (40 percent of potential), but he is below average in attention to clothing (17.5 percent). This may be just a reflection of his basic interest. He may prefer to talk about skis, bindings, and poles rather than about pants and parkas. The sales manager should mention to Joe that he should be doing a bit better in his sales of clothing. However, Joe is not sufficiently below par in any category for the sales manager to be unduly concerned.

Gus's Sales Performance

Probably the first thing the sales manager would note about Gus's sales performance is his apparent inability to sell to ski shops. He is closing only 37.5 percent of the calls he makes on them, whereas the company average is 76.9 percent. On the other hand, he has an extremely high batting average in getting orders from sporting goods stores (90 percent). The sales manager may conclude that Gus speaks the language of the nonskiing owner of a sporting goods store but does not communicate well with a ski expert. The sales manager may consider a conference with Gus to talk over the problems of the ski shop owner and how they differ from those of the sports shop. Gus may not be sufficiently trained in the technical aspects of skiing to answer the questions and gain the confidence of the ski professional. Gus's expenses seem to be in line with the company average, and his calls per day are satisfactory. While Gus is not achieving par as far as a share of the market is concerned, the deviation is not significant enough to warrant any conference on the matter.

Paula's Sales Performance

Paula seems to do fairly well in getting orders from both sporting goods stores and ski shops. But her average order ($612) is significantly below the company average ($1,231). This indicates a problem area. The sales manager probably first wants to determine if these low average orders are a function of the size of Paula's customers or whether this truly reflects her inability to sell merchandise. That Paula made 1,100 calls with the smallest market potential indicates that her average customer is considerably smaller than those of the other reps. The sales manager may become alarmed at Paula's relatively high expense of sales. However, he should realize that this is caused by the limited sales potential. Paula's cost per call and cost per order are the lowest of the three reps, indicating that her expense accounts are not out of line with her efforts.

It should be obvious to the sales manager that Paula is working hard; she is making almost five calls per day. This factor helps to explain several of the others. Her high call rate probably is the explanation for her low cost per call, and it explains the relatively large number of calls she makes. It also may explain why she is not selling so much per order. Perhaps she is not spending sufficient time with each customer. On the other hand, the number of miles per call (32) indicates that her territory is relatively dense, and this alone may be the reason she is able to make almost five calls per day. She does not have to spend as much time traveling between calls as the other two reps.

While a sales manager may at first seriously consider discharging Paula, a detailed analysis shows that she is doing as well as, if not better than, the other two reps. Her costs for efforts undertaken are lower. Also, she is achieving a larger percentage of the business available to her. Her only problem seems to be that her territory has limited market potential.

The Sales Manager's Decisions

In conclusion, the sales manager probably will undertake several different projects. First, he may try to get Joe to work a few more days in the year. It is understandable that this rep is tempted to do a little loafing. He has an annual income of $60,000 and is leading the sales force in sales. However, Joe's territory has a tremendous sales potential. If he does not want to service it properly, the company can cut it in half, giving each rep a $3 million potential to work with. This would still result in two territories of larger potential than that worked by Paula. Also, the sales manager may investigate why Joe is not selling to more sporting goods stores.

With Gus, the sales manager probably will focus his entire attention on why ski shops are such an obstacle. Gus is not able to sell to ski shops as well as the others. He probably needs additional instruction on the technical aspects of skiing.

The sales manager may want to ask Paula why she does not sell more skis to sporting goods stores. That is about her only real weakness, outside of her low average order. Certainly, the sales manager should investigate the reasons for Paula's low average order. However, as previously noted, this may not be the result of poor selling ability.

Summary

A fair and accurate evaluation of the company's sales force is a critical, yet unappreciated, task. The manager's appraisal of the sales people is important not only because pay and promotions should be based on such rating, but because good supervision and training should be based on an objective evaluation of the sales rep's performance. However, the task is difficult. Subjective methods leave much to be desired as managerial biases distort the ratings. Most firms do little in formal objective evaluation of their people.

The factors affecting a person's performance are many and varied. Moreover, many of those factors are beyond the person's control. Yet, it is critical that a person be evaluated only on factors over which he or she has control.

First, management should set some basic policies on the evaluation of the sales personnel. It should establish who will do the rating, when and how often it will be done, how the results will be used, and what bases people will be rated on. As much as possible, quantitative bases should be used in preference to qualitative ones. Quantitative bases are divided into output and input factors. Output factors such as sales, orders taken, gross margins realized, new accounts, and lost accounts are then compared to such input factors as calls made, days worked, expenses, and varied nonselling activities. From such comparisons, various efficiency ratings can be developed. Company records are the basic source of information needed for such evaluations.

Next, some standards must be developed. Relative standards such as what other groups are doing are widely used. However, there is a place for some absolute standards such as total selling costs and days worked.

The basic performance equation is:

Sales = Days worked $\times$ Call rate $\times$ Batting average $\times$ Average order

By factoring each element in that equation, the sales manager can obtain a good picture of what each rep is doing and why they are successful or not. Subjective ratings are fraught with danger. Yet, most managements still use them widely.

Questions and Problems

1. How can a sales manager determine accuracy of sales people's reports?
2. How can a sales manager determine the differences the reps encounter in the severity of competition in each territory?

3. What are some of the indexes a sales manager can use in evaluating the prospecting ability of his reps?

4. What are some of the indexes a sales manager can use to evaluate the degree to which each sales person is covering the assigned territory?

5. As sales manager for a baby food concern, you want to evaluate the ability of your reps to attain good shelf space in grocery stores. How would you do this?

6. How can a sales executive determine the ability of each rep to regain lost customers?

7. An owner-manager of a medium-size apparel manufacturing company proclaimed, "Don't bother me with all that evaluation hogwash. Just give me sales volume and a good bottom line and I'm as happy as a horse in clover. I am making so much money now that I can't spend it all. So why should I waste my time and effort massaging such numbers?" How would you reply to this owner?

8. Your firm's sales force is producing outstanding results. Yet after careful study of several months' sales reports, you conclude that most of them are fictitious. Reps reported calls they never made and imaginary conversations that never took place. As the firm's sales manager, what would you do about the situation?

9. The importance of sales force evaluation increases with the size of the sales force and management's distance from it. Comment.

10. Are sales people more sensitive to criticism than other types of workers?

Case 22–1

Kent Company

Diagnosis of Sales Rep's Problem

Jim Albert, sales manager for the Kent Company of New Haven, Connecticut, studied the file on Ed Gower carefully. He knew the time was ripe for him to do something to help Ed's performance come up to company expectations. Ed had been hired two years ago on the strong recommendation of one of the Kent Company's best customers. Ed had been selling a line of goods competitive to the Kent line for four years with apparently good results. After initial training in the Kent line, Ed had been given a good territory. However, he had failed to produce up to company standards.

The Kent Company sold a line of high-quality sportswear to traditional menswear shops. The upsurge of the "preppy" look in the early 1980s had given the Kent line a big boost in sales. Over the years the company had developed a set of standards it expected its sales people to achieve. The company's sales management policies differed significantly from other firms in the industry in many respects. One of the main differences was in its compensation plan. Most firms in the industry paid their people a straight commission— usually from 6 to 10 percent of sales—and the reps paid all of their own expenses. The Kent Company paid a salary with performance bonuses; moreover, it paid all legitimate selling expenses.

Naturally, management knew it could afford to spend only so much for the execution of the selling function. But it felt that it wanted to retain all of the advantages that accompanied salary plans. Management depended on other motivational tools to provide needed incentive that did not come from the salary plan. The sales representatives knew what was expected of them if they wanted continued employment with the company.

Each rep was expected to sell $1.25 million worth of goods at wholesale. Expenses were expected to be less than $25,000 a year on the average. The reps were expected to work 200 days a year and make 400 calls. The company accounts were divided into two classifications—A stores and B stores. A stores (those with more than $1 million in sales) were to be called on at least monthly; B stores (those with less than $1 million in sales) were to be called on at least four times a year. The average rep had 15 A stores and 58 B stores to call on. Naturally, these figures varied considerably from territory to territory depending on circumstances. Customers often mailed or called in orders when they ran short of inventory. Most reps kept in close telephone contact with their good accounts.

In reviewing Ed's performance for 1985, Jim saw that his sales volume was $910,000, a most unsatisfactory amount. His expenses of $16,500, however, were most modest. Ed's sales reports indicated he had made 435 calls on his accounts. Jim wondered if it was true, and, if so, just how meaningful those calls really were. Ed had 11 A accounts and 66 B accounts in his territory. Ed's sales to A accounts were $190,000; to B accounts, $720,000. Clearly, his performance was unsatisfactory. If it could not be improved quickly, it seemed to Jim that Ed should be terminated. But Jim wanted to investigate the situation thoroughly. He was proud of his managerial record; up to this time he had never had a failure.

Questions

1. What does an analysis of Ed's sales indicate?
2. Exactly what should Jim do to complete his evaluation of Ed's performance?

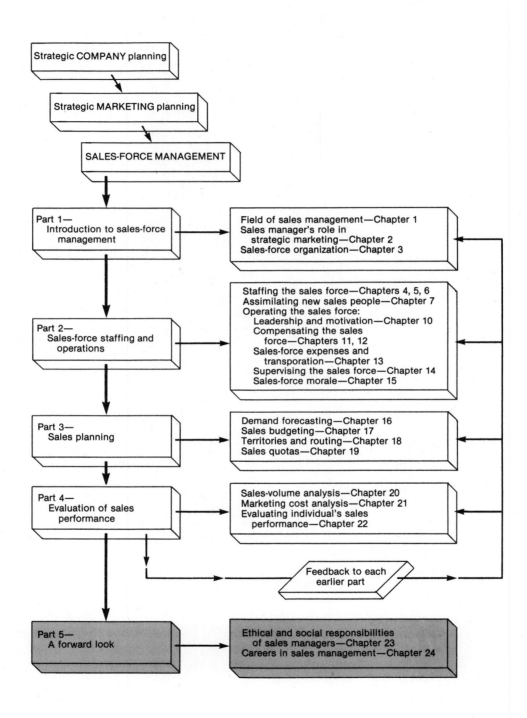

PART 5

A Forward Look

This final section of the book is a combination of two topics—a macro view of sales management in our socioeconomic system and a look ahead at your possible career in sales management. Chapter 23 is a discussion of the ethical aspects of sales management and the social responsibilities of sales executives. The topic of government regulation of business as it applies to sales managers is also covered. Chapter 24 is a discussion of various aspects of a career in sales management.

23

Ethical and Social Responsibilities of Sales Managers

I believe that every right implies a responsibility; every opportunity, an obligation; every possession, a duty.
JOHN D. ROCKEFELLER, JR.

Business is often criticized even by its strongest supporters. There is a popular argument that the giant corporations should be broken up. People grossly overestimate corporate profits and favor a ceiling on them. They want industry to stop polluting and to clean up the environment. This wave of consumer discontent—popularly labeled *consumerism*—is not likely to abate. It has attracted too much political attention.[1]

The main target of consumerism is generally the marketing activities in a firm and the function of marketing in the total economy. This is understandable because marketing is usually the part of a company's total program that is closest to the consumer. Within a firm's marketing program, the area most likely to arouse consumer comment is promotion (personal selling and advertising). It is visible and in direct contact with the consumer. Its avowed goals are attracting attention and generating consumer action.

Concept of a Social Audit of Business

In response to this climate of criticism, there is a growing interest in the idea of a *social audit* of a business firm's activities. This interest is found both among business executives as well as in some nonbusiness segments of society. In essence, a social audit is an evaluation of a firm's social and ethical policies, performances, and

[1] See Paul N. Bloom and Stephen A. Greyser, "The Maturing of Consumerism," *Harvard Business Review*, November–December 1981, pp. 130–39.

responsibilities. A social audit is designed to do the same job in social matters that an accounting audit performs in financial and economic areas.

Unfortunately, the concept of a social audit is still vague. There is no general agreement on exactly *what* it is, precisely what should be audited, or even *who* would do the job (a company itself or an outside agency). We speak of auditing a company's social responsibilities, but there is no consensus as to (1) exactly what these responsibilities are in a given firm or (2) to what expense the firm should go in meeting them. Nevertheless, the increasing interest in the concept suggests that a social audit is an idea whose time has come.[2]

In the literature on social responsibilities of business leadership, much attention has been devoted to the performance of *top* executives. Top management is often aware of these responsibilities, but unfortunately some lower level executives may be avoiding them. The purchasing agent may be placing undue pressure on a small supplier in order to get an extra low price. Or the sales force may be using comparative prices in a misleading fashion.[3]

The various sales managers must share in the social responsibilities and ethical considerations of their companies. Consequently, in this chapter our discussion will center on two topics—the ethical problems facing sales managers and the social responsibilities of sales managers and sales people.

Business Ethics and Sales Management

Webster's New Collegiate Dictionary defines ethics as the science of moral duty or the science of ideal human character. Ethics are moral principles or practices. They are professional standards of conduct. Thus, to act in an ethical fashion is to conform to some standard of moral behavior. Sales managers face the problem of translating this definition into a meaningful model that can serve as a workable guide in their daily activities. In any given situation, they must be able to differentiate between what is ethical and unethical. They should forgo the unethical, regardless of any possible short-run gain.

Some sales executives might question the idea of including a dis-

---

[2] For some suggestions as to what should be included in a social audit and who should do this job, see Raymond A. Bauer and Dan H. Fenn, Jr., "What *Is* a Corporate Social Audit?" *Harvard Business Review,* January–February 1973, pp. 37–48.

[3] For a framework to help marketing managers prepare for their part in a corporate audit, see A. H. Kizilbash, Carlton A. Maile, William O. Hancock, and Peter Gillett, "Social Auditing for Marketing Managers," *Industrial Marketing Management,* January 1979, pp. 1–6.

cussion of ethics in a book dealing with the practicalities of running a sales force. It is realistic and quite relevant, however, to connect the concepts of business ethics with the management of a sales force. If sales managers recognize their moral responsibilities as administrators, they are only operating in their own self-interest. The truth of the matter, however, seems to be that sales managers are not aware of the *practical* value of ethical conduct. Judging by their practices, too many still seem to believe in a caveat emptor philosophy when dealing with customers.

The Pressure to Compromise Personal Ethics

It is easy to be ethical when no hardship is involved—when you are winning and life is going good. Undoubtedly, most sales managers prefer to act ethically. The test comes when things are *not* going so good—when the competitive pressures build up. These pressures are not limited to sales-management situations; they appear in all walks of life. Would you cheat on an exam in this course if the alternative is to flunk the course? In professional football, assume that an offensive lineman cannot control his opponent on defense. Should the offensive player then resort to holding the defensive player (and hope that it goes undetected by the officials)? The alternative for the offensive lineman may be for his team to lose, or even worse, for him to lose his job.

Do business managers feel pressure to compromise their personal ethics for company goals? In many cases the answer is yes, even in firms that profess to be leaders in the campaign for business ethics. Surveys continue to show that business executives believe that, in order to advance in an organization, a person occasionally must indulge in unethical practices. Personal values often have to be set aside in order to advance. Also, to climb the ladder in an organization, executives believe that it may be necessary to aggressively "clear the path" of those who stand in the way.[4]

These questionable ethics in business tend to reflect the general public's ethical behavior. Permissive attitudes seem to prevail regarding sexual mores and the use of drugs, for example. Business executives and the general public agree that ethical behavior in the United States has declined sharply since the 1970s. This conclusion was reported in a study conducted jointly by *The Wall Street Journal* and the Gallup Organization.[5] This survey reported, for example, an in-

[4] See Douglas J. Lincoln, Milton M. Pressley, and Taylor Little, "Ethical Beliefs and Personal Values of Top Level Executives," *Journal of Business Research,* December 1982, pp. 475–87.

[5] Roger Ricklefs, "Executives and General Public Say Ethical Behavior Is Declining in U.S.," *The Wall Street Journal,* October 31, 1983, p. 27. Also see "Morality," *U.S. News & World Report,* December 9, 1985, pp. 52 ff.

crease in lying and stealing, and 80 percent of the executives admitted to driving their car while drunk.

At the same time, a large majority of executives support the idea of a company code of ethics and the teaching of ethics in business schools. Interestingly enough, *almost all executives believe that business ethics, however imperfect, are as good as, or better than, the ethics among the public at large.*[6]

The Problem of Determining Ethical Standards

It is easy to say that a sales executive should act in an ethical fashion, but it is far more difficult to put this axiom into practice. Sales managers as individuals usually have their own standards of conduct they believe to be ethical. And, usually they abide by these standards in the management of their sales forces. It is doubtful if many people, sales executives included, consciously commit unethical deeds with any degree of regularity. Most of us believe we are acting ethically *by our own standards.* However, ethical standards are set by a group—by society—and not by the individual. Thus, the group evaluates what you as an individual think is ethical.

The problem is that the group (society) lacks commonly accepted standards of behavior. What is considered ethical conduct varies from one industry to another and from one situation to another. The dictates of personal conscience are an individual matter, even among people with a common ethical tradition. Looking to the law or corporate policy for guidance leads only to more gray areas rather than to clearly defined, specific guidelines.

The moral-ethical-legal framework presents special problems for sales executives, more than for most other managers. The rules for sales work are neither clear-cut nor hard and fast. Entertaining customers in a gambling house, for example, may be either moral or immoral from an individual's point of view. This entertainment may be considered acceptable (ethical) or not depending on the industry's practice. And, it may be legal or illegal depending on whether it happened in Nevada or California.

As further examples of a sales executive's problem, consider these situations:

1. A box of golf balls may be a reasonable Christmas gift to give a $5,000-a-year customer. But is a $2,000 personal computer a gift or a bribe when given to a million-dollar customer?
2. It is acceptable practice and legally okay for a manufacturer to

---

[6] See Roger Ricklefs, "Executives Apply Stiffer Standards Than Public to Ethical Dilemmas," *The Wall Street Journal,* November 3, 1983, p. 27.

give a department store's sales clerks "push money" to promote the manufacturer's brand. But can this manufacturer rightfully give the head buyer a little something extra for first getting the product into the store?
3. It is customary for appliance manufacturers to reward their distributor-customers with an all-expense-paid incentive trip to the Bahamas. But is it acceptable for a pharmaceutical company to invite its doctor-"customers" to Jamaica for an all-expense-paid seminar?

An Attempt at Setting Ethical Guidelines

The problem of determining what is right and what is wrong is an extremely difficult one. Yet, it is one that, to a degree, is soluble. It is not realistic for a sales manager to construct a two-column list of practices, one headed "ethical" and the other labeled "unethical." A better approach is to depend on time and conscious examples to point out the difference between acceptable and nonacceptable standards of performance. The same philosophy may be adopted as that followed in the writing and subsequent administration of Section 5 of the Federal Trade Commission Act. The act outlaws unfair competition, but it does not state what that term means. The legislators wisely left the task of definition to the commission and the courts. Thus through the years, examples have accumulated as the law has been administered case by case.

As another approach to defining ethical practices, a sales executive may evaluate the ethical status of each proposed action by answering such questions as the following. Also see Figure 23–1 for additional questions.

Is this sound from a long-run point of view?
Would I do this to a friend?
Would I be willing to have this done to me? (The Golden Rule.)
Would I want this action publicized in national media?

Take a long-run point of view. Sales executives should take the *long-run* point of view regarding the ethics of a given situation. They should understand that ethical behavior not only is morally right but, over the long run, realistically sound. Too many sales administrators are shortsighted. They do not see the possible repercussions (the boomerang effect) from their activities and attitudes. Whether or not the buyer was deceived or high-pressured may seem unimportant as long as the sale is consummated. Management often does not recognize that such practices can lose customers or invite public regulation. Executives must consider the ultimate consequences of their

---

Figure 23–1

Ethics without a Sermon—or Twelve Questions for Examining the Ethics of a Business Decision

---

1. Have you defined the problem accurately?
2. How would you define the problem if you stood on the other side of the fence?
3. How did this situation occur in the first place?
4. To whom and to what do you give your loyalty as a person and as a member of the corporation?
5. What is your intention in making this decision?
6. How does this intention compare with the probable results?
7. Whom could your decision or action injure?
8. Can you discuss the problem with the affected parties before you make your decision?
9. Are you confident that your position will be as valid over a long period of time as it seems now?
10. Could you disclose without qualm your decision or action to your boss, your CEO, the board of directors, your family, society as a whole?
11. What is the symbolic potential of your action if understood? if misunderstood?
12. Under what conditions would you allow exceptions to your stand?

Source: Laura L. Nash, "Ethics Without the Sermon," *Harvard Business Review,* November–December 1981, p. 81.

---

acts. The brushmark of one immediate sale is unimportant when the entire canvas is examined. As Ohman said, ". . . the job is the life. *This* is what must be made meaningful. We cannot assume that the end of production justifies the means. What happens to people in the course of producing may be far more important than the end product."[7]

Put guidelines in writing. In the mid-1970s many executives were shaken by disclosures of such business practices as bribery of foreign officials by American firms and large-scale bribery in domestic business affairs. Spurred by these revelations, many companies developed written ethical guidelines to be followed at all levels of management. One example of such statements is presented in Figure 23–2. It is a 10-point set of ethical guidelines designed specifically for sales-force managers.

Writing a code of ethical conduct is no easy task. The company may end up with a set of platitudes. Each company should develop its own statement because, as one executive said: "Writing a code that would be universally accepted means you would end up with a motherhood sort of thing." Critics claim that such a statement usually is public-relations window dressing that covers up a bad situation and corrects nothing.

---

[7] O. A. Ohman, " 'Skyhooks' (with Special Implications for Monday through Friday)," *Harvard Business Review,* May–June 1955, p. 37. This classic article was reprinted in *Harvard Business Review,* January–February 1970, pp. 4–8 ff.

Figure 23–2

Ten Ways to Keep Your Sales Force on the Straight and Narrow

1. Get assurance from your board chairman and your president that they expect you to follow both the letter and the spirit of the law.

2. Develop and circulate a sales-ethics policy. Of the companies hit by the SEC in the foreign payoff scandals, 75 percent reported that they had no formal policies on commercial bribery.

3. Set the proper moral climate. One management consultant suggests that the marketing staffs most likely to commit bribery are in companies in which (a) new ideas are discouraged, (b) "the top person does everything himself," or (c) officers don't attend trade association meetings and feel that "nothing can be learned from the competition."

4. Set realistic sales goals. The sales rep who is pressured by the need to meet an arbitrary, unfair quota is the one most likely to rationalize his way into a bribery or kickback scheme.

5. Institute controls when needed. For example, don't hesitate to keep close tabs on a sales rep whose lifestyle exceeds his known income.

6. Encourage employees to call for help when they face an ethically troublesome sale.

7. Resist a prospectively shady deal. You'll sleep better.

8. Meet with your competition if payoffs are an industry problem. Thankfully, no antitrust law ever barred competitors from hammering out a code of ethics.

9. Blow the whistle when you must. Yes, it's the hardest of these suggestions to follow. A *Harvard Business Review* survey reports that four out of seven executives would rather cover up a bribery or price-fixing revelation than suffer the cost and conspicuousness of a prolonged legal battle. So, yes, you'll be bucking convention. You may also risk censure by your peers for "squealing" on the team or damaging the reputation of the company.

10. Keep your perspective. An anonymous author may have had bribery in mind when he said, "Following the path of least resistance is what makes men and rivers crooked."

Source: "It's Time to Repeal the Right to Do Wrong." *Sales & Marketing Management*, October 11, 1976, p. 42. Reprinted with permission.

Nevertheless, there is growing agreement that these formal written statements are desirable. They lessen the chance that executives will knowingly or unknowingly get into trouble. They strengthen the company's hand in dealing with customers and government officials who invite bribes and other unethical actions. They strengthen the position of lower-level executives in resisting pressures to compromise their personal ethics in order to get along in the firm.

Enforce the ethical codes. There is also general agreement that effective *enforcement* of ethical codes is a major key to their success. The penalties should be severe, especially when top management is involved in the violations. Firing a few top executives, assessing stiff fines to be paid personally, or putting them in jail can be a strong deterrent to unethical action. Other executives may then think twice before engaging in such practices because "Everybody else is doing it," or "We must do it to make the sale," or "When in Rome, do as the Romans do."

Ethical Situations Facing Sales People and Sales Executives

In their everyday selling activities, sales people often face situations with ethical overtones. In these situations, the sales reps must make decisions that conform both to company standards and to the reps' own ethical and moral standards. Frequently this is no easy task. It is no wonder that sales people readily admit that they want more guidelines to help them answer ethical questions.[8]

Interestingly enough, the people that sales reps often have to deal with in an industrial sale—that is, purchasing agents—also face many situations that pose questions of ethical behavior.[9]

Finally, ethical questions are involved in many of the relationships that sales managers have with their sales people, their companies, and their customers. A few of these situations are discussed here.

Relations with the sales force. A substantial portion of sales managers' ethical problems relates to their dealings with the sales force. Ethical considerations may be involved, for instance, when management splits a sales territory. Assume that the sales person has put a large amount of effective effort into building a territory into a highly profitable district. The rep may even have worked under a straight commission compensation plan and paid his own expenses. When management sees this sales person's relatively high earnings, an executive may decide there is too much territory and split it. It this ethical? On the other hand, is it sound management *not* to split the district, if the sales executive believes there is inadequate coverage of an overly large district?

In some companies, management takes over the very large, profitable accounts as *house accounts*. (These are customers who are sold directly by some executive. The sales person in whose district the account is located usually receives no commission on the account.) Is this ethical, particularly if the sales person spent much time and effort in developing the account to a profitable level? Yet, management may feel that the account is now so important that the company cannot risk losing it. Thus, executives handle it.

Ethical questions often arise in connection with promotions, termination, and references. If there is no likelihood that a sales repre-

---

[8] For a report on some ethical questions faced by sales people, see Alan J. Dubinsky, Eric N. Berkowitz, and William Rudelius, "Ethical Problems of Field Sales Personnel," *MSU Business Topics*, Summer 1980, pp. 1–16. See also Lawrence B. Chonko and John J. Burnett, "Measuring the Importance of Ethical Situations As a Source of Role Conflict: A Survey of Salespeople, Sales Managers, and Sales Support Personnel," *Journal of Personal Selling & Sales Management*, May 1983, pp. 41–47.

[9] For a report on the ethical beliefs and behavior of members of one state purchasing association, see John Browning and Noel B. Zabriskie, "How Ethical Are Industrial Buyers?" *Industrial Marketing Management*, October 1983, pp. 219–24.

sentative will be promoted to a managerial position, should the rep be told? If the sales manager knows that the rep is working in expectation of such a promotion, to tell him means to lose him. In another instance, when a managerial position is open in another region, a sales manager may keep a star sales rep in his present territory. This is done despite the rep's obvious qualifications and desire for promotion. And what is management's responsibility in giving references for a former sales person? If the rep was incompetent but a nice guy, an executive may be tempted to cover up for him. To what extent is this manager ethically bound to tell the truth, or to give details, about former employees?

Relations with the company. Changing jobs and handling expense accounts illustrate the ethical problems involved in sales executives' relations with companies. When changing positions, a manager may want to take customers with him to the new employer. These may be key accounts which he himself has been selling, but they are also quite important to the former employer. Ethical and legal questions may arise if this executive tries to move those customers to the new firm.

Many times a sales manager possesses information that could be highly useful to a competitor. Naturally, it is difficult to control the information a manager gives to a new employer. But beyond certain limits, such behavior is clearly unethical. One sales manager resigned to accept a similar position with a smaller competitor. He took with him material in his files including important marketing research information on the former firm's customers.

In dealing with sales expenses, expense accounts should not be padded, and the expense policies set by top management should be followed. Ethical questions may arise, however, in the interpretation of these policies. Suppose that top management states it will pay only 22 cents a mile to sales reps or sales managers who use their personal cars for company business. Yet, a sales manager knows that actual expenses are 28 to 30 cents a mile at the minimum. He may be tempted to pad his mileage and encourage the reps to do so also to make up the difference. He may justify this action on the basis that the money is really being spent for business purposes, and the spirit of the expense account is not being violated. Ethical questions include the following: Should sales personnel manipulate expense accounts in order to protect themselves from the stingy policies of top management. In so doing, they are only recovering money honestly spent in the solicitation of business for the firm. Or should they attempt to get policies changed? Or, failing that, should they change employers rather than commit what they believe to be unethical acts?

Relations with customers. Perhaps the most critical set of ethical questions facing sales managers is associated with customer relations. The major problem areas involve bribes, gifts, and entertainment.

Bribes. Bribery in selling is an unpleasant fact of life that apparently has existed, in varying degrees, since time immemorial. However, bribery is not limited to selling. It exists in many other areas of social interaction. It can start with parents bribing their children: "If you kids are good today, we'll take you to the beach tomorrow."

Bribery is found in many (perhaps all) cultures and political systems. It is so implanted in many cultures that various languages have slang words to designate it. In Latin America it is called the *mordida* (small bite). It is *dash* in West Africa and *baksheesh* in the Middle East. The French call it *pot de vin* (jug of wine). In Italy there is *la bustarella* (the little envelope) left on a bureaucrat's desk to cut the red tape. In Chicago, people call it "a little grease."

A complicating factor is that bribery is not a sharply demarcated activity. Sometimes the lines are blurred between a bribe, a gift to show appreciation, and a reasonable commission for services rendered. Blatant bribes, payoffs, or kickbacks may be easy to spot. They are patently wrong. Unfortunately, today much bribery is done in a more sophisticated manner and is less easy to identify.

Bribery may involve a small fee for fixing a speeding ticket, or it may be a multimillion-dollar payoff to get a large government contract. In sales, the bribe offer may be initiated by the sales person, or the request may come from the buyer. Usually the buyer's request is stated in a veiled fashion, and the sales representative has to be perceptive to understand what is going on.

Bribery in selling erupted as an international scandal in the mid-1970s. There were revelations of payoffs to foreign officials by American companies engaged in selling abroad. The resultant political sensitivity in the United States and in several foreign countries undoubtedly has done much to clean up a bad situation. The furor also has served to spotlight and discourage bribery in domestic marketing.

Undoubtedly, however, bribery will continue to put sales managers and sales people to the ethical test. It would be naive to conclude that the foreign scandals will mark the end of bribery in selling. In fact, in many foreign countries there is no way a company can hope to make sales without paying fees or commissions (translate that as bribes) to agents in those countries.[10]

Nevertheless, the scandals should strengthen the ethical resolve of

---

[10] See Jack G. Kaikati and Wayne A. Label, "American Bribery Legislation: An Obstacle to International Marketing," *Journal of Marketing*, Fall 1980, pp. 38–43.

A day-to-day operating problem in the
Majestic Glass Company (L)

Deceptive Packaging by Majestic's Customers

One morning Mr. Brion's secretary placed on his desk a copy of a widely-circulated consumer magazine. It contained an article exposing fraudulent and deceptive packages in which some drugs and toiletries products were being sold. The article was profusely illustrated with photographs. In two of them, the Majestic Glass Company's mark showed plainly on the bottoms of the bottles. The mark, a letter "M" in a circle, probably did not identify Majestic to many consumers. But it was well known in the container industry. Majestic was not mentioned in the article, but some of its customers were.

In one case, the makers of a perfume had inserted a long tapering plastic stopper in the neck of a Majestic bottle. The stopper occupied almost 20 percent of the space inside the bottle, and forced the level of the liquid to appear higher than it was. Majestic had not supplied the stopper. In another case, Majestic's standard pale blue transparent bottle was used to package a colorless liquid labeled and advertised as "Blu-Cool" after-shave lotion.

Mr. Brion knew of other cases not mentioned in the article, in which customers had employed Majestic containers to deceive consumers. He had once refused an order that would have required stamping the word "IMPORTED" in the glass of a perfume jar. The jars were bought by an Indianapolis firm which, Mr. Brion knew, imported nothing. The order was readily accepted by a competing glass company. More than once, Majestic had been asked to imprint bottles with false labels of capacity, such as "SIX FULL OUNCES" on a standard 4½-ounce bottle. Majestic did not print labels or wrappers for the containers it sold. This work was done by the customer or by some other firm.

Question

How should Mr. Brion respond to these situations of deceptive packaging?

Note: See the introduction to this series of problems in Chapter 3 for the necessary background on the company, its market, and its competition.

---

sales executives. They should not offer bribes. They should resist demands or suggestions for bribes from purchasing agents and encourage their sales people to do the same. If nothing else, sales executives should realize that the idea "Everyone else is doing it" is no longer a valid excuse. The penalties can be stiff for proven takers or givers of bribes.

Gifts. The practice of sales executives and sales people giving gifts to their customers, especially at Christmas, is time-honored in American business. The practice of gift-giving under some conditions also may be related to bribery. Today, perhaps more than ever before, the moral and ethical climate of gift-giving to customers is under careful scrutiny in many firms. The practice is being reviewed by both the givers and the receivers of gifts. Some firms put dollar limits on the business gifts they allow their employees to give or receive. The Internal Revenue Service places a limit of $25 a year on the amount that may be deducted for business gifts to any one person. Other firms have stopped the practice of giving Christmas gifts to customers. Instead some of these firms are offering to contribute (in amounts equal to their usual gifts) to their customers' favorite charities.[11]

It is unfortunate that gift-giving to customers has become so complicated and so suspect in our society. A reasonably priced, tastefully selected gift can express appreciation for a customer's business. Today the problem lies largely in deciding what constitutes "reasonably priced" and "tastefully selected."

Fortunately, sales executives do have some time-tested guidelines to help them in avoiding gift-giving that is unethical or in bad taste. For example, a gift never should be given *before* a customer does business with a firm. That is, the gift should not put the recipient under obligation to the giver. It may be all right to give a gift to a purchasing agent's children, but not to the agent's spouse. Inordinately expensive gifts or those with blatant advertising messages are generally in poor taste. A little common sense mixed with some social intelligence can go a long way toward keeping sales gift-giving within ethical boundaries.[12]

Entertainment.   Entertaining customers is very common in selling today, but it, too, can pose ethical questions. Good sales representatives usually learn to tailor their entertaining to the type of customer and potential value of the account. In fact, some customers do not want to be entertained for fear of being obligated, or because their companies do not permit it. Business entertainment is definitely a part of sales work, and a large portion of the expense money often is devoted to it. If reps spend this money unwisely on accounts with little potential, they are wasting time and their selling costs will be out of line. Indeed, a contributing factor in sales people's success may be their ability to know the right person to entertain and the nature of the entertainment called for.

Over the years some useful generalizations have been developed that may guide sales representatives in their use of customer enter-

[11] For a survey of purchasing executives regarding their organization's attitudes and policies toward gift-taking, see "How Purchasing Execs View Taking Gifts from Suppliers," *Purchasing,* February 1985, pp. 23 ff.

[12] For a summary review of gift-giving practices in business, see Walter Kiechel III, "Business Gift-Giving," *Fortune,* January 7, 1985, pp. 123–24.

tainment. Entertaining usually is done to develop long-term business relationships, rather than to get a one-time order. Ordinarily it is *not* a good idea to rely too heavily on entertaining. It is no substitute for a good product or the effective servicing of an account. If reps try to buy business through entertaining, some seller can always outbid them by entertaining more lavishly.

What Is Social Responsibility?

A sales administrator has a three-part responsibility as follows:

1. A *revenue* responsibility to the company. In this respect, an executive's job is to provide a satisfactory income over the long run by buying revenues at a reasonable cost in the marketplace.
2. A *human* responsibility to the sales force. In this sense, an administrator's function is to provide a good working environment by proper management of the sales force and by adequate planning and control of sales operations.
3. A *want-satisfaction* responsibility to the market. Here an executive's task is to maximize the customers' standard of living by delivering the desired products at the lowest feasible cost. See Figure 23–3.

In all three of these relationships, any *ethical* considerations are quite frequently viewed on a person-to-person basis. However, the substance of *social responsibility* is much broader. It emphasizes an executive's institutional (company) actions and their effect on the entire social system. Without this broader viewpoint, personal and institutional acts tend to be separated. Sales executives can lead model

Figure 23–3
Responsibilities of a Sales Manager

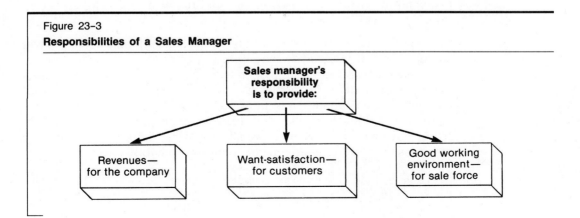

personal lives but continue to justify their company's pollution of a river because there they have no direct personal involvement. To them, river pollution is a public problem to be solved by government action. The concept of social responsibility requires them to consider their acts within the framework of the whole social system. Thus, executives are held responsible for the effects these acts may have anywhere in that system.

> When a man's . . . values are limited primarily to a certain group or organization, he tends to become a partisan acting for that group. But, if he thinks in terms of a whole system, he begins to build societal values into his actions, even when they are for a certain organization. *This is the essence of social responsibility.* For the manager it means realizing that the business system does not exist alone and that a healthy business system cannot exist within a sick society.[13] (Italics added.)

Reasons for the Sales Manager's Responsibility to Society

Sales managers should conduct their affairs in an ethical and socially desirable manner in order to justify the privilege of operating within our relatively free socioeconomic structure. No freedom or privilege that is worth much comes without a price. Just as our precious political freedoms sometimes have a high price, so do our economic freedoms.

Minimize government intervention. If sales managers fail to perform in a socially desirable fashion, society will restrict their freedom of operation. Most of the governmental limitations placed on sales activities throughout the years have been the result of management's failure to live up to its social responsibilities. Once some form of governmental control is established, it is rarely removed. The wise course of action, therefore, is to understand and fulfill a social responsibility, thus minimizing any additional government intervention.

The power-responsibility equation. The concept that social power equals social responsibility may help to explain why business executives have a responsibility to society. Sales managers have a considerable amount of social power as they influence markets, speak out on matters of economic policy, and so on. The lessons of history suggest that the social responsibilities of business people arise from social power they have. If responsibility arises from power, then we may reason that the avoidance of social responsibility will lead to an

---

[13] Quotation and adaptation in preceding paragraph from Keith Davis, "Understanding the Social Responsibility Puzzle," *Business Horizons,* Winter 1967, p. 46.

erosion of social power. That is, "in the long run, those who do not use power in a way that society considers responsible will tend to lose it."[14]

Sales department represents the company. Sales executives and their sales forces represent the company to the people. Some years ago, Procter & Gamble put this point nicely in an annual report: "When a Procter & Gamble salesman walks into a customer's place of business—whether he is calling on an individual store or keeping an appointment at the headquarters of a large group of stores—he not only represents Procter & Gamble, but in a very real sense, he *is* Procter & Gamble." Therefore, the way the public sees these people and their activities is the way it will judge the concern.

Ordinarily, people do not judge a concern by its office or plant workers, because they rarely see these groups. In fact, the sales force is frequently blamed for inefficiencies by office and production employees. If a product is defective or a bill is incorrect, the sales department bears the brunt of the customer's anger. Furthermore, the way the sales department handles the complaint can determine whether the customer will continue to patronize the organization.

Sales department represents our economy. In many instances, our system of free enterprise is appraised by the public in light of their impression of selling activities. Many people are strongly opposed to certain current marketing methods. Television commercials and telephone soliciting are often the targets of consumer dissatisfaction. Often the critical reaction is: "There ought to be a law against such practices," or "This is what happens when business is allowed to go unrestrained."

In other words, the lack of social conscience in selling hurts not only the company involved, but also the entire economic system. Hence, anything a sales administrator can do to develop a socially desirable sales operation will help to perpetuate our basic socioeconomic structure.

Positive Action Regarding Social Responsibilities

Before sales executives (or any person, for that matter) can demonstrate social responsibility, they first must acknowledge that they have such an obligation. Many sales executives seem to believe their responsibility is solely to their companies and the stockholders. They must be aware that they also have responsibilities to society, or

[14] Keith Davis and William C. Frederick, *Business and Society,* 5th ed. (New York: McGraw-Hill, 1984), p. 34.

any further suggestions will fall on barren ground. There are several courses of action for those sales executives who are aware of, and want to shoulder, their social responsibilities.

Manage sales force effectively. A sales executive should manage the sales force in such a way that its business practices are approved by society. In a sense, the bulk of this book has been devoted to this one point—the intelligent and sound management of a sales force. Specific examples could be drawn from most chapters. A socially responsible sales administrator designs a compensation plan that considers the best interests of the customer. A sales quota should be set so that it is not necessary to high-pressure or overstock customers. Sales people should be properly selected and placed so that human resources are not wasted.

The *Sales Manager's Creed* (see Figure 23–4) can serve as a good summary of a sales executive's social responsibilities and some practical ways to meet these obligations. This creed was developed many years ago by the Sales and Marketing Executives—International and continues to be relevant today. There are marked similarities in the spirit of the creed and the 10-point program outlined in Figure 23–2, to stimulate ethical behavior in a sales force.

Sales executives also have another, perhaps broader set of responsibilities regarding sales people. Fundamentally, a sales manager is a manager of people. Thus, a sales manager should help sales people realize their personal and professional goals. He should minimize, or try to offset, the disagreeable parts of their job. Too many people merely work for a living. They do not enjoy their jobs, as witness the TGIF (Thank God It's Friday) and the "Blue Monday" sentiments in our society. Many people count the hours until quitting time, the days until the weekend, and the weeks until vacation. A sales manager's goal should be to generate a climate where sales people can derive satisfaction from the work they do. Perhaps this goal is too idealistic and is too much to expect, but at least we can try.

Play a stronger role in the strategic marketing planning process. Top management can help sales-force managers perform in a more socially responsible manner by involving them more in the strategic marketing planning process. Sales managers' participation in the strategic planning process is essential (1) if the company's product and market plans are to reflect the customers' needs, and (2) if the company is to get maximum commitment from the sales managers in implementing these plans.

Field sales managers are responsible for achieving assigned performance levels. They will come closer to reaching these goals in a socially responsible manner if they are given a real voice in the development of the goals.

Figure 23–4
Sales Manager's Creed

A CREED

I SUBSCRIBE TO THIS SALES MANAGER'S CREED, PREPARED BY THE NATIONAL FEDERATION OF SALES EXECUTIVES, WHICH I BELIEVE TO BE IN THE BEST INTERESTS OF AMERICAN BUSINESS:

All salesmen shall receive fair compensation during their initial or subsequent training periods.

While recognizing changes in compensation or territory to be functions of sales management, salesmen shall be consulted prior to establishing such changes and given reasonable notice of the effective date.

Earnings of commission or bonus salesmen shall be unlimited, unless otherwise specified at the time of their employment. Should basic changes in a business justify modifying this policy, all salesmen affected shall be advised of the fact a reasonable time prior to establishing such ceilings as become necessary.

When evaluating the ability of salesmen, conditions beyond their control, such as differences in the sales potentials of their territories, shall be given full consideration.

Salesmen shall be offered the same vacation, job or income security, and other employee benefits as are enjoyed by other employees in comparable positions in the same company.

The only "house" or "no commission" accounts shall be those clearly defined in advance of solicitation.

The paper work required of salesmen shall be held down to a minimum and its value clearly justified.

Salesmen's expense reimbursement policies shall be uniform, after taking all variations of conditions into consideration.

A sharp distinction shall be drawn between salesmen's earnings and expense allowance, and any system which affords salesmen either a substantial profit or loss on expense accounts, shall be corrected.

Salesmen shall be given either a contract, agreement, or letter covering those conditions of his employment which might otherwise be the basis for later misunderstandings.

If quotas are used—
(a) Salesmen should know how their figures have been determined, and
(b) The quotas shall be based on reliable seasoned personal evaluation of accurate and adequate criteria.

A salesman whose health or well being gives evidence of being prejudiced by the nervous tensions involved in his work, shall be given such relief as may be possible.

Pressure to achieve results shall be of a constructive nature, avoiding the use of "fear" psychology or threatened loss of employment.

No matter where a salesman may be located, he shall be provided with a simple means of stating his grievances, which shall be promptly considered and answered.

Interpret consumer demand.   A major responsibility of a sales executive is to determine what the consumers want and then supply products and services to satisfy these wants. It is *not* the consumer's responsibility to invent new products. Consumer demand for a product may be latent or dormant. That is, the demand is present, but unrecognized by the consumer until a product appears to fulfill the want. For example, consumers seemed to get along well with standard transmissions, silk hosiery, and the old-fashioned paintbrush. However, when automatic transmissions, nylon hosiery, and roller paint applicators appeared on the market, they were eagerly accepted. Apparently, the demand was present even before the new products were marketed, but it was dormant.

If management refuses to accept the responsibility for interpreting consumer demand, the public will look elsewhere to have its wants satisfied. The institution they usually seek out in this case is some agency of the government.

Keep intelligently informed.   Sales executives can help themselves by reading on a wide variety of subjects. They owe it to themselves, to their companies, and to society to take advantage of this storehouse of knowledge. Some of the purposes for which sales executives may read are as follows.[15]

1. *For fun and amusement.* Reading the comics in the daily newspaper or a joke book keeps alive our sense of humor. We can smile at other people's foibles and laugh at our own. Humor levels people and makes the encroachment of dictatorship difficult.
2. *For idle curiosity.* A hurried glance at the newspaper can provide a glimpse of the actors on the stage of life. We keep up with the times superficially with this type of reading. It may be done over the breakfast table, on a commuter train, or at home in the evening. It also may be complemented by radio and television news reports and analyses.
3. *To keep up with their jobs.* Sales managers may also read for immediate practical purposes. This probably accounts for the bulk of the reading done by most sales executives. They may read periodicals of general business interest such as *Business Week, Fortune,* or *The Wall Street Journal.* They read journals of general marketing and sales interest, such as *Sales & Marketing Management* or *Industrial Marketing.* They also usually examine the trade journals in their own industries.
4. *To learn to write and speak better.* Careful reading, paying atten-

---

[15] For the idea and content of this list, we are indebted to Henry A. Burd, professor of marketing at the University of Washington until his retirement.

tion to the mechanics of expression, can help us improve our command of the language. To some extent, this overlaps several other types of reading. People may read trade journals to keep up with their jobs, for example, while at the same time they are conscious of the writing style and other aspects of expression.

5. *For a broader understanding of their living conditions.* This requires the reading of good magazines and books on economic, political, and social conditions.

6. *To learn to live more successfully.* This type of reading enters the realm of philosophy and religion. Consciously or unconsciously, we all have a philosophy of life. It may be sheer imitation, or it may be developed and modified by reading the Bible and other serious works.

7. *To satisfy a deep inner curiosity about the universe.* This involves reading about astronomy and the world of modern science, including the nuclear and space age.

8. *For appreciation.* Sales managers, however practical, may want to read the world's masterpieces to enhance their appreciation of these classics.

Work closely with outside organizations.   As part of their jobs, sales managers usually come in contact with various organizations outside the company. By working closely with these outside groups, sales managers frequently are helped in fulfilling their social responsibilities.

Trade associations.   Sales executives often find their societal intentions are thwarted by competitive conditions. Consequently, they may find their efforts will be more effective if they are handled on an industrywide scale by a trade association. Usually, such agreements governing all firms in an industry are voluntary. Often the trade association provides the machinery for arbitrating any differences or grievances. The arbitrators may lack enforcing power, but their decisions usually carry considerable moral and ethical persuasion.

By working through their trade association, sales managers can also take advantage of the Trade Practice Conferences offered by the Federal Trade Commission (FTC). A trade association, working with the FTC, can draw up a set of trade practice rules relating to competitive conduct in the industry. Usually the rules are divided into Group I and Group II. Group I rules prohibit only those practices that the FTC considers illegal under the laws it administers. Group II rules are additional statements of ethical conduct that are not necessarily related to any law the Commission administers. The Trade Practice Conferences are entirely voluntary. The FTC simply offers an opportunity to define in a specific fashion what are considered fair or unfair competitive trade practices in a specific industry.

Labor unions. Sales managers whose sales forces are unionized have the responsibility of working as closely and harmoniously as possible with the union. The goal is not only to improve the material lot of the reps, but also to upgrade the ethical standards they follow in their work. Sales managers with a unionized sales force ordinarily are making a mistake if they ignore the union. They may have fought vigorously against unionization. However, once the union is recognized as a bargaining agent, they can gain little, and stand to lose much, by continuing to fight it.

Better Business Bureaus. A well-operated Better Business Bureau in a city can be a strong voice representing the consumer's interest. Sales managers should encourage the sales force to know the bureau and its operations. This is especially true of sales reps who sell directly to the consumer. The sales executive should cooperate with the local bureau in its efforts to maintain fair competitive selling conditions in the community.

Chambers of Commerce. A sales manager should be active in the local Chamber of Commerce. Also, a company should have a membership in as many of the communities as possible where it sells. Chambers are usually the voice of executives at the local, state, and even national level. A good sales manager has much to offer the chamber and, at the same time, much to gain through active participation.

Participate in community affairs. Every citizen has the social responsibility of participating in civic affairs. Sales managers should willingly accept the task of spearheading community projects such as a United Fund drive or a building expansion program in a local school district. Managers who shirk this responsibility run the risk of hurting their company's reputation, because to the public they *are* the company.

Participate in politics. To the question, "Should marketing executives take part in politics?" the answer is yes. Many marketing executives are coming to realize that such activity is desirable, if not mandatory, for the country's welfare. Top management is encouraging people in the middle and lower executive echelons to engage in political affairs. Sales-force managers particularly are in a good position to take part in politics at the state and local levels. Not only can this participation help to fulfill their responsibilities as citizens, but it also offers them a means of explaining the vital role of selling in our economy.

Public Regulation and Sales Managers

Public regulation at any level of government—federal, state or local—touches a company's marketing department more than any other phase of its operations. This does not imply that regulation of nonselling activities is unimportant. The Securities Exchange Commission affects corporate financing; the Taft-Hartley Act and minimum wage legislation influence several aspects of personnel and labor relations; various measures establish safety regulations for offices and factories; local zoning laws affect plant location, and so on. However, the various regulatory measures that affect areas of marketing, such as pricing, advertising and personal selling, generally have a greater impact on a company's success.

Reasons for Government Intervention

American business history shows rather clearly that legislation regulating business is passed usually in response to one of two situations. Either (1) business acts in a manner that is contrary to the public's interest or (2) a special-interest group promotes the legislation to benefit that group. Let's look at some examples of legislation resulting from these two situations.

Because business did not meet its social responsibilities, we have antitrust legislation, laws prohibiting unfair competition, and legal restrictions on advertising. For example, when society felt that the abuses engendered by monopolies were contrary to the public interest, the Sherman Antitrust Act (1890) was passed. When private industry ignored its responsibilities in matters of labeling and selling food and drugs, the government intervened with the Pure Food and Drug Act (1906). As the years went by and short-sighted, antisocial businessmen found ways to circumvent this law, it was strengthened by amendments in 1938.

Early in the 20th century, business practices had degenerated to the point where the Federal Trade Commission Act was passed in 1914 to restrict unfair competition. Through the years that followed, the advertising done by many firms was misleading and deceptive. Industry self-policing was ineffective or was not attempted. Once again the government stepped in, this time with the Wheeler-Lea Amendment (1938) to the Federal Trade Commission Act. The 1960s and 1970s brought in a wave of regulatory legislation. Much of this dealt with consumer protection. It was passed in response to consumerism—that is, consumer protests against perceived injustices on the part of business firms.

The second general situation resulting in regulatory legislation occurs when one business group actively seeks government regulation to protect its own interests. In this vein, at the state level we have legislation, such as the unfair practices acts, chain-store tax laws, and laws restricting interstate trade. We also have municipal ordinances regulating door-to-door selling by companies not located in the given city.

Before leaving this topic, we want to mention two categories of government involvement in business that are *not* of the regulatory type. One occurs when a task is simply beyond the ability of any single company. For example, the government has built the large dams to generate electricity and control floods.

The other category includes the many services provided by the government in an effort to foster business competition and to increase business efficiency. For example, several states offer courses in distributive education, with federal support through the George-Dean Act. Much of the statistical information used by firms in setting quotas and territories comes from the Bureau of the Census. The United States Department of Agriculture publishes a considerable amount of marketing information that is useful to farmers, middlemen, and manufacturers.

Areas Where Public Regulation Touches Sales Executives

Let's look briefly at four areas where sales executives are affected by government regulation of business. These four are price discrimination, unfair competition, the Green River type of municipal ordinance, and cooling-off laws.

Price discrimination. The Clayton Antitrust Act (1914) and its Robinson-Patman Amendment (1936) are federal laws that generally restrict price discrimination. Sales administrators, for example, cannot allow members of their sales force to indiscriminately grant price concessions. Some customers may demand larger discounts than are normally allowed and threaten to take their business elsewhere if their demands are not met. If the seller grants the unusual discount, assuming no corresponding cost differential to justify the transaction, he (and the buyer) may be violating the Robinson-Patman Act.

In another situation, in order to make a sale it may be necessary for a seller to absorb some or all of the freight ordinarily paid by the buyer. Care must be taken to ensure that the move is made in good faith to meet an equally low price of a competitor. Firms normally cannot make price guarantees to some customers without making the same guarantees to other competing customers. Let's assume that a firm wants to grant allowances to customers for such things as cooperative advertising or demonstrators. Then these attractions must be offered to all competing customers on a proportionately equal basis.

Unfair competition. Unfair trade practices that may injure a competitor or the consumer are generally illegal under the Federal Trade Commission Act and its Wheeler-Lea Amendment. No specific examples of unfair competition are spelled out in these laws. However, a large body of illustrations has built up through the years as the Federal Trade Commission administered these legislative acts. A few examples of unfair competition as they may relate to a sales manager are as follows:

- Making false, deceptive, or disparaging statements about a competitor or his products.
- Bribing employees of customers in order to acquire or hold an account.
- Representing as new products those that are rebuilt, secondhand, or seconds in quality.
- Using bribery or espionage to learn the trade secrets of competitors.[16]
- Making false or misleading claims about services that accompany the purchase of a product.
- Misleading the customers into thinking they are getting a bargain, a reduced price, or some sort of free deal when such is not actually the case.[17]

Green River ordinances.[18] Many cities have ordinances restricting the activities of sales people who represent firms located outside the city. These representatives may sell door to door (in-home), or they may call on retailers or other business establishments. Ostensibly, most of these laws were passed to protect local consumers and businesses from the fraudulent, high-pressure, and otherwise unethical selling practices of outlanders. Actually such measures not only serve this purpose, but they also tend to insulate local firms from external competition. Generally, these ordinances require sales people to have a local license to do business in the town. But often it is difficult for representatives from some types of outside firms to get the necessary license. While the constitutionality of these laws is highly questionable, they do serve as a deterrent to unethical sales activity.

[16] For some legal, and even ethical, ways that a company can gather intelligence about its competition, see Steven Flax, "How to Snoop on Your Competitors," *Fortune,* May 14, 1984, pp. 28–33.

[17] For additional examples of what sales people legally can and cannot do or say, see two articles by Steven Mitchell Sack in *Sales & Marketing Management*—"Watch the Words," July 1, 1985, p. 56, and "The Risk of Dirty Tricks," November 11, 1985, p. 56.

[18] These legal measures derive their title from Green River, Wyoming, the location of one of the earliest of such acts.

Cooling-off laws. Legislation at the federal, state, and local levels protects consumers against the sales activities—sometimes unethical—of door-to-door sales people. Much of the state legislation and FTC administrative rulings is of the "cooling-off" type. That is, the regulations provide for a cooling-off period (usually three days). During this period the buyer in a door-to-door sale (in-home) may cancel the contract, return any merchandise, and obtain a full refund.

The Federal Trade Commission rulings (1972) apply to all sales of $25 or more. They require the sales person to inform the customer orally and in writing about the opportunity to "say no to the company even after you have said yes to the sales person." By 1973, close to 40 states, as well as several cities, had passed some type of cooling-off law. This poses real problems of compliance for national direct-selling companies, who may find themselves dealing with many varieties of laws and sales contracts.[19]

Conclusion

Undoubtedly, the amount and severity of public regulation are increasing at all levels—federal, state, and local. The important question concerns the reactions of sales executives to this encroaching social control. Are they aware of the trend? Do they care about it? What can they do about it?

Most sales managers are probably concerned only secondarily with the public interest. Instead, they are primarily concerned with practices that serve their short-run interests. They sometimes encourage activities by sales people that are similar to those that brought on public regulation in the past. It is a bit discouraging to note how little some sales administrators learn from history.

Sometimes, sales executives foster public regulation in another way. Outwardly they advocate free competition. However, when they face strong but fair competition, they may run to their elected representatives to seek a tariff, a trade barrier, or some other type of protection. In many cases, a sales manager's concept of fair competition means being able to beat a competitor. It is unfair competition when the competitor wins. Sales executives must realize that it is not possible to regulate part of one segment of the economy and let the other part go unrestrained. Regulation begets more regulation.

---

[19] For an analysis of the role of cooling-off legislation and its effectiveness in protecting consumers, particularly those with low incomes, see Orville C. Walker, Jr. and Neil M. Ford, "Can 'Cooling-off Laws' Really Protect the Consumer?" *Journal of Marketing,* April 1970, pp. 53–58.

Summary

Many people in our society have an unfavorable attitude toward business, especially the larger companies. This consumer discontent—labeled *consumerism*—is not likely to abate because it has attracted too much political attention. The main target of consumerism usually is a company's marketing activities—especially the firm's personal selling and advertising. In response to this climate of criticism, there is a growing interest in the idea of a social audit of a company's activities. We believe that sales managers must share in their companies' social responsibilities and the ethical considerations.

Ethics may be defined as moral standards of behavior. It is easy to be ethical when it does not cost you anything—when you are winning. The test comes when things are *not* going well. Then there may be real pressure to compromise your personal ethics. The problem is to determine what the ethical standards are. Society lacks commonly accepted standards of behavior. One good ethical guideline to follow is to do what you would feel comfortable explaining to your family, your friends, or even to the public at large on television. A key consideration for anybody (including sales executives) is to take the long-run point of view regarding the ethics of a given situation.

Ethical considerations are involved in many of the relationships the sales executives have with their sales forces, their companies, and their customers. Customer relations involving bribes, gifts, and entertainment especially can have serious ethical overtones.

A sales executive has a three-part responsibility—(1) a revenue responsibility to the company, (2) a human responsibility to the sales force, and (3) to customers, the responsibility to maximize their standard of living. In these three relationships, *ethical* considerations are often viewed on a person-to-person basis.

However, the substance of *social responsibility* is much broader. And sales executives do have a social responsibility. There are several practical reasons for sales executives to act in a socially responsible manner. And there are several courses of action that sales executives can take that are socially responsible.

Public regulation touches a company's marketing department more than any other phase of its operations. History tells us that government regulation of business has occurred either because (1) business has not acted in a socially responsible manner or (2) special interest groups lobbied for the regulations. Government intervention in business also occurs when a job is too big for private industry to handle by itself. The government also provides information and aid to business on a voluntary basis.

Public regulation affects sales executives especially in the areas of price discrimination, unfair competition, Green River ordinances, and cooling-off laws.

Questions and Problems

1. A sales manager is faced with the problem of whether to approve practices of his sales force that will result in profitable sales, but that are also slightly unethical. By sanctioning these practices, the executive meets his responsibility to his company and its stockholders, but fails in his social responsibilities. Is management's social responsibility thus incompatible with its responsibilities to its stockholders?

2. Discuss the problem of determining ethical standards, especially as your ideas may differ from those presented in this chapter.

3. Is ethical conduct always good for business in total, and unethical conduct always bad for business in total? Is your answer the same for the individual firm?

4. Are unethical practices always illegal? If not, cite specific examples of practices you feel are unethical, but are not outside the letter of the law. Are illegal practices always unethical?

5. As sales manager, you have been asked to recommend someone for a job as sales manager with another, noncompetitive firm. You have several sales people who would be excellent for the position, but you don't want to lose them. The other position would be a definite improvement for them. They will never be able to do so well within your own firm. Would you tell them about the opening? Would you recommend them to the other firm?

6. You are a sales manager of a firm that makes printed electronic circuits. You have been requested to write down your policies on entertaining customers, giving gifts, and handling bribery. State your policies in clear, specific terms so that all people concerned know exactly how you will handle each situation.

7. What are some implications in the power-responsibility equation with respect to a sales manager's responsibility to society?

8. Should a sales manager have more social responsibility than a production manager or an accountant in a firm?

9. *The Sales Manager's Creed* in Figure 23–4 was written over 40 years ago. Does it include any points you feel are now outdated and should be revised? Are there additional points you would add to the creed if it were to be rewritten today?

10. Should participation in community affairs be made part of the

job description for a sales executive? If so, should this factor be considered when his compensation is being reviewed? Is your answer the same for a sales person on straight salary? On straight commission? Does the nature of the product sold have any bearing on your decision?

11. Discuss the question of whether sales managers and their reps should actively participate in politics.

12. In what ways are sales-force managers affected by each of the following laws:
   a. Federal Trade Commission Act.
   b. Robinson-Patman Act.
   c. Green River ordinances.
   d. Cooling-off laws.

Case 23-1

Norton Electronics

Pirating Sales Reps from Former Employer

Mark Caplaw had just accepted the presidency of Altatec Electronics, a direct competitor of Norton Electronics where Mark just resigned as sales manager. During his five years as sales manager for Norton, Mark had made quite a name for himself in the industry. He was a highly able marketing executive who built a large, hard-hitting sales force that had taken Norton to the top of the industry. It was a most profitable operation. His record attracted the attention of Mr. Martinez, the owner of Altatec. Altatec's sales were floundering in spite of a good product line. Mark looked to be just what Altatec needed to lead it out of the doldrums.

The key to Mark's success at Norton was his ability to attract a group of exceptionally able young people who were adept at selling the company's wares. Mark treated them quite well, and they were most loyal to him. In particular, seven men and one woman were considered to be his team. Upon accepting the presidency of Altatec, Mark immediately faced the question of whether to ask his team to come with him to the new firm. He needed their skills badly to turn the operation around.

Questions

1. Should Mark attempt to take his team of sales people with him to Altatec?
2. If he does, should they go?

Case 23-2

Some Incidents Involving Ethical Considerations

Incident 1

You are a sales rep selling industrial conveying equipment, and you are paid a 7 percent commission on your sales volume. Recently you entertained the plant executive who will be making the final decision on an order for $850,000 of your goods. During that pleasant evening meal with the executive and his wife, you talked about the fall's new television programs. Your host's wife mentioned that they had been having a lot of trouble with their old television set. The plant executive laughingly said to his wife, "Careful now, Nell, before you know it, Bill here will be giving us a new set from all that money he'll be making if he gets our order." You laugh uncomfortably because you know it is against company policy to do such things. However, you also know that many of your peers buy gifts with their own money.

Once you questioned a sales rep who had given an expensive gift to a customer. She replied, "Why do you think the company pays us a higher commission than other companies pay. They expect us to take care of things like that without letting them know anything about it."

Questions

What would you do in this situation?

Incident 2

On a flight to New York you find yourself sitting next to a sales executive of a leading competitor. He is drinking and in a talkative mood. He has not identified himself, or asked who you are, but you recognize him from a trade show. He begins talking about some things his company is doing that are interesting to you. Then, he says he is going to New York to make a sales presentation to a potential account. Your firm was not aware of this possible new customer.

Questions

1. Should you identify yourself?
2. Should you pump the talkative executive for more information?

Incident 3

A purchasing agent who can give your firm a large contract has let you know he wants to leave his present employer. He strongly hints that if your firm hires him, he will give you a large contract before he leaves.

Question

What would you do?

Incident 4

You are calling on a new company whose founder becomes impressed with your selling skills and knowledge of the industry. He proposes that you sell his products to potential accounts in the territory you now cover. He will not only pay you a 10 percent commission on all orders, but will give you stock options to buy up to 20 percent of his firm, depending on how much business you bring in. There is no overlap in products and customers between your present employer and the new company. You now make $35,000 a year but feel a real need for more income to meet some pressing obligations. There is little future in management with your present employer. You feel that the products of the new concern are worthy and that they have good market possibilities.

Questions

What would you do?

24

Careers in Sales Management

First say to yourself what you would be; and then do what you have to do.
EPICTETUS

The sales manager of an industrial fasteners company explained the satisfactions of his job as follows.

> I wasn't at all certain that I wanted to be sales manager when it was offered to me. After all, I was making real good money in the field, I liked the freedom and the customer contact. I wasn't all that sure I would like managing, let alone be able to do so. Now, as I look back, I can't understand my reluctance to go into management. Working with these people, building the organization, getting things done—I really get a kick out of it. For instance, take a green kid, turn him into a real producer, and you'll know what accomplishment feels like.

Unfortunately, the satisfactions provided by the sales manager's job are not widely known. This chapter considers the advantages and disadvantages of a career in sales management and demonstrates what a sales manager must do to become successful.

The Challenge

People of ability thrive on challenge. Jobs that do not utilize their capabilities to a significant degree quickly bore them. A key question you should ask about an anticipated career is: "Will it offer sufficient challenge to sustain my interest in doing a continually better job?" A sales manager's job has such a challenge.

For example, an old-line publishing company with $14 million sales volume was floundering. Its 1983 losses exceeded $4 million.

672

The firm hired a proven executive from another publishing company. His experience was largely in the editorial side of the business, although he had started his career in sales and was widely known in the industry for his selling skills. He was given control over the firm's 40-man sales force with the mandate to remake it into a reasonably productive unit. While the company's average annual sales per sales person was $350,000, it was generally felt that a $600,000 average would be more in line with industry standards.

The new sales manager went into the field to work with each of the reps for one day in order to evaluate their talents. He found most of them not only lacking sales skills but also lacking the desire and ability to develop them. He spotted 20 people he could use; the others were asked to find other employment. With overhead reduced, he set about molding his new crew into a hard-hitting sales force. They met for a week in Acapulco to mend fences and to put together a new sales plan; it worked. As the manager later explained, "I used to think that getting out a new book was a challenge. But it's nothing compared to turning a sick operation into a profitable one while giving 20 people more successful careers. It's the toughest job I've ever had, but it made me grow!"

The sales manager is in the front lines, where performance is easily appraised by peers and superiors. While the abilities or contributions of a bookkeeper, personnel manager, or a design engineer may be difficult to assess, the sales manager's effectiveness is quite evident. Such measurable indexes as sales volume, selling expenses, turnover of the sales force, and percentage of market share are potent arguments either for or against the manager's performance. There is no place to hide.

The Wide Variety of Sales Management Positions

Most firms have no such thing as *the* sales executive or *the* sales manager. The role of a manager in sales work can vary from top-management planner to little more than super sales person. Authority can range from that of a top manager to that of an office clerk. The sales force commanded may be large or small. Each sales managership is unique, and the aspiring executive should consider all such positions separately.

Principal Classes of Sales-Force Executives

Chief sales-force executive. Chapter 1 defined the duties of the chief marketing executive in charge of a firm's entire marketing program. However, another type of administrator—the chief sales executive—is far more numerous. This is the administrator who has charge of the sales force. The exact role varies among companies, but usually he is given some responsibility for product, price, and distribution policies. The degree of authority over these decision areas varies, depending on the firm's policies. If top management is marketing oriented, it will probably retain a great deal of authority over marketing policies. But if it has little interest or ability in the marketing field, it may rely heavily on its chief sales executive for guidance.

Assistant sales managers.   Frequently, the chief sales force executive has under his direct command one or more assistants to aid him in executing the details of operating the sales force. A subordinate to the chief sales executive who has direct line authority over the sales force usually is given the title of *assistant sales manager.* One who does not have direct authority over the people in the field is usually called *assistant to the sales manager.*

Usually the assistant sales manager works directly with sales force operating problems. The assistant *to* the sales manager may be given staff work, such as forecasting, budgeting, sales correspondence, marketing research, sales promotion, or other technical duties. In larger organizations, several people may be employed in these capacities.

Product sales managers.   Many firms that distribute a wide line of products find it advisable for one person to assume specific responsibility for a given product or group of products. Usually, these people do not exercise line authority over the sales force but serve strictly in a staff capacity. Since they deal with product policy, pricing, and promotion of particular products, they have little contact with sales-force management. Other companies segregate their sales forces on a product basis. At the head of each division is a product-operating executive who is responsible for managing those who sell one line of products.

Market sales managers.   Often firms organize their sales forces by markets or types of customers. One company selling heavy duty compressors has one sales force that calls on building contractors while another calls on mining operators. Each has its own sales manager.

Territorial sales managers.   A large firm may have a number of territorial sales executives—as many as three levels of them, each with responsibility for a specified geographical area. Often a firm is organized in regions, divisions, and districts. Management may divide the nation into five large regions, with a regional sales manager in charge of each. Each region may be divided into 5 to 12 divisions, depending on the circumstances, with a divisional sales manager in charge of each. Under each division head may be several districts, each with a district sales manager.

Throughout this book we have been primarily concerned with these various types of territorial sales managers. They usually are in direct-line authority over the sales force and perform most sales management functions. In large organizations, most of the recruiting and selection of sales people is done by these territorial sales executives. They are also most directly involved with the supervision, stimulation, training, pay, expenses, and control of the sales force. Moreover, a successful sales person will likely become some type of territorial sales manager.

Geographic Coverage

The amount of territory the sales manager controls can vary from the whole world to a small city. The prospective sales executive can choose the size of area he prefers. A person who wants to minimize traveling should join an organization whose distribution is limited to a small geographic area. Many such opportunities exist in automobile dealerships, appliance distributorships, business-machine branch organizations, office supply houses, insurance agencies, and local radio, television, and newspaper firms—in general, any retail or wholesale organization that serves a local trading area. Positions with small firms can be as desirable or challenging as those with companies that distribute nationally.

Geographic Location

Sales management positions are located in every section of the country. Prospective sales executives can determine their living environment by getting a job in the area where they want to live. Of course, this limits their bargaining power and choice of firms. However, most sales management positions are located in larger cities and in the more densely populated areas of the country where corporations have their home offices, branches, and sales offices. This does not suggest that there are no firms with headquarters in small towns. The home offices of Maytag Company and W. A. Sheaffer Pen Company are both located in small towns in Iowa.

Types of Selling Activities

The sales executive can also choose the type of selling activity to be administered. Each type of sales job requires a varying degree of pressure, different personal qualities, and varying efforts. The job of managing a door-to-door sales organization is different from the task of guiding individuals in selling large industrial installations to top executives. The task of managing a group of automobile salesmen is different from that of administering the activities of a manufacturer's sales force.

The sales job in each industry is unique and has its own characteristics and demands. In planning a sales management career, you should give considerable thought to what you will be happiest selling. Experience indicates that there are great advantages to staying in one industry throughout a sales career. The person who jumps from one industry to another creates problems for himself. Much of his knowledge and many of his contacts are of little value in a new industry.

The Life of a Sales Executive

While it is true that each sales manager's job is unique, there are some common elements.

Travel

Some traveling is required for the performance of any sales-management job. However, the amount can vary from an occasional convention trip to an extensive amount of field work with the sales branches or with customers.

The amount of traveling sales managers do somewhat depends on their attitudes toward traveling. Many enjoy being on the road. They seize every opportunity to get out of the office and into the field because they love it. One man enjoyed the road so much that he failed to spend sufficient time in his office doing the necessary paperwork. In the end his boss divided the job by hiring an inside man to take care of the office tasks, thus leaving the manager full time in the field.

Paperwork

Inherent in modern management is the nuisance called paperwork. No one relishes it, but "it goes with the territory." However, few people who are lax in handling the paperwork connected with a job advance very far in management. Business systems rely heavily on documents for communicating information among the various units. A manager who neglects the paperwork input to the company's information system places a burden, sometimes a difficult one, on other executives who need the information.

What constitutes doing paperwork properly? First, paperwork should be done accurately and completely, not haphazardly. Second, it should be done on time; the manager who is habitually late getting things done seldom lasts long or goes very far. Finally, it is done discriminately; the talented manager learns when to create documents and when not to. Useless reports or memos are one mark of an inefficient administrator.

Conferences

Next to paperwork, administrators seem to complain most about the seemingly endless conferences they must sit through. The conference is a favorite administrative communication and decision-making technique. But it is frequently overused in the name of participative management. Nevertheless, a capable administrator learns how to participate effectively in conferences.

Work with People

While all administrators must deal with people, this point is particularly true for sales managers. They have one more interface with people than most of the other executives in the company. The sales manager also deals directly with customers.

If there is one common denominator among sales managers, it is that they must deal with people at all levels. In one day, the sales manager may hold conferences with both the sales force and the board of directors or may contact both top executives and a customer's operating staff.

Sales

Most sales managers continue to sell to customers to some extent. Some retain certain key accounts. Others go into the field for important sales. Few sales managers ever get very far away from selling—it is the name of the game.

Picking People—Talented Ones

We have stressed in this book that the sales manager's most important job is selecting sales personnel. The knack of picking winners is critical to the sales manager's own success.

Fire Fighting

All sorts of problems continually arise that require immediate attention. A customer calls to voice a complaint; something must be done. Corporate counsel requires a deposition in a lawsuit. A sales rep is injured while skiing and cannot cover the trade for a month.

The office football pool is busted by the local vice squad. There is no anticipating what is going to happen. However, the sales manager must somehow handle each problem presented.

Above All, They Are Managers

Many supersalesmen have failed as sales managers because they did not realize that, above all, they were expected to be managers. A manager *manages!* A manager leads a group to accomplish its mission. A manager gets things together and makes things happen. Responsibility is a key concept. The manager is *responsible* for what happens to the group.

One man whose tenure as sales manager was short seemed to consider his promotion to the position to be an honor recognizing his years of successful service. His concept of the job was badly distorted. He evidently thought that a manager spends a couple of hours in the morning in a paneled office, then retires to the golf course for an afternoon round. Meanwhile, the sales force would take care of itself. "Just let them alone and they'll get the job done!" was his managerial philosophy. It seldom happens that way.

The Rewards of a Sales Management Job

Reward systems are important in shaping the behavior of the people in an organization. In several direct and many subtle ways, how much people are paid and the way it is distributed determines what they will produce. The rewards awaiting a sales manager are an important consideration in your job choice.

Direct Monetary Rewards—The Money

Few current studies disclose the earnings of the average sales manager. However, bear in mind that the idea of the average sales manager is difficult to pin down. The variations in the data are such that statistics on central tendencies are not very meaningful.

The pay you can expect in sales management depends on the industry and the company you work for. There are industries that notoriously underpay their people. Similarly, some companies try to get a lot of mileage from the payroll dollar.

Indirect Monetary Payments

Little is known statistically about the extent of indirect monetary payments for sales managers. These payments include company-paid insurance plans, pension systems, country club memberships, company-owned airplanes, and other company-furnished additions to a manager's standard of living. However, such indirect payments are important and widely used. At some point in their career, sales managers may place a high value on deferred compensation, such as stock option plans, pension plans, and insurance policies, which are nontaxable or are taxed at lower rates than ordinary income. A $10,000 country club membership would be worth about $14,000 if it were paid as regular compensation.

These considerations are of particular importance to the sales manager. It is easier to justify to the Internal Revenue Service that the sales manager needs such things as a company-owned airplane or a country club membership than it is to build the same case for the production manager. It is far more likely for the sales executive to be given these benefits than it is for any other executive on the same level in the organization.

What It Takes to Be a Successful Sales Manager

Education

Not too many years ago a sales manager only needed successful sales experience to qualify for the job. Today, perusal of the job specifications for a wide range of sales management positions indicates that applicants for these jobs should have college degrees. It is disheartening to see mature people with long, successful sales records whose careers are at a dead end for lack of a degree—not lack of talent, just the degree. It is usually impractical for them to return to school, so they remain stuck in their jobs.

Career advancement is easier if the proper credentials are acquired along the way. A career in management calls for requisite training and certification.

Experience

Sales experience is necessary, but you do not have to be an outstanding sales producer to be promoted into a management position. Nevertheless, you have a brighter future as a sales manager if you have performed successfully in a selling job. Such a background provides several advantages.

First, the sales force will have more respect for you than if your sales experience has been limited or unimpressive. They will know that you have been in the field and know the problems they face each day. When you tell them to do something, they will have confidence that you know what you are talking about.

Second, sales experience enables you to be realistic in planning activities and in your supervision and control efforts. You are not likely to expect the impossible of the sales force, but you will be able to recognize a loafer when you see one.

Third, the customer contact provided by selling is valuable for any top policy-making executive. Knowing the problems of the customer is essential in developing sound marketing plans. Having personal acquaintances among the firm's customers is also helpful.

More important than sales experience, however, is managerial experience. If you have had no experience as a supervisor or in some other administrative position, it may be difficult for top management to determine whether you have executive talent.

"But how can I prove I have management skills if I am not given the opportunity to show them?" is a common complaint of sales reps who are continually passed over for promotion because they have had no managerial experience. The person who really has management talents, however, will find ways of showing them to the boss.

Development of Administrative Skills[1]

One member of the Young Presidents' Organization, when questioned about how he had developed his administrative skills, advanced this idea:

> After I got out of college and settled down into my first job, I made it a point to get involved in all sorts of community activities, any group that would take me. Little League, church, neighborhood, you name it and I joined it. I volunteered to do whatever it was that had to be done. I found out that you can learn a great deal about how to get people to do what it is you want them to do—managing them, if you will—in just such activities.
>
> At first I found I was terrible at it. I remember that first year. It was awful. Everything was messed up, nothing flowed right, and I couldn't organize my people. I didn't do a very good job of it, but with experience I learned the ropes. I learned how to organize projects, how to line up things, and how to get things done. I attribute a large part of my success in business to those early years in community activities where I learned to manage people.

That is the way one person developed administrative skills. He learned by doing. He projected himself into situations that required administrative skills and then was perceptive enough to learn them.

Another individual, the vice president of manufacturing for a large machine tool company, used another approach to develop administrative skills.

---

[1] This section is adapted from Richard H. Buskirk, *Your Career* 2d ed. (Boston: Cahners Books, 1981), p. 51.

In my first years with the company I seized every opportunity I could to show some management skills. I remember that first year the boss wanted someone to organize the company picnic. I stepped forward and knocked myself out to make sure that was the best run picnic the company ever had. And it was! The boss never forgot that. For the next 10 years he was continually reminding me of the great job I did on that picnic. Then there was the time we had all of the confusion when the workers struck. We were trying to keep the plant open to get out critical orders and run the place on a skeleton staff. I worked round the clock organizing that effort, and I think more than anything else that was responsible for getting me where I am now. The boss was really impressed with how I held things together during that strike.

A sales manager relates:

I always wanted to be in sales management, and I spent a lot of time thinking about how I was ever going to prove to Mr. Howard (the boss) that I had management skills. One day he hired a new salesman, and I saw an opportunity. I walked into his office and volunteered to help train the new man. He was so happy to get rid of the responsibility that he agreed. I really trained that young man, and he was immediately successful in the field. Time after time Mr. Howard would comment about how much he liked my ability to train new sales people. I think that's what was responsible for my promotion.

The moral of these stories seems clear: You must aggressively seize every opportunity to use administrative skills. You will only develop these talents if you use them. You will never be a manager if you duck the responsibility for making things happen.

A young junior engineer was able to develop his position rather admirably when he volunteered to open a liaison office for his company—an electronics manufacturing concern—at Las Cruces, New Mexico. This office would work closely with the people at White Sands Testing Station. He went to the city alone, set up shop, and successfully did business there. At the same time, he received his Ph.D. in electrical engineering at New Mexico State University. That developmental program did wonders for a career.

Desire

Probably more than anything else, you must *want* to be a successful sales manager if you are to become one. Your desire must be great enough so that you will apply yourself diligently to all the difficult tasks that lie ahead of you. Many otherwise successful sales people do not become sales managers simply because they have no desire to do so. If you really want to be a sales manager, you probably will have the opportunity at some point in your career.

Women in Selling

One of the significant current trends in selling is the rapid influx of women into the sales field, both as sales people and managers. While their impact is now being felt in the field, the future is even more impressive. A study of the industrial sales women and their sales managers reported that they were enjoying success beyond their expectations. Moreover, their managers were most satisfied with their performances and planned to hire more women for their sales forces.[2]

One reason sales is an attractive field for career women is that it offers pay in proportion to results. According to the women sales managers interviewed, the biggest problem they faced with saleswomen is the reps' unwillingness to move to another area. Such immobility has limited somewhat the promotability of the successful sales woman. The woman who does not want to move would be wise to work for local concerns where a promotion would not mean a transfer.

One woman felt that being a woman is more of an asset than a liability because her husband's salary freed her to take risks that a male breadwinner might duck. It is clear that women are rapidly advancing in the field of selling and sales management. They will undoubtedly make whatever adjustments are required for success in the field.

Your Strategic Career Plan

Throughout this book we have included at the beginning of most chapters a section on the role of the chapter topic in the firm's strategic market plan. Now it is time for you to think strategically. What is your strategic plan for yourself? What are your goals? How do you plan to achieve them? The members of one of the author's M.B.A. classes were asked about their strategic plans. Their puzzled looks disclosed that few of them had given such plans much thought. Guess what the next assignment was!

The Matter of Goals

It would be folly to suggest that you can now foresee what you will be doing and who you will be at age 50. All evidence clearly shows that fate plays a heavy hand in your career game. Nev-

[2] Richard H. Buskirk and Beverly Miles, *Beating Men at Their Own Game—A Woman's Guide to Successful Selling in Industry* (New York: John Wiley & Sons, 1980).

ertheless, you need goals. You can change goals as you discover new information about yourself and the markets you're dealing in. But you still need ultimate and intermediate goals. Some career specialists suggest that you set goals each year. What do you want to accomplish by this time next year? What do you want to be doing?

One advantage of having goals is that it helps you resist temptations that will lead you into unacceptable situations. For example, assume that you know that you want to end up at age 35 with your own business. Then you might refuse attractive job offers that would provide you little opportunity to acquire the skills you need to be your own boss. If one of your goals is to live in the Sun Belt, then you might shun offers from firms whose bases of operation are in the Northeast. Success with such firms might mean living somewhere you don't want to live.

The bottom line is that you should know what you want in life if you want to maximize your chances of getting it.

What Do You Need to Do to Achieve Your Goals?

We are all imperfect, and our imperfections may block the path to our goals. If you are to achieve your goals you will have to develop yourself in diverse ways. Identify what you need to learn and what skills you need to acquire to become what you want to be. Then, formulate a plan to remedy your deficiencies. If you see a need for selling skills, go to work for a firm that can give you excellent sales training and sales experience. Think in terms of who knows what you want to know, and then tap that source of knowledge.

What Is Your Level of Aspirations?

Many of you will want to play in the "Major Leagues"—whatever that may mean to you. It means different things to different people. Others want no part of the fast track. It is best to identify what level of competition you seek early because it is difficult to climb in "Class." Coaches wanting to coach in professional football usually do not start out coaching in high schools.

What Is Your Timetable?

You need to achieve a position by a certain time lest you fall behind your competitors. In the military, if an officer has not made a certain rank by a certain age, his career is over. To a somewhat lesser degree, the same thing is true in business. You can become too old for a job just as you can be too young, at least in the mind of the person making the decision about you.

If you are not making normal progression toward your goals, you need to reassess what you are doing. If your boss likes your work and intends to promote you, you will be given some very tangible evidence of that intention. If nothing good is happening on your job, your firm is sending you a message. Look for tangible rewards.

Summary

A career in selling offers the college-trained person essentially four advantages:

- An opportunity to make relatively high earnings.
- Freedom of movement and control over one's time.
- Good mobility between firms.
- Extensive contact with people.

However, there are people for whom selling offers little. Some people are uncomfortable in the role of calling on people to ask them to buy something. They are unable to accept a high rate of failure. Others do not like being rejected. The sales person is continually involved in interactions with people who feel socially superior to them. In contemplating a sales career, you should give considerable thought to how well you can deal with these pressures.

While you will have little difficulty finding a sales job, getting one that meets your particular requirements is another thing. The really good sales jobs do not usually come looking for you. You must exert considerable effort finding them and then being hired.

Questions and Problems

1. If you were applying for the job of president of a corporation and had been a sales manager for a competing organization, what statistics and factual data would you present to prove your abilities?
2. What aspects of the sales manager's job are distasteful to you?
3. Suppose that you wanted to become a sales manager. Formulate a detailed plan for realizing this goal.
4. How does the job of managing a door-to-door sales organization differ from that of administering the activities of people selling business machines to commercial organizations?
5. If you wanted to work as a sales manager in Miami, Florida, how should you go about achieving this goal?

6. The statement has been made that, in general, sales personnel are far more mobile than any other people at the same level in the organization. Why is this so?
7. How should an individual go about preparing to be a sales manager? What type of experience is best? Would a graduate degree be an aid?
8. While sales managers are usually relatively free to arrange their own schedules, many of them find it impossible to break away from their jobs and enjoy themselves. Why is it that some people seem to be able to do their jobs and spend relatively little time doing so, while others seem to become prisoners of their work?
9. If you were seriously considering the field of sales management as a lifetime career, what should you do in order to arrive at a final decision on the matter?
10. As the president of a small, recently established tool company making a new type of crescent wrench, how would you go about finding a top-notch sales manager?

Case 24-1

Bill Banks

Where to from Here?

"Can I talk with you for a few minutes?" Bill Banks asked the professor in his sales management course. It was Bill's last semester at a West Coast business school. "I have a problem and I don't know what to do about it."

"It wouldn't be much of a problem if you did know what to do about it, would it?" Professor David responded. "Come in now. We have a few minutes before class."

Professor David knew Bill was a good student with a promising future in business. He related well with people and made a good impression. "Tell me about your problem!"

Bill began, "I have three ways to go after I graduate. Right now I have a firm offer from Xerox that's attractive. It pays well and there's a good future with them. They want me to sell a wide line of their equipment. I know I need some good sales experience. It will look good on my resume."

"Then, my father wants me to go to graduate school. He'll pop for the full ride if I go on and get my M.B.A. He's with TRW and says that no one in the future will go to top management without an

M.B.A. He says that I should get one just as insurance. He says, 'You can't have too many credentials.' It's just that I am tired of school. I want to get out and do something. When I tell him that I can always go back to school later, he shakes his head and says that it doesn't work out that way too well."

"And then there is Tom, my roommate. He has this little company he started two years ago that sells beachwear. He gets the stuff made by several other firms and sells it to retailers. He has sold over $500,000 of it this year and has made a profit of about $100,000. He's paid his way through school. Well, he is also graduating and wants me to join him in the deal. I'll get a good piece of the company and can really make some money if I get out and sell. He wants me to be the outside man while he runs the company and works with the suppliers. We have worked it out many ways on paper this past year and if things go as planned, I can be rich in a few years."

The professor asked, "And if they don't, what then?"

"I can worry about that if it happens that way. Who knows?" Bill responded.

"Sounds to me like you have already made up your mind about it. Why are you asking me? You're a big boy now. Do what you want." Professor David said.

"It's not that easy. Tom and I are really good friends. We've been roommates for four years and have dated the same girls. We really get along. It would tear me up to lose his friendship. I've been told that you should stay out of business with friends. It's a good way to lose them. I've helped Tom out several times by selling to some big dealers so I know that I can do the job."

Professor David smiled as he said, "Now we have the non-economic motives coming to the surface. It would be foolish for me to pass judgment on your relationship with Tom. That's something you'll have to work out. As for your going on to graduate school, many people do return for their M.B.A. after working for a few years. It is a preferred pattern because they are more mature and better able to profit from the education. As for Xerox, it's a good company. You would learn much from working for them. You'll have to pound out this problem. Talk with Tom some more about your fears. Talk with your father and about how you feel. Let's go to class now."

Bill nodded but felt he was no where closer to a decision than when he walked into the office. He said to the professor, "You professors sure do know how to avoid giving any definitive answers to problems."

The professor could not allow that statement to stand uncontested. "And that, lad, is your problem. You think that there is one right answer to your dilemma. Perhaps all of them or none of them are right for you."

Question

What advice would you give Bill?

Case 24–2

Forbes Company, Inc.*

Declining Sales and Morale in the Heating Equipment Division

It was the beginning of the new year, and Roger Matthews, the marketing manager of Forbes Company, was becoming increasingly concerned with the performance of the heating equipment division (HED) of his company. Not only were its sales declining, but the division appeared to be losing its share of market as well. Also, there appeared to be significant internal turmoil in terms of employee turnover and unrest. In seeking a solution to these problems, Roger realized that he would be hampered by strong and knowledgeable competitors as well as by internal personnel complexities. He decided to schedule a meeting with Tom Forbes, the manager of the heating equipment division, in order to gain further insight into possible reasons for the sales and organizational problems. Roger believed that this would lead to a more workable solution. Prior to the meeting, he reviewed the background of the division, both current and historical, in order to place it in the overall company framework.

Forbes Company was a wholesale distributor of heating and plumbing equipment. Its 1981 sales were approximately $20 million, and 1982 sales were expected to top $22 million. The heating equipment division sales were $1,596,000 in 1981 and were forecasted to be approximately the same for 1982. Exhibit 1 shows annual gross sales since 1978.

Exhibit 1
Gross Sales of the Heating Equipment Division

Year	Total Sales	Monthly Average
1981	$2,193,517	$182,793
1980	1,906,909	158,909
1979	1,702,109	141,842
1978	1,595,875	132,989

---

* Case prepared by Professor Thomas H. Stevenson, University of North Carolina at Charlotte. Reproduced with permission.

HED specialized in sales of heating equipment, such as furnaces and associated products. The parent company sold the entire range of plumbing equipment from simple home valves and washers to a complete industrial plumbing installation. HED represented well-known manufacturers, such as Crane, American Standard, and others. Customers were original equipment manufacturers as well as such industrial users as plants, stores, and hospitals.

Forbes operated from its main headquarters in a medium-size northeastern city. The Heating Equipment Division was located in the same town, although in a separate building. The company's major markets were located within a radius of approximately 150 miles of its headquarters. The company was family-owned and had grown from its beginning in the 1940s to a position of prominence in its marketing area. The president and owner was particularly concerned that the HED not continue to reflect poorly on the entire operation of the company.

The day-to-day activities of Forbes Company were supervised by an executive vice president. The president concerned himself mainly with corporate financial affairs. Recently the president's son, Tom Forbes, had been appointed as manager of the heating equipment division. Tom had worked for the company in various jobs during his summer vacations from school and since his graduation from college. As manager of HED, Tom reported to the executive vice president.

Roger Matthews joined the firm about 10 months previously as a sales representative. Recently he was moved from his sales position to the newly created marketing manager's position. He was informed that the promotion was because of his outstanding performance and his strong managerial capabilities. The HED problem was delegated entirely to Roger by the executive vice president. His words to Roger were: "This is your baby. You are responsible for getting HED back on target. You have the authority to make whatever changes you feel are necessary to do so."

Roger scheduled an afternoon meeting with Tom Forbes at a time that would normally be free of interruptions and that would allow for a detailed conversation. The meeting began with Roger explaining that he was aware that HED sales were not satisfactory and that they needed to work together to resolve the problem. Then Roger asked Tom if he had any ideas as to the reasons for the poor performance in HED.

Tom stated that the present situation was due somewhat to the fact that two years earlier the then manager of HED quit and opened his own business in direct competition with HED. He took with him four of the Forbes' inside sales people, plus a secretary and many of Forbes' important customers. Since then, the competitor's business had prospered as had the businesses of other competitors in the area. Further, that competitor was recently bought out by a larger national firm that seemed to be intent on buying even more business in the immediate area. They now appeared to be selling at 5 percent less than other major suppliers in the area.

Tom also noted that Forbes people (including HED) were all compensated on a straight-salary basis. The former manager had wanted to switch to a salary-plus-commission plan but was not allowed to do so because other divisions were not compensated in this manner. He quit primarily over this issue, but also because he felt he could make more money elsewhere. Evidently many of the staff felt the same, since they went with him and were compensated with salary and commission.

Tom also told Roger that the fact that HED was physically separated from the parent company appeared to be a cause of problems. Up until 12 years ago all divisions operated from the same building, but space pressures forced a separation. Tom mentioned that he had heard sales people say such things as, "Why is HED always left out?" and "What we do isn't that important to the overall operation."

Tom showed Roger an organization chart of HED (see Exhibit 2).

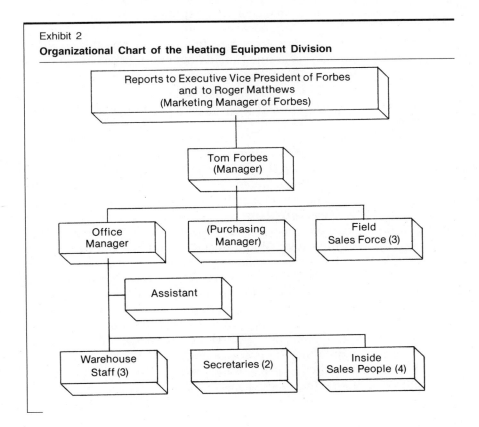

Exhibit 2

Organizational Chart of the Heating Equipment Division

Reports to Executive Vice President of Forbes and to Roger Matthews (Marketing Manager of Forbes)

Tom Forbes (Manager)

Office Manager

(Purchasing Manager)

Field Sales Force (3)

Assistant

Warehouse Staff (3)

Secretaries (2)

Inside Sales People (4)

The division employed 15 people: 3 outside sales reps, Tom Forbes (manager), an office manager (who also was purchasing agent) and his assistant, inside counter sales people, secretaries, and warehouse clerks. Most of the people had worked their way up through HED to their present positions, many having started as hourly help in the warehouse. All training was on-the-job, since there was no formal training program.

Elaborating on the organization chart, Tom explained that he administered the entire operation of HED, performing the functions of division manager as well as sales manager. However, he noted that he really had more to do than he could handle since he wanted to travel with and train the sales force. Yet, he also felt that it was necessary to supervise the inside operation.

Tom was aided by the office manager who was in charge of the internal operations of the division and who also had responsibility for purchasing. Since purchasing was a new responsibility for him (it was formerly handled by another person who had since been promoted to outside sales), it distracted him from other duties. He also had responsibility for pricing orders for billing purposes, but the return of a former employee had reduced the pressure here somewhat. The office manager had expressed an interest in moving into a field sales position because he felt that the chances for financial gain were greater there. However, this request was turned down because of the shortage of trained inside people. Further, the office manager seemed to resent his isolation (both in physical distance and status) from the parent organization across town.

Roger noticed that the inside/counter people had both phone sales and counter sales responsibility. Tom noted this frequently resulted in confusion over who should do what. In busy periods there was chaos—with either long lines at the counter or ringing telephones. And during slack periods, time was wasted. During one such busy period, Roger noted a warehouseman and a secretary drinking a soft drink together, seemingly unaware of, or uninterested in solving, the overload problem. Tom and his assistant were too busy to notice this, and the secretary and warehouseman did not take any initiative on their own. When Roger mentioned this to Tom, the reply was that each person in the organization appeared interested only in doing his or her own job—teamwork was not practiced.

While Roger and Tom were having that afternoon meeting, Tom had to answer the telephone. At that point, Roger noticed that two of the outside sales people were in the office. When Roger asked them about this, they replied that they wanted to be sure that the inside people did their jobs correctly. Therefore, they frequently came in to the office to price orders, wait on the counter, and to check the warehouse for product availability.

Tom told Roger that he worked with both the outside sales force and the inside staff to develop new business. However, his other duties and his lack of experience in his managerial role limited his time and effectiveness as a leader for the field sales force. Tom was aware of the declining sales figures shown in Exhibit 1. However, he felt that these results were about all that could be expected under the present circumstances, particularly with the apparent lack of teamwork and motivation. As a result, new-customer prospecting was virtually nonexistent. The sales force spent its time trying to maintain present business with old accounts, and even in that market there were problems.

After the meeting, Roger was pondering the information given to him by Tom, as well as that obtained through his own observations. Since this situation was his first real managerial problem as marketing manager, he felt that the president was watching closely to see how well he handled this matter. He also felt that there was much business to be acquired, both from old customers and new, and that present business must be maintained. He also wanted to avoid any more turmoil because of turnover, and he wanted to improve morale and teamwork in general.

Roger knew that the resolution of the problems would not be easy, but he was optimistic that he would be able to improve the situation at HED.

Question

What courses of action should Roger Matthews put into effect in order to resolve the problems facing the heating equipment division?

Case 24-3

Mike Woods

Big Company or Small?

"I just don't know what to do. First I lean one way, then I lean the other. I thought that a talk with you might help me make up my mind." Mike Woods, about to graduate from a large private university with a double major in marketing and entrepreneurship, was asking for some help from Professor Stowe, a member of the marketing faculty.

"Tell me what your alternatives are," the professor asked.

"I have two excellent offers from large companies, both of which really appeal to me. Arco has offered to put me into their new solar energy subsidiary at a higher-than-market wage and with all the benefits that go with such companies. I would be working with some of their new products in a capacity that depends on their needs at the time. I just start out in training and go from there.

"And then there is Merrill Lynch. They are going every which way in the financial field and in real estate, so they're hiring all sorts of marketing capabilities. Again, they have the usual 'bennies,' and it's a top-notch organization." Mike paused, waiting for some reaction from Dr. Stowe, but all he got was a knowing nod with the implicit message for him to continue.

"Now on the other side of the picture is the deal Jack offered me. You know Jack Counter, my mentor in the program."

Professor Stowe knew Jack quite well—he was one of the outstanding business people who served as a mentor to students in the school's entrepreneur program. Mr. Counter, a multimillionaire, was owner and head of a large construction company engaged mainly in real estate developments in southern California.

Mike continued, "Jack has made me a funny proposition. He says that he'll pay me a salary of $1,800 a month for six months. Then, if all goes well, we'll negotiate some sort of deal when we both make up our minds what it is I'll do with him. He emphasizes that word *with*. My first task is to put together a package on an industrial property he has in Carson and go sell it to some investors. He wants to develop the land soon. I don't know about it. We didn't even get around to talking about any benefits. I have the feeling that if I had asked about them, the conversation would have ended." Mike paused.

"You are a bit afraid of Jack's offer. Is that it?"

Mike nodded in agreement. He did not like to hear himself say so, but that was the bottom line. He said, "I really like Jack and he's helped me a lot, but those other two offers are really solid opportunities."

"You don't think Jack's offer is an opportunity?"

"Oh, it's a great opportunity, but . . ." Mike failed to finish his thought.

"But what? But you're afraid you can't do the job Jack expects of you. Is that it? You're afraid of failure and feel more secure in the training programs of the larger firms. Is that what you're saying?" Professor Stowe watched Mike wince at those hard words. Mike knew the professor's contempt for people who feared failure.

Mike felt he was cornered and had to defend himself. He countered, "I know where you're coming from. You don't like the big corporations. But you've got to admit that these two companies have a lot going for them. And their offers are good. The Arco job could lead to something really exciting, and they have the money to back their play. And Merrill Lynch is moving fast, so there's plenty of opportunity for advancement. Besides, they provide great training."

"Well, then why are you talking with me if you know what I would tell you? You want me to order you to go to work for Jack? What is it you want me to tell you?" The professor then suggested that Mike outline the pros and cons connected with each job, which they did together. It did not seem to help matters—all three opportunities looked good.

"Tell me, what is the worst thing that could happen if you went to work for Jack? What is the best thing that could happen? How about the same information for Arco and Merrill?" Professor Stowe asked.

"You've made your point, as usual," Mike replied.

The two sat silent for a moment each waiting for the other to speak. Then the professor told Mike to go to the beach for the afternoon and look at the ocean while contemplating his dilemma. "Just sit and think about it for several hours with no one to bother you. Try to focus on what is really bothering you about each offer."

Mike protested, "But nothing is really bothering me about any of the offers. They're all great."

"If you really feel that way, toss a coin. You can't lose." The professor continued, "I suggest that something really is bothering you about each, so try to define your feelings. Come back tomorrow at 11. I can't wait to find out if you can be honest with yourself."

Mike left the office wondering which beach he should go to.

Questions

1. What are the advantages and disadvantages of each of Mike's job offers?
2. What do you think is really bothering Mike about each of the jobs offered him?

Index

*This book has been set Linotron 202 in 10 and 9
point Melior, leaded 2 points. Part numbers and
titles are 48 and 30 point Helvetica Bold; chapter
numbers and titles are 48 and 30 point Helvetica
Regular. The size of the type page is 33 by 47
picas.*